Scotland's Parliament Site and the Canongate: archaeology and history

Scotland's Parliament Site and the Canongate: archaeology and history

Holyrood Archaeology Project Team

Edinburgh 2008
SOCIETY OF ANTIQUARIES OF SCOTLAND

COVER IMAGES
View of the Scottish Parliament (© Stuart Reynolds);
Detail from painting by G Walker of Edinburgh from St Anthony's Chapel, c 1823 (© City Art Centre);
Detail from John Slezer's engraved panorama of Edinburgh from the north, c 1680 (© National Library of Scotland)

ENDPAPER IMAGE
Reconstruction of Queensberry House in the late seventeenth century (© David Simon)

Published in 2008 by the Society of Antiquaries of Scotland

Society of Antiquaries of Scotland
National Museum of Scotland
Chambers Street
Edinburgh EH1 1JF
Tel: 0131 247 4115
Fax: 0131 247 4163
Email: administration@socantscot.org
Website: www.socantscot.org

British Library Cataloguing-in-Publication Data
A catalogue record for this book is available from the British Library.

ISBN 978 0 903903 45 5

The Society gratefully acknowledges grant-aid towards the publication of this volume from Historic Scotland.

HISTORIC SCOTLAND

The Scottish
Parliament

Typeset by Waverley Typesetters, Fakenham
Design and production by Lawrie Law and Alison Rae
Manufactured in Spain

Contents

PART 1 Introduction

PART 2 The Parliament site in the medieval burgh c 1128 to the 1660s

**PART 3   The 'urban palace': the 'Great Lodging', Hatton House
and Queensberry House**

Tom Addyman and John Lowrey

Tom Addyman and John Lowrey

Tom Addyman and John Lowrey

Preface

The project of archaeological excavation, documentary history, building analysis and scientific research undertaken in advance of the building of the new Scottish Parliament building at Holyrood was the largest of its kind in Scotland. The decision to site Scotland's new Parliament building in the heart of the medieval burgh of Canongate, and adjacent to Scotland's primary royal palace, provided an opportunity, because of the sheer scale of the development, to explore a large proportion of an important medieval town that had lain at the centre of the history of Scotland. This was also an area that had been witness to an extraordinary change in fortune, from a 16th-century quarter of rich aristocratic dwellings and the infrastructure needed to support them, to a 19th-century industrial suburb with some of the highest levels of poverty and deprivation in Europe.

This fine book, put together by a skilled and dedicated team of archaeologists, historians, architectural historians and scientists, provides a series of snapshots of the initial settlement, development and eventual decline of the burgh and the great house at the heart of the site.

The project included a ground-breaking analysis of Queensberry House, a major urban 'palace'. The removal of all the internal plaster as part of the architectural conservation provided an unrivalled opportunity for archaeologists to unravel the development history of this vast, complex and fascinating, if controversial, building. It began as the relatively modest Grand Lodging of a minor member of the gentry and developed into one of the great houses of Scotland, before, like the burgh around it, descending the social scale to become tenements, then a barracks, a poorhouse and finally a hospital.

Integrating the complex archaeological project into the parliament-building project was a major achievement. Behind this achievement lie the skills of my own staff, who managed the archaeological project, the staff of the Parliament's building project management team and the archaeological contractors and their sub-contractors.

The site of the new Scottish Parliament has been at the heart of Scotland's history. This book places the new use of the Parliament site in that long historical context. I hope that you find it both enjoyable and useful.

JOHN GRAHAM
Chief Executive
Historic Scotland

Acknowledgements

This report is the product of many hands and the contributing authors, many of whom had very significant roles in the fieldwork. We are very grateful to all of them for their labours over the last decade. The project was managed by Historic Scotland (HS) on behalf of, first, the Scottish Office and then the Parliament Corporate Body (PCB), according to the protocols for the management of government projects then in force. The HS project manager was Gordon Barclay, with major contributions within the agency by (Inspectorate) David Breeze, Richard Emerson, Noel Fojut, Doreen Grove, John Hume (who also provided assistance to the Parliament Corporate Body after his retirement), Aonghus Mackechnie, Rod McCullagh, Olwyn Owen, Graham Reed and Andrea Smith; (Procurement) Keith Downie; (Communications and Media) Pat Connor and Isla Macleod. The project benefited during its fieldwork phase from the untiring support of the then Director of Heritage Policy, the late Frank Lawrie, and the then Chief Executive, Graeme Munro.

The work on site was only possible because of the active engagement of the team managing the construction of the Parliament for, first, the Scottish Office and then the Parliament Corporate Body. Alan Ezzi and Sarah Davidson were the Project Directors in the later stages, but during the major part of the fieldwork the responsibility for balancing the needs of the archaeology and the wider project fell to Barbara Doig, as Project Sponsor, Martin Mustard as Project Manager and John Gibbons; all were very positive and supportive. Bill Armstrong, as the first project manager, helped put in place the structure within which the archaeology took place. Day-today contact with the Holyrood Parliament Project Team was through Paul Grice, Eric Kinsey, Shona Lines, and especially, John Paterson, who made major contributions to the efficient running the project. John Hyne and Alan Mack, of what was Bovis Europe, the construction management contractor helped co-ordinate our work with the construction.

The work on site was ably undertaken by a consortium of Headland Archaeology and SUAT Ltd. The archaeological work on site was directed by Colm Moloney for Headland Archaeology and Russel Coleman for SUAT Ltd. Particular mention should be made of the considerable skill with which Colm and Russel and their team fitted their work around the increasingly complex demolition and construction work.

When it was determined by the Holyrood Parliament Project Team that the internal 19th- and 20th-century plaster finishes of Queensberry House had to be removed, this work was undertaken with great skill by the firm of Kinsley & Bolton, supervised on site by Stuart McGeachie. Invaluable assistance was given in the early stages of the project by the demolition contractor, Demolition Services Ltd. Liaison with the architects EMBT/RMJM over Queensberry House, where the archaeology project provided information about the building to assist design work, was handled very effectively by Nira Ponniah. The initial assessment of Queensberry House was undertaken by Simpson & Brown Architects in 1997, and subsequent analysis by Addyman & Kay Ltd (aided by Kenneth Macfadyen and Shelley Brown).

The task of drawing all the parts of the report together into the first full draft was undertaken by Gordon Barclay. Thirteen distinguished referees, inside and outside Historic Scotland, then read and commented upon the draft text, and we are very grateful to them for their invaluable help. The co-editor of the report, Anna Ritchie, then undertook the daunting task of preparing the final draft, with the assistance of Jackie Henrie, who undertook the rigorous task of copy-editing the final text.

Assistance was afforded by individuals and organisations throughout the project. Gordon Ewart of Kirkdale Archaeology undertook early archaeological survey and trial trenching. Alistair Knowles, Office Premises Manager for Scottish & Newcastle Brewers, allowed access to the eastern part of the site and to the S&N archives in the early weeks of the project, when S&N were still in occupation. Mark Collard, then Edinburgh City Archaeologist, was supportive throughout the fieldwork. David Hogg and David Simon provided reconstruction drawings and visualisations during the project. Morag Cross contributed to the historical research.

We are very grateful for assistance with illustrations to Christopher Fleet (National Library of Scotland, Map Library), Gordon Ewart (Kirkdale Archaeology) and David Henrie. Chingman Chan undertook picture research, Catriona Armit created the index and Kevin MacLeod scanned and manipulated the digital images, and we are very grateful for their help. Inlingua Language Centre, Edinburgh, provided the French and German translations of the Summary, and Donald Stewart kindly undertook the Gaelic translation.

Individual author acknowledgements are made in the Notes to each Chapter.

Detailed reports on the artefacts were provided by Adrian Cox, Dennis Gallagher, Derek Hall, Nicholas Holmes, Robin Murdoch, Effie Photos-Jones and Clare Thomas and on the environmental remains by Ruby Ceron-Carrasco, Stephen Carter, Tim Holden, Mhairi Hastie and Catherine Smith, and these reports will be published in full elsewhere.

We are very grateful to the Society of Antiquaries of Scotland for exceptional help with this publication, in particular to Alison Rae as Production Manager and her team, Lawrie Law, Graham Lumsden and Kevin Hicks.

The following institutions were kind enough to supply artwork and to give permission for its use: Royal Commission on the Ancient and Historical Monuments of Scotland, Trustees of the National Library of Scotland, Edinburgh City Archives, National Gallery of Scotland, British Library, National Trust, Scottish Record Office, Edinburgh City Art Centre, SCRAN and Scottish Brewers Association. Except where otherwise attributed in the captions, all illustrations are Crown Copyright: Historic Scotland.

The project received interest and support from Scotland's first and second First Ministers, Donald Dewar and Henry McLeish, both of whom visited the site (fig 1.2), and the lead architect of the Holyrood complex, Enric Miralles.

GORDON J BARCLAY and ANNA RITCHIE
Edinburgh, 2008

List of figures

Summary

The choice in 1998 of the Holyrood area for the site of the new Scottish Parliament involved as a first stage of its development both archaeological excavation and architectural analysis, the results of which are described in this volume. Situated in Canongate at the foot of the Royal Mile in Edinburgh, the site encompassed the former Scottish & Newcastle Breweries (which were demolished) and Queensberry House (which was to be part of the new Parliament). The area was known to have been part of the medieval burgh of Canongate and in the 17th and 18th centuries to have included two other major townhouses, Haddington House and Lothian Hut, in addition to Queensberry House. Excavations were carried out in 1998 and 1999 by Headland Archaeology Ltd and SUAT Ltd, and the recording and analysis of Queensberry House by Addyman & Kay Ltd took place in 1999, 2000 and 2001. Running in tandem with the practical work on site was intensive historical research by Patricia Dennison and John Lowrey. The history of the site explored by these means spans nine hundred years of busy urban life from the 12th to the 20th centuries.

When Holyrood Abbey was established in the 12th century, the abbey was allowed to found a burgh in order to attract commerce and create wealth: the burgh of Canongate, which was separate from the burghs of Edinburgh and Leith. Once Holyrood developed as a royal palace, Canongate became a fashionable place for Scotland's leading noble families to build townhouses and remained so until the later 18th century, when its fortunes declined and the fine houses were gradually replaced by slums, hospitals for the poor and breweries. The archaeological evidence for all this activity has been divided into five broad periods and is presented in Chapter 3: Period 1 covering the 12th to 14th centuries, Period 2 the 14th and 15th centuries, Period 3 the 16th to 18th centuries, Period 4 the 17th and 18th centuries and Period 5 the 19th and 20th centuries. The earliest major feature was a substantial ditch dug in Period 1 probably to enclose an area used for cultivation by the abbey, which was redeveloped in the 14th century as long narrow burgage plots that ran from the Canongate street downslope to the line of the modern Holyrood Road. Compared to burgage plots in other burghs such as Perth and Aberdeen, the Canongate plots showed a surprising, and interesting, low level of usage for craft-working and cultivation, which may relate to the high social status of their owners. Iron-working and possibly tanning of hides were among the activities that appear to have taken place here in medieval times. Leading from glazed windows was discovered, along with part of an inlaid floor tile which implies the presence of a prestigious building, and a bone die reflects the board games that were played by the inhabitants. The bulk of their pottery was local Scottish White Gritty ware, but they were also buying pottery imported from the Rhinelands and France, and jars of olives from Spain. From Period 3 in the 16th century came part of a tile from the sort of ceramic stove most commonly found in religious buildings. Metal pins and a thimble suggest that among the shops along the Canongate were the premises of a tailor, but the construction of Queensberry House has largely obliterated the structural traces of the medieval frontage. Incorporated into the fabric of Queensberry House are, however, building materials derived from earlier buildings on the site, including dressed stone from windows and fireplaces, roofing material and structural timbers.

Soil analysis confirmed that coal had been the dominant source of fuel from very early on until the 17th century, when the area was turned into formal gardens, and this radical change in land-use is also reflected by the fact that carbonised grain was found only in the early levels. The influence of the nearby abbey may perhaps be seen in the animal bones recovered from the site, in which sheep dominate over cattle, unlike most other east coast burghs where cattle is the dominant component. Wool and sheepskins were the staple goods of the Scottish economy in the medieval period, and abbeys maintained large flocks of sheep. In terms of protein, the Canongate diet appears to have consisted of mutton and lamb, beef, pork, rabbit, hare, poultry, partridge, red grouse, cormorant, fish and shellfish, particularly oysters.

After the Union of the Crowns in 1603, the royal court moved from Holyrood to Westminster, but the burgh of Canongate continued to thrive, despite the disruptions caused by warfare and epidemics of disease. A fashion for smoking pipes grew rapidly during the 17th century and most of the broken pipes found in the excavations date from between about 1630 and 1680. Holyrood Palace was reconstructed in the 1670s and became the focus once again of Scottish politics, with the result that Canongate recaptured its status as a very desirable place to live. Leading noble families wished to acquire residences as close to the Palace as possible, and Queensberry House is a survivor of a group of fine 17th-century mansions at the Holyrood end of the burgh.

Queensberry House remains today an imposing townhouse with a complex architectural history. It began as Balmakellie's Great Lodging, built in 1667–70 by Dame Margaret Douglas of Balmakellie, and became Hatton House when it was acquired and renovated by Lord Hatton from 1679, later becoming Queensberry House when it was taken over by the first Duke of Queensberry in 1688. About two thirds of the house as it survives date from the Balmakellie phase. It was designed as a T-shaped building with three stories above a double-level ground floor, its exterior harled and lime-washed, and Lord Hatton added a belvedere, or viewing tower, the remains of which were discovered in the attic during the archaeological investigations. All plaster wall coverings were removed and this has enabled a detailed history of the practical use of the building to be matched to its documented history. The design of the rear façade of the house was enlivened by two large shaped gables of Dutch type, a feature in common with many houses of this period in Scotland that reflects important mercantile links with the Netherlands. Formal gardens are documented to the rear of the house, and the excavations revealed remains of a raised terrace with a central stair leading down into the garden. In many respects the Balmakellie house combined contemporary urban architecture with that of country houses.

Apart from alterations to the house itself, Lord Hatton acquired neighbouring properties in order to create space around the house for service courts and stables. Invaluable information about Hatton House and its furnishings survives in a document dated 22 March 1681 and titled *Instructions for my hous in the Canongait with the Courts yrof etc*, including a description of two rooms in the tower, and a painting by Thomas Sandby around 1746 depicts the tower with a parapet.

By the mid-1680s, Lord Hatton, by then the Earl of Lauderdale, faced political failure, allegations of corruption and crippling debt, and he sold Hatton House to the Queensberry family. Major renovation was undertaken by the second Duke of Queensberry from 1695, when the first of a series of detailed inventories was drawn up which has provided much useful information about the furnishing and function of the house. The architect in charge of the rebuilding was James Smith, who had worked for the first Duke at Drumlanrig Castle, and at Queensberry House he added a new west wing, a single-storey vestibule on the Canongate façade and two closet towers at either end of the garden façade. William Edgar's survey of Edinburgh in 1742 depicts the formal gardens of Queensberry House in their heyday, when they seem to have been used as nursery grounds for the Drumlanrig gardens, and it is clear from the inventories that the gardens were embellished by gilded flowerpots and statues. One of the more unusual items found by excavation in the soil of the gardens is an 18th-century wig curler. At the foot of the gardens was an orchard, which was enlarged and became the major feature of the grounds by the later 18th century.

Haddington House was built at the south-west part of the Parliament site in the 18th century, between Reid's Close and Haddington's Entry. Two walls survived above ground and had been incorporated into the perimeter wall of the later Queensberry House Hospital, and traces of the other walls and a contemporary well were found during excavation. Parlour games such as carpet bowls would have been popular in wealthier Victorian households, and fragments of one made in a glazed ceramic were retrieved from deposits within the footprint of Haddington House.

The 18th-century townhouse known somewhat incongruously as Lothian Hut, belonging originally to the Marquis of Lothian, occupied the eastern part of the Parliament site and was redeveloped as a brewery in the later 19th century. Excavation revealed that the old medieval backlands had been replaced by large structural plinths and foundations for buildings that were later demolished.

The development of the New Town of Edinburgh seems to have led to a decline in the prestige of Canongate as a fashionable place to live in the 18th century. Queensberry House was rented out and no major renovation was attempted, indeed after it was sold to William Aitchison in 1801 the house was stripped of its fine interior fittings. Major alterations were undertaken by the Board of Ordnance around 1808–11 in order to turn the house into a military hospital and barracks, and the old gardens became a parade ground with a quartermaster's store to one side. Among the alterations was the remodelling of the attic floor into a full third floor with the consequent loss of the belvedere and the Dutch gables. Minor changes were made as the house became accommodation for the destitute as a House of Refuge from the 1830s, and the process of modernisation continued as its role gradually evolved into that of a hospital for the care of the elderly in the 20th century. Thus the development of Queensberry House mirrored that of the Canongate through all these centuries, and this volume sets the house and the new Parliament site into their wider historical context as part of the capital of Scotland.

Résumé

Le choix de Holyrood en 1998 pour le site du nouveau Parlement écossais, a fait intervenir au stade initial de son développement, des fouilles archéologiques et une analyse architecturale dont les résultats sont décrits dans ce volume. Situé à Canongate, au pied du Royal Mile à Édimbourg, le site couvre les anciennes Brasseries Scottish & Newcastle (qui ont été démolies) et Queensberry House (qui allait faire partie du nouveau Parlement). On savait que le quartier avait fait partie du bourg médiéval de Canongate et au XVII et XVIIIe siècles, il comprenait deux autres importants hôtels particuliers, Haddington House et Lothian Hut, en plus de Queensberry House. Les fouilles ont été effectuées en 1998 et 1999 par Headland Archaeology Ltd et SUAT Ltd, et l'enregistrement et l'analyse de Queensberry House par Addyman & Kay Ltd ont pris place en 1999, 2000 et 2001. Parallèlement au travail pratique sur le site, d'intenses recherches historiques ont été menées par Patricia Dennison et John Lowrey. L'histoire du site exploré par ces personnes couvre neuf cent ans de vie urbaine foisonnante du XIIe au XXe siècle.

Lorsque l'abbaye de Holyrood fut établie au XIIe siècle, celle-ci eut le droit de fonder un bourg afin d'attirer le commerce et créer des richesses : le bourg de Canongate, qui se distinguait des bourgs d'Édimbourg et de Leith. Lorsque Holyrood fut transformé en palais royal, Canongate devint un lieu très à la mode pour les principales familles nobles d'Écosse qui construisirent des hôtels particuliers et restèrent là jusqu'au XVIIIe siècle, époque à laquelle leurs fortunes déclinèrent et les belles maisons firent progressivement place aux taudis, aux hôpitaux pour les pauvres et aux brasseries. Les preuves archéologiques de toute cette activité ont été réparties en cinq vastes périodes et sont présentées au chapitre 3 : la Période 1 couvre le XIIe au XIVe siècle, la Période 2 le XIVe et le XVe siècles, la Période 3 le XVIe au XVIIIe siècle, la Période 4 le XVIIe et XVIIIe siècles et la Période 5 le XIXe et XXe siècles. Le plus ancien élément majeur découvert fut un fossé important creusé à la Période 1, sans doute pour entourer une zone utilisée pour les cultures de l'abbaye, qui fut redéveloppée au XIVe siècle pour devenir des terrains à bâtir longs et étroits qui s'étendaient de Canongate street jusqu'à la moderne Holyrood Road. Comparés aux parcelles à bâtir d'autres bourgs tels que Perth et Aberdeen, les parcelles de Canongate faisaient preuve d'un faible niveau d'utilisation d'artisanat et de culture ce qui est à la fois intéressant et surprenant, et est sans doute lié au statut social élevé de ses propriétaires. La ferronnerie et peut-être le tannage de peaux faisaient partie des activités qui semblent avoir pris place au Moyen-Âge. Des plombures de vitraux ont été découvertes, ainsi que des fragments de carreaux incrustés pour le sol indiquent la présence de bâtiments prestigieux et un dé en os montre que les habitants jouaient à des jeux de société. L'ensemble de leur poterie était d'origine locale mais ils achetaient également des poteries importées de Rhénanie et de France, et des pots d'olives d'Espagne. De la Période 3 au XVIe siècle on a trouvé un fragment d'un carreau de la sorte de poêle en céramique essentiellement trouvé dans les bâtiments religieux. Des épingles en métal et un dé à coudre suggèrent que parmi les boutiques de Canongate se trouvait un tailleur, mais la construction de Queensberry House a en grande partie effacé les traces structurelles de la devanture médiévale. Incorporés à la structure de Queensberry House, toutefois, se trouvent des matériaux de construction dérivés d'anciens bâtiments du site, notamment des pierres dressées provenant de fenêtres et de cheminées, du matériau de toiture et des poutres structurelles.

L'analyse du sol a confirmé que le charbon avait été la principale source d'énergie depuis très longtemps et jusqu'au XVIIe siècle, époque à laquelle le quartier fut transformé en jardins à la française, et ce changement radical dans l'utilisation du sol est également reflété par le fait que des céréales carbonisées ont été trouvées uniquement dans les couches anciennes. L'influence de l'abbaye voisine est peut-être constatée dans les ossements d'animaux retrouvés sur le site, où les montons dominaient par rapport aux bovins, contrairement à la plupart des autres bourgs de l'Est où les bovins représentaient l'élément dominant. La laine et les peaux de moutons étaient les marchandises de base de l'économie écossaise à l'époque médiévale, et les abbayes possédaient de gros troupeaux de moutons. Il semble que l'alimentation du quartier de Canongate, en termes de protéines, se composait de mouton et d'agneau, de bœuf, de porc, de lapin, de lièvre, de volaille, de perdrix, de coq de bruyère, de cormoran, de poissons et crustacés, notamment d'huîtres.

Après l'Union des couronnes en 1603, la cour royale quitta Holyrood pour Westminster, mais le bourg de Canongate continua de prospérer, malgré les perturbations causées par les guerres et les épidémies. La mode de fumer la pipe se développa rapidement au XVIIe siècle et la plupart des pipes cassées trouvées durant les fouilles datent d'entre 1630 et 1680. Le palais de Holyrood fut reconstruit dans les années 1670 et devint à nouveau le point central de la politique écossaise, ce qui rendit à Canongate son statut de quartier d'habitation très prisé. Les grandes familles de nobles souhaitaient acquérir des maisons aussi proches du palais que possible, et Queensberry House est un vestige d'un groupe de grandes maisons du XVIIe siècle, proches du palais de Holyrood.

Queensberry House demeure aujourd'hui un hôtel particulier imposant avec une histoire architecturale complexe. Son histoire commença par Balmakellie's Great Lodging, construit entre 1667 et 1670 par Dame Margaret Douglas of Balmakellie, et devint Hatton House lors de son acquisition et rénovation par Lord Hatton à partir de 1679. La maison devint Queensberry House lorsqu'elle fut rachetée par le premier Duc de Queensberry en 1688. Les deux tiers environ de la maison telle qu'elle a survécu, datent de la phase Balmakellie. Elle fut conçue comme un bâtiment en T avec trois étages au-dessus d'un rez-de-chaussée double, et son extérieur était crépi et passé à la chaux. Lord Hatton ajouta un belvédère, ou tour de guet, dont les vestiges ont été découverts dans le grenier durant les fouilles archéologiques. Tous les plâtres des murs ont été retirés et ceci a permis un historique détaillé de l'usage pratique du bâtiment qui correspond à son historique documenté. La conception de la façade arrière de la maison était enjolivée par deux larges pignons de type hollandais, élément commun à de nombreuses maisons de cette époque en Écosse et qui reflète les importants liens marchands avec les Pays Bas. Les jardins à la française sont documentés à l'arrière de la maison et les fouilles ont révélé les vestiges d'une terrasse surélevée avec un escalier central donnant dans le jardin. À de nombreux

égards, Balmakellie house associait une architecture urbaine contemporaine et celle des manoirs ruraux.

En dehors des modifications apportées à la maison même, Lord Hatton devint propriétaire de plusieurs propriétés voisines afin de créer de l'espace autour de sa maison pour les communs et les écuries. Des informations inestimables sur Hatton House et son ameublement survivent dans un document daté du 22 mars 1681 et intitulé *Instructions for my hous in the Canongait with the Courts yrof etc*, comprenant une description de deux pièces de la tour, et un tableau de Thomas Sandby datant de 1746 environ qui décrit la tour avec un parapet.

Au milieu des années 1680, Lord Hatton, qui était alors devenu Comte de Lauderdale, connut l'échec politique, des soupçons de corruption et des dettes insurmontables. Il vendit donc Hatton House à la famille Queensberry. Une rénovation très importante fut entreprise par le second Duc de Queensberry à partir de 1695, époque à laquelle la première série d'inventaires détaillés fut rédigée ce qui a fourni des informations très utiles sur l'ameublement et la fonction de la maison. L'architecte en charge de la reconstruction était James Smith, qui avait travaillé pour le premier Duc au château de Drumlanrig, et à Queensberry House, il ajouta une nouvelle aile ouest, un vestibule à un seul étage sur la façade côté Canongate, et deux tours à cabinets de chaque côté de la façade côté jardin. L'étude topographique d'Édimbourg par William Edgar en 1742 décrit les jardins à la française de Queensberry House durant leur âge d'or, où il semble qu'ils aient servi de pépinières pour les jardins de Drumlanrig, et il est clair d'après les inventaires que les jardins étaient embellis par des vasques dorées et des statues. L'un des objets les plus inhabituels trouvé lors des fouilles dans le sol des jardins est un fer à friser pour perruque datant du XVIIIe siècle. Au pied des jardins se trouvait un verger, qui fut agrandi et devint une caractéristique majeure des jardins de la fin du XVIIIe siècle.

Haddington House fut construite dans la partie sud-ouest du site du Parlement au XVIIIe siècle, entre Reid's Close et Haddington's Entry. Deux murs ont survécu au-dessus du sol et ont été incorporé au mur d'enceinte de l'ancien Hôpital de Queensberry House, et des traces des autres murs ainsi qu'un puits contemporain ont été découverts durant les fouilles. Les jeux de salon tels que le jeu de boules sur tapis étaient sans doute très populaires dans les demeures victoriennes cossus, et des fragments d'une boule en céramique vernissée ont été extraits de gisements au pied de Haddington House.

L'hôtel particulier du XVIIIe siècle connu de manière quelque peu incongrue sous le nom de Lothian Hut, qui appartenait à l'origine au Marquis de Lothian, occupait la partie est du site du Parlement et fut transformé en une brasserie à la fin du XIXe siècle. Les fouilles ont révélé que l'ancien parc médiéval avait été remplacé par de larges socles structurels et fondations de bâtiments qui furent démolis par la suite.

Le développement du quartier de New Town à Édimbourg semble avoir entraîné un déclin dans le prestige de Canongate en tant que quartier d'habitation à la mode au XVIIIe siècle. Queensberry House fut louée à des particuliers et aucune rénovation importante ne fut tentée. En fait, après sa vente à William Aitchison en 1801, la maison fut dépouillée de tous ses éléments intérieurs de luxe. D'importants travaux furent entrepris par le Board of Ordnance (*Bureau d'intendance militaire*)

aux alentours de 1808–1811 afin de transformer la maison en hôpital militaire et en caserne, et les anciens jardins devinrent un champ de manœuvres avec un magasin d'intendance sur un côté. Les travaux ont impliqué notamment la transformation des combles en un troisième étage complet, ce qui a entraîné la perte du belvédère et des pignons hollandais. Des changements mineurs ont été apportés au moment où la maison nommée House of Refuge fut utilisée pour loger les pauvres dans les années 1830, et le processus de modernisation continua au fur et à mesure que son rôle évolua pour devenir un hospice au XXe siècle. Ainsi, l'évolution de Queensberry House reflète celle de Canongate à travers les siècles, et ce volume place la maison et le site du nouveau Parlement dans son contexte historique plus large en tant qu'élément de la capitale de l'Écosse.

Zusammenfassung

Als die Wahl 1998 auf Holyrood als Standort des neuen Schottischen Parlaments fiel, waren in seiner Entwicklungsgeschichte zuerst einmal archäologische Ausgrabungen, jedoch auch architektonische Analysen nötig, mit deren Ergebnissen sich dieser Band beschäftigt. Es liegt im Canongate, am Fuße der Royal Mile in Edinburgh und an seiner Stelle befanden sich früher die Scottish and Newcastle Brauereien (die abgerissen wurden) sowie Queensberry House (das nun Teil des neuen Parlaments ist). Von der Gegend ist bekannt, dass sie Teil des mittelalterlichen Burghs von Canongate war und sich dort im 17. und 18. Jahrhundert, zusätzlich zu Queensberry House, noch zwei weitere bedeutende Stadthäuser befanden, nämlich Haddington House und Lothian Hut. Headland Archaeology Ltd. und SUAT Ltd. führten 1998 und 1999 die Ausgrabungen durch und 1999, 2000 und 2001 wurden die Einzelheiten von Queensberry House durch Addyman & Kay Ltd. aufgezeichnet und analysiert. Zeitgleich mit den praktischen Arbeiten vor Ort, stellten Patricia Dennison und John Lowrey intensive historische Nachforschungen an. Die so erforschte Geschichte dieses Orts umfasst neunhundert Jahre regen städtischen Lebens, vom 12. bis hin zum 20. Jahrhundert.

Als Holyrood Abbey im 12. Jahrhundert erbaut wurde, erlaubte man es der Abtei, um Handel anzuziehen und Wohlstand zu schaffen, ein Burgh zu gründen, das Burgh Canongate, das sich von den

Burghs Edinburgh und Leith abgrenzte. Als Holyrood sich zum königlichen Palast entwickelte, galt es für Schottlands wichtigste adlige Familien als modern, im Canongate Stadthäuser zu bauen. Dieser Status änderte sich erst im späteren 18. Jahrhundert, als der Wohlstand dort nachließ und die herrschaftlichen Häuser nach und nach durch Elendsviertel, Armenkrankenhäuser und Brauereien ersetzt wurden. Die archäologischen Beweise für all diese Aktivitäten wurden grob in fünf Zeitabschnitte eingeteilt und werden in Kapitel 3 dargelegt: Abschnitt 1 – 12. bis 14. Jahrhundert, Abschnitt 2 – 14. und 15. Jahrhundert, Abschnitt 3 – 16. bis 18. Jahrhundert, Abschnitt 4 – 17. und 18. Jahrhundert und Abschnitt 5 – 19. und 20. Jahrhundert. Das früheste bedeutende Merkmal war ein in Abschnitt 1 ausgehobener, beachtlicher Graben, der höchstwahrscheinlich einen Bereich abgrenzte, der von der Abtei zur Bewirtschaftung genutzt wurde und im 14. Jahrhundert als lange schmale Bürgerlehen vergeben wurde, die sich von der Straße im Canongate bis hin zum Verlauf der modernen Holyrood Road hinab erstreckten. Im Vergleich zu Bürgerlehen in anderen Burghs, wie z.B. Perth und Aberdeen, wiesen die Anbauflächen im Canongate einen erstaunlich geringen Grad der Verwendung für Kultivierung und Bewirtschaftung auf, was vielleicht im Zusammenhang mit dem hohen sozialen Status deren Besitzer steht. Zu den im Mittelalter scheinbar hier ausgeführten Aktivitäten zählen Kunstschmiedearbeiten und möglicherweise das Gerben von Häuten. Es wurden Verbleiungen verglaster Fenster sowie ein Stück einer eingelegten Bodenfliese entdeckt, was auf das Vorhandensein eines prestigeträchtigen Gebäudes schließen lässt. Ein Knochenwürfel lässt Aufschlüsse über die Brettspiele zu, denen seine Bewohner nachgingen. Beim Großteil ihrer Steinzeuge handelte es sich um schottisches White Gritty aus der Region, sie kauften jedoch auch Tonwaren, die aus dem Rheinland und aus Frankreich importiert wurden. Des Weiteren fand man Gefäße spanischer Oliven. Aus Abschnitt 3 im 16. Jahrhundert stammt der Teil einer Kachel, die für jene Keramiköfen verwendet wurden, die am häufigsten in religiösen Gebäuden anzutreffen waren. Metallstifte und ein Fingerhut weisen darauf hin, dass sich unter den Geschäften entlang des Canongate auch die Werkstatt eines Schneiders befand, jedoch wurden die baulichen Spuren der mittelalterlichen Straßenfront durch den Bau des Queensberry House weitgehend verwischt. In das strukturelle Gefüge des Queensberry House wurden jedoch auch Baumaterialien, wie z.B. von Fenstern und Feuerstellen stammende Bruchsteine, Bedachungsmaterialien und Bauholz miteingeschlossen, die aus sich früher an diesem Ort befindlichen Gebäuden stammten.

Bodenanalysen haben bestätigt, dass seit sehr früher Zeit bis in das 17. Jahrhundert hinein Kohle die vorherrschende Brennstoffquelle war. Danach wurde das Gebiet in Barockgärten umgestaltet und auch dieser radikale Wandel der Landnutzung spiegelt sich in der Tatsache wider, dass sich nur in den frühen Schichten Spuren von Kohle fanden. Der Einfluss der nahegelegenen Abtei lässt sich möglicherweise aufgrund der vor Ort gefundenen Tierknochen erahnen, bei denen Schafe die Oberhand über die Rinder hatten. Dies steht im Kontrast zu den meisten anderen Burghs der Ostküste, bei denen Rinder die dominierende Komponente darstellten. Wolle und Schaffelle zählten im Schottland des Mittelalters zu den Grundbedarfsgütern und Abteien hielten zumeist große Schafherden. Im Hinblick auf Proteine schien die Ernährung im Canongate sich aus Hammel- und Lammfleisch, Rindfleisch, Schweinefleisch, Kaninchen, Hasen, Geflügel, Rebhühnern, Moorschneehühnern, Kormoranen, Fisch und Schalentieren, insbesondere Austern, zusammenzusetzen.

1603, nach der "Union of the Crowns", zog der königliche Hof von Holyrood nach Westminster um. Das Burgh Canongate florierte jedoch, trotz den durch kriegerische Auseinandersetzungen und Krankheitsepidemien verursachten Störungen, nach wie vor. Im Laufe des 17. Jahrhunderts entwickelte sich das Rauchen von Pfeifen schnell zur Mode und die meisten der bei den Ausgrabungen gefundenen, kaputten Pfeifen, datieren aus dem Zeitraum zwischen etwa 1630 und 1680. In den 1670ern wurde Holyrood Palace wieder aufgebaut und entwickelte sich erneut zum Mittelpunkt schottischer Politik. Dies hatte zur Folge, dass das Canongate seinen Status als sehr begehrte Wohngegend zurückeroberte. Wichtige adlige Familien wollten Domizile so nahe wie möglich am Palast erwerben und Queensberry House blieb, aus einer Gruppe sich am Holyrood-Ende des Burghs befindlicher herrschaftlicher Wohnsitze des 17. Jahrhunderts, erhalten.

Queensberry House bleibt bis zum heutigen Tag ein eindrucksvolles Stadthaus mit einer komplexen architektonischen Geschichte. Seine Anfänge nahm es als, 1667–70 von Dame Margaret Douglas of Balmakellie erbautes, Balmakellie´s Great Lodging und wurde ab 1679, nachdem es von Lord Hatton erworben und renoviert worden war zu Hatton House. Nach der Übernahme durch den ersten Duke of Queensberry, 1688, erhielt es den Namen Queensberry House. Etwa zwei Drittel des Hauses in seiner heutigen Form stammen aus der Balmakellie-Phase. Es wurde als T-förmiges Gebäude mit drei Stockwerken über einem Erdgeschoss auf zwei Ebenen entworfen. Seine Aussenfassade wurde mit Rauputz versehen und getüncht. Lord Hatton fügte ein Belvedere, oder einen Aussichtsturm, hinzu, dessen Überreste im Rahmen der archäologischen Nachforschungen auf dem Dachboden gefunden wurden. Der gesamte Wandputz wurde entfernt. So konnte eine detaillierte Geschichte der praktischen Nutzung des Gebäudes mit seiner dokumentierten Geschichte in Einklang gebracht werden. Die Gestaltung der rückwärtigen Fassade des Hauses wurde durch zwei große, nach holländischer Art geformte Giebel aufgelockert. Dieses Merkmal wiesen viele schottische Häuser dieser Epoche auf, wodurch die wichtigen Handelsbeziehungen mit den Niederlanden zu erkennen waren. Es ist belegt, dass sich auf der Rückseite des Hauses Barockgärten befanden und die Ausgrabungen förderten Überreste einer erhöhten Terrasse zutage, von der aus eine mittig angelegte Treppe in den Garten hinunterführte. In vielerlei Hinsicht vereinte das Balmakellie House zeitgenössische städtische Architektur mit jener von Landhäusern.

Zusätzlich zu den am Haus selbst vorgenommenen Änderungen, erwarb Lord Hatton auch noch angrenzende Liegenschaften, um Platz für Dienstbotenunterkünfte und Stallungen um das Haus herum zu schaffen. Ein auf den 22. März 1681 datiertes, erhalten gebliebenes Dokument mit dem Titel „*Instructions for my hous in the Canongait with the Courts yrof etc*", liefert äußerst wertvolle Informationen über Hatton House sowie dessen Innenausstattung. Unter anderem findet sich darin eine Beschreibung zweier Räume im Turm und ein Gemälde von Thomas Sandy von etwa 1746 stellt den Turm mit einer Brüstung dar.

Mitte der 1680er fand Lord Hatton, damals bereits Earl of Lauderdale, sich mit seinem politischen Versagen, Korruptionsvorwürfen und lähmenden Schulden konfrontiert und verkaufte Hatton House an das Geschlecht derer von Queensberry. Ab 1695 ließ der zweite Duke of Queensberry großangelegte Renovierungsarbeiten durchführen. Seinerzeit wurde auch die erste einer Reihe detaillierter Inventarlisten erstellt, die äußerst nützliche Informationen über die Innenausstattung sowie die Funktion des Hauses lieferte. Der für die Erneuerung verantwortliche Archititekt war James Smith, der bereits für den ersten Duke an Drumlanrig Castle gearbeitet hatte. Dem Queensberry House fügte er einen neuen Westflügel, ein einstöckiges Vestibül an der Canongate-Fassade sowie zwei Wohntürme an den jeweiligen Enden der Gartenfassade hinzu. Die von William Edgar angestellte Studie Edinburghs im Jahre 1742 beschreibt die Barockgärten des Queensberry House in Ihrer Blütezeit, während derer sie offensichtlich als Anzuchtstätte für die Gärten von Drumlanrig benutzt wurden und aus den Inventarlisten geht hervor, dass die Gärten mit vergoldeten Blumentöpfen und Statuen geschmückt waren. Einer der eher ungewöhnlicheren, bei den Ausgrabungen im Erdreich der Gärten zutage geförderten Gegenstände, ist ein Lockenwickler für Perücken aus dem 18. Jahrhundert. Am Fuße der Gärten befand sich ein Obstgarten, der im späteren 18. Jahrhundert vergrößert und zum bedeutendsten Merkmal der Anlage wurde.

Haddington House wurde im 18. Jahrhundert im südwestlichen Bereich des Standorts des Parlaments, zwischen Reid´s Close und Haddington´s Entry, erbaut. Zwei über der Erde liegende Mauern blieben erhalten und wurden in die, das spätere Queensberry House Hospital umgebende Mauer miteingearbeitet.

Des Weiteren stieß man im Laufe der Ausgrabungen auf Spuren der anderen Mauern sowie auf einen aus der damaligen Zeit stammenden Brunnen. Gesellschaftsspiele, wie z.B. Rasen-Bowls, waren in wohlhabenderen Haushalten der viktorianischen Zeit sehr beliebt und man fand Teile eines solchen, aus glasierter Keramik bestehenden Spiels, in den Überresten auf dem Gelände von Haddinton House.

Der östliche Teil des Standorts des neuen Parlaments wurde von dem etwas unpassend als Lothian Hut bezeichneten Stadthaus des 18. Jahrhunderts eingenommen, das sich ursprünglich im Besitz des Marquis of Lothian befand und im späteren 19. Jahrhundert zu einer Brauerei umgebaut wurde. Die Ausgrabungen machten deutlich, dass die mittelalterlichen Ländereien durch große tragende Sockel und Fundamente später abgerissener Gebäude ersetzt worden waren.

Die Entwicklung von Edinburghs New Town scheint im 18. Jahrhundert dem Prestige von Canongate als begehrter Wohngegend abträglich gewesen zu sein. Queensberry House wurde vermietet und es wurden keine größeren Renovierungen in Angriff genommen. Ganz im Gegenteil wurde es nach seinem Verkauf an William Aitchison, 1801, seiner herrlichen Innenausstattung beraubt. In etwa zwischen 1808–11 wurden vom *Board of Ordnance* (militärischen Ausschuss) bedeutende Veränderungen vorgenommen, um das Haus in ein Lazarett sowie eine Kaserne umzuwandeln. Die alten Gärten wurden zu einem Exerzierplatz umfunktioniert, an dessen einem Ende sich ein Versorgungslager befand. Die Änderungen umfassten unter anderem die Umgestaltung des Dachbodens in einen vollständigen dritten Stock, wodurch das Belvedere sowie die holländischen Giebel verloren gingen. Als sich das Haus ab den 1830ern als House of Refuge zu einer Unterkunft für Mittellose entwickelte, wurden weitere kleine Veränderungen vorgenommen und die Modernisierung setzte sich fort, als ihm im 20. Jahrhundert nach und nach die Rolle eines Krankenhauses zur Altenpflege zufiel. Daher spiegelte die Entwicklung von Queensberry House jene des Canongate über all diese Jahrhunderte hinweg wider und dieser Band bringt das Haus und den Standort des neuen Parlaments in ihren weiteren historischen Kontext als Teil der schottischen Hauptstadt.

Giorrachadh

As dèidh do dh' àrainn Thaigh an Ròid a bhith air a taghadh mar làrach Phàrlamaid ùr na h-Alba, thòisicheadh air an obair an dà chuid le cladhach airceòlach agus le rannsachadh ailtireachd. Anns an leabhar seo thathas a' toirt tuairisgeul air na toraidhean. Suidhichte anns a' Canongate aig bonn na Mìle Rìoghail ann an Dùn Èideann, bha làrach a' gabhail a-steach sheann Taighean-Grùide Scottish and Newcastle (a chaidh a leagail) agus Taigh Queensberry (a bhiodh 'na phàirt den Phàrlamaid ùir). Bha uair ann a bha àrainneachd seo mar phàirt de bhorgh meadhan-aoiseach Chanongate. Anns an 17mh agus an 18mh linntean, a thuilleadh air Taigh Queensberry fhèin bha dà thaigh-baile mòr eile rim faighinn an seo: Taigh Haddington agus Bothan Lòdainn. Ann an 1998 agus 1999 chaidh cladhaichean a dhèanamh le Headland Archaeology Earr. agus SUAT Earr., agus rinneadh obair-clàraidh agus obair-rannsachaidh ann an Taigh Queensberry le Addyman & Kay Earr. ann an 1999, 2000, agus 2001. Ann an co-bhuinn ris an obair phraictigich seo rinn Patricia Dennison agus John Lowrey mion-rannsachadh eachdraidheil. Tha an eachdraidh a chaidh sgrùdadh leo a' sìneadh tro naoi ceud bliadhna de bheatha dhripeil a' bhaile mhòir, eadar an 12na linn agus am 20mh.

Nuair a chaidh Abaid Thaigh an Ròid a stèidheachadh anns an 12na linn, thugadh cead don abaid borgh a chur air bhonn gus malairt a thàladh thuice, agus ionmhas a chruthachadh. B' e siud borgh Chanongate, a bha uair air leth bho bhuirgh Dhùn Éideann agus Lìte. Aon uair's gun do rinneadh àros rìoghail de Thaigh an Ròid, dh' fhàs Canongate fasanta 's e 'na àite far an togadh mòr-uaisleachd na h-Alba taighean-baile. Mhair e mar seo gu ruige anmoch 's an 18mh linn, nuair a thàinig earra-dhubh air an àite. Mean air mhean chaidh slumaichean, ospadail do dhaoine bochda, agus taighean-grùide a thogail an àite nan taighean spaideil a bh' ann. Tha na th' ann de dh' fhianais airceòlaich airson a' phròiseis seo air an roinn ann an còig mòr-earrainnean, a thèid riochdachadh ann an Caibideil 3: Trèimhse 1 a' gabhail a-steach an 12mh gu ruige a' 14mh linn; Trèimhse 2 an 14mh agus an 15mh linntean; Trèimhse 3 an 16mh gu ruige an 18mh linn; agus Trèimhse 5 an 19mh agus an 20mh linntean. An comharradh mòr as tràithe a fhuaireas, b' e siud dìg dhomhainn a chaidh a chladhach ann an Trèimhse 1, a-rèir coltais gus talamh-àiteachais a bhuineadh don abaid a phàirceachadh. Chaidh an talamh seo a chur gu feum ùr anns a' 14mh linn mar lotaichean fada cumhang aig na bùirdeisich, lotaichean a shìn eadar sràid a' Chanongate sìos gu ruige far a bheil Rathad Thaigh an Ròid an-diugh. An taca ri lotaichean bhùirdeasach ann am buirgh eile leithid Pheairt agus Obar Dheathain, tha e iongantach, agus inntinneach, a thoirt an aire cho ainneamh 's a chaidh an cleachdadh airson obair-chiùird agus àiteachais. 'S dòcha gum b' i àrd-inbhe an fheadhainn a bha an urra riutha bu choireach. Bha obair-iarainn an seo anns na Meadhan Aoisean, ge-tà, agus 's dòcha cairteadh sheicheannan cuideachd. Thathas air pìosan luaidh bho uinneagan gloinne a lorg, còmhla ri bloigh de chrèadh-lic chùmhdaidh a chuireas an cèill gu robh togalach cliùiteach ann uaireigin, agus cuideachd dìsinn-cnàimh a sheallas na geamaichean-bùird a bhiodh muinntir an àite a' cluich. B' e bathar Geal Garbh Albannach a bh' anns a' mhòr-chuid den chrèadhadaireachd a bh' aca, ach bhathas cuideachd a' ceannach crèadhadaireachd bhon taobh a-muigh, bhon Rheinland agus bhon Fhraing, cho math ri crogain de dhearcan-ola às an Spàinn. Bho Thrèimhse 3 anns an 16mh linn thàinig pàirt de chrèadh-lic bho nàdar de stòbha crèadha a gheibhear mar is trice ann an toglaichean cràbhaidh. Tha prìneachan meatailt agus meuran a' cur air shùilean dhuinn gu robh aig aon uair tàillear ag obair ann an tè de na bùithtean air a' Chanongate. Nuair a thogadh Taigh Queensberry, ge-tà, chaidh cur às don mhòr-chuid de na ballachan-aghaidh meadhan-aoiseach. Co-dhiù, am broinn an taighe seo gheibhear stuth-togail bho thoglaichean na bu thràithe air an làraich, leithid chlach-snàidhte bho uinneagan agus teallaichean, pìosan den mhullach, agus fiodhrach structarach.

Dhearbh rannsachadh-ùir gum b' e an gual an connadh bu chumanta bho gu math tràth gu ruige an 17mh linn, nuair a rinneadh gàraidhean foirmeil den àite-sa. Tha an t-atharrachadh bunaiteach seo ann an obair-fhearainn soilleir ri fhaicinn, leis mar nach lorgar gràn gualaichte ach a-mhàin anns na breathan as tràithe. 'S dòcha gum faicear buaidh na h-abaide faisg air làimh anns na cnàimhean a chaidh a lorg anns an làraich. Tha barrachd chnàimhean-chaorach na cnàimhean-cruidh innte, eu-coltach ris a' mhòr-chuid de na buirgh air an taobh sear far a bheil nas motha de chrodh. B' e a' chlòimh agus craicnean chaorach am bathar bu chudromaiche ann an eaconamaidh na h-Alba anns na Meadhan Aoisean, agus bhiodh treudan mòra de chaoraich an seilbh nan abaidean. A-thaobh protain, a-rèir coltais bhiodh muinntir a' Chanongate a' tighinn beò air feòil-chaorach agus feòil-uain, mairt-fheòil, muc-fheòil, coineanaich, geàrran, sitheann-circe, cearcan-tomain, cearcan-fraoich, sgairbh, iasg, agus maorach, gu seachd àraidh eisirean.

As dèidh Aonadh nan Crùn ann an 1603, rinn a' chùirt rìoghail imrich bho Thaigh an Ròid gu ruige Westminster. Bha cùisean fhathast a' soirbheachadh le borgh Chanongate, ge-tà, a dh' aindeoin buairidhean cogaidh agus ghalairean. Tron 17mh linn bha barrachd fèill air smocadh, agus 's ann eadar 1630 agus 1680 a rinneadh a' mhòr-chuid de phìoban briste a fhuaireas anns na cladhaichean. Chaidh Àros Thaigh an Ròid ath-nuadhachadh anns na 1670an, 's e a-rithist aig teis-meadhan poileataics na h-Alba. Mar sin, bha Canongate aon uair eile 'na àite gu math fasanta. Bha teaghlaichean àrd-uaisle ag iarraidh taighean a cheannach cho faisg air an Àros 's a b' urrainn dhaibh, agus tha Taigh Queensberry air fear de bhuidhinn de thaighean-mòra brèagha bhon 17mh linn a sheas aig ceann Thaigh an Ròid den bhorgh.

Tha Taigh Queensberry 'na thaigh-baile urramach fhathast, le eachdraidh iom'-fhillte 'na ailtireachd. Chaidh a thogail bho thùs ann an 1667–70 mar Thaigh-Loidsidh Mòr Bhail' Mo Cheallaich, leis a' Bhana-Ridire Mairghread Dubhghlas Bhail' Mo Cheallaich. Rinneadh Taigh Hatton dheth nuair a chaidh a cheannach agus ath-nuadhachadh le Tighearna Hatton bho 1679, agus thugadh Taigh Queensberry air nuair a ghabh a' cheud Diùc Queensberry thairis e ann an 1688. Tha mu dhà thrian den taigh mar a tha e an-diugh a' dàtachadh bho linn Bhail' Mo Cheallaich. Rinneadh an togalach ann an cumadh T le trì làraichean bhos cionn ùrlair dhà-rangaich, an taobh a-muigh dheth le còmhdach sgreabhagan agus aoil. Chuir Tighearna Hatton tùr-seallaidh ris an taigh, agus ri linn an rannsachaidh airceòlaich chaidh a làrach a lorg anns an lobhtaidh. Chaidh am plàsd gu lèir a thoirt far nam ballachan. Mar sin, chaidh mion-eachdraidh mu mar a chaidh an togalach a chleachdadh gu praictigeach a chur ri fianaisean nan làmh-sgrìobhainnean. Mar bu trice a thachair le taighean mòra ann an Alba aig an àm, chaidh cùl an togalaich a bheòthachadh le dà gheibheal mòr dealbhte air nòs Duidseach, comharradh a chuireas an cèill cho cudromach 's a bha ceanglaichean-malairt an uair sin leis an Ìsil-Tìr. Tha sgrìobhainnean a' toirt fianais air gàraidhean foirmeil aig cùl an taighe, agus dhearbh na cladhaichean gu robh làrach de bharraid àird ann, le staidhre anns a' mheadhan a' dol sìos don ghàradh. Ann an iomadach dòigh bha Taigh Bhail' Mo

Cheallaich 'na cho-chur de dh' ailtireachd cho-aoisich a' bhaile mhòir agus ailtireachd thaighean-dùthcha cho math.

A thuilleadh air na h-atharrachaidhean a rinn e air an taigh fhèin, fhuair Tighearna Hatton seilbh air fearann timcheall air an togalach ach am biodh àite ann mun taigh airson chùirtean-seirbhis agus stàbaill. Tha fiosrachadh air leth luachmhor mu Thaigh Hatton agus an àirneis 'na bhroinn ri fhaighinn an dà chuid ann an làmh-sgrìobhainn bho 22 Màirt 1681 air a bheil *Instructions for my hous in the Canongait with the Courts yrof etc*, anns a bheil tuairisgeul mu dhà sheòmar anns an tùr, agus cuideachd ann an dealbh le Thomas Sandby mu 1746 a sheallas an tùr le barra-bhalla.

Ann am meadhan nan 1680an bha Tighearna Hatton, no Iarla Lauderdale mar a bh' air a-nis, a' fuiling air sgàth thrioblaidean poilitigeach, chasaidean cealgaireachd, agus ainbhfhiach. Reic e Taigh Hatton ri muinntir Queensberry. Rinn an dàrna Diùc Queensberry ath-nuadhachadh mòr air an taigh bho 1695 air adhart, a' bhliadhna nuair a chuireadh ri chèile a' cheud fhear ann an sreath de mhion-chunntasan a tha air a bhith uabhasach feumail a-thaobh àirneis agus feumalachdan an taighe. B' e Seumas Mac a' Ghobhainn an t-ailtire a bha bhos cionn an ath-nuadhachaidh seo. Bha e air obrachadh mar-thà don cheud Diùc aig Caisteal Dhruim Lannraig, agus aig Taigh Queensberry chuir e ris sgiath iar ùr, for-dhoras de dh' aon ùrlar air balla-aghaidh a' Chanongate, agus dà thùr clòsaid air gach taobh de bhalla-aghaidh a' ghàraidh. Tha an t-suirbhidh a rinn Uilleam Edgar de Dhùn Èideann ann an 1742 a' sealltainn mar a bha gàraidhean foirmeil Thaigh Queensberry aig àirde an seise, nuair a bhathas 'gan cur gu feum, a-rèir coltais, mar liosan-àraich do ghàraidhean Dhruim Lannraig. Tha na cunntasan ag innse gu robh na gàraidhean air an sgeadachadh le poitean-fhlùran òraichte agus ìomhaighean-cloiche. Am measg nan nithean as neònaiche a chaidh a lorg ann an ùir nan gàraidhean, bha inneal-toinnidh pioraraig bhon 18mh linn. Aig bun nan gàraidhean bha ubhal-ghort a chaidh a leudachadh agus a dh' fhàs, anmoch anns an 18mh linn, gu bhith mar shuaicheantas den talamh seo.

Anns an 18mh linn chaidh Taigh Haddington a thogail ann an cuibhreann an iar-dheas de làrach na Pàrlamaid, eadar Clobhsa Reid agus Innteart Haddington. Mhair dà bhalla 'nan seasamh bhos cionn na talmhainn, agus na b' anmoiche chaidh an toirt a-steach gu balla-crìche Ospadal Thaigh Queensberry. Ri linn a' chladhaich chaidh làraichean bhallachan eile a lorg, cho math ri tobar cho-aimsireach. Tha fhios gu robh fèill air geamaichean-seòmair leithid bòbhlaireachd brait-ùrlair am measg nan teaglaichean Bhictòrianach na bu bheairtiche, agus fhuaireas bloighdean de dh' aon bhall dèante de chrèadh gloinichte bho fhuigheall am broinn làrach Thaigh Haddington.

B' ann aig Marcas Lòdainn bho thùs a bha an taigh-baile den 18mh linn air an robh an t-ainm car mì-chliùiteach Bothan Lòdainn. Bha e a' lìonadh cuibhreann taobh sear làrach na Pàrlamaid, agus chaidh ath-thogail mar thaigh-grùide anmoch anns an 19mh linn. Sheall an cladhach gun deach bunaitean structarach mòra agus làraichean do thoglaichean a chaidh a leagail a-rithist a stèidheachadh air na seann lotaichean meadhan-aoiseach.

Nuair a chaidh Bail' Ùr Dhùn Èideann a chur air adhart anns an 18mh linn, tha e coltach gun tàinig crìonadh air cliù Chanongate mar àite-còmhnaidh fasanta. Chaidh Taigh Queensberry a leigeil a-mach air mhàl, agus cha do rinneadh oidhirp tuilleadh gus ath-nuadhachadh mòr a chur an gnìomh. Gu dearbh,

nuair a chaidh a reic ri Uilleam Aitchison ann an 1801, chaidh an taigh a rùsgadh den àirneis bhrèagha a bha 'na bhroinn. Rinneadh atharrachaidhean bunaiteach le Bòrd an Ordanais mu 1808–11 gus ospadal armailteach agus gearastan a dhèanamh den taigh, agus bha na seann ghàraidhean a-nis 'nam faiche le taigh-stòr stiùireadair-airm air aon taobh. Am measg nan atharrachaidhean chaidh làr an lobhtaidh ath-dhealbhadh mar treas ùrlar slàn, agus chailleadh an tùr-seallaidh agus na geibheil Dhuitsich. Rinneadh atharrachaidhean na bu lugha don taigh bho na 1830an air adhart, nuair a bha e 'na Thaigh Teàrmainn, àite-còmhnaidh nan dìol-dèircean. Lean am pròiseas nuadhachaidh seo air adhart, agus an taigh ag atharrachadh mean air mhean gus an robh e 'na ospadal do sheann daoine anns an 20mh linn. B' ionnan na h-atharrachaidhean a thàinig air Taigh Queensberry agus na dh' èirich don Chanongate fhèin tro na linntean sin gu lèir. Tha an leabhar seo a' cur an taigh, agus làrach na Pàrlamaid ùir, anns an t-suidheachadh eachdraidheil fharsaing aca fhèin, mar phàirt de phrìomh-bhaile na h-Alba.

PART 1

Introduction

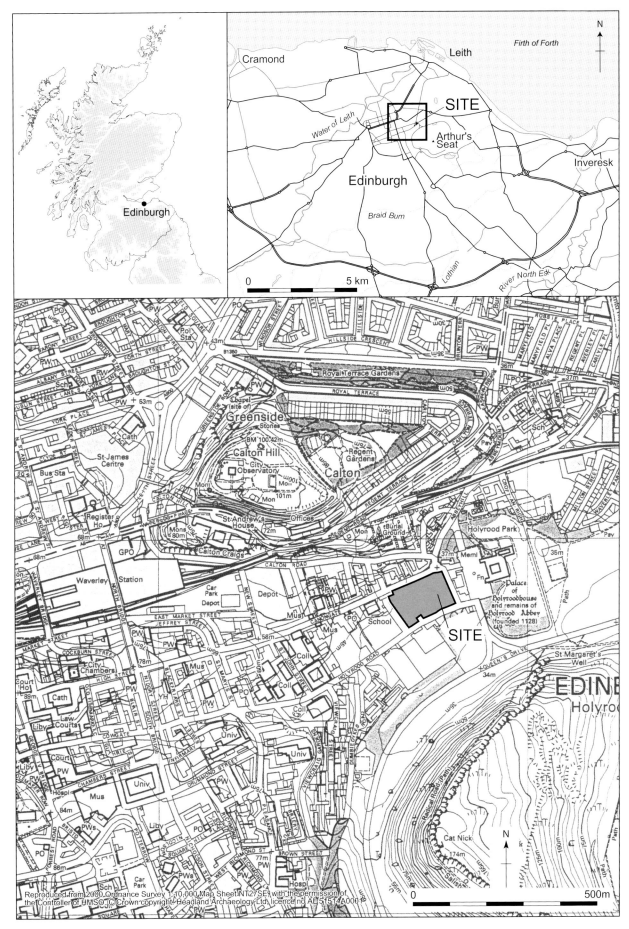

Figure 1.1
Location map of the site (based on a facsimile of Ordnance Survey maps © Crown copyright)

Chapter 1

The Scottish Parliament archaeology project

RUSSEL COLEMAN and SIMON STRONACH

1.1 Introduction

The UK General Election in 1997, and the subsequent choice of the Holyrood site in Edinburgh for the new Scottish Parliament building – a site steeped in history – prompted a major historical and archaeological project.

The site chosen for the new Parliament lies at the tail end of a long and narrow ridge that runs down from Edinburgh Castle to the palace of Holyroodhouse – key places in Scotland's history (fig 1.1). In 1998, the eastern part of the site was occupied by the offices of Scottish & Newcastle Breweries (brewing had ceased in the 1960s), and the western part by Queensberry House Hospital and Gardens. In the new design for the site the brewery was to be demolished, but Queensberry House, a much neglected but listed 17th-century urban palace and the scene of many important political events of the 17th and 18th centuries, was to be retained.

In the early 1980s, a survey had been undertaken of the archaeological implications of development in the Canongate as part of the Scottish Burgh Survey (Stevenson *et al* 1981). A desk-based assessment of the history and archaeology of the Parliament site and its environs, undertaken in 1998 soon after the site was chosen, showed that it offered considerable potential for further historical research (Dennison & Ewart 1998). An opportunity was also afforded in April 1998 to excavate a single trial trench within the garden area of Queensberry House Hospital, an event marked by a visit by Donald Dewar, then Secretary of State for Scotland (fig 1.2). In the years between the two surveys, there had been few opportunities to test the archaeological potential of this part of Canongate as there had been little development in the area. Nevertheless, the site, which covered an area of around 15,000 sq m, was known to include several complete properties that once lay within the medieval burgh of Canongate, a settlement separate from both Edinburgh and Leith, which bordered onto the precinct of Holyrood Abbey (fig 2.1). The abbey, which was founded in AD 1128 and later developed

into the palace of Holyroodhouse, had been granted its own settlement (the burgh of Canongate) by David I (1123–54) from which it could draw an income in the form of rents from properties and tolls from the market place. The people of Canongate would also have provided goods and services to the abbey. Investigating and understanding the relationships between the burgh of Canongate and the abbey of Holyrood, between the burgh and its neighbours, Edinburgh and Leith, and the architectural development and role of Queensberry House in the politics of the day were to be the main research aims of the historical and archaeological project.

The work reported in this volume was put out to competitive tender and the contract awarded in 1998 to a consortium formed between SUAT Ltd and Headland Archaeology Ltd, based respectively in Perth and Edinburgh. Dr Pat Dennison, Edinburgh University, who undertook the initial desk-based assessment, continued as the project historian. The first months of the project focused on evaluating the site and dealing with the potential impact of the new building on the below-ground archaeology. However, as the project progressed and details of the new building design emerged, the recording of Queensberry House in advance of major refurbishment and extensive landscaping works around the Parliament site became significant additions to the project. The recording of Queensberry House was led by Tom Addyman and William Kay, of Addyman & Kay Ltd (now Addyman Associates), with support from Headland Archaeology Ltd/SUAT Ltd and from the Royal Commission on the Ancient and Historical Monuments of Scotland (RCAHMS). Addyman & Kay Ltd and John Lowrey, Edinburgh University, who undertook research into the history of Queensberry House itself, were appointed directly by Historic Scotland. The project was managed by Historic Scotland on behalf of, first, the Scottish Office (now the Scottish Government), and then the Parliament Corporate Body, both of which organisations funded the work as part of their responsibility as the developer of the site; these responsibilities are set out in published government policy in *The Care of Historic Buildings and Ancient Monuments by Government Departments in Scotland* (1995).

The fieldwork element of the project began in September 1998 and comprised the excavation of a series of trial trenches across the site (fig 1.3; Trenches 1–20, 23–5). Not all areas of the site were immediately available for investigation as the area occupied by the brewery was not vacated until spring 1999. Gradually,

Figure 1.2
Donald Dewar's visit to the trial excavation in 1998

a model of the underlying archaeological deposits was developed which identified areas where archaeological levels survived but also allowed parts of the site to be written off as archaeologically sterile due to past disturbance, notably much of the brewery area and the Canongate street frontage. Once the details of the development emerged, particularly the design for the foundations, it was possible to devise a strategy, timetable and costs for the excavation of a potentially very large area within a tight timetable and while sharing the site with other contractors. The main open-area excavations took place between February and April 1999 in tandem with the demolition contract, with a return visit by a smaller team to deal with the brewery area in June. All of the set-piece excavation outside Queensberry House was completed in August 1999. The bulk of the post-excavation analysis was undertaken over the next 12 months.

Extensive alterations planned for Queensberry House, in order to convert it for use within the new Parliament, prompted a return to the site, and a major programme of building recording was undertaken between September 1999 and March 2000, together with some limited trial excavations in the basement. The team returned to Queensberry House once more in April and May 2001 to undertake further excavations in the basement in advance of the floor levels being lowered. There then followed a programme of watching briefs throughout Queensberry House, including monitoring of the removal of the 19th-century top floor to lower the wall-head to the level of the Queensberry phase; worked stones were marked before removal, then recorded before being transferred to storage off-site for future reuse in conservation work within the building.

The report is set out largely in chronological order. The archaeology was interpreted within a framework of periods and sub-phases:

Figure 1.3
Plan of the site showing the locations of excavation trenches (based on the Ordnance Survey plan © Crown copyright)

Period 1   12th–14th-century ditch and earlier features

Period 2   14th–15th-century burgage plots

Period 3   16th–17th-century tenements and gardens

Period 4   17th–18th-century townhouses and formal gardens

Period 5   19th-century barracks and modern features

1.2 Research objectives

A number of research objectives were specified at the outset of the project in order to guide the historians, archaeologists and other specialists. These were expressed as a series of questions and can be grouped chronologically as follows:

Pre-burghal settlement, pre-1128

The area was exploited from the earliest times; did pre-burghal settlement remains exist below medieval levels?

The medieval period, 1128–1580

If early settlement was discovered, was there continuity of settlement from the pre-burghal to the medieval period?

What did the early burgh look like and how did the natural topography of the surrounding area influence the layout?

What was the relationship between the abbey and the burgh?

The post-medieval period, 1580–1707

What was the nature of the buildings and gardens associated with the urban precinct that developed around the palace of Holyroodhouse?

The early modern period, 1707–1825

Documentary evidence records that the Canongate declined in status in this period; did the archaeological evidence reflect this?

The modern period, 1825–present day

The conversion of Lothian Hut, an 18th-century townhouse, to a brewery after 1825 marked the beginnings of brewing on an industrial scale on the site. What remains survived relating to the early development of the site as a brewery, and was there any evidence for continuity in brewing from the medieval period?

1.3 Methodology

1.3.1 Evaluation

At the outset of the project the nature of any buried archaeology on the site was largely unknown and there was too little information to form an appropriate excavation strategy. It was decided to undertake evaluation trenching at the earliest possible opportunity in September 1998 (fig 1.3; Trenches 1–8, 16–19, 23–5; small test-pits in and around Queensberry House are not shown because of scale). However, this evaluation was constrained by several factors, including continued partial occupation of the site. The trenching, therefore, had to be augmented by watching briefs on numerous engineering test pits and boreholes. The results indicated that modern development had destroyed archaeological levels over much of the eastern (brewery) part of the site, including the Canongate frontage. A proposed basement car park in the western half of the site prompted the full archaeological excavation of two areas (fig 1.3; Trenches 22 & 26).

1.3.2 Excavation

As soon as demolition contractors had cleared these two main areas, the archaeological team moved in and, using machine excavators, removed all the modern overburden (fig 1.4). Deep homogeneous garden soils were also removed by machine after features cutting into them had been recorded and bulk soil samples had been taken for finds retrieval and environmental information (the nature and structure of these soils are discussed in Chapter 3.10). Once these extensive spreads had been removed, all archaeological features

Figure 1.4
Work in progress clearing the western part of the site, viewed from the north

were recorded and hand-excavated down to the level of undisturbed natural subsoil.

Once this first main phase of archaeological investigation was completed in the summer of 1999, the site passed into the control of Bovis Lend Lease, the construction managers for the construction programme. The archaeological team returned later that same summer to excavate some further trenches in the brewery part of the site, an area that was not available earlier in the programme (fig 1.3; Trenches 31–3).

1.3.3 Queensberry House

The investigation of Queensberry House was not included in the initial specification for the archaeological project (fig 1.5). A limited amount of work was undertaken in 1998–9 by Addyman & Kay under a separate contract from Historic Scotland, funded by the Scottish Office. As the scale of the structural interventions to be undertaken became clear, the amount of archaeological and recording work was increased, and in July 1999 the work on the house formally became part of the Holyrood Parliament Site Archaeology Project.

It was recognised that the building had a complex history and that the restoration of the house should be based on good evidence. For structural reasons the building project architects decided to remove all plaster wall coverings within the house. This provided an opportunity to record information preserved in the walls, such as slappings for doors, blocked-up doors and windows, different phases of wall construction and the incorporation of earlier fabric. The plaster removal was done between September 1999 and

Figure 1.5
Aerial photograph of the site and its surroundings in 1999, from the east. Queensberry House is in the top right corner of the site. Holyrood Palace is just out of sight at the bottom of the frame

March 2000, under archaeological supervision, by the specialist company Kingsley & Bolton. During this period, RCAHMS recorded the main external elevations, with detailed recording where necessary by Addyman & Kay.

The need for the ground level of the basement to be lowered necessitated further archaeological work in Queensberry House. A number of test-pits (Trenches 34–40, not illustrated) had been excavated during the 1999/2000 programme and established that archaeological remains associated with Queensberry House and previous phases of the building survived beneath more modern floor levels. In advance of the lowering of levels, full excavation was carried out in the rooms with the best preservation (Trenches 63–5, not illustrated) between April and May 2001, and an intermittent watching brief maintained during contractors' work in several other rooms and corridors. A significant depth of archaeological deposits still survives in these rooms preserved beneath the new floors as all excavations terminated at the construction formation level.

1.3.4 Landscaping works

In addition to the main excavation areas and the building recording in Queensberry House, a programme of evaluation, limited excavation and watching brief was undertaken around the Parliament site. Much of this was prompted by the rerouting of services, notably in Horse Wynd and Holyrood Road, and by the upgrading of Queen's Drive in Holyrood Park. The results of this work will be reported on separately as elements of it were still ongoing when this volume was being prepared.

Chapter 2

Edinburgh before the burgh: the pre-medieval evolution of the Parliament site to c 1128

STEPHEN CARTER, E PATRICIA DENNISON and RICHARD TIPPING

2.1 Introduction

STEPHEN CARTER & RICHARD TIPPING

Standing at the Scottish Parliament today, it is difficult to appreciate fully its natural setting. Views of surrounding hills are partially blocked by tall buildings and the actual ground surface has been altered by nearly 1000 years of urban life. In places this has added 2–3m of sediment to the natural ground surface, and elsewhere a similar depth has been cut away. Despite this, the natural landscape and its history remain an outstanding feature of central Edinburgh, controlling the way the town evolves and providing a dramatic setting for the modern city. The medieval burghs of Edinburgh and the Canongate (fig 2.1) along with the castle and Holyrood Abbey were not established in virgin territory in the 11th and 12th centuries. Their creation followed 9000 years of natural and cultural landscape evolution and, more specifically, at least 1000 years of development of Edinburgh as a centre of economic and political power.

2.2 Sources of evidence

STEPHEN CARTER & RICHARD TIPPING

Evidence for the pre-burghal evolution of Edinburgh and its environs comes primarily from the archaeological and palaeoenvironmental records. Documentary references are limited to a very few sources in the latter part of the first millennium AD.

The archaeological record of present-day greater Edinburgh is greatly influenced by the extent of built-up areas and the location of the surviving islands of open ground. In the built-up areas, archaeological records for prehistory are limited to accidental discoveries of artefacts and burials. The discovery of human remains tended to excite interest and therefore was reported. Similarly, recognisable artefacts, in particular bronze objects, were noteworthy and robust enough to stand rough handling during excavation. These discoveries generally occurred during the construction of houses, roads and railways and the precise location or context of the discovery is often only poorly recorded.

Prehistoric settlement remains, structures and other sites have only been recorded in areas of open ground that include Arthur's Seat and Blackford Hill. Both of these are rocky hills and archaeological remains have been preserved as earthworks. Other areas of open ground, including land to the south-east around Prestonfield and Craigmillar, was or still is agricultural land and no above-ground archaeological features have survived. Sub-surface features could be present and appear as cropmarks on aerial photographs but none has been recorded in these particular areas.

Interpretation of the distribution of archaeological sites and findspots should be treated with caution as it must, in part, reflect the period in which different parts of greater Edinburgh were developed.

2.3 The natural setting of the Parliament site

STEPHEN CARTER & RICHARD TIPPING

2.3.1 Topography

STEPHEN CARTER

The setting of the Parliament site is best viewed from the south, from Salisbury Crags. From this high vantage point it is possible to appreciate the pronounced natural topography that dominates this part of Edinburgh (fig 2.1). We see the site located at the eastern end of the long ridge that is followed by the High Street and Canongate, the principal axis of the two medieval burghs. There are well-defined valleys to the north and south, now followed by Calton Road and the Cowgate/Holyrood Road, and sweeping into the foreground from the south-west is the deep depression that separates Salisbury Crags from St Leonard's. All of these features merge onto a level area that now lies within Holyrood Park.

These valleys and slopes are the product of processes of erosion and deposition during recent glacial periods acting on a complex pattern of different rock types. In summary, a huge ice-sheet crossed this area some 20,000 to 18,000 years ago, moving from the Highlands in the west to the North Sea in the east.

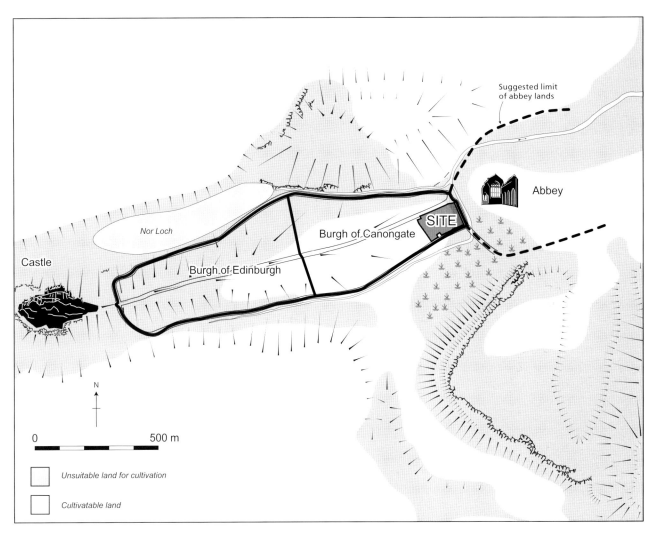

Figure 2.1
The medieval setting of the excavation site: the boundaries of the burghs of Canongate and Edinburgh; the locations of the Abbey and castle,
and the probable drainage pattern

The ice dug into the ground and exposed the relatively resistant rocks of former volcanoes that make up the Castle Rock, Calton Hill and Arthur's Seat. Deflection of ice round the volcanic plugs at these three points protected rock immediately to the east from erosion but caused the excavation of deep troughs on the western face and northern and southern sides of the hills in a streamlining effect. Thus, the High Street/ Canongate ridge was created in the lee of the Castle Rock with pronounced linear depressions eroded out to the north and south (a classic glacial crag-and-tail formation). At Arthur's Seat, erosion created the deep trough to the west of Salisbury Crags (now followed by the Queen's Drive), and basins on the north and south

sides. The southern basin survives to the present day as Duddingston Loch; the northern basin ('Holyrood Loch' to geologists) has now filled with sediment and lies beneath the Queen's Drive to the south of the Palace of Holyroodhouse.

The original topography of the excavation site has been extensively modified and masked by human activity over the past 800 years but it can be reconstructed, at least in part, from levels recorded on the surface of the natural subsoil at the base of the archaeological sediments. The contour map that can be generated from these levels is incomplete for two reasons: first, parts of the site were inaccessible during the archaeological fieldwork and therefore remained

Figure 2.2
The contours of the subsoil surface, which give a better impression than the modern surface of the original topography of the site
(based on the Ordnance Survey plan © Crown copyright)

unexcavated; second, other areas had been reduced to below the natural subsoil level by earlier building works thus the natural topography has been destroyed. Despite these limitations, the information presented in fig 2.2 is sufficient to understand the original appearance of the site.

Three topographic zones can be defined: a steep slope underneath Queensberry House, a level terrace across the centre of the site, and a more gentle slope in the south-east corner of the site. There is a steep, rock-controlled slope underneath Queensberry House which is part of the south side of the ridge that is followed by the Canongate. The slope runs at an acute angle to the Canongate, therefore buildings like Queensberry House are set at an angle to the slope. Much of this area has been heavily terraced for the construction of buildings fronting onto the Canongate, and original ground levels cannot be determined with any precision. Most of the archaeological excavation trenches lay to the south of this slope within an almost level area at around 35m OD. This 60m-wide terrace is part of a more extensive surface that can be identified eastwards past the palace of Holyroodhouse and out into Holyrood Park (fig 2.1). In the south-east corner of the site there is a gentle slope down to below 34m OD. This area was generally not accessible during the archaeological excavation therefore this slope could not be followed to the limits of the site. However, levels on subsoil in the park immediately to the south of Holyrood Road are at 34m OD until the edge of the former Holyrood Loch is reached.

2.3.2 Ancient rivers and lochs

The natural watercourses in this part of Edinburgh have been radically altered by the development of the city and little evidence survives at the surface to indicate what formerly existed. Springs have been tapped, watercourses redirected and buried in pipes, and a loch has infilled and then been drained. However, sufficient evidence is available from topographic, documentary and archaeological sources to attempt a reconstruction of the original pattern (fig 2.1).

Land to the north of the High Street/Canongate ridge drained into a burn which ran eastwards from the former Nor' Loch along what is now Calton Road. At the foot of the Canongate, by what was formerly the Watergate, it turned to the north-east and passed to the north of the palace at Croft an Righ. This watercourse is recorded on maps from the 17th century onwards but was progressively covered over and is now entirely

contained within sewers. The south side of the High Street/Canongate ridge and the land now occupied by Edinburgh University drained into the Cowgate. No evidence has yet been found for a natural watercourse in the Cowgate but archaeological monitoring in 1993 at the foot of Holyrood Road identified a 16m-wide channel that may be part of this missing burn (City of Edinburgh Council Archaeology Service, unpublished data). This channel flowed eastwards but the course followed by the burn below this point is uncertain.

Holyrood Loch is an infilled basin roughly 500m long and up to 150m wide at its western end. The maximum depth of the basin is not known but nearly 3m of deposits have been found on the northern side of the loch, suggesting a former loch level to roughly 34m OD. The catchment of the former Holyrood Loch included the area to the west of Salisbury Crags as far south as St Leonard's and possibly also the Cowgate Burn. No outflowing streams from the loch have yet been identified because of artificial alterations to the landscape, but it is assumed that there was sufficient flow to create and maintain a permanent channel. Archaeological evaluation in the park to the east of the palace in 2000 did not locate a natural watercourse leading north-east from the former east end of the loch, although more than one artificial drain now takes this route. This suggests that the outflow lay somewhere further to the west. A north/south aligned ditch or channel was identified to the west of the palace garden during archaeological evaluation in 1985 (Ewart, unpublished data). This is a candidate for the outflow (albeit modified in the medieval period), but it could equally be a channel flowing into the loch, possibly the Cowgate Burn.

2.4 Evolution of the human landscape
STEPHEN CARTER & RICHARD TIPPING

2.4.1 The prehistoric origins of medieval Edinburgh: 0 BC to AD 1000

The creation of medieval Edinburgh with its burghs and abbey reflects the patronage of Scottish monarchs who held Edinburgh Castle as a significant royal residence from at least the 11th century. It has long been recognised from scraps of information in early documentary sources that Edinburgh Castle has origins that significantly pre-date its earliest surviving medieval fabric. Archaeological excavations in Edinburgh Castle in 1988–91 (Driscoll & Yeoman 1997) produced substantial evidence for the continuous existence of a settlement on the Castle Rock from the early Iron Age onwards (c 750 BC). It is probably this settlement that is first documented as *Din Eidyn* in the *Gododdin* (a collection of poetic elegies referring to events around AD 600).

The site on the Castle Rock appears to have been one of many enclosed settlements that came into existence in the Lothians from the Early Iron Age. It is clear that at some point in the later Iron Age the status of the Castle Rock changed from being one of many local centres of settlement to a centre of regional power. Driscoll & Yeoman (1997) have argued that the high concentration of Roman finds from the excavations on the Castle Rock indicates the site was already a centre of authority in the 2nd century AD. The degree to which the short Roman military occupations had any lasting impact in Lothian is debatable, but the prolonged proximity of southern Scotland to Roman political and economic forces in northern England may well have shaped the political geography of the Lothians in a more fundamental manner at this time.

Archaeological evidence for the nature and status of the settlement on the Castle Rock for the remainder of the 1st millennium AD is less substantial but continued occupation seems likely. Lothian was a disputed zone on the border between the Anglian kingdom of Northumbria and the Pictish (latterly Scottish) kingdom between the 6th and 10th centuries AD. Brief entries in contemporary chronicles record a siege of *Etin* in AD 638, possibly by the Angles, and in the mid-10th century the fortress of *Eden* was abandoned to the Scots (Driscoll & Yeoman 1997, 227).

These scraps of evidence are sufficient to suggest that the Iron Age settlement on the Castle Rock gained the status of a regional power centre before the 2nd century AD and retained it during successive periods of Anglian and British control before emerging as the regional centre of Scottish royal power in the 11th century. The history of medieval and later development in the Canongate, which is the principal focus of this volume, is a record of the continued political and economic significance of Edinburgh in Scotland.

2.5 Pre-burghal settlement before 1128

E PATRICIA DENNISON

The foundation legend of Holyrood Abbey, attributed to David I, is in fact a late medieval adaptation of a well-known miracle legend of St Hubert, and probably transferred to St Hubert by St Eustace. There is nothing whatsoever to link King David I (1124–53) with this tale. According to this late medieval apochryphal legend, in 1128 on the feast of the Holy Cross, King David I was out hunting. Temporarily separated from his followers, the king was confronted by a large white stag, which unhorsed and threatened to kill him. A vision of the Holy Cross, however, encouraged and reassured the king and the stag took flight. In thanksgiving for this deliverance David I, acting in the name of Christ and in honour of the Holy Rood and of St Mary the Virgin and of all the saints, established an abbey dedicated to the Holy Rood.[1]

In support of this new foundation, David I granted that the abbey should have a burgh, later called Canongate (meaning the 'gait', 'road' or 'walk' of the canons), sited between the church of Holyrood and the burgh of Edinburgh. It is clear that the church that was to form the nucleus of the Augustinian priory was already built.[2] Some historians have argued that this was on the site of a pre-existing ecclesiastical foundation (Anderson 1938, 117).[3] Whether or not this is correct, the fact that there was already a church built implies an essential workforce resident nearby; and if this was a pastoral, rather than monastic, church there were probably also lay people nearby to whom the church ministered.

Some 19th-century historians have taken this implicit settlement further and have argued that the founding of the burgh was merely a formalisation of legal rights to an already existing community.[4] It has been argued that the choice of the Latin words, *herbergare quoddam burgum*, in the charter of confirmation, supports this theory, since *herbergare* means to 'settle' or 'build up'.[5] This could imply an already existing settlement, which was now being elevated to the status of a burgh. Burghs were rarely founded on 'green-field sites', and there is no compelling argument for Canongate to be in any way different from burghs such as Dunfermline and Linlithgow.

Excavations at Ronaldson's Wharf, North Leith (Reed & Lawson 1999), have shown that established settlement pre-dates, by at least a hundred years, the 12th-century port that served the Augustinian priory of Holyrood.[6] It is just possible that similar ties may have existed also between an 11th-century (or earlier) North Leith and a settlement, possibly with an ecclesiastical nucleus, on the wide plain at the foot of Salisbury Crags and Calton Hill.

This form of an ecclesiastical settlement at the foot of a long linear approach from a royal site (Edinburgh Castle) has certain parallels in Scotland, for example at Aberdeen (Old Aberdeen, the religious centre;

New Aberdeen, the lay) and possibly Cambuskenneth (religious) and Stirling (lay). It is noted also in Ireland, for example, at Clogher in County Tyrone and possibly also in northern England at Carlisle and York. David I's decision formally to found an Augustinian house may also be a reflection of an already existing situation, perhaps an ecclesiastical site serviced by a priesthood, with a related lay settlement,[7] as was the case, for example, in Dunfermline, when David I's mother, Queen Margaret, founded the Benedictine monastery there.

Augustinian priories were intended, amongst other things, to function as support for lay communities. The establishment at Holyrood was clearly to be a prestigious house, and it is possible that David I envisaged the community that was to be served by the abbey was already in existence and living in the area that was to become called Holyrood and Canongate.[8] It is unlikely that the community was that of the burgh of Edinburgh (where the canons were housed during the construction of their abbey and associated buildings), which was served by its parish church of St Giles.

Certainly, with the foundation of an associated burgh, an honour bestowed on only one other religious house – that of Arbroath – in the 12th century, a new urban parish appears to have been carved out of the existing parish at Edinburgh. Canongate was detached from the *parochia* of St Cuthbert under the castle of Edinburgh, the mother church of the shire of Edinburgh, which itself had been annexed to Holyrood at its foundation, and the burgesses of Canongate were henceforth to worship in the parochial aisle within the nave of the abbey, served by a canon of the abbey (Cowan 1995, 39) (fig 2.1).

Notes

1 Barrow (ed) 1999, no. 147. E Patricia Dennison has benefited from discussions on these points with Professor Barrow.
2 The Augustinian order of regular canons was under the rule of St Augustine, this rule being based on that of St Augustine of Hippo who died in 430. Not becoming fully recognised until the mid-11th century, by 1125, there were already over 30 monasteries in England and Wales, but only one in Scotland at Scone.
3 Professor Barrow knows of no such foundation.
4 *Liber Cartarum Sancte Crucis* (Bannatyne Club 1840), p lxxxvi.
5 Barrow (ed) 1999, no. 147. The idea that the burgh was once called 'Herbergare' is based on a misinterpretation of the verb *herbergare*. The original was misread and misunderstood.
6 As yet unpublished archaeological research by Mark Collard, previously City of Edinburgh Council archaeologist.
7 E Patricia Dennison has benefited from discussions with Alex Woolf on this point.
8 E Patricia Dennison is grateful to Professor Barrow for his views.

PART 2

The Parliament site in the medieval burgh
c 1128 to the 1600s

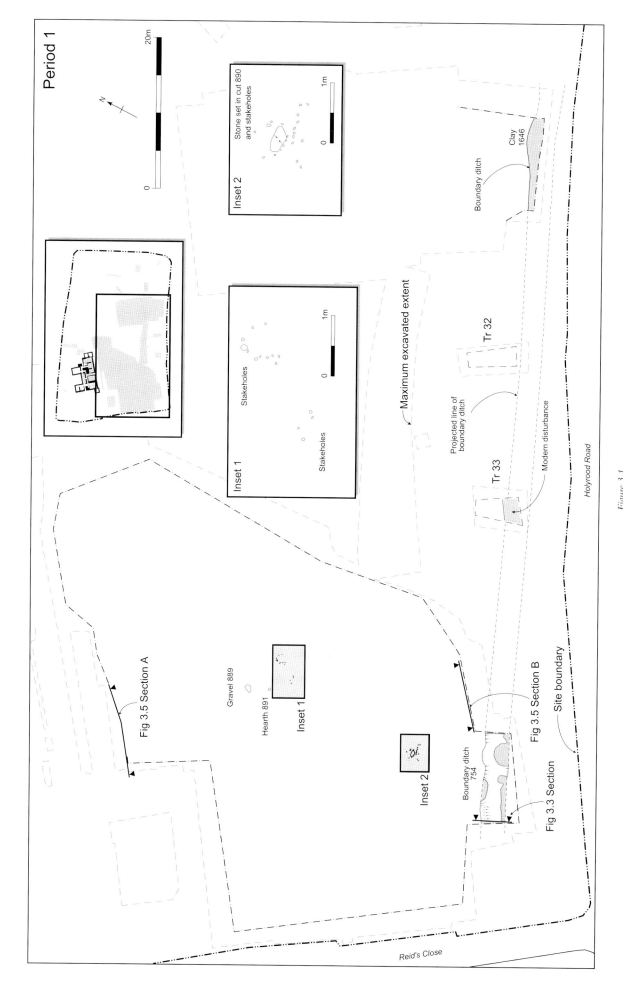

Period 1

20m

Inset 2

Stone set in cut 890
and stakeholes

1m

Clay
1646

Boundary ditch

Inset 1

Stakeholes

Stakeholes

1m

Maximum excavated extent

Projected line of
boundary ditch

Tr 32

Tr 33

Modern disturbance

Holyrood Road

Fig 3.5 Section A

Gravel 889

Hearth 891

Inset 1

Boundary ditch
754

Inset 2

Fig 3.5 Section B

Fig 3.3 Section

Site boundary

Reid's Close

Figure 3.1

Plan of the site in Period 1: undated features, some of which may be prehistoric and some are pre-burghal

Chapter 3

The archaeological evidence from the Parliament site

SIMON STRONACH, ADRIAN COX, DEREK HALL and STEPHEN CARTER

3.1 Introduction

SIMON STRONACH

This chapter describes the main archaeological features encountered during the excavation, and the artefactual and environmental evidence where appropriate. The results are prefaced by a summary of the main archaeological findings. At the end of the chapter is a brief discussion of how the archaeological results shed light on the main research questions posed at the beginning of the project.

A recurring issue for archaeologists working in historic towns is how to deal with 'dark earth' or 'garden soils'. These are deep accumulations of well-mixed homogeneous loams often containing isolated stone features such as walls, stone-lined wells, drains and kilns which appear to be 'floating' within the soils. This phenomenon is common to many of Scotland's historic towns and Canongate was no exception. There were two distinct spreads of these soils at the Parliament site: one of medieval date and the other post-medieval. During initial post-excavation work, features were grouped together into nine stratigraphic phases based on whether archaeological features were sealed beneath, contained within, or cut into these deposits from above. With subsequent analysis of the structure and content of the soils it became clear that the dating provided by pottery and other artefacts did not support chronological separation of the phases beyond a broad association with the medieval or post-medieval horizons. The phases, however, conveniently fitted within the wider chronological periods (Periods 1–5) used to structure the narrative of the report (Chapter 1), which weaves together the history, archaeology and architecture of the site and its environs. It was decided, therefore, to work with these same periods in order to provide continuity. The original phases have been expressed as sub-periods where more than one were subsumed within a period. Each period description is preceded by a summary of its stratigraphic background related to sub-periods.

In each period, the text and the drawings have been structured around the identification of burgage plots (properties established in the medieval period) and vennels (paths between plots). Where there was some physical evidence for the boundaries that marked these plots (fence lines, ditches and gullies), the properties they defined have been labelled according to period and plot. Through historic processes such as amalgamation, and the archaeological bias of preservation, the plot boundaries were not static. To avoid confusion the plot numbers are prefaced by their period, for example Period 2, Plot 1 is referred to as Plot 2.1. All the evidence for plot boundaries was found in the southern half of the site, but these properties would originally have extended the whole distance from the Canongate street frontage to the end of these plots on what is now Holyrood Road. Property boundaries, where visible, have therefore been projected northwards and southwards.

Fig 1.3 shows all of the areas which were investigated during both the main excavation and earlier phases of evaluation, except areas inside, or immediately outside, Queensberry House (for example, Trenches 9–15, 20, 30) for reasons of scale. In each of the period plans that follow (Periods 1–5; figs 3.1, 3.4, 3.9, 3.14, 3.19) there is an inset showing the area of archaeological interest (shaded) in relation to Queensberry House (a useful reference point on an extensive site such as this), a large-scale plan showing features attributed to that period, and additional insets showing individual features enlarged to provide more detail. Photographs and section drawings of key features support the information contained in the period plans.

3.2 Summary of the archaeological evidence

SIMON STRONACH

It appears that the site was the location for prehistoric human activity, perhaps from the earliest period of habitation in Scotland. Several features, such as a hearth, that may have derived from this activity were preserved, although the only certain evidence came from a residual assemblage of struck stone scattered around the site. Whether this ephemeral evidence reflects the transient nature of prehistoric use or the removal of more substantial remains by later activity is difficult to say.

A substantial ditch was cut at the south end of the site at an unknown date. Sometime after the 13th century it was left to silt up for a while and then deliberately filled. No other features could be attributed to this period and it is presumed that the ditch was defining an area that lay to the north, since marshes lay to the south. For reasons that are explored fully in Chapter 3.11 this feature seemed more likely to have acted as a boundary within the precinct of Holyrood Abbey than within the burgh. Given a paucity of finds and features associated with the ditch, it may have defined an area used for cultivation or horticulture.

After the ditch was filled in, the land was reorganised by cutting a series of gullies running at right angles to Canongate. These divided the site into characteristic medieval properties or burgage plots. The pattern was not wholly regular and it seems that amalgamation of some plots may have occurred immediately. The backlands of some plots contained simple stone tanks and drains, probably associated with flimsy structures constructed of wood, turf or thatch, which have not left visible traces. The features are likely to have been the focus for craft activities. In other plots there were no features of this kind and perhaps these areas were used as gardens or stockyards. Buildings lined

the Canongate and these comprised clay-bonded stone wall footings, presumably supporting timber superstructures.

During the later medieval and post-medieval periods most of the site was given over to decorative gardens. Tightly-packed tall tenements lined the Canongate until such time as many were cleared to make way for grand townhouses. A complicated system of underground culverts was used to provide drainage. By the Early Modern period, the numerous narrow medieval properties had been replaced by two large properties: Queensberry House and grounds occupied the western half of the site, and Lothian Hut, another grand townhouse, occupied the eastern half before this area was progressively developed as a brewery.

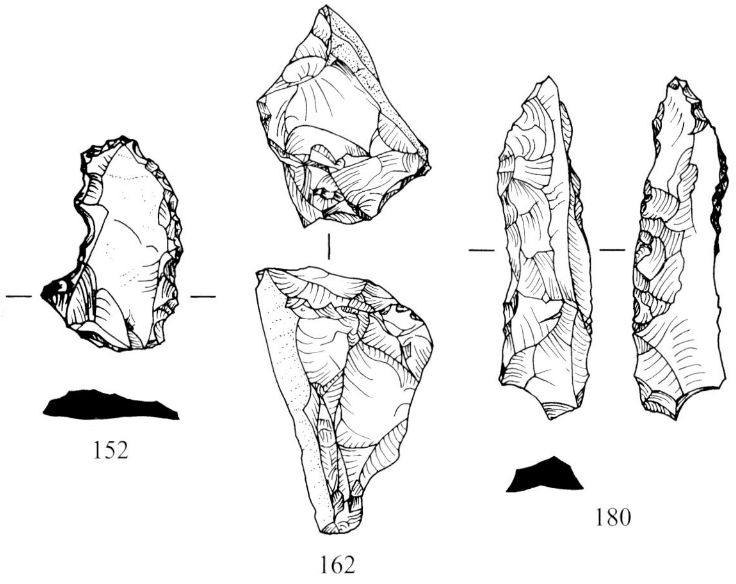

3.3 Early features

SIMON STRONACH

With the possible exception of one feature (890) all contexts in this period were truncated and survived below the level of subsoil (fig 3.1). The topsoil, which must have originally covered the area, had since been incorporated into a thick loam that was sealed in the late medieval period.

The homogeneity of the loam indicated that it had been thoroughly mixed by both human and natural processes. In these circumstances it is not surprising that the earliest archaeological deposits survived at and below the level of subsoil. The fact that later medieval activity may have destroyed traces of earlier settlement was highlighted by the recovery of a small lithic assemblage, although all of this should probably be regarded as residual (fig 3.2). These waste flakes from the making of stone tools and some finished tools came from two technological traditions and indicate that the site saw sporadic activity from the Mesolithic to the Bronze Age. In the earlier period the site would have been covered by a mixed forest of oak, hazel and elm, occupied by communities who survived by hunting and gathering. Later, it would have been suitable to develop as farmland. Several features that may have been prehistoric were discovered on the Parliament site, such as clusters of stakeholes that may have formed small windbreaks. These were not

Figure 3.2
Some of the flaked stone recovered from the site (scale 1:1)

152

162

180

in a concentration that might suggest that an early settlement was located here, but there may have been a settlement nearby, perhaps on top of the ridge where more level ground and better drainage would have contributed to a more attractive location.

It is currently impossible to be sure where the settlements inhabited by the prehistoric people who occupied the area were located, but the foot of the Canongate ridge, with lower, wetter ground on either side, would have been a suitable spot. Although no conclusive evidence for prehistoric remains was identified during the excavation, several isolated features could be described as prehistoric rather than medieval in character. An apparently natural patch of gravel (889) in the subsoil was associated with stone working and was close to a simple hearth (891) located in a shallow scoop. Elsewhere were undated groups of stakeholes, which are more easily interpreted as relating to small shelters or windbreaks rather than fence lines. One group was clustered around a smooth, rounded metre-long stone in the subsoil (890), the only stone of this size noted during the excavation. A section excavated against the stone showed that it might have been set within a cut. The stone was not flat and had a shallow groove running from east to west along its length. If this was not a natural feature, then it was designed for rubbing or grinding rather than supporting something above ground. Both this feature and the hearth could only have functioned if the topsoil around them was very thin, and it could be argued that this supports a prehistoric association.

3.4 Period 1: 12th–14th-century ditch

SIMON STRONACH

The most substantial feature in this period was a large ditch (754) cut into subsoil and running from north-east to south-west close to Holyrood Road (fig 3.1). Over 1m of fill survived and the ditch had a wide and irregular profile (fig 3.3), which should probably be viewed as the product of erosion and weathering of the sides of an originally much narrower boundary. Certainly the primary fills in the ditch were silts and clays derived from the surrounding natural soil, which suggested that it had been substantially eroded.

Anthropogenic material was rare in the primary weathering accumulations, but some sherds of White Gritty pottery (Pot no. 58), as well as a type of ware used up to the 13th century, and some charred grain seeds were present. One of the sherds of White Gritty (Pot no. 13) was thought to be from a vessel that imitated Yorkshire wares imported in the 13th and 14th centuries. It is difficult to estimate how quickly the weathering fills accumulated, but assuming that the Canongate ridge had been cleared of trees, this amount of material could have washed into the ditch in a very short time and the date of the pottery can be assumed to relate closely to that of disuse.

Further east a deposit of malodorous clay (1646) was noted to lie along the southern edge of excavation, possibly within a cut into subsoil. Unfortunately not enough was exposed on plan to establish that this was a fill within the same ditch, and it could only be excavated to a depth of 0.4m. However, low amounts

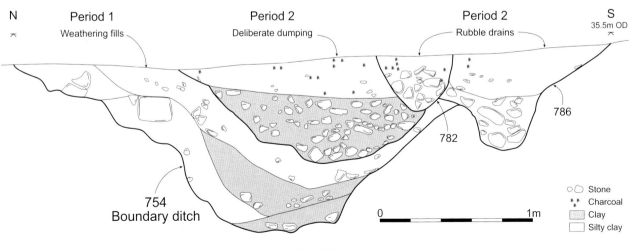

Figure 3.3
Section through the town boundary ditch

of anthropogenic material (bone, shell, coal/cinders and charred wheat grain) were recovered from samples, and it did run on exactly the same line as the feature further west.

Two further areas (fig 1.3, Trenches 32 & 33) were excavated roughly on the line of the ditch between the two larger areas of excavation. This was undertaken at a late stage in the project following demolition of Queensberry Lodge, and their positioning was very much constrained by construction work. The southern end of one, which would have been expected to cross the line of the ditch, had been subject to modern disturbance, which extended below the level of subsoil. Although speculative, the location of this disturbance suggested that it may have been occasioned by the need to remove the soft fills of the ditch during construction of Queensberry Lodge to avoid later subsidence. Trench 32 needed to be stepped for safety reasons and consequently the exposed area of subsoil probably did not extend far enough south to encounter the ditch.

3.5 Period 2: 14th–15th-century burgage plots

SIMON STRONACH

Stratigraphically this period comprised three separate sub-periods (fig 3.4). Sub-period 2.1 exclusively comprised features sealed beneath the loam deposit (612) (fig 3.5). Sub-period 2.2 comprised some features beneath the loam, but also some which had been cut from within it, and some cut through it, but thought to be earlier due to stratigraphic relationships to other features. Sub-period 2.3 exclusively comprised features cut into the surface of the loam. The associated artefacts suggested that all should be interpreted as relating to late medieval use of the site.

3.5.1 Medieval accumulation

Up to 0.5m of homogeneous loam (612, fig 3.5) spread across all of Trench 22 (fig 1.3), except where truncated by later activity. It was evident that this deposit had partly derived from the dumping or accumulation of domestic, building and industrial waste, which had been combined into a homogeneous loam by mixing over a period of time. The soil contained a variety of artefacts including English and German pottery. Other items that suggested a relatively prosperous medieval community in this part of the Canongate were: a copper alloy lace tag (no. 10); a cruciform copper alloy mount (no. 16) possibly originally attached to a waist or sword belt; and a medieval horseshoe (no. 53). There

was also evidence for leisure activities with the find of a possible game counter (no. 136); another feature (1506, Period 2, Plot 4) from this period contained a bone die (no. 189).

During excavations in the basement of Queensberry House it became apparent that the exterior loam deposit had formerly spread beneath it (410 = 7154, 7130, not illustrated). However, in the east this contained post-medieval artefacts and is likely to have been disturbed during later construction activity, which seemed to have been more intensive here. As ground level rose toward the Canongate it was found that the basement of Queensberry House had been cut into the subsoil, and this must have removed all earlier deposits.

In Period 2, Plots 5 and 6, two equivalent deposits (1634 & 1684, not illustrated) were identified. These were similar in colour and composition to deposit 612, but were thinner and contained far fewer artefacts, perhaps reflecting much less activity in these plots. In the north of the site, beyond the later (Period 4) terrace wall, three later medieval loams (652, 667 & 671, fig 3.5) were preserved. It is thought that these survived here because they were outside the area cultivated in Period 3 and therefore had not been mixed into a homogeneous deposit.

3.5.2 Boundaries and backlands

Despite some filling with weathered soil, the large Period 1 ditch (754) must still have been an open and muddy channel by the beginning of Period 2. Around this time it was filled with a dump of rubble, probably quarried from a local rock outcrop, which was then sealed with silty clay (fig 3.3). This would have functioned as a rubble land-drain and for a while probably helped keep the surrounding area dry. Elsewhere the site was divided into long narrow plots, typical of a medieval town, by the cutting of ditches. The alignment expressed by these was not at right angles to the Period 1 ditch, and the end of one (759), between Period 2, Plots 1 and 2, cut its upper fills (fig 3.4). For these reasons this division of the site is interpreted as part of a reorganisation.

The minimum width of the plots did not vary significantly within the site and appeared to be around 13m (Period 2, Plots 1, 2 and 5); as discussed below, a yet thinner strip (between Plots 2.2 and 2.3) may have been a vennel. It would seem that Plots 2.3 and 2.4 had both been amalgamated into double-sized ones, albeit with one (Plot 2.3) generously sized at the expense of the other. The larger plots may merely reflect use

of a different type of boundary, which has not been identified archaeologically, such as a hedge. However, boundary ditches would have been a sensible option here, given the poor drainage and there are some historical references that have suggested that ditching was common practice (Chapter 4).

Period 2, Plot 1 (Plot 2.1)

The eastern side of Plot 2.1 was defined by a ditch in the southern part (759), and more formally, toward the frontage, by a drystone wall (004). The western side of the plot was not encountered within the area of excavation but may have been roughly below the eastern side of Reid's Close. The property contained a couple of pits (336, 323) dug into subsoil, which was very clayey here. They may have been intended to extract some clay for building or waterproofing, rather than being primarily for rubbish disposal. A rectangular cut (333) was preserved within the plot. It contained stakeholes in its base and impressions of planks in its sides. If the cut originally held a wooden lining, it could have functioned as a trough or something similar. Its backfill was indistinguishable from the surrounding loam and contained an array of artefacts that did not help in any diagnosis of function. A very regular cut (680) was found to have neatly held the base of a barrel (fig 3.6). Presumably this would have held water, perhaps for supplying animals or some craft activity. The wood was in such poor condition that its species could not be identified. The backfill (681) contained many iron nails and fragments, one designed for a horseshoe (no. 57), and a flax seed.

Figure 3.6
Pit containing the base of a barrel

At the south end of Plot 2.1 a rubble drain (786, fig 3.4) was cut on the same alignment as Holyrood Road, perpendicular to the plot boundaries. It contained a red and white clay floor tile (no. 122), which suggests that at least one building of high status had been constructed in the vicinity. The drain suggested that the area remained poorly drained and it fed a sump (767) to the east. The sump had a secondary channel sloping from the south, suggesting that this area was also in need of drainage, although perhaps outside the property. A later rubble drain (782) replaced 786 (fig 3.4) after it had ceased to be effective.

There was a concentration of later rubbish pits (669, 728, 722–4 & 720) close to the southern edge of the site beside Holyrood Road, on the boundary between Period 2, Plots 1 and 2. Mainly these appeared to contain domestic refuse such as a whetstone (no. 141), pottery and animal bones, but also fragments of Dutch and Maiolica floor tile (nos 127 & 131), which confirmed the nearby presence of high-status buildings. One of the fills (694) contained grape seeds. Grapes must have been transported to the Canongate dried, and their presence indicated that the inhabitants were wealthy enough to import foreign food as well as building materials.

Period 2, Plot 2 (Plot 2.2)

Plot 2.2 contained a stone-lined circular feature interpreted as a cistern (764, figs 3.4 & 3.7), which extended 1.4m into subsoil. A stone drain (768) was built into its lip and ran downslope to the south-east toward Holyrood Road, where it extended outside the trench (figs 3.4 & 3.5B). A shallow post setting (884) lay to the immediate west. Both this feature and the ditch (759), which formed the western boundary of the plot, contained a concentration of metalworking debris, and the ditch also contained a significant amount of magnetic residue (hammerscale). This suggested that part of the plot might have been used for ironworking. The stone-lined cut did not hold water during the excavation, but it would have done so if it had been waterproofed in some way. It is hard to interpret it as anything other than a cistern, since a drain seems to have been designed to carry liquid away from it to the south. As the base had filled with loose rubble, it seems likely that it had some sort of stone structure above the level to which it survived. Above the rubble was a loam, which contained much White Gritty ware pottery, a stone gaming counter (no. 137) and an iron horseshoe (no. 54). The last is perhaps suggestive of the type of smithing activities that could have been undertaken in this rear area of the plot which was safely removed from frontage buildings.

In the south of Plot 2.2, was a large pit (746). The first layers within it contained much midden material. This material had been dumped into the feature from the north and again indicated that metalworking

Figure 3.7
Cistern (764) and drain (768), seen from the north
(located on fig 3.4)

activity had been undertaken here. The pit was not filled to its brim and the soil that subsequently washed in from the north did not contain metalworking waste, but it included a dog bone with cut marks, which might indicate skinning. It may be that this large disposal pit was excavated to clear the plot following a change in ownership and consequent change of use. A small pit (753) to the north also contained metalworking debris and also seemed to have been for disposal of waste.

POSSIBLE TANNING TANKS

Plot 2.2 contained two features, which were interpreted as having been designed to hold liquid. One formed a double tank made of roughly shaped slabs bonded with watertight clay in a rectangular cut (775, 775, figs 3.4, 3.5, 3.35). The base was formed from large flagstones. The fills contained a copper alloy thimble (no. 21), dog bones with cut marks, probably the result of skinning, and an iron knife blade (no. 61). A couple of postholes in the vicinity (817 & 827) suggested that there may have been some sort of above-ground structure associated with the tank, although this would seem to have been very flimsy and perhaps was just a lean-to shelter.

To the south was a circular double cut (843), of which the northern cut was stone-lined. The southern cut contained a stake thrust hard against its side, and this may indicate the original presence of a wooden lining. The presence of clay at the point at which the two pits were connected confirmed the impression that these tanks were associated with two, presumably different, liquids. The backfilled material in the cuts contained horse bones with skinning marks and the head of a large fork (no. 60). Other domestic refuse was found in the backfill, notably a fragment of rare French Sgraffitto pottery, possibly from a drug jar (Pot no. 58).

These two features have most in common with tanning pits, especially some twinned examples found at Northampton and dated to the 16th century (Shaw 1984). The location of the tanks could be used to argue against an association with tanning, since it was an antisocial activity and they are not located at the very rear of the plot. However, they are at least some distance from the frontage and located in a plot close to the edge of the burgh. In view of the use of alkalis in the tanning process it is probably relevant that a pit (815) neighbouring the rectangular stone tank contained mostly lime. Elsewhere in Plot 2.2 were three pits (702, 706 & 796), all of which contained a mixture of domestic midden and building material.

POSSIBLE VENNEL

A ditch (810) defined the east side of Plot 2.2. It was post-dated in the middle part of the site by a sandstone culvert (703), leading away from the frontage. It was also earlier than another ditch (772). The fill of ditch 810 (809) was rich in artefacts and included ceramic roof tiles, another indicator of high-status buildings existing on the Canongate frontage, together with pottery that suggests a later medieval date for disuse of this boundary. The fill of the later ditch (772) was comparatively very clean. Also located in the vicinity of this boundary were several pits (411, 428, 808, 851), two of which were discovered beneath the basement of Queensberry House. The west side of Plot 2.3 was defined by a drystone wall (figs 3.4 & 3.8; 845 & 653), which had been reduced by subsequent robbing, and at another time a ditch (913 & 805). The ditch fill (912) contained a copper alloy buckle and two lace tags, which have been dated to the 15th/16th century (nos 4, 11 & 12).

The gap left between the boundaries appeared too small to have accommodated another plot and it may have functioned as a vennel. It did contain a feature (673) which, because of its form, was interpreted as the former location of a tree. This was post-dated by a large pit (fig 3.4; 854), which seemed to have filled gradually with weathered material. The apparent closing of the vennel at this point might suggest that it was designed to provide access to the rear of the plots from Holyrood Road, or as it then was 'The Strand', rather than from the Canongate frontage.

Period 2, Plot 3 (Plot 2.3)

Plot 2.3 contained a few truncated features (847, 858 & 959). They had been backfilled with domestic refuse, namely fishbone, shell and some building material such as plaster. Two pits (975 & 994) containing clay and lime mortar were identified below the remnants of a clay-bonded wall foundation (965). The foundation seemed to represent the south-east corner of a building, which would have extended beyond the northern limit of the excavation trench. This is taken to be the southernmost extent of buildings lining the Canongate.

Within Plot 2.3 a north/south-orientated wall (7060) was discovered around a metre beneath the floor of a room in the east of the Queensberry House basement. At the time of excavation the wall was noted as unusual because it was the only example seen in the basement that did not contain any lime mortar bonding; it pre-dated the large tenement foundations, which had been constructed here during the next period. The wall had been sealed by the dumping of a deposit (7046) containing 15th/16th-century pottery fragments.

Period 2, Plot 4 (Plot 2.4)

Plot 2.4 contained, at its northern end, the only preserved area of Canongate frontage exposed during the excavation. Although several remnants of clay-bonded walls survived (195, 1084, 1099 & 1105),

Figure 3.8
Drystone wall defining the western side of Plot 2.3

they were very poorly preserved because of later building activity and probably did not relate to a single structure. Clay (1104 & 1108) and gravel (1106) surfaces were also preserved; the former contained a complete horseshoe (no. 56) and fragments of 16th-century jars from Seville, probably used to import olive oil (not illustrated). The surfaces were dominated by a high concentration of metalworking debris, coal and cinders. This and the horseshoe suggested that ironworking was undertaken here, and perhaps even more specifically that it was a farriery. Several other features including hearths (206, 1110 & 1115) were also recorded.

Further south in Plot 2.4 was a group of channels and backfilled pits to the east of the boundary ditch between Plots 2.3 and 2.4 (1555) and the later drain (983). These were interpreted as a single group of industrial features, which had been replaced or renewed on at least one occasion. They included two stone-lined wells (1567 & 1571); finds from the backfill of 1567 included a rare sherd of green-glazed Siegburg stoneware (Pot no. 86), dated to the 14th/15th century and one of only three sherds yet found in Scotland, and a decorated stone spindle whorl (no. 140). The group was bounded to the north by a badly preserved lime mortar-bonded stone building (1510) containing a cobbled floor (1509), which had been extended (1515) to the west; it is presumed the building and pits were related. The features consisted of three large subrectangular cuts with depths of around 0.4m (1522, 1537 & 1539) and several subcircular features with a similar depth (997, 1518, 1527, 1531, 1545 & 1565). Among them ran at least four linear features (1506, 1520, 1541 & 1574), which may originally have been gullies designed to connect some of the larger features, as was certainly the case between cuts 1518 and 1527. The backfills within them all appeared to contain midden material, which was not particularly diagnostic as to function. The most common inclusions in samples retrieved from these were hammerscale, small fragments of bone, and coal and cinders. However, none was particularly concentrated and, given the presence of probable metalworking at the front of this plot, could have derived from elsewhere. One of the pits contained impressions that suggested it might have held a stone lining. Both the gullies connecting the features and the nearby presence of the well suggested that, whatever the function of the features, water was involved. If all these features had at one time been lined, they would perhaps fit the bill of the 'steipstanes' mentioned in the documentary sources. These were hollowed stone troughs, possibly used for soaking flax or malt. This can be no more than speculation, however, in the absence of further evidence.

Period 2, Plots 5 and 6 (Plots 2.5 and 2.6)

The eastern Plots 2.5 and 2.6 were defined not only by boundary ditches (1631, 1695 & 1698), but possibly also by fences (1692 & 1712). These slight features may have been preserved here because the loam accumulations were thinner and shallower cuts consequently extended into subsoil. On the boundary was a well (1727), which contained a horse bone that may indicate that skinning had been carried out here. The most varied assemblage of waterlogged plant remains recovered from the excavations was found in the backfill of the well. It contained hazelnut shells, the remains of edible fruits such as pear or apple, blackberry or raspberry, and strawberry. These could have been homegrown, but other species such as fig and grape must have been imported as dried fruits. A poppy seed was also present and may reflect use for flavouring food. The seeds are likely to have found their way into the well as part of faecal material and imply that the well was used as a

cesspit toward the end of its life. Also present were considerable numbers of seeds of plants that inhabit damp waste ground.

Several features had been dug within the plots; one was truncated but appeared very regular (1755) and, along with a stone-lined example (1778), seemed likely to have been more than a mere disposal pit. The large cut (1691), resembled the large cut in Plot 2.4 (1522) and might have served the same purpose. Other features may simply have been excavated for waste (1633, 1639, 1686, 1716, 1762 & 1775). Two sections of rubble drain (1655 & 1759) separated by modern disturbance seem likely to have been part of the same feature. This, taken with a ditch (1725) leading to a couple of sumps (1756 & 1736), suggests that drainage was a problem, a situation confirmed by two separate finds of amphibian bone from the fills of the rubble drain and sump, as well as the plant remains mentioned above.

The number of artefacts and the quantity of anthropogenic material recovered from samples taken from these features was low. The type of material was typical for medieval midden deposits, including coal, charcoal, metalworking debris, pottery, bone, shell, and charred cereal grains. None was in a concentration to suggest what the plots were predominantly used for; and at least in this part of the site the ground may have been damp and therefore relatively undeveloped.

3.6 Period 3: 16th–17th-century tenements and gardens

SIMON STRONACH

At this point in the site's history (fig 3.9) there appeared to have been a major change in the way the backlands were treated. Dark loams rich in artefacts built up across the area (fig 3.5B, 563), although in the eastern part of the site they were both lighter and less substantial (1620 & 1670, not illustrated). The difference in colour from the lower medieval loam is probably best explained as being a result of manuring with nightsoil and domestic rubbish including coal and ash, and it seems likely that most of the area was turned over to horticulture as depicted on Gordon of Rothiemay's perspective of 1647 (fig 6.1). This period comprises the dark loams and several late features that were sealed below them; it has no sub-periods.

The extensive spread of dark loam (563) contained a large assemblage of artefacts including a post-medieval bone die (no. 188), 17th-century glass and fragments

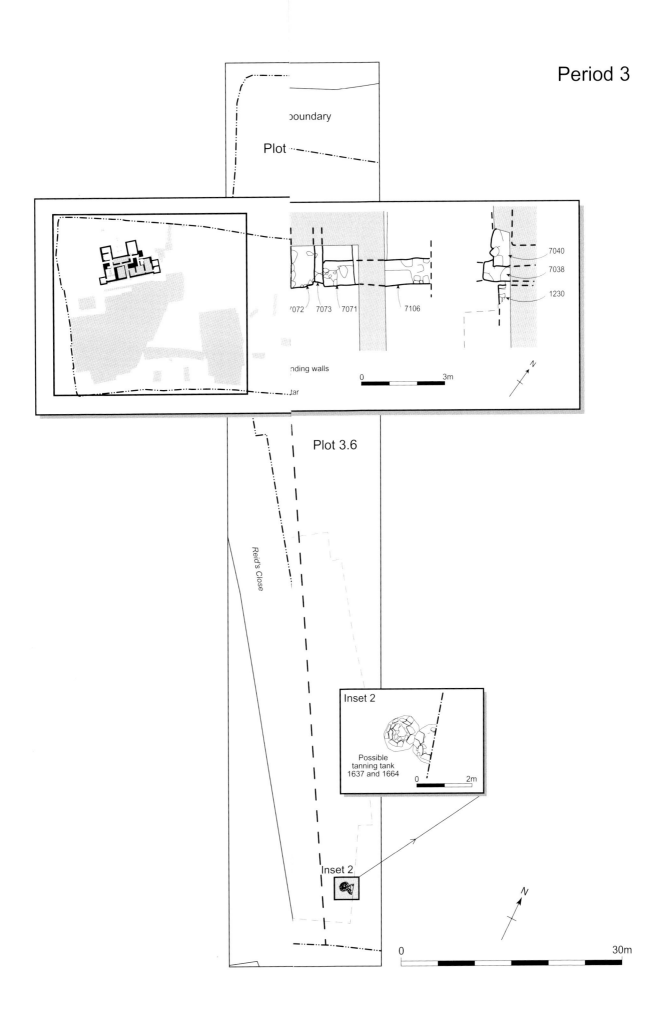

Period 3

boundary

Plot

7040
7038
1230

7072 7073 7071 7106

nding walls

tar

0   3m

N

Plot 3.6

Reid's Close

Inset 2

Possible
tanning tank
1637 and 1664

0   2m

Inset 2

N

0   30m

Figure 3.10
Termination of culvert 692

western boundary at the southern end (804), which seemed primarily designed to bury a large tree stump. This would have been very awkward to move and was probably just disposed of in the hole left when the tree was uprooted. The wood was identified as rowan, which is often used as an ornamental tree, but the fruits and bark also have practical uses. The bark can be used in tanning and for dyeing fabrics black, the berries can be made into jelly and both bark and berries are used in herbal medicine (Grieve 1992, 70). Superstition also held that the rowan provided protection from witches. The location of the tree suggested that the vennel was no longer needed to provide access to the rear of the plots after they were converted into gardens.

The southern part of Plot 3.3 contained no archaeological features that were assigned to this period; however, within the Queensberry House basement several substantial wall foundations that ran under the standing building were preserved beneath the modern

Figure 3.11
Early wall 849 forming the boundary between the vennel and
Plot 3.3, preserved under later wall 635

of clay tobacco pipes (nos 73, 268 & 324), bones from a wide variety of animals, and a range of pottery.

Period 3, Plots 1–3 (Plots 3.1–3) and possible vennel

A rubble drain (665) ran along the boundary between Plots 3.1 and 3.2 (fig 3.9). A large sandstone slab culvert (692, fig 3.11) probably ran along the eastern boundary of Plot 3.2. It might have provided drainage for a frontage building, although there was no evidence that it carried effluent. The culvert appeared designed to drain into the possible vennel established in the previous period, as did a stone culvert (757) on the eastern side. This boundary (between the vennel and Plot 3.3) was also defined by a drystone wall (750 = 849, fig 3.11). These culverts ended midway down the plot, and presumably drainage to the south was left to less formal means, such as open ditches and natural drainage. The possible vennel contained a large pit close to its

Figure 3.12
Wall of a tenement building surviving under Queensberry House

floor. The east wall of the south-west corner tower (7134) had been built on an earlier foundation, which contained an arch below ground level. A corner (7155) was revealed beneath the doorway of the neighbouring room.

Wall foundations revealed elsewhere indicated the edges of tenement buildings (1230, 7038, 7040 & 7071–5; figs 3.9 & 3.12). All these walls had been very disturbed by later construction and demolition, but several observations could be made. Foundation 7071/7106 appeared to be part of the same building, separated by later construction. Otherwise, the foundations were not all built at the same time, but where relations could be identified it was clear that they had functioned together for a spell. The walls usually had faces on the parts exposed above contemporary ground level and their substantial nature suggested that they had supported multi-storey tenements. They frequently used earlier walls for support, and it would

seem that construction was something of an *ad hoc* process, with different sides of buildings often reusing different walls. Little more can be said on the form of the buildings given the limited evidence. Overall they are consistent with the crowded terraces of tenements lining the Canongate on Rothiemay's plan of 1647 (fig 6.1).

Period 3, Plots 4–6 (Plots 3.4–6)

There were no identified plot boundaries further east than the west side of Plot 3.4 during this period. However, given that the boundary between Plots 2.4 and 2.5 was replicated in Period 5, it seems likely that this represents a lack of visibility rather than a temporary amalgamation. Similarly, it seems logical that the amalgamation of Plots 2.5 and 2.6 should be attributed to the documented purchasing of neighbouring properties during the development of the townhouse of Lothian Hut (Chapter 13.2.5) during

Period 5 rather than this period. Therefore, Plots 3.5 and 3.6 are assumed to have existed and are shown on fig 3.9 using dashed lines.

In Plot 3.4, the drain, which ran along its western boundary in the previous period, was robbed out (1507) and replaced, although much of this structure (1524) had also been robbed later. Several pits, of different form from those of the previous period, were located within this plot (1512, 1534, 1553, 1561 & 1562). They appeared to have been used to dispose of waste, in particular pit 1512, which contained a horse carcass. The bones did not exhibit any butchery marks and it would seem that the horse was a natural casualty. Metal objects and metalworking debris were common in the fills of several of these features and it may be that the association of this plot with metalworking of some description continued into this period. The structure 1510 continued in use and an accumulation of burnt material was preserved over the cobbling and within

a niche in the wall. This contained one of the few concentrations of chaff found during the excavation, consisting of barley and oat chaff dominated by culm fragments, which probably originated as straw.

POSSIBLE TANNING PIT

In the area assumed to have lain within Plot 3.6 one feature extended into the east baulk of the excavated area and consisted of two interconnected subcircular cuts (fig 3.13, 1637 & 1664). Both were stone-lined. The eastern cut (1664) contained remnants of an inner wood lining and was larger and deeper than 1637. Superficially this feature has much in common with the possible tanning pit 843 (Plot 2.2). No bones with skinning marks were found within either tank but there was a complete small unglazed bowl with a spout on the rim (Pot no. 99). The form of this vessel suggested that it may have been used for measuring out liquid, and its disposal without any evident damage

Figure 3.13
Possible tanning pit within Plot 3.6

may imply that this liquid was unpleasant, rendering the vessel useless after its primary function ceased. Measuring quantities of unpleasant liquids would certainly have been necessary as part of the tanning process. The location of the twin cuts in the backlands, as far away from the frontage as possible and at the edge of the burgh, would also be consistent with use for a noxious process. The stone lining in one of the cuts showed signs of mineralisation, which might have occurred if the pit had held tanning liquor.

Elsewhere in Plots 3.5 and 3.6 only four truncated features (not illustrated) were assigned to this period. Most appeared to be small disposal pits; one (1683) produced a glazed fragment of 16th-century stove tile (no. 74), a very rare find in a Scottish context that indicates the presence of high-status buildings in the vicinity.

3.7 Period 4: 17th–18th-century townhouses and formal gardens

SIMON STRONACH

Haddington House

The previous Plot 3.1 appears to have been subdivided into two properties by the building of a lime-mortared stone wall running north-west/south-east (218, figs 3.14 & 3.15). During the earlier part of this period the new subdivision (Plot 4.1) contained a series of north-east/south-west-aligned slots, each around 2m wide and up to 0.4m deep. The slots were quite closely

Figure 3.15
Excavation of the surviving walls of Haddington House and garden wall, looking north-west

spaced and had steep sides reaching flat bases. All had apparently been backfilled immediately with a mixture of rubble and loam. Their fills contained a variety of finds which suggested that they had been created in the 17th century. Above the slots was a dark loam (222, not illustrated) which also contained a variety of finds, including a fragment from a small bell (no. 1) and a decorative gilded buckle (no. 2). The lack of disturbance within these slots suggested that they were not used directly as planting beds. It seems more likely that they were intended to provide drainage below the loam, in which were planted formal floral beds and designs.

Later in this period the western subdivision was developed at its southern end, and the first building within the site to be located at the Holyrood Road end of the plots was constructed. This was not apparent on Edgar's plan of 1742 but was by the time of Lizars' survey of 1778 (fig 3.16). Within the excavated area the exterior wall (286, figs 3.14 & 3.17) was built on a deep, clay-filled foundation trench; an internal wall (284) was also identified. Pottery associated with the foundation trenches confirmed a construction date in the 17th or 18th century, which was consistent with an identification of the building as the documented Haddington House. The west and south walls had been incorporated into the perimeter wall of Queensberry House Hospital and survived to a height of around 2m. Originally the structure had been set back from Holyrood Road and was located between Reid's Close to the west and Haddington's Entry to the east. Its Holyrood Road façade was 8m wide (fig 3.17) and contained at least two windows at either end. This side did not appear to have contained the main doorway, and it is more likely that the building was accessed through Haddington's Entry. Later the building was extended to the south, the former façade became an internal wall, a fireplace was inserted, one former window was converted into a door and the other blocked.

To the north of the building was a large well (231, fig 3.18). Historical records relating to 12 Haddington's Entry, built before 1860, mention rights of access to a pump well, which was associated with a nearby malt works. A couple of disposal pits (281 & 290) were located between the well and the building.

Balmakellie and Queensberry House

Plot 4.2 was formed from the amalgamation of Period 3, Plots 1 (eastern part), 2, the vennel, 3 and 4.

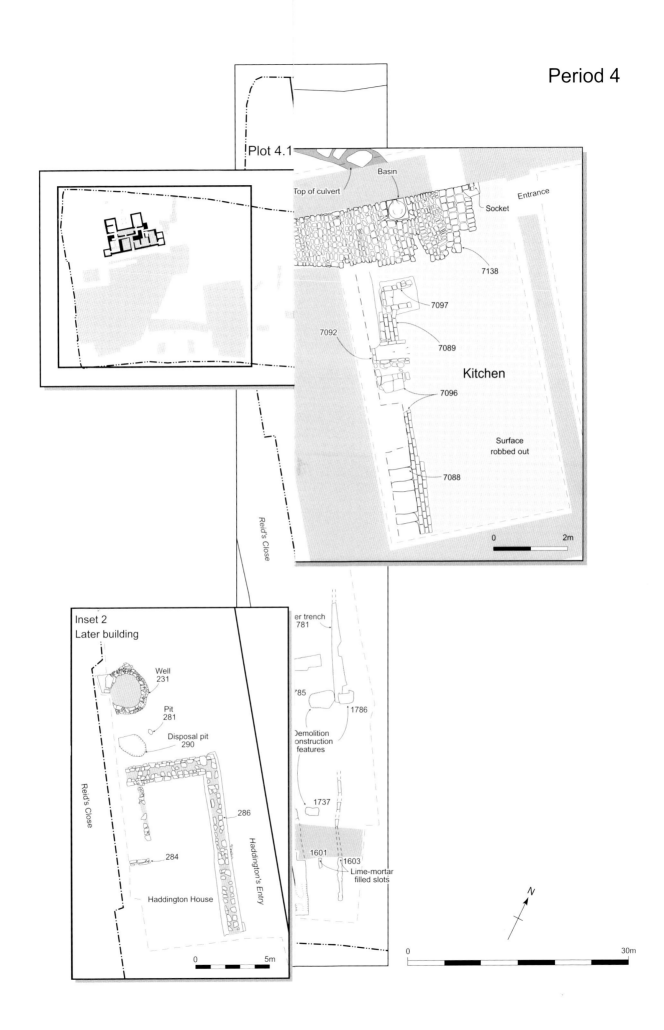

Period 4

Plot 4.1

Top of culvert
Basin
Entrance
Socket
7138
7097
7092
7089
7096
Kitchen
Surface robbed out
7088

0   2m

Inset 2
Later building

Well
231

Pit
281

Disposal pit
290

Reid's Close

286

284

Haddington House

Haddington's Entry

0   5m

er trench
781

785

1786

Demolition
construction
features

1737

1601
1603
Lime-mortar
filled slots

N

0   30m

Figure 3.16
Lizars' survey of 1778, showing the presence of Haddington House (© NLS)

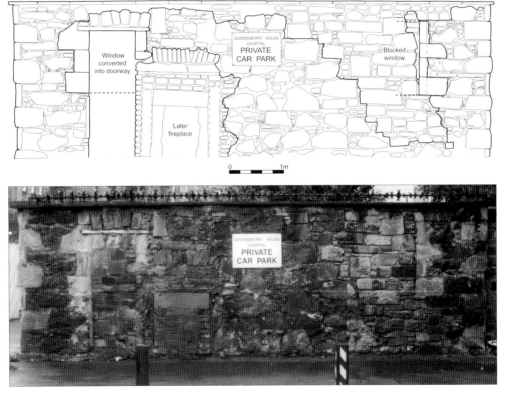

Figure 3.17
The Holyrood Road elevation of Haddington House wall

In it was a further series of drainage slots, similar to those in the plot containing Haddington House, but distinguished by running from north-west/south-east (fig 3.14). These also contained 17th-century artefacts, many of which indicated an increase in wealth, such as fragments of a decorated glass bottle (no. 85) which was probably Venetian and designed to carry a luxury such as perfume, and an ornate French ceramic bowl (Pot no. 65). A larger cut (618, fig 3.14) on the same orientation and holding more rubble, may have been hardstanding for a path. The very dark loam (540, not illustrated), which sealed these features and functioned as a cultivation soil, contained a variety of finds including an initialled wig curler (no. 121), iron shears (no. 62) and an early 18th-century medicine phial fragment (no. 84).

In the north these garden features appeared to respect a south-west/north-east-aligned wall (635, fig 3.14); the wall returned to the north along the line of the presumed property boundaries associated with the Balmakellie phase of building. The wall had later been extended east and west (629 & 988). The wall was likely to have formed a raised terrace overlooking the formal gardens. The extensions clearly reflected the expansion of the Canongate property, such as was carried out from the Balmakellie phase to that of the 2nd Duke of Queensberry. A gap in the centre of the wall accommodated a set of steps leading down from the terrace.

Layers of loam were dumped to raise the ground level within the terrace (643, 888, 974 & 992). One of these sealed a large pit (935), which appeared to have been created to dispose of surplus construction or demolition material such as rubble, both sandstone and true roof slates, glazed tiles and mortar. One of the fills contained a coin (no. 199) dating to the reign of James II or III (1437–88). Due to the underlying topography of the site the terrace did not need to be created in the west, as the ground level was already high enough. Here the retaining wall had been cut into the underlying loams. A small regular gully (650) filled

with stone in this area may represent the base of a garden feature.

Immediately to the south of the terrace wall in its western extension was a very large, shallow scoop (717), filled with crushed sandstone, which may have been mason's debris from the construction of the extension. Adjacent to the wall to the east were two pits (674 & 922) filled mainly with lime mortar, and these may also have been related to construction.

Some irregular features (916, 923 & 927) were present to the south of these pits. All were fairly irregular and had fills similar to the neighbouring drainage features. For this reason they are interpreted as features within the formal gardens. A linear spread of lime mortar (708) was located close by, and seems likely to have represented another feature within the gardens. To the east were several irregular features (943, 950 & 960). These were not very well preserved but exhibited a similar fill and alignment to those in

Figure 3.18
Excavation of a well behind Haddington House

the west, and are also interpreted as garden features. Later in this period two simple rubble-filled land-drains (666 & 670) were created to the immediate south of the terrace wall.

The terrace was remodelled towards the end of this period. A robber trench (644) removed part of the original wall 635, and several layers of rubble and earth (623–5) were dumped to raise the level of the terrace by around 0.5m. A wall (610 = 127, not illustrated) was then built on an east/west alignment within the raised terrace. This was a very crude structure built from roughly dressed stones loosely bonded with lime mortar. It suggested a much less formal garden, perhaps as a result of the decline in the Canongate's prestige toward the end of this period.

Close to the southern boundary with Holyrood Road was a truncated drain (601) leading to a sump (633), which must have drained the area to the south of a possible boundary ditch (661).

Sunken-floored kitchen and culverts

Two culverts discovered within the basement of Queensberry House may have related to two interconnected culverts outside. In a sunken-floored room identified as the kitchen a capped sandstone drain (7096) was of the same build as culvert 919 outside to the south and one seen between the two in an evaluation trench (132); these have all been interpreted as part of the same drainage system, which was joined by culvert 928, which was of the same build and seemed to be heading toward culvert 7017, discovered beneath the floor of a room in the east of the basement. Culvert 7096 ran beneath the south wall of the standing building, while 7017 had been cut by the construction of the wall. It is assumed that this wall was constructed during development of the site in the later half of the 17th century by Dame Balmakellie, and culvert 7096 must have functioned as part of this. Culvert 7017 must relate to a late phase of tenement use. However, both appear to have functioned within the same drainage system. Adaptation and retention of an existing system fits in well with the way in which Balmakellie's construction work reused existing foundations rather than clearing them and starting afresh.

A brass jeton from Nuremberg dated to 1490–1550 (no. 215) was retrieved from the backfill around culvert 919, while some silt (921) within it contained four copper pins (nos 24 & 25). Additionally, two pins came from a levelling deposit into which this

drain was cut, and another from the deposit overlying its stone capping. The entire excavation only yielded a total of 11 pins, which makes this concentration appear very significant. It was recorded that one of the properties in the area acquired as part of development by Lord Hatton (around 1680) was that of a tailor (Hume & Boyd c 1984, 57) and the pins may have derived from his premises. Culvert 919 had been constructed to pass through the terrace wall 635, while in the west culvert 628 was truncated by the wall's extension (629).

The level of the old tenement foundations immediately below the floor of Queensberry House Hospital indicated that the floor level of Balmakellie's building could not have been very different. Between and around the foundations were dumps of rubble and loam, deliberately used for levelling and composed of waste from the demolition process. Clay pipe fragments from these deposits fell within the date range 1630 to 1660, immediately prior to Dame Balmakellie's development.

The room identified as the kitchen had been created with a sunken floor lower than the rest of the basement, and later levelling had led to the preservation of early surfaces and features. The room was originally larger and incorporated what had later become part of a corridor to the immediate north. Here one of the capstones of culvert 7096 was a stone basin set within a cobbled surface 7138 (fig 3.14). The basin sloped northward, where it had a spout that extended beneath the north standing wall of the room. On the other side of the wall, on what was the exterior of the early building, the top of a culvert could be seen some half a metre higher, and this may have fed the kitchen culvert. Practical reasons for making this room sunken-floored would include having a ready supply of water flowing through its culvert. Silt within the culvert (7105) contained the waterlogged remains of apple or pear and some grape pips, which probably arrived as sewage and suggested that, at least latterly, the culvert was probably not used for supplying fresh water.

A socket discovered set into the cobbling in the east of the room might have been connected to a stairway or entrance. Further south in the room, beyond the later wall used to create a corridor and at the same level, a handmade brick and flagstone surface (7088) was used instead of cobbling. Presumably the cobbling or brick had originally stretched over the rest of the room. The bricks had also been used to form two rectangular features (7097 & 7092). Analysis of some

Period 5

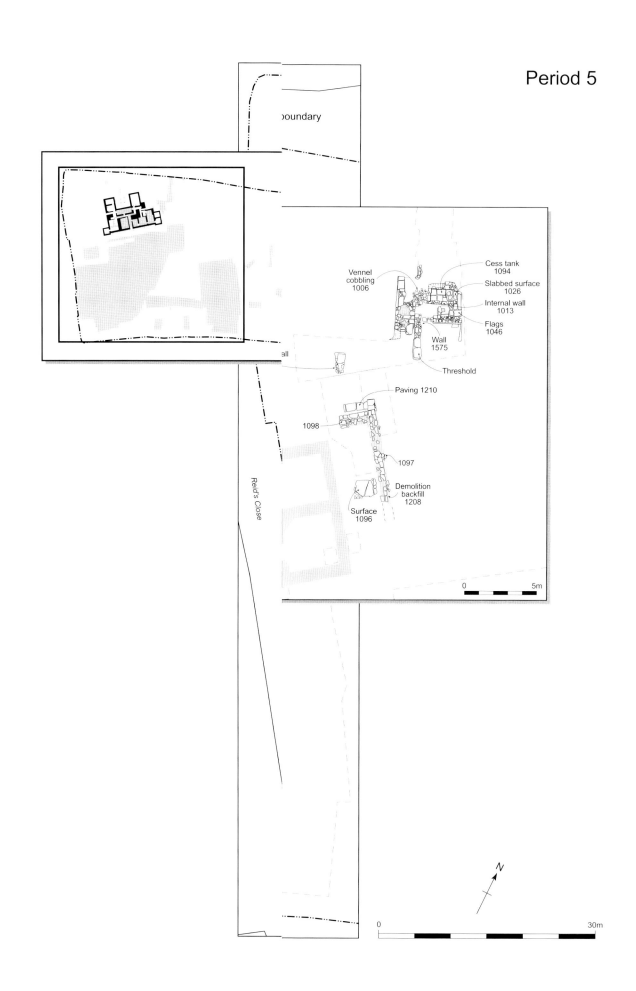

boundary

Reid's Close

Vennel
cobbling
1006

Cess tank
1094

Slabbed surface
1026

Internal wall
1013

Flags
1046

Wall
1575

Threshold

Paving 1210

1098

1097

Demolition
backfill
1208

Surface
1096

all

0   5m

N

0   30m

3.8 Period 5: 19th-century military barracks and modern features

SIMON STRONACH

Haddington House

In the building identified as Haddington House a very disturbed brick feature (282) appeared to have formed the base of a rectangular structure. A drain (265, fig 3.19) with a pronounced bend sloped away from this and exited the building through a gap in wall 222, which was the only place where any fill was preserved in the drain. This contained many fish bones, which suggested that the building might have been domestic. However, the next most common inclusion was metalworking debris and fragments of slag. This contrast may represent a change in use from a domestic building into an industrial one, perhaps when taken over by the military early in the 19th century (Chapter 14.3). Further north along Reid's Close a structure (213) was constructed, and then extended to the south (212), up to Haddington House.

Quartermaster's store and military features

Further east was a rectangular building with dividing walls, which corresponded to the location of a quartermaster's store (figs 3.19 & 3.20) constructed during military use of the site and planned by Kirkwood in 1817 (fig 3.21) but not by Lizars in 1778. The quartermaster's store was converted into a canteen late in its history. A number of internal walls, surfaces, drains and an extension were added in order to achieve this. Also as part of military use, rubble and hard standing (622, not illustrated) were dumped over the terraced gardens to create a parade ground, and two large conduits (952 & 957) were constructed to service barracks. The excavation revealed foundations likely to have been for the western gatehouse depicted on Kirkwood's plan adjacent to Holyrood Road.

Tenement and Queensberry House

The tenement immediately to the east of Queensberry House, still standing as no. 60 Canongate at the start of the project, was built around this time (fig 3.19, inset). To the rear were foundations (1097 & 1098), which were interpreted as relating to a slightly later building. Several features associated with these were preserved, including a stone cesspit (1094), several flagged surfaces (1026, 1046, 1096 & 1210) and a well-laid cobble floor (1006). Less substantial internal walls (1013 & 1068) were also recorded.

Within Queensberry House, material was dumped within the sunken-floored kitchen in the 19th century to bring the floor level into conformity with the rest of the basement. A range of crockery fragments from this make-up is thought to have related to the building's use as a House of Refuge from 1853 (Chapter 14.4). They have provided a valuable insight into conditions within the institution.

3.9 Summary of the artefactual evidence for Periods 1–5

ADRIAN COX & DEREK HALL

3.9.1 Period 1 (12th–14th centuries)

Few finds were associated with this period, although there was some evidence of metallurgical activity. Among other artefacts recovered was a horseshoe nail (no. 58), of a form generally thought to have been in use until the 13th century, although finds from Perth indicate that similar nails may have remained in use into the 14th century. The excavations yielded a total of 44 pieces of struck stone (mainly flint), although probably none was in a primary context. Two bipolar flakes of quartz (nos 143 & 144) came from the natural silting in the boundary ditch 754 located along the southern edge of excavation, and a hard-hammer flake (no. 145) was found in a gravel deposit in this period.

This period produced a small amount of pottery (24 sherds in total), comprising jugs and cooking pots of Scottish White Gritty ware, presumably of local production. Of most interest is the single sherd that is apparently from a local copy of a Yorkshire seal jug (756; Pot no. 13). If this identification is correct, the context that produced this sherd, namely backfill within the large boundary ditch 754, can date no earlier than the 13th or 14th centuries.

3.9.2 Period 2 (14th–15th centuries)

Period 2.1

Even fewer finds were associated with Period 2.1, when the site was formally divided, than was the case in Period 1. Among those recovered was the earliest of a number of iron horseshoe fragments (no. 54). Other horseshoes were recovered from Periods 2.2, 2.3 and 4.1.

Period 2.2

Associated with the accumulation of medieval 'garden soil' deposits and associated features in this period is a

Figure 3.20
Excavation of the quartermaster's store (centre); to the right (west) are the remains of Haddington House and Haddington's Entry

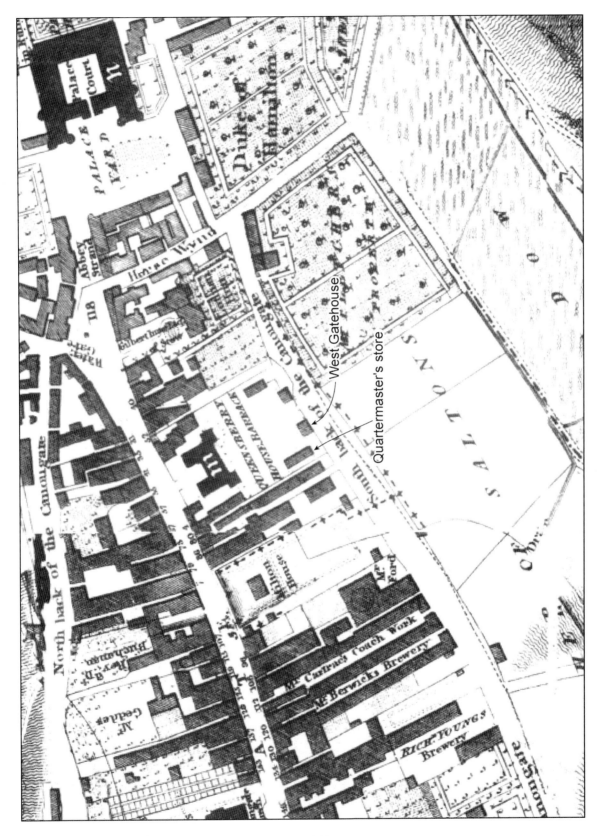

Figure 3.21
Kirkwood's map of 1817, showing the locations of the quartermaster's store and the west gatehouse (© NLS)

varied assemblage of artefacts, representing a diverse array of craft activities and domestic pursuits. As also in Period 1, a number of finds provide tentative evidence of the types of buildings which existed on or near the site. Among this evidence are two lead alloy window came fragments, indicating glazed windows. Found in the upper fills of the Period 1 boundary ditch 754, a fragment representing the edge of an inlaid floor tile (no. 122) probably came from a prestigious building, possibly with a religious function.

There is some limited artefactual evidence of non-ferrous metalworking. A fragment of lead alloy waste, rolled up and possibly intended for recycling (no. 51), came from one of the garden soil deposits, and a possible lead alloy offcut (no. 47) was found with the window came fragments referred to above. As well as being in demand to make cames, workers in lead would have been involved in the fabrication of roofs for ecclesiastical buildings and other large structures, and in the manufacture of pewter tableware, tokens and other artefacts (Ewan 1990, 34). Evidence for the cold working of sheet metal survives in the form of a riveted fragment of copper alloy sheet, probably representing a vessel repair patch (no. 35), which was found in the fill of the boundary ditch 810 on the east side of Plot 2.2. This may have been fabricated on the site, although the vessel may possibly have been brought to the site in its repaired condition.

Analysis of the industrial debris from the site revealed a sustained accumulation of iron smelting/smithing waste in an area to the south of Queensberry House in Periods 2.2–2.3 and Period 3 (Section 18.3.4), possibly indicating that metallurgical activities were concentrated in this area during the medieval and post-medieval periods.

Many town-dwellers probably produced much of their domestic requirements themselves. Indeed, documentary sources reveal that many people owned spinning wheels and other weaving equipment. Many would have clothed themselves with home-produced textiles. A decorated spindle whorl (no. 140), found in the fill of a well (1567, Plot 2.4) in this period, represents one of the artefact types associated with this kind of activity most likely to survive in the archaeological record. Generally, textiles and organic components of weaving equipment are only preserved on waterlogged sites, where anaerobic conditions occur. No. 140 is paralleled by finds from 13th- to 15th-century contexts elsewhere in Scotland. Spindle whorls were used in the production of fairly small quantities of yarn by the drop spinning method. As

Peter Yeoman (1995, 75) notes, the evidence recovered from Scottish urban excavations, in terms of spinning and weaving equipment, and of textiles, suggests that most domestic cloth production was simple and small-scale.

Limited evidence of costume survives in the form of dress accessories, such as a double-looped buckle from this period (no. 3), again recovered from a cultivated soil deposit, and dating from the mid-14th century or later. This buckle may have been used in conjunction with a spur. The individual who wore it may therefore have been someone of at least moderate means, and perhaps the same can be said of the person who owned a copper alloy mount of cruciform shape (no. 16), which may have been worn on leather or textile clothing.

Alongside subsistence and any commercial activities, the site's inhabitants must have found time for leisure pursuits. The smallest of four stone discs from the site (no. 136), again recovered from a cultivated soil deposit, may represent a gaming counter. The earlier of two bone dice (no. 189) was also found in Period 2.2. Dice could be used in different ways, either by themselves in games of chance, or to determine the movement of pieces on a gaming board.

This period marks the first appearance of sizeable quantities of pottery on the site (1979 sherds). Scottish White Gritty ware is the most common fabric with smaller quantities of the later local fabrics, Reduced Gritty ware and Oxidised Redware. The largest number of sherds of Yorkshire Type ware was recovered from this period, including sherds from the fill of a slot (333, Plot 2.1) and a pit (746, Plot 2.2) which were located in the property running adjacent to Reid's Close. Rhenish Stoneware (14th/15th century) first appears in this period with sherds from Raeren and Siegburg vessels from industrial feature 1520 (Plot 2.4) and sump or feeder channel (767, Plot 2.2) respectively. Industrial feature 1520 also produced a single sherd of 16th/17th-century Weser Slipware, which would place the backfilling of this feature towards the end of this period. The only sherd of green-glazed stoneware (15th century) from the excavation was found in the fill of a well (1567, Plot 2.4). It is of interest that even at this early stage the imported pottery present includes high-status stoneware and slipware.

Period 2.3

Scottish White Gritty continues to be the most common fabric in this period, with Reduced Gritty ware and Oxidised Redware also well represented. The proximity of high-status buildings is suggested by a single sherd of Beauvais Double Sgraffitto ware from the backfill of a stone tank (843) in Plot 2.1 and four sherds from Spanish olive jars from surface 1104 on the Canongate frontage in Plot 2.4.

Based on the diagnostic fragments recovered, the glass assemblage from Periods 1 to 2.2 dates from the 15th century or earlier, whereas that from Period 2.3 dates from the late 15th to the early 16th century. The evidence from documentary sources indicates that, by the late 15th century, there were some wealthy and substantial dwellings bordering Canongate's main street.

Finds of costume accessories become more numerous in this period. Two copper alloy lace tags (nos 11 & 12), designed to prevent the ends of clothing and shoe laces and thongs from fraying, came from a ditch 913 on the west side of Plot 2.3. The same feature produced a small, copper alloy, D-shaped buckle of 15th- or 16th-century date (no. 4).

Documentary records reveal that workshops, wells and gardens were situated to the rear of many burgage plots. Skinners, tanners, shoemakers, cutlers, masons and brewers all held property on the south side of Canongate. The frontages of the plots offered opportunities for commercial enterprises, with booths serving as retail outlets. Some recovered artefacts may have been associated with industrial or craftworking activities, although there were no diagnostic concentrations of artefact types. Clay-lined stone tank 775 (Plot 2.2), thought to have been used in a tanning process contained a possible knife blade (no. 61) in its fill. The primary fill of stone-lined tank 843, also in Plot 2.2, contained the heavily corroded iron head of a large, three-pronged fork (no. 60). The fork may simply represent a component of discarded waste material, thrown into the feature once it had gone out of use. However, given its location in the primary fill, a connection with the feature's primary function is a possibility. Perhaps the fork was used to agitate the contents of the tank. On the boundary between Plots 2.1 and 2.2, a possible hone fragment (no. 142) was found in the fill of rubbish pit 722.

Documentary evidence points to an abundance of gardens and orchards in the medieval burgh, and many people kept their own livestock. Artefactual evidence for the keeping of animals is scarce, although the only complete horseshoe recovered from the site (no. 56) was found in clay surface 1104, located near the frontage in Plot 2.4.

3.9.3 Period 3 (16th–17th centuries)

During the 16th century, Canongate may have gained in prestige due to the presence of royalty, although it suffered at the hands of the Earl of Hertford's expeditionary forces in the years after James V's death in 1542. Artefact evidence, such as the different types of decorated floor tiles recovered, indicates the presence of prestigious buildings in the vicinity of the site during the medieval and post-medieval periods. The floor tiles were not concentrated in a particular area, but found in different parts of the site, and therefore are difficult to relate to particular buildings.

There is still a large group of Scottish White Gritty ware present in this period which must suggest that a lot of the features and deposits producing it are more likely to date to the earlier end of the medieval period. Imported wares are represented by sherds of Low Countries Tin-glazed Earthenware from the fill of drain 757, located on the west side of Plot 3.3, and a sherd of Siegburg Stoneware from drain 1524 (Plot 3.4). All these sherds are from features associated with the burgage plots that run back from the Canongate. Of most interest in this period is the piece of 16th-century ceramic stove tile from the fill of garden feature 1683 (Plot 3.5, Pot no. 74, fig 18.3). This feature lies in the part of the Parliament site that may originally have been part of the monastic precinct of Holyrood Abbey and, as these ceramic stoves are more commonly found related to religious buildings, this may imply the proximity of such a building on this part of the site.

Documentary sources reveal that young men from all parts of Scotland were sent to Canongate in the 16th century to serve as apprentices among the burgh's hammermen, who included blacksmiths, cutlers, lorimers, braziers and jewellers. Merchants and craftsmen would have derived benefits from living close to Holyrood Palace, where they could readily have found outlets for their various skills. Among the assemblage of copper alloy artefacts there appears to be some evidence of tailoring activity. Such finds include a thimble of open form (no. 20); a type used for specialised tasks such as sewing canvas and in tailoring, and generally preferred by tailors for heavier work. Copper alloy pins were also found in this period, as was a probable needle fragment, although a greater concentration of pins appeared in Period 4.1.

Although 16th-century Edinburgh suffered from overcrowding, the burgh of Canongate was not so built-up, and fine private residences were being constructed at that time (Turner Simpson & Holmes 1981, 49). The presence of two Nuremburg jetons, one of late 15th- to mid-16th-century date (no. 215), the other of late 16th- to early 17th-century date (no. 216), lends support to the notion of at least moderately wealthy residents on the site at this time.

Along with increasing evidence of wealth, there is increasing evidence of recreational activity. Part of a disc or counter, derived from a sherd of Reduced Greyware pottery (no. 120), found in rubble overlying stone-capped culvert 757 in Plot 3.3, was probably used as a gaming counter. The fabric of this object indicates that it dates from the 15th or 16th century, and it was found with window glass of a similar date. A small bone die (no. 188) was also found in this period.

The earliest clay pipes from the excavation date from the period c 1620–40, and can be compared with examples found in a pre-1637 context beneath Edinburgh's Tron Kirk (Gallagher 1987a). One of the stratigraphically earliest is a polished bowl from a garden soil deposit in this period (no. 225). Other early examples come from Period 4.1. Of over 900 pipe fragments recovered from the site, the majority were manufactured between c 1630 and 1680, a period in which there was a rapid growth in the fashion for pipe smoking in Edinburgh.

3.9.4 *Period 4 (16th–18th centuries)*

Period 4.1 (16th–17th centuries)

The amounts of Reduced Gritty Ware and Oxidised Redware finally overtake Scottish White Gritty ware in this period. Interestingly, the most common ceramic cooking vessel represented in the Oxidised Redware fabric is the handled skillet (Pot nos 37–41). A wide variety of imported wares are present in this period, largely dating to the 16th or 17th centuries; many of these are from cultivation features and soils within the formal gardens of Queensberry House (Plot 4.2) and Haddington House (Plot 4.1).

These fabrics include a second sherd of Beauvais Double Sgraffitto ware, sherds of Frechen Stoneware and a small group of slipwares that may be locally produced. The garden features (1610, 1616) associated with Lothian Hut (Plot 4.3), contain sherds from Loire jugs. This period produced the only two sherds of Mediterranean Green and Brown Redware and Saintonge Palissy Type ware from a levelling deposit within a terrace (643, Plot 4.2), and the backfill of boundary ditch 661 (Plot 4.2). Both sherds are from very ornate pottery vessels and it is tempting to suggest

that they both originate from Queensberry House itself. A unique vessel in an unidentified fabric (Pot no. 99), present in the backfill of stone-lined industrial tank 1637 (Plot 3.6), appears to be an apothecary's cup, presumably used for measuring small quantities of liquid into the tank.

The Confession of Faith, signed in 1638 by a large number of Canongate's residents, indicates a broad cross-section of craftsmen living locally. For example, more than 50 tailors signed, along with 32 wrights, 25 weavers, 15 dyers and eight saddlers (Turner Simpson & Holmes 1981, 50). There is tentative artefactual evidence from the excavation to support the presence of craftsmen, and also evidence of increasing wealth and sophistication, although many poorer and less fortunate residents would have lived alongside the wealthier members of society.

Of the 11 copper alloy pins recovered from the site, all but two are from Period 4.1. Their form indicates a probable 17th-century date. Four of the pins came from the fill of a stone-capped culvert 919 (Plot 4.2) likely to have led from the kitchens of a house fronting onto Canongate. Other pins came from the underlying and overlying deposits. This concentration of pins would appear to be significant, and may indicate tailoring activities, either in the house from which this drain led, or in a property occupying the vicinity of the drain, probably in the second half of the 17th century. Part of a small pair of iron shears (no. 62), from a garden soil deposit, may have performed a variety of household functions or been used by a tailor working on or near the site.

Among the coins recovered from the site, the largest group is of 17th-century copper coinage. The burgh's location, on the main routes from the port of Leith to both Holyrood and Edinburgh, encouraged thriving commercial activity.

Finds from the Period 4.1 garden soils include a fragment of a copper alloy rumbler bell (no. 1), probably of 16th- or 17th-century date, which may have been worn as a costume accessory, on horse harness, or on the collar of an animal. A decorative buckle (no. 2), dating from the mid-17th to 18th century, was also recovered, along with numerous clay pipe fragments dating from the second half of the 17th century and glass of similar date. Overall, the glass assemblage from Periods 3 and 4.1 dates from the early 16th to the early 18th century. One of the garden soil deposits produced a ceramic wig curler of probable 18th-century date (no. 121).

Two decorative copper alloy mounts of domed form were found in this period. No. 14 was found in a garden soil deposit, while No. 15 came from a levelling deposit for a terrace (Plot 4.2). Two copper alloy studs of the kind used on furnishings in the 16th and 17th centuries were also found.

The earliest clay pipes from this period date from the period 1630–50 (for example, nos 226 & 228). One of these (no. 226) came from a garden soil deposit under Haddington House (Plot 4.1). Closely dated clay pipes from primary contexts provide particularly useful dating evidence, for example, a pipe bowl dating from c 1660–1700, found in the packing for terrace wall 629 (Plot 4.2).

Period 4.2 (18th century)

Numbers of artefacts decline in Period 4.2, possibly as a result of changes in the use of the site at this time. Despite being present throughout Periods 2, 3 and 4.1, almost all evidence of the deposition of ironworking waste disappears at this point.

The glass recovered from Period 4.2 dates from the later 18th to the 19th century. There is a surprising scarcity of glass (both vessel and window) of 18th-century date in the assemblage. Wine bottles, in particular, were manufactured and used in very large numbers in the middle of the 18th century, yet a relative lack of fragments of this date has been noted from this site, possibly indicating a change of site usage after the 17th century.

Very few clay pipes from the site post-dated 1700. Snuff taking appears to have replaced pipe smoking as the usual method of tobacco consumption after c 1730, and pipes dating from the remainder of the 18th century are uncommon in much of Scotland. Twenty pipe bowls dating from c 1640 to 1680 were found in a make-up deposit inside Haddington House (Plot 4.1) in this period.

By this period the amount of pottery present has begun to decline, possibly reflecting a change in the rubbish disposal pattern and the use of the southern part of the site as gardens. Of most significance are the sherds from Loire jugs in a feature associated with the construction of Lothian Hut in Plot 4.3 (1785) and a rimsherd from a late 16th-/early 17th-century Weser ware dish from drain 601 (Plot 4.2).

3.9.5 Period 5 (19th–20th centuries)

Period 5.1

In Period 5 the pottery assemblage is dominated by 18th- and 19th-century china, possibly associated with the military occupation of the site. Apart from a small group of Low Countries Tin-glazed Earthenware from the floor make-up of the quartermaster's store (536), all the remaining pottery is liable to be residual.

Among the finds from Period 5.1 were two conjoining fragments of a glazed ceramic carpet bowl (no. 119). These were found in the fill of a shallow pit within Haddington House. This represents further evidence of leisure pursuits on the site, which appears to be a continuing small-scale theme throughout its occupation since medieval times. Parlour games such as carpet bowls would have been popular in wealthier Victorian households.

The carpet bowl fragments were accompanied in the pit fill by a flat-bottomed, iron hanging vessel (no. 67), probably of 19th-century date, which may have served a partly ornamental function. Also found in this fill was a leather shoe of riveted construction, probably dating from the 1850s or later. Boots or shoes of riveted construction usually had front lacing, and three further leather fragments with lace-holes from this period are from footwear of a similar style and method of construction.

Smaller quantities of clay pipes came from make-up deposits in this period than came from Period 4.2. Pipes from the make-up of the floor of the quartermaster's store have a date range of c 1680–1710. The glass assemblage from Period 5 dates from the 19th and 20th centuries.

Period 5.2

Canongate's fortunes had declined through the 17th and 18th centuries, and by the 19th century the burgh contained derelict and overcrowded slums (Turner Simpson & Holmes 1981, 50). Nevertheless, one particular find from this phase may be an indicator of the presence of a prestigious household: this is a German porcelain tobacco pipe bowl, of 19th-century date, depicting a young woman resting on a plinth and reading a book (no. 348). This find came from the backfill of a Period 4 well to the rear of Haddington House (231, Plot 4.1), which also contained two copper alloy buttons and a ceramic alley (no. 116).

Alleys such as no. 116 formed components of the closure mechanisms for glass bottles in the 19th century, but they were also often claimed as marbles by children, once the bottles had been used. By this time many manufactured items bore the maker's or seller's name. A stoneware bottle top (no. 118) bearing the mark of J Stewart & Sons, a firm based on Canongate,

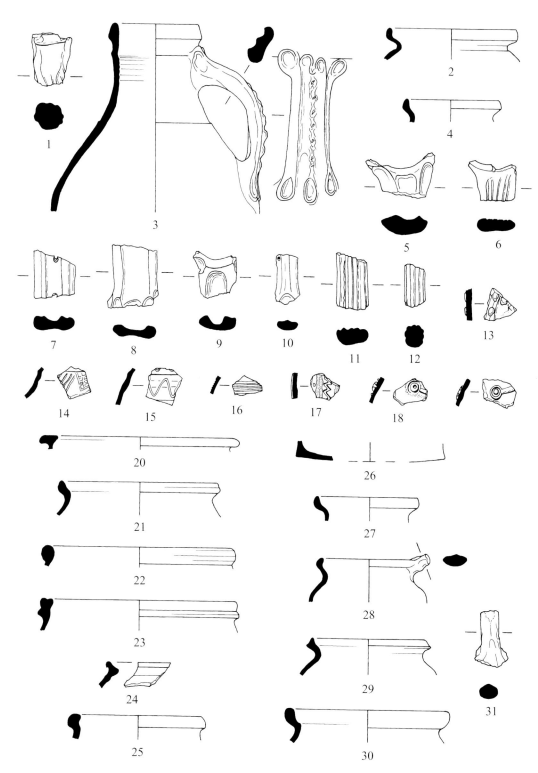

Figure 3.22
Pottery (scale 1:2)

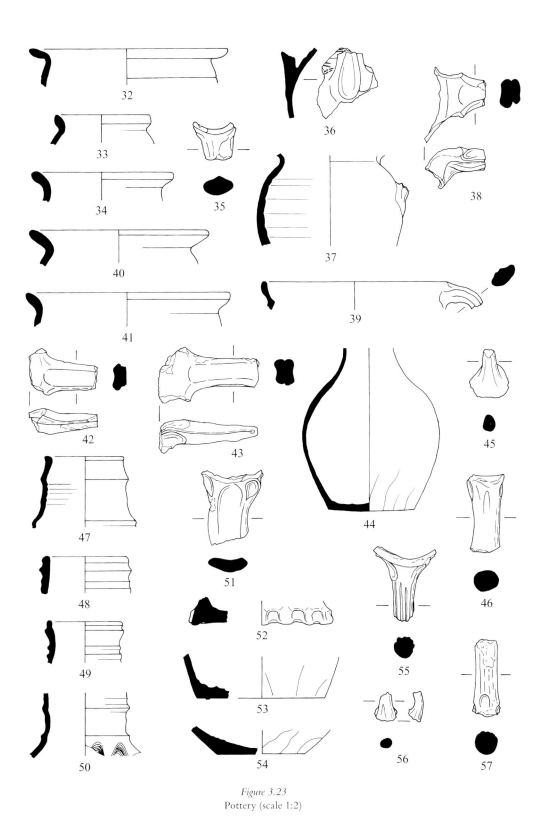

Figure 3.23
Pottery (scale 1:2)

was found in a service trench in this period. Among the finds from the kitchen of Queensberry House is the body of a mineral water bottle embossed with a legend indicating a connection with Dr Struve's mineral waters business (QH no. 10).

Physical evidence for the nature of structures on the site in this latest phase of its occupation includes an iron strap hinge, of 19th-century date, from a cupboard or shutter (no. 59). This too, came from the fill of a service trench.

3.9.6 Artefact catalogue (selected items mentioned in the main text)

Period 1

POTTERY

Pot no. 13 Bodysherd from green-glazed jug with remains of applied seal including incised letter 'K'
Context 756 (fig 3.22)

IRON

54 Horseshoe. Length 58mm; max. width 24mm; thickness 3mm.
Fragment representing part of one branch, heavily corroded, and with part of the outer edge missing. Parts of three rectangular nail holes survive.
Context 760; IADB 2680

58 Horseshoe nail. Length 29mm; width of head 13mm; thickness 4mm.
Almost complete horseshoe nail, missing only its tip, in three conjoining pieces. The head is of lobed, semicircular form. X-radiography indicates that the nail tip was clenched.
Context 790; IADB 2325 (fig 3.32)

LITHICS

143 Bipolar flake, quartz. 13 × 15 × 8mm.
Phase 1, Context 790.
144 Bipolar flake, quartz. 16 × 12 × 4mm.
Phase 1, Context 790.
145 Hard-hammer flake with oblique distal truncation, flint. 24 × 17 × 6mm.
Phase 1, Context 889.

Period 2

SIEGBURG STONEWARE

Pot no. 86 Frilled base from small unglazed vessel.
Context 763 (fig 3.24)

COPPER ALLOY

3 Buckle. Diameter 18mm; thickness 2mm.
Double-looped annular buckle, bisected symmetrically by the pin bar. The frame is plain, with subrectangular cross-sectioned edges. The pin is in the form of a plain, rectangular cross-sectioned, tapering strip, simply looped around the central bar. Distorted.
Context 667 (Sample 1106); IADB 3636 (fig 3.26)

4 Buckle. Length (including pin) 15mm; width 17mm; thickness 3mm.
Small buckle of approximately D-shaped form, with a serrated outer edge and a narrow flange along the pin bar. The pin is in the form of a plain, rectangular cross-sectioned, tapering strip, simply looped around the buckle frame. Slightly distorted.
Context 912 (Sample 2789); IADB 2855 (fig 3.26)

10 Lace tag. Length 33mm; max. diameter 2mm.
Almost complete lace tag, made from thin sheet, with an edge-to-edge seam. A possible remnant survives of the lace or thong it enclosed. There is slight breakage at both ends and the tag is corroded. Undecorated.
Context 612; IADB 2463; Phase 3

11 Lace tag. Surviving length 21mm; max. diameter 2mm.
Lace tag fragment, made from thin sheet, broken at both ends. It has an overlapping seam. Undecorated.
Context 912; IADB 2853

12 Lace tag. Surviving length 16mm; max. diameter 2mm.
Lace tag fragment, made from thin sheet, broken at both ends. It has an edge-to-edge seam. Undecorated.

16 Mount. Length 20mm; surviving width 19mm; thickness 1mm.
Mount in the form of an equal-armed cross, with arms of approximately D-shaped cross-section and small pellets in the angles between the arms. The object was formerly secured by iron rivets through small perforations (<1mm) through the rounded, expanded terminals. A remnant of one of the rivets survives and another two are attested by the presence of corrosion products. Parts of all four terminals survive, although two are broken across their rivet holes. The rear of the mount is flat. Corroded.
Context 612 (Sample 1615); IADB 3627 (fig 3.26)

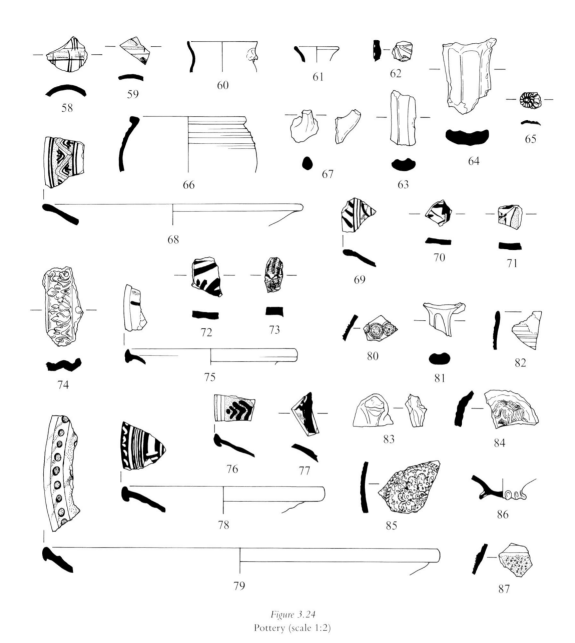

Figure 3.24
Pottery (scale 1:2)

21 Thimble. Surviving height 18mm; original max. diameter c 15mm.

Thimble of slightly tapering, domed form, with broadly spaced, possibly punched, indentations on the surviving upper part of the body, with a plain band below. The top of the thimble is largely missing, although a small, detached fragment survives and appears to bear indentations. The object has been crushed almost flat and is heavily corroded.

Context 812; IADB 2282

IRON

53 Horseshoe. Length 54mm; max. width 24mm; thickness 4mm.

Horseshoe fragment representing part of one branch, including the terminal. X-radiography reveals that the object has broken across a rectangular nail hole.

Context 612; IADB 2635

54 Horseshoe. Length 58mm; max. width 24mm; thickness 3mm.

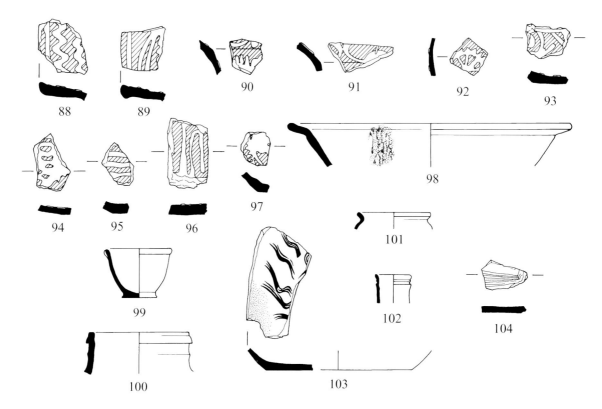

Figure 3.25
Pottery (scale 1:2)

Horseshoe fragment representing part of one branch, heavily corroded, and with part of the outer edge missing. Parts of three rectangular nail holes survive.

Context 760; IADB 2680

56   Horseshoe. Length 121mm; max. width 30mm; thickness 7mm.

Complete horseshoe. X-radiography reveals seven rectangular nail holes, arranged asymmetrically. There is a calkin on one branch only. Heavily corroded.

Context 1104; IADB 3427

59   Strap hinge. Length 153mm; width 77mm; max. thickness 6mm.

Strap hinge with a tapering arm, with three nail holes, one of which it has broken across. The arm narrows and then is broken across the beginnings of an expansion.

Context 1042; IADB 2941

60   Fork. Length c 420mm; max. width c 205mm; max. thickness c 65mm.

Head of a large fork, with three parallel prongs of equal length, rounded shoulders and an approximately circular-cross-sectioned handle. One of the prongs is broken but all parts survive. Very heavily corroded.

Context 837; IADB 2373

61   Knife blade? Length 84mm; max. width 13mm; thickness 3mm.

Possible knife blade with part of the tang. The back is straight, and the edge follows a smooth curve, rising to meet the missing tip. Only a small fragment of the tang survives. The object is very heavily corroded and at no point does a complete cross-section of the blade survive.

Context 806; IADB 2496

CERAMIC

122   Inlaid floor tile. Thickness 26mm.

Fabric sandy and micaceous, orange with a grey core. Decoration stamped and filled with white clay. Clear yellow lead glaze, showing yellow on a brown ground.

Context 785; IADB 2329 (fig 3.27a)

131 Maiolica floor tile. Thickness 23mm.

Fine cream-coloured fabric. Tin-glazed, though this is mostly missing. The remaining fragments are hand-painted with a ?floral design in blue, dark blue, green, yellow and orange.

Context 668; IADB 1513 (fig 3.27b)

132 Delft tile. Thickness 8mm.

Cream fabric with sandy back, glaze white with pin hole in corner. Decoration in blue and dark blue.

Context 222; IADB389 (fig 3.27c)

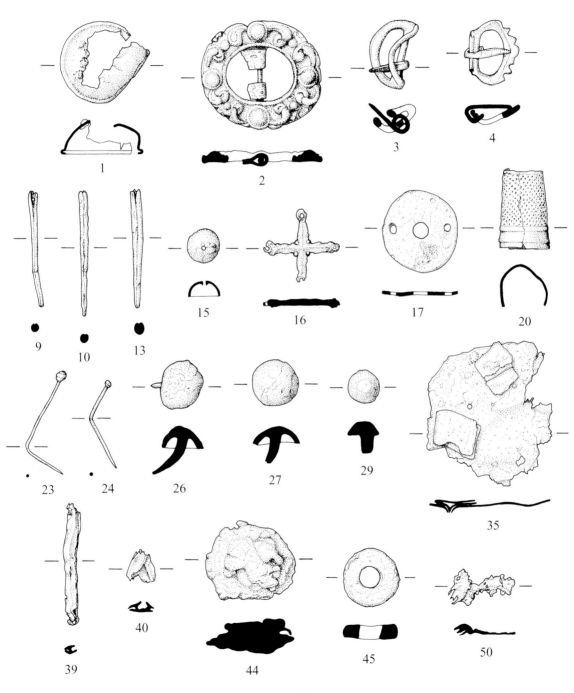

Figure 3.26
Metal artefacts (scale 1:1)

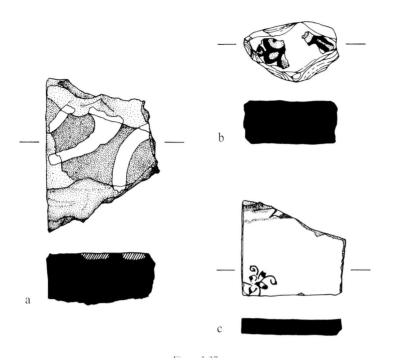

Figure 3.27
Ceramic tiles (scale 1:2)

two faces means that a number of the motifs are missing.

Context 1505; Sample 3075 (retent) (fig 3.29)

Period 3

POTTERY

Pot no. 74   Border fragment of stove tile decorated with floral pattern and glazed brown.

Context 1682 (fig 3.24)

Pot no. 99   Complete unglazed measuring vessel or crucible.

Context 1638 (fig 3.25)

COPPER ALLOY

20   Thimble. Height 20mm; original max. diameter c 15mm.

Tapering thimble of open form, with machine-knurled indentations on the upper

STONE

140   Spindle whorl. Diameter 29mm; thickness 15mm.

Spindle whorl derived from fine-grained, grey stone, with a central, circular hole and slightly convex faces. Both faces are decorated by a series of incised radial grooves, some of which are slightly oblique. On one face these appear to be shallow and/or more greatly worn than on the other. The outer surface is similarly decorated by roughly equidistant incised diagonal grooves. Slightly abraded.

Context 1568; IADB 4093 (fig 3.28)

BONE

189   Die. Length 8mm; max. width 8mm; max. thickness 8mm.

Die, probably derived from a large ungulate long bone shaft. Originally of cuboid form, the object is missing a wedge-shaped piece which has broken away. In addition, other corners and edges are damaged and abraded. Each face bears ring and dot motifs (each c 2mm in diameter), although damage to

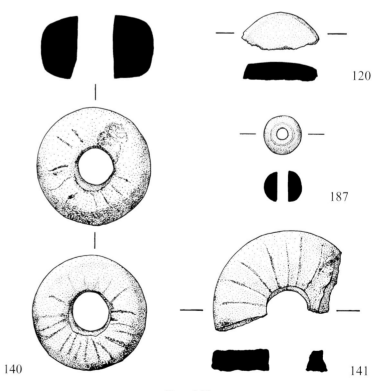

Figure 3.28
Stone whorls (scale 1:2)

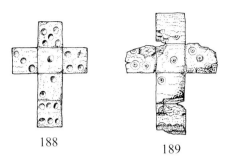

Figure 3.29
Bone dice (scale 2:1)

60–70 per cent of the body, with a plain band below. The object is distorted and part of the wall is missing.

Context 660; IADB 1184 (fig 3.26)

CERAMIC

120   Disc or counter. Projected diameter 48–50mm; thickness 8mm.

Fragment of a circular disc or counter, derived from a pottery sherd in a dark-grey, reduced fabric with an external dark-green glaze. Slightly abraded.

Context 738; IADB 1995 (fig 3.28)

BONE

188   Die. Length 7mm; width 7mm; thickness 7mm.

Die of cuboid form, probably derived from a large ungulate long bone shaft. Each face bears small, drilled circular indentations (with diameters ranging from 1.1mm to 1.4mm), arranged to represent the numbers 1 to 6.

Context 563; Sample 2957 (retent) (fig 3.29)

COINS

215   Brass jeton. 26 × 25.5mm; 2.4g; die axis 9.5.

Nuremberg anonymous 'ship penny' type (c 1490–1550); cf Mitchiner types 1168–76; cracked and chipped at 1.5 obverse); slightly damaged green patina; slight to moderate wear.

Context 89; IADB 274

216   Brass jeton. 22 × 21mm; 1.33g; die axis 12.

Hans Krauwinckel II, Nuremberg, rose/orb type (1586–1635); as Mitchiner type 1539; slight wear.

Context 120; IADB 275

Period 4

POTTERY

Pot no. 37   Sidewalls and handle junction from skillet, internally glazed green and externally smoke-blackened.

Context 807 (fig 3.23)

Pot no. 38   Rimsherd and handle junction from skillet, internally glazed green-brown and externally smoke-blackened.

Context 215 (fig 3.23)

Pot no. 39   Rimsherd and handle junction from skillet, glazed green internally with traces of external smoke-blackening.

Context 129 (fig 3.23)

Pot no. 40   Rimsherd from skillet, internally glazed brown with patch of external brown glaze and smoke-blackening.

Context 222 (fig 3.23)

Pot no. 41   Rimsherd from skillet, glazed brown internally and externally smoke-blackened.

Context 1572 (fig 3.23)

Pot no. 65   Fragment of applied rosette decoration, glazed yellow with green border, from scalloped bowl? Saintonge Palissy Type.

Context 643 (fig 3.24)

COPPER ALLOY

1   Bell fragment. Original diameter c 21mm; thickness of wall 1mm.

Fragment of a rumbler bell, representing a single hemisphere, roughly broken at the flanged edge and around the originally dumbbell-shaped perforation. Traces of ferrous corrosion products adhering to the interior surface may represent a remnant of an iron pea. The exterior surface is undecorated. Heavily corroded.

Context 242; IADB 558 (fig 3.26)

2   Buckle. Length 37mm; width 29mm; thickness 3mm.

Two-piece buckle with a broad oval frame, bisected by a slender pin bar of trapezoidal cross-section. Fragments of a buckle plate survive where they were looped around the pin bar, although no trace of a pin survives. The frame is decoratively moulded, with circular bosses at the ends of the pin bar and the ends of the frame, with smaller bosses between these, interspersed with foliate or scrolling ornament, all in relief. Traces of gilding survive between the raised elements on one part of the frame.

Context 227; IADB 1243 (fig 3.26)

14 Mount. Height 4mm; length 18mm; width 12mm.

Fragment of a plain, oval mount of hollow, domed form, with a circular perforation (diameter 2mm) positioned slightly off-centre. Part of a horizontal flange, 2mm wide, survives on one edge.

Context 540; IADB 669

15 Mount. Height 4mm; diameter 9mm.

Plain, circular mount of hollow, domed form, with a circular perforation (diameter 1 mm) at the apex.

Context 888; IADB 3160 (fig 3.26)

24 Pin. Length if straightened 25mm; width of head 1mm; diameter of shaft 0.7mm.

Pin with a pinched, wound-wire head and a circular cross-sectioned shaft, which is bent just above mid-shaft.

Context 921 (Sample 2825); IADB 4724 (fig 3.26)

25 Pin. Length 23mm; width of head 1mm; diameter of shaft 0.6mm.

Pin with a pinched, wound-wire head and a circular cross-sectioned shaft. Traces of a white metal (probably tin) plating appear on the shaft.

Context 921 (Sample 2825); IADB 4725

35 Riveted sheet. Length 41mm; width 38mm; thickness (including rivets) 2mm.

Sheet fragment of irregular outline with roughly broken edges, perforated by two paperclip rivets, only the upper (rectangular) parts of which survive. Heavily corroded.

Context 809; IADB 2332 (fig 3.26)

LEAD

39 Came. Length 66mm; width 7mm; thickness 3mm.

Window came fragment with an H-shaped cross-section, broken at both ends and flattened.

Context 1654; IADB 4823a (fig 3.26)

40 Came. Length 18mm; width 16mm; thickness 5mm.

Window came fragment representing a corner join.

Context 1654; IADB 4823b (fig 3.26)

IRON

62 Shears fragment. Length 46mm; max. width 14mm; thickness 7mm.

Fragment representing overlapping parts of the blades of a pair of shears, along with parts of the handle arms. The latter are of approximately circular cross-section.

Context 540; IADB 674 (fig 3.32)

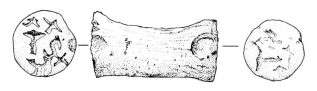

121

Figure 3.30
Ceramic wig curler (scale 1:2)

CERAMIC

121 Wig curler. Length 35mm; max. diameter 17mm.

Object made from buff to white clay, in the form of a cylinder with expanded terminals. Each terminal has a flat face, into which the legend 'T S' has been roughly incised, with diagonal crosses above and below. The edges of both faces are chipped and abraded.

Context 540; IADB 427 (fig 3.30)

CLAY PIPES

226 Bowl, rim bottered; 6/64 inch; 1630–50, cf Tron Kirk, Edinburgh (Gallagher 1987c, 270, no. 2). 307/1ADB 1551.

228 Bowl, rim bottered and milled; 7/64 inch; 1630–50, cf Tron Kirk, Edinburgh (Gallagher 1987c, 270, no. 2) 1789/1ADB 4981.

STONE

136 Disc or counter. Diameter 27mm; thickness 4mm.

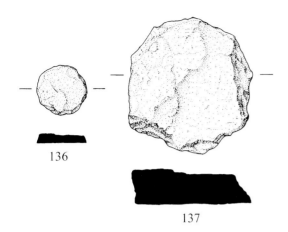

136

137

Figure 3.31
Stone discs (scale 1:2)

20mm; 1.62g; die axis 11.0; uneven striking; some accretion; moderate wear.

Obv.: + % I0c [ ] DeI [ ] 0 [ ] ReX; orb upwards and to right

Rev.: [ ] × % [ ] iIT % Oi [ ]; pellets on cusps; nothing in spandrels

PAR 98, Context 859, IADB 2558

CLAY PIPES

225   Plain polished bowl, rim bottered; c 1620–40; 7/64 inch.

215/1ADB 401.

Roughly circular disc or counter, derived from micaceous stone. Undecorated.

Context 612 (Sample 1605); IADB 2133 (fig 3.31)

137   Disc or counter. Diameter 72mm; max. thickness 18mm.

Object with a roughly circular outline and one roughly flat face. Undecorated.

Context 760; IADB 2677 (fig 3.31)

BONE

189   Die. Length 8mm; max. width 8mm; max. thickness 8mm.

Die, probably derived from a large ungulate long bone shaft. Originally of cuboid form, the object is missing a wedge-shaped piece which has broken away. In addition, other corners and edges are damaged and abraded. Each face bears ring and dot motifs (each c 2mm in diameter), although damage to two faces means that a number of the motifs are missing.

Context 1505; Sample 3075 (retent) (fig 3.29)

COIN

199   James II–III copper 'Crux Pellit', type IIa (c 1450–82)

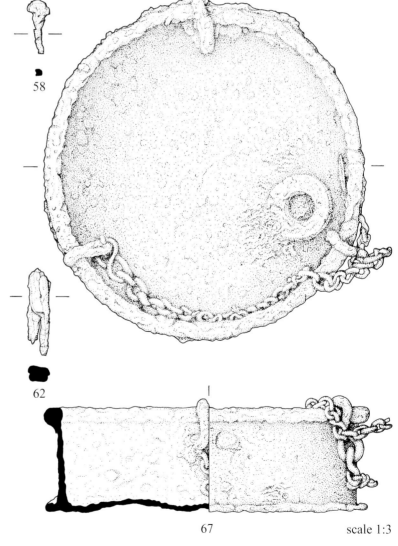

58

62

67

scale 1:3

Figure 3.32
Iron artefacts (scale 1:3)

49

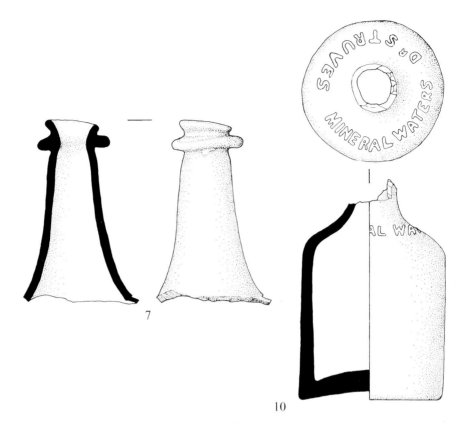

Figure 3.33
Glass from Queensberry House (scale 1:3)

286   Heavy-walled bowl with mould-imparted W/Y, rim bottered and partly milled; 8/64 inch; 1660–80, William Young.
211/1ADB 1060.

324   Bowl and stem fragment in buff fabric with orange surface, bowl damaged, indistinct impression of a castle-type basal stamp; 7/64 inch; 1640–60.
563/1ADB 3349.

Period 5
IRON
67   Vessel. Diameter at rim 171mm; diameter at base 176mm; depth 56mm.
Circular, flat-bottomed vessel with approximately vertical sides and a rounded rim. The base appears to have been made separately and its edge projects from the vessel sides in the form of a narrow flange. At equal intervals around the rim, chains are secured by means of broad, S-shaped links. Several detached chain links were found in close association with this vessel, and recorded as IADB 714.

Context 294; IADB 718 (fig 3.32)

CERAMIC
116   Alley. Diameter 20mm.
Spherical alley made from stoneware, with a pale brown glaze.
Context 214; IADB 288

118   Bottle top. Diameter 30mm; length 28mm.
Stoneware bottle top, incorporating a discoid cap and a centrally set screw-threaded shank. The top of the object bears an off-centre stamp bearing the legend 'J.STEWART & SONS, 62 CANONGATE EDINBURGH'.
Context 1042; IADB 2939

119   Carpet bowl. Diameter 72mm.
Spherical carpet bowl in two conjoining fragments. The stoneware fabric is fine, buff to grey in colour and has an irregular fracture. A pattern of rounded triangles with central dots, executed in green, decorates the entire external surface.

Context 294; IADB 757

CLAY PIPE

348 Porcelain pipe with spur, deep blue with an oval showing a young lady reading seated on a plinth, with trees in the background. The plinth, which bears a garlanded urn, has the inscription 'Denkmal der Jugend' (Monument of Youth). The interior of the bowl has a painted mark, possibly a 3, near the rim. German, 19th-century.

Context 214; 1ADB 286

LEATHER

193 Ball. Diameter 41mm. Ball with a cover made from four equal-sized pieces of leather, sewn together along edge-to-edge seams with thread. Internal filling of tightly packed scraps of leather or textile.

QH; Fireplace (FF1); IADB 5359 (fig. 3.34)

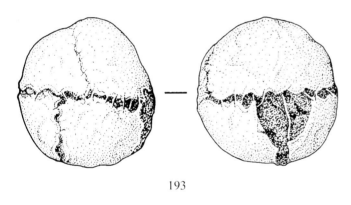

193

Figure 3.34
Leather golf ball (scale 1:1)

GLASS

QH 10 Bottle base. Surviving depth 106mm; diameter at base 76mm. Base and a small part of the neck, of a moulded bottle with a circular cross-sectioned body and a flat base. The body narrows sharply at the shoulder, which is embossed with the legend 'DR STRUVE'S MINERAL WATERS'. The bottle is broken at the junction of neck and shoulder (Illustrated).

Context 7069; IADB 5507; Period 5.2

3.10 Summary of the environmental evidence

STEPHEN CARTER

Analysis of the soils and sediments focused on the relationship between the natural topography of the site and how this has influenced settlement patterns, the soil processes which have shaped this part of the Canongate to the present day and how these processes have enabled us to interpret the history of past settlement here.

The strange angle at which Queensberry House sits in relationship to the Canongate street frontage, for example, is due to the odd angle of the underlying slope which runs from north-west to south-east across the site. This frontage area has also been significantly terraced over the centuries to such an extent that no archaeological levels survive here. In fact, the topography of the whole area has been subject to much alteration, particularly of the natural drainage channels which have been diverted to create areas suitable for settlement (fig 2.1). These channels are thought to have taken water down past the tail end of the plots that extended both north and south from the Canongate street frontage to what are now Calton Road and Holyrood Road respectively. The process of draining this area was almost certainly undertaken by the abbey in order to improve what must have been marginal land. Elsewhere on the site, the level terrace that forms the central area of the site was clearly an attractive place to establish the formal gardens that occupied this area in the post-medieval period.

The analyses of the soils and sediments and the carbonised plant remains both confirm that coal was the dominant source of fuel from very early on. This also supports the evidence from the study of the metalworking debris. Only in the very earliest period (Period 1) was coal absent. This coincides with the use of wood as both fuel and constructional material, and perhaps also with the use of turf. The disappearance of coal from the archaeological record in the 17th century neatly marked the end of the use of these properties for light industrial use and the establishment of formal gardens, as individual plots were bought up and larger properties created, a process which started with Dame Balmakellie. This radical change in use is also reflected in the carbonised plant assemblage. Here, grain was concentrated in the early levels only. Much of this grain is thought to have come in from East Lothian and the barley in particular is thought

51

to have been used in brewing, an industry which became synonymous with this area from the late 18th century onwards.

Coal ash, thought to have derived from domestic and light industrial middens subsequently dumped across the site, was the single largest component in the accumulation of soils on the site. Analysis of these soils and their deposition confirms the archaeological findings that the western half of the site has a very different history from the eastern. This may relate to the eastern half being part of, or at least associated with, the abbey until quite late in the medieval period. Even if this area was laid out as properties from which rent was derived as income for the abbey, it would seem that they were not used for light industrial or craftworking as the western plots were.

The influence of the abbey may also be seen in the faunal remains recovered from the site. The dominance of sheep/goat over cattle in the assemblage is a pattern that has been identified in the Borders and is unlike most other east coast burghs where cattle is the dominant component. In the Borders, the dominance of sheep/goat is thought to have been due to the large flocks of sheep maintained on the vast estates of the four great abbeys – Melrose, Dryburgh, Kelso and Jedburgh. Wool and woolfells (whole skins) were the staple goods of the Scottish economy in the medieval period and were exported through the many ports on the east coast of Scotland (most notably Berwick-upon-Tweed) to the great Flemish cities of Bruges and Ghent. The meat itself would have been a lesser by-product.

The diet did not only consist of beef, mutton and lamb however, for pork, rabbit, hare, poultry, partridge, red grouse, cormorant, fish and shellfish were also on the menu. There appears to have been consistent consumption of mainly white fish (cod, haddock, whiting), herring and mackerel, with some freshwater fish (salmon or trout) and shellfish. Shellfish were significant from the earliest times, particularly oysters, for which the Firth of Forth was famous until they were overexploited in the 18th century.

In terms of craftworking, there appears to have been a tradition of leather workers in this part of the Canongate. A number of the animal bones recovered from the site showed knife cuts consistent with skinning, but, interestingly, these were foxes, dogs, cats and horses, which perhaps suggests that they were not processed in a commercial tannery.

3.11 Conclusions

SIMON STRONACH

This section considers how the archaeological excavations have contributed to answering the research questions set out at the beginning of the project (Chapter 1).

Pre-burghal settlement, pre-1128

The area was exploited from the earliest times; did pre-burghal settlement remains survive below medieval accumulations?

Some possible prehistoric features were recorded and a small assemblage of lithics recovered. The remains are not really substantial enough to suggest that a long-lived prehistoric settlement once existed on the site. However, their presence implies that the site was perhaps peripheral to a settlement, located on the level surface of the ridge, which would have remained well drained all year.

The medieval period, 1128–1580

Was there continuity of settlement from the pre-burghal to the medieval period?

Some early features were discovered during the excavations but cannot be securely dated to any period. It is possible that they are pre-burghal, but they could date to many centuries earlier. In any event, the activity they represent would seem to be transient rather than settled. The cutting of the Period 1 ditch represented the earliest division of the site. This matched the alignment of Holyrood Road in the eastern part of the site, but not in the west because of a kink in the road. This can be readily seen on an aerial photograph of the area (fig 1.5). The ditch did not form a right-angled end to the property boundaries identified in Period 2. Nor did it line up with a ditch discovered during excavations to the west (Gooder 1999), which was likely to have defined the southern limits of medieval burgage plots extending back from the Canongate. The ditch seems to have returned, presumably to the north, somewhere on the line of Reid's Close, and reflected a layout at odds with the extant plots. The excavations suggested that this layout pre-dated the medieval division of this part of the Canongate into plots.

The alignment of the ditch is closer to that expressed by gardens within the abbey, or as it then was palace, grounds as shown on Lizars' plan (1778; fig 3.16) and Kirkwood's plan (1817; fig 3.21). On balance, the feature is probably best interpreted as defining an abbey enclosure and, moreover, the edge of the monastic precinct itself, which was later divided into individual properties. The ditch should probably not be thought of as truly defensive, although it would have made an impressive boundary, especially when combined with a bank, as well as helping to drain higher ground to the north. Given the absence of archaeological features that would have suggested more intensive use, it seems likely that the putative enclosure defined a cultivated area. The limited number of artefacts within the ditch's primary fills offered some support for this interpretation.

It is likely that the ditch had been maintained by cleaning for many years before it became redundant in the 13th or 14th century. Unfortunately, the archaeological deposits were only relevant to abandonment and did not suggest when the feature was first created. However, the earliest pottery from the loam that covered the site was made in the 12th century. The pottery recovered from the soil probably reflected use of waste from the abbey for manuring and, significantly, a fragment of inlaid floor tile (no. 122) from the ditch fill was of a type that might have come from a religious building. In all probability the enclosure was created around the time of David I's foundation of the Augustinian priory in 1128. To conclude, the excavations did not recover any evidence for continuity of settlement from pre-burghal to medieval times. It should be noted however, that although no supporting evidence was found in this part of the medieval precinct, this does nothing to challenge suggestions that the priory occupied the site of an earlier church.

What was the relationship between the abbey and the burgh?

From the abbey's point of view, the conversion of ecclesiastical land into plots for sale or rent must have represented one of the quickest and easiest ways to obtain funds. Urban encroachment onto former abbey grounds has been noted in Coupar Angus (O'Sullivan 1995, 1056), where the demand for space must have been much less.

To judge by the date of pottery fragments in the infilled early ditch, the conversion into plots occurred during the 13th or 14th century. A similar date was suggested for the infilling of a ditch within the abbey precinct discovered during earlier excavations (Bain 1998, 1074). This was interpreted as reflecting a major reordering of the abbey as a result of increasing royal patronage in the 14th century. The presence of the

monarch in the abbey would have created a need for nearby townhouses of suitable rank for the attendant court and perhaps a demand for new plots.

It is possible that conversion into plots was a piecemeal process. The possibility that the abbey precinct may once have extended onto the site has been suggested previously (Dennison & Ewart 1998, 44) because of the position of the girth cross as marked on Rothiemay's plan (fig 6.1). This marked the edge of the Abbey Sanctuary and implied that the boundary was some distance further west than Horse Wynd and within the Parliament site. There was no evidence from the relative plot widths to suggest that those on the east were created later than those in the west. However, a contrast becomes apparent between east and west of the vennel in Period 2 when considering the number of finds that the plots contained: the plots to the west (Plots 2.1 & 2.2) contained more artefactual material and may have been created first. This conclusion is supported by the presence of the vennel itself, as a thoroughfare can often mark a temporary edge of plot development.

A second contrast becomes apparent when considering the depth of deposits across the site, and this may suggest another temporary edge of plot development between Plots 2.4 and 2.5, corresponding to a marked drop in the amount of accumulated material. This conclusion is also supported by a decrease in the amount of artefactual material to the east, within Plots 2.5 and 2.6. If we assume that Plots 2.3 and 2.4 were created with a double width, as would seem to be the case, then the abbey may have been responding to quite specific demands. Given that the plots were being laid out on land that the abbey was in all probability already using, this approach is understandable.

What did the early burgh look like and how did the natural topography of the surrounding area influence the layout?

As noted in Chapter 4.2, it is likely that the abbey created the first burgage plots next to the Holyrood precinct. If the interpretation offered above is correct, the earliest plots are likely to be those immediately west of the excavated area. As shown by Spearman (1988a) in Perth, corroboration of different dates of plot creation can be sought by examining their relative widths, which should be standardised within each contemporary block. Measurements taken from the 1st Edition (1854) Ordnance Survey plan of the area suggested a plot width of around 7m to the west and further upslope in the Canongate. The later plots on the Parliament site would seem to have been almost twice as wide, at around 13m. Presumably the area remained as a cultivated part of the abbey precinct until plots occupied all the available space on the ridge between it and the burgh boundary with Edinburgh. The evidence from the excavations suggested that this part of the precinct began to be developed into plots around the 14th century and it would seem that the Canongate's main period of growth, from the precinct to the Netherbow Port, was completed by this time.

With regard to topography, the tail of the Canongate ridge becomes rather constricted as it descends toward the abbey and the area may not have been ripe for plot development until demand led to exploitation of the growing town's margins. The conversion of an area of abbey grounds into plots suggests pressure on, or at least demand for, land. However, the archaeological evidence from within the properties on the site did not suggest that they were subdivided. On the contrary, the backlands of some of the plots appeared to have been amalgamated from the earliest period of division (Plots 2.3 & 2.4). The lack of buildings in the backlands is apparent on Rothiemay's plan of 1647 (fig 6.1) and contrasts starkly with the burgh of Edinburgh. Excavations within Edinburgh have shown the presence of substantial stone buildings in the backlands from at least the 14th century (Schofield 1976).

This apparent contradiction is not readily explained by any intensive industrial use of the backlands, which would have precluded building. On the contrary, the archaeological evidence suggested that these backlands might only have seen small-scale craft or subsistence activities (a reconstruction of the site during the medieval period is shown in fig 4.2). Certainly, considering that the time span expressed by the features and deposits in Period 2 may have lasted 200 years, it is the lack of features in comparison to other burghs, such as Perth and Aberdeen, that is surprising.

There is some evidence to suggest that the amalgamation of backlands may not necessarily have meant that the corresponding frontages were a single property. Certainly, the tenement wall foundations discovered below Queensberry House (Period 3) suggested divisions where none was evident outside, to the south, in the backlands. It was perhaps the nature of these properties, and the special status of the Canongate, which led to a lack of development in the backlands. They may have been a rather peripheral

concern in comparison with the social status to be gained by owning a highly visible frontage, or near-frontage, property. Keeping the backlands as gardens rather than selling them for development may also have been part of expressing status. The artefacts recovered from the plots complement this interpretation, suggesting an increasing level of wealth and conspicuous consumption.

Although in general there was a lack of backland activity within the site, there were significant variations between the plots that should not be ignored. In Period 2 two plots (2 & 4) were much 'busier' in terms of archaeological features than the others. With Period 2, Plot 2, this distinction was reinforced by a concentration of artefactual remains. This seems likely to have reflected the occupation of the owners. It seems that craftworking was concentrated in these plots, with much less evidence of activity in the others, which also tended to be wider, presumably as a result of amalgamation.

Ironworking waste was concentrated at one time during Period 2 in Plot 2 and suggested that both smithing and smelting were undertaken here. Perhaps this activity was the impetus behind the creation of the vennel providing access from the rear, although an alternative explanation is offered above. There may also have been another craft undertaken in this plot, with some evidence for small-scale skinning. Two twin-tank features located within the plot have been interpreted as tanning tanks (fig 3.35). The tanning process involves both the long-term soaking of hides in a solution of water and vegetable matter (for example, bark) and their daily agitation in an acid or alkaline solution (for example, water with urine, stale beer, lime or dung). The twin tanks could have been used for both. As noted above, the tanks could also have been used to steep barley or flax; neither of these uses is preferred as an interpretation because it is difficult to see why either would require twinned tanks. Dyeing is not considered likely because it usually seems to require some kind of heating.

A medieval tannery has been identified in St Andrews where a series of pits was identified side by side (Lewis 1996). Several tanning pits discovered in Aberdeen had similar dimensions to those identified on the Parliament site and were also rectangular or circular (Cameron & Stones 2001, 108). However, in contrast to these examples, the small number of tanks on the Parliament site suggested that only a small number of hides could have been processed at any one time. The remains are difficult to interpret as any kind of commercial tannery and they may represent tanning to meet specific needs. The animal bones with cut marks indicative of skinning were consistent with this idea, for they came from foxes, dogs, cats and horses, rather than animals commonly used in commercial ventures. Also the presence of bones with cut marks suggested that the animals were skinned here, rather than at the professional skinners of the medieval burgh. Whether these were being processed as part of some kind of specialised leatherworking or for household requirements is difficult to say.

In general, Plot 2.4/Plot 3.4 was the most intensively used for industrial processes throughout the medieval period. Ironworking waste was found toward the front of Plot 2.4. The nature of the metalworking seems to have involved primary smelting and smithing, a surprising discovery given its location on the crowded frontage. Part of this activity may have involved farriery. Horses were probably more common than usual because of the high concentration of nobles in the area. The burial of a horse and also the presence of burnt straw in a structure within Plot 3.4 could even suggest the presence of a stable.

Further to the south, to the rear of the frontage buildings in Plot 2.4, were several large, probably lined, pits joined by channels whose function was not elucidated by any artefactual or environmental remains. The process appeared to have required a nearby source of water. It is possible that the pits were used to steep barley or flax, although it is not clear why this would require more than one pit joined by channels.

The contrast between the plots emphasised the mixed nature of land use in the medieval burgh. Canongate may have contained high-status dwellings, with open back gardens, but these were scattered amongst the workshops and yards of craftworkers. However, as royal patronage of Holyrood continued to rise, the tendency toward high-status properties with gardens became more pronounced.

This leaves an impression of the Canongate as a rather unusual burgh, with a very crowded and grand frontage with relatively open uncluttered space to the rear. Comparison with the width of plots in other towns, from 5m in Perth to 10m in St Andrews, bears this out, for those excavated on the Parliament site were significantly wider. It is also worth noting that the earlier plots outside the excavated area to the west are comfortably within the expected range. This difference suggests that transformation of the Canongate into an atypical burgh can be traced to around the 14th century, when the site was divided into plots. The process seems likely to reflect increasing royal patronage of Holyrood. It should, of course, be remembered that the Canongate did not operate in isolation, and what became greater Edinburgh evolved out of the growth of three separate settlements (Edinburgh, Canongate and Leith). It was thus possible for Canongate to become the burgh of choice for the wealthy, with the other settlements serving complementary roles: Edinburgh as the commercial centre and Leith as a busy port.

The post-medieval period, 1580–1707

What was the nature of the buildings and gardens associated with the urban precinct that developed around the Palace of Holyroodhouse?

Canongate's prestige reached its zenith in the early 16th century with the construction of Holyrood Palace. The archaeological remains suggest that this had a rapid and radical impact on the surrounding townscape. Neighbouring properties were purchased and tenements on the frontage were cleared to make space for the grand townhouse that evolved into Queensberry House. The Holyrood Road frontage was developed for the first time with the construction of Haddington House.

What was to become Queensberry House had its genesis in 1667 as Dame Margaret Balmakellie began to buy up neighbouring properties in order to create her 'great lodging'. Although obscured by later alterations, this structure still survives in remarkably well-preserved form within the later house. This T-shaped building was cleverly designed to maximise the impact both of the Canongate façade and the open views to Holyrood Park at the rear. Expressing aristocratic status amongst the crowded buildings that sprang up around Holyroodhouse was a competitive business and prompted major renovations and extensions of the structure carried out by Lord Hatton from 1679 and the second Duke of Queensberry from 1695. Hatton's most notable addition was the viewing tower or belvedere, the remains of which were discovered in the attic of the building. Queensberry gave the building much of its current appearance, notably the addition of closet towers.

To the rear, archaeological remains of the formal gardens that accompanied these buildings were discovered. A large raised terrace with central

Figure 3.35
Twin tanks that may have been tanning pits

staircase was constructed to the rear of Balmakellie/ Queensberry House. This would have afforded the owners and their guests a fine panorama over the patterned hedges and plants in the garden, and would have elevated them above neighbouring properties. The artefacts found within the garden included items that reflected importation of luxury items such as wine and perfume, as well as personal items associated with the nobility, especially a wig curler.

Even though the townscape had been dramatically altered, it still retained some medieval character. In particular, it is worth noting the line of a garden path on the route of a vennel during Periods 2 and 3, and the location of Balmakellie House within what had been Plots 2.3 and 3.3, a seemingly amalgamated area of backlands from the earliest phase of plot division.

The remains from Period 4 included a remarkable discovery that allowed a glimpse beyond the nature of the buildings to that of one of the owners. Within the basement of the predecessor of Queensberry House were the surviving remnants of a floor, made somewhat eclectically from handmade brick, sandstone flags and cobbles. It is rare to be able to associate any group of archaeological finds with a particular individual, but it is known from documents that Lord Hatton, the owner from 1679, paid for a cobbled floor to be laid in the kitchen. The excavation revealed metalworking remains likely to relate to the assaying and refining of silver and other precious metals and what appeared to have been the base of an assaying forge associated with this cobbled floor. Lord Hatton was a Master of the Scottish Mint (Chapter 9.4) and refining the quality of silver and other metals would have been relevant to such a position. Given that the room was recorded as a kitchen during Hatton's tenure, it can be questioned whether this was a bona fide workshop. The evidence might be interpreted to suggest that Hatton, on purchasing the house, converted the erstwhile kitchen into a workshop illegally to cream off money from the Royal Mint. The dumps of levelling material that sealed these remarkable remains contained pottery consistent with the date of Queensberry's acquisition of the house following Hatton's disgrace.

The early modern period, 1707–1825

Did the archaeological evidence reflect the decline in status of the Canongate during this period?

The opening of the New Town, and consequently the availability of more fashionable places to live, seems to have caused an exodus of the wealthy and a decline in the Canongate's prestige. During this period, Queensberry House ceased to be the principal residence of the dukes and became rented accommodation, albeit initially for the upper echelons of society. Very little below-ground archaeology from this period was identified, presumably because very little disturbance or development was carried out. Queensberry House did not undergo major renovations and the most significant, and somewhat poignant, event was the stripping of the interior by William Aitchison after he bought it in 1801. In this sense the absence of all the interior fittings, such as wooden panelling and fine fireplaces, provided the most marked reflection of this decline.

The modern period, 1825–present day

What remains relating to the site's early development as a brewery survived, and was there any continuity in the use of wells from the medieval period?

The eastern half of the site became a brewery in the second half of the 19th century. The archaeological remains showed, for the first time, extensive development of the old medieval backlands in the form of large structural plinths and foundations. These related to 19th- and 20th-century buildings, but no surfaces or other above-ground elements survived. The medieval and post-medieval wells that survived on the site had not been used in the modern period. The modern brewery wells were large and must have removed completely any medieval predecessors that might have existed. Therefore there was no evidence for any continuity in the use of wells.

In the western part of the site the transformation of the Canongate was typified by the conversion of Queensberry House to a barracks and later to a House of Refuge. Analysis of the finds from the House of Refuge allowed a glimpse into the impoverished lives of the inhabitants, in stark contrast to their privileged post-medieval antecedents.

Chapter 4

The medieval burgh of Canongate

E PATRICIA DENNISON

4.1 The founding of the burgh

Burghs are first documented in Scotland early in the 12th century, although there is no doubt that a number of small settlements were already, before this time, exhibiting characteristics that might be defined as 'urban'. At least Berwick-upon-Tweed and Roxburgh, and possibly also Dunfermline, Stirling, Perth and Edinburgh, were privileged with the grant of burghal status even before David I became king of Scots in 1124 (Pryde 1965, 3; *Registrum de Dunfermelyn*, no. 26). His reign saw the bestowal of status of 'burgh' on more, probably some 13 or 14, small townships and urban settlements, including Canongate.

Burghs were made legal entities by the granting of burghal status by the Crown or by the Crown giving the right to found a burgh to an important magnate. The Scottish burgh was basically a community organised for trade (Dickinson 1945–6, 224; Maitland 1897, 193; Barrow 1981, 85). The percentage of clauses dealing with mercantile matters in early burghal legislation (Ballard 1916, 16) suggests that it was recognised as such from the 12th century. In practice and in time, this brought several advantages, but perhaps of most significance to burgesses was the freedom from payment of toll, or dues, to the owner of a market, thus enabling a burgess to travel at will around the country buying and selling. Another advantage was that the burghal community gained the right to have its own market, at which it could exact toll on others.

When establishing the burgh of Canongate in 1128, David I also endowed the abbots of Holyrood with the barony of Broughton, the lands of Pleasance and adjacent areas, and part of Leith (Cowan 1924, 79), an extensive area, or regality, which also gave Canongate a port. Those living in the regality were obliged to attend the Canongate market, pay the market dues and obey its rulings.

The new burgh of Canongate was given the specific right to buy and sell at the market of Edinburgh, a quite significant concession, as this meant that the burgesses of Canongate might share in the profits of Edinburgh's market.[1] In time, however, the burgesses

of Canongate held their own markets in their burgh, and the two physical symbols of the burgh's market appear in the medieval records: the tolbooth is first mentioned in 1471, and the market cross was certainly in existence by 1572, and in all probability very much earlier (*RMS*, ii, 217).

But it was not only the burgesses who benefited financially. It was in the Crown's interests to promote burghs in this way, as the royal burghs, through their economic activities, provided revenues for their overlord, the king, just as the burgesses of Canongate supported the Abbey of Holyrood financially. The tolls that were paid by outsiders to attend the burgh market, even if originally paid in kind, could be transmuted to cash and supplied the Crown, or in the case of Canongate, the Abbot of Holyrood, with a regular income. Burgh rents were a further source of revenue. Indeed, these burghal sources of revenue provided much of David I's known income (Duncan 1978, 475) and Canongate's rentals must also have financially benefited the abbey. Moreover, all burgesses had the duty to watch and ward, or protect, their burgh, so ensuring not only the security of the town, but also the safety of an excellent source of income to the burgh superior.

The granting of burgh status further assured fundamental rights for its privileged inhabitants.[2] Most striking was the relative freedom of a burgess: while recognising the authority of the burgh and its superior, other feudal ties were severed. The harshest punishment under burgh law was banishment from the community, for this meant loss of all personal rights and privileges. Allied to this personal freedom went the right to burgage tenure, that is the right to hold a burgage plot in the burgh and build on it. This was inalienable if inherited, except *in extremis*, and was, moreover, protected by the king's peace and later by burgh law.[3]

Twelfth-century evidence shows clearly that there already existed a body of law, both legislative and customary in origin, which applied to all burghs (MacQueen & Windram 1988, 209). Whether these should be equated with the *Leges Burgorum*, the Laws of the Four Burghs, reputedly formulated in the reign of David I, is less secure, but it was during the reign of David I's grandson, William I (1165–1214) that royal recognition was confirmed,[4] and the *Leges Burgorum* may well have been compiled gradually from William I's reign (Duncan 1978, 481). The *Constitutiones Regis Willelmi*, laid down in William's reign, while dealing with a number of wider issues, were largely concerned with burghal regulations.[5] With the borrowing, or copying, of burghal charters one from another, there was also established a common code, which offered general guidelines, but which each individual burgh might adapt to its own circumstances. The important factor is that burghs had an accepted corpus of law from early in their history.

There was a further jurisdiction in Canongate. The girth, or sanctuary, cross stood in the middle of the High Street of Canongate and acted as a marker. All who passed to the east of the cross, and entered within the sanctuary boundary, which ran southwards in a straight

Figure 4.1
Photograph of town ditch

line from the Watergate until turning westwards at the meadow at the foot of Salisbury Crags, regardless of any crime they may have committed, would receive the safekeeping, or sanctuary, of the abbey.

A burgh was, however, much more than a legal body. It was also the home, refuge and workplace of the townspeople. As described in Chapter 2, the geology of the site constrains the burgh's layout (fig 2.1). Canongate's ridge was bordered both to the north

and to the south by waterlogged land, the areas near what are now Calton Road and Holyrood Road being, in effect, small rivers or burns. Even into the late 15th and early 16th centuries these routeways were both called 'Strand', indicating their proximity to water. What is not clear is whether, on reaching the hollow at the foot of the present Canongate, these two small rivers formed a lagoon, with access to the Holyrood Abbey site being by means of a narrow pass on raised ground. There was certainly a 'Holyrood Loch' that had to be drained in the early 16th century to make way for James IV's (1488–1513) new south gardens in Holyrood.[6]

4.2 The laying out of the burgh and the emerging town plan

There is no documentary evidence as to exactly how the first burgesses delineated and protected their township. Ditching was an obvious first step, but, by the time records are extant in the 16th century, ditches are also associated with walling, which varied from something as slight as wooden palisading that was regularly blown down in winds, as at Linlithgow, to stone walling as at Perth. Stone walling was less common, and rarely in Scotland was there great walling of the type associated with, for example, York, Carlisle or Carcassone.

The early burgh ditch, or fosse, has been discovered by archaeological research on both the Parliament site and further west on other areas of the early burgh of Canongate (Chapter 3.3; fig 4.1). The ditch became associated with walling some time during the Middle Ages. There are few documentary references to the Canongate ditches (one to the north of the settlement and one to the south), as contemporaries were more interested in the town walls than the ditches, and therefore recorded them more often. This was because, as noted above, medieval burgesses were required by burgh law to maintain the wall and thus protect the town. In some cases in the sources, the notaries recorded 'dyke' while more correctly meaning 'dyke and/or fosse'. The ditch was definitely in use to the north of the Canongate as late as 19 June 1492 and was referred to as *capitalis fossa* (main/great ditch), implying that lesser ditches were also in existence.[7]

Fifteenth- and 16th-century protocol books, which record the transfer of property, give an insight into the nature of townscape in this area. Clearly, where permitted by geology and natural features, burgage plots were laid out in the traditional pattern running at right angles to the main street, called the High Street of Canongate (fig 4.2). The plots were bordered to the south by the 'heid dyke', or small wall,[8] often with a gate, and a back lane, consistently called the Strand.[9]

The numerous references to the town walls, both north and south of the Canongate properties, gave these walls various names: 'yard dykes'; 'dykes of the orchards'; 'heid dykes'. In most property descriptions, however, the boundary to the south of the properties on the south side of Canongate is merely referred to as the 'Strand' and, later, 'South Back of Canongate'. Some of these references may be to the walls that divided the long burgage plots, replacing by the late Middle Ages the earlier delineating ditches. The walling to the north and south of the burgh was not substantial even well into the Middle Ages, a complaint being made that the burgesses neglected to 'fosse, bulwarke, toure, turate and itherwise strengthen' their town, other than having insignificant 'civil' walls in 1513 (Kinnear 1969, 4). This was, however, not unusual, as it was a common complaint in many towns.

It is relatively safe to assume that once the formal laying out of the burgh had commenced, burgage plots would have been set down as close as possible to the abbey. This is confirmed by documentary sources. One property in the 1480s, on the south side of and fronting Canongate High Street, lay immediately to the west of 'Abbey Cloise'; but to its south it was bordered by a garden of the monastery.[10]

In most burghs there was a quite deliberate planning of streets and burgage plots, often respecting natural features such as rivers, marshes and hills. For Canongate, the delineating features were, inevitably, the two strands to the north and south, the burgh of Edinburgh to the west and the abbey to the east. St Andrews (founded 1124 x 1144 by Robert, Bishop of St Andrews) was laid out by Mainard the Fleming, who had probably planned Berwick-upon-Tweed, and Glasgow (founded 1175 x 1178 by the Bishop of Glasgow) was laid out by Ranulf of Haddington, to precise plans, both men specifically introduced for this task.[11] Evidence of early land use has been found by archaeological research in Perth, St Andrews and Aberdeen. Reinforced with documentary and

cartographic information, it may be concluded that a high degree of precision went into both the initial dividing up of available street frontage, and also into the subsequent maintenance of these delineations by the appropriate town officers, the liners, appointed by the burgess community.[12] The identity of the first town planner of Canongate is unknown, but it is not unlikely that he was a canon or closely associated with the abbey, although other boroughs are known to have been laid out by laity.

Archaeological excavations have shown that Canongate's burgage plots were initially divided one from another by ditching, which, by the later Middle Ages, had been replaced by stone dykes. These property boundaries suggest that the width of each burgage plot at the west end of the site was about 6m, while those to the east were larger, being approximately 13m wide. This implies that the east end of the burgh was laid out at a different time from the west end. It has been suggested that there was a common standard throughout Europe of between 28ft (8.62m) and 32ft (9.85m) (Brooks & Whittington 1977, 288). In St Andrews, also an early (12th-century) burgh, there were numerous variants, the most common being 36–8ft (11.1–11.7m) and 28–32ft (8.62–9.85m). But there were variants throughout many Scottish burghs. The *Leges Burgorum*[13] reflect in several chapters the mid-12th-century 'customs' of Newcastle and, to a lesser degree, of Winchester, Northampton and Nottingham.[14] These specified that the standard was to be 'one burgh perch', said to be 3m (Bateson 1904, 110). The *Fragmenta Collecta*, a drawing together of a number of early laws and regulations, suggests a standard double this.[15] Excavations at Perth have suggested a frontage of 20ft (6.2m); and at Dunfermline cartographic and sasine evidence indicates frontages of 22ft 6in (6.9m), sometimes rising to 25ft (7.7m) (Spearman 1988a, 55–6; Torrie 1988, 40–1).

4.3 The homes of the burgesses and indwellers

The dwellings of the burgesses were built at the front of the plot, or toft, abutting the street, now part of the Royal Mile. Their homes were originally simple wooden buildings, many of the first being only single rooms. Many 12th- and 13th-century dwellings were basically huts made of stakes and interwoven wattle with free-standing posts to support the walling. Roofs were normally thatched with cut heather or turves of growing plants that offered water resistance, doors were often straw mats or wattle, and there is no evidence of

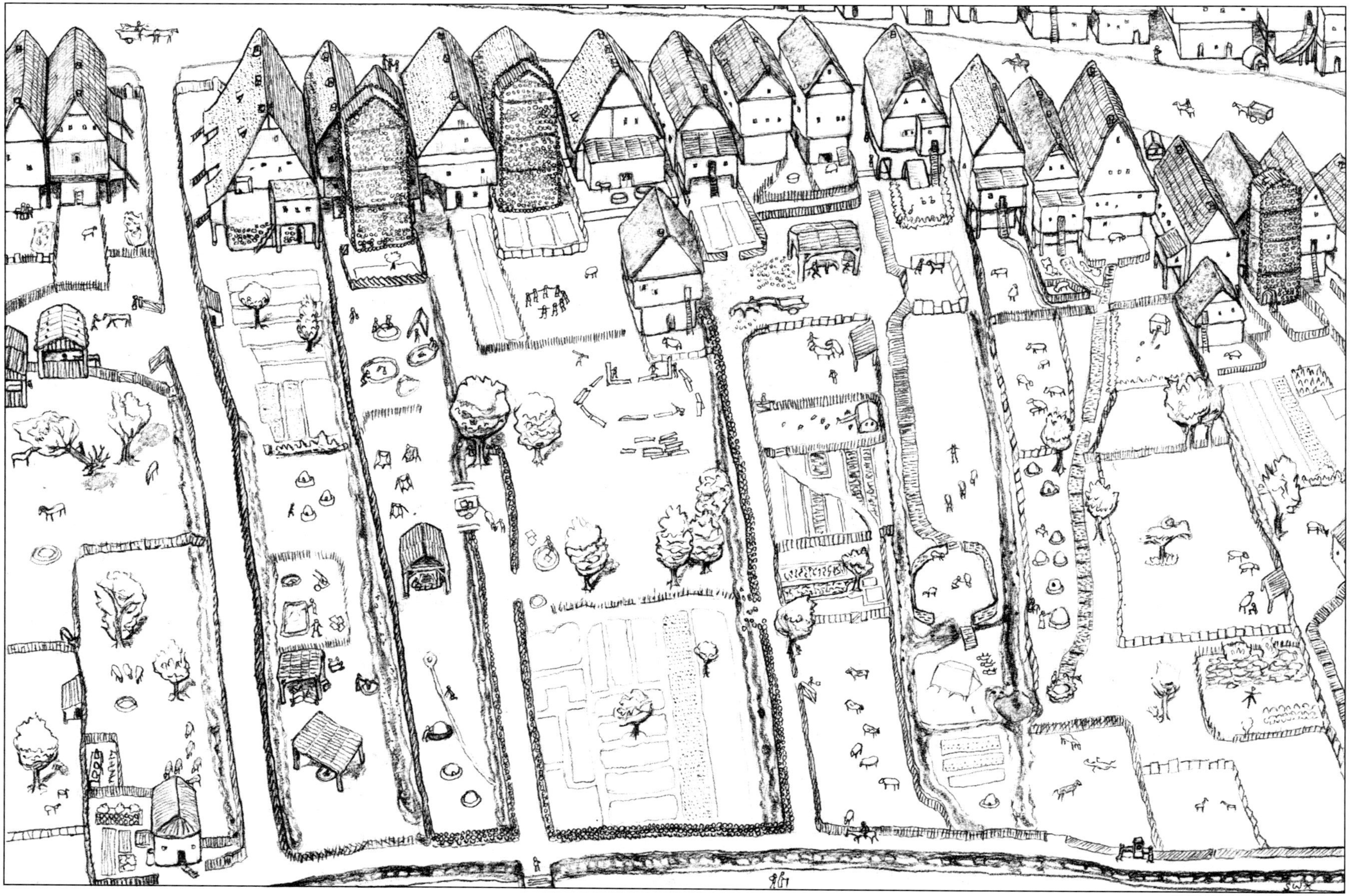

Figure 4.2
Reconstruction drawing of the site in the medieval period

windows in these early houses. Floors were sand, clay or silt, probably scattered with litter such as heather, bracken or cereal straw. Most homes had a hearth for warmth and cooking, which was set directly onto the floor as a clay-lined hollow or a stone slab, and smoke would percolate out of the house through a small hole in the roof. From the late 13th century most town dwellings showed a growing sophistication. Instead of walls supported by free-standing posts, stakes were set into ground sills of wood, which, in turn, were often superseded by stone foundations for ground sills. Walls were reinforced with heavy clay, dung, mud or peat cladding; and interior partition walls indicated different functional areas, the larger being for living or working quarters and the smaller for storage or animal shelter.

Stone buildings were not unknown but were exceptional and prestigious, the occupants in all probability being closely associated with the abbey. The first firm documentary evidence for stone dwelling houses comes as late as the 14th century: three in Ayr, one in Edinburgh and one in Aberdeen (Ewan 1990, 17). A reference to a burgh house with a solar in what is now Abbey Street, St Andrews, in a document of the 1240s might strongly suggest a stone building, at least on the ground floor, even though the upper floors may have been timber (Bullough & Storey 1971, 129–30). A suspect Bull, purported to be that of Pope Celestine III, refers to a stone dwelling in Perth in 1198, but this is in all probability a later forged or tampered-with translation (Easson 1947, i, 29, 33).[16] By the end of the medieval period, however, a number of houses were constructed of stone at ground level, with upper stories of timber, and larger wooden houses were roofed with tiles or slates, each tile or slate overlapping and fixed to the wooden sarking by nails at the top corners. The tiles surmounting the ridge were often decorated and finished in a yellow, green or brown glaze (Stones 1987, 12). The earliest slates on this site date from the late medieval period and were made of sandstone, rather than true slate, although slate types from both Aberdeenshire and the West Highlands have been found on the Holyrood Parliament site. Although sandstone was harder to work than slate, proximity of supply probably proved more economical.

The large clay-bonded stone medieval building, set back a little from the street frontage, excavated at 58–60 Canongate (once Cumming's Close) is probably typical of many that once existed in Canongate. It is to be expected that prestigious stone housing would have lined the Canongate at the east end, in all

probability associated closely with the abbey. Stone buildings were almost solely for the exclusive use of the wealthier members of society. Interestingly, in 1487, Robert Lauder, bailie of Canongate, gave permission for a house or houses to be built in a garden, using stone taken from a garden dyke to the west.[17] The archaeological evidence of decorated floor tiles, not common in this period, and of imported tiles from the Netherlands also indicates the presence of prestigious housing on this site.

The fine imported pottery (French White ware) found on the site at 58–60 Canongate and the evidence of trade in luxury items such as a Spanish olive jar also reinforces the fact that stone houses were for the wealthier members of society. Dating as it does to at least the 15th, but possibly as early as the 13th century, this building was one of the earliest medieval, urban, stone domestic dwellings in Scotland. Evidence of industrial activity, possibly smithing, being carried on in a flimsy wooden structure at the front of the building, and a horseshoe to the rear of the property are reminders that abbey complexes housed many essentials, both industrial, including smithies, and agricultural.

4.4 The early royal presence in the burgh

Another reason why prestigious housing would be expected in this area of Canongate was that this small burgh saw many important people, including royalty, passing along, and inhabiting, its main street throughout the Middle Ages. Although a palace was not constructed at Holyrood until early in the 16th century, the abbey complex was host to the Crown on numerous occasions. A colloquium, for example, was held in the church of Holyrood in 1285, following the death of Alexander III's (1249–86) heir and raising the question of the remarriage of the king (Watt 1987, v, 417). Parliaments were held in Edinburgh in 1321 and in 1328, and possibly the venue was Holyrood. If so, exactly where in the abbey the Parliaments of Robert I (1303–29) met is unclear. The refectory, sited in the south cloister range, was possibly sufficiently substantial to be converted in the 16th century into the great hall for the adjacent royal palace (Dunbar 1999, 61), and there was also probably a late 13th-century chapter house, 12.2m in diameter (Fawcett 1994, 101). Either of these buildings might have been able to accommodate parliamentary sessions, although the likelihood is that Holyrood Abbey church housed these meetings. Edward Balliol also favoured Holyrood for his second

Parliament in 1334 (*APS*, i, 500). Holyrood was the venue for the General Council held in 1384, when royal justice was removed from the hands of King Robert II (1371–90) and entrusted to John, Earl of Carrick, later Robert III (1390–1406), as guardian (Boardman 1996, 124). Indeed, a number of the meetings of Parliament recorded between 1373 and 1406 as being held in Edinburgh might, in fact, have been held at Holyrood. That held in 1389, for example, although initially summoned to Perth, concluded at Holyrood (*APS*, i, 556–7). Robert III stayed in the abbey guest house, as did all Stewart monarchs in medieval times. Indeed, Holyrood, albeit as an expedient alternative to Scone, witnessed the coronation of James II (1437–60) in 1438 (McGladdery 1990, 11; *APS*, ii, 31).

It was, therefore, inevitable that the dwellings that bordered the main street, called the High Street of Canongate, were substantial, housing not only ecclesiastics but also important laymen connected to the royal court. This picture is confirmed by evidence in extant protocol books. In 1489, Dene John Wricht, vicar of Kirkcudbright and canon of Holyrood inherited a property on the south side of the Canongate from his parents,[18] and the vicar of Baro (Bara) also held a tenement on the same side of the street.[19] A 'great mansion' stood on the north side of the High Street of Canongate, beside the gate to the monastery. In 1493, Abbot Bellenden granted this property to the chaplain of the chapel and almshouse of St Leonard, which lay within the regality of Broughton, along with an annual rent of 20 shillings from a tenement on the south side of the High Street, to pay for the provision of fuel and other essentials for the six poor and infirm inmates. The chaplain also enjoyed an annual income of 33s 4d, raised on the rental of another property to the south of the High Street (Smith & Paton 1940, 116). The level of these rentals indicates prestigious properties.

4.5 The rural atmosphere in the medieval town

The strong impression is that there was no pressure for space in the burgh, unlike some burghs: gardens, orchards and barns were abundant, and many people often tended their own livestock (Blanchard 1987a, 45). A large number of the properties ran without subdivisions from frontage to heid dyke,[20] while other burgage plots were parcelled into smaller units.[21] References to 'inner lands' of tenements[22] and 'myddil mansiones'[23] are indications of the origins of the narrow closes, typical of much of early modern Canongate and Edinburgh. Many of the properties must have been prestigious, with a number of chambers, ranging from 'upper halls' to vaults and cellars.[24]

The rear of many burgage plots housed middens, wells, workshops, gardens and animals. The records contain evidence of these backland activities. A number of the properties had their own personal wells, but a significant proportion also housed kilns and 'steipstanes' (hollowed stone troughs for steeping malt, flax, etc).[25] This would indicate an element of industrial activity. Skinners, tanners, masons, brewers, shoemakers and cutlers all held property on the south side of Canongate, and some would have plied their craft in their own backlands, possibly using the source of water at the foot of their burgage plots. Indeed, even the frontages of the burgage plots offered a commercial opportunity: there was a brew house and a number of the properties housed booths, which functioned as retail outlets.[26]

While the records make it clear that many burgage plots retained open garden spaces in the backlands, the division of the property of Marion Robesone on the south side of the Canongate, on her death in 1501, to her three daughters gives an indication of the complex arrangements of certain tenements. The property was divided three ways: firstly, the foreloft, the kiln, the steipstane under the stair and the piece of the yard lying between the kiln and the well of the tenement, with the obligation to keep the forebooth watertight and pay one-third of the annual dues; secondly, the forebooth, the barn with the nether end of the yard from the well down to the head dyke, also paying one-third; thirdly, all the backhouses from the foreland descending down to the north end of the barn with a piece of land at the south end of the barn, descending down to the kiln, again paying one-third of the annual dues. All three were to have free 'ische and entrie', that is exit and entrance, over the others' properties and use of the well.[27]

Gradually, over time, and certainly by the early 16th century, the burgage plots extended up to the boundary with the burgh of Edinburgh, at the Netherbow Port.[28] It is clear, also, that by the 15th century, if not before, Canongate was developed right up to the abbey gates. There were, for example, two tenements sited between the 'abbay yet' and a wasteland and certain houses pertaining to the abbey in 1498.[29] A further tenement is recorded as 'lying near the gate of the monastery of Holyrood', with a 'common wynd' on the west, the garden of the monastery on the south and the highway on the north.[30] This 'common wynd' ran from north to south. 'Abbay Cloise' also appears in the records as having two tenements immediately to its west.[31] This impression of built tenements hard up against the abbey precinct at the east end of Canongate is also supported if the 'canon-corse', beside which a cordiner's (leatherworker's) tenement was sited, was one and the same as the girth cross,[32] which it may have been. Certainly, one William Young, a cutler, held property near the 'girthe croce' in 1567.[33]

In spite of the fact that Canongate stretched from the abbey gates to Edinburgh's Netherbow Port, it was still a very small town. Population figures for most towns in the Middle Ages are very difficult to determine. The vast majority would have housed only a few hundred people. The first remotely accurate assessments for most towns belong to the 17th century: of 44 burghs paying tax in 1639, it is estimated that 33 had a population of 2000 or less (McNeill & MacQueen 1996, 320). It is safe to assume that Canongate housed only a very few hundred people, at most. All would have known each other.

4.6 Lifestyles in the town

From knowledge of other medieval burghs, it is clear that the interiors of most houses would have had few luxuries. Beds were usually of the box variety and in the poorest homes bedding would have been straw. By the 15th and 16th centuries better-quality homes would have had sheets, blankets, bolsters and coverlets, and, in the most prestigious dwellings, feather bolsters and feather beds, sometimes draped with curtains, might have been found.[34] Straw was also the traditional medieval floor covering – it was cheap and could be replaced easily. Only the most luxuriously appointed homes would have had rugs or tiles. Tables were of one of two types: the compter, a reckoning table, marked out in squares, although it is possible, according to medieval paintings, that the table might be covered with a squared tablecloth, or the more common form of table, the trestle table – a board with trestles to support it. This had the great advantage of being removable at the end of a meal, so releasing precious space in cramped living conditions. Chairs would have been found in only the wealthiest houses, and the form, or bench, and the stool were the usual types of seating. Storage was also essential. Barrels stored salted meat and fish and dried goods; and some homes might even have had a meat 'army' (cupboard, armoury) and bread 'army' to keep food clean. Wooden kists were the normal form of general storage – they could also be used as seating – and well-

appointed homes might even have had a 'towel burd' (cupboard) for bedlinen, tablecloths and serviettes, and a wall press. The stone houses lining the Canongate would have been luxuriously appointed with such amenities.

The utensils used in the majority of homes were, in general, simple, but efficient. Plates and dishes were usually made of wood or pewter, jugs and drinking vessels normally of pottery and cooking utensils, such as goose pans, fish pans, kale pans, girdles, spits and ladles, of iron. Only in the wealthiest households would items such as silver spoons, mirrors, clocks or books have been found.

All homes needed lighting at night. The most usual forms were candles, supported by brass candelabra in the wealthiest homes, or lamps which burned oil (Holdsworth 1987, 206), probably from flax imported from abroad or grown in the backlands of the tofts. Heating was essential in the colder months. Archaeological evidence indicates that the most common fuel was coal, although peat and wood may also have been used.

Clothing would have varied greatly according to wealth. The most common materials used were coarse cloth, of wool, canvas or of fustian, a type of rough linen, fastened with small brooches, lace tags and buckles. Jackets and shoes were made of leather. From documentary records it is known that many households possessed spinning wheels and carding combs, and shuttles and ancillary equipment for weaving. The majority of medieval town dwellers probably dressed themselves in domestically-produced cloth (Blanchard 1987a, 45).

Also produced at home were many of the foodstuffs eaten by the ordinary townspeople. Cereals, mainly wheat and barley and oats, with some rye, were the staple of the diet, as has been shown by archaeological evidence. These were usually grown in the town's crofts, or arable lands, though the location of Canongate's crofts is not clear. The land immediately adjacent to the burgh was possibly too waterlogged for cultivation. The burgesses probably rented lands from the abbey in the Pleasance and the regality of Broughton. Surrounding rural parishes would have been tied to marketing cereals, meat, other foodstuffs, and wool through the burgh market. After a bad harvest, grain might have been imported from nearby areas such as the fertile lands of East Lothian or from overseas, in particular the Baltic region, via the town's port at Leith. For home consumption, the grain might be ground on domestic handmills but, if for sale, the townspeople had to take their grain to the abbey's own mill, the Canon Mill, situated to the north of the burgh, at what is now called Canonmills. Similarly, bread might be baked at home for personal consumption in a private oven, but the sale of this bread was forbidden, as production of bread for profit was the prerogative of the baxter, or baker.

Archaeological evidence has shown that beef, pig, sheep and goat were all butchered and eaten, most commonly sheep and goat. Dog, cat, roe deer, fox and rabbit bones were also found on-site. Chickens and geese were reared in the backlands, and small wild birds were trapped for the table. Some properties also had dovecots in their gardens, for the supply of pigeons/doves for the table.[35] Fish and shellfish were readily available at the market, as were any dairy products not produced at home.

Archaeological evidence has revealed the level of cultivation in the backlands. Most vegetables, such as leeks, fat hen (a 'weedy' plant – *Chenopodium album*), syboes and kale, were probably grown in the backlands, although more exotic produce, such as apples and onions, was imported. To supplement this, wild berries were collected. Archaeological evidence in other towns points to the consumption of brambles, blaeberries, raspberries, wild cherries, rowans and elderberries (Stones 1987, 30; Holdsworth 1987, 206). As long as famine did not hit Canongate, this was a relatively well-balanced and nutritious diet.

Water was readily available in the two strands and in wells, but the strands tended to become polluted, thus the usual drink for most, including children, was ale. The wealthier classes favoured wine.

Archaeological evidence, both in Canongate and other burghs, suggests that although there was a certain inevitable squalor, attempts were made to introduce an element of cleanliness. The culverts excavated at the Canongate site are merely one example of attempts by medieval people to counteract contamination from the build-up of dirt on the public thoroughfares and in the backlands. Certain diseases were rife, some endemic and chronic, in the medieval town. Leprosy was common throughout western Europe but the need for isolation was understood. Many towns had their own leper house outwith their boundaries. Where the lepers of Canongate were exiled to is unclear. Edinburgh had a leper house to the north-east of the town near Trinity College (Cowan & Easson 1976, 175–6) and lepers from Canongate may have been accepted here.

The greatest fear was plague or 'pest'. In fact, plague was several diseases, the bubonic form being the most noted. But 'pest' in the records may have concealed other diseases, such as typhus, which hit communities when resistance was low, as after famine. Pneumonic plague was prevalent in Scotland, both as a secondary infection to bubonic plague and as a primary disease, and the cold and rain that Canongate experienced, as did many other towns along the Forth and Tay valleys, would have tended to encourage it. Towards the end of the medieval period, increasing spatial mobility brought contact with new types of bacteria and viruses, many perhaps concealed in the records as 'pest', including syphilis, cholera, tuberculosis and smallpox. Care of the sick was largely a matter of self-help, and herbs were grown and collected for their medicinal and restorative properties.

Labour was interspersed to some extent with pastimes: foot and hand ball, dicing (a substantial number of gaming pieces and ceramic and stone counters have been found on the site) and pennystanes, for example, as well as drinking, storytelling and gossiping. The wealthier members of society might also enjoy archery, hawking and hunting; and those who were close to the king might even partake of a little jousting in the royal grounds or hunt in the deer park at Holyrood. Children had little toys, such as pottery or carved dolls and animals. All ages could enjoy the visits of travelling jesters, tumblers, pipers, drummers, minstrels and actors. But medieval life was hard.

4.7 The town market

Wine and exotic fruits and vegetables were imported and bought at the town's market. Produce that could not be grown in the backlands and burgh crofts might also be purchased there; and there was a close interdependence between the burgh and the surrounding countryside. There was also a close physical relationship with the neighbouring burgh of Edinburgh. Whether this was always cordial the medieval records do not make clear. At its foundation, Canongate was given the right to buy and sell at the market of Edinburgh. This meant that the burgesses of Canongate might share in the profits of Edinburgh's market.[36] It is very likely that this was resented by the Edinburgh merchants, who also probably dominated the merchants of the smaller burgh. As noted above, however, the burgesses of Canongate in time held their own markets in their own burgh (*RMS*, ii, 217). The abbey was an important consumer of goods and services, thereby encouraging the commercial growth of the burgh.

Animals were brought into the town on the hoof on market days and slaughtered on the public thoroughfare. Little was wasted from the carcasses: the skins were tanned and used by the leather workers, or cordiners, most of the carcass became meat, intestines and stomach linings were converted to sausage- and haggis-type foods and tripe, and fats were rendered down for candles and soap. Any rejected bones would have been boiled for glue or removed by scavenging dogs. The result was inevitable squalor, and this was added to by the common practice of fishmongers gutting the catch at the market.

Although market days were bustling, noisy occasions, a close watch was kept on selling and buying by the burgh authorities. Both quality and quantity control were monitored. Tasters of ale and meat ensured that these commodities achieved an accepted standard, and set prices for differing qualities of ale and weights of bread were laid down. The only weights permitted at the market were those of the town (Torrie 1990, 42); and anyone found abusing this ruling, or selling short measure was punished – usually with a fine and the 'dinging out' (banging out) of the bottom of the pot or barrel that held the commodity, so that it was of no further use. That all such dealings could be seen to be open and fair, selling was allowed only at the market cross or official booths near the cross and tolbooth, not at the port (Leith) or in 'myrk [murky] howsis and quiet loftis' – that was, secret places.[37] The two greatest offences against the good rule of the market were forestalling – the purchase of goods before they reached market, so avoiding the payment of toll to the burgh – and regrating – buying in bulk and possibly hoarding in order to sell at an advantageous price when prices were high. Both of these met stiff penalties: very strict fines or even banishment from the burgh.[38]

4.8 The influence of the Church

A hospital existed to the south of Canongate, at St Leonard's. Already in existence by the 13th century, it was granted to Holyrood Abbey by David II (1329–71). In 1493, Robert Ballantyne, Abbot of Holyrood, reconstituted the hospital and established six beds for poor or old men in the almshouse to the south of the chapel of St Leonard's (Cowan & Easson 1976, 177). An almshouse for poor women, dedicated to the Virgin Mary, stood in St Mary's Wynd. Though outside the Netherbow Port of Edinburgh, St Mary's Wynd fell within the jurisdiction of Edinburgh, and

it is uncertain whether it would have been open to women of Canongate (Geddie 1930, 23; Cowan & Easson 1976, 177). The same may be true of the Hospital of St Mary and St Paul, situated near Trinity College and described in 1470 as a poor hospital, which was dedicated to St Paul and had an adjacent chapel dedicated to St Mary. Another hospital for the poor (12 men), dedicated also to St Mary occurs in the record in 1485. This probably united with the St Paul Hospital, forming one establishment (Cowan & Easson 1976, 177). St Thomas Hospital in the Canongate existed in 1541. These were typical of medieval hospitals, which were, in reality, more in the nature of almshouses for a few poor people, or more often for select groups such as widows of important merchants or places of rest for pilgrims, housing very few beds.

In spite of the best efforts of townspeople and the Church, death was always close at hand for medieval people. Archaeological research elsewhere suggests that the normal medieval lifespan was short. The most vulnerable groups were babies, young children and women of childbearing age. To reach the forties was to achieve a good old age, although a few hardy individuals might survive much longer.

Death was tempered by the teachings and support of the Church. Death must have held less terror for the wealthier members of Canongate society who could afford to pay for masses, or even establish chaplainries, for the saving of their souls by reducing their time in purgatory. Many of those who worshipped in the parochial aisle in the abbey could not afford this luxury, and therefore because of poverty could not alleviate their fear of death.

The Church dominated life from birth and baptism to death and burial in the burgh graveyard to the north of the abbey. A few fortunate boys benefited from attendance at school, run by the Church. For all the townspeople, the daily routine was marked by the sounding of the church bell at dawn and when labour ended and again when the town gates were closed at curfew. The liturgical cycle also regulated the yearly secular life of the town, with the timing of head courts at Easter, Michaelmas and Christmas.

Holy days were days for veneration of the saints, but also days of rest from routine – the only holidays. Religious plays and processions through the High Street of Canongate must have brought not only the opportunity for reverence of the saints but also for a bit of fun and amusement.

Notes

1 *Liber Cartarum Sancte Crucis*, 6.
2 There are no extant charters to burghs before 1160, and many of those known to have existed soon after this, such as those to Edinburgh, Perth and Berwick, are lost or destroyed. It is, therefore, necessary to extrapolate from surviving evidence, such as the charters to Inverness or Rutherglen, reiterating the rights bestowed by David I, *RRS*, ii, no. 213; *RRS*, ii, no. 224.
3 *Leges Burgorum*, c ic, for example, in Innes (ed) 1869.
4 *Leges Burgorum*, c xciv.
5 A number of manuscripts survive, the earliest being BL, Add. Ms 18111.
6 'Edinburgi Regiae Scotorum Urbis descriptio, per Alexandrum Alesium Scotum, S.T.D., 1550', *Bannatyne Miscellany*, i (1827), 187. John Dunbar, personal comment.
7 *Protocol Book of James Young*, no. 533.
8 *Protocol Book of James Young*, no. 1120.
9 Ms. 'Protocol Book of Vincent Strathauchin', i, no. 37, for example.
10 *Protocol Book of James Young*, no. 207.
11 Lawrie 1905, no. 169; *Charters and Other Documents Relating to the City of Glasgow* 1894–7, Glasgow, i, pt. ii, 5.
12 *Protocol Book of James Young*, nos 35 & 221, for example. See also Torrie 1990, 53.
13 NAS, PA 5/1, fo. 62r; *APS*, i, 178.
14 The detailed assessment of borough customs in Bateson 1904 highlights these similarities.
15 *Fragmenta Quaedam Veterum Legum et Consuetudinum Scotiae Undique Collecta* in *APS*, vol. i.
16 I am grateful to Professor G W S Barrow for his views.
17 *Protocol Book of James Young*, no. 82.
18 *Protocol Book of James Young*, no. 277.
19 *Protocol Book of James Young*, no. 1160.
20 *Protocol Book of James Young*, no. 71, for example.
21 *Protocol Book of James Young*, nos 50 & 410, for example.
22 *Protocol Book of James Young*, nos 836 & 404, for example.
23 *Protocol Book of James Young*, no. 754, for example.
24 Ms. 'Protocol Book of Vincent Strathauchin', i, no. 50, for example.
25 Ms. 'Protocol Book of Vincent Strathauchin', i, nos 866, 867 & 774, for example.
26 Ms. 'Protocol Book of Vincent Strathauchin', i, no. 1061, for example.
27 *Protocol Book of James Young*, no. 1120.
28 Ms. 'Protocol Book of Vincent Strathauchin', i, no. 51.
29 *Protocol Book of James Young*, no. 990. I have benefited from discussions on this period with Dr E Ewan.
30 *Protocol Book of James Young*, no. 1041.
31 *Protocol Book of James Young*, no. 207.
32 *Protocol Book of James Young*, no. 853.
33 'Extracts from the records of the burgh of Canongate near Edinburgh, MDLXI–MDLXXVIII', *Miscellany of the Maitland Club*, ii (1840), 27 November 1567.
34 Ms. Dundee Burgh Head Court Book, 4 June 1521; 12 June 1521; 13 July 1552; 19 October 1554; 22 December 1556; 13 July 1552; & 4 February 1557, for example.
35 *Protocol Book of James Young*, no. 72.
36 *Liber Cartarum Sancti Crucis*, 6.
37 Ms. 'Dundee Burgh Head Court Book', 5 October 1556.
38 Beveridge (ed) 1917, 64, 81, 33, 184; Torrie (ed) 1986, fos 2v. & 3v.

Chapter 5

The royal presence in Canongate c 1500–1603

E PATRICIA DENNISON and JOHN LOWREY

5.1 Introduction

E PATRICIA DENNISON

Royalty had been frequent visitors to the guest house of the Abbey of Holyrood throughout the Middle Ages, but from the 15th century there is increasing evidence that the Stewart kings found the abbey precincts, with their gardens and orchards, a commodious place to stay. James II (1437–60), for example, was born, crowned and buried in Holyrood Abbey and here it was that James III (1460–88) married. With the reign of James IV (1488–1513), however, the royal lodging at Holyrood was to be converted into what was called in 1503 'the king's palace near the abbey of Holyrood' and, ten years later, the 'palace of Edinburgh' (Dunbar 1999, 56; *TA* IV, 528; Sinclair 1904–5, 352–63). The palace underwent major remodelling and refurbishment in the reign of James V (1513–42) (Paton 1957, vol. 1, xiii) and, again, in 1554 when the Queen Mother, Queen Regent Mary of Guise, restored Holyrood. The building works encompassed not only prestigious accommodation for royalty and its entourage, but also gardens (Paton 1957, vol. 1, xliii, 192, 222) and courtyards and the more mundane essentials such as stables, workshops and storerooms for hay for the king's carthorse (Paton 1957, vol. 1, 7).[1] Edinburgh had become effectively the sole capital of Scotland, and the small burgh of Canongate would be increasingly drawn into the limelight of national politics.

5.2 Holyrood Palace 1500–1603

JOHN LOWREY

5.2.1 Introduction

The development of the royal palace at Holyrood can be seen as part of a process both of absorption of the monastic fabric into an increasingly sophisticated royal building and of secularisation of the Augustinian institution. The strategic position of Edinburgh, the fact that the abbey was a royal foundation, and the monastic duty of hospitality all combined to make Holyrood a natural place for a royal residence.

In architectural terms there is a clear relationship between abbey and palace. The royal residence developed from the monastic guesthouse that was to be found in all monasteries. The guest house was one of the 'worldly' parts of a monastery in that it dealt with non-religious, albeit in some cases royal, visitors or travellers. For that reason, the guest house was placed as far away as possible from the sacred parts of both church and cloister, that is to the west of the main abbey layout. That is certainly the case at Holyrood and early views, such as the so-called English spy's view of Holyrood of 1544 (fig 5.1),[2] although difficult to interpret, certainly indicate a developing palace complex in that position. Moreover, there is no doubt that, as the palace developed, that basic relationship with the cloister became something more cohesive as parts of the monastic complex were taken over for royal needs or cloister buildings formed the starting point for western extensions. By the mid-16th century the result was a courtyard which lay alongside but also overlapped with the cloister layout of the abbey.

Although this new palace was essentially a 16th-century creation, it had its roots in the 15th century and its development was clearly a matter of great importance to the royal household. For whereas royal accommodation had been a matter for the abbey's resources throughout most of the Middle Ages, from the 1470s alterations and improvements became a matter for the exchequer. So, in 1473 we find repairs being carried out in 'the queen's chamber' and by the 1490s there are a number of references to the 'king's chamber' and the 'king's closet' (Dunbar 1999, 56; *TA*, I, 46, 355).

5.2.2 James IV's palace

As part of the preparations for his marriage to Margaret Tudor in August 1503, James IV planned a series of major improvements to Holyrood, which was referred to as 'the king's palace near the abbey of Holyrood' (*TA*, IV, 528, quoted by Dunbar 1999, 56). Evidently some kind of accommodation lay in an independent block a little to the west of the west cloister range of the abbey (Dunbar 1999, 58). These two elements were linked

Figure 5.1
Detail of English 'Spy map', 1544 (© British Library; Cotton Augustus I.ii.56)

by two further ranges, a northern range containing a new chapel and a southern range containing apartments for James's English bride. The west cloister range, the old guest house, may have provided further accommodation, although it is possible that it was still used by the religious community at this time (Dunbar 1984, 17).

Although the detail of the planning of James's palace is uncertain, what is clear is that Holyrood, with an existing extensive and complex range of buildings and a comparatively spacious site on which to expand, allowed for the development of a palace that was more differentiated in planning. Public and private space, service and recreation, congregation and separation could all be accommodated far more easily at Holyrood than, for example, at Edinburgh Castle. Certainly, medieval planning, based on the great hall, used for reception and for dining for the entire royal

household, was no longer entirely adequate and part of James's motivation was to expand the planning sequence beyond the hall. That does not mean that the hall was entirely superseded and James's new palace also included a new hall. This was almost certainly the refectory of the abbey, that is to say, the south range of the monastic cloister. For this reason, presumably at around the same time, the Augustinian community expanded that same range to the east to create a new refectory and 'croce house' (Gallagher 1998, 1090; Dunbar 1964, 250).[3] James IV's palace was therefore based on the essential elements of the medieval royal household: hall, chamber and chapel, but in an extended format, with the chamber expanded into a suite of rooms and with the hall reduced in importance.

In this way a palace was created by a process of linking together old and new and by usurping a certain amount of the space of the monastery. This was done in such a way as to produce a quadrangular plan that echoed and slightly overlapped with the existing building and it has influenced the layout of the palace ever since.

If the broad layout is reasonably clear, the detail of this building is rather more difficult to discern. Details of the royal apartments are very sketchy, but the *Accounts of the Lord High Treasurer for Scotland* for the period contain a number of references to chambers for both king and queen (*TA*, II, 33, 270), with the additional information that the king's chamber had some kind of 'bos' or bow window (*TA*, II, 270). Both king and queen also had an oratory (*TA*, II, 417, III, 375), the king had a closet (*TA*, II, 419) and we can assume that the queen had likewise.

The main builders were Walter Merlioun, the king's master mason, assisted by William Turnbull and John Brown (Dunbar 1999, 57). Michael Wright was responsible for the erection and fitting out of the queen's chamber and it has been suggested, given his name and the likelihood that this indicates his trade, that this structure may well have been largely of timber construction (Dunbar 1999, 57).[4] While Merlioun no doubt had overall charge of the works and is specifically connected with the chapel (Dunbar 1999, 57), Turnbull is mentioned in connection with a new, windowed gallery (Dunbar 1999, 57), although the precise location of this is unknown.

Away from the palace itself, Merlioun started work on a new forework or gatehouse in 1502, with a vaulted pend, and an upper floor accessed from a stair turret on the south-east corner of the building. Evidently, this was never finished during James IV's reign because work continued in the 1530s (see below). The building was demolished in 1753, although some traces of it can still be seen in Abbey Strand.

By the time the marriage took place in August 1503, the new palace was substantially complete (Dunbar 1999, 57). The work involved not only the creation of royal accommodation that was appropriately stately, yet comfortable and properly serviced, but also external ceremonial space in the creation of a large 'basse courte' or outer court between the palace and the new gatehouse. This was used during the wedding festivities, for example, as the venue for a tournament (Dunbar 1999, 59).

More substantial work also continued at Holyrood in the years after the marriage as further improvements were made. Merlioun was responsible for the construction of a new tower, possibly what was later known as the south tower, in 1505. This seems to

have formed an extension to the king's apartments and certainly it was used as such by 1529, when the accounts of the Masters of Works start and mention the wardrobe in the south tower, as well as 'the king's grace own chamber in the south tower where his grace lies instantly' (*MW*, I, 27). The suggestion that this would have been near the junction of the two royal apartments, overlooking new gardens to the south of the palace, seems reasonable and adds to a picture of increasingly sophisticated royal accommodation that was as concerned with comfort and recreation as it was with stateliness and security. The focus on regal recreation is also enhanced in the period 1511–13 with the construction of the Queen's Gallery and the development of a menagerie, including the construction of a lion house (Dunbar 1999, 59; Jamieson 1994, 21–4).

5.2.3 The palace of James V

When James V assumed power in 1528, after the calamity of Flodden and its aftermath, his intervention at Holyrood was at first in sharp contrast to the developments of the previous reign, with an emphasis on strength and protection rather than expansiveness and leisure.[5] He almost immediately began building work at Holyrood (figs 5.2, 5.3) as the first step in a royal building campaign that encompassed Holyrood, Linlithgow, Falkland and Stirling. The first phase of this was focused on Holyrood alone and involved the construction of an apparently free-standing tower, with corner towers and battlements, standing immediately to the north of the western range built by James IV (Dunbar 1964 and 1999 are the best sources for this). By August 1529, the work had reached first-floor level, with the ironwork for the windows of the principal rooms being supplied at that time (*MW*, I, 3). By the following August, the two main floors were complete and by September 1531, preparations were underway for the installation of the great platform roof (*MW*, I, 58), which seems to have been at least partly prefabricated before installation in November (Dunbar 1999, 63; *MW*, I, 64).

Thereafter, the parapets, crenellations and upper parts of the two western corner towers were completed by the following March, when Alexander Chalmers and Sir John Gylgour were paid for gilding parts of the building and painting 'the tua lyonis and torris upon the heid of the tua west roundis' (*MW*, I, 79). The structure of the eastern corner towers was finished shortly after May 1532, when the quarriers supplied 'tua peis aslar lang stuf for lyntalis to the ii durris of

Figure 5.2

The west front of Holyrood Palace c 1647 (after Gordon of Rothiemay) (© Edinburgh City Libraries. Licensor www.scran.ac.uk)

Figure 5.3
Holyrood Palace with James V tower on the left (© Crown copyright: RCAHMS)

the est roundis abone the battelling' (*MW*, I, 85). The lining and plastering of the corner towers was completed over the summer, with the eastern towers being plastered by early August (*MW*, I, 93)

Given the vicissitudes he had faced since his father's death at Flodden, perhaps it is not surprising that James V was, at least at first, concerned with protection and security in his Edinburgh palace. The accounts show that the main entrance to the new tower was via a drawbridge and through a strong iron yett at first-floor level (*MW*, I, 18). William Hill, the smith who supplied the ironwork for this, was kept very busy throughout this period, notably on internal yetts and on bars for most of the windows. In addition, excavations in the early 20th century seem to suggest that the tower might originally have had a moat either around it or at least on the north side (Harrison 1919, 58). It was also defended by ordnance; with splayed gun loops still

visible at ground level and guns mounted on the roof (*TA*, VII, 1907, 350; VIII, 1908, 236, 307).

Exactly how this new tower related to the existing buildings is uncertain. Evidently, some demolition was required to accommodate it and it has been suggested that the north-west corner of the king's apartment was demolished, although conclusive proof is missing.[6] However, there is no doubt that the north-west corner of the chapel roof was dismantled in June 1530 to accommodate the south-east angle tower of the new work (*MW*, I, 45). The disengagement of the new work from the old that this implies, along with the evidence of the entrance via a drawbridge, which would have little real defensive purpose if it were also possible to access the new work from within the existing palace, is certainly suggestive of an independent structure.

The exact location of this entrance is somewhat mysterious, although the most recent research suggests

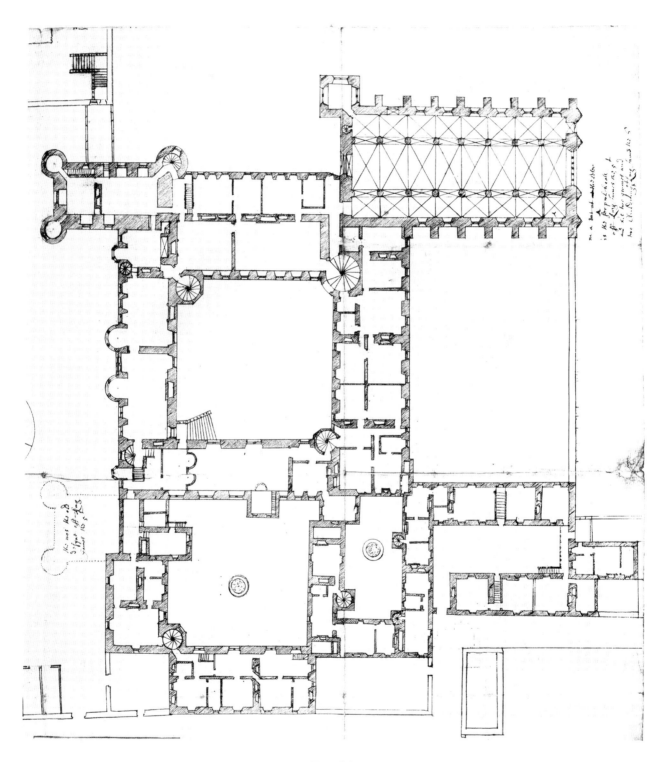

Figure 5.4
John Mylne's plan of Holyrood Palace in 1663 (© Crown copyright: RCAHMS)

it was on the east side of the tower, facing back towards the abbey church (Dunbar 1999, 60, 64).

In terms of the accommodation, the purpose of the new tower was to provide royal apartments. Those prepared for Margaret Tudor in the south range by James IV were converted into a hall 'quhair now the household eittis' (*MW*, I, 76) and the two main floors of the new tower became the royal apartments, comprising an outer and inner chamber, with closets in the rounds and the main turnpike stair in the north-east round (fig 5.4). The function of the south-east round, which was subsequently removed (see below), is uncertain.

However, the independence of this structure did not last long and again, the prospect of a royal marriage seems to have been the catalyst for a more lavish and extensive building programme, which was started almost as soon as the great tower was completed. With negotiations underway for the marriage between James V and Madeleine de Valois, work resumed on the palace in 1535 with the demolition of the old west range, its replacement with a new one and a reorganisation of the existing courtyard layout to create a new and integrated palace (*MW*, I, 153–67, 170–5; Dunbar 1999, 65–72). All of this was complete by the time the king brought his new bride back to Edinburgh in May 1537.

The reorganised south range of the courtyard was adapted yet again, this time to create a new chapel. The servants' hall that was thus lost may have been replaced by the great hall that James IV had made from the old monastic refectory, which was repaired at the same time but had been effectively superseded by this time. The old chapel range on the north range was probably expanded into a double pile structure and the chapel itself was replaced by two large rooms looking into the courtyard, the one at the south end being designated the council chamber. The most significant change, however, was in the construction of the new west range, which reconnected the great tower to the rest of the palace, allowing the apartments there to function as the private quarters of the king and queen but providing it with a suitably grand approach. The processional approach to the royal apartments started where the main entrance to the palace is now situated, in the south-west corner of the inner court. Here, a platt and scale forestair, 12ft wide (*MW*, I, 140, 166) led from the courtyard to the chapel in the south range, but also to the new west range. This contained three rooms, an outer chamber, mid chamber and inner chamber or wardrobe (Dunbar 1984, 17; Dunbar 1999, 143,

MW, I, 190–1). By the 17th century, the terminology had changed and the first two rooms are referred to as guardroom and presence chamber, the third room as a lobby. Certainly, whatever the terminology, it does seem that this third, smaller room, was a more private space, belonging properly to the space of the tower itself. Similarly, it has been suggested (Dunbar 1999, 143) that the room next to the new council chamber, at the west end of the new north range, may also have formed part of this extended reception suite. The new west range, the expansion of the north range and the crossing of the royal apartments from west range to tower, to north range, emphasises very strongly how the great tower was reintegrated with the developing palace and also suggests that it was probably at this time that the south-east round tower was demolished in order to facilitate this expanded and more integrated plan, although there is no definite proof of this. Ultimately, the reintegration of the tower with the rest of the palace was complete by the late 16th century, when the north range was expanded and connected to James V's tower.

Two other aspects of this phase of James's work are also of interest. The first, somewhere within the palace, possibly along the east range (Dunbar 1984, 18), was a great gallery. The accounts for this period include a number of references to this being supported on stone pillars with carved capitals (*MW*, I, 140). At the same time, the forework or entrance gate built under James IV was either completed or further elaborated because the mason's accounts indicate that the 'grete house' was built above the gate at this time, along with the tower containing the turnpike to access the upper level, and the battlements on the top (*MW*, I, 166; Gallagher 1998, 1095). On completion, between 1535 and 1537, it provided accommodation for the redoubtable Thomas Peebles, the glazier who had worked for James IV and continued to work at the palace in the 1530s (*MW*, I, 166; Gallagher 1998, 1095).

Evidently, James V's ambitions for Holyrood were not entirely satisfied by the time he died in 1542. According to John Mylne, who surveyed the palace in 1663, the king had intended duplicating his great tower at the south end of the new west range, to create a symmetrical façade (fig 5.4). It was this that provided an important starting point for Sir William Bruce in his remodelling of the palace in the 1670s.

5.2.4 The later 16th century

After the death of James V, both palace and abbey suffered badly as a result of English invasions and

Scottish internecine warfare (Harrison 1919, 81). The light artillery and 'small munitions' situated on the great tower and elsewhere in the palace between 1540 and 1544 were clearly no match for the well-equipped and well-trained English troops (*TA*, VII, 350; VIII, 236, 307). In Hertford's invasion of 1544 the abbey and palace were looted and burned (Harrison 1919, 76–80), although the palace seems to have survived better than the abbey and the great tower in particular seems to have been strong enough to withstand the onslaught (Harrison 1919, 80). The 1547 invasion was more unequal in its depredations. In this case, the palace was specifically excluded from English attention, but the abbey was 'suppressed' exactly as an English abbey would have been under Henry VIII's policy of the time: its lead roofs were stripped and its bells removed (Harrison 1919, 82). This particular aspect represents an overlap between the 'rough wooing' and the Reformation that, on the one hand, hastened the absorption of the abbey into the palace and, on the other, saw the gradual removal of the religious community and the decline or destruction of the specifically monastic fabric of the complex.

The church itself survived the invasions of 1544 and 1547, although its octagonal chapter house, which lay alongside the choir, to the east of the cloister, was destroyed in 1544 (Gallagher 1998, 1087). After 1560, the abbey was disbanded, but the church, as the parish church of the Canongate, was retained. However, the east end was redundant and gradually fell into such a state of disrepair that by 1569, it was demolished and the stonework used to repair and adapt the nave as a reformed parish church (Gallagher 1998, 1084).

The palace was gradually repaired, especially during the regency of Mary of Guise (1554–60) when it once again became the main royal residence. The use of the palace continued during the reign of Mary Queen of Scots and James VI, although little of great importance was carried out within the palace itself. It is in this post-Reformation period, however, that the palace came entirely to dominate the abbey. The monastic life ended, although the canons were allowed to live out their lives with a pension, and they retained a hold in some areas, including some of the gardens (Gallagher 1998, 1093), but the abbey buildings were increasingly used for court purposes. Thus, the new frater and cross house were gifted to Patrick Lord Ruthven in 1564 as his residence and remained in his family until 1584, when it was forfeited to the Crown

(Gallagher 1998, 1090). In the same period, the complex of courtyards to the south of the palace and cloister, containing service areas, kitchens, and so on, was further developed to include Chancellor's Court and, as a continuing ecclesiastical presence in the 17th century, Bishop's House, which lay to the south of the cloister (Gallagher 1998, 1092).

The old abbot's house, to the east of the abbey, was taken over in the 1630s as the lay commendator's house and this, from what we can tell of it from Gordon of Rothiemay's map of 1647 (fig 6.1), was a substantial courtyard dwelling, although it does not seem to have survived much beyond this time.

Both abbey and palace were, of course, part of a much larger complex of courts, gardens and parkland and this, like the abbey itself, was gradually annexed to lay and specifically royal use. There were gardens associated with the abbey, including a series of fish ponds to the south of the cloister. Both James IV and James V were involved in developing the gardens and, by the end of the 16th century further substantial developments had been made. One of the complications in the arrangement of the gardens was that there were two roads through the palace complex. The first was the route to the abbey church and churchyard, which was essential as the abbey church served as the parish church; the other was the vennel that cut east and then south on the south side of the palace. Both of these are clearly visible on the 1647 plan and are divided off from the gardens by a series of dykes which contribute to the compartmentalisation of the gardens.[7] In addition to the cultivation of fruit, flowers and herbs, the gardens and the wider park were developed to cater for specifically royal activities. The image of the gardens and park at Holyrood as the setting for courtly pageantry and regal display comes across very strongly even from the fragmentary accounts that survive. Under James IV, for example, a lion house was built to accommodate a beast acquired in 1506 (Jamieson 1994, 24, 29; *TA*, III, 200; IV, 275, 372, 377). The 'Lyones yaird' can be found in the accounts right through until 1615, although by that time the name probably commemorated the original function of the place (*MW*, I, 342, 345, 360). In the later 16th century, however, not only is a lion mentioned, but also a tiger, a lynx, and even an ape are all associated with the palace and its gardens (Jamieson 1994, 29–30).

If regal animals were important to the sovereigns and regents who lived at Holyrood, so were regal pastimes. Foremost amongst these, of course, were hunting and hawking. A hunting park had existed at Holyrood since medieval times, but this was expanded and enclosed within the 16th century even though Falkland was certainly a more important hunting park than Holyrood (Jamieson 1994, 31–2). Similarly, archery was clearly an important activity and references to the butts are found throughout the records of the time. The accounts also contain references to what was probably the ultimate in regal recreation, namely the tournament. This concern with a ritualised and, by the 16th century, somewhat antiquated display of military prowess was extremely popular in Renaissance courts across Europe, and James IV and his immediate successors were no exception to this trend (Edington 1995, 102–3). The tournament at the time of James IV's marriage has already been noted and this interest in chivalry was demonstrated again in 1507 when he staged the 'Tournament of the Black Knight and Black Lady' in which the setting of the garden was crucial to the understanding of the conceit behind the tournament which was focused on 'the tree of Esperance, which grows in the garden of Patience, bearing leaves of Pleasure, the flower of Nobleness, and the fruit of Honour'.[8] This was such a success that it was held again in 1508. In this case, and no doubt in others, the importance of the event was not only in the jousting and other forms of combat but in the pageantry that accompanied it and provided the framework for the action. A similar tournament, called the Siege of Troy, mentioned in a 1582 charter, is almost certainly commemorated in the small garden near the commendator's house (Gallagher 1998, 1092). No doubt the combination of classical erudition with noble and chivalrous single combat and courtly love, which the story of Paris and Helen might have suggested to 16th-century sensibilities, made this an attractive subject both for a pageant and for a garden. That it was attractive to James IV is certain because in 1503 he purchased a set of tapestries with just this subject matter for his apartments (Gallagher 1998, 1092; RCAHMS 1951, 144). On a considerably larger scale, but in a related vein, was the famous picnic of Mary Queen of Scots in 1564, when, as part of the celebration of the nuptials of the Lord High Chamberlain, she arranged for Hunter's Bog, a valley between Arthur's Seat and Salisbury Crags, to be dammed to create an artificial lake in the royal park as a setting for the celebrations, which no doubt included entertainments on the water (Jamieson 1994, 32).

5.3 Politics and religion

E PATRICIA DENNISON

The untimely death of James V at the age of 30 on 14 December 1542, six days after the birth of his daughter Mary, heralded unrest not only for Scotland, but also for Canongate. The king's body was transported from Falkland Palace to Holyrood Abbey for the funeral rites. The young queen was to become a pawn in the political and dynastic ambitions of Henry VIII of England (1509–47), in his 'rough wooing' of this child on behalf of his son Edward. In May 1544, a report on the expedition to Scotland by Edward Seymour, Earl of Hertford, gives a flavour of the impact of national events on the capital: for three days, 'neyther within the wawles, nor in the suburbs was lefte any one house unbrent … Also we brent the Abbey called Holy Rode, and the Pallice adjoynyge to the same' (Laing 1851–4, 102).

This laconic understatement conceals a mass of misery and destruction for Canongate. Although Edinburgh Castle was the principal target, English intelligence determined that the weakest defensive point of the capital was from Calton Hill via the Watergate, so avoiding the assault of cannon that would have greeted a more direct offensive on the castle. A contemporary plan (fig 5.5), executed by Richard Lee, builder, architect and surveyor, who was knighted for his services in this campaign, or one of his staff, shows the massed ranks of Hertford's men assembled below Calton Hill, with one section already in the process of forcing the Watergate on 4 May. The troops then proceeded to fire their way up Canongate High Street, described in a contemporary account of the expedition as 'a brode strete', towards the Nethergate Port. The castle did, indeed, prove impregnable, and troops returned the following day to wreak further incalculable damage on the lives and homes of the people of Canongate and Edinburgh. The abbey was desecrated and the palace sacked (Dalyell 1798, 6–7). Other smaller, but important, features of the townscape suffered. The hospital of St Thomas Martyr, said to have been founded in 1541, stood in the Watergate. The seven almsmen received annual rents from property in Bell's Wynd, but this tenement and the manses and chambers associated with the hospital were also destroyed (RMS, v, no. 1242). The hospital itself, however, survived not only Hertford's attacks, but, also, the Reformation (Cowan & Easson 1976, 178; Wood 1937, 181–2). Hertford predicted ten days later that the destruction was such that 'the enemy

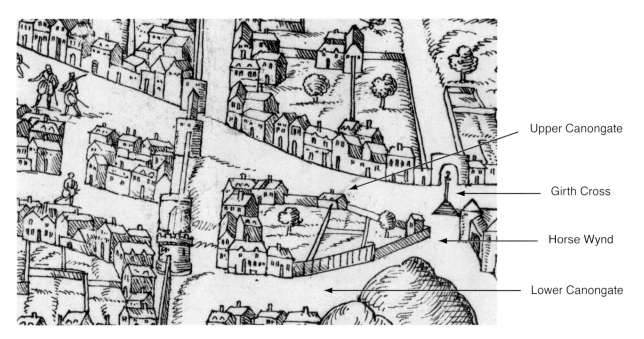

Upper Canongate

Girth Cross

Horse Wynd

Lower Canongate

Figure 5.5
English engineer's drawing of Canongate, 1573 (© NLS)

shall neither recover this damages while we live, nor assemble any power this year in these parts, whatsoever aid come to them' (Merriman 2000, 149).

Three years later, as the Duke of Somerset and Protector to the young Edward VI (1547–53), Hertford defeated the Scottish troops, under James Hamilton, Earl of Arran, near Musselburgh, at the Battle of Pinkie. Leith was occupied (Merriman 2000, 248), and Edinburgh and Canongate awaited a further assault. The English leader, however, chose to turn south via Soutra, avoiding the stronghold of Edinburgh Castle, though Holyrood was ransacked.

The records of the burgh of Canongate confirm that properties that had once existed close beside the abbey had become derelict. What the records do not clarify is whether these properties had become waste when fired in Hertford's raid of 1544, or later, during the political and religious civil wars of 1568–73. What is clear is that Canongate burgh may have gained in prestige by the presence of royalty, but it was also to suffer from its proximity to Edinburgh, the capital of Scotland.

Further damage was done to the ecclesiastical fabric of the town either in the name of religion or from neglect. As early as December 1520, Edinburgh Town Council granted a site at Greenside and the keys to the Rood Chapel there to the Carmelite friars of Queensferry. Their actual possession did not take

place for another five years, but their presence was not welcome to the monks of Holyrood. Whether this was because it was felt to impinge on the Holyrood rights in the barony of Broughton, or on the Carmelites' proximity to the important routeways to the Canon Mills and the port at Leith, the documents do not make clear. Friction was so acerbic that in March 1530 it resulted in the 'downcasting' of the house where the friars lived.[9] The 'downcasting' cannot have been total, for the Greenside friary had become a leper hospital by 1591.

A number of religious establishments in Canongate were affected in the Reformation crisis of 1559–60. In August 1560, Parliament adopted a reformed confession of faith, rejected papal authority and outlawed the mass (*APS*, ii, 526–35). But, typical of the lukewarm conversion to Protestantism at the outset, even in the capital, was the selective damage to the religious fabric. Only a mile away from Canongate was Restalrig, a royal chapel, which was largely dismantled. Within the burgh, however, initial damage was minimal. The hospital of St Leonard stood to the south-west of the burgh and continued to function for a time after the Reformation. The manse of the chaplain of St Leonard's was sited within the burgh, for it was referred to as 'the great mansion lying beside the gate of the monastery on the north side of the high street of the Canongate'.

The Treasurer's Accounts in 1541 give some clues to its construction, which was probably similar to many of the prestigious dwellings known to have lined the Canongate. 6s 6d. was spent on 'grathing' [making ready] the house and breaking down two walls of mud and clay in it. Interestingly, two locks for the doors of the manse cost 8s (Smith & Paton 1940, 122). In the following year, 1542, the manse was referred to as a 'tymmerhous', which implies a considerable quantity of wood in its construction (Smith & Paton 1940, 123).

Another hospital to survive the Reformation was that of St Mary and St Paul. Its exact location is not certain, although Vincent Strathauchin's 'Protocol Book' in 1521 (no. 347) refers to a land near the Hospital of the Blessed Virgin Mary, formerly called the hospital of St Paul, as being near the port of St Andrew, with the stream of water called the Strand to the north. This at least places the hospital on the north side of the High Street, and it is thought to have stood east of Waverley Station. The interest by Edinburgh magistrates in the affairs of Canongate, however, was to be a growing facet of burgh government and one that was not always welcome to the Canongate burgesses.

One time-honoured feature of the burgh partially to disappear at the Reformation was the right of sanctuary within the precincts of the girth cross. A test case came in 1569, with a supplication to the Lords of Privy Council by Adam, Bishop of Orkney, Commendator of Holyrood and the convent, and Mr John Spens of Condie, advocate. William Barrie, messenger, had searched with armed men the houses of Thomas Hunter, Andrew Chalmer and Sir John Stevenson, which were all within the girth. It was confirmed that the privileges of right of sanctuary had been abolished at the Reformation. Only debtors might henceforth claim this protection (Mackay 1879, 158–60).

Although the official religion might have changed, many traditional features of burgh life continued. Canongate had had for some time at least one school, a grammar school, and possibly also a song school. It was probably sited close to the abbey and the reference to the schoolmaster – Master Hary Henryson – in 1529 rather implies that at this point there was only one school functioning (*RMS*, iii, no. 918). In 1554, Master Robert Dormond was appointed to this post. In the 1568 ratification of his appointment it was specifically stated that he was entitled to hold a grammar school wherever he wanted in the burgh (Anderson 1935, 4). Other schools, however, were by then in existence in Canongate: in March 1565, the kirk session minuted

that all masters of schools in the parish should convene (Calderwood 1961, 40). In 1606, the grammar school was specifically referred to as being 'beside the abbey' (Anderson 1935, 7), although it would move again by the late 17th century.

The Canongate church continued to function as the parish church, and, indeed, as the Catholic parish church for Edinburgh during the amnesty drawn up between Mary of Guise and the Protestant Lords of the Congregation between July and October 1559 (Lynch 1981, 26). The return of the young Queen Mary (1542–67) from France in August 1561 epitomised the dichotomy of thinking. On the first Sunday after her return, the queen attended mass in her chapel of Holyrood, to be countered the following Sunday with John Knox preaching at St Giles' Church in Edinburgh that one mass was more dangerous than a thousand enemies.

Throughout Mary's personal reign (1561–7), the ambiguities of a realm which had a Catholic queen and a largely Catholic household but which had also officially adopted Protestantism were closely mirrored within the Canongate: the queen's private chapel within the palace became a haven for those disaffected from the infant Protestant church, and Canongate found itself in the odd situation of having a Protestant parish church sited close to the only legal Catholic chapel in Scotland. Even legally, there were inconsistencies and lacunae: the Reformation Parliament of 1560 had banned the mass, but not all seven Roman sacraments (Lynch 1991, 210). Canongate, initially, became noted for a less zealous opposition to Catholics than its neighbour, Edinburgh. Consequently, a number of Edinburgh burgesses found the smaller burgh more commodious for worship, even in the absence of the queen, and, if the Canongate kirk session also proved tiresome, those with the right credentials might find protection within the households of significant members of the court or central administration (Lynch 1981, 43).

That many were in time prepared to conform to the new regime is, however, indicated by the presence of 1000 communicants in early 1564 and a further 200 two years later (Lynch 1981, 97; *CSP Scot*, i, no. 967). This, from a population that probably numbered between 2000 and 3000, including children not eligible to take communion, would appear to indicate strong support for the Protestant order and may well also be a comment on the forcefulness of the Protestant minister of Canongate, John Brand. Quite how much the ordinary, mainly illiterate, townspeople of Canongate, however, understood the political and religious implications of the Reformation crisis is not documented. The same church building continued to function as their spiritual focus, albeit stripped of some of its altars and symbolic trappings. Queen Mary had the proclamation of her marriage to Henry Stewart, Lord Darnley, made by John Brand (Calderwood 1961, 25), although her marriage took place in the chapel of Holyrood according to the Catholic rite. The following year, 1566, she attended the marriage of James Hepburn, fourth Earl of Bothwell, in Canongate Church, according to the Protestant rite.

The celebrations at Holyrood of Candlemas 1566 (2 February) marked an attempt by Mary to attract her Catholic nobility back to open celebration of the mass at court, which coincided with the formal investiture of Darnley into the French chivalric order of St Michel. The effect was explosive. Darnley and his drunken supporters swaggered up the Canongate into Edinburgh, boasting that he had returned Scotland to the mass. A month later, he was part of the gang of Protestant assassins who murdered the queen's Italian servant, David Rizzio, within the precincts of the palace. During Easter week in the same year, it was reported that 9000 Catholics attended the mass at Holyrood.[10] And at Easter 1567, Mary's own Spanish confessor claimed that Catholic worshippers exceeded 12,000. Yet the more open celebration of the mass by Catholics coincided with a slippage in the queen's own position.

The mysterious death of Darnley in February 1567 brought about a political crisis, which was exacerbated by Mary's marriage to Bothwell on 15 May. When the queen married Bothwell, Brand refused to publish the banns, a courageous move as Edinburgh was in the hands of Bothwell's supporters; but it was according to Protestant rite that the marriage took place on 15 May. Within a matter of a month, Mary had been confronted by the Confederate Lords, a formidable coalition of nobles, at Carberry, near Musselburgh. Bothwell was forced into exile, and the queen was imprisoned in the island fortress of Lochleven and, in July, forced to sign a deed of deposition. Just days after her imprisonment on Lochleven, the Earl of Glencairn broke into the royal chapel and destroyed all its Catholic furnishings, statues and images.[11] The 'stripping of the altars' at Holyrood signalled the end of both Mary's reign and the possibility of a Catholic counter-Reformation. With her escape in May 1568, defeat at Langside and ultimate enforced 19-year stay in England, the focus for Catholicism in Scotland was lost.

Civil war raged in Scotland from 1568. By 1571, Edinburgh was the cockpit. Canongate inevitably was drawn in. The queen's men held Edinburgh, with a council and a kirk session, and the king's men, the young prince's supporters declaring him James VI (1567–1625), were based in Leith, also with a council and kirk session. Dual government even extended to the holding of two parliaments. The Marian party convened a parliament in the Edinburgh tolbooth on 14 and 16 May. In response, the king's men held a parliament in Canongate, in the house of one William Cocker according to the diarist Robert Birrel (Dalyell 1798, 19), but technically within the precincts of Edinburgh:

> at a place called St Johnis Croce; and fearing that soldiers of the town would disturb them thay forteifed two places, the ane at the 'Dowe Crayg' [later occupied by Calton jail] the other at a house belonging to Lawson in Leith Wynd; and there shot in violentlie at the east port and slew soldiers and inhabitants; which lasted all the time of that parliament, which was called the 'croping parliament'. After this those of the town sortit and burnt divers houses near the town walls where their enemies resortit.[12]

This 'creeping parliament', which lasted less than 15 minutes, was little more than a brave show, although it did enact mass forfeitures of Marian supporters in that brief time. Edinburgh's defences were now so strong that cannon and gun fire could have little impact, but cannon fire from the castle bombarded the smaller burgh. The townspeople of Canongate near the Netherbow Port paid for this symbolic gesture. It was claimed by some that damage caused by both sides was even greater than that inflicted during the 'rough wooing' (Lynch 1991, 221). And the king's men at Leith could control exports and imports and, consequently, prices. To further exacerbate this war of attrition, all mills and granaries, including those of Canongate, were burned. Although Edinburgh had been taken in 1572, it was only with the final fall of Edinburgh Castle in May 1573 that the young king's men gained control, and some semblance of peace descended on the two neighbouring burghs.

5.4 The craftsmen of Canongate

E PATRICIA DENNISON

In spite of warfare, the growth of Edinburgh as a capital had a profound effect on the Canongate: nobles and their retinues, lawyers and their clients, and a growing infrastructure of service industries resulted from the increasing resort to the Court of Session after its formal constitution as a College of Justice in 1532, the more frequent meetings of both Privy Council and Parliament and the requirements of the royal court. Both commerce and the trades or crafts in Canongate thrived. Food supplies from crafts such as bakers and fleshers and the services of tailors and seamstresses were essential to all. Less in demand, but necessary for the wealthier classes, were the makers of quality products. It is known, for example, that one Baldwin Glasinwright (glassworker) was living in the town in 1512.[13]

During this century there was a formalisation of the rights of a number of Canongate's crafts by the granting of seals of cause, or charters of incorporation, to their respective guilds. In 1538, the bailies of Canongate granted a seal of cause to the cordiners, or shoemakers, of the burgh, thus bestowing on them all the rights and privileges enjoyed by similar incorporations throughout Scotland. This included the power to levy dues in Canongate from both shoemakers and cobblers, who were the vendors as well as repairers of old boots and shoes, but were not members of the incorporation. In 1554, this right was extended to outlying parts of the barony of regality, namely North Leith ('North' being the part of Leith granted to the abbey), the Pleasance or St Leonard's Gate, and part of St Ninian's Row – an extensive concession. Permission was also given for them to build an altar in the parish church, dedicated to their patron saint, Crispin (Malcolm 1932, 101–2).

The earliest documentary evidence of the incorporation of tailors is their seal of cause granted in 1546 by Robert, Commendator of Holyrood and bastard son of James V, to 'Thomas Allanson, Dekyn and Kirk Master of the Tailzeiour craft within our brugh of Canongate and certain masters of the same craft'. As with the cordiners, rules were laid down and endorsed by the commendator in 1554 (Marwick 1938, 91–2). He also, at the same time, gave permission for the provision of 'augmentation of divine service at ane altar biggit within our said Abbey, quhair Sanct An, thair patrone now stands' (Ross 1922, 127).

The hammermen craft included many seemingly different trades, from wealthy goldsmiths and jewellers to blacksmiths, gunsmiths or dagmakers, cutlers, lorimers or harnessmakers, locksmiths, saddlers, pewterers and also coppersmiths, hookmakers, sheathmakers and braziers or white-ironmen, who were less wealthy. Armourers also were subsumed within the hammermen craft, but by the 16th century their

skills were becoming almost obsolete (Wood 1935a, 2). It appears from the 'Book of the Hammermen' that watchmakers were attached (Wood 1935a, 10). As with the other crafts, a deacon was appointed to head the incorporation, in the case of the hammermen being elected at Beltane, usually 1 May, and from 1560 a treasurer also held office. The lists of apprentices show that young men from all parts of Scotland were sent to Canongate to acquire the secrets of the craft, with the intention of returning home to practise (Wood 1935a, 9). The goldsmiths were the most prestigious of the hammermen craft, their earliest mention in Canongate being in 1569. Amongst their numbers were Jerome Hamilton, who rented his house in Canongate from a burgess of Edinburgh, John Achesoun, who for several years was 'master cunyear' (coiner) to the king and whose son was also a goldsmith, James Gray and Adam Haw or Hall. A clockmaker, Abraham Wanweyneburgh, was recorded in the craft in 1592 (Wood 1935a, 11).

One of the main advantages of this formalisation of the standing of the crafts was the authority bestowed on the masters to control all aspects of a craft, from regulations laying down requirements from apprentices, internal discipline, control of price and quality of goods produced, to protection of the monopoly and privileges of the craft. A further intrinsic character of guild life was the notion of fraternity linked to religion. All crafts supported their altars dedicated to their patron saints in the parish church; all processed, in order of importance, on saints' days carrying aloft their banners representing their saints and craft allegiances; and all worshipped together while living and escorted the bodies of members on death at their funerals in preparation for their journeys into the next life. This formal corporate worship was continued after the Reformation, albeit without altars dedicated to patron saints, but from pews or lofts allocated specifically to certain crafts where solidarity was expressed in physical form. 'Free' or privileged craftsmen were visibly set apart from 'unfree' members of an intensely hierarchical society.

The old right giving permission to Canongate burgesses to use Edinburgh's markets still caused dissension. Canongate had its own market and a new tolbooth was erected in 1591, probably on the site of the previous one, the court of the regality of Broughton and the burgh of Canongate being held here from at least the 1560s (Wood 1937; Anderson 1949). The Edinburgh markets, however, were lucrative. On 20 March 1595, the bailies and council of Canongate supported George

Foullair, an armourer burgess, in an appearance before the Privy Council. The Edinburgh inhabitants had begun to molest Canongate men at their three weekly markets. Goods which had been taken from Foullair were returned to him while the matter was considered by the Court of Session. Significantly, pending their decision, it was declared that there was to be freedom to Canongate people to trade in the Edinburgh market (Wood 1935c, 103–4). This was, however, merely one incident in a series of harassments and ill feeling between the craftsmen of the two burghs that was to continue into the next century.

5.5 The transformation of the townscape

E PATRICIA DENNISON

Documentary evidence, most notably from contemporary protocol books, gives a certain insight into the urban setting of the burgh in the 16th century. The town still consisted of one main street, the High Street of Canongate, with back lanes, still both called the Strand. The alignment of burgage plots was carefully monitored by the burgh liners, and the main street was probably wider than that which may be seen today. Although properties lined both sides of the High Street, some lay waste.[14] This could have meant that the burgage plots had never been developed, but it is more likely that the dwellings on the plots had fallen into such a state of disrepair that they were, in effect, derelict. There was a certain advantage in claiming property to be 'waste' – it was not liable for burgh taxation. Not all property owners, however, were seeking to evade their dues. Some tenements had most certainly suffered fire or bombardment in the times of political and religious unrest.[15]

The general impression, however, is of a single-street town with properties stretching from the abbey gates up to the West Port, or Netherbow, which was the east and main port of Edinburgh. There were, for example, two tenements on the south side of High Street, bordered to their east by 'portam vocatam le abbay zet' (the port called the abbey gate), a wasteland and certain houses pertaining to the abbey and, on the west, other properties.[16] This port was probably that which gave access to the townspeople to their parish church.[17] The boundary between abbey precinct and working town was indistinct, despite the existence of a precinct wall. There was, for example, a brew-house to the south side of the abbey, which was mentioned in 1569 in a charter of feuferme on 'waste houses' and

lands called of old the brewhouse, with a croft of land attached on the south side of Holyroodhouse.[18] Nearby was a cluster of houses with gardens, which would later be called St Ann's Yards and be tenanted by both nobles and commoners. The Duke's Walk, which would also develop between these and the palace, extended in an eastwards direction to Clockmylne House or Cloicksholm (Mackay 1879, 154). References to tenements on the south side of the High Street are also firm indication that canons of Holyrood lived on the High Street and not solely within the abbey precincts (Wood 1937, 181–2).[19]

The 'Protocol Book of Vincent Strathauchin' for 1507–24/5 indicates that burgage plots stretched right up to the West Port, even though the area here to the south of High Street was technically within the precincts of Edinburgh, albeit outside Edinburgh's town walls. In 1512, a burgess was instructed to build his west wall on the line of 'the auld dik betuix his lands and James of Poltonis by the west port'.[20] Interestingly, there was a certain realignment at this end of the town. The south dykes of the properties here were now closed up and posts had been set up by the liners indicating the line of burgage plots down to the south port. This 'south port' seems to have been an official entry and exit for all, but in all probability, most burgage plots, both to the north and south of the High Street, had their own personal small gates in the back dykes, giving access to the Strands and the countryside, including the Pleasance, beyond.

The Water Yett (Watergate), to the north, was the principal gate into the town, giving access to and from the important route to Leith. This was locked at night during curfew and served to prevent tradesmen entering the town illegally to market goods without payment of market dues, thereby protecting the rights of the town's own craftsmen. It was also made fast at times of approach of peril, be it in human form, for example, the troops of the Earl of Hertford or something less tangible, such as plague.[21] The gate also gave access to the burgh lands. An incident between the servants of an Edinburgh tailor burgess and a Canongate burgess highlights the rural atmosphere that might still pervade the town in the 16th century. Just outside the gate the two men fell into disagreement and one was injured; his main defence was that he was going about his business in an orderly fashion – 'riding his master's horse to the plough in sober manner' (Wood 1937, 178).

By the latter half of the 16th century, it seems that the town was demarcated with stone walls. The arrival at Edinburgh in 1590 of James VI's new queen, Anne of Denmark brought her along a route 'to the south side of the yards of the Canongate, along the party wall ...'.[22] This gives the impression of a substantial wall bounding the southern side of the burgh. Already, by 1588, the wall to the north of Canongate was stone-built. It was of sufficient structure for one William Stewart, a writer (that is, a lawyer), to have a privy built into the stone wall and an access route through the garden to reach it. This was well sited, as it could drain or soak away into the town ditch. This was probably not an unusual practice by the late 16th century and the same may be expected to have occurred on the south side also.[23] Other features of the townscape were the canon cross (girth cross),[24] St John's Cross (Wood 1937, 122) and the 'loplie stane' (Wood 1937, 57, 221, 278, 401),[25] all considered sufficiently notable landmarks to be quoted in property transactions. The most important cross was the market cross, for it was here, as in the Middle Ages, that important business transactions took place. Another medieval custom to survive was the use of the jougs attached to the market cross (Wood 1937, 164), although in post-Reformation years much of the disciplining of the populace was shared with the kirk session; its records reveal an insistent desire to stamp out such habits as fornication, adultery and harlotry (Calderwood 1961). The girth cross also functioned as a place of punishment.

In 1591, the tolbooth was replaced, probably on the site of the medieval tolbooth. Still standing, albeit with later alterations, it was an important building, constructed of stone. Its roofing material was wooden shingles, which were replaced with slate only in the late 19th century. A panel of the shingles was preserved at that time and is still in the keeping of the National Museums of Scotland (Walker 2001, 169–70).

While much of the evidence suggests an essentially rural atmosphere, there are also firm indications of the desirability of possessing property in Canongate and, in consequence, the development of subdivision of the backlands of plots and the emergence of closes giving access to the properties to the rear of the forelands. Tenements with High Street frontages to the north might still be bounded to the south by the dyke of an orchard. But many of these, even if still possessing large gardens to the rear, might consist of an upper hall, a vault and two cellars, with a further hall and chamber occupied to the north – a not insubstantial property.[26] Brodie's Close, one of the many closes that were to proliferate in Canongate in the modern period, has now disappeared within the new Parliament complex, but had its origins in this century. Its earlier name was Little's Close, so named from the mansion of William Little built c 1570. Two such closes that stood to the north of High Street were Scott's Close (Wood 1937, 23, 28) and Pais' Close, named after one Pais with an unrecorded Christian name (Wood 1937, 56).

This increased building activity is evidenced in the archaeological record. Medieval and post-medieval stone-lined culverts which carried domestic waste from structures fronting High Street began to be constructed during this period (Chapter 3.5). A concentration of industrial features is indicative of greater use of the backlands of properties.

A seemingly rare reference to 'Buthraw' comes in the 'Protocol Book of Vincent Strathauchin'.[27] A merchant booth lay within a tenement of land 'in buthraw' on the south side of High Street. Although, unlike the incorporated crafts, there is no evidence of a merchant guild in Canongate at this time, there were sufficient of their number clustering together in their booths to merit a place name of 'Booth Row'. It is not stated, but it is possible that Booth Row stood very near to the site of the tolbooth and the market cross. Booths, however, probably stretched along most of the length of High Street. The 'Protocol Book of Alexander Guthrie snr', dating from 1579 to 1581, locates booths, easter and wester, in a fore-tenement of the Hospital of St Thomas, beside Holyroodhouse, on the east side of Bell's Wynd, on the south side of High Street.[28] A further volume of Alexander Guthrie snr's 'Protocol Book', which dates from 1582 to 1585, refers again to the east and west booths as being the property of Jonet Adamesoun.[29]

On 16 October 1572, the market cross had to be repaired.[30] All towns had such a responsibility for the maintenance of public buildings and roads. In 1593, a significant 'act for the mending of the calsay o' the Canongait and outwith the Water Yett' was passed. This was an extensive repair job, stretching along the High Street from the Water Yett to the foot of Leith Wynd and especially between the 'clock myln' and the Water Yett. To fund this two pence was levied on every full cart and one penny on every horse load coming through the Water Yett with goods to be sold at the market (Mackay 1879, 115).

There was, however, to be a far greater investment in the townscape of Canongate, although it came not from the burgesses of Canongate, but from the growing importance and physical expansion of the precincts of the royal court at Holyrood, especially after the young king, James VI, took up near-permanent residence

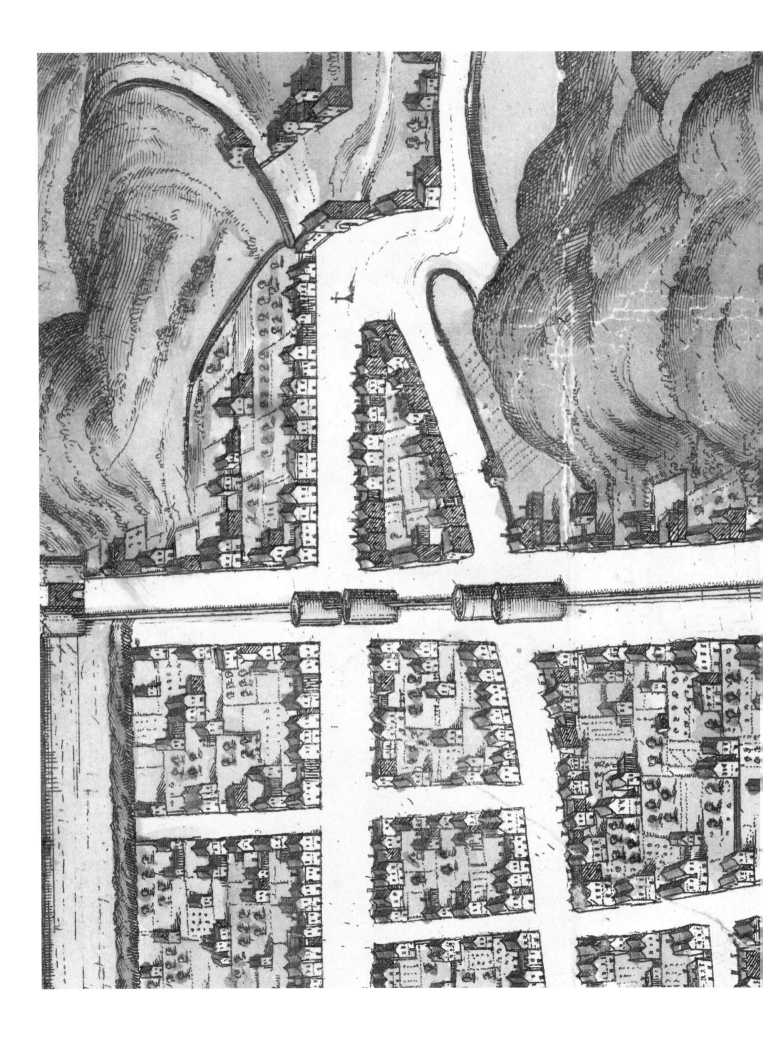

there in 1579. Sixteenth-century maps and illustrations give very firm clues that a radical transformation of the townscape was in process at this time.

The 1544 view drawn from Calton Hill by an English soldier is considered to be a relatively accurate portrayal of Canongate and Edinburgh, although certain small elements are stylised (fig 5.2). Known buildings and topographical features of 16th-century Canongate are delineated. The Water Yett is clearly noted, being the main entrance into the burgh and the route the English troops used in 1544 to enter Canongate before passing up the High Street to the Netherbow Port of Edinburgh. Holyrood Palace, the parish church and properties close to and associated with the abbey and palace appear accurately, as do the Salisbury Crags and even the routeways passing at their feet. Importantly, the plan suggests a distinct lack of development to the rear of properties at the east end of the burgh, both to the north and the south, but to the south-west of the burgh, in the area outwith the town walls of Edinburgh, but technically part of the precinct of Edinburgh, there is considerable subdivision in the backlands. Documentary sources reinforce the view that this is a highly accurate delineation. Even more importantly, from the perspective of this plan drawn from the north, after having entered into the burgh by the Watergate, the visitor was faced by the south side of the High Street totally built up along the frontage; to move south out of the burgh, it was necessary to turn left, or east, a short way down the High Street passing beyond the girth cross, before turning right to follow the small routeway south which was just in front of the palace/abbey walls.

It is important to compare this plan with an English military engineer's drawing of 1573 (fig 5.5). This particular drawing has been proven to be very exact in features depicted in both Edinburgh and the dry dock at Newhaven, used for the building of James IV's warship, the 'great' *Michael*, and it is not unreasonable to accept its accuracy for Canongate. This view is from the south and, because of this different perspective, the alignment of the routeway leading to Watergate in relationship to the High Street and other physical features appears different. The narrowing of the built extent of the burgh is portrayed again, as in 1544, at the east end of the burgh. Archaeological evidence has shown that the southerly part of the east end of the

site would have been waterlogged, forming, as it did, part of the loch at the foot of the crags (Chapter 3.2), which would support the accuracy of this view. The overall impression is one of a burgh that still retained many of the characteristics of an 'organic' settlement, that is one that, although officially laid out in burgage plots, respected very much the geology and natural attributes of the site.

What is significant is that, delineated as it is from a different perspective, this 1573 drawing shows no building to the south of the Water Yett and girth cross. The line of sanctuary had from medieval times run through the Watergate, via the girth cross, and southwards into the 'King's meadows', which also supports the general accuracy of this drawing. What also appears more clearly than in the 1544 plan is the siting of the girth cross in relationship to the abbey/palace walls. The precinct wall is clearly delineated on the map, running north–south, just to the east of the girth cross.

This view of the girth cross standing in isolation might seem to be supported by Braun and Hogenberg's map of 1582 (fig 5.6), but a number of other features on this plan are recognisably incorrect. The map is highly stylised, as are many of Braun and Hogenberg's plans of towns in Europe and, in consequence, little faith should be placed in it, for these purposes. Nevertheless, the 16th-century cartographic evidence does, in general, support the theory that, until into the second half of the 16th century, development was marginal at the east end of Canongate, the girth cross probably stood in isolation and the abbey precinct wall stood immediately to the east of the cross and the small routeway, the line of sanctuary, that gave access to the 'King's meadows'.

Cartographic evidence of the following century shows a totally new picture. Gordon of Rothiemay's plan of Edinburgh of c 1647 has long been acknowledged as a highly accurate representation of site and boundaries (fig 6.1). According to this plan, the girth cross, as would be expected, still stood in its traditional position, to the south of the Watergate. These are the only two urban features at the east end of Canongate that bear any relationship to the 16th-century topography. Most strikingly, the palace walls no longer lie immediately to the side of the girth cross. They are significantly distant. If compared with the 16th-century cartographic evidence and supporting documentary information, it can only be concluded that the medieval wall surrounding the abbey had been removed and replaced with another further east.

Figure 5.6
Braun & Hogenberg's view of Canongate, 1582 (© NLS)

Furthermore, the girth cross is now surrounded by properties, and the narrowing of settlement at the east end of Canongate is no more. In place of this narrowing are developed backlands and formally laid-out gardens. A radical reconstruction of the east end of Canongate had taken place.

What is also highly telling is that Rothiemay's map retains, embedded, one further 16th-century feature – the imprint of the previous sanctuary precinct. Following a line through the Water Gate and the girth cross, the delineating marker, the precinct line may still be traced moving south through the 17th-century burgage plots, before skirting closely to the west wall of the erstwhile monastic gardens south of the Strand.

There is no evidence of extensive building works at Holyrood Palace in the early 17th century, with the king largely resident in England from 1603. It therefore seems safe to assume that this transformation of the townscape took place in the 16th century, either during the minority of James VI or, more likely, in his personal reign.

After the Reformation and the passing of religious houses, including Holyrood Abbey, into secular hands, King James and his agents were in a position to redefine Holyroodhouse and its associated lands. This secularisation of ecclesiastical property in the post-Reformation years probably served well James VI's elegant transformation of Holyroodhouse and its grounds. The result was a sophisticated royal court, focused, as it had been in the past, on Holyrood, but with a neighbouring urban enclave that offered a formal burghal setting of grand and commodious housing for the court.

5.6 A royal court with an urban precinct

E PATRICIA DENNISON

Whether the realignment of Holyroodhouse occurred during the personal reign of King James VI or earlier, it was certainly during the latter part of the 16th century that this site became truly prestigious. The whole area became transformed into an urban precinct of grand and commodious housing for the royal court. Rothiemay's map (fig 6.1) shows clearly the insertion of a new roadway, to be called Horse Wynd, possibly respecting an original pre-Reformation feature, whether abbatial or royal, through the newly established, very regular, burgage plots. These were to become the nucleus of a new urban court, along with the important housing to the east of Horse Wynd. They did not look to the wynd,

but rather, were mostly furnished with courtyards opening into the outer courtyard of the palace.

The king's household, alone, numbered some 350, not counting the associated menial services of such as laundrywomen, cleaners and general labourers.[31] These officers included masters of the wine cellar, ale cellar, pantry, wardrobe and stables (ten of the latter) to keepers of the silver vessels (six personnel), great larder and small larder, an aviary man, a coal man, the tailor of the wardrobe, and the cook of the court kitchen, all supplemented by their essential back-up staff.[32] The court would be swelled well beyond such numbers when Anne of Denmark, the queen of James VI, was in residence, or when visiting ambassadors and diplomats, often from England, arrived with their entourages. Increasingly, prolonged attendance at court by nobles and their retinues became expected and the norm. Accommodation had to be provided for all of these. Rothiemay's map and Hollar's 17th-century view define vividly the metamorphosis (fig 6.2).

It was not only the establishment of this urban court that characterised the latter decades of the 16th century, but also the transformation of Holyrood Palace itself. The fine detail of exactly how James VI brought about this transformation is largely unknown for the earlier part of his reign. The Accounts of the Masters of Works are lacking for the pre-1579 years, but those extant for the following decade reveal much activity in and around the palace. From the autumn of 1579, there were extensive repairs and minor building works to prepare for the residence of the young king and work continued for several years.

The records make it clear that in addition to the royal personages and their household there were many dwelling in and near the palace. With the shift eastwards of the gateway to the royal palace and the insertion of the new thoroughfare, Horse Wynd, through the newly established burgage plots, the nucleus of a new urban court was formed.[33] Inevitably, Edinburgh's role as the 'capital' of Scotland attracted aristocrats and lairds, as well as the personnel of government. It was, for example, in 'my Lord Seytoun's hous in the Canegait' that the French ambassador resided as a guest in 1582 (Mackay 1879, 146). The details of the preparations in 1589 for the marriage of the king to Anne of Denmark mention the splendid furnishings that graced many of the prestigious houses in Canongate.[34]

The properties at the east end of the High Street were clearly highly prestigious, in a number of cases having courtyards facing towards the palace, and there is little doubt that those to the west of Horse Wynd, on the site of the new Parliament, were equally elegant.[35] One example to illustrate this is the mansion built for William Little in c 1570, in what became called Little's Close. This same close may once have been called Tailliefer's Close, since William Little inherited land in Tailliefer's Close from his brother Clement Little, the distinguished lawyer and benefactor of the town college.[36] It is, however, possible that more than one property was inherited on the south side of the High Street. Little's house survived until 1836. Little, from an Edinburgh establishment family, had reached the Town Council as early as 1567, immediately on being granted burgess-ship and guildry and had a long career in civic office, culminating in his term as Lord Provost of Edinburgh in 1591 (Kirk 1989, 34). His position, and that of his family, in society is a good indication of the quality of this building in what was becoming an urban court precinct.

Property transactions recorded in protocol books give a clear indication of the desirability of residence in the Canongate during the reign of James VI. A 'great mansion' or 'great tenement', for example, stood on the east side of Bell's Wynd, and other houses were owned by prominent burgesses. Bell's Wynd was highly desirable because it was close to Holyrood Palace. But, equally, many other wynds were so placed and the interest in property in Bell's Wynd was merely a cameo of what was happening in other parts of Canongate. Many, naturally, settled near the palace not merely for social reasons but to benefit their own livelihoods. Bakers, butchers, tailors, goldsmiths and many other crafts could find a ready outlet for their skills. Archaeological finds from the site confirm the sophistication and wealth of many within Canongate at this time: late medieval pottery which includes north German slipwares, Spanish olive jars, and a single fragment of glazed stove tile that may be from the Baltic (Chapter 3.9). Wild duck, grey partridge, red grouse, gulls and pigeons also probably found their way to the table.

Canongate was not, however, solely the preserve of the wealthy and prestigious. There were always the poor at the gates of the influential and in those backlands that were not laid out as gardens and orchards. In June 1581, for example, the treasurer's expenditure benefited the poor of Canongate, when James VI authorised a payment of £20 for them.[37] In January 1583, however, 10s was given to a messenger, George Horne, to take letters to the provost and bailies of Edinburgh and Canongate, requiring them to execute their duty in ridding the towns of idle beggars and wastrels. This was repeated in the following March at a cost of 13s 4d, as presumably the instruction was being ignored.[38] But, in April, the poor at the foot of Canongate were again given financial assistance, along with those at Leith and Newhaven.[39] The poor were not, however, to be disorderly and disturb the peace of the palace and its hundreds of occupants; in June 1585, David Forester, the bellman of Canongate, was paid 40s for his troubles in removing the poor from Holyroodhouse gate and restoring order.[40]

Royal policy may appear to have been inconsistent, but, in fact, there was a distinction drawn between the idle beggar and layabout, who made no attempts at self-help, and the genuine poor, who might at times be lucky enough to benefit from royal generosity. The Scottish 'Act anent the punysment of strong and ydle beggars, and provision for sustenance of the poor and impotent' of 1574 (merged into a permanent Act in 1579) provided that the poor, aged and impotent of parishes or towns were to be supported by a local tax in proportion to the payer's financial resources. What the Act did not lay down, however, unlike the English Act of 1572, was the necessity for the local authorities to provide work and work materials for those needing employment. Problems also arose in enforcing the Act, and decisions as to who was genuinely poor and who was merely idle were often subjective, inconsistent and arbitrary.

The overwhelming impression, however, is one of grandeur, wealth and display. Formal entries of the monarch or his spouse into Edinburgh and Canongate reached the heights of splendour, magnificence and symbolism during the reign of James VI. It was Renaissance convention that the formal entry of a monarch, particularly to the capital, should be full of symbolism and display – of the splendour of the monarch and the obedience and love of the subjects. Margaret Tudor on her arrival in Edinburgh in 1503, for her marriage to James IV, set the tone of magnificence, to be emulated by Mary of Guise, Mary Queen of Scots and James VI (MacDonald 1991, 101).

Notes

1 'Edinburgi Regiae Scotorum Urbis descriptio, per Alexandrum Alesium Scotum, S.T.D., 1550', *Bannatyne Miscellany*, 1 (1827), 187.

2 The drawing, attributed to an English spy, shows a view of Holyrood from the north with the positions of some of the English troops nearby. It is associated with the 'rough wooing' by the Earl of Hertford in 1544.

3   For more generally on the role of great halls, see Dunbar 1999, Chapter 4.

4   On the other hand, it was not unknown, certainly in the following century for wrights to have charge of stone constructed projects.

5   There was a general upsurge in defensive, albeit specifically military, building in this period, noted in Glendinning *et al* 1996, 16–17.

6   Dunbar 1999, 63. This demolition is suggested as an explanation for the king taking up temporary residence in the south tower. No documentary evidence is given and while this explanation is possible, it must be just as likely that the king moved simply to avoid the disturbance caused by the building work. The suggested demolition must therefore be open to some doubt.

7   The best source for Holyrood palace gardens in this period is Jamieson (1994).

8   Quoted by Jamieson (1994, 30) from Treasurer's Accounts, vol. 3, 46.

9   *Edinburgh Recs*, i, 203 & 222; *Protocol Book of John Foular, 1501–28*, W Macleod & M Wood (eds) (SRS, 1930–53), iii, no. 461; *Acts of the Lords of Council in Public Affairs, 1501–54*, R K Hannay (ed.) (Edinburgh, 1932), 325.

10 *John Knox's History of the Reformation in Scotland*, W C Dickinson (ed.), 2 vols (Edinburgh, 1949), ii, 5; *Papal Negotiations with Mary Queen of Scots during her reign in Scotland, 1561–1567*, J H Pollen (ed.) (SHS, 1901), 496.

11 Knox, *History*, ii, 213.

12 'Historie and Life of King James the Sext, 1566–1596', *BOEC*, xvi (1928), 18–19; collated by Thomas Thomson for Bannatyne Club, 1935.

13 'Protocol Book of Vincent Strathauchin', no. 111.

14 'Protocol Book of James Young', vii, 24v, no.854; 'Protocol Book of James Young', vii, 88v, no. 967; 'Protocol Book of Vincent Strathauchin', 1507–24/5, no. 338.

15 'Protocol Book of Alexander King', (1548–50), fo. 107 11 Dec 1549, for example.

16 'Protocol Book of James Young', 8 November 1497, 88v; no. 967.

17 'Extracts from the Records of the Canongate', ii, 316.

18 'Extracts from the Records of the Canongate', 322–3.

19 'Protocol Book of James Logane', 1576/7–80/1, 49–49v. NAS B22/22/25.

20 'Protocol Book of Vincent Strathauchin', no. 96 (March 1511/12).

21 'Extracts from the Records of the Canongate', ii, 330.

22 *Papers Relative to the Marriage of King James the Sixth of Scotland, with the Princess Anna of Denmark, AD MDLXXXIX and the Form and Manner of Her Majesty's Coronation at Holyroodhouse, AD MDXC*, collated by J T Gibson Craig (Bannatyne Club, 26, 1828).

23 'Extracts from the Records of the Canongate', ii, 356–7.

24 'Protocol Book of James Young', 21 Jan 1496/7, 24r, no. 853.

25 'Protocol Book of Vincent Strathauchin', 1507–24/5, nos 508 & 111.

26 'Protocol Book of Vincent Strathauchin', 1507–24/5, no. 50 (1510).

27 'Protocol Book of Vincent Strathauchin', no. 241.

28 'Protocol Book of Alexander Guthric snr', 1579–81, 60.

29 'Protocol Book of Alexander Guthrie snr', 23 March 1582–12 June 1585, 6. She might well be the Jonet Adamsoune who was banished along with the wives of the exiled ministers in the autumn of 1584 (Lynch 1981, 366; Calderwood 1961, iv, 200).

30 'Extracts from the Records of the Canongate', ii, 326.

31 The household figures have resulted from the researches of Dr Amy Juhala ('The household and court of King James VI of Scotland, 1567–1603', unpublished PhD thesis, University of Edinburgh, 2000).

32 NAS, E21/63, Treasurer's Accounts, 1582, 130–130v.

33 The accounts of the Masters of Works are missing throughout most of this reign. They would, in all probability, have highlighted this transformation. There is an old, unproven tradition that Horse Wynd takes its name from the royal stables once sited there. If correct, this, too, would suggest that the area of Horse Wynd was once within the palace precincts.

34 *Papers Relative to the Marriage of King James the Sixth of Scotland, with the Princess Anna of Denmark, AD MDLXXXIX and the Form and Manner of Her Majesty's Coronation at Holyroodhouse, AD MDXC*, collated by J T Gibson Craig, 29, for example (Bannatyne Club, 26, 1828).

35 It should be noted that Horse Wynd was widened by some 11ft to the west in the 20th century.

36 'Protocol Book of Alexander Guthrie, snr', 1579–81, 89 & 100; 'Protocol Book of Alexander Guthrie, snr', 1587–88, 134; Lynch 1981, 261, 304; Boog Watson 1996, 16–17.

37 NAS, E21/61–61, Treasurer's Accounts, 1579–81, 135v.

38 NAS, E21/63, 108v & 120.

39 NAS, E21/63, 127.

40 NAS, E21/64, 71v.

Chapter 6

The absentee Crown and court 1603–c 1660

E PATRICIA DENNISON and JOHN LOWREY

6.1 Introduction

E PATRICIA DENNISON

After the Union of the Crowns, in 1603, when James VI of Scotland also became James I of England, the royal court was removed to Westminster. Many Canongate people considered this to be a loss of status. Indeed, the residents petitioned the Privy Council in 1629 over their perceived poverty after the Crown's departure (Wood 1956, 34). The Privy Council was regularly meeting in the capital,[1] however, and, although Crown and immediate court had largely departed, Canongate was, in reality, by no means an abandoned town. This is indicated, for example, by the response of the Canongate bailies to James VI, preparing for a return visit to the capital in 1617. The king sought lodgings for his vast retinue and stabling for their horses in Canongate. The bailies were forced to reply that they were unable to comply as 'Canongate was full of noblemen, gentlemen and officers of His Majesty's forces'. Whether this was strictly true, the retort that the bailies were to 'tak present order with the persons disobeying and refusing the said billets, and to punish them to the terror of others' (Malcolm 1932, 121) did produce results.

Preparations for the royal homecoming in 1617 also, significantly, included the rearrangement of the Chapel Royal (relocated from Stirling to Holyrood in 1612) for episcopal worship. This was all part of James VI's centralising ecclesiastical policy. A common Church in his unified realm would be a major step towards a reunited Christendom (Lynch 1991, 242). Sectional differences were to be removed by conformity – private baptism, confirmation by bishops, private communion, kneeling at communion and observance of Holy Days were to be practised. These were the so-called Five Articles, rejected by the General Assembly in 1617 but pushed through at the next General Assembly in Perth in 1618, and ratified by Parliament in 1621, but with a small majority. The potential for major dissension in the reign of his son, Charles I (1625–49) had already hatched.

6.2 James VI and the royal visit to Holyrood Palace in 1617

JOHN LOWREY

Under James VI and Charles I, Holyrood received less attention than other Scottish royal palaces, but, nevertheless, the general trend towards the consolidation of the palace complex amidst the rambling structure of the palace/abbey complex continued.[2]

King James, having declared on his departure to London in 1603 his intention of returning to Scotland every three years, made only one trip, in 1617. The 1616 proclamation of this visit speaks of the 'salmonlike instinct of our mind' that made his 'hamecoming' essential. (Harrison 1919, 171; *RPC*, vol. 10, 685). Huge and costly preparations, including work on Holyrood Palace, were undertaken. James Murray, the Master of Works at the time, was instructed to:

> tak down the haill roof and thaske of the ludgeing above the ulter yett callet the Chancellaries Ludging with sa meikle of the stain worke as is requisite and to caus the same to be buildit up ane perfyte of new (Harrison 1919, 173; *RPC*, vol. 10, 517).

Other work was in a similar vein: demolition and rebuilding in some areas, including a gallery, and complete demolition of others. Through demolition the idea was to create more uniformity in parts of the palace, thus the bakehouse yard had a number of buildings removed in order to create a 'perfyte close'. Probably the most notable work, and certainly the most controversial in Presbyterian Edinburgh, was the fitting up of the chapel in the south range of the palace as a chapel royal, the fixtures and fittings for which were made in London and transported to Edinburgh (Harrison 1919, 174).

One result of the 1617 visit was an increased role for the palace. James used the visit to reaffirm Holyrood as the centre of his Scottish realm and instructed the Privy Council to meet only in the palace to keep up the 'face of a court' (Harrison 1919, 170; *RPC*, vol. 11, 203). Similarly, in this same post-1603 period, the palace was adopted as the home of the king's representative in Scotland, the Commissioner to the Scots Parliament. In this way, Holyrood Palace started to take on a symbolic role that culminated in the 1670s, under the Duke of Lauderdale as Commissioner, in the great reconstruction of the palace by Sir William Bruce and Robert Mylne (see 6.7.2 below). That symbolism, at least in the pre-1688 period, was not only about kingship and royal government but also about religion and its relationship with government. James VI not only insisted that the Privy Council met at Holyrood but also that they and the city councillors attended services in his expensively fitted out and essentially Anglican chapel (Harrison 1919, 179), which had been officially designated the Scottish Chapel Royal, superseding Stirling, in 1612 (Harrison 1919, 207).

6.3 Charles I's coronation 1633, and after

6.3.1 Changes at Holyrood

JOHN LOWREY

For the coronation in 1633, it was decided that the abbey church, rather than St Giles, was the most suitable venue (Harrison 1919, 180). Concern had been voiced about the condition of the church for a number of years and James Murray had produced a report on it as early as 1629, which seems to have formed the basis for the alterations (MacKechnie 1993, 248, 251). In a period of only a few months, Murray and his assistant Anthony Alexander carried out extensive works at the abbey kirk. Much of this involved essential repairs, but the work also substantially altered the character of the medieval work with major reworkings of both the east and west fronts. They built a new east gable, with a large window containing reticulated tracery. Work on the west front was even more significant in that it involved remodelling the original medieval façade above first-storey level (the original east front had been demolished after the Reformation). This included the remodelling of the gable itself and rebuilding the two flanking turnpikes with ogee domes replacing the medieval pyramidal tops. The southern flanking tower of the medieval façade had been subsumed within the north range of the palace in the late 16th century, but the northern tower was substantially remodelled, with a square plan and tall bell-cast roof, reminiscent of Flemish architecture of the same period and immediately influential on both St Ninian's manse in Leith and the Tron Kirk in Edinburgh (Gifford *et al* 1984, 138). The paired central windows were also remodelled: the upper ones were replaced by two much

simpler and smaller ogee-headed lights and the tracery of the lower ones was replaced by elaborate fleur de lys cusping in the segmental window-heads. MacKechnie (1993, 253–4) has pointed out both the immediate influence of this detail (on the Tron Kirk and on the new Parliament House) and, more importantly, its source at James V's Stirling palace block and in the hood moulding over the eastern entry to Linlithgow. In other words, its use at Holyrood was 'a conscious reference to the old Scots royal palaces, made for the eagerly-anticipated coronation of the new king of Scots' (MacKechnie 1993, 254).

A similar concern with the achievements of his 16th-century predecessors may have been behind the larger-scale enterprise alluded to by John Mylne in his 1663 survey (fig 5.4), in which he referred not only to James V's intention to build a second great tower to balance the existing on the north, but also to Charles I's intention, in 1633, possibly to repeat the whole James V west front, including the tower, as a mirror image to the south, creating a new and vastly extended, symmetrical palace façade (Mylne 1893, between 148 & 149) (fig 6.4).

6.3.2 Charles I in Canongate

E PATRICIA DENNISON

Charles I's coronation in the Abbey Church of Holyrood on 15 June 1633 was conducted amidst much splendour. Preparations had been energetic to ensure that the town was in a seemly state for the event. The Canongate bailies had been instructed by the Privy Council to rid the town of 'sturdie, clamarous and raling' beggars before the king's arrival. Their response was that, while eager to comply, it would be a difficult task unless Canongate's own poor were removed from the streets and, to that end, a warrant was sought so that a collection might be made from the Canongate people to provide for the poor out of sight of the king (Wood 1956, 10). The reaction of the poor is not documented. Another group who felt the brunt of the king's presence were ministers, who, by now accustomed to plain black gowns, were ordered to wear surplices and bishops' rochets, close-fitting surplices assigned to abbots and bishops (Donaldson 1971, 306). This assertion of the royal prerogative to prescribe apparel for clergymen was resented by many. For the coronation, Holyrood Palace was refurbished. The abbey kirk was once again transformed, its east gable being given its present giant traceried window and the west gable likewise dramatically altered, with a bell-cast cupola over the north-west steeple. But it was not in the kirk, but in 'his owne chappell royall' that Charles I held his devotions and where Archbishop Laud of Canterbury preached before him on Sunday 30 June (Selby Wright 1965, 17).

In an attempt to further his father's desire for uniformity in church worship, a new prayer book was prescribed by Charles I. The Scottish response was to produce the National Covenant in 1638. Those who signed bound themselves to maintain the forms of religion most in accord with the will of God, the Presbyterian road, and, if necessary, by force.

In the meantime, the Abbey Church was undergoing a number of changes to make it more suitable as the parish church of the Canongate. In 1639, permission to erect seats, or lofts, for the populace and, also, the payment of seat rents for the poor were instituted in Canongate Church. In 1641, a deputation of Canongate hammermen appealed to the kirk session for space for new seats for their craft between the two pillars at the east end of the king's erstwhile position of state. Two years later, a confirmation was granted by the bailies and the council of the permission granted by the kirk session for a 'high loft' between the pillars east of the pulpit pillar, in addition to the low seat already possessed by the craft. This immediately prompted the tailors and weavers to ask for, and obtain, similar concessions (Wood 1935, 103). Although in a much changed format, with no altars to maintain nor religious pageants in which to cooperate, the crafts were perpetuating an aspect of their pre-Reformation function – that of worshipping together and, in particular, offering spiritual and moral support at the funerals of their brother craftsmen, their wives, children or apprentices (Cameron 1925, 32).

Other pre-Reformation institutions found a new lease of life. The Hospital of St Mary and St Paul was rebuilt in 1619 and it developed in the 17th century as a workhouse or house of correction. It was said to have continued as such until 1750, although the building survived longer – in 1805 James Ballantyne established his press there and the Waverley novels were printed (Cowan & Easson 1976, 177). And on 2 February 1637, the magistrates of Edinburgh made over to the minister and kirk session of Canongate the ground annuals, pittances and pittance silver due from properties, including possibly some that were mortified or transferred to St Leonard's chapel and hospital, in Canongate, St Leonard's and environs for pious uses, in consideration of their undertaking to pay 300 merks (£200) of salary to Mr Alexander Gibson, the master

of the grammar school of Canongate (Smith & Paton 1940, 127).

6.4 Civil war and Commonwealth

6.4.1 Background

E PATRICIA DENNISON

It was not merely over religious matters that Charles I, as a largely absentee ruler, clashed with his Scottish subjects. From the late 16th century, Parliament increasingly met in Edinburgh. But Edinburgh's tolbooth was becoming too cramped for parliamentary meetings and, in 1632, with encouragement from the king, the construction of the first purpose-built Parliament building was started, on a section of the former St Giles' graveyard. The great hall with its impressive open-timber roof is a standing reminder of the grandeur of the building, which was originally adorned with paintings, tapestries and sculpture. The allegorical figures of 'Justice' and 'Mercy', two of the adornments, still survive. The Parliament building was ready for its first session in 1639, and, significantly, at this same session Parliament quite specifically opposed the king's policies. This, and the aversion of the Scots to absentee and absolute monarchy, whether in religious or lay matters, would result in civil war throughout England, Wales, Scotland and Ireland and, ultimately, the deposition and execution of the king by the English, in 1649.[3]

The effect of the king's execution by what became the English Commonwealth regime had the effect of drawing together many in Scotland who had opposed each other, and also opposed the king, for religious or political reasons. It also highlighted the discrepancies between the Covenanters (the supporters of the two National Covenants) and their English allies: the dead king's son was proclaimed Charles II by the Scottish Parliament, whereas the monarchy was abolished by the English Parliament. By June 1650, the Scottish king was in Scotland, having signed the Covenants. With banners proclaiming 'For Religion, King and Kingdome', the king's new, heavily purged, army suffered a humiliating defeat at Dunbar on 3 September, with 4000 Scots killed and 10,000 captured (Lynch 1991, 279). The reaction in the capital was swift – Edinburgh's Council and kirk sessions fled, the kirk's ministers fleeing to the safety of the castle (Lynch 1991, 282). By December, the English troops of Oliver Cromwell, who had now assumed power in the supposed absence of a king, took the castle, which offered little resistance. On 1 January 1651, Charles II was crowned at Scone.

Summer and early autumn were to see the denouement. The Battle of Inverkeithing on 20 July[4] and the capture of Perth on 2 August persuaded the new king to make for England, only to be caught up with by Cromwell. With the overwhelming defeat of the king's men at Worcester and the utmost devastation perpetrated in Scotland, particularly in Dundee, which suffered appalling atrocities (Torrie 1990, 105–6), by the forces of Cromwell's senior officer, Monck, the king fled to France. The Wars of the Covenant were over.

6.4.2 *Holyrood during the Civil War and Commonwealth*

JOHN LOWREY

After the work carried out for the coronation, the conflict that marked Charles I's reign had extremely destructive consequences for his royal palace of Holyrood. In 1642, with the Covenanter party in control in Scotland and the outbreak of Civil War in England, the Chapel Royal with its 'popish' trappings and Episcopalian layout was dismantled. A few years later, in 1650, Holyrood once again fell victim to an invading army, this time led by Cromwell, whose troops, possibly inadvertently (Harrison 1919, 195), set fire to a portion of the palace. It is very difficult to be certain of the damage inflicted on the palace at this time, but certainly by the time of the Restoration the building, once again, seems to have been in a pretty poor state (MacIvor & Peterson 1984, 259). This was despite the fact that a substantial addition had actually been made to the building in the form of a two-storey, ashlar-fronted structure on top of the old west range.[5] This was the so-called 'usurper's building'[6] erected but apparently never finished during the interregnum (MacIvor & Peterson 1984, 260).

6.5 Life in 17th-century Canongate

E PATRICIA DENNISON

In spite of revolution, warfare and occupation, a semblance of normality was maintained in the burgh. Inventories and archaeological evidence indicate an increasingly high standard of living. In 1619, for example, the widow of Robert Tailfeir, a cutler, was ordered to give to a nephew certain heirship goods. Certainly, the fact that such a dispute had arisen would suggest relative wealth, but the documentary evidence

offers an interesting insight into personal possessions. The heirship goods included a copper cauldron of 24-gallon size and brewing utensils, valued at £100 – a clear indication that more than the cutler trade was being pursued; a silver piece valued at £42; a furnished feather bed, an almery (cupboard) and a long oak settle, valued at £20; 12 plates and 12 trenchers worth £24; a suit of black clothes of Scots 'seybombasie',[7] a brown cloak of English cloth, a pair of woven worsted 'shanks' (stockings) and a Scots hat with crape band, all valued at 80 merks; 12 shirts, a sword and other arms, a chest, a chair, six stools, a brass pot of two-gallon size and a brass candlestick, together worth £20 (Wood 1935b, 102).

Life had to continue for the craftsmen, no matter what the political or religious situation. An agreement was formulated in 1610 between the four incorporated trades – the hammermen, tailors, baxters and cordiners. The hammermen included their deacon and 19 master freemen, amongst whom were a pistol maker, a goldsmith, a pewterer, a cutler, an armourer and a blacksmith. There were the same number of tailors, but fewer baxters, possibly as they were still thirled to Canonmills (Cameron 1925, 29). The representatives solemnly contracted 'for the haill remanent members and bodie' of their respective trades to maintain 'ane mutuall band of amitie luif and bretherheid'. It was agreed that there would be an appointment annually of a Deacon Convener from each craft in rotation, and a convenery court to maintain discipline (Cameron 1925, 30). The fifth article agreed was that, on pain of a fine of 10s, all craftsmen would support their brethren at funerals. The sixth article of agreement forbade, under the pain of a £10 fine, that any craftsman dispossess another of the 'hous or buith quhairin he duellis or workis'. This may be hinting at an influx of discontented artisans from Edinburgh and, in consequence, a class of unpropertied freemen (Cameron 1925, 33).

Certainly, the increasing prosperity of the Canongate cordiners was a source of irritation to the Edinburgh cordiners. In 1568, the Canongate cordiners had already appealed to both the Commendator of Holyrood and to the Privy Council against their treatment by the Edinburgh craft. Again, in 1607, the bailies of Canongate joined with the Deacon of Cordiners in appeal against his imprisonment in the tolbooth for buying hides at public market and successfully obtained his release (Malcolm 1932, 113–14). The Edinburgh records in this century indicate that the crafts of Canongate were a thorn in the side of the larger burgh, even though numerically Canongate had market forces stacked against it. Indeed, it has even been claimed that Canongate 'competed with Edinburgh on quality rather than price' (Makey 1987, 196). Probably also resented was the fact that in Edinburgh the crafts had to submit to choosing their deacons from a leet nominated by the Town Council, but in Canongate the principal crafts were strong enough to oppose their bailies and were, in consequence, uncontrolled in the nomination of their officers (Wood 1935, 98).

This 1610 agreement holds further interest, as it gives an indication of the level of literacy in the burgh, in so far as the ability to sign one's own name unaided is a very crude indication of literacy. The signatures of the craftsmen of Canongate suggest that the ambition of the Reformed Church's First Book of Discipline of an educated, godly society was not yet reality. Only one deacon, James Symsoun of the baxter craft, signed his name unaided. Of the hammermen, 11 signed, though seven could not do so without assistance and two were missing; of the tailors, out of 20 only five signed with their own hand unaided. The rest received the assistance of a notary public, marking 'with our handis at the pen led be the noteris undersubscryveand at our command becaus we cannot wreit our selffis' (Cameron 1925, 34, 42–4). Interestingly, the poor level of literacy is confirmed again in 1638. Those in Canongate who signed the Confession of Faith in March 1638 included many of differing social standing and educational background, from advocates, writers and schoolmasters to gardeners, coopers and stablers: 310 signed their own names and 330 could not write (Wood 1956, 10–16).

It is perhaps not surprising that the hammermen appeared to have a higher level of literacy in 1610, as their numbers still included the more prestigious crafts of goldsmiths, or jewellers, and watchmakers. In 1613, James Hart was a goldsmith master for one year at least, but after that no goldsmith appears to have been elected as a master for many years and during this period no freemen or apprentices were admitted (Wood 1933, 12). The reason for this may probably be sought in the lack of trade, but it is also possible that Edinburgh, with its many goldsmiths, who were wealthy enough to serve as bankers as well, monopolised the trade. Clock and watchmakers were rare both in Edinburgh and Canongate. Indeed, at one time, William Smith of Canongate was employed by Edinburgh since the larger town had no one of sufficient skill to regulate their town clocks (Wood 1933, 12).

The rivalry between the Canongate and Edinburgh craftsmen had been heightened when Edinburgh's increasing dominance over its smaller neighbour was aided by a 1565 charter granted by Robert Stewart, Commendator of the monastery of Holyrood. In this charter Sir John Bellenden of Auchnowl (Auchnoule) (the justice clerk and a powerful figure at court), and his male heirs, were appointed as heritable justiciars and bailies of the barony and regality of Broughton and the burgh of Canongate. On the resignation by the commendator and the convent, Sir John's son, Sir Lewis, obtained on 28 July 1587 a charter from the king of all the lands and barony, excluding the abbacy and the monastery and the district immediately adjoining. The Bellendens of Auchnowl were the maternal ancestors of the ducal family of Roxburgh, whose head in 1636 was Robert, Earl of Roxburgh. Both Charles I and the Earl of Roxburgh were heavily in debt to the town of Edinburgh, Charles I on account of loans by both Edinburgh and the wealthy goldsmith George Heriot, Roxburgh for loans by Heriot only. In commutation of these sums of money, the whole superiority of Canongate and North Leith was transferred to Edinburgh, and the lands of Broughton to the administrators of Heriot's legacy, consisting of the Town Council and the ministers of Edinburgh. (There was one exception – the lands of Holyroodhouse, which had been disponed to John Bothwell, first Lord Holyroodhouse. By 1646 the second and last Lord Holyroodhouse had been dead for 11 years and in consequence a charter was granted by the Crown in favour of James, Duke of Hamilton, appointing him and his male heirs Heritable Keepers of Holyroodhouse. By virtue of this guardianship, Holyrood Palace and the abbey sanctuary appear to have become vested as hereditary in the Dukes of Hamilton.) As superiors of Canongate and North Leith, Edinburgh no longer needed to fear the rivalry of its neighbour, which until 1856 continued its existence as a separate burgh of regality with officials chosen by Edinburgh Town Council (Wood 1974, 29).

Natural disasters also hit Canongate. Many of the medieval diseases, both endemic and epidemic, still afflicted the populace. Plague was, as ever, greatly feared, and with reason, as it continued to hit throughout the 16th century and the first half of the 17th century. The summer months were when it hit hardest, according to the contemporary diarist Robert Birrel, as for example in the heat of July 1604 (Dalyell 1798, 61). In 1645, there was a devastating outbreak of plague, which started in Canongate in June and lasted almost a year. The authorities had major problems keeping the epidemic under control and such was the lack of manpower that prisoners were set free from the tolbooth. Many suffering from the disease were put in huts and tents in the park of Holyrood. In due course the majority of the Canongate dead were also buried there, just as the victims from Edinburgh were interred in the Meadows, rather than in the churchyards (Selby Wright 1965, 21). The Canongate school could not reopen until March 1646, and the death rolls, according to the kirk session, extended to 2000. It is possible that mortality resulted also from typhus, hunger and hardship; but this was a vast proportion of a parish, the population of which probably numbered fewer than 4000 (Flinn 1977, 138–9).

But it was probably warfare, revolution and occupation that had the greatest effect on the lives of the people. Indeed, throughout the 17th century, there were grumbles in Canongate against the authorities regarding the practice of quartering troops on them (Malcolm 1932, 121). During the period of the Commonwealth and of the Protectorate of Oliver Cromwell (1653–8), Canongate was particularly hard hit; the Canongate magistrates in many ways made their own lives more difficult by their refusal to acknowledge the rule of Cromwell and his officers, as the Edinburgh magistrates did.

An indication of the troubled times came in 1651, when the hammermen expressed concern over the safety of their valuables. They ordered the titles of their new house to be built up in one of the rooms, confided other papers to the deacon, with the express condition that he was not to be held responsible in the event of their loss, and placed the craft mortcloths in the custody of another member. But, on 26 May 1651, it is recorded that 'thair lockit book quhairin wes all thair acts and statuts for reiding of the traid and the samyne acts and statuts being reft spoiled and all lost', the said acts were to be rewritten and bound in the old boards. The book had been 'wronged by the suldiers'. But there is little evidence of interference in the life of the craft otherwise. Freemen continued to be admitted to the craft, swearing allegiance to uphold the king and government of the realm until 1658, when they swore obedience to the supreme magistrate of the burgh (Wood 1935, 32).

On his first visit, in 1648, Cromwell resided in 'Lady Home's Lodging in the Canongate' (which had been built some years before Charles I visited the same property in 1633). This sumptuous dwelling house was later called Moray House, as Lady Home's elder daughter married James, fourth Earl of Moray, who died in 1653, and Alexander, fifth Earl of Moray, came into possession of the house that year. The occupants of this house, and all other residents of Canongate, would see both victor and vanquished of the Battles of the Covenants. On 18 May 1650, James Graham, Marquis of Montrose and King's Lieutenant in Scotland, having been defeated and captured at Invercarron, was brought from Leith via the Water Gate and taken up the High Street of Canongate in a cart on his way to execution at the market cross of Edinburgh. At this very time, Lord Lorne, the son of his enemy, Archibald Campbell, Marquis of Argyll, was in Moray House for his marriage to Lady Mary Stewart, the sister of Alexander, fifth Earl of Moray (Cowan 1995, 293).

After his resounding success at the Battle of Dunbar on 3 September 1650, Cromwell returned to Moray House and wintered there from 1650 to 1651. Town life was disrupted. The kirk session minutes note that, 'There was no session kept because of the defeat of the Scottish army at Dunbar by the Inglishe army. The ministers, elders, and whole honest men in the toun being removed'. Church life was at a standstill for fully a year (Selby Wright 1965, 23).

The homes of the ordinary townspeople were also requisitioned. In November 1650, John Nicoll recorded in his diary that life was disrupted because of 'the body of the Englische airmy being ... quarterit in Edinburgh, Cannongait, Leith, and in severall uther pairtis of Lowthiane'.[8]

The palace was used as barracks during the Cromwellian era and, as a result, was extensively damaged by fire in 1659. A nearby property was of sufficient size to house a military hospital for Cromwellian troops. On occupying Edinburgh, Colonel Monck, the leader of the Commonwealth forces, quartered his sick and wounded soldiers in the barely completed Heriot's Hospital in Edinburgh. In 1658, however, the governors of the hospital persuaded Monck to remove the troops, in exchange for other premises with all conveniences for sick soldiers, upkeep of the premises, grants towards the salaries of the physician, the surgeon apothecary, the surgeon's mate and the gardener. These premises were, in all probability, on the site of the new Parliament at Holyrood. Certainly, there was in the possession of Heriot's Hospital archives a document setting out an agreement 'betwixt my Lady Lauderdaell and the Commissioners for the Commonwealth of England for ane house at the foot of the Canongait, called

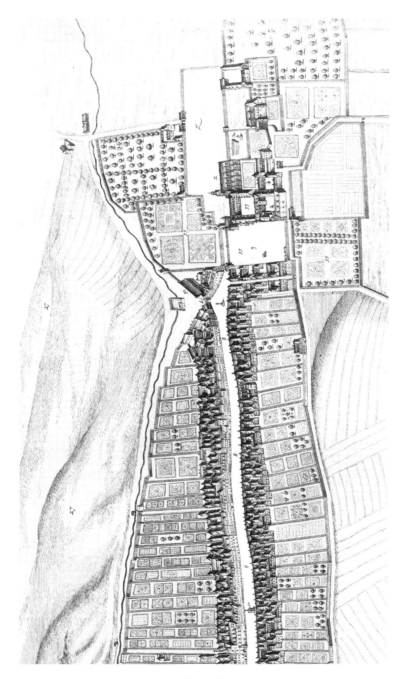

Figure 6.1
Rothiemay's view of Canongate (© NLS)

Kinloch's Land, 20 December 1652' (Thin 1927, 138). A section of Brodie's Close, later removed to build brewery buildings, was called 'of old' Kinloch's Close, after Henry and John Kinloch, and the governors of Heriot's Hospital are known to have owned property here until into the 18th century. Both these factors further support the view of a 17th-century hospital on the site (Boog Watson 1923, 124–5). Given that there was a garden attached, the hospital was probably one of the properties on the south-east of the Parliament site, clearly visible on Rothiemay's map (fig 6.1).

6.6 The developing townscape

E PATRICIA DENNISON

A visitor's impression of Canongate in 1618 is significant:

> the buildings on each side of the way [Canongate] being all squared stones five, six, and seven stories high, and many by-lanes and closes on each side of the way, wherein are gentlemen's houses, much fairer than the buildings in the High Street [Edinburgh], for in the High Street, the merchants and tradesmen do dwell; but the gentlemen's mansions and goodliest houses are obscurely founded in the ... lanes.

He continued that the walls were 8ft or 10ft (2.5m or 3m) thick.[9]

Such a view accords with what is known of the prestigious noble houses that lined the Canongate. Moray House, Huntly House and Acheson House are all standing reminders of the fine mansions that provided the townhouses of the nobility.

This visitor's impression of important dwellings lining the closes is confirmed by evidence from a number of closes, including Bell's Wynd. It is known from archaeological research that a medieval frontage building on the south side of High Street was demolished by the 17th century, and a close was established (Chapter 3.6). This close would become named 'Cumming's Close' by at least the 18th century. Such development was probably typical of many frontages on the Canongate and is an indication of multiple occupation spreading back from the High Street. Vallance Close, for example, could date as far back as c 1610 when there is record of a 'maister hammerman – John Vallange'.

Sir William Brereton, a visitor in 1636, drew attention to another characteristic of Edinburgh and Canongate houses. Commenting on the height of the stone houses lining the main thoroughfare, he continued that they were:

> lined to the outside and faced with boards ... towards the street [which] doth blemish it and derogate from glory and beauty; as also the want of fair glass windows, wherof few or none are to be discerned towards the street. This lining with boards, wherin are round holes shaped to the proportion of men's heads, and this encroachment into the street about two yards [1.8m], is a mighty disgrace (Hume Brown 1891, 139–40).

The high incidence of fire in the contemporary records, such as the diary of Robert Birrel, confirms that not all properties were totally of stone. Many were still built of wood, although some had a ground floor or solum of stone. To counteract the spread of fire, the townspeople were alerted by the ringing of the common bell and the beating of the town drum (Dalyell 1798, 55, 61). An account of 1608 gives a clear impression of good-quality housing surrounded by smaller dwellings, all of which suffered. It is recorded that it:

> being ane maist tempestuus and stormie nicht be accident yair arrais in ye cannongait ane grite and terribill fyre Be ye quhilk yair wes ane fair ludging distroyit and brunt with sum laich houses and mekill insicht plenissing and mechand guidis quhilkis wer within ye said ludging for ye tyme.[10]

Interestingly, both Rothiemay's c 1647 map (fig 6.1) and Hollar's later 17th-century view (fig 6.2), while displaying clearly the closes running back from the High Street, also record that to the rear of the properties were largely open spaces, typical of the medieval backlands.

The gardener's inventory for the Earl of Moray's house in 1646 gives an interesting insight into the gardens of the wealthy in the Canongate. It itemised two dozen apple trees, about 60 plums and 80 cherry trees, five apricot trees, a damson, a quince and a fig tree. Many of these trees were described as 'great', suggesting that some were quite old (Robertson 2000, 128). Such prestigious policies probably go far to explaining the relatively high numbers of gardeners in Canongate (Lynch 1987, 23).

Many of these orchards and parterres are delineated carefully on the two contemporary illustrations. The stone wall that enclosed the burgh to the south can also clearly be seen on both Gordon of Rothiemay's map and on Hollar's view. Whether the ditch was still intact, however, is unclear on these views, and the

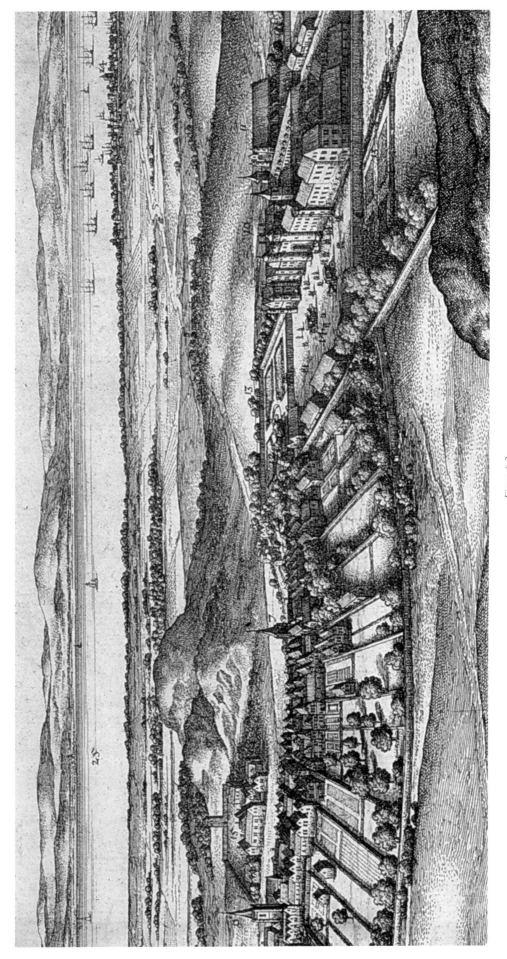

Figure 6.2
Hollar's view of Canongate, 1645 (© NLS)

documentary evidence is equally reticent. The Water Yett and many of the features noted in 16th-century protocol books (Chapter 5.5) are portrayed as still standing.

It was not merely the nobility and gentry who invested in the urban fabric. The cordiners possessed a number of properties in this area, and it is clear from the rentals of 1647 that they varied from dwelling houses, some with lofts and cellars, to industrial premises, brewhouses, stables and yards.[11] One of their properties, which consisted of three tenements on the north side of Canongate, gave its name to Shoemakers' Close and Dark Shoemakers' Close (Boog Watson 1923, 97). The eastmost property was known as the Bible Land from the Bible carved below the insignia of the cordiners' craft. In spite of owning property, until the convening house of the cordiners was built in 1653, the annual meeting at which office-bearers were elected was held on Calton Hill on Beltane Day (usually 1 May, see Chapter 5.4), or if this fell on a Sunday, on 2 or 3 May. Other meetings took place in the Abbey Kirk, Canongate tolbooth or on MacNeill's Craigs (Calton Hill) (Malcolm 1932, 109).

Another craft to see the potential for investment in property was the hammermen craft. On 23 September 1647, property was purchased, but for letting out rather than for their own use (Wood 1935, 79). The following year, a decision was taken to make part of this property into a convening room (Wood 1935, 80). Until this house was bought, the hammermen, like the cordiners, met in the open air on MacNeill's Crags, or in Trinity College Church, the Abbey Church or Canongate tolbooth (Wood 1935, 90).

This investment in property by many varying classes of society and the growing evidence of closes with multiple occupation was a result not merely of economic factors, but also of significant population growth.[12] In spite of the complaints by Canongate at the departure of the king and court, the billeting of troops, and mercantile competition from Edinburgh and, what was to become an increasing grievance, foreign craftsmen, the evidence suggests that this was a growing townscape. An unusual tax was imposed by the Covenanting regime in 1639 based on valued rents. Not only is this probably a fairer indicator of size than the more usual tax rolls, it is also important as it includes six baronial burghs not usually, as yet, subject to normal tax. One of these burghs was Canongate. While the rentals can give only a rough notion of population size, it is significant that the valued rent of £7533 suggests that Canongate had just over 4000

people within its bounds. This places it within the top seven medium-sized burghs, not counting the four large burghs of Edinburgh, Aberdeen, Glasgow and Dundee, and suggests that it was more populous than Ayr and Stirling. This was no tiny insignificant town. But its constant sense of threat from its larger neighbour can perhaps also be better appreciated when Canongate's valued rent of £7533 is compared with Edinburgh's £130,000.[13]

6.7 The late 17th century: wider context

6.7.1 The impact of political events

E PATRICIA DENNISON

The restoration of the monarchy in the person of Charles II (1660–85) in 1660 meant far more than the return of a king. By the time that Charles had arrived in Scotland in 1661, also restored were the Privy Council, the Scottish Parliament and the judiciary. Politics became even more closely intermingled with religion. By the Rescissory Act of March 1661 virtually all legislation passed since 1633 was declared void – that is, both Covenants were renounced, and the official religion was once more episcopal. Significantly, as early as 3 September 1661, a letter was sent from Covent Garden, London, to Robert Douglas, the minister of Old Greyfriars, Edinburgh, informing him of the intended move of Jesuits to a house in Canongate. Clearly, after the restoration of Episcopalianism, the Jesuits felt the religious climate sufficiently calm in Scotland that even their presence would be tolerated.[14] With the new episcopal state religion would come confusion – opposition to religion might imply opposition to government and moderate dissent suggest radical Covenanting views. And, perhaps most symbolically for the people of Canongate and Edinburgh, a sign that times had indeed changed was the digging up of the disarticulated body of Montrose, the removal of his head from a spike on the tolbooth of Edinburgh, which it had adorned since 1650, and a reverential process of the remains down the High Streets of Edinburgh and Canongate to a formal state funeral at Holyrood.

For many, however, the return of the monarchy must have been a time of hope – an end to occupation by troops, an end to warfare and material loss, and an end to religious dissension. With the benefit of hindsight, these were, of course, unrealistic expectations. Normality and the Stewart monarchy had returned, but the latter had not necessarily learned from the mistakes of its fathers.

THE ABSENTEE CROWN AND COURT 1603–c 1660

The palace had suffered great damage during the Cromwellian occupation. It had been occupied by the English and extensively damaged by fire in the 1650s,[15] and plans were now set in place to restore Holyrood to its former glory. Sir William Bruce was appointed as the architect. One of the seemingly small, but highly significant, schemes involved in this restoration of the building was to remove the private chapel of the king, the Chapel Royal, and, in consequence, in 1672, the Privy Council decreed that the church of Canongate, the abbey church, was to be 'his majesty's chapel in all time coming'.[16]

Harsh though this may have seemed to the Canongate parishioners, suffering in the name of religion was greater in other parts of Scotland. The crudity with which episcopacy was reimposed caused about a third of the establishment clergy to leave (Hutton 1997, 87), and

gave rise to secret meetings in conventicles. Religious beliefs pushed many of the more radical Presbyterians into political rebellion against the perceived wickedness of episcopal government. Although the people of Canongate suffered little compared with other areas of Scotland in these times, Canongate tolbooth saw a number of prisoners incarcerated for meeting in conventicles, including five who in November 1685 managed to escape (Fountainhall 1928, 146). Many others were martyred for their cause in these 'killing times', and, after 1679, this was at the hands of James, Duke of York and Albany, a convert to Catholicism and brother of the king.

It was he who, on the death of Charles II in 1685, became James VII of Scotland and II of England (1685–8). Signs of the times were already both openly and covertly in place. In 1681, James, as Duke of York,

Drawn Eng.d & Pub.d by J & H.S. Storer Chapel Street Pentonville Jan.1 1819.

Figure 6.3
New parish church of Canongate by James Smith (© Crown copyright: RCAHMS)

99

wrote to Lord Dartmoor from Holyroodhouse that, 'I live here as cautiously as I can, and am very careful to give offence to none'. But he had already requisitioned the Long Gallery in the palace to serve as his private Roman Catholic chapel (Selby Wright 1992, 133). In December 1687, orders were given that the Chapel Royal, established in the nave of the Abbey Church since 1672, should be adapted to Roman Catholic worship and as a chapel of the Knights of the Order of the Thistle. The previous year the king had established James Watson as 'printer to our household in our ancient Kingdom' and from the Holyrood Press in a shop erected in the central court of the palace Watson and his successor Peter Bruce distributed books and pamphlets of a Catholic persuasion (Selby Wright 1992, 133; Donaldson 1971, 382). A Jesuit college, also set up at Holyrood, offered free education to all regardless of religious inclination.

This new college was probably resented by some as being in direct competition with the town college. In reality, however, from the arrival of James in Holyrood in 1679 until the collapse of his personal government, royal patronage favoured not only the established college, but many other intellectual pursuits. This patronage was not entirely innovatory, for many of the advances in learning that James encouraged had their origins in the earlier part of the century and before; but as Duke of York and as king, he responded to the demands and interests of the professional classes, in particular those of Edinburgh. New charters were prepared for both the college and the city of Edinburgh; the Royal College of Physicians, the Advocates' Library and the Order of the Thistle were established; the Royal Company of Archers and the Physic Garden were supported; and royal patronage was bestowed on varied intellectual pursuits from cartography, medicine, surgery, numismatics, mathematics, and engineering to weather recording. Most of this intellectual activity was centred in Edinburgh and Canongate (Ouston 1982, 133–4 & throughout).

The people of Canongate, having lost their parish church and with no building in which to worship, found temporary accommodation in Lady Yester's Kirk, which was to become, in 1691, the parish church for the part of Edinburgh along the south side of Cowgate from Cowgate Port to Lady Yester's Kirk. But, by 1688, the new Canongate parish church was completed, at a cost of 43,000 merks, with the great assistance of a bequest of Sir Thomas Moodie of Sauchtonhall, with the proviso that all who had had the right to attend the Abbey Church of Holyrood should be certain of

accommodation in the new building (Daniel 1854, 22) (fig 6.3). In spite of this proviso, accommodation was at times at a premium. After the Restoration, Canongate was again the hub of elite society. The kirk session and the trades met, therefore, to discuss 'the urgency of present accommodation of nobles and gentlemen now resident in the parish'. It was agreed that, for the meantime, the front two pews would be set aside for nobles and gentry.[17] In 1692, the kirk session took the further measure of posting two elders, 'to wait upon the kirk door and not to suffer any persons to enter but such as [had communion] tickets and pensions of known quality'.[18] Lack of space was, however, to be a recurring problem into the 18th century. For over a year, from 1758 until 1759, the Canongate tailors were in legal dispute with the kirk session for depriving them of one of their pews.[19]

Other events impacted on Canongate at this time. James VII's efforts to gain toleration for Roman Catholics and the restriction of royal favour to those of this faith received much opposition. Such was the concern, that in January 1686, rioting took place in Edinburgh at the celebration of mass in the house of Lord Chancellor Perth. The birth of his son, James Francis Edward Stewart, bringing the possibility of another Roman Catholic monarch, tipped the balance against James VII. Once the news reached Edinburgh of the landing in Britain of William, Prince of Orange, on 5 November 1688, with the intention of claiming the thrones of Scotland and England, the Marquis of Atholl was swift to use the tumultuous Edinburgh rabble with a view to removing the Roman Catholic Lord Chancellor. In spite of the attempts by the Edinburgh provost to lock the town gates in order that the mob could not get out and attack the king's palace and the Catholic residents of Canongate (Fountainhall 1928, 171–2), the mob set off for the smaller burgh. A picture of the Earl of Perth was taken down from a building at the back of the Canongate weighhouse and the mob then marched down Canongate High Street, to the beat of a drum. Captain John Wallace and 120 men were defending Holyrood Palace. On refusal to disperse, the mob was fired upon and a number were killed – three or four, according to one source (Fraser 1890, ii, 102), approximately a dozen, according to another (Balcarres 1841, 15–17), 36 or 38 according to a third (Wodrow 1836, iv, 474) – and many others were wounded. This merely inflamed matters, drawing more malcontents to their numbers. Holyrood Palace was taken, the Jesuits were driven out and their house plundered, the Chapel Royal was sacked and royal tombs were desecrated. On completion of the rampage, a contemporary letter relates, the chancellor's cellars were opened and the mob inflamed itself further with his wine. The next two or three days were then spent scouring the town, entering private houses, such as Huntly House, plundering and harassing Roman Catholics and removing rosaries, images and Catholic literature (Balcarres 1841, 15–17; Wodrow 1836, iv, 474).[20]

In spite of the rabble-rousing in Canongate and Edinburgh, the 'Revolution' of 1688 was basically peaceful, and largely instrumental to its success was the king's flight to France. Scotland declared that the king had 'forefaulted' the Scottish Crown, and that he had broken 'the knoune lawes, statutes and freedomes of [the] realme' (*APS*, ix, 33–4; 38–40; Glassey 1997, 9). Britain replaced a monarch who ruled by divine right with joint rulers, William of Orange and Mary II, whose authority was based on the power of those they governed (Murdoch 1998, 40). For Scotland, this meant a reassertion of the constitutional and political power of Parliament and, almost conversely and perversely, the road to Union with the English Parliament. In Scotland, also, this was essentially a religious revolution. Presbyterianism finally ousted Episcopalianism.

6.7.2 Lauderdale and Bruce: the great reconstruction of Holyrood, 1671–8

JOHN LOWREY

A key document in understanding Holyrood Palace is the plan produced by John Mylne, Master Mason to the Crown, in 1663 (Mylne 1893, between pages 148 & 149; fig 5.4) Although there is some question about the degree to which it indicates an intention by Charles II (Mylne 1893, 148; MacKechnie 1993, 236), it seems most likely that it provides a fairly accurate picture of the form of the palace in the immediate post-Restoration period. The south and west ranges accord closely with what we know of James V's palace; the expanded, double-pile north range and the complex, though 'tidied-up', series of courtyards to the south, both reflect the known work of the late 16th and early 17th centuries.

While Mylne's plan is our best indication of the arrangements of the principal floor plan in the 1660s, William Adam's plan in *Vitruvius Scoticus* of c 1728 (Adam 1980, 27) summarises the changes and rebuilding of the palace by Sir William Bruce in the 1670s (fig 6.4), which produced the palace substantially

as it is now, although the building to the north-east, a rather ecclesiastical looking kitchen block designed to balance the remains of the abbey church (*Vitruvius Scoticus*, plate 4) was not executed and possibly not designed by Bruce (Adam 1980, 27).

This new Holyrood Palace was a considerable architectural achievement, combining traditional and modern elements (fig 5.3). On the one hand, Bruce's design represents an appropriate continuity for the Stewart monarchy, taking as it does the basic idea of James V's proposed west front with a tower at each end of the façade. Indeed, in his original design, this connection with the 16th-century palace would have been even stronger because the initial intention was to retain the whole James V west range. On the other hand, in terms of planning, style and decoration, the palace was very much in tune with modern European developments, drawing on French, Dutch, Italian and English influences.[21]

Bruce's original design for Holyrood was sent to Windsor at the beginning of June 1671, along with a 'Small mapp of his majesty's palace of Hallyrudehouse with the grounds lying about the samen', which was produced by Mylne (Mylne 1893, facing 169), showing the palace in its immediate context. From this it is clear that Bruce's highly ambitious conception for the palace included a huge outer court, in the manner of the recent work at Versailles, which would have involved the demolition of the 16th-century gatehouse, the stables and a substantial area of housing at the foot of the Canongate, roughly up to the girth cross and overlapping with the eastern edge of the modern Scottish Parliament site. This was rejected, but the king was keen to consolidate further his holdings in the vicinity of the palace. In particular, he wanted to connect Bruce's proposed new formal garden, on the site of the monastic buildings, to the park beyond, by acquiring the properties that lay to the east, primarily those of the Dean of Edinburgh, comprising an L-plan house, possibly that visible on the Gordon plan of 1647, with a yard, orchard and what is referred to on Mylne's plan as a bowling green.[22] A start was made on the demolition of this property in 1675.[23]

Along with the site plan, Bruce also sent to Windsor for the king's consideration a set of detailed drawings that contained two key elements of the design as executed. Firstly, in accordance with the apparent intentions of both James V and Charles I, the great tower at the north end of the west quarter was repeated at the south end, producing a symmetrical façade that shows a concern with classical trends, but at the same

SCOTLAND'S PARLIAMENT SITE AND THE CANONGATE

time emphasises the important theme of continuity with the past. Secondly, in the inner court, Bruce suggested a covered arcade at ground level and façades ordered and ornamented by the classical orders: Doric at ground level, rising to Corinthian at the upper floor, and with a pediment marking the centre of the east quarter. This design sets Holyrood within the context of European classical architecture since the Renaissance and can be taken at one level to represent 'modernity' juxtaposed by 'tradition' as represented by

the new tower. However, the idea is more complex than that because, of course, Scotland had not been immune from European influence and ideas since the Renaissance and the courtyard design also has an echo in earlier Scottish work, such as Heriot's Hospital in Edinburgh, of the 1620s and 1630s. It has even been plausibly suggested that a fragment of the inner court had already been built earlier in the 17th century that provided Bruce with his starting point and model. Certainly, the main building contract clearly refers

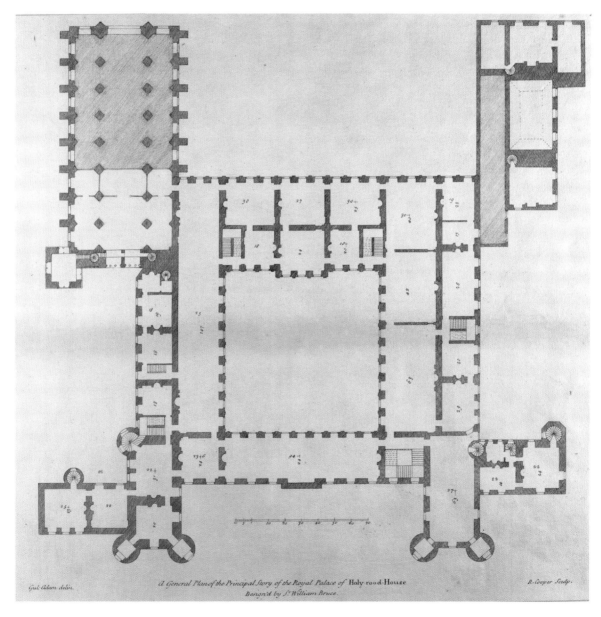

Figure 6.4
William Adams's plan of Holyrood Palace (*Vitruvius Scoticus*) (© Edinburgh City Libraries. Licensor www.scran.ac.uk)

to the north-west corner already in existence in 1672 (Mylne 1893, 180).[24]

The main floor plan that accompanied Bruce's elevation of the inner court contained key elements of both the contract and final design, but also had significant differences. The west quarter was retained, although the terminology of the planning was modernised. The north and east quarters required substantial remodelling, but the south quarter was to be entirely demolished and substantially deepened by expansion to the south and to the north. The new south tower was to contain a double-height Chapel Royal, with a royal pew at the upper level. Two major apartments were accessible from a large platt-and-scale staircase at the south end of the old west quarter. To the east, this gave access to the king's apartment through a series of ceremonial spaces set across the line of the building. To the north, through the old west quarter, the sequence led to the old tower, the culmination of the queen's apartment. However, Bruce also included a third, smaller royal apartment in the east quarter, accessed from a stair in the north quarter. A small gallery ran across the front of the east quarter.

The response from the king was not entirely positive, and in particular he did 'much dislike' the small gallery (Mylne 1893, 170). As far as the outside of the building was concerned, the king made two significant points. Firstly, he admired the design of the inner court, but thought it would be far too expensive. He suggested instead that the façades should be finished in plain ashlar. Secondly, although he was in favour of the demolition of the Cromwellian building on top of the west quarter, he was not in favour of leaving this space merely as a terrace, which was what Bruce favoured, but insisted that it should be raised to the full height of the towers and finished with a slate roof (Mylne 1893, 170).

Between June 1671 and the contract of 1672, Bruce redesigned the palace with the retention of his classical façades, not only in the inner court, but also on the east façade of the east quarter, looking out over a new privy (private) garden with a stone basin and statue or fountain (Mylne 1893, 179). Bruce's solution to the proposed heightening of the west quarter was to retain but remodel the Cromwellian building (Mylne 1893, 179). In the interior, the revised plan was far simpler than the original. The main stair was the pivotal element, giving access to both royal apartments and the Privy Council Chamber. The approach to the king's apartment was far more satisfactory, with the main

rooms arranged along the length of the building and subsidiary spaces on the south side. The guardroom, presence chamber and privy chamber filled the entire length of the south quarter, with the rest of the apartment in the east quarter. The antechamber led to the royal bedchamber, overlooking the new privy garden, and the dressing room filled the equivalent space on the court side, beneath the pediment. The puny gallery in the east quarter was replaced by a huge gallery that filled the whole courtside of the north quarter and linked the king's and queen's apartments.

Most of this work was completed by 1675, but the design continued to evolve and early in 1676 attention was turned to the west quarter of the palace. Perhaps Bruce had used the argument that building the west front to the same height as the rest of the palace would darken the courtyard. In February, the decision was taken to demolish the 'Usurper's building' (Mylne 1893, 189–91).[25] It was later still, however, in July 1676, before the decision was taken to replace the entire west quarter with new façades both to the west and the east, producing the final version of the design (Mylne 1893, 193).[26]

The final version of Holyrood encapsulated a number of important architectural and political themes. It was, as discussed, both modern in terms of its planning and decoration (inside and out) and also concerned with tradition and continuity. This was not simply a matter of harmonising with the existing ancient fabric but was also concerned with providing a clear link to the Stewart past. This was done not only through the repetition of the James V tower but also in features like the great gallery with its series of 110 portraits by Jacob de Wett. These were commissioned in 1684 and showed every Scottish king from the mythical Fergus I (4th century BC) to Charles II (and later James VII and II). In this way, the Stewarts were presented as the culmination of an unbroken line of kings stretching back into the mists of time so that their antiquity and, more importantly, their legitimacy, was unquestionable.

The final form of the palace also reiterates and modernises the French influence that was evident in the palace of James V, albeit other influences are also evident in both that building and in Charles II's palace. The courtyard plan was a given, but the lowering of the west quarter, its flat lead terrace and great *porte cochère* are all reminiscent of the French chateau as it developed in the 16th century and, more immediately, the aristocratic Parisian *hôtel particulier,* as it developed in the 17th century. That influence also extended to the planning. Features like the gallery filling one wing of the palace and Bruce's initial design with a chapel filling the end pavilion or tower are both features that can be found in French planning of this period.

One final aspect of this great project also deserves a mention. Bruce's grandiose plan for a huge outer court, as we have seen above, was rejected by the king. However, Bruce clearly was a persuasive man and several aspects, originally rejected, were ultimately executed. The court, of course, never was, but the commissioners who approved the redesign of the west front also supported the resurrection of this original idea. In this case, however, the Treasurer Depute, Charles Hatton, did not concur (Mylne 1893, 193).[27]

Notes

1 On occasion the Privy Council met at Holyrood, but more normally in Edinburgh (location unspecified). The Court of Session met in the tolbooth of Edinburgh. Many Court of Session judges were also Privy Councillors until after 1625, so it is probable that the council also met in the tolbooth, at least until this time. E Patricia Dennison is indebted to Dr J Goodare for his views.

2 Work on other palaces included Dunfermline in the 1590s, for Anne of Denmark, the Chapel Royal at Stirling (1594), Edinburgh Castle Palace Block (1615–17), and Linlithgow north quarter (1618–20s)]

3 For details of the revolution years see Donaldson 1965, 317–42; Lynch 1991, 263–81; Cowan 1995.

4 For full details of the campaign that led to this disastrous defeat, see Bensen 1978, 125–35.

5 A conjectural reconstruction of the west front of the palace, including this feature, is shown in MacIvor and Peterson 1984, 251, fig 116.

6 NAS. E33/9

7 'Bombasie' was an alternative word for 'bombazine' – a twilled worsted dress material. 'Sey' was a woollen cloth resembling serge, often woven by families for their own use. 'Sey' might also mean, however, a trial or test piece; so there may be an extra meaning of an apprentice's cloth.

8 'The diary of John Nicoll, 1650–1667', *BOEC*, xvi (1928), 36.

9 'Extract from John Taylor the Water Poet's Pennylesse Pilgrimage to Scotland in 1618', *Bannatyne Miscellany*, ii (1836), 403.

10 NLS, Wodrow Ms. Quarto ix, 50r.

11 NAS, GD 1/14/1, Minute Book of the Cordiners of Canongate, 1584–1773.

12 An example of property investments of this time still stands in Canongate. A man named Andrew Gray had escaped the gallows and done well in the service of the Emperor of Morocco. He returned to Scotland where he supposedly healed the daughter of his old enemy the provost, Sir John Smith of Groathill, with a Moorish medication. Being banned from Edinburgh, he settled as a wealthy and respectable man in Canongate and built Morocco Land, still remembered by the statue of a Moor on the wall (Boog Watson 1923, 92).

13 Lynch in McNeill & MacQueen (eds) 1996, 320.

14 NLS, Ms. Wodrow Ms. Fol. xxvi, ff. 137–8. E Patricia Dennison is indebted to Dr Louise Yeoman for this interesting information.

15 'The Diary of John Nicoll, 1650–1667' in the *Book of the Old Edinburgh Club*, xvi, 36 suggests that the date of burning was 13 November 1650; Bonar 1856 *The Canongate, Ancient and Modern*, 7, argues for 1659.

16 *Register of the Privy Council of Scotland*, iii (1669–72), 594.

17 NAS, CH2/122.4, 324.

18 NAS, CH2/122/9, fo. 55.

19 NLS, MS1961 122–3, 138.

20 E Patricia Dennison is grateful to Dr L Glassey for assistance.

21 Baroque palace planning is discussed by Baillie (1967). However, although Baillie's article is wide-ranging in its discussions of palaces all over Europe, it omits Holyrood and instead uses earlier and less sophisticated examples of Scottish royal planning.

22 No. 15 on the key is 'a present bowling green which the dean pretends right unto'.

23 NAS, E36/33/404: Account of John Drummond for 'casting doune of the dean's lodging be east the pallace', 23 June–23 August 1675.

24 MacKechnie 1994, 235 makes the suggestion that this might have been a pre-existing element that was developed by Bruce, although there are other possibilities. One of these is that the corner in question was built between the production of the drawings in 1671 and the building contract in 1672. The contract itself makes it clear that some work was already underway by the time the document was drawn up. However, the more general point, that early 17th-century Scottish architecture provides examples of arcaded courtyards with applied orders, is certainly relevant in considering Holyrood.

25 Mylne prints three documents: a royal warrant to the Lord Commissioners, instructing the work to be demolished, 21 February 1676; a warrant from the commissioners to Bruce to the same effect, 28 February 1676; and a contract between Bruce and Robert Mylne for the demolition of the work.

26 Again, a warrant is followed by a contract, at the end of July 1676.

27 'We recommend to his Majesties Thesaurer deput to setle and agrie with the heretors of the several tenements and yards necessar to be brought in for making of a large and convenient passadge for the designed direct entry to the said pallace for which thir presents shall be to them a sufficient warrant'.

PART 3

❦

The 'urban palace': the 'Great Lodging', Hatton House and Queensberry House

Chapter 7

The site of the 'urban palace'

TOM ADDYMAN and JOHN LOWREY

7.1 Introduction

TOM ADDYMAN

Queensberry House has long been known as a major, if much abused, survivor of a group of aristocratic town mansions that occupied the lower Canongate in the 17th and 18th centuries. As the largest of these, in its heyday it dominated this area of the Edinburgh townscape.

The chapters in Part 3 outline the principal findings of the programme of archaeological building recording and analysis at Queensberry House and antecedent structures. The approach taken to the renovation of Queensberry House (for example the removal of all internal and external plaster and harl) allowed an unusual level of recording of surfaces. The recording exercise was a complex process that involved many parties, whose results are incorporated into this section of the report. RCAHMS prepared plans at each level, a number of exterior elevations, sections, and a general photographic record of the building. Addyman & Kay Ltd, with additional support from Headland Archaeology, undertook (under the direction of Tom Addyman) a wider programme of recording of the internal elevations of each room and floor structure throughout the building following the general stripping out and removal of internal wall plaster, which had been undertaken as part of the renovation works. This record was updated, amended and annotated (by Tom Addyman) during subsequent building works on Queensberry House. Anne Crone of AOC Archaeology carried out an assessment of the potential for dendrochronological analysis, which proved to be limited. Analytical studies such as the evidence for roofing materials were carried out (Tom Addyman). An archaeological/historical study was made of the evidence for the belvedere tower, the remains of which were identified within the roof space (Tom Addyman). A general review of historical sources for Queensberry House was carried out (John Lowrey assisted by William Kay). An individual assessment was carried out of historic visual source material for Queensberry House (Tom Addyman

and William Kay). An assessment was made of the evidence for historic paint schemes (William Kay) and historic mortars and plasters were analysed (The Scottish Lime Centre, with the on-site assistance of Tom Addyman).

The plans and internal and external elevations have been analysed in detail, allowing the preparation of complex digital drawings in which the fabric assigned to each phase resides on a different 'layer' of the drawing, and can be colour-coded. It is thus possible to 'edit away' later interventions from a drawing to display only that fabric that can be assigned to a specific phase.

7.2 Background

TOM ADDYMAN

Queensberry House, no. 64 Canongate, is located on the south side of that thoroughfare, a short distance to the west of Holyrood Palace (NGR: NT 267 738). The building is set back from the general Canongate frontage.

The description that follows is of Queensberry House prior to the works undertaken to prepare it for its role in the new Scottish Parliament complex. *Note that anything referred to here in the past tense has subsequently been removed or changed in the building itself.*

A substantial pair of axially-placed stone entrance-piers within the street-fronting boundary wall led into a small paved court in front of the mansion. On this side the frontage of Queensberry House encloses the rear part of the court on three sides. Two tall jambs (each four bays long by two wide) extend northwards from a principal east/west aligned range that is three bays wide within the court. On the Canongate frontage the whole structure rose to four stories. To the rear of the inner court area and occupying its entire width there is a single-storied porch, the frontage of which is detailed with rusticated ashlarwork and a prominent central entrance. The two projecting jambs, which are detailed with rusticated quoins, rose to plain straight-gabled heads surmounted by chimneys.

The Canongate frontage of Queensberry House, as in all other exterior areas, was harled in a coarse cement roughcast when survey work began, with only the stone dressings of windows and other features exposed, though painted. The numerous symmetrically placed windows on each elevation bear surrounds of polished freestone (sandstone) detailed with a raised margin, up to which the harl extended, and an internal chamfered aris.

The principal east/west range, forming the south side of the 'U', also extends further to the east, and from its south-facing garden elevation the scale of this 80-room mansion is more readily apparent. Here its façade rose five stories (a basement level is not apparent on the north side) and extends for some 45m in width, terminating at closet towers at its south-east and south-west corners. The garden area, subsequently a parade ground and more recently a car park, extended down to the Cowgate to the south. This area is now occupied by the buildings of the Scottish Parliament.

At the time of survey the mansion comprised five full stories – the *Lower Ground* floor level (the 'basement' level referred to above, the original entrance level, containing kitchens, cellars, garden-facing rooms, etc), the *Upper Ground* floor level (the later/existing entrance level (the ground floor level entered from the Canongate, containing the *piano nobile* or sequence of principal rooms), and the *First, Second* and *Third* floor levels. The last originally consisted of loft accommodation but was subsequently raised to a full storey in the early 19th century. There had also existed a series of mezzanine spaces within the *Upper Ground* floor; at the time of the survey the only relict of this level existed in the form of an additional level within the east stair. The upper parts of the east stair had also formerly extended up for yet another storey above *Third* floor level in the form of a belvedere or viewing tower. This had subsequently been partly demolished.

At the time of the survey, the building also contained three staircases, one at the junction of the east jamb and the principal range (the east stair), one within the central part of the principal range (the central stair) and one within the central part of the west wing (the west stair). Each of these accessed all five principal floor levels.

Before the present survey, the architectural history of Queensberry House had only been examined in outline, although plans by the military c 1810 were redrawn by the city architect in 1943 and contain considerable analytical detail. These earlier studies were hampered by the general inability to examine

in detail the masonry fabric of the structure. As a consequence, and despite it being one of the larger historic buildings in the Edinburgh townscape at the time of the initial investigation in 1998, the structural evolution of the Queensberry House was remarkably little understood.

In summary, the core of the existing building is formed by the town mansion constructed by Dame Margaret Douglas of Balmakellie in the period c 1667–70, hereafter termed the Balmakellie phase. Following his purchase of the property Charles Maitland, Lord Hatton, undertook a number of modifications in 1680–1, some of which have left direct physical evidence, others that are documented; this is the Hatton phase. Although purchased in 1688 by the first Duke of Queensberry it was under the second Duke that what had now become Queensberry House saw major modification and extension in the period c 1695–1700, the Queensberry phase.

Queensberry House saw only minor additional modification in the 18th century and it was not until the period c 1808–11 that further major alterations took place under the auspices of the Board of Ordnance, the Military phase.

7.3 Ownership of the site of Queensberry House and its predecessors

JOHN LOWREY

All of the main archival sources contain very rich information on the site of Queensberry House (Lowrey 1999, 29–40). Some of these relate directly to the house and its site, others, the majority, to contiguous properties which help to describe its boundaries. Overall, this material provides a useful insight into the history of the site from c 1480 to c 1710.[1] The main sources are charters, writs, sasines and so on in the Lauderdale and Buccleuch papers. The latter in particular has a fairly systematic legal record of the site of the house. On the acquisition of Hatton's mansion, a complete inventory of the 'writs and evidents' was drawn up in 1688. This is arranged in four bundles which appear to correspond to some of the individual plots and properties that made up the building and its gardens.[2] In addition to these private archive sources, Edinburgh City Archive contains a number of relevant items, mainly charters.[3] Some analysis of the site had already been carried out by Boog Watson, based substantially on the Edinburgh City Archive material.[4] Watson identifies at least seven separate properties, on the street and in the backlands, that made up the property on which Charles Maitland of Hatton erected his house. In fact, taking into account the other evidence, it seems to have been nearer nine or ten and it is possible, in some cases, to compile a history stretching back for at least a hundred years before the building of Hatton's mansion.[5]

There are three main areas that are relevant to this discussion. Two of them seem to comprise most of the site of the house and gardens as it was eventually developed by the end of the 17th century. The third is important mainly because it establishes a known eastern boundary to the site, the property of the Glen family, that continued to exist as Glen's Land right up until the beginning of the 19th century when it too was subsumed by Queensberry House.[6]

A useful starting point is the property that was handed over by Charles Maitland, by then Earl of Lauderdale, to the Duke of Queensberry in 1686. This is described in a charter dated 1688 which lists the properties acquired by Maitland in order to build his house. Nine properties are listed in all, belonging to:[7]

Dame Margaret Douglas of Balmakellie, and
    Alexander Douglas, her husband
George Glen, tailor, burgess
Robert Gray, writer in Edinburgh
John Wauchope, one of the macers of the Court of
    Session
William Hepburn, shoemaker
William Johnston, merchant in Edinburgh
Jasper Johnston, farmer in Restalrig
Alexander Kay, former Bailie of the Canongate
Thomas Serjeant, upholsterer

What is immediately striking about this list is the kind of person who owned property in this area at this time: on the whole from service trades and professions, but with the gentry, in the person of Dame Margaret, prominent amongst them. It is not possible to trace the history of every one of these nine sites, nor is it possible to locate each of them with respect to the present arrangement of the house. However, in some cases it is possible to trace something of their history and to locate them with some degree of certainty. This evidence can then be combined and compared with cartographic and archaeological material to provide a picture of the setting of the house as it developed in the late 17th century and the urban context in which it sat.

One of the key properties that made up Hatton, and later Queensberry, House was that disponed to Charles Maitland of Hatton by Dame Margaret Douglas of Balmakellie on 22 December 1679.[8] The history of the Balmakellie property itself is complex and touches on a number of properties which seem to lie at the core of Queensberry House.

The story can be traced continuously in the record from 1581. At some point before that date, Gilbert Cleugh (or Cleuch) disposed of two adjoining properties (probably through his will) on the south side of the Canongate. The property on the west was inherited by Margaret Cleugh and that on the east by Helen Cleugh. The women were presumably Gilbert Cleugh's daughters. They married, respectively, Peter Wood, maltman and burgess, and William Gray, burgess. In 1581, Cleugh and Gray signed a charter of alienation of the backlands of the east tenement to Jerome Bowie, 'servant to the king'.[9] This started a long involvement of the Bowie family, who appear to have been in charge of the wine cellars at Holyrood Palace, with this key site, at the heart of what was to become Queensberry House.[10] In 1588, Margaret Cleugh made a precept in her son Thomas's favour of the:

> west tenement of the two tenements of the late Gilbert Cleugh … between the backlands of the east tenement formerly of Helen Cleugh now of Jerome Bowie, with free ish and entry by the fore gate of the said tenements on the east, the land of James Fraser on the west and the yard of the said west tenement belonging to the said late Helen and now to the said Jerome on the south.[11]

Despite some slight inconsistencies between and within these two documents, they do seem to be talking about the same properties and, although the real situation was probably more complex, it is possible to draw some conclusions about the relative locations of the different properties. Figure 7.1a is a summary of the two documents, showing Wood's property hemmed in by what was originally Helen Cleugh's. The latter certainly lay to the south and east and, since Wood's access to the street lay through Cleugh's property, the implication is that he was also hemmed in on the north.

The 1588 charter indicates that Jerome Bowie acquired the backlands of Cleugh's property but not the whole property, which, at least diagrammatically, suggests the division of the Cleugh property into a northern and a southern portion. The Bowie property therefore lay immediately to the east of Wood's tenement, as indicated in the 1588 charter, and the Bowie family later seem to have acquired that property also. In 1617, James Bowie, 'servant to the king' and presumably a descendent of Jerome's, was granted a sasine of property formerly owned by Wood comprising 'a tenement of land with yeard and coble [cess pool or trough] on the south side of the Canongate' (fig 7.1b).

Fig 7.1b, based strictly on the evidence of the charters, suggests that by 1617, the Bowie family had acquired a band of property, formerly in the hands of the Cleughs, initially through marriage (in the case of Jerome Bowie), and later by other means. Later, it seems that the Bowies acquired much more of this and the surrounding properties. In 1642, a precept was granted to Anna Bowie, 'daughter of the late James Bowie, servant of the king' of the:

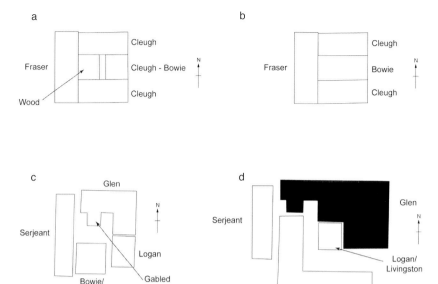

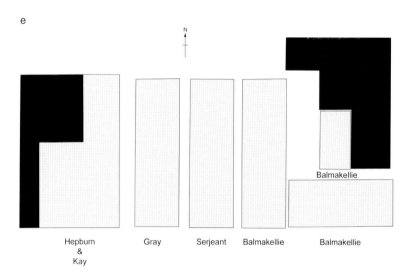

Figure 7.1
The relationship of property holdings suggested by documentary sources
(not to scale) (© John Lowrey)

> backlands of the east tenement of the late Gilbert Cleuch's two tenements with those two yards and coble, which were conquest by the late Jerome Bowie from the heirs of the said Gilbert, with a yard conquest by the said Jerome from the late Gilbert Geichan, being a part of his tenement, and of the fore tenement with those backlands, on which were once a barn, kiln and coble conquest by the said late James Bowie from the late Thomas Wood, all lying contiguous on the south side of the High Street between the lands of the late Hector Cranston, then of the late John Glen, burgess of Edinburgh, now of Robert Logan and the lands of the late Alexander Blair and the said late Gilbert Geichan, then of the late Patrick Urquhart, stabler, and now of George Glen, tailor, on the east, the lands of the late James Frissell and the heirs of [...] Watson, now of Agnes Blair, wife of William Sergeant, on the west, the strand and the lands of Dishflatt on the south; whereupon the said Anna Bowie resigned the same for conjunct infeftment to be given to herself and her husband, John Scott of Spenserfield.[13]

A number of important issues arise here. Firstly, the acquisitive Bowies appear by this time to have acquired all or most of the original Gilbert Cleugh properties.

Secondly, Jerome Bowie's holdings were slightly larger than the documents already considered had indicated, including as they did, the property of Gilbert Geichan. Thirdly, we learn that the site to the east was quite complex, being divided between two parties, Robert Logan and George Glen. The implications of this will be explored more fully later. Fourthly, we are given more of the genealogy of property ownership for the sites on the east and west of the Bowie property. This is not in itself particularly significant except that the picture that emerges in 1642 is very close to the final profile of ownership in 1679 when properties started to be acquired by Charles Maitland of Hatton. For example, on the west, a property that until 1642 was simply that of James Fraser had passed from Fraser (or Frissell) to Watson, to Blair and, through marriage, to Serjeant. Serjeant is one of the names of those who disponed property to Hatton. Similarly, the Bowie property itself, through Anna's marriage, also became the property of John Scott of Spencerfield, the final owner before the upgrading of the whole site. On the east, we also learn that Gilbert Geichan not only owned part of what became the Bowie property but also part of what became the Glen property (another name in our initial list), suggesting perhaps quite a complex boundary between those two, a suggestion borne out by other documents from around the same time. One of these, a Complaint of Neighbourhood, taken out by Anna Bowie against George Glen on 5 March 1642, locates his property at east and north of Bowie's: on the south side of the burgh, on the east side of the complainer's great lodging and on the north side of her yard. The said George proposes to build upon the south dyke marching between him and the complainer's yard, encroaching within the complainer's bounds, and is guilty of other grievous wrongs.[14]

Very shortly afterwards, the Bowie/Spencerfield family complained once again to the Council:

> notwithstanding the former decreet the said George has struck out lights and windows of the south gable of his lands towards the complainers lands from which he or his tenants may throw out filth.[15]

These two documents give us some important additional information. Firstly, we learn that Glen's property lay to east and north, suggesting that Logan's land, alluded to in the 1642 charter, must have lain to the south of Glen's, while still forming part of the eastern boundary of the Bowie/Spencerfield property. Secondly, we learn that the latter property was a 'great Lodging', suggesting a substantial dwelling on the site. This is the same terminology that was used to describe the later Balmakellie house, implying perhaps that this, like the Hatton and Queensberry houses that followed it, was based on an existing structure. Thirdly, we learn that it lay withdrawn from the street, with a yard to the north but with the gable of Glen's

extension sitting on the boundary wall, with windows looking into their yard and presumably their house. Glen's extension therefore was clearly running north/south. All of this is expressed in fig 7.1c.

Further information on the relationship between the Bowie/Spencerfield property and the lands to the east comes in the form of a charter in favour of William Livingston, an Edinburgh merchant burgess who was owed money by Logan, with his Canongate property as security. The property is defined as:

> on the south side of the High Street between the lands formerly of Sergeant James Bowie, now of John Scott of Spencerfield on the south and west of the lands formerly of Patrick Urquhart, now of George Glen, tailor on the east.[16]

With the information that Glen's property lay to the east as well as to the north, we are now presented with a picture of Logan's property being almost engulfed by Glen's on two sides. The further information that the Bowie/Spencerfield property lay to the west but also to the south of Glen's (and therefore also of Logan's) presents us with the picture presented in fig 7.1d of a very complex pattern of interlocking properties.

Most of the discussion so far has been based on the evidence of the Canongate Chartulary with only a few references to documents elsewhere. Research in the Edinburgh City Archive found very little between 1650 and c 1685, the crucial period during which the properties were amalgamated into the dwellings of Charles Hatton and later the Duke of Queensberry.[17] To continue the tale of the Douglas of Balmakellie property, we must turn to the evidence of the Lauderdale Papers.

Dame Margaret's property was made up of two main parcels of land/property. The first of these was the whole of the Bowie/Spencerfield tenement and the second was part of the property of George Glen, almost certainly the part to the north that overlooked the Spencerfield property. The Spencerfield property as described in 1642 consisted of 'the two dwelling houses or backlands of two tenements of land and a fore tenement of land and yards thereof and pertinents lying in the Canongate'.[18]

It was essentially this property that was acquired by Dame Margaret Douglas early in 1668, after negotiations with Spencerfield and his son (who was acting as his father's factor) starting in October 1667.[19] She paid 6300 merks, plus 40s feu duty per annum (and other public burdens).[20]

The property acquired from the Glens (George and his son James) consisted of:

> a laigh house and house above the same … and together with ane other laigh house and house above the same … possesst by Matthew McGrain indweller in the said burgh as thatched with straw, together also with that piece of waste ground lying on the west of the said thatchen.[21]

In order to make a complete plot, this was probably the part of the Glen property immediately to the north, presumably including the extension the Bowies had complained about in 1642. For this they were paid 850 merks.[22]

This exploration of what became a key part of Queensberry House casts a great deal of light particularly on the eastern boundary of the site and it is worth exploring this in a little more detail. As fig 7.1c and fig 7.1d show, the large Glen property was not the only property to the east of Balmakellie's house. Robert Logan's property, squeezed in between the Glen and Spencerfield lands, is first recorded in a sasine in his favour in 1635.[23] Logan is identified as an 'indweller', to whom, with his wife Elizabeth Matheson and their son, also Robert, John Glen, an Edinburgh merchant, made a disposition of 'the three parts of a foretenement of land of old belonging to William Gray and others'. This is also borne out by a charter in the Canongate Chartulary which does not mention William Gray but does confirm that the property passed from Glen to Logan and also that it had belonged to Hector Cranston some time before that.[24]

The rest of the papers in the Buccleuch inventory show the property passing, not entirely smoothly, from Robert Logan (probably junior) to Alexander Logan; to George Logan (1657); to John Boyd, merchant in Edinburgh (1662); to Dame Margaret Boyd, daughter and heir to John (1679); and finally, the property was disponed by Dame Margaret and her husband, Sir James Foulis, to Charles Maitland of Hatton on 20 April 1681.[25] As we shall see, this played a key part in defining the eastern boundary of the site.

The western side of the site is rather more difficult to define, although, again, the examination of the Balmakellie property does throw some light on this. Figures 7.1a–d, and the documents on which they are based, tell us something of the site immediately to the west of the Balmakellie site. The Buccleuch inventory of Queensberry writs allows us to trace the site back to 1600, and beyond that to 1553.[26] On 29 October 1600, Michael Fraser signed a contract with William

Little, agreeing to sell, 'his tenement of land, back and fore with the yaird and pertinents'.[27] Fraser had been in possession of the property since 1553, when he took sasine of it.[28] William Little quickly passed the lands on to Patrick Watson and Christian Nicholson (his wife) in October 1603,[29] and the property was inherited by William Watson, Patrick's brother, in 1611.[30] Oddly, although both the retour and sasine confirming William's status and ownership are dated 1611, a disposition of the property was granted by him to James Fogo of Calingsay on 18 March 1608 and his sasine, like Watson's, is dated 18 April 1611.[31] In 1628–9, James Fogo's son, Henry, found himself the subject of a decreet of Apprysing which resulted in the property being passed to Janet Galbraith and her daughter, Agnes Blair. The 1642 precept granted to Anna Bowie already discussed above, casts further light on this. In 1642, Agnes Blair and her husband, William Serjeant, an upholsterer, owned the property immediately to the west of that belonging to Anna Bowie (which became the Spencerfield and later Balmakellie property). Their son, Thomas Serjeant, inherited in 1666 and eventually sold the property to Charles Maitland in 1680.[32]

From the evidence available, it would appear that these two, consolidated properties, Balmakellie in the east and Serjeant in the west, comprised the core of the site used by Hatton for his house. However, whereas we have a lot of information about what lay to the east of the Balmakellie property, the area to the west of the Serjeant property is a little more difficult to ascertain and the precise edge of the Hatton property consequently more vague. There is, however, quite a lot of other detail available on the west side of the site, much of it relating to those properties identified in the 1688 charter.

According to this charter, the western boundary of Queensberry House was defined by:

> the lands of the heirs of William Hepburn on the west, the lands of the said Alexander Kay and the backlands and yard of John Straitton on the west of the yard and buildings formerly belonging to the Earl of Lauderdale.[33]

This somewhat complicated description suggests a combination of properties lying along the western boundary and a further investigation of these adds considerable detail to the picture.

By 1688, the heirs of William Hepburn were Mungo Malloch and his wife Janet Litster. They acquired the property in 1686 and the charter in their favour lists a long line of property holders on the site as well as information about the neighbouring sites.[34] The most important of these for our purposes was the property immediately to the east of Malloch's. By 1686, this belonged to the Earl of Lauderdale but formerly had been the property of Samuel Gray. This property seems, therefore, to have sat between the Sergeant and Hepburn (later Malloch) property, all to the west of the Balmakellie property. Gray's property can be traced right back to the 15th century. On 10 February 1480, Andrew Kennedy granted a charter to Richard Bennerman 'of a forland in the Canongate'.[35] Over the following decades the property changed hands, through sale and inheritance, to the Sanderson and later the Gray family, and seems to have grown from a foreland to a foreland and backland, and with a cellar also being added.[36] It was this property that was inherited in 1624 by Samuel Gray, who in turn passed it on in 1665 to Thomas Gray, whose son, Robert, inherited shortly thereafter. Robert is presumably the person mentioned in the 1688 charter, but he did not sell direct to the Earl of Lauderdale; instead he sold to James Crombie, 'Smith in Canongate', who sold on to Lauderdale in 1679.[37]

A more detailed description of some of these western properties can be gleaned from the Canongate Chartulary and these documents give us some clues as to the physical boundary of the site. A precept of Clare Constat, dated 17 July 1700, itemises a series of properties in different parts of the city inherited by Barbara and Ann Kay, daughters of Alexander Kay, 'sometime Bailie of the Canongate'.[38] This is the same man mentioned above with property to the west of 'the yard and buildings formerly belonging to the Earl of Lauderdale'.[39] Here the property is described as: between the tenement of James Bell's heirs on the west, the tenement of the late James Gib, now of Kentigern Malloch and the Duke of Queensberry on the east and south.[40]

A more detailed discussion of the adjoining properties makes it clear that this building was withdrawn from the street, because the main property on its northern boundary was a foreland and oven built by William Shivas, a baker.[41] To the south lay property owned by the Duke of Queensberry, formerly owned by Henry Fenton, maltman and in addition to the previously mentioned property which also formed part of the southern boundary. This latter is something of a puzzle because it is referred to as the property of Kentigern Malloch and the Duke of Queensberry. One possible explanation for this is that it was one property divided into two, with Malloch owning the piece to the east

and Queensberry to the south. Some support for this interpretation can be found in the inventory of writs at Drumlanrig, which itemises the disposition of 'a backland in the Canongate' by William Hepburn to Charles Maitland in 1681. Since the Hepburn land eventually found its way to the Mallochs, it could be that this indicates that the southern portion of their plot had already been sold to Hatton, thus splitting the property between the two.[42] On the other hand, the more detailed breakdown of the Barbara and Ann Kay property suggests that the Queensberry/Malloch property was actually two, probably adjoining, properties, one to the east and south, the other to the east.[43]

Whatever the precise arrangement was, it seems unlikely that there was any kind of joint ownership of property between Queensberry and Malloch. What there certainly was, however, was a very close connection between the two properties, the intimacy of which was occasionally to cause disputes. In addition, it is also clear that on the west, just as on the east, the Hatton property included backlands of properties that stood on or near the street, that is to say it ran behind existing properties, specifically, the Malloch and the Kay properties. A later charter, of 1705, confirms but also simplifies the arrangements discussed so far. Malloch and his wife, Elizabeth Smith, owned a property to the east of the Kay sisters and to the west of that property formerly owned by Samuel Gray and purchased from him by Charles Maitland of Hatton. To the south, were the stables and offices built by Maitland (as well as the strand and the Dishflatt).

At the beginning of this chapter, the nine properties that made up Queensberry House were listed. Most of them have now been accounted for and most of the rest can be dealt with fairly quickly.

Dame Margaret Douglas of Balmakellie: a substantial site on the east of the Hatton property.

George Glen: also to the east, forming part of the eastern boundary but also parts of it subsumed within the Balmakellie property and part purchased by Maitland.

Robert Gray: a property to the west of the site, between Serjeant's and Malloch's.

John Wauchope: possibly a property to the east of the site, since the 1688 charter opens its description of the eastern boundary with 'a small yard belonging to the heirs of John Wauchope'.[44]

William Hepburn: almost certainly to the west of

the site. This is the property that is later acquired by the Mallochs but is bounded on the south by Queensberry House because Hepburn sold off 'a backland in the Canongate' to Maitland in 1681.[45]

William Johnston and Jasper Johnston: the Johnston family held property to the east of Glen's land in the early 18th century,[46] but entered a contract with Charles Maitland in 1681, in the following terms:

Contract between the said Charles Maitland and William Johnston, merchant in Edinburgh, and Gaspar Johnston, farmer in Lastalrig, whereby the said Gaspar is obliged that so soon as the said William should attain to the age of 14 years that he should dispone the two stables and a burnt land lying in the Canongate, dated 3rd December 1681.[47]

Leaving aside the evident precocity of the 14-year-old entrepreneur, the precise location of these buildings is unknown, although, given the other evidence of the Johnstons' possessions, they may have been towards the east side of the site.

Alexander Kay: an important site on the western boundary of the site but which also overlooked it to the south. Again, this was probably because part of the backlands had been sold off to Maitland and there is one record of the sale of 'a tenement of land in the Canongate' which may refer to this.[48]

Thomas Serjeant: an important site immediately to the west of Lady Margaret Douglas of Balmakellie's property.

Not all of this can be accommodated within a diagram, but fig 7.1e attempts to summarise in very simple form all of the site information discussed so far.

Having established, therefore, the broad outlines of the history of the site, and having indicated that there is some relationship between this analysis and the shape and structure of the site, and possibly the building, the issue to be considered now is what we can conclude about the site and

the building from the evidence of the legal documents when combined with other archival, illustrative and cartographic evidence.

The first point to make is that the properties so far discussed appear to comprise the entire Queensberry House site but were all acquired by Charles Maitland of Hatton, not by any of his Queensberry successors. This is borne out by the 'Inventar of Writs' referred to on a number of occasions, which summarises all of the properties, indicating that they were all acquired by Hatton and transferred to Queensberry. The same is true of the other main source, the Canongate Chartulary, in which even those documents that long post-date the Queensberry acquisition of the property, are nevertheless ultimately referring to transactions involving Hatton. The importance of this is that it indicates that Queensberry did not need to purchase extra land in order to build his western extension of the house and that there must have been a substantial piece of ground available on the west side of Hatton's property, perhaps raising the possibility that he might have expanded the house himself had he held on to the property for longer. Certainly the Slezer drawing of Hatton's house (fig 7.2) seems to indicate a substantial space to the west on which building work could have occurred.

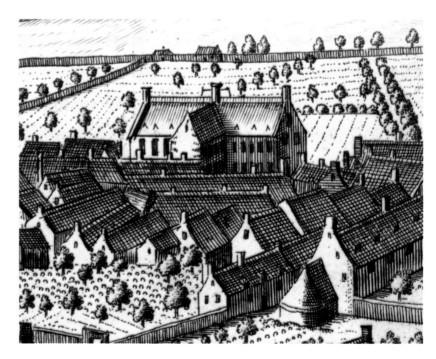

Figure 7.2
Detail from John Slezer's engraved panorama of Edinburgh from the north showing Hatton House c 1680 (© NLS)

1647 Building Layout

metres

0   50   100

ABBEY STRAND

HORSE WYND

CALTON ROAD

GALLOWAY'S ENTRY

Forsyth's Close

CANONGATE

Valleyfield's Entry

REID'S CT

BROWNS CLOSE

REID'S CLOSE

Figure 7.3
The plan of the lower Canongate from Gordon of Rothiemay's 1647 superimposed by the modern OS map, showing the overlap of earlier structures with those existing in modern times (© Kirkdale Archaeology Ltd)

In terms of cartographic evidence, the Gordon of Rothiemay plan of Edinburgh (fig 6.1) is of crucial importance in our understanding of the site of Queensberry House. In this area of research, we can helpfully combine the archival and the cartographic to deepen our understanding of the site and, ultimately the building itself. The Dennison and Ewart report employed a technique of overlaying, in block plan form, the structures visible on historic maps on a modern Ordnance Survey 1:1250 plan in order to see the relationship between ancient and modern structures and boundaries (Dennison & Ewart 1998, 10–28). Figure 7.3 shows this same technique applied to the whole Parliament site. The first thing that is striking about this is the difference between the majority of buildings

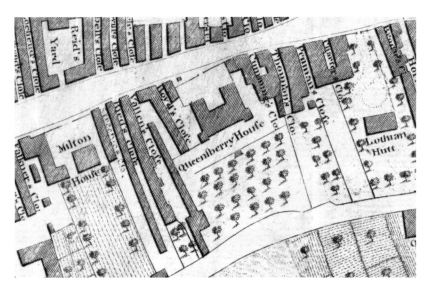

Figure 7.4
Detail of Kincaid's map of Edinburgh, 1784 (© NLS)

on the Parliament site, to the east of Queensberry House, and those on the site of Queensberry House itself. It has been shown that the majority of these buildings were tenements separated by pended closes with secondary tenements, at a lower level, behind the main ones (Dennison & Ewart 1998, 14). It has also been suggested that the very different structures at the east and western ends of the site surveyed suggest either multifunctional buildings or grander dwellings; the material discussed above certainly suggests the latter and it is quite easy to equate the structures visible in the Gordon of Rothiemay view with the kind of 'Grand Lodging' purchased by Dame Margaret Douglas.

However, clearly the area was very mixed and there are also several indications in those documents and elsewhere that suggest multifunctionalism and multi-occupancy.[49]

The first thing that the overlay tells us is the extent of the Queensberry House site in relation to the plots on Gordon of Rothiemay's plan. Queensberry House appears to take up two full plots and part of a third plot on the west. The division of this western plot may well ultimately be related to the boundary between Queensberry and Malloch discussed above. Similarly, although the precise arrangement of the western boundary remains fairly obscure, the previous discussion makes it clear that the property acquired by Hatton was partly overlooked from the north and therefore a trace of this site history can still be seen in the modern tenement that overlaps the north-west boundary of the site.

If the western edge of the site remains fairly obscure, the detailed study of the eastern edge seems to provide a clearer connection between the documentary record, the later cartographic history and the existing fabric of the building. There are two main aspects to this. First, although the diagrams illustrated here (figs 7.1a–d) do not represent maps or plans, they are consistent in suggesting a particular stepped form to the north-east boundary of the site that recurs in every map of the area from the 18th century to the present day (fig 7.4). It seems reasonable to suggest therefore that the complex legal history outlined here, and the strenuous efforts of a succession of property owners, most notably the Bowies, Balmakellie and then Hatton, to create an increasingly grand space and lodging for themselves, have left a clear physical trace on the townscape of this area that has survived until the present day and is still, to some extent, celebrated in the Parliament building design.

The second area of connection between documentary history, archaeology and built fabric is in the eastern portion of Queensberry House. The existing east wing of Queensberry House has clearly been altered to bring it into conformity with the latest phase of the building work carried out by James Smith for the second Duke of Queensberry in the late 1690s. Ewart's analysis of the Gordon of Rothiemay plan suggests very strongly that this east jamb overlaps very precisely with a south-facing jamb of a building on the main street. The most likely candidate for this is the gabled extension erected by George Glen, which caused Anna Bowie to complain so bitterly to the Dean of Guild in 1642. This suggests that when Dame Margaret Douglas bought the series of properties that made up her house, notwithstanding the fact that the Bowies had a 'Great Lodging' of their own, she must have created a new building that at least partly overlapped with the foundations of some of the earlier ones, including the offending jamb.

7.4 Physical evidence for pre-existing structures at Queensberry House

TOM ADDYMAN

With one possible exception, the structural investigation revealed no evidence for the incorporation of *in situ* structural remains earlier than 1667–70 into the standing fabric of the building. This is in spite of the fact that the east jamb would appear, as noted above, to be located upon the site of an earlier tenement range of similar dimension depicted in Gordon of Rothiemay's engraving of 1647 (fig 6.1). Rothiemay's engraving also suggests the presence of a three- or four-storied square tower that would have approximately occupied the site of the western part of the principal range. Again there was no clear indication of incorporated fabric.

However, there was abundant evidence for the recycling of materials from earlier buildings, the majority of which can be reasonably supposed to have been recovered from pre-existing structures on the site. This material appears most commonly in the existing building fabric of the Balmakellie phase mansion (c 1667–70), and to a lesser degree within the Queensberry phase extensions (c 1695–1700). In the Military phase (1808–11) there is considerable reuse of materials which generally derive from the earlier phases of Queensberry House itself.

Of greatest frequency are reused dressed stones that display a variety of tooling detail. Of these the more significant are stones that display architectural details that derive from features such as windows, entrances and fireplaces. Other categories of building material seen include various types of roofing material, early bricks and isolated examples of structural timberwork.

While little specific can be learned of the actual form of the structures previously on the site

(Rothiemay guides us here), much can be learned of their general character. The majority of moulded window and entrance dressings (jamb stones and lintels) are detailed with chamfered arises, and less frequently with relatively narrow, quirked angle rolls. The majority are of polished ashlar (that is, displaying no actual tooling on their presentation faces). Those detailed with chamfered surrounds have both raised and plain margins. Many of the lintel and cill stones display seatings for vertically set diamond-section iron stanchions. From this evidence it is reasonable to deduce that many of the former buildings on the site were well-built masonry structures probably dating to both the 16th and 17th centuries. This comes as little surprise and is consistent with the pictorial evidence of Rothiemay.

Roofing materials incorporated into the general fabric of the Balmakellie phase mansion (and therefore probably indicating reused materials) included over 60 recorded instances of sandstone roofing tile throughout the structure and 11 instances of pantile fragments within three isolated groups on the lower stories of the north exterior wall of the principal range, to the east. All were clearly derived from earlier buildings. The sandstone tiles were generally about 2–2.5cm thick and of a hard somewhat micaceous purplish-brown stone, possibly of Carmyllie type, imported from Angus. Each had chipped edges and a single drilled hole (generally 8–12mm diameter) towards the head. The broad diameters of these holes and consistent absence of iron staining demonstrated that they must have been for wooden pegs. The pantile fragments, where recorded, were mostly curved, but the fragments were too small to ascertain a complete profile; they were of an orangey-red, low-fired terracotta fabric and generally about 10–14mm thick. No instance of the incorporation of slate in the fabric of the Balmakellie mansion was recorded.

In the same area where the pantiles were identified, a number of fragments of brick were also seen. These were of notably small dimension, approximately 70mm by 35–40mm (length not seen). They were of two colours: a creamy medium-yellow and a dark purplish hue, the latter apparently high-fired and very hard. It is possible that these are imported Dutch bricks, as the 17th-century English and Scots east coast brick industries generally produced terracotta bricks of reddish hue.

The material represents a great variety of architectural detail and style clearly suggestive of complex multiple and multiphase property units typical of the

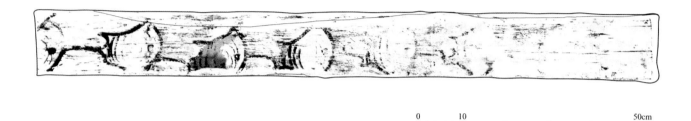

0   10   50cm

Figure 7.5
Reused section of ceiling joist decorated with polychrome tempera scheme, probably from a later 16th-century domestic interior. This had probably been incorporated into the Balmakellie phase mansion but had seen secondary reuse as an entrance lintel in the Military period.

Edinburgh Old Town and Canongate of the 16th and 17th centuries. This material forms an important and direct link to the pre-existing buildings on the site.

Within the Balmakellie phase fabric, or reliably having come from that fabric, were a number of instances where sections of structural timberwork had been incorporated either as window or entrance lintels, or, in the case of the mezzanine level of the eastern stair, ceiling joists. A number of these (all of pine) bore some degree of diagnostic detail relating to their former use. Of particular interest was a short section of ceiling joist that retained painted decoration in the form of a repeated polychrome fruit motif (fig 7.5). Other sections, perhaps also former ceiling joists, were detailed with narrow angle chamfers and then painted with a dark grey-brown-black oil-bound paint. Within the easternmost chamber of *Upper Ground* floor level a number of dooks clearly represented sawn sections of timberwork that perhaps derived from window frames or other interior framed woodwork, although their exact nature remained uncertain. The wood was identified as oak (A Crone, pers. comm.).

Notes

1   The earliest document is a charter dated 10 February 1480, listed in the *Inventar of writs and Evidents of the Duke of Queensberry's house in the Canongate*, Buccleuch Mss NRA(S) 1275/vol. 12/ff. 120v–124v. The actual items to which this inventory refers have not been found in the archive. The latest document is a Precept of Clare Constat in favour of James Malloch, dated 30 November 1709 (although describing boundaries that existed pre-1686), ECA, Canongate Charters, vol. 5, 1683–1711, no. 868.

2   Buccleuch Mss, NRA(S) 1275/vol. 12/ff. 120v–124v.

3   ECA, Canongate Charters, vol. 5, 1683–1711, no. 868.

4   *Some Notes on Queensberry House, Canongate, Edinburgh by Charles B Boog Watson, one of the Directors thereof, December 1926*, Edinburgh Central Library, Edinburgh Room, qYHV1481H.

5   The 17th-century inventory of writs in the Queensberry archive at Drumlanrig Castle (see note 1) covers nine separate properties.

6   According to Boog Watson (1923, 13), when William Aitchison sold Queensberry House in 1803, he included Glen's land in the sale, described at that time as 'taken down and ruinous'.

7   ECA, Canongate Charters, vol. 5, 1683–1711, no. 745 (available in transcript book in Search Room).

8   *Inventar of writs and Evidents of the Duke of Queensberry's house in the Canongate*, Buccleuch Mss NRA(S) 1275/vol. 12/ff. 120v–124v; this item is listed under bundle 3, item 95.

9   Lauderdale Papers, NRA(S) 832/64/52. A glazier's and a smith's account for work at Holyrood Palace in 1679 both mention work in the chamber of one 'Gyrie Bowey', who may well be the same person (Paton 1957, 305–6).

10   The documents discussed below show continuous royal service by the Bowies over three generations, the last of whom, James, is described in a 1642 charter as 'Rijand of his Maj. wine cellaris', Lauderdale Papers, NRA(S) 832/25/4.

11 ECA, Canongate Charters, vol. 5, 1683–1711, no. 231 (available in transcript book in Search Room), 13/11/1688. A similar document, a precept of Clare Constat, of the same date, records the same transaction, except this time Thomas Woods inherits the property 'as hare to Peter Wood, burgess of Edinburgh, his father …', Lauderdale Papers, NRA(S)832/64/52.

12 Lauderdale Papers, NRA(S)832/64/52. Sasine dated 22/1/1617.

13 ECA, Canongate Charters, vol. 5, 1683–1711, no. 417, 2/12/1642 (available in transcript book in Search Room). On the same day an instrument of sasine was made in favour of Anna Bowie and John Scott of Spenserfield, along with a resignation by Anna Bowie to her husband. Lauderdale Papers, NRA(S)832/64/52.

14 ECA, Acts of Bailies of Canongate, 1623–1652, vol. II, 41, 5 March 1642 (available in transcript book in Search Room).

15 ECA, Acts of Bailies of Canongate, 1623–1652, vol. II, 41, 9 June 1642 (available in transcript book in Search Room).

16 ECA, Canongate Charters, 1683–1711, vol. 5, no. 568, 8/4/1650.

17 The research project concentrated mainly, though not exclusively, on transcribed material. This was partly because it was much easier to use than the original documents and partly because there is no index to the Ms material, making systematic research extremely time-consuming.

18 Sasine in favour of John Scott of Spenserfield, 2/12/1642, Lauderdale Papers, NRA(S) 832/64/52.

19 Minute of contract is dated 12/10/1667 and indicates that a number of tenants lived in or operated from the property, including William Nicol, vintner; Dougall Macfarlane; Bartholomew Smith, barber; Agnes Kerr, widow. Lauderdale Papers, NRA(S) 832/25/4.

20 Lauderdale Papers, NRA(S) 832/64/6. The same bundle contains the Instrument of Resignation (15/1/1668), which refers to a disposition of 3/12/1667; a sasine in favour of Dame Margaret dated 17/1/1668, registered 10/2/1668.

21 Lauderdale Papers, NRA(S) 832/25/14, 'Copy dispositions and renunciations of a tenement on the south side of the Canongate 1717–69'.

22 Lauderdale Papers, NRA(S) 832/25/14, in a disposition dated 4/3/1669.

23 Dated 9 June 1635 and Registered 16 July. *Inventar of writs and Evidents of the Duke of Queensberry's house in the Canongate*, Buccleuch Mss, NRA(S) 1275/vol. 16/ff. 120v–124v; this item is listed under bundle 2, item 65. The records for this property in total are covered by items 65–77.

24 Precept following upon a retour in favour of Anna Bowie, 2/12/1642. ECA, Canongate Charters, vol. 5, 1683–1711, no. 417 (available in transcript book in Search Room).

25 As 23 above.

26 *Inventar of writs and Evidents of the Duke of Queensberry's house in the Canongate*, Buccleuch Mss, NRA(S) 1275/vol. 12/ff. 120v–124v; bundle 3, items 78–91.

27 As 26 above, item 78.

28 As 26 above, item 79.

29 As 26 above, item 82.

30 As 26 above, item 83.

31 As 26 above, item 85.

32 As 26 above, items 90 & 91.

33 ECA, Canongate Charters, vol. 5, 1683–1711, no. 745, 1688.

34 As 33 above, no. 727, 2/7/1686. The list is Elizabeth and Anna Ronald; William Malloch; James Cuthbertson; James Gib; Robert Gib; William Hepburn and Gavin Hepburn. To the west lay the property of Adam Barton, inherited by his widow, Euphame Smith.

35 *Inventar of writs and Evidents of the Duke of Queensberry's house in the Canongate*, Buccleuch Mss, NRA(S) 1275/vol.16/ff.120v – 124v; this item is listed under bundle 1, item 1. The records for this property in total are covered by items 1–64.

36 As 35 above. Most of this seems to have happened in 1566.

37 As 35 above, item 64. This was the first property acquired by Hatton.

38 As 33 above, no. 820.

39 ECA, Canongate Charters, vol. 5, 1683–1711, no. 745, 1688.

40 As 33 above, no. 820, 17/7/1700.

41 As 40 above.

42 As 35 above, item 99, 10 March 1681.

43 As 40 above. Both properties seem to follow the same route of ownership from the Mallochs to the Gibs and, eventually, back to Kentigern Malloch.

44 ECA, Canongate Charters, vol. 5, 1683–1711, no. 745, 1688. Wauchope is also mentioned in the *Inventar of writs and Evidents of the Duke of Queensberry's house in the Canongate*, Buccleuch Mss, NRA(S) 1275/vol.16/ff.120v – 124v, item 101, which is an inserted item 'Contract between the Lord Haltoun and John Wauchope, Macer, dated 20 September 1681'.

45 *Inventar of writs and Evidents of the Duke of Queensberry's house in the Canongate*, Buccleuch Mss, NRA(S) 1275/vol.16/ff.120v – 124v, item 99, 10 March 1681.

46 ECA, Canongate Charters, vol. 5, 1683–1711, no. 830, 5 March 1703, and no. 850, 24 April 1706. The latter refers to a property of the Glens, 'between the lands of the late William Johnston on the east, the great mansion of the Duke of Queensberry on the west, and the yards of the said duke on the south'.

47 *Inventar of writs and Evidents of the Duke of Queensberry's house in the Canongate*, Buccleuch Mss, NRA(S) 1275/vol.16/ff.120v – 124v, item 100, 3 December 1681.

48 *Inventar of writs and Evidents of the Duke of Queensberry's house in the Canongate*, Buccleuch Mss, NRA(S) 1275/vol.16/ff.120v – 124v, item 98, 24 April 1681

49 Dennison & Ewart 1998, 11. The multifunctional character of some of the buildings is hinted at in the references to ovens, barns, stables, etc, in documents already discussed.

Figure 8.1

John Slezer's engraved panorama of Edinburgh from the north

Chapter 8

The Balmakellie 'Great Lodging'

TOM ADDYMAN and JOHN LOWREY

8.1 Introduction

JOHN LOWREY

The archaeological evidence strongly suggests that the original house constructed by Dame Margaret Douglas of Balmakellie was substantially the same as the house later purchased by Charles Maitland of Hatton, although he improved and somewhat extended it. For this reason, some mention is made of Hatton's house in this chapter and the plans mostly apply in his case also, although his house is examined in the next chapter. It seems most likely that the motivation in acquiring and developing the house was different in each of these two cases, and the significance of the house to each of them consequently differed.

8.2 Architectural symbolism in the Canongate in the 1670s

JOHN LOWREY

By the late 1660s the south end of the Canongate was beginning to regain much of its old importance. Throughout much of 1668, Holyrood Palace was undergoing repairs and redecoration for the opening of Parliament in October 1669 (MacIvor & Petersen 1984). Holyrood was once again to be the centre of attention and accommodation in that area was at a premium. Even after the departure of the commissioners in 1670, the area retained its cachet because, from that time on, the palace was completely remodelled by Sir William Bruce and was the focus of Scottish politics throughout the 1670s and early 1680s. This was not simply because of its symbolic importance, but also because the palace was used as the residence first of the Duke of Lauderdale, and, between 1679 and 1682, of the future James VII. The southern end of the Canongate became a very desirable place to live in the late 17th century.

For Charles Maitland of Hatton and, indeed, for his Queensberry successors, the motivation to build was at least partly political. The desire among the nobility to have a residence in or near Holyrood Palace (or sometimes both) was based on both practical considerations (the need to be close to the seat of power) and on considerations of status and prestige. The great families would therefore seek to be visibly and ostentatiously close to the residence of the king. The fact that, after 1603, the king was elsewhere was irrelevant. Edinburgh was still a capital city, with a Parliament and Privy Council, and there was still the practical need to have a base there. There was also the real expectation in the Restoration period that the king would return to Scotland and this was increased by the rebuilding of the palace. Moreover, the presence of the king was symbolised by the new palace and the need to be represented in or close to it was still important. Indeed, it could be argued that the symbolic role played by the palace in the 17th century made architectural symbolism in general all the more important, and the need to have houses that very clearly signalled the power and prestige of their owners became all the more acute. Certainly, this could be one reason for the emergence of larger and more lavish 'lodgings' such as Moray House in the 1620s and Queensberry House in the post-Restoration era. These two were the largest, but there were a number of others; for example, roughly contemporary with Queensberry, and in the immediate vicinity, were Roxburgh House and Panmure House (the latter, admittedly, a rather modest L-plan).

After the remodelling and expansion of Holyrood Palace by Sir William Bruce in the 1670s, it could be argued that this symbolic role of the royal residence, as representative of the monarch himself, was being emphasised and that Holyrood came to take on a symbolic function in relation to Edinburgh not unlike that enjoyed by the Louvre in relation to Paris in the same period.

8.3 Margaret Douglas of Balmakellie

JOHN LOWREY

Dame Margaret's house pre-dated the new work on the palace and her own position and motives were very different from those of either Hatton or the Queensberrys. Nevertheless, the general background of the increasing importance of the palace area in the post-Restoration era forms part of the context for her house and made it an extremely desirable place to live.

Margaret Douglas was the daughter of Patrick Douglas of Spott in East Lothian. She married the brother of the second Earl of Panmure, Colonel Henry Maule of Balmakellie, after the death of his wife, Lady Jean Wemyss. This second marriage was a clandestine affair and would probably have been disapproved of by the powerful Panmure family (Douglas 1910, 21; Maule 1874, 375). When Henry died in 1667, it is unlikely that his widow could have looked to the Panmures for much help and the acquisition of the Canongate properties shortly afterwards might be seen as her attempt to resettle herself, with her young daughter, in Edinburgh.

About ten years later she married Alexander Douglas of Gogar and, around the same time, in 1677, decided to let out her Canongate property. From the ragbag of disparate tenements and yards that she had acquired in the 1660s (Chapter 7), Dame Margaret in 1676/7 leased to Katherine, Countess of Erroll, 'all and haill of the Great Lodging, high and laigh and haill office houses belonging thereto with the yeards pertaining to the same …'.[1] The Countess took a three-year lease at the end of 1676, with effect from Whit 1677, for a rent of 700 merks, but with £80 Scots retained as annual rent on a debt that the Gogars owed to her.[2] Clearly, this was a residence suitable for a woman of her station. Katherine was the daughter of the second Earl of South Esk and married Gilbert, eleventh Earl of Errol. She was widowed in 1674 and lived in Edinburgh until c 1680, where she became part of the circle of Sir Robert Sibbald who used her artistic talents to produce natural history plates for one of his publications.[3] Later, in 1689, she became governess to James Francis, Prince of Wales, and followed the Stewarts into exile in St Germain, Paris, where she died in 1693 (Douglas 1910, vol. 3, 579). It was Katherine's residence that was disponed to Charles Maitland of Hatton at the very end of 1679. As Hatton's main lands were in the Ratho area, it is possible that Dame Margaret Douglas's new husband, Alexander Douglas of Gogar, who was a neighbour and almost certainly known to Hatton, was instrumental in arranging the sale.

8.4 The house and its urban context

JOHN LOWREY

The Gordon of Rothiemay map of 1647 (fig 6.1) provides a useful tool in understanding the nature of the Canongate in this period. On the Parliament site there are three distinct zones: firstly, the houses around Horse Wynd, dating from the later 16th century, which clearly provided highly prestigious accommodation, some of it, especially towards the palace itself, organised around spacious courts (Dennison & Ewart 1998, 46). To the west, there is a series of buildings running at right angles to the street and representing very well the classic pattern of overbuilding of the narrow burgage plots that dictated the pattern of land ownership and building practice. That clear system of narrow buildings bounding narrow access closes is, however, somewhat interrupted in the area immediately to the west where some of the plots have buildings in the backlands that run across the site, probably because the plots are slightly wider at this point, allowing the creation of small courtyard houses. It was in this third zone that Dame Margaret Douglas built her house and it was here also that Lord Hatton extended the site to create still more open space around the house.

The form of Balmakellie Lodging was, therefore, very closely related to the grain of the townscape in which it was built. The gabled jamb towards the street picks up the pattern of narrow gabled structures running perpendicular to the main thoroughfare and indeed, as suggested in Chapter 7.3, sits on the foundations of one that was built around 1642.[4] Beyond that, the more expansive main block of the house sits across the plot thus creating a dominating and important façade towards the gardens rather than towards the street. Within the context of the Canongate, this was a fairly unusual, though not unique, characteristic of the house and was to have some importance for its design.

8.5 The historical evidence

8.5.1 The house and its site

TOM ADDYMAN & JOHN LOWREY

The little surviving archival evidence concerning the Great Lodging relates entirely to the site and is concerned with the acquisition of the various buildings and parcels of land that made up the property. The charters relating to these contain little positive architectural evidence, other than the information that some of the structures were thatched (although with what material is not clear). The picture that emerges from that study is of a substantial lodging belonging to the Bowie/ Spencerfield family, encroached upon to the north and east by a number of poorer and sharply contrasting buildings. It was important for Dame Margaret to acquire these poorer quality buildings as well as the more substantial property immediately to the south so that she could both build a suitably impressive lodging and also provide it with an appropriate setting. This involved clearing the buildings to the north and, as far as possible, opening up to the street, although it is possible that she was not entirely successful in achieving this desirable aim. What is clear from an engraving by the military engineer, Captain John Slezer (fig 8.1), however, is that her house was the most substantial building in that part of the Canongate and it stood out quite dramatically among the poorer buildings around. When she sold on to Lord Hatton, Dame Margaret was the owner of a 'Great Lodging', which encompassed the majority of what was to become Hatton House (the house was passed on to William, first Duke of Queensberry). The implication, therefore, is that this building was substantially erected in the late 1660s by Dame Margaret on the site of the various properties she had purchased.

The term 'Great Lodging' had been applied some decades earlier to the Dowager Countess of Home's Canongate residence, latterly Moray House, which is referred to as her 'great ludging' (Dunbar 1966). The Balmakellie building was certainly deemed suitable for an aristocratic dwelling, not only by Dame Margaret herself, but also by the Countess of Erroll.

The earlier parts of the present Queensberry House are clearly identifiable as being part of Balmakellie's Great Lodging and account for about two-thirds of the present volume of the building. This is confirmed both by the archaeological assessment of the mansion and the evidence of Slezer's engraving (fig 8.1).

8.5.2 Slezer's panorama (c 1676–88) (fig 8.1)

TOM ADDYMAN

In his engraved panorama Slezer depicts the lower parts of the Canongate from the north. As the Canongate Parish Church does not appear, his view can clearly be dated to before the construction of the church in 1688. The remodelling of the exterior of Holyrood House was completed by 1676 and is illustrated by Slezer. The execution of the original drawing upon which the engraving was based can thus be confidently dated to within the period 1676–88. It is documented that a prospect tower was added to the Balmakellie building in c 1680–1 for its second owner Lord Hatton (see Chapter 9). The engraver depicts what appears to be a structure above the junction of the north wing and the main body of the house (the correct position for the

tower) but it is apparently shown within the gardens *beyond* the mansion. Whether this is a misreading on the part of the engraver of the depiction of the prospect tower in the original drawing or some other unrelated feature cannot now be known and as a consequence it is dangerous to further refine the dating of the view to before 1680–1.

Whatever its precise dating, the engraving clearly illustrates Dame Margaret's 'Great Lodging' before the major subsequent modification of the Queensberry phase. The building is shown as a tall T-plan structure consisting of a large east/west-aligned principal range with a less substantial northwards-running jamb, and the structure dominates this area of the Canongate. While its lower storey is obscured by the roofscape in the foreground, its upper two floors and roofline are clearly illustrated. Accepting the limitations of a secondary, engraved representation, it is apparent that the structure had steeply pitched roofs that were gabled to the north, east and west, and the overall massing of the building and its general impression agrees with the archaeological evidence.

However, most other details of the view must be treated with considerable caution. For example, the fenestration of the north elevation of the principal range cannot be reconciled with the archaeological evidence, for there appears to be one bay too many on either side of the jamb. An archaeological test-excavation at the north-east corner of the range failed to provide any indication that the east gable wall had formerly extended further to the east, although admittedly there was extensive later disturbance in this area. The principal range is surmounted by three, rather than four, chimneys, and the two chimneys that had surmounted the jamb are wholly omitted. The apparent cresting at the ridge also remains unexplained. However, the suggestion of small gabled dormers along the principal roof probably is accurate. It is not possible to interpret from the engraving the nature of the roofing material employed, whether stone, pantile or slate.

In summary, therefore, there are significant problems in reconciling the representation of the drawing and the house itself, as recorded by the archaeologists, and the Slezer drawing cannot be relied upon as accurate.

8.6 The archaeological evidence – exterior

TOM ADDYMAN

The archaeological analysis of Queensberry House has confirmed that the Balmakellie 'Great Lodging' forms

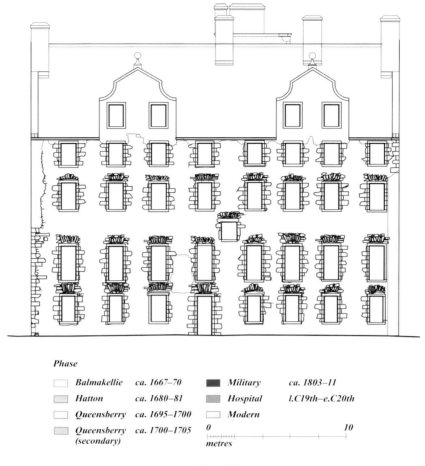

Phase

☐	*Balmakellie*	*ca. 1667–70*	■ *Military*	*ca. 1803–11*
▨	*Hatton*	*ca. 1680–81*	▨ *Hospital*	*l.C19th–e.C20th*
☐	*Queensberry*	*ca. 1695–1700*	☐ *Modern*	
▨	*Queensberry (secondary)*	*ca. 1700–1705*		

0   10
metres

Figure 8.2
South exterior elevation of the Balmakellie phase

the core of the present building and that its principal elements are essentially well preserved.

The earlier structure corresponds to the eastern eight bays and the full depth of the existing principal range, an area of 26.5m (east/west) by 11m, and almost the entirety of the northward-projecting east jamb (7.6m by 12m). The structure was of four full stories with an attic level, its overall height to the original eaves about 13.75m, and about 19.5m to its ridge. The eaves of the east jamb lay at about 1.7m above those of the principal range.

8.6.1 General construction – exterior

The Balmakellie mansion was rubble-built, apparently for the most part constructed from the remains of demolished tenement buildings, as suggested by the reuse of numerous dressed stones previously described.

It appears to be of a single programme of building as its general construction and architectural features are of similar character throughout. The masonry fabric is essentially a homogeneous random rubblework of mixed stone types bedded in a coarse, cream-coloured lime mortar employing river sand as an aggregate.

With the exception of the exposed sandstone dressings, as defined by their raised margins, the entirety of the exterior had evidently been surfaced with a thrown lime harl that was then lime-washed. Very little of this finish survived later resurfacings; traces of exterior harl were only identified upon the original west gable wall of the principal range where the later west wing either sealed the original surface or protected it from weathering (as in the roof space). Where it survived, this surface comprised a reasonably even harl, not pressed back or otherwise smoothed.

Figure 8.3
Thomas Sandby's drawing of Queensberry House garden elevation in 1746

Dressings are of a high-quality, light yellow to light grey fine-grained sandstone. Although there is no surviving documentation to indicate a quarry source, other contemporary structures, including the 1680s' additions to Holyrood Palace, employed a similar stone quarried near South Queensferry.

The majority of window surrounds survive from this phase; each is detailed with a 4cm chamfered arris within a surrounding raised margin up to which the exterior harl must have been taken. The lintels of most of the surviving original windows were protected by relieving arches over them, formed of unworked sandstone slabs set between springers. The windows were consistently 1m wide, but varied in height according to floor. Rising up the building, window heights measure 1.82m at *Lower Ground*, 2.28m at *Upper Ground*, 1.72m at *First* and 1.5m at *Second* floor levels. The wall-head cornice of the principal range seems to have rested directly upon the lintels of the

upper level windows. While the wall-head of the east jamb lay at a higher level, it was also finished off with a cornice course that was periodically interrupted by dormer windows whose cills lay below the cornice.

At the four angles of the principal range are neatly tooled quoins that are otherwise unadorned and over which lime harl must have died out. In contrast, the northern angles of the east jamb were detailed with raised margins, a small area of which survived behind a later remodelling of the north gable at the lower east side of the north-east angle indicating an 18cm-wide margin at the corner.

Little survived of the original cornice stones *in situ*, but truncated stones were identified at the south-east corner of the principal range and on the north elevation of the same range to the east of the jamb. Only at the original north-west corner of the principal range was the full profile of the cornice moulding preserved in the form of a single stone at the north-west

125

corner. This had been embedded within the abutting masonry of the later, western parts of Queensberry House. Here, the top of the cornice stone sloped down to accommodate the eaves' slates; below this the projecting part of the stone was detailed with a simple *cyma recta* profile above a single fillet, the whole cornice measuring about 17cm in height. Throughout, the cornice stones had been laid on a course of oyster levellers, a late medieval practice that continued in this region well into the 17th century, oysters presumably being brought up from Leith, the by-product of domestic consumption. These tended to survive even where the overlying stones had disappeared. There is every reason to believe that the original cornice of the east jamb was of identical form. The height of the wall-head was confirmed and a number of *ex situ* cornice stones had been built into the later top storey at the beginning of the 19th century, although these may equally have come from the main range.

While the gabled head of the east jamb is now wholly lost, much of the masonry of the east and west gable heads of the principal range did survive. To the east, two of the skew stones remained *in situ*, revealing the gable-head to have been straight, the only direct confirmation of the Slezer engraving. These remaining skews were tied back into the masonry of the gable-head but had clearly held in place intermittent flat skews. Although the exterior face of the two surviving stones had been clawed back, it seems likely that they had been detailed with a projecting margin up to which the exterior harl had been taken; this was apparently confirmed by recorded *ex situ* stones bearing this detail.

Little remained of the original four principal range chimneys except for the lower parts of the westernmost. This had been very substantial, containing the major flues from the kitchen fireplaces at *Lower Ground* floor level. The lower dressings on the south side of the chimney still survived, including an *in situ* thackstane and four tooled quoins above. These are of similar neatly tooled character to the general quoining at the corners of the range and it is again probable that the exterior harl extended over these.

8.6.2 Masons' marks

A single *in situ* mason's mark was recorded for the Balmakellie phase, upon the dressings of one of the east gable windows. Three further marks were found upon a single reused stone that may have come from one of the Balmakellie phase window dressings in the original west gable wall. One or more of these may

have been masons' marks, but the reason for three on a single stone was not apparent.

8.6.3 Exterior detail – principal range

South elevation (fig 8.2)

The south-facing garden elevation was monumental in scale even as originally constructed, eight bays wide over four principal stories. The bay spacing is subtly unequal, for the outermost bays are set slightly further away from the neighbouring three on either side, and the latter are in turn located on either side of a broader gap on the apparent centre line. An armorial panel was constructed between the *Upper Ground* and *First* floor levels at this point, a relieving arch over, all evidently of the original build. Its surround was formed of reused dressings that defined an aperture of 1.25m high by 1.05m wide; the recessed carved panel within has long since been removed. However, the western part of the building is considerably broader than the eastern part, and the windows to the west are somewhat more broadly spaced than their counterparts to the east. A garden entrance was formed, in place of a window, at the fourth bay from the west.

At two points along the south elevation the surviving general masonry of the first phase extended a little above the line of the wall-head as defined by the surviving course of oyster levellers. This provided firm evidence that at the Balmakellie phase there had been features rising above the general line of the wall-head. Eighteenth-century illustrations that show the south frontage, most notably a pencil and wash panorama of Edinburgh by Thomas Sandby executed in 1746 (fig 8.3), depict two shaped gables, each two bays wide. These were detailed with pedimented heads above concave sections of walling. The gables were symmetrical to the Balmakellie phase façade and, with the archaeological evidence of the surviving masonry, confirmed as an integral part of the original design of the south façade. They were retained even when the mansion was subsequently extended to the west thus rendering them off-centre, but were finally removed during the rebuilding by the Board of Ordnance at the beginning of the 19th century. These features provided both order and further vertical emphasis to the façade. They also performed the more prosaic role of lighting the attic rooms on the south frontage.

North elevation to west

The arrangement of windows on the Canongate-facing north elevation of the principal range is somewhat irregular despite its aspect facing the principal street approach (fig 8.4). At *First* and *Second* floor levels there are three more or less symmetrically arranged windows. This regularity was upset by further windows close to the east re-entrant with the east jamb. Later disturbance rendered it impossible to elucidate the exact arrangement in this area at either level. The original fenestration of the *Upper Ground* floor level that now forms the rear wall of the existing entrance porch was wholly disrupted by extensive later slappings. Only a pair of internal relieving arches remained to indicate the former presence of windows in the western two bays; presumably there had been at least one more further to the east. At *Lower Ground* floor level the lower parts of two windows were exposed, one slightly east of centre and the other close to the eastern re-entrant. Neither of these aligned with the windows at higher levels. At the re-entrant itself there had been a small angle loop.

North elevation to east

The remainder of the north elevation, on the east side of the east jamb, is two bays wide, which is in contrast to the Slezer representation, which shows three. There is some structural complexity in this area even at the Balmakellie period. This led to an early hypothesis that the east gable wall had been reduced by a bay since Slezer's time. An apparent vertical construction break exists slightly offset to the west along this section of façade that corresponds to an internal narrowing of the wall by about 0.3m to the west of the break. Superficially it would appear that the masonry to the east of the break is the earlier fabric, or was alternatively thought to reflect episodes within one building programme. However, the lower walling to the east contains two apparently anomalous features. The first are the lintel and west jamb of a small opening close to the north-east corner quoining of the range between *Lower Ground* and *Upper Ground* floor levels. The east jamb

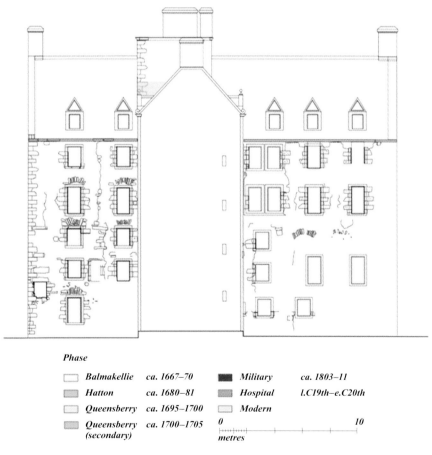

Phase

☐ *Balmakellie*	*ca. 1667–70*	■ *Military*	*ca. 1803–11*
▨ *Hatton*	*ca. 1680–81*	▨ *Hospital*	*l.C19th–e.C20th*
☐ *Queensberry*	*ca. 1695–1700*	☐ *Modern*	
▨ *Queensberry* (secondary)	*ca. 1700–1705*		

0   10
metres

Figure 8.4
North exterior elevation of the Balmakellie phase

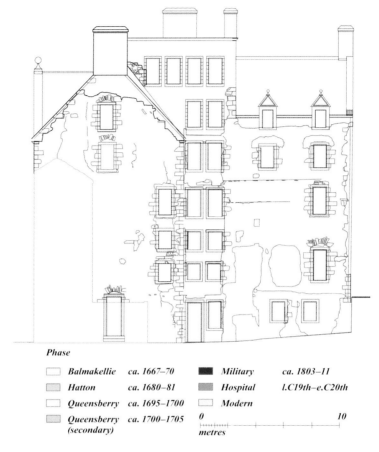

Phase

☐	*Balmakellie*	*ca. 1667–70*	■ *Military* *ca. 1803–11*
☐	*Hatton*	*ca. 1680–81*	■ *Hospital* *l.C19th–e.C20th*
☐	*Queensberry*	*ca. 1695–1700*	☐ *Modern*
☐	*Queensberry (secondary)*	*ca. 1700–1705*	

0   10
metres

Figure 8.5
East exterior elevation of the Balmakellie phase, including the east elevation of the jamb

of the feature appears to have been broken away. The second feature is a small centrally placed *Upper Ground* floor level opening that appears to bear little relation to the windows on either side and whose function is unclear. These features and the extensive presence of reused building materials in this area, particularly brick and pantile that occur nowhere else, suggest that this area of walling may in fact incorporate a fragment of an earlier building. Alternatively, it is perhaps possible that the opening at the north-east corner represents an outlet for a substantial kitchen fireplace that lies within the basement room close to this point (it was not possible to examine the interior of the fireplace).

East gable wall (fig 8.5)

The broad east gable wall contained relatively few openings, all subsequently blocked. At *Lower Ground* floor level there was a centrally placed entrance but no fenestration. At *Upper Ground* and *First* floor levels

windows existed towards the north-east corner, including an *Upper Ground* floor level mezzanine window. At *Second* floor and *Attic* levels single large windows were centrally located. Internal entrances associated with the subsequent addition of a closet tower to the south-east have removed any evidence for possible windows at that point if any had existed.

West gable wall (fig 8.6)

The former west gable wall of the principal range is now overlain by the later west wing. A number of features were preserved internally. At *Lower Ground* floor level there was a window towards the north-west corner, at *Upper Ground* floor level there were large windows towards each corner, while at *First* and *Second* floor levels there were large, centrally placed windows that mirrored those to the east. At *First* floor level the remains of a small window existed at the south-west corner. The area of the north-west corner was heavily impacted by later slappings at *First* floor level and above and no evidence survived for earlier windows in this area.

8.6.4 Exterior detail – east jamb

West elevation and principal entrance (fig 8.6)

The western elevation of the east jamb facing the entrance court contains windows arranged in four bays. The three northern bays are equally spaced and that to the south at a slightly greater distance. At *Lower Ground* floor level, now for the most part buried below the raised courtyard, but visible internally, there had been three small cellar windows and beyond these to the south, the principal street entrance to the mansion. The remains of the street entrance survived within the existing vaulted cellar beneath the later porch. Following plaster removal, the clawed-back outline of a substantial bolection-moulded entrance surround

was revealed. It was not possible to determine whether there had been an armorial panel set above because of the abutting vault structure above, but perhaps none was present, given the small space between the entrance-head and a window directly above. A small window was located close to the south jamb of the entrance and beyond this, at the angle, a small loop of quasi-defensive nature, commanding the entrance approach. At *Upper Ground* floor level the two central bays are occupied by substantial windows, while the outer bays contain much smaller upper and lower windows that relate to an internal mezzanine arrangement. Close to the north-west angle of the jamb were recorded three small, vertically aligned light openings that had served the back stair that occupied the angle.

The wall-head of the east jamb, being at a higher level than that of the principal range, supported a series of four dormer windows constructed directly upon the walling below. Of these, parts of the internal ingos and

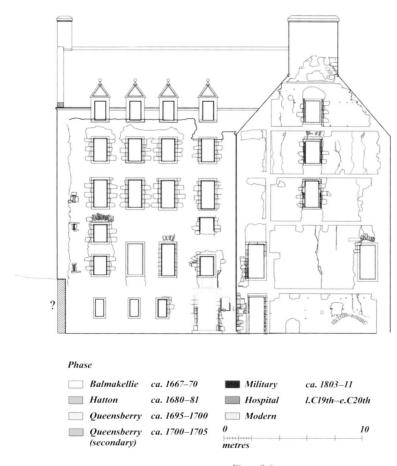

Phase

☐	*Balmakellie*	*ca. 1667–70*	■ *Military*	*ca. 1803–11*
▨	*Hatton*	*ca. 1680–81*	▨ *Hospital*	*l.C19th–e.C20th*
☐	*Queensberry*	*ca. 1695–1700*	☐ *Modern*	
▨	*Queensberry (secondary)*	*ca. 1700–1705*		

0   10
metres

Figure 8.6
West exterior elevation of the Balmakellie phase, including the west elevation of the jamb

the external cill stones remained *in situ* to demonstrate that this had been the case. These were omitted from the Slezer view although they were clearly part of the first phase of construction.

North gable

The original masonry of the north wall of the east jamb is now almost wholly obscured by a later refacing and it is only at the north-east corner that much-mutilated quoining was recorded. The line of the original gable wall can be seen internally and is set at a pronounced angle, the walling projecting considerably further to the north at its north-west corner. There is little indication from the scant surviving internal evidence for the presence of features such as windows within the wall. It is perhaps possible that this gable had had little or no fenestration as it is clear from documentary evidence that it faced directly onto the rear gable of a pre-existing frontage property. The existence of this adjacent property may well relate to the curious angle of the gable of the Balmakellie building. No part of the early gable-head survived the later reconstructions. From the evidence of both the opposite internal cross-wall and the Slezer engraving, the gable had clearly been steeply pitched; Slezer does not show a chimney, but evidence of fireplaces to the interior demonstrates that a chimney must have existed. Slezer also suggests the presence of a single small *Attic* level window, but none for lower floors.

East wall (fig 8.5)

The eastern wall of the east jamb had only limited fenestration and, hemmed-in by pre-existing adjacent properties, there was little requirement for a formally designed composition. Its most notable feature was paired windows at each level to the south, including diminutive mezzanine-level windows, close up to the re-entrant angle with the principal range. These provided the only light source at each level for the main stairwell within. There seems to have been a back entrance at *Lower Ground* floor level in this area, although it is now much mutilated by subsequent modifications. On the north side of this was a stairwell window and beyond that at least two cellar windows. At each level above there is an original window towards the north-east corner, including a dormer rising from the *Attic* level wall-head, but a central window only at *Second* floor and *Attic* levels (a further dormer). The cills of the dormers remain *in situ* and are of identical form to those on the west wall of the jamb.

The arrangement of fenestration here is perhaps related to the surrounding properties, notably the main part of Glen's property to the east. The fact that windows appear at the upper levels might suggest that Queensberry House was higher than its neighbour and that the windows would not have been overlooked by a close neighbour as they would have been lower down.

Within the general masonry of the east wall a number of horizontal construction breaks were recorded that clearly represented individual episodes within one programme of construction, suggesting that general walling in this area was constructed in 1.5m lifts.

8.7 Stylistic analysis: exterior

JOHN LOWREY

8.7.1 *The Canongate façade*

Although very little of the Great Lodging is now discernible, much of it still survives within the fabric of Queensberry House and has been elucidated by the archaeological investigation. It was clearly an important building in its own right, not simply because it formed the core of the later and more lavish dwellings of Lord Hatton and the Duke of Queensberry.

Stylistically, very little survives of the original house, but it is possible to piece together a picture of a house that combined both traditional and some rather advanced elements, and in that respect it can be related to trends in Scottish architecture of this period, in which history and tradition were extremely important and were increasingly combined with new elements. Some of what we know of the Balmakellie Lodging fits in well with other examples of major house building in town and country at this time. The projecting jamb created a re-entrant angle, which contained the entrance to the house. The remains of the great bolection-moulded doorcase still survive, with a small window alongside and a peephole or gunloop providing a pseudo-defensive *enfilade* from the main block. Certainly, all of these features were commonly found in Scottish houses both prior to this period and also in the later 17th century. For example, Acheson House, in Bakehouse Close further to the west, built in 1633, has a double gunloop on the entrance/ staircase tower. A link with the tradition of tower house architecture can also be seen in a comparison with Old Leckie, outside Stirling, dating from the 1570s, which has an arrangement even closer to that of the Balmakellie Lodging. Here, the re-entrant angle entrance is also overlooked by a peephole and has a very real gunloop alongside the door.

There are elements even of this entrance arrangement that are slightly more unusual, however. The entrance jamb is commonly found in many Scottish buildings, but is often associated with circulation and service, that is to say, it takes these important elements away from the main body of the house in order to allow the maximum space for the main rooms of the plan. Without going into the detail of the plan at this point, it is worth noting that the jamb of the Balmakellie Lodging seems always to have contained important accommodation. The gable that it presented to the Canongate was almost blank, with only very small windows on the right-hand side that lit a service stair. This may perhaps suggest that the building continued to be overlooked and hemmed in towards the street, but, on the other hand, the Slezer view (fig 8.1), as indicated above, certainly indicates that it was the dominant structure in the area. Relatively blank gables were fairly common even in country houses that were certainly not overlooked. The reasons for this were partly structural and related to the location of flues and, especially in the case of projecting jambs that contained rooms, partly related to the planning of the rooms. Local examples of this can be seen at Peffermill, from the 1630s, and Bruntsfield, from the beginning of the 17th century. The fact that the quoins of this gable appear to have been treated in a slightly more elaborate fashion than the others on the house, with a simple stone margin, might suggest that the gable was indeed visible, or at least partly visible, from the street, implying that it was not completely hemmed in on that side.

8.7.2 The garden façade

The garden façade has already been alluded to and here again a plain harled rubble façade was enlivened by two large, shaped gables rising well above the wall-head (fig 8.2). Leaving aside the implications of this for the plan, the form of these gables raises some interesting questions about the building and its role in Scottish architecture of this period.

The use of such gables became fairly common in Scotland in the 17th and early 18th centuries. The earliest recorded instance was by the Royal Master Mason, William Schaw, who built a house in Dunfermline with a 'Dutch' gable. The date of this is uncertain, although it may have been when he was working on the palace at Dunfermline for Queen Anne

of Denmark around 1590 and again in 1600. Certainly this building must pre-date his death in 1602 (Mylne 1893, 61–2; Howard 1992, 48, n36; Noad 1928, 109).

In general, the use of this feature in burgh architecture related to mercantile houses and to the front gable of the house, facing the street. In this way, the building could make an important statement of the owner's prestige and possibly also bore some connection to the source of the owner's wealth. Trade in 17th-century Scotland, especially on the east coast, tended to be over the North Sea, and the Dutch trade was so important that in 1681 the Committee of Trade referred to the mercantile links with Holland as 'the marrow of our trade' (Lowrey 1996, 33). The Netherlands was Scotland's biggest trading partner. Even so, the urban buildings that demonstrate this tend to be from a slightly later period, around 1700 or even slightly later (Dysart, Macdouall Place; Edinburgh, West Bow; Greenock, William Street are all from the early 18th century).

The shaped gable was found, however, at a much earlier date in lairds' houses, especially in the east of Scotland. Pitreavie, near Dunfermline, was built possibly as early as 1614 for the Wardlaw family (McKean 2001, 204)[5]. Sir Henry Wardlaw was the Queen's Chamberlain and remained in Scotland with Queen Anne when the court departed to London in 1603. He was later knighted and made Baron of Pitreavie in 1614. The house was built some time between then and his death in 1637. MacKechnie makes the connection between the Pitreavie gables and the curvilinear gable added to the James V tower at Holyrood (fig 5.3) c 1624 (MacKechnie 1993, 244, 246). The Holyrood gable certainly still existed in the 1660s when the Balmakellie Lodging was built and, although its form is different, it may have exerted some influence on it.

Pilrig House, Edinburgh (fig 8.7), built around 1638 for Gilbert Kirkwood, has an almost identical gable to Pitreavie (although RCAHMS 1951, 220, suggests it is later 17th-century). In both cases, the gable is on the garden side of the building. Pitreavie is almost centrally placed and Pilrig is central on that façade. Again, in each case, the gable marks an important area of the house, covering the dominant room of the principal floor. There are interesting differences between the two buildings, however. For, whereas Pilrig, whatever the date of the gable, was certainly reordered at the end of the century to make the garden façade look like a small classical mansion, with the gable replacing the pediment, Pitreavie's garden façade is much more

Figure 8.7
Pilrig House (© Crown copyright: RCAHMS)

readable in terms of its plan. The sequence is of three rooms of differing sizes, the two outer rooms with a single window and the middle, larger room with two. Another issue relevant to the use of the curved gable in Scotland is that they are nearly all combined with a chimney, as at Pitreavie and Pilrig. It is also true, certainly of the surviving gables, of the most lavish example of a house with this feature in Scotland: Prestonfield in Edinburgh. The estate of Priestfield (its original name) was purchased by the Edinburgh merchant Sir James Dick in 1676. The original house was burned to the ground in 1681 and the current house was built from 1686, apparently with the advice of Sir William Bruce (Forbes 1897, 40; Baird 1898, 92). Unfortunately, it is not certain to what extent the house replicates the original, although the idea that

Bruce would have designed such a building in 1687 seems unlikely. In this case, a basically U-plan house has very elaborate gables on the front and a trio of similar gables on the back of the house. In each case, they support a chimney.

Prestonfield is roughly contemporary with the earlier phases of Queensberry House, but the detailing of the two is completely different. The shaped gables on the back of the Balmakellie Lodging are really very modest compared with any of the examples discussed so far and especially Prestonfield. These other examples are useful for comparison, however, and they show a number of similarities as well as clear differences. The differences are firstly in form. All of the other examples discussed have elaborate, at least two-part, curves and terminate in chimneys. The Balmakellie examples do not support chimneys and instead rise to a triangular point. Their elaboration is the very simple one of a single concave moulding on either side of a two-bay extension of the wall-head. They are almost an elaborate and rather large form of wall-head dormer and in that respect they can be linked with burgh architecture of the same period, where sometimes fairly large gablets, occasionally of two stories, rise above the wall-head. Gladstone's Land, Edinburgh, is an example of this. However, they are also connected with the rural lairds' houses we have been discussing. As at Pitreavie and Pilrig, they are placed on the garden façade – away from the prying eyes of the street. They provide welcome relief on a façade that is eight bays long and four stories high, but they also help to articulate and order that façade. Unlike Pitreavie, the gables do not bracket an important space in the plan. Instead, their two bays each straddle two different rooms on the principal floor. Like Pitreavie, the façade is not symmetrical in the sense that the garden door divided it into five- and three-bay sections. However, in each case, the gables bring balance to the façade. In the Pitreavie case, they divide the façade into a one, two, one pattern. In the case of Balmakellie's house, the gables isolate two bays in the centre and one on either side. In this way the Balmakellie gables produce both variety and balance on an otherwise rather plain façade. Along with the armorial panel that appears to have been in the centre of the façade, they overcome the inevitable asymmetry caused by the insertion of the garden door (inevitable because the façade is an even number of bays in length).

8.8 The archaeological evidence – interior

TOM ADDYMAN

8.8.1 Structure

In common with the external walls, all other walls within the mansion were constructed of mortar–bonded rubblework. This had been neatly faced-up throughout, the coarse surface texture being the result of scraping the mortar flush with the edge of the trowel. In many areas, particularly on the upper levels, remains of wall plaster onto-the-hard were noted. By contrast, in the principal chambers and reception rooms it was apparent that the walls had been lined, most likely with wooden panelling. This was attested in many areas by the presence of wooden dooks, in many cases reused sections of moulded timber (many identified as oak as previously noted).

Most openings (entrances and windows) were detailed, with multiple wooden inner lintels, over which were relieving arches formed of rough sandstone slabs. Many entrances retained major parts of their dressed surrounds, although these were usually clawed-back. Some particularly well-preserved surrounds survive within the main stairwell. Most of these were detailed with 40mm chamfered arises and raised margins, up to which the interior wall plaster was taken. The masonry newel of the main staircase was similarly detailed. Some entrances were formed of tooled, squared blocks with no other detail; it is apparent that these must have been lined with woodwork. A number of entrances within the more utilitarian areas of the mansion, particularly the basement and the upper floors, were simply formed up with plastered jambs.

Fireplace surrounds in the Balmakellie phase seem to have been formed of sandstone, and varied considerably in size and richness of ornamentation in relation to the status of the room in which they were located. The majority had clearly been detailed with a robust bolection moulding, of which the silhouette occasionally survived. It is a great misfortune that every fireplace enriched in this fashion had had its moulding dressed off, primarily during the refurbishment works at the beginning of the 19th century. In the majority of cases fireplaces were formed of two large vertically set jamb stones and a lintel above. Instead of relieving arches over, most were provided with over-lintel stones, usually reused architectural fragments.

Floor structures were universally formed of close-set common joists of pine, many of which survived at *Upper Ground* and *First* floor levels. The joists were generally only lightly squared and many retained their wany edges and even bark. Although no roof structures survived *in situ*, it is probable, from the evidence of a number of reused sections of roofing timber, that the rafters and other timbers were of similar roughly squared character and species to the floor joists (fig 8.8).

Despite a very detailed survey and sampling exercise, very few examples of Balmakellie phase painted plaster surfaces survived. Those that did were generally whitewashed.

8.8.2 Layout of interior

The general plan form of the Balmakellie mansion was influenced by external factors. With existing buildings obscuring the Balmakellie plot to the north-east it was only to the north-west that there was space fronting

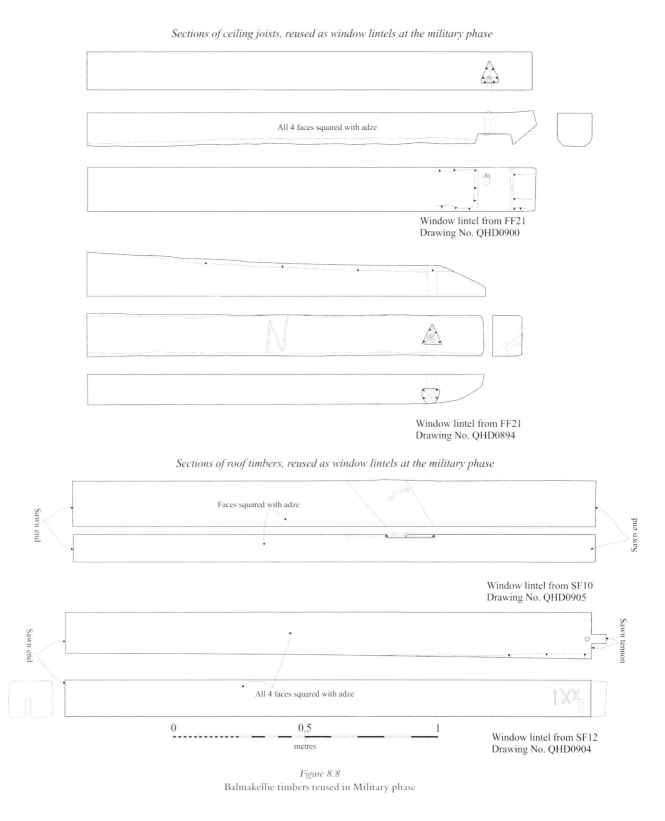

Sections of ceiling joists, reused as window lintels at the military phase

All 4 faces squared with adze

Window lintel from FF21
Drawing No. QHD0900

Window lintel from FF21
Drawing No. QHD0894

Sections of roof timbers, reused as window lintels at the military phase

Faces squared with adze

Sawn end

Sawn end

Window lintel from SF10
Drawing No. QHD0905

Sawn end

Sawn tennon

All 4 faces squared with adze

0   0.5   1
metres

Window lintel from SF12
Drawing No. QHD0904

Figure 8.8
Balmakellie timbers reused in Military phase

onto Canongate. The structure was further constrained to the north-east by the irregular outline of the adjacent property boundaries and the existence of a high, south-facing gabled wall immediately to the north of the site of the east jamb. The resulting T-plan of the Balmakellie building appears to be an intelligent use of the available space, closely infilling the irregular plot boundary to the north-east. It seems also to explain the apparent absence of windows in the north gable of the east jamb, the few on its east side, particularly lower down, and again the fact that there were few low down on the east gable of the principal range.

The west gable of the principal range must lie close to the west boundary of the Balmakellie phase plot (before being greatly extended in that direction by purchases by Lord Hatton in c 1679–80). This would suggest a street frontage of about 11m. Clearly there was a requirement for a more or less imposing frontage to the Canongate, the principal public approach to the structure, and maximum use was made of this available frontage area. A small entrance court was formed in the angle between the east jamb and the principal range, and the walls that fronted onto it contained a full complement of fenestration that was both visually impressive and maximised the available light.

It is clear that within the constraints of the Balmakellie plot the most advantageous aspect was the open ground sloping gently down to the south to the Cowgate. Beyond this lay the broad expanse of Holyrood Park and the dramatic scenery of Salisbury Crags. It was perhaps inevitable that the principal suite of reception rooms should take full advantage of both this vista and the south-facing aspect of the site. As a consequence the principal range was laid out across what must have been almost the entire width of the rear of the property.

The arrangement of interior space was governed by the requirements for a gracious state apartment that was laid out at *Upper Ground* floor level (the *piano nobile*) and effectively the remainder of the building was designed about this space. The superficially awkward location of the central stair, at the junction of the east jamb and the principal range, and extending into both, was in fact the most pragmatic location. Its central position permitted direct access to all parts of the building and considerable scope for internal service access and the formation of a network of closets that occupied awkward corners of the building once the principal chambers had been laid out.

The general disposition of space on the floors above and below the *piano nobile* was primarily governed by

the internal cross-walls that defined rooms of the state apartment, and by the walls surrounding the main stairwell. All other rooms represent permutations construed within this basic framework.

8.8.3 *Interior detail* – **Lower Ground** *floor (fig 8.9)*

The original entrance from the Canongate side, now buried by the infilling of the court at the Queensberry phase, was revealed within the present basement in the west re-entrant angle of the east jamb and main body. This had had a substantial moulded architrave, now cut back. The truncated remains of a threshold slab 0.8m above the present floor level suggests that there had been a short flight of steps up to the entrance. The entrance was flanked by a window on its south side beyond which there was a narrow corner 'loop'. Within the north rybat of the entrance there exists a well-formed drawbar cavity, 1.6m deep. The angle loop and drawbar behind what was in most probability a substantially constructed door must reflect a concern for a moderate degree of security that was in no way exceptional in the 17th century.

The lower chamber of the east jamb may have functioned in part as a cellar, as suggested by the three high, narrow windows to the west (presumably these had been barred). The remains of at least two more substantial windows with ingos extending to the floor were recorded to the east, although their dimensions were not recoverable because of later disturbance. The only other surviving early feature within this chamber are the remains of the lowest level of what had been a wooden turnpike stair countersunk into the walling of the north-west corner. This rose up to the closets behind a principal bedchamber on the floor above, and thence to the upper floors.

No evidence for internal subdivision survived within the cellar. However, given that the entrance to the cellar area and the larger windows are located to the east, it is likely that the cellar chambers proper lay to the west where the more secure smaller windows are located. The eastern area may therefore have been a passage that provided access to each cellar. The back stair to the north-west had therefore directly entered a cellar chamber; thus it is possible that the chamber was reserved for the storage of wine.

The basement level of the principal range was arranged into four basic subdivisions, each two bays wide and defined by internal north/south masonry cross-walls. The western chamber contained the kitchen, the floor level of which lay about 1m below

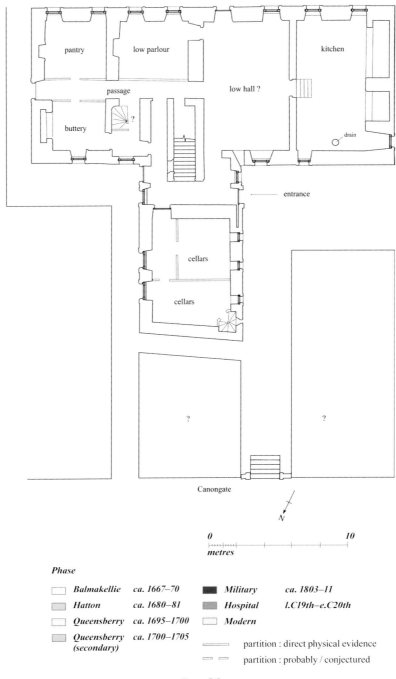

Figure 8.9
Plan of *Lower Ground* (original entrance) level of Balmakellie phase

that of the rest of the range. This chamber was lit by two windows to the south, one at the north end of the west wall and a fourth window at the east end of the north wall. The major features of the kitchen interior are a pair of substantial low arched fireplace recesses in the west wall, the southern arched opening being much the larger (at 2.1m and 3.5m wide respectively). The fireplaces were formed with low segmental arched heads and jambs of polished sandstone. These dressings are detailed with chamfered arrises and ruled out joints that provide an impression of greater regularity. Along the north side of the room an area of cobbled paving survived, in the centre of which was a large, circular slop sink that fed into a major stone-lined drain that ran southwards below floor level, between the two windows and out to the gardens. Archaeological trenching to the exterior revealed the substantial stone-lined drain at about 2.5m below the present exterior ground surface. The kitchen has a single original entrance in the centre of the east wall that can only have been accessed by a short flight of steps up.

The chamber beyond to the east is also two bays wide and the full depth of the principal range. This area was entered by means of a broad opening from the entrance vestibule to the north-east. While no evidence of internal partitions survived, it is possible that the north-west part of the room, to the north of the kitchen entrance, had formed an individual chamber. Certainly this was the case by the 1680s as demonstrated by a document relating to Lord Hatton's modifications to the building. The document also indicates that there had been a well within this space, a feature that had presumably existed previously. The north-west area was lit by a single window to the north, and if this had been central to the chamber, the small angle loop on the east would also have lain within its bounds.

The east wall contained two entrances, one at its south end with a surround of dressed stone facing to the west and the second in the centre of the wall. The first entrance leads into a well-lit chamber, to the east of two bays, that looks south over the gardens. This chamber contained a fireplace in the centre of its east wall and was the only major chamber to retain its plastered ceiling, in this case wholly unornamented. The second entrance had plastered jambs and no elaboration as it was the entrance to a service passage.

A service passage led eastwards from the central entrance in the east gable wall, running through the eastern half of the principal range along its central east/west axis to the east gable wall where there existed an entrance to the exterior. The passage linked through to the kitchen entrance to the west. As one moves along the passage from west to east, there is a small under-stair press immediately to the left (north), followed by a passage connecting to the stairwell itself. Beyond this is a broad entrance north into a small chamber lit by a single window in its north wall. This chamber was provided with entrances back to the stairwell to the north-west and north-east into the room occupying the north-east corner of the principal range. It is possible that this area, of no obviously apparent function, had contained a small timber-framed service stair of

turnpike form rising to a similar closet-like chamber on the floor above. In this respect a sequence of vertically-aligned dooks on the east wall may indicate the location of the stair partition on its north side.

The axial passage extended across the last two bays of the principal range as demonstrated by scars for former partition walls on either side. The chamber thus formed on the north side of the passage is lit by a single central window to the north and contains a very substantial, 1.95m-wide arched fireplace to the east. The fireplace is of identical general character to those in the kitchen and indicates a similarly utilitarian function, perhaps the bakery or buttery at this phase. The room to the south of the passage had a single small fireplace near the centre of its east wall and is lit by two garden-facing windows.

Stair

The main stairwell lies at the junction of the east jamb with the principal range and extends into both. It is rectangular on plan, measuring 6.75m north/south by 3.3m, and has a substantial masonry newel that rises through to the *Second* floor landing. The stairwell is well lit from the north-east by paired windows at each level. These are separated by a narrow pier, little more than a substantial mullion, and deeply splayed internally to admit maximum light. As the only light source for the stairwell, it was necessary to pierce the newel with paired openings at each level so as to admit borrowed light to its west side; the jambs of these were purposefully splayed. The ends of the newel are detailed with raised margins and chamfered corners, and the newel openings are also bordered with a raised margin. The stair rises in straight flights on the west side of the newel. The stair risers are detailed with projecting rounded treads that return below at either end. Each stair slab has a rounded underside that was plastered over.

8.8.4 *Interior detail* – Upper Ground *floor (fig 8.10)*

The *Upper Ground* floor level contained the principal apartments of the Balmakellie phase mansion and thus represents the *piano nobile*. The principal access to this area was from the head of the first flight of the main staircase where a broad entrance leads westwards into what must have been a low-ceilinged antechamber or lobby with a mezzanine chamber above. The antechamber occupied the third and fourth bays of the principal range from the west on its north side and must have been lit by a window in its north wall. Entrances within partition walls, now lost, must have led into the principal chambers to the west and south.

The principal rooms of the range ran along the south frontage, constituting a state apartment of four high-ceilinged rooms of considerable pretension. Each room corresponded to two bays of the south frontage, and the paired windows within each were of substantial proportions (although even these were subsequently raised). The rooms were arranged *enfilade*, their interconnecting entrances to the south permitting an unimpeded east/west view along the length of the range, a total distance of 24.1m. The function of each of these rooms is well understood from a series of early 18th-century inventories of the dukes of Queensberry, who, despite major modifications elsewhere, retained their original use and arrangement. The visitor perambulated the rooms from west to east and upon entering each room was first faced with the wall containing a central fireplace. The surviving evidence demonstrates that these rooms were arranged with a high degree of symmetry, with openings, whether windows, entrances or press doors, arranged opposite one another, usually towards the end of each wall, and fireplaces centrally located. Where direct evidence does not survive, these principles permit a reliable conjecture to be made as to the location of lost features in most cases.

To the west lay the state dining room, the largest of the group of four, measuring 9.2m by 6.0m. This was well lit by the paired windows to the south, by corresponding windows in the north wall and by two further windows at the north and south ends of the west wall. A substantial fireplace was centrally located in the west wall. Its surround, which is now much mutilated, seems to have been bolection-moulded in sandstone opposed to a planted fascia. The east wall of the room is now almost wholly lost with the exception of a north/south wall plate demonstrating the former

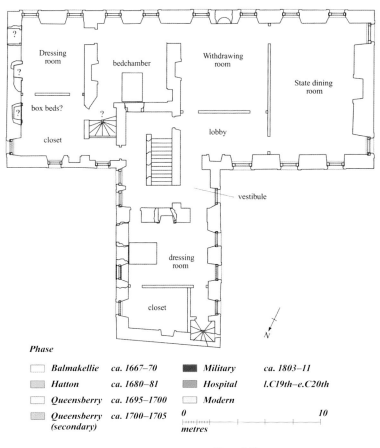

Figure 8.10
Plan of *Upper Ground* floor (*piano nobile*) level of Balmakellie phase.

presence of a studwork partition structure. This beam was inspected during demolition, revealing traces of adhering wall and ceiling plaster that preserved the impression of lost cornice work that had extended some 20cm onto the ceiling. The entrance from the antechamber must have been located close to the north-east corner of the room, symmetrically arranged with the entrance to the south-east and mirroring the location of the window openings in the west wall. The absence of wall plaster onto-the-hard on the masonry walls to the north, west and south indicates that the room had either been lined out and plastered onto lath or, much more likely in this context, panelled.

To the east of the state dining room lay the drawing or withdrawing room, a chamber square on plan (approximately 6.2m square). Lit from the south, this chamber had had a large fireplace in the centre of its east wall and clearly there had been an east/west partition wall to the north that may have contained entrances from the antechamber.

Proceeding eastwards the next chamber had been the state bedchamber, and beyond was the dressing room. Evidence for an east/west partition wall demonstrated that this chamber had measured 4.6m by 4.8m (north/south). There had been a fireplace in the centre of the east wall. Beyond, to the north, there had been a closet or closets with mezzanine rooms above. Both levels in this area were provided with low square windows in the centre of their north wall and at the north end of the east wall. The lower level was provided with a press at the west end of the north wall. In the west wall at each level there were two entrances. The northern of each of these connected through a further closet to the *Upper Ground* and *Mezzanine* levels of the main stairwell respectively. The southern entrance may have connected to a back stair down at the lower level.

The east jamb was accessed from the north side of the main stairwell. The area within was subdivided into a larger, two-bay, full-height chamber to the south and an arrangement of closets that incorporated a further *Mezzanine* level to the north. The main chamber seems to have functioned as a further grand bedchamber, for one of the inventories of the early 18th century refers to the space as the 'Old Duke's bedchamber' – that is, its function in the 1690s immediately before a major programme of extensions. There is no evidence to suggest that this function had changed since the original construction. The absence of structural features in the east wall would suggest that the bed had been centrally located on that side. Evidence survived to suggest that there had been a

fireplace in the centre of the south wall. The principal entry to the chamber had evidently been at the west end of the south wall, where a broad entrance led from a small low-ceilinged vestibule (there is a *Mezzanine* level chamber above) lit by a small window to the west. This vestibule connected through to the larger antechamber to the west of the stair-head previously described. The entrance from this into the vestibule was also broad.

There seem to have been paired closets to the north of the bedchamber in the east jamb, each presumably accessed by an entrance opposite those in the south wall. The substantial window at the north end of the east wall suggested that the closet to the north-east had been full height. There may have been a fireplace in the north gable wall to serve this chamber (as on the floors above). There is also evidence for a feature extending into the same wall at the north-east corner whose nature was not determined – perhaps a press or stool closet recess. The north/south partition separating the two closets was not located but may have been offset to the west as is the suggested case on the floor above. The closet to the north-east was lit by a low square window in the west wall and provided access to the back stair, a wooden turnpike arrangement partly countersunk into the walling of the north-west corner and lit by small stair lights to the west and, presumably, the north. This provided access to levels above and below, including a small *Mezzanine* level closet immediately above, the principal evidence for which is a low *Mezzanine* level window in the west wall.

Enough physical evidence survived, supported by historic documentation of varying quality, to permit an understanding of the access arrangements to both the east jamb apartment and the main state apartment. Following entry at *Lower Ground* floor level, one immediately took the single stair flight to the right up to the *Upper Ground* floor level then turned right again into the antechamber. From this one first entered the state dining room to the west where the most public of functions occurred. One could either exit by the same route or proceed through the first of the *enfilade* entrances along the south frontage to the withdrawing room. It is probable that the visitor then had the option of either leaving by an entrance into the antechamber to the north or proceeding through the state apartment to the east. The state bed presumably occupied the centre of the north wall and one faced this to the left as one entered the chamber. The entrances on either side permitted any visitor to exit to the north-west directly to the head of the stair down, or to permit the occupant or servants a discreet exit to the north-east. Alternatively, intimates might be permitted access to the innermost chamber at the east end of the state apartment, the dressing room. The visitor would have had to retrace their steps to effect an exit, while the occupant or servant could either retreat to the closet room to the north-east or to the back stairs or main stairwell via the room to the north-west.

The visitor would have approached the great bedchamber in the east jamb from the antechamber at the head of the stairs, north through the vestibule and beyond into the bedchamber proper, where one faced the foot of the bed to one's right. In the bedchamber the door to the south-east permitted household access to the main stair.

8.8.5 Interior detail – Mezzanine (fig 8.11)

TOM ADDYMAN

The Balmakellie phase mansion was designed with a sophisticated arrangement of *Mezzanine* level chambers, all of which were located within the upper part of the *Upper Ground* floor level. The main stair itself was constructed with a low *Mezzanine* stage. This permitted access to a chamber above the entrance antechamber, the north wall window of which overlooked the entrance area within the Canongate-facing court. The room also contained a small fireplace in the north wall. An entrance to the north-east led to a small subsidiary room above the vestibule into the east jamb. This room was lit by a low window to the west and contained a small fireplace at the north-east angle. It is suggested that this small apartment was occupied by a senior servant. The ability to monitor the main entrance may well have been part of the function of these rooms.

The *Mezzanine* level of the stair also permitted access into the series of closets to the east. This area was divided into at least three rooms, the first directly accessed from the stairwell and lit by a single low window to the north. This connected through to rooms at the north-east corner of the principal range, the first lit by a low window in the north wall and the second by a similar window at the north end of the east gable.

8.8.6 Interior detail – First floor (fig 8.12)

TOM ADDYMAN

At the *First* floor landing of the central stair a broad entrance opened into the rooms to the west. The internal arrangement of this area, the western half of the principal range, was not fully elucidated, although various features on its exterior walls suggested that there had been some subdivision. It is probable for instance that there had been a principal north/south partition that had bisected the area, lying most favourably in structural terms above the line of the framed wall between the state dining room and the withdrawing room on the floor below. It is difficult to see how the ceiling structures would have been supported if this had not been the case. This suggestion is further supported by the presence within the east and west walls of fireplaces that are not symmetrically opposed. It is probable that a single room occupied much of the south-west part of the space. A partition running eastwards from the over-wide north jamb of the central window within the west wall would render the fireplace on its south side central to the suggested chamber. With the central north/south partition the resulting space would be almost exactly 6.2m square. This would appear to be confirmed by the slight remains of a second original fireplace further north on the west wall; this in turn becomes symmetrically disposed within its own chamber. Accepting this combined evidence, the south-west chamber was lit by the two substantial south wall windows as well as the window already described to the north-west. The latter was balanced visually by a press or stool closet recess at the south-west corner. The smaller chamber to the north-west may also have been two bays wide, lit by windows in the north wall. It is possible that a further press existed at the north-west corner of the room, although all evidence in this area has now been lost.

The internal arrangement of the eastern part of the space is more problematic. A large fireplace exists in the centre of the east wall suggesting a single unified space, perhaps some form of gallery. However, the various windows and entrances in the three masonry walls to the north, east and south are not symmetrically arranged, although in design terms this factor appears to have been less of an issue further away from the principal apartments. To the north the fenestration is necessarily offset to the west so as to be clear of the adjoining east jamb. The outer jambs of either two windows or one very broad, and presumably mullioned, window still survive, but the detail within the intervening space is now lost. There also exists a narrow entrance at the north-east corner that provides access into the east jamb, and a further more substantial entrance at the south end of the east wall. The dressed

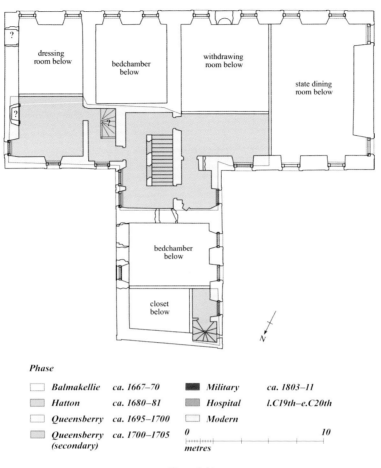

Phase

☐	*Balmakellie*	*ca. 1667–70*	■ *Military*	*ca. 1803–11*
▨	*Hatton*	*ca. 1680–81*	▨ *Hospital*	*l.C19th–e.C20th*
☐	*Queensberry*	*ca. 1695–1700*	☐ *Modern*	
▨	*Queensberry (secondary)*	*ca. 1700–1705*		

Figure 8.11
Plan of the *Mezzanine* level of the Balmakellie phase

surround of the latter faces west, suggesting that this had been the intended direction of approach.

The next room to the east was accessed at its south-west corner by the entrance just described. This room, defined by original masonry walls, retains a number of early features. A fireplace is located in the centre of the east wall and there is a press towards the north end of the opposite west wall. The chamber was also accessed by a door off the landing of the central stair to the north-west and there were further small service entrances on the north and east walls at the north-east corner. One led into a closet room to the north and the other, which was framed and lined with wood internally, through to the east. A further more substantial entrance exists at the south end of the east wall, its dressed surround facing west.

The easternmost two bays of the principal range seem most likely to have been subdivided into two rooms by an east/west studwork partition wall. The slightly larger southern room had a fireplace central to its east wall. It was lit by two large windows to the south, between which was located a narrow press. A service access entrance existed at the north-east corner of the room. The northern chamber was lit by a single window in the centre of its north wall and by a second window at the north end of its east wall. A fireplace may have existed to the south of this second window, although this area of walling was not exposed during the survey. The west wall of the room appears to have been a studwork partition, beyond which lies a small closet room lit by a single window to the north and with an entrance to the stairwell at the north end of the west wall. The north wall steps back by about 0.3m on the west side of the point where the suggested partition wall had met.

An entrance at the north-east corner of the stairwell opened into a substantial room within the east jamb. Partition scars demonstrated that there had been a

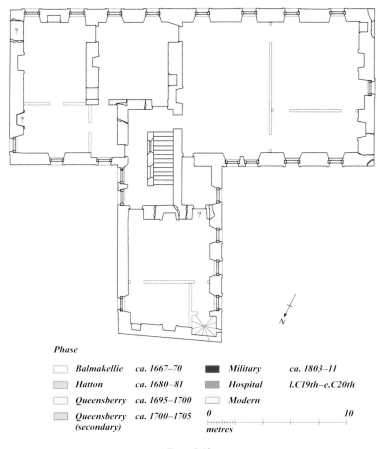

Phase

☐	*Balmakellie*	*ca. 1667–70*	■ *Military*	*ca. 1803–11*
▦	*Hatton*	*ca. 1680–81*	▨ *Hospital*	*l.C19th–e.C20th*
☐	*Queensberry*	*ca. 1695–1700*	☐ *Modern*	
▨	*Queensberry* *(secondary)*	*ca. 1700–1705*		

0   10

metres

Figure 8.12
First floor plan of Balmakellie phase

principal chamber to the south (6m by 4.5m north/south) and closets to the north, closely reproducing the arrangement on the floor below (although no direct evidence for the presence of a north/south partition survived). The principal chamber was similarly lit by two large windows to the east and heated by a fireplace in the centre of the south wall. At the south-west corner the remains of an entrance into the small closet room to the south were exposed. The closet room was lit by a window to the west and had also been entered by a narrow entrance to the south-east; there was no indication that the room had had a fireplace. Within the area of the closets to the north of the main chamber, the remains of the back stair were traced at the north-east corner. Within the flooring to the north-west survived the only evidence for the framing of the stair, a north/south bridle beam supporting common joists on its east side. Other features for which evidence survived, despite major subsequent remodelling on the north wall, included the hearth

framing for a fireplace in the centre of the wall and a continuation of the east wall face into the thickness of the north gable – apparently a press or similar such feature. Large windows lit the closets to the east and west. It is suggested that the north-east closet had been the larger, perhaps a dressing room, encompassing the possible press, the east window and the fireplace, and that the partition had been offset to the west.

8.8.7 Interior detail – Second floor (fig 8.13)

TOM ADDYMAN

The planning of the *Second* floor closely reproduces that of the first. A broad entrance at the head of the *First–Second* floor flight of the main stair, which itself terminated at this level, leads into the western half of the principal range. The former rooms within the western part of this area have features – fireplaces, presses, etc – that are identical to those on the floor below and a similar arrangement is proposed, namely a larger room to the south-west with a smaller one to the north-west. The eastern half of the space may itself have been subdivided. In contrast to the evidence on the floor below, the slight remains of a fireplace within the east wall are well offset to the south and not centrally located. The room had probably been two bays wide, lit by the windows in the south wall, and had been enclosed to the north by a partition wall. It is not clear whether the space to the north had been further subdivided. A small fireplace at the east end of the north wall could perhaps suggest this. Further to the west similar evidence for fenestration survived to that on the floor below, namely outer jambs that could indicate one broad window or two closely set smaller windows.

In the centre of the east wall, just to the south of the presumed partition, exists a broad entrance into the room to the east, its jambs formed not of dressed stone but plastered. A second entrance led through to the east at the south end of the same wall, in this case provided with a dressed surround facing to the west.

The chamber beyond to the east is roughly square and contains an original fireplace in the centre of its east wall, two large windows to the south and an entrance with dressed west-facing surround at the south end of the east wall. The room also contains what appear to be broad service access entrances at the north end of the west and east walls (the west entrance has been described above). Why it was necessary to make these so broad was not determined, although the arrangement suggests an east/west service passage. However, no direct evidence for a partition wall was revealed and, if one had existed, the fireplace to the east would not have been centrally situated. The purpose of this arrangement was not resolved. At the west end of the north wall there is an entrance from the stairwell landing. The entrance to the south-east leads to the easternmost rooms of the principal range.

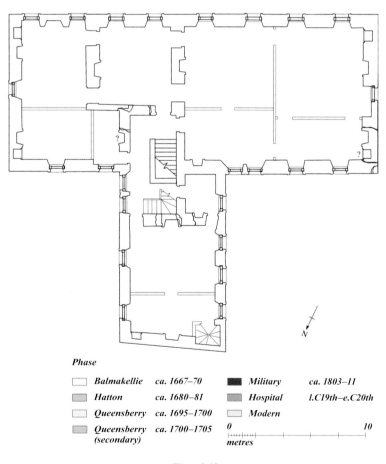

Phase

☐ *Balmakellie*	*ca. 1667–70*	■ *Military*	*ca. 1803–11*
▨ *Hatton*	*ca. 1680–81*	▨ *Hospital*	*l.C19th–e.C20th*
☐ *Queensberry*	*ca. 1695–1700*	☐ *Modern*	
▨ *Queensberry (secondary)*	*ca. 1700–1705*		

0   10

metres

Figure 8.13
Second floor plan of Balmakellie phase

The final two bays of the principal range to the east had apparently been subdivided in a similar fashion to that suggested for the corresponding rooms immediately below, namely an east/west partition wall dividing the space into a larger southern chamber and a smaller room to the north. While no actual scars of the wall itself survived, the fact that the east wall contains two original fireplaces would suggest this to have been the case. The southern chamber thus formed contains a fireplace offset to the south of its east wall; to the north of this is a large window that is central to the east gable wall. It is possible that an east/west passage, if it had existed, had also extended into this area, and had been lit by the large window. If a second east/west partition wall had existed, forming the south side of the passage, the fireplace in the southern chamber would have been located centrally within its east wall. The southern chamber also contained two presses or recesses, one to the south-east and one between the two windows in its south wall.

The chamber to the north of the suggested passage contains a fireplace in its east wall and to the north of this a press. The space was lit by a single window to the north. The east wall of the northern chamber may have been formed by a further partition wall and, as on the floor below, the north wall steps back by about 0.3m at this point. The only surviving features of the small closet-like room thus formed beyond to the west are a single window in the north wall and an entrance from the stairwell landing to the north-west.

At the north-east corner of the stairwell there is an entrance with a dressed surround facing into the stairwell, which leads into the east jamb. As on the floors below, the space within the east jamb appears to have been subdivided, forming a large rectangular southern chamber and a smaller northern space. The southern chamber was two bays wide, lit by two west wall windows and a further single window to the east on the centre line of the chamber. A fireplace had existed in the centre of the south wall, balancing the

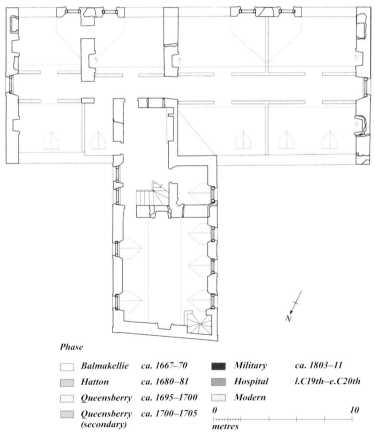

Phase

☐	*Balmakellie* ca. 1667–70	◼	*Military* ca. 1803–11
▨	*Hatton* ca. 1680–81	▨	*Hospital* l.C19th–e.C20th
☐	*Queensberry* ca. 1695–1700	☐	*Modern*
▨	*Queensberry* ca. 1700–1705 (secondary)		

0   10
metres

Figure 8.14
Third (Attic) floor plan of Balmakellie phase

entrance to the south-east and the similar entrance to the south-west. The entrance to the south-west led into a small closet. This contains an eastern entrance from the stairwell landing and was lit by a large window to the west. There was also evidence to demonstrate that there had been a small fireplace in the centre of the north wall.

The northern end of the east jamb contained the upward continuation of the back stair. Evidence for hearth framing in the floor structure demonstrated that there had been a fireplace in the central part of the north wall. The northern room or rooms was lit by single windows in the east and west walls. No direct evidence for a north/south partition was located.

8.8.8 Interior detail – **Third** *floor – attic and roof structures (fig 8.14)*

TOM ADDYMAN

The great width of the principal range was spanned by one very substantial roof structure, although no direct evidence of its framing survived. The *Attic* level rooms were clearly coombed and most probably lit on the north pitch by small framed dormers rising from the pitch of the roof itself. This would appear to be confirmed by the Slezer engraving, which shows small dormer windows part-way up the north pitch of the roof – that is, not rising directly from the wall-head. This is further likely to have been the case because the eaves of the roof lay close to the floor level of the *Attic* level, rendering the construction of wall-head dormers awkward. Given the absence of tie beams, there must have been collar beams that in turn supported the flat ceiling areas of the *Attic* rooms, and some form of sole-piece/ashlar-piece assembly at the wall-head.

It was deduced that the principal access to the *Attic* level rooms had been by a wooden stair that rose up from within the northern 1.6m of the main stairwell. There was certainly no evidence for a further flight of stone steps up to the *Attic* level and the central newel terminated at *Second* floor level. The back stair at the north-west corner of the east jamb also extended up to the *Attic* level.

At the north end of the east wall of the chamber at the top of the main stair there exists evidence for a vertical continuation of the wall-head that had contained a pair of large windows, replicating the arrangement of stair windows on the floors below. Had this formed part of the 1680s period construction or was it as originally intended? If it was not the original arrangement, the chamber could only have been lit by dormer windows

in the same location. The principal feature of the chamber is a very substantial fireplace and associated chimney breast towards the south end of the west wall. Vertical jambs of tooled ashlar culminate at corbels that in turn supported a projecting lintel and the masonry of the chimney breast above. On the south side of the fireplace is a large aumbry. This is the only instance of such a feature within the Balmakellie mansion and suggests a very specific function for the space. Given that the primary access to the *Attic* level lies within this chamber and that there are three early entrances, this could hardly have been either a private chamber or general upper level reception room whose purpose was to view the prospect to the east. It is suggested that this had been a heated communal area for servants. Along the south side of the principal range it is probable that there had been four chambers, each lit by one of the two windows in each of the shaped gables that formerly rose above the wall-head of the south elevation. In the western half of the range this would again suggest, as on the floors below, that there had been a principal north/south partition wall bisecting the area. There are almost no surviving early features within the west gable wall and the internal cross-wall to the east to provide further evidence of the internal arrangement of the space. The only surviving feature to the west is the remains of a large central window. To the east the only feature is a passage-like entrance in the centre of the wall. Indeed, this may suggest that there had been a central axial east/west passage running to the west gable wall and lit by the window already described. Logically, the *Attic* rooms would then have been arranged in pairs on either side of the passage. The suggested passage may also have continued to the east gable, where there is a window on the same axis, and an intervening entrance into the eastern parts of the loft space.

The space within the east jamb was lit by dormer windows rising from the east and west wall-heads, and two and three windows respectively. Of these the plastered ingos survive and, as already noted, their cill stones to the exterior. The cill stones lie about 0.85m below the top of the wall-head cornice. As on the floors below, there may have been an east/west partition wall that had formed a larger southern and smaller northern chamber. The south wall of the southern chamber contained a central fireplace and a second entrance to the south-west that led into a small closet room. The upper parts of the face of the south wall retained early lime wall plaster that preserved the silhouette of the plastered ceiling of the room, which in turn demonstrated the location of a collar beam.

Eight individual flues were recorded in the masonry above the apex of the south cross-wall.

8.9 The planning of the Balmakellie Lodging

JOHN LOWREY

The detail of how the plan functioned is more properly dealt with in the later Hatton and Queensberry phases of the house because there is documentary evidence that gives us an insight into the way it worked in those later periods. However, some general remarks on the planning of the Balmakellie phase are possible because the archaeology of the building has established the basic form of the plan and it is clear that the Balmakellie Lodging established the essential principles of the plan throughout the subsequent Hatton and Queensberry phases.

As in other aspects of the house, the Balmakellie Lodging had planning characteristics that linked it to the past but also contained modern elements. The entrance level of the house was also the functional basement of the house, with storage cellars, kitchens, etc. Although the detail of this is now uncertain, the general pattern was the norm in laird's houses and in urban dwellings at this time. Similarly, the disruption of the main floor levels by the insertion of a mezzanine in the eastern part of the house around the staircase links the house with the kind of vertical circulation patterns characteristic of the Scottish tower house tradition.

On the other hand, the most striking thing about the plan of the Balmakellie Lodging is its modernity, with the emphasis mainly on the horizontal and on the sequential. The principal floor, reached by the staircase just beyond the basement entrance, gave access via a lobby to a full state apartment of dining room, drawing room, bedchamber, dressing room and closet. Moreover, these rooms were arranged in the classic Baroque *enfilade* plan, with the doorways of the rooms aligned with one another on the south, garden side of the house (fig 8.10). This allowed a controlled and uninterrupted view from one end of the house to the other and also allowed views from each of those rooms over the formal gardens that would certainly have been intended on the south side. This was a pattern that grew increasingly common all across Europe from the mid-17th century, drawing its inspiration ultimately from royal planning (Baillie 1967). It was a system that was not only formal but also hierarchical and even absolutist, since, in theory at least, progress along the *enfilade* and admission to and reception in its various

rooms was related not only to the rank of a visitor but to the relative ranks of visitor and owner (Girouard 1978, 144). In a period when the nuances of rank and power were of great importance, this kind of planning was significant and even, in a certain sense, functional. By the 1660s, in the post-Restoration period, it was gaining ground in houses all over Britain. This was especially true of country houses but also of the great aristocratic townhouses that were being built in London in the years after 1660, most notably Clarendon House, by Sir Roger Pratt, in 1664–5.

The Balmakellie Lodging was not, of course, on the scale nor had it the grandeur of houses like these. Neither was it alone among Scottish houses in having an apartment plan. Such a development can be found as early as the 16th century, especially in royal planning and notably at Holyrood (see Chapter 5). As far as townhouses were concerned, the apartment was also the basis of the planning of Argyll's Lodging in Stirling from the 1630s, although the terminology and perhaps some of the functions were not developed until the 1670s (Fawcett 1996, 16). In the countryside, new houses like Panmure, built by George, second Earl of Panmure (brother of Henry Maule of Balmakellie) in the 1660s, adopted the apartment plan, and the state apartment and, as far as possible, the *enfilade*. The significance of the Balmakellie plan is not, therefore, that it was unique or that it was the first, but that it was very thoroughgoing in its application of these planning principles. The state apartment at Balmakellie has five rooms, six if the lobby at the top of the stairs is counted as an antechamber. That is considerably more elaborate than any other Scottish townhouse, and indeed most country houses, up to this date. All of the main rooms are arranged in *enfilade*, something which even Panmure does not manage. Moreover, this arrangement seems to have been carried on even into the two upper floors of the building, where, even though we do not know how they functioned at this time, the potential for further apartment planning was certainly present. The archaeological evidence suggests that, on the third level of the building, that is the floor above the state apartment (fig 8.11), a slight variation was introduced where the main public room, running the whole depth of the building, lay immediately to the west of the staircase and suggests that the plan did not work sequentially from west to east on this floor. The detail of how this might have worked is discussed below (where there is some evidence from the 1690s), but suffice it to say at this point that this room suggests a continuing connection with the Scottish practice of putting a gallery at the upper levels, and in a dominating position, of the house. This practice can also be seen at Panmure, already cited as an important contextual building for Balmakellie. It also provides a connection with Gallery House, in Angus, that will be discussed below.

The plan is not only concerned with formality and grandeur and, indeed, is probably more concerned with functionality and comfort. There is a great concern with the servicing of the main spaces of the house and with comfortable private accommodation. Thus, it has picked up on the combination of bedchamber and closet as the basic units of planning for personal accommodation. This is seen not only in the main body of the house but also in the projecting jamb which, at each level, appears to combine a main chamber with a closet beyond. In addition, there is an important element of vertical circulation towards the north and east end of the house (where most of the bedchambers were situated). In the jamb itself, there was a turnpike stair that ran the whole height of the building, connecting the closets with the basement. In the region of the main stair, the mezzanines provided the possibility of personal service, from a maid, footman or page, into the rooms of the state apartment on the floor below. Again, the archaeological evidence suggests a timber stair alongside the main stair running from basement to mezzanine, allowing discreet service in this most important part of the house. The insertion of the mezzanines might be seen as providing a link with a Scottish tradition of vertical and mural planning. However, the mezzanines in this building were well organised, on a single level and at a useful and appropriate point on the modern plan. In this way, it could be argued that they have more in common with modern planning practices, showing a concern with servicing the most important, private areas of the plan, and are thus part of a trend in sophisticated 17th-century planning that culminates in the mezzanines at Kinross House in Perthshire in the 1680s.

8.10 Balmakellie and Gallery House

JOHN LOWREY & TOM ADDYMAN

Although no direct archival evidence on the building of the Balmakellie Lodging has been traced, the archaeological investigation has noted a significant number of similarities with Gallery House in Angus (fig 8.15; Addyman 2001). So strong are these connections that it seems almost inconceivable that

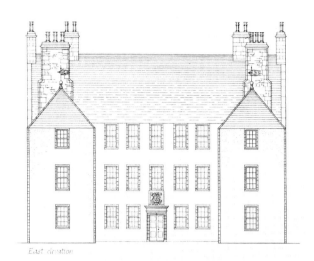

East elevation

Figure 8.15
Gallery House, Angus (© Crown copyright: RCAHMS)

they were not executed by the same hand, therefore the survival of important documents relating to Gallery House, including the original building contract, is of great significance for the Balmakellie Lodging (Dunbar & Davies 1981, 295–9). What this and other documentary evidence suggest is that there are a number of connections between the two buildings.

The Gallery contract, dated 30 April 1677, is between Sir John Falconer of Balmakellie, Master of His Majesty's Mint, and Thomas Wilkie, mason burgess of Edinburgh. Falconer had followed his father, the third son of Sir Alexander Falconer of Halkerston, into the Royal Mint (Douglas 1908, 248). The Balmakellie estate provides a clear link between him and Dame Margaret Douglas, and it may be that he acquired the Balmakellie lands after the death of her husband. If Gallery House was in this way connected with the first owner of the house in the Canongate, it also had a link to the second owner, Charles Maitland of Hatton, who, as Treasurer Depute was effectively Falconer's superior within the Treasury.

Thomas Wilkie was apprenticed to the Edinburgh mason, Thomas Corse (or Cross), in 1658 (Register of Apprentices 1906, 198). By 1667 he was a burgess of the city (Watson1929, 526) and by 1674 he was appearing on the leet for election as Deacon of the Masons (an honour that went to Robert Mylne), and was eventually elected to that position in 1679/80 (Wood 1950, 174, 377, 379, 380, 407) and again in 1681 (Wood & Armet 1954). By the late 1670s, Wilkie was a prosperous and important mason and building contractor and was able, according to the contract, to act as undertaker of the Gallery project, coordinating and no doubt financing work across several trades. Moreover, Wilkie was involved with Falconer at the Mint also, since he is recorded as working there from 1676 until 1682.

If, as the archaeological evidence suggests, the similarities between the two buildings are architecturally significant, it implies that Wilkie must have worked on the Edinburgh house around 1667 and later was awarded the job in Angus. This could have come about through his work at the Mint and his rising importance within the Edinburgh mason community. However, if he had worked on the Balmakellie Lodging, his later involvement at Gallery House might have come about partly through the connection between Falconer and Dame Margaret. This could have been through the direct connection of the Balmakellie estate and also, via her new husband, indirectly through Lord Hatton. Whatever the exact truth of the matter, Gallery House and Balmakellie 'Great Lodging' seem to be inextricably linked at a number of levels that cannot have been entirely coincidental.

8.11 Conclusion

JOHN LOWREY

The Balmakellie Lodging successfully combined a number of fairly traditional and some rather advanced elements. The T-plan house was very directly related to the grain of the townscape with the narrow gabled extension running towards the street and the more expansive oblong block in the backlands. In the 1670s, this was one of the largest townhouses in Edinburgh. Although it was still severely circumscribed by its neighbours, the Balmakellie Lodging marks a real attempt to create a spacious urban *hôtel*, free-standing between court and garden. Stylistically little survives, but we are able to piece together a picture of a house that in its detailing looked much like others being built in town and country at this time: the great bolection-moulded doorcase, the protective gunloop by the door, the simple moulded margins at quoins and the pedimented dormer-heads (inferred) were all fairly typical details. Add to that, features such as the extensive use of mezzanines, and a picture emerges of a building that is drawing on a long tradition of Scottish architecture. There are also some fairly unusual features. The paired curvilinear gables on the back of the house link the Balmakellie Lodging

with a growing interest in such features in the 17th and early 18th century in Scotland, perhaps deriving ultimately from the influence of the Netherlands on Scottish architecture. However, these gables are of interest not just because of their shape but also because of their form. They are effectively large, double wall-head dormers and are the kind of detail, with curvilinear, straight or crow-stepped gables, that were being seen increasingly in Scottish urban architecture, often in mercantile buildings, such as Gladstone's Land in Edinburgh. Less obvious but even more curious is the detail of the planning of the east jamb of the building that contains a turnpike service stair connecting a series of apartments for the entire height of the building, but which connects those spaces not to a footman's room but to a storage cellar. Again, merchants' houses (and Gladstone's Land) come to mind here. Thus the Balmakellie Lodging is closely related to developments in urban architecture, but in its scale and overall plan form it is closer to country house architecture. Of particular interest in this connection is the way in which this house displays at a relatively early date modern country house planning practices. The archaeological evidence strongly suggests that the *enfilade* apartment plan that came to characterise the later development of this house was established in the late 1660s in Dame Margaret's building programme. This would link the house with the most recent developments in Scottish country house planning and with the modern, Parisian urban *hôtel*. In this context, even features like the mezzanine rooms take on an added significance and can be seen not as survivals of a tower house architecture but rather as elements in modern planning, concerned not only with formality but also with discreet service.

Notes

1 Lauderdale Papers, NRA(S)832/25/4, 'Tack betwixt Gogar and his Lady and the Countess of Erroll of the Great Lodging in Canongate for three years after Whit 1677 for 700 merks yearly', 28/11 and 6/12/1676.
2 As 1 above.
3 NLS, Ms. Adv. 6.1.14.f12. Drawing by John Adair for Sibbald's *Scotia Illustrata* project. Prepared from a drawing by the Countess of Erroll.
4 The complaints by the Bowies against the Glens that talk about this structure are at ECA, Acts of Bailies of Canongate, 1623–52, vol. 2, 41, 5 March 1642 (available in transcript book in Search Room) and Acts of Bailies of Canongate, 1623–52, vol. 2, 41, 9 June 1642.
5 However, Howard (1995, 65) dates the building to the 1630s.

Chapter 9

Hatton House

TOM ADDYMAN and JOHN LOWREY

9.1 Charles Maitland of Hatton

JOHN LOWREY

After the death of her husband, Dame Margaret Douglas was clearly wealthy enough to build a new house in one of the most prestigious parts of the city, in which to bring up her young daughter. Ultimately, after her remarriage, the house became a source of rental income and by the time she sold it in the late 1670s the lower Canongate was enjoying a prestige akin to that of the pre-1603 period. For a rising politician like Charles Maitland, it was a highly desirable address. Moreover, for Lord Hatton, Holyrood Palace was not merely a symbolic seat of power, it was the actual seat of the political power of his family. Since 1661, his brother, John Maitland, first Duke of Lauderdale, had been Charles II's main instrument of policy in Scotland.[1] As Secretary of State 1661–80, Lord High Commissioner to the Scots Parliament 1669–74 and 1678, and President of the Privy Council from 1671, he was virtually Governor of Scotland, acting on behalf of the king and residing at Holyrood Palace in some style, especially after Bruce's rebuilding work (MacIvor & Peterson 1984).[2] As Lauderdale rose, so too did his brother:

> he was, beyond his own merits, influential in Scottish affairs, and both by his own conduct as well as on account of the Government, aroused the enmity of all classes (Douglas 1908, 307).

He had a strong interest in architecture. As Treasurer Depute he was involved in the management of the Holyrood rebuilding, including the design changes that saw the old west quarter replaced by a new one in 1676. He was acknowledged as someone with knowledge and taste in architectural matters, certainly by his brother who sought his advice, along with that of Sir William Bruce, on the remodelling of the family seat at Thirlestane Castle (Dunbar 1975, 204–6). By that time, he had already substantially remodelled Hatton House at Ratho, acquired as a result of his marriage to the wealthy Elizabeth Lauder of Hatton. This rebuilding also involved extensive architectural gardens (terraces, pavilions, etc) which were well known in late 17th-century Scotland for their lavishness and elaboration. The work at Hatton seems to have been carried out around the late 1660s to the early 1670s. At this time he also owned Dudhope Castle in Dundee and again, apparently using the same workmen who had converted Thirlestane for his brother (ie the same workmen who were responsible for Holyrood Palace), he modernised the building in a luxurious fashion around the mid-1670s. This was a successful period for Hatton both politically and architecturally and it was at this time, in 1675, that he was given the prestigious honour of his own apartments at Holyrood Palace (evidently quite substantial because they included a kitchen).

As a significant member of the Scottish government, Hatton had both the resources and the political motivation to build a substantial dwelling at the foot of the Canongate. He had also, through his work at Ratho and Dudhope, considerable experience of house building and garden construction.

9.2 The acquisition of the site

TOM ADDYMAN & JOHN LOWREY

The history of the legal titles to the site of the house has been dealt with in Chapter 7, and these show the properties acquired by Hatton to make his own house. Some of this is worthy of a little further investigation because it draws a very interesting picture of how Hatton went about acquiring his property and possibly has implications for what he was able to do to the house. The most important acquisition was, of course, that owned by Dame Margaret Douglas of Balmakellie, which was disponed to Hatton on 22 December 1679.[3] However, Hatton had started buying up property around the house as early as February 1679, when he purchased a fore and back tenement from Robert Gray, who had only just acquired the property from his father's estate earlier the same month and, indeed, his sasine is dated on the same day, 26 February, as his disposition to Hatton.[4] This was a site that lay to the west of Balmakellie's but was not contiguous to it. The site that lay immediately to the west of the house belonged to Thomas Serjeant, an upholsterer, who was prevailed upon to sell after Hatton's acquisition of the house, in November 1680.[5] By this time, Hatton had already received a 'Jedge … for building and enlarging his lodging',[6] presumably from the Dean of Guild Court. Without reading too much into the title of a document that does not survive, it does seem to suggest a fairly substantial project involving an expansion of the house. The archaeological evidence has suggested, however, that this did not happen.

Beyond the 'Jedge' mentioned above, a further key historical document in the Lauderdale Papers was prepared for Lord Hatton, titled *Instructions for my hous in the Canongait with the Courts yrof etc* and dated 22 March 1681 (the individual items contained in the

Instructions are discussed below).[7] This provides the first detailed architectural information about the structure and the planning of its immediate surroundings. It outlines a series of instructions by Lord Hatton for the completion of works to the Balmakellie phase 'Great Lodging' that had already been ongoing since March of the previous year. Given that the works to the house were nearing completion only a year after they commenced, they could hardly have involved very major works of construction. Rather the impression given is of a comprehensive refurbishment of the earlier building and a few modest alterations. This appears to be supported by the study of the building fabric where there is little identifiable stratigraphic evidence for secondary intervention at this stage. It is

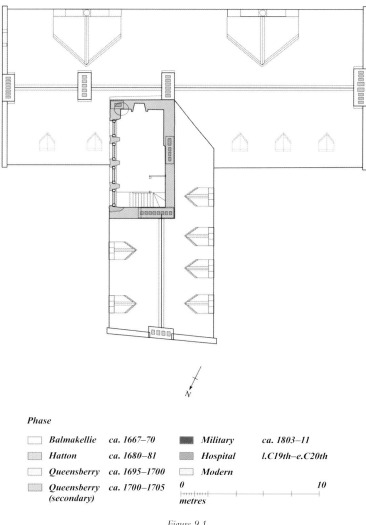

Phase

☐ *Balmakellie*   *ca. 1667–70*
▨ *Hatton*   *ca. 1680–81*
☐ *Queensberry*   *ca. 1695–1700*
▨ *Queensberry*   *ca. 1700–1705*
    (secondary)

■ *Military*   *ca. 1803–11*
▨ *Hospital*   *l.C19th–e.C20th*
☐ *Modern*

0   10
metres

Figure 9.1
Roof and belvedere upper level plan in the Hatton phase

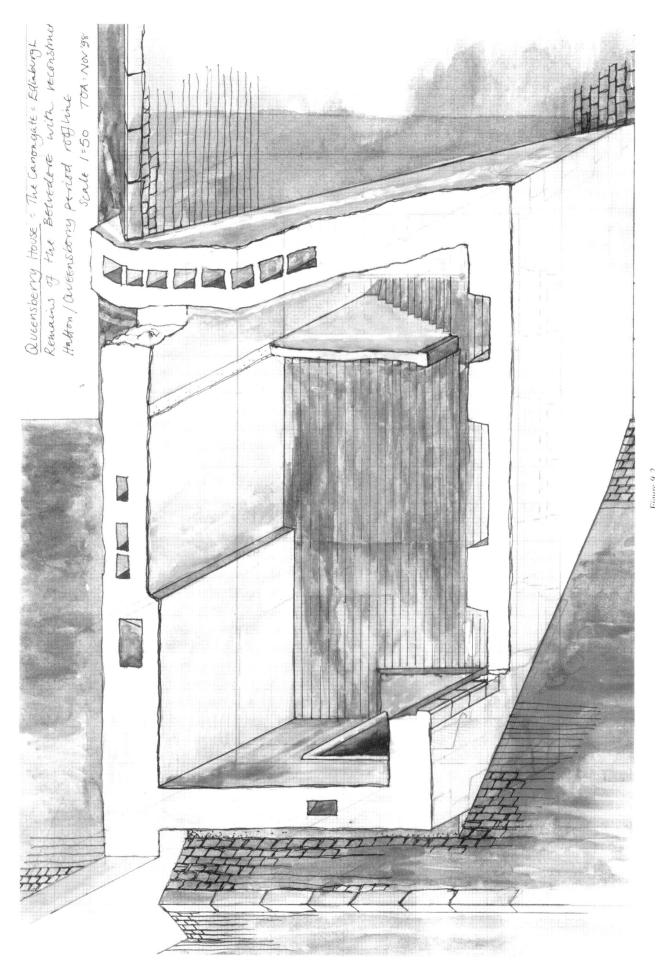

Queensberry House = The Canongate = Edinburgh
Remains of the Belvedere with reconstructed
Hatton / Queensberry period roofline
Scale 1:50   TOA: Nov '98

Figure 9.2

Perspective drawing of the surviving remains of the belvedere tower (floor level and stair reconstructed)

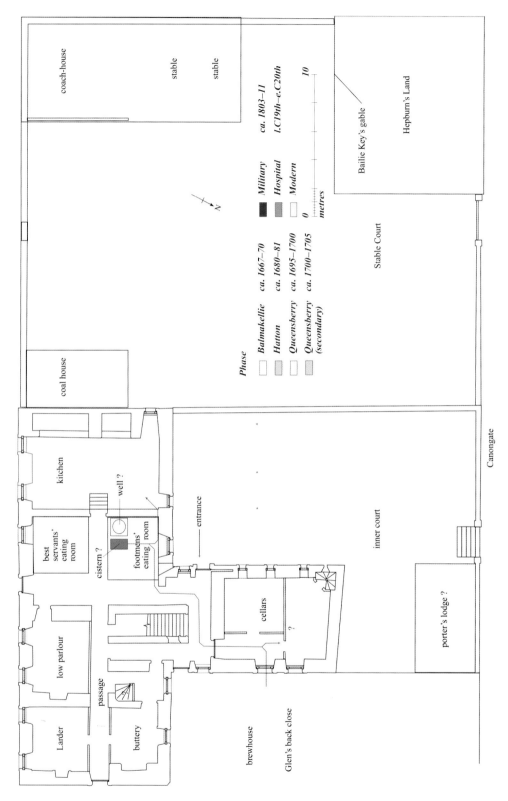

Figure 9.3
Lower Ground (original entrance) level plan, with surrounding courts in Hatton phase

possible that Hatton had originally intended a more complete rebuilding, but that time and circumstances were against this. It was November 1680, several months after work started on the house, before he acquired the Serjeant property and there was little possibility of major expansion of the fabric of the building itself.

What was possible, however, was the continuation of a trend started by Dame Margaret Douglas of creating space around the house and freeing it from the close embrace of its crowded neighbours. In the case of Hatton, part of this concern was related to the need to create much more service space, for courtyards, stables, and so on. Certainly the smaller parcels he seems to have purchased even after the work was well underway were probably necessary to create this service space. Thus, presumably at around the time work started in the spring of 1680, he purchased some 'backhouses' from George Glen, whose main property lay to the east of his but may still have encroached slightly to the north-east and towards the street.[8] This purchase, therefore, could either have been related to the creation of courtyard space towards the street or, perhaps more likely, freeing space on the east side of the house, which was overlooked by Glen's property. Another small group of purchases went through the following spring[9] and a further purchase involving two stables and a burnt land[10] was agreed as late as December 1681. These do not sound like properties on the street and it may have been that Hatton was consolidating court and garden space by this time.

9.3 The physical evidence and the belvedere tower

TOM ADDYMAN

If it were not for the surviving documentation, it would be very difficult to distinguish any Hatton phase alterations from the physical evidence. With individual exceptions, it would seem that the alterations of 1680–1 constituted remodellings of the existing interior spaces, and specific items refer to alterations to the interior wall linings, installation of panelling and interior painting.

One of the more significant finds during initial investigative works in 1998 was the truncated masonry remains of a prospect tower or belvedere that remarkably survived within the existing space below the early 19th-century (Military phase) roof structure above the east stairwell (figs 9.1 & 9.2).

The tower, which had been a vertical extension of the walls that define the Balmakellie phase stairwell, was thus asymmetrically placed to the east side of the east jamb, its east wall on the same plane as and contiguous with the exterior east wall of the jamb itself. Its principal aspect was thus to the east. Securely dated by Hatton's 1681 *Instructions*, this feature is one of the key elements in the architectural and cultural history of the building. Lord Hatton's *Instructions* clearly describe the progress of the tower's construction and some of its details:

> at the Roof the stonework of the platforme is finyshed, And it is set the timber that bears the load be laid on And that the lead be properly laid on, & then the two Roums beneth it with the Closet & the timber stair that is to be the passag to them must be maid & ended.

The 'platforme' indicates a flat roof structure that was to be leaded as specified. Further details and reconstructions are provided in section 9.4 below.

Exterior courts (fig 9.3)

Lord Hatton's *Instructions* also specify major works immediately to the north and west of his mansion. A new inner court was laid out to the north. Its specified dimensions, 72ft (22m) north/south by 60ft (18.3m), correlate well with the distance from the north wall of the principal range to the street frontage and the distance from the north-east corner of the east jamb to the line of the west gable wall of the principal range. This was designed with a 7ft (2.1m)-wide entrance fronting to the Canongate to the north and adjacent to which was a porter's lodge. The gateway was to be built by James Smith, with gate piers on either side to a suitable height. The court walls were to be no higher than the cills of the *Upper Ground* floor windows. Stairs ran down from the gate to the court surface, and this in turn sloped down by 2ft (0.6m) from north to south.

A stable court was laid out along the west side of the mansion and the west wall of the inner court. Its south side was bounded by the garden wall that ran westwards from the south-west corner of the mansion. The court had a broad, 9ft (2.74m) street frontage entry close-set against the boundary with the neighbouring property, Hepburn's Land, to the west. This entry was detailed with plain rybats and was open above; the gate within was to be double-leaved.

The stables and coach house occupied the south-west sector of the court, with entrances opening eastwards. The building measured 24ft (7.3m) wide by

73ft (22.2m) and ran northwards from the garden wall, with which it was contiguous. The north gable was apparently contiguous with that of Bailie Kay's gable (presumably his south gable wall), and the latter was to be reconstructed as part of the works. The building was to be one and a half stories including a loft above, and 15ft (4.6m) to the eaves. The coach house occupied the south end of the range, containing continuous doors to the east, measuring 24ft (7.3m) from the south-east corner. On the north side of this lay two stables. With the sloping ground of the court the floors between each subdivision dropped successively in increments of 1ft (0.3m).

A sewer is described passing under the south end of the coach-house, 'to convey the water both from the Inner Court and the Back Court'.

9.4 The layout of Hatton House

9.4.1 Lower Ground *floor – interior (fig 9.3)*

TOM ADDYMAN

The *Instructions* provide considerable information about the *Lower Ground* floor, some of which can be directly associated with the recorded building fabric:

> As to the ground Storie The roume beneath my waifs Closet is to be the buttrie and the roume beneath her dressing roume is to be the larder …

The buttery and larder are evidently the *Lower Ground* floor rooms at the north-east and south-east corners of the principal range, lying on either side of the axial passage. The former contains the substantial arched fireplace to the east, previously described:

> The roume beneath my waifs bedchamber is to be the low parlor, and to be paved with blackwhait marbles by Mr Ja: Smith and to be of the largest marbell that I got from Sir Wm Binnies.

The low parlour can only be the garden-facing room occupying the third and fourth bays from the east. No remains of a black and white marble floor had survived later remodelling. Elsewhere:

> all the rest off the ground Storie is to be paved with freestone, exsept the Kitchin which is to be calsayed in the same manner as the inner court off Holyroodhous is, the Kitchen being sunk 2 fit lower than the rest off the ground Storie is, having a sayver holl [?] or two to ward the garden which is alreadie maid in that South wall off the Kitchin on or two stone the gav Holl is to be on the

South Sid off the West bak off the gretest Chimby to pass thrugh the South sid off the Colhous & from that to the back Court.

This extract from the *Instructions* apparently describes a new sewer or drain that is to extend westwards from an existing north/south sewer then pass along the south side of the greater of the two kitchen fireplaces, through the west gable wall, along the south side of the coal house and thence into the back (stable) court. The north/south sewer was identified during archaeological investigations as were the remains of a *calsayed* or cobbled floor along the north side of the kitchen chamber (Chapter 3.7).

Following instructions for the removal of earth within the *Lower Ground* floor (that could be the residue of the flooring operations or excavation for a well), there are extensive modifications to be made to the large chamber immediately east of the kitchen:

> The passage that entereth the garden from the low storie on the South West sid thereof most be a roam for the best servants to eat in to be deveided with a plaster wall and on the North West Sid of that passage most be a roam for the footmen to eat in heir to the draw well and the passage to the well to be deveided from it by a timber partition.

This would appear to indicate that there was to be a passage running south to the garden entrance (identified archaeologically; Chapter 3.7) and that an eating room with plastered partition walls was to be created for the best servants in the south-west part of the remaining space. Within the north-west part of the space was to be a further eating room for the footmen. Details of the well-house and associated water system follow:

> And the well most be built with stone the hight of the stone pavement of that roam most be Contracted to be foursquer with a brest work of timber having a gallery & a pulley & Bukooks. The entrie to the well to draw water most be in that roume wher the footmenis to eat – The burkets most emtie in to a lead sisterne & to – have on peip to goe to the Kitchins to Cross the north wall of the foot mens roume & an other peip to goe to Glens batk Closs to serve the seller & the Brewhous & all these most be contrived conveniently [?] befor the pavement stone be laid …

In summary, there was a well-house entered from the new footmen's eating room. The well-head was to be 4ft (1.2m) square with a raised breastwork of timber and gallery for drawing the water by means of a pulley and buckets. The water was to be emptied into a lead cistern from which lead pipes ran out, one along the north wall of the footmen's room into the kitchen to the west, and a second below the floor paving through to the cellar (east jamb) and out to the brew-house situated at Glen's back close (between the east side of the east jamb and the property boundaries beyond).

Kitchen

It is possible that with the formation of the stable court beyond the west gable wall of the Balmakellie mansion at this stage, it was necessary to provide direct access to the exterior in this area. An entrance at this point was also required in the Queensberry phase scheme of extension of the later 1690s and it may alternatively date from that time. The entrance remained open thereafter. Within the kitchen the cill of the window at the north end of the west gable wall was broken away and formed into an entrance with the insertion of new dressings to match the existing below.

A well-preserved area of the cobbled kitchen floor – possibly the remains of the 'calsayed' one instructed by Hatton in 1681 – survived to the north, sealed below a raising of the floor level within what appears to be a passage of the Queensberry phase along the north side of the room (Chapter 3.7).

9.4.2 Upper Ground *floor* (piano nobile)

In March 1681 work was still ongoing within the *Upper Ground* floor level:

> As to the 2nd Storie it is all finyshed except the dining roume, and my roume and litel closet, As to the dining roume it being to be trew Wanescot it most have no ynlaid mullars upon the Edges of the panells, but most be off the same order of workmanship as the drawing roum is, bot if it be thought fit the doors & window shutters may have ynlaid mouldings or mullars …

It is clear from this that work had been undertaken elsewhere on the *Upper Ground* floor level. The works still to be completed in the dining room appear to be restricted to completion of the wall linings, specifically panelling. It also confirms that the drawing room had been panelled, at least by this stage. It is also possible that this activity had included the raising of the window-heads of the state apartment windows along the south frontage, if not part of the 1690s' alterations. Here there is direct evidence that the lintels were lifted by about 0.45m. It is probable that this operation also extended to the principal range windows at this level that fronted onto the entrance court.

In relation to 'my roume and litel closet', presumably the chambers within the east jamb, the *Instructions* continue:

> & I desayer my closet to be trew Wanscot & to be so finished as the dining roume is in the same order of work, with a press off 16 inshes deep on the partition wall nixt my dressing roume, according as I have instructed Alex, Isat …

While no physical evidence survives for this work, this reference appears to confirm the presence next to the bedchamber of both a dressing room and closet. As suggested for the previous phase, these most likely lay to the north-east and north-west respectively.

The *Instructions* also provide incidental information that confirms the function of the rooms at the east end of the state apartment where mention is made of 'my waifs Closet' [to the north-east], 'her dressing roume' [to the south-east] and 'my waifs bedchamber' [third and fourth bays from the east overlooking the garden], functions they subsequently retained.

9.4.3 First *and* Second *floors*

The *Instructions* state that [work to the] 'forth Storie is nier perfected: so is the 3d Storie' (counting from the *Lower Ground* floor). No physical evidence was identified that could be directly related to this work, which may simply have consisted of interior remodelling and minor modifications.

The house functioned with the already existing state apartment on the *Upper Ground* floor level, which was also the apartment of Lady Hatton. Lord Hatton's quarters were at the same level, in the east jamb.

9.4.4 *Belvedere tower – evidence (figs 9.1–9.8)*

Exterior

Externally the tower had measured 8.1m (north/south) by 4.55m. Its surviving remains, which still rise to varying degrees above the original level of the surrounding roofs, are constructed of mortared rubble masonry with sandstone dressings that include neatly tooled quoins that survive at the south-east, north-east and north-west corners, over which lime harl had apparently died out. Soot-encrusted remnants of harl still adhered to the north wall, too perished to determine the desired finish with certainty.

The mortar employed, the general character of construction and the details of the dressings are identical in character to that of the surrounding Balmakellie

Figure 9.4
The exterior south wall of the belvedere tower with three projecting corbels to support the roof of the principal range

pitch of this roof had extended along the side of the tower. Three corbels just below this line had apparently been intended to support the abutting roof structure. The subsequent truncation of these and the formation of new sockets suggest that the corbels had been badly positioned.

On the south wall three sub-stantial socketed corbels survive (fig 9.4). These were intended for a horizontal beam to support the abutting north pitch of the roof structure of the principal range. Where this roof met the south side of the tower, a valley was formed that served to take run-off from the flat roof of the tower itself. The valley drained to the east. A socket was cut into the quoins at the south-east corner of the tower to support part of the timber substructure of the valley itself.

mansion. It was not possible to define construction breaks between the pre-existing Balmakellie phase fabric and that of the tower.

On the east side towards the south-east corner survives the south jamb of a window, which is detailed externally with raised margin and chamfered arris. The truncated remains of its cill survived and the ingo within dropped to the former floor level. The window jamb was rebated internally for a frame. Evidence for the height of the lintel did not survive. However, a socket for a lost upper jamb stone suggested that the window had been at least 1.35m in height, but probably more; no evidence survived to demonstrate the width of the window.

The lower parts of the north wall incorporate a principal cross-wall of the Balmakellie building. The profile of the roof of the east jamb can still be seen in the form of an offset wall-head within the *Attic* level room immediately to the north. The Hatton tower may simply have been built off this wall-head.

To the west a lime mortar fillet indicates the point at which the west

At the south end of the east wall an offset sloping wall-head indicated the line of the north pitch of the roof of the principal range. A sloping lime mortar fillet at a considerably higher relative level above the offset suggested that the roofline swept upwards as it met the tower, thus ensuring that rainwater from the valley gutter was directed away from the tower itself. The

Figure 9.5
On the interior north wall of the tower, a silhouette survives of the tower stair

purpose of a second, vertical lime fillet just below the first remained unclear.

Interior

The *Instructions* describe, 'two Roums … with the Closet & timber stair that is to be the passag to them'. From the archaeological evidence and the deducible logic of the internal planning of the structure it is clear that that the two 'roums' refer to upper and lower chambers within the tower (each measuring 3.15m by 5.15m), that the stair was located against the north wall, and that the 'Closet' was the existing room located on west side of the lower tower chamber.

Figure 9.6
The interior south wall of the tower shows the remains of a fireplace and the outlines of shelving

Stair

Direct evidence for the tower stair survived in the form of a silhouette defined by the surrounding wall plaster on the north wall of the upper chamber. Here nine steps were evident, rising up in a flight from east to west (fig 9.5). The impression of the riser of the uppermost step near the north-west corner lay at a pronounced angle demonstrating that the stair had begun to turn anticlockwise around the angle of the north-west corner at that point. The underside was straight-edged, presumably representing the supporting beam.

A vertical scar defined by plaster towards the north end of the west wall demonstrated that there had been an east/west partition at that point. While this was initially thought to have formed a wall segregating the stair from the chamber to the south, it may simply represent a small vestibule at the head of the flight of steps rising from the *Third* floor. No evidence was found for a corresponding partition on the floor below, although wall plaster did not survive in this area.

The main stair of the Balmakellie–Hatton phase mansion only rose to *Second* floor level. It is thus most likely that a wooden stair rose from the *Second* floor at the north side of the stairwell to provide access to the lower tower chamber and *Third* floor level, followed by a second flight to the upper level of the tower. Indeed, the internal planning of the lower chamber permits little room for any other arrangement.

Upper chamber

The upper chamber of the belvedere was plastered internally, substantial areas surviving to the west, south and east. The interior also retains evidence for a number of features, the most significant of which are the remains of a fireplace central to the south wall (figs 9.1 & 9.6). This had had a bolection moulding, which had subsequently been clawed back. Wall plaster also preserved the outlines of shelving within each of the three surviving corners of the chamber. A trail of wax ran down the upper part of the west wall 1.45m from the south-west corner. This probably indicates the location of a sconce just above.

Evidence for the ceiling level of the upper floor of the tower did not survive, but the highest surviving wall-head to the north must have been very close at 58m OD. The floor level of the upper chamber was clearly defined by the edges of the surviving wall plaster on the west wall above and below. Later patching of this area suggested the presence of sockets for east/west joists. The south side of the ingo of the window to the south-east was also traceable down to this level, where it terminated.

Flues

The south, west and north wall-heads were found to contain flues. To the south a single flue served

Figure 9.7
Over-door painting at Dyrham Park showing Queensberry House on the far right (© National Trust)

the fireplace within the upper room of the tower; the flue sloped sharply towards the south-east corner. Four flues were in evidence to the west. The southernmost of these was larger than the others and had served the substantial fireplace within the lower tower chamber. The existence of this flue necessitated a thickening of the southern part of the west wall to form a chimney breast that projected into the chambers at both levels by some 0.15m.

The north wall contains a bank of eight narrow flues, offset to the west. These served fireplaces within the south wall of the principal chambers of the east

jamb at each level and their associated closets to the south-west.

It can thus be inferred that flue outlets, if not actual chimneys, had to exist central to the west wall, at the south-east corner and at the western end of the north wall. In terms of roofscape, the fact that the north wall flues were offset to the west would indicate an attempt to place them symmetrically in relation to the ridgeline of the roof of the east jamb, thus making a chimney at that point a probability. The flue to the south-east and possibly those to the west may simply have opened from the head of the parapet. In the reconstruction drawings, however, a chimney is represented to the west.

9.4.5 Representations of the belvedere tower

While the tower is not a feature of Slezer's view (fig 7.2), it does appear in two contemporary views: a painting at Dyrham Park, Gloucestershire, of c 1688–95, and in Thomas Sandby's 1746 panorama of Edinburgh (detail shown in fig 8.3).

Painting at Dyrham Park, Gloucestershire (after Slezer?), c 1688–95 (fig 9.7)

An over-door panel painting at Dyrham Park contains a polychrome oil painting that depicts Holyrood Palace and the lower part of the Canongate from the north. It lies above the entrance running south from the Cedar Staircase into the East Hall, within the eastern parts of the house that were built for Sir William Blythwait to the designs of William Talman between 1698 and 1702. Little is known about the provenance of the painting although it has been at Dyrham since the beginning of the 18th century, apparently mentioned in an inventory of c 1703.

A date of 1688–95 has been established for the drawing upon which the painting was based, which clearly represents the Hatton phase building on the extreme right of the painting, the only contemporary view that unequivocally illustrates the building at this stage. The detail in it appears to be topographically correct. The east and north sides of the Hatton building, including the belvedere tower, are clearly depicted, although shown in block form, without details such as fenestration. Thus the tower is depicted as a solid parapeted structure seen to rise to a level just above the main roofline.

It is probable that the painting was executed from an original monochrome drawing and painted remotely in a studio or on-site at Dyrham, not necessarily by anyone familiar with the actual scene. This is suggested by the colouring of the urban roofscape where, with the exception of Holyroodhouse, red is universally employed to indicate roofing material. A number of buildings so depicted could not have had such a roof, most notably the steeply pitched Queen Mary's bathhouse.

Thomas Sandby c 1746 (fig 8.3)

The Sandby panorama provides the most reliable contemporary illustration of the belvedere tower, which makes its appearance above the roof of the principal range as a plain, parapeted structure. Unfortunately its eastern side is obscured by a chimney in the foreground. A further chimney surmounts the

parapet at its north-west corner; there is no indication of further flue openings or chimneys on the west or south wall-heads. The parapet-head is depicted as very plain, the double line used perhaps suggesting a simple stone cope.

18th-century documentary sources

Later documentary sources from the Queensberry period make only the most tangential allusions to the tower, referring to it as the 'bartizan'. In 1729, an account by Thomas Wallace, smith, mentions work to the 'bartiesen door' (NRAS 1275/1556), while an estimate for roughcasting Queensberry House in 1758 includes, 'To 57 yards of the walls of the Bartizan' (NRAS 1275/ 479/A/13). Soot-encrusted remnants of harl still adhered to the north wall, too perished to determine the desired finish with certainty. This probably represents a later harl coat applied to the tower and perhaps relates to harl repairs carried out in 1758. It most probably replicates the original finish.

This definition of a bartizan is not consistent with modern usage, but appears to be standard terminology in the early/mid-18th century for any parapeted structure surmounting a tower (and had been in Scotland from at least the 16th century). Contemporary references in Stirling Burgh Records, for example, routinely use the term 'bartizan' when referring to the maintenance of the towers of the tolbooth and church.

Reconstruction of the design (figs 9.2 & 9.8)

There is enough physical and documentary evidence to reconstruct the design of the belvedere tower with some accuracy. From Hatton's description of the stonework of the platform, two rooms and stair beneath the leads, it would appear that the essential layout of these survives.

On the east exterior side it is suggested that the upper chamber had had four windows. The south jamb of the southernmost window survives. There is no reason to suppose that the paired stairwell windows were not simply reproduced in the same alignment for the upper tower chamber. The resulting spacing permits one further window between these and the surviving window remains to the south. No windows are possible to the west or south, nor does it seem likely that there were windows to the north.

The main questions that arise concern the height and treatment of the walls of the tower as they rose above the roof. It is very likely that Sandby's view and the 1758 document specifying '57yds of harling'

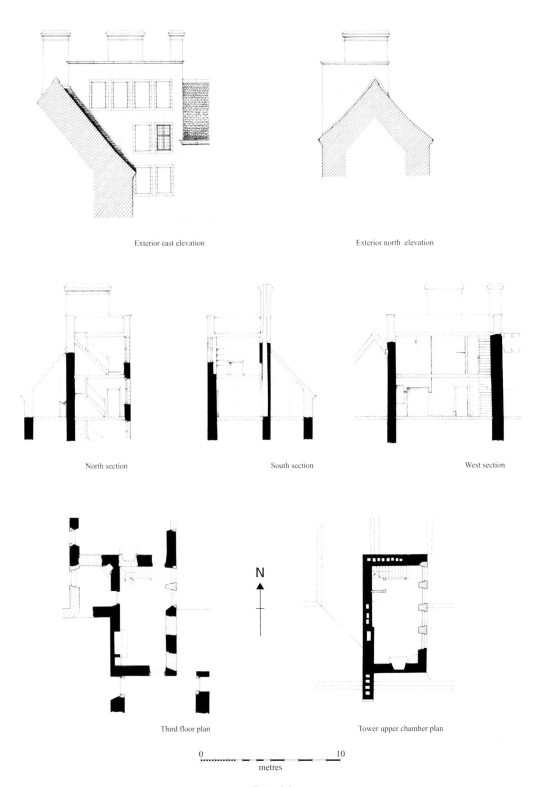

Exterior east elevation

Exterior north elevation

North section

South section

West section

N

Third floor plan

Tower upper chamber plan

0   10
metres

Figure 9.8
Reconstruction plans, sections and an elevation of the belvedere (surviving masonry in black)

to the walls are evidence enough for appearance and wall area. It seems entirely possible that the surviving fabric was reduced to just below the original joist level that supported the lead platform. The reconstruction assumes that the upper chamber was of a similar height to that known for the lower tower chamber. A reasonable parapet over this would bring the structure up to a level consistent with that depicted by Sandby, a reliable source for other details.

One problem, however, is the existence of flues in the wall-head of the tower. Sandby depicts a slightly uneven wall-head a mere 65 years after construction – could this suggest that it had been reduced by then? He only depicts a single flue on the north side of the tower. It is possible that the other flues had vented directly from the wall-head, especially if the tower platform was used only occasionally in summer when no fires were lit. Most notably, Sandby does not show a chimney on the west side. Certainly, if one had existed there, the symmetry of the roofline from the Canongate frontage would have had a notable disruption (a west chimney is shown in the reconstruction).

All the available evidence points to a very plain and simple treatment of the belvedere, with unornamented harled walls and parapet without balustrade. The flat lead terrace roof or 'platform' is attested by the documentary references, Sandby's view, and precedent. A simple hatch is suggested for roof access as there is no evidence (principally Sandby) for anything more elaborate.

The only ornamentation applied to the reconstruction consists of a simple moulded parapet cope and more heavily moulded chimney copes. These details are loosely based on other contemporary houses by James Smith (who is documented to have been employed by Hatton at Queensberry House). Sandby shows such chimney copes, while his uneven parapet head may actually depict the cope itself.

9.5 Analysis of Hatton House

JOHN LOWREY

9.5.1 Internal planning

Very little information survives about the building work at Hatton's new house. As far as accounts are concerned, only a precept for payment of £794 4s Scots survives. This was for, 'the price of 198 punshions [barrels] and ane load of sand at 8/- per punshion ... to my Lord Treasurer Deput's new building in the Canongate' between 21 August and 6 November 1680.[11] This confirms at least when the building work was carried out, but does little more than that.

The key document is the *Instructions for my hous in the Canongait . . .* of March 1681.[12] This, combined with the archaeological investigation, has provided the basis for the reconstruction of the plans and elevations of the house at this stage. With one notable addition, this house was substantially the same as that built and occupied by Dame Margaret Douglas, already discussed, although the *Instructions* document allows us to be a little more precise in discussing the plan during the Hatton phase of occupation and much of what is suggested here is also borne out by the fuller documentation of the Queensberry phases.

As far as the planning of the principal floor (fig 8.10) is concerned, the requirement here would have been for apartments for Hatton and his wife and, overlapping with that, a number of reception rooms. The pattern of the plan already existed and has already been discussed in relation to the earlier phase of the house. Almost certainly, this principal apartment, with the grand *enfilade* and rooms overlooking the gardens, would have been that of Lady Hatton, in her role as hostess, while the jamb towards the street would have been the apartment of Hatton himself. This broad division is borne out by the documentary evidence. In the *Instructions*, Hatton, in discussing the arrangements of the inner court, talks about the height of the wall being 'no higher than the selle of the window of my dressing roome which is on the second storey ...'. This locates his apartment reasonably precisely to the front of the building on the principal floor. It could really only have been in the jamb and it is difficult to imagine any other plan form that would square with this evidence. It follows, therefore, that his wife's apartment must have been on the garden side. This logical conclusion is also borne out in the same document in an admittedly somewhat ambiguous passage that describes the arrangements of the ground floor (that is the service floor) (fig 9.3) and links them to the grander rooms on the floor above:

> As to the ground storie the roome beneath my wife's closet is to be the buttrie and the roome beneath her dressing room is to be the larder, the room beneath my wife's bedchamber is to be the low parlour.

These arrangements can only be made to square with the east end of the house, meaning that the larger spaces of the west end made up the main rooms of the state apartment and, again, this is borne out by both the archaeology and the later Queensberry documentation.

There remain, however, two important questions regarding this proposed arrangement. Firstly, how does the state sequence work, given that the staircase arrives at principal floor level well away from the beginning of the sequence? Secondly, why are the arrangements for Lady Hatton's dressing room and closet so generous, with the dressing room being almost as large as the bedchamber and drawing room? The answers to these questions lie in the way the house functioned. It was necessary to combine the stately and the domestic, the public and the private, which of course is a fundamental aspect of 17th-century planning, but here it had to be carried out within a very tight space.

On arrival at the top of the stairs, the visitor was confronted by a blank wall. To the left, access was possible to the more private spaces of the apartment and to Lord Hatton's quarters in the jamb. To the right (fig 8.10) lay the formal route to the great dining room via a lobby or antechamber that looked out from the main block of the house over the main entrance and courtyard. The dining room is the first room in the state sequence and the rest of the plan unfolds along the *enfilade*. Although this relatively small house contained a full state apartment, it was equally important that it functioned easily and that service could be provided to all of the major spaces both in an ostentatious and ceremonial way and in a more discreet and private manner. The plan is very well adapted to achieve this in that it is arranged so that every major room can be separately serviced from the stair, lobby and passages around. Added to that were the service stairs and mezzanine rooms built into the house that greatly aided discreet service of the more private areas. The service stairs allowed servants to go quickly and invisibly directly to bedchambers or closets from basement or mezzanine. The mezzanine rooms themselves would undoubtedly have allowed personal servants to be on hand without encroaching on the privacy of Lord and Lady Hatton.

As to the issue of Lady Hatton's private apartments, the size of her dressing room and closet is perfectly compatible with the duality of her and her house's function, that is both public and private. Since the principal apartment was essentially a public apartment and no separate apartment was possible within the space available, it is reasonable to suggest that Lady Hatton enjoyed a more substantial suite of private rooms than might otherwise have been the case.

It is even possible that her dressing room actually contained a bed, as closets and dressing rooms sometimes did, and certainly did in this house in the later Queensberry phase. In this way, her apartment is both the culmination of the public house and also a private space equal to the space offered to her husband in the north jamb. In terms of French *hôtel* planning, which is not entirely irrelevant to an urban mansion house of this kind and was certainly an influence on royal and aristocratic architecture in Edinburgh at this time, this arrangement is rather like those plans which contain both a *chambre* and a *chambre à coucher*, the dressing room taking on the role of the latter, while the bedchamber retains a mainly ceremonial role. There is at least one other significant example of this type of planning in Scotland around this date, at Panmure House (discussed in Chapter 8). For our purposes, it is also important because not only the broad arrangements but also some of the detail of Hatton's plan persist in the expanded house built by the Duke of Queensberry.

Precise information about how the upper floors of the house were used is lacking, but, of course, the archaeological evidence for the Balmakellie phase holds good for the Hatton phase also. Most of the specific information in the *Instructions* relate to the service basement and have been incorporated into the *Lower Ground* floor plan (fig 8.9).

Furniture and furnishings cannot be analysed for either the Hatton or Balmakellie phase, although it seems clear that Lord Hatton's improvements included a general upgrading of the fixtures and fittings, and no doubt the furniture, of the house. The black and white marble floor of the garden parlour, the only grand room in the service basement, can be linked to the use of this material in other Scottish houses of the same period. Leslie House, Fife, which belonged to the Duke of Rothes', was supplied with the material from Holland in 1670 with the help of Sir William Bruce (Macaulay 1987, 3). Slezer's view of Thirlestane Castle, the main Lauderdale seat in Berwickshire, depicting the house after its improvements of the 1670s, also shows a chequered black and white pattern on the terrace at the main entrance to the house. Of course, Slezer's view shows a number of features that may have been intended but were never executed and this may well have been one of them (there is certainly no sign of the marble now), but it demonstrates a Maitland connection for such patterned floors.

The *Instructions* document also gives us the information that a number of rooms were panelled (quoted in Chapter 9.4.2). It suggests that all of the main rooms on the principal floor were panelled, although only Lord Hatton's own rooms and the dining and drawing rooms are mentioned. Alexander Eizatt was a wright closely associated with the royal works, having worked at Holyrood and at other projects involving Sir William Bruce. He is one of only two craftsmen mentioned in the document, the other being James Smith, at this stage also associated with the royal works and with Sir William Bruce as a master mason and sculptor. He was quickly to emerge as Bruce's replacement in the royal works, under the patronage of the Marquess of Queensberry (Colvin 1978, 755), as an architect in his own right and as the major figure in the subsequent development of Queensberry House.

9.5.2 The significance of the belvedere (figs 9.2, 9.8)

JOHN LOWREY

In his recasting of the Balmakellie house, the most obvious addition by Charles Maitland of Hatton was the viewing platform or belvedere rising just behind the east jamb. This was an important and, in the context of an urban house, an unusual feature whose significance lay partly in its juxtaposition with Holyrood Palace and in the ambition of Hatton himself.

Fitting out the relatively small townhouse in the Canongate was not a huge undertaking for Hatton and it is not very surprising, in that context and given his work elsewhere, that he should have sought to aggrandise it with the belvedere tower. By the 17th century these features were becoming increasingly important in Scottish houses. McKean (2001, 73–4) links both the viewing platform (as he terms it) and the gallery with a concern for the view:

> Early examples were usually at the top of the entrance tower – the one with the public stair in the ground storey. Adorned with the finest detail – balustrades, finials, parapets and carvings – the viewing platform was the climax of the design. From between five and seven stories up a laird and his guests could gaze down upon the yards, plantations and agricultural improvements.

Indeed, the positioning of the viewing platform at the top of the stair tower was not restricted to the early period (the 16th century in McKean's terms) and it certainly continued in that position up until the mid-17th century (for example, Auchans in Ayrshire, 1644). There are a number of examples of these types of structure in the Edinburgh area. Woolmet in Midlothian has a projecting stair tower with a balustraded lead flat on top. The same is true of Gogar Castle. It has already been suggested that Hatton's purchase of the house may have been facilitated through his proximity to Alexander Douglas of Gogar, who married the widow Balmakellie, and Hatton would certainly have known Gogar Castle. Winton is also a good example of this type and was in close proximity to Hatton's house in Edinburgh. Perhaps of added significance is that the Earl of Winton's townhouse lay almost opposite Hatton's on the Canongate.

In each of these cases, the 'belvedere' is on top of a projecting tower containing the staircase and usually has a single storey with a chamber, or in the case of Winton, two levels with chambers, immediately below the viewing level. However, that is not the case with Hatton's house. Here the single chamber floor and the platform appear to emerge from the roof of the house and do not form any part of a projecting tower. It does, however, relate to the main stair of the house, thus the positioning of Hatton's belvedere is clearly linked to a strong tradition of such features, but it is also conditioned by the substantial change in house design which has seen the stair become an integral part of the main fabric of the building, rather than a projecting appendage.

There is, of course, another example, which is unlike any of the others but provides quite a strong link with Hatton's Canongate lodging, and that is Hatton House near Ratho. The modernisation undertaken by Hatton involved wrapping a new building around the original and very ancient tower on the site. This tower effectively became the belvedere for Hatton's new house. It rose up above the new house and was especially dominant from the main front (which was lower than the garden front).

The belvedere at the Canongate Hatton House is therefore related to a strong theme of prospect found in Scottish houses throughout the 17th century. It encompasses both the tower, although within a modernised context of the internal stair, and the terrace, albeit the latter is in a somewhat vestigial form. Overall, it adds to the picture that is emerging of Hatton/Queensberry House as a building that draws together many themes from 17th-century architecture. Most of these belong properly to the country house, rather than the urban house, but the urban aspects of the building will also be explored in more depth in analysing Queensberry House itself.

9.6 The political significance of Hatton House

JOHN LOWREY

Proximity to the palace and to the ear of his brother was not the only motivation for Hatton's building work in the Canongate. From acquisition to completion the house took from 1679 until 1681 or possibly 1682. These dates coincide exactly with the return of royalty to Holyrood, with James, Duke of York, future monarch, coming north to influence affairs in Scotland directly. The prestige of the lower Canongate area had never been higher in the 17th century and a grand and imposing residence alongside the royal palace certainly betokened a person of great importance. If, however, Hatton's hope was for preferment, he was to be sadly disappointed. The arrival of the future James VII in Edinburgh, whatever else it achieved, actually indicated the end of the Lauderdale dominance of Scottish politics (Ouston 1982). The Duke's handling of the Covenanter issue in particular had been under close scrutiny and criticism and after the murder of Archbishop Sharp and subsequent battle of Bothwell Bridge, both in 1679, Lauderdale was forced into retirement, to be replaced by the Duke of Hamilton's party and the Duke of York himself, who became the King's Commissioner to Parliament. Hatton could not survive his powerful brother's fall from favour. In 1682, after the death of Lauderdale, Hatton succeeded to the earldom of Lauderdale and immediately found himself under investigation for his handling of the nation's financial affairs as Treasurer Depute. The discovery by the archaeologists working on Queensberry House that the kitchen was used for the smelting of mint-grade silver within Hatton's time suggests that, among his other shady practices, the Treasurer Depute was not averse to clipping the royal coinage (Chapter 3.7). The result was his removal from all offices and, in March 1683, his personal liability, along with his son and others from his office, for £72,000 sterling (Douglas 1908, 307). Although this was later commuted to something rather more manageable, Hatton was forced into serious debt.

It is against this political context that Hatton's Canongate house should be seen. Hatton seems to have been a very ambitious man, but, even as he started to build his new house, and certainly by the time he had finished it, his family's star was on the wane and he found himself struggling with heavy debts. The combination of these two factors lies behind his decision to sell the house in 1686 to William, first Duke of Queensberry.

All of this political background has significance for the building itself. In addition to the general symbolism of having the grandest house in the most prestigious part of the city, declaring wealth and political power, there is significance also in some of the specifics of the building. This is particularly true of the belvedere, which suggests that Hatton was well aware of the political significance of his house and made efforts to enhance it. Both the room in the tower and the platform above seem to have been oriented towards Holyrood Palace, the residence in Hatton's time of the future James VII. In the room, there are windows only on the east side and although at platform level views all around were of course possible, there were flues on the north, south and west sides, leaving only the east completely free and unencumbered. This favoured view, therefore, is directly towards Holyrood and looks straight into the inner court and at the centre of the royal apartment (although the actual room below the pediment was the dressing room rather than the state bedroom). This visual link to the royal power was also reciprocated. Holyrood also had lead platforms on the towers on the front and, since the tower of Hatton's house would have been most prominent when viewed from the east, because of the fall of the ground and the dominance of his house over those that surrounded it, it could not fail to have been the most prominent incident in the urban landscape. It could be argued, therefore, that Hatton was not only drawing attention to himself but was also emphasising a connection between his house and the king's, between his family and the royal power.

9.7 Conclusions

JOHN LOWREY

It is unfortunate that the March 1680 judgement is missing. This document would perhaps define the extent of the work to the Balmakellie mansion and possibly confirm James Smith, whose name is mentioned in connection with the continuing works in the *Instructions*, as its architect. The probable association of James Smith with the building in the early 1680s is significant given his later involvement in the major extensions he undertook for the second Duke of Queensberry in the mid/late 1690s. At the time of this initial programme of work Smith was at the beginning of his career. Having recently returned from Italy and worked under Sir William Bruce at Holyrood, he received his first important commission in 1680, significantly for the first Duke of Queensberry at Drumlanrig Castle. The work he carried out for Lord Hatton at the Canongate may well have been part of a larger commission, but, even if that is not the case, it certainly marks the beginning of a long association with the house.

Notes

1 Dukedom conferred in 1672 but not passed on to his successor Charles, who inherited the Lauderdale titles in 1682 as third Earl. (See Douglas 1908, 306–8.)

2 More generally, for a summary of Lauderdale, see Lynch 1991, 291–5. Lynch suggests a very direct link between the politics and architecture of this period, with the assertion that houses like Queensberry were built with the ill-gotten gains of political corruption.

3 Queensberry writs, NRA(S)1275/vol. 16, item 96.

4 Queensberry writs, NRA(S)1275/vol. 16, item 64. See also items 59–61.

5 Queensberry writs, NRA(S)1275/vol. 16, item 91.

6 NRA(S) 1275/Vol. 16, Folios ff.120v–124v: Inventory of writs c 1696, no. 105 (Drumlanrig Archive). Unfortunately, it has not been possible to locate this document.

7 'Instructions for my house in the Canongate with the costs thereof, etc' Lauderdale Papers, NRA(S) 832/61/68.

8 Queensberry writs, NRA(S) 1275/vol. 16, item 93.

9 Queensberry writs, NRA(S) 1275/vol. 16, items 77 and 98.

10 Queensberry writs, NRA(S) 1275/vol. 16, item 100.

11 Lauderdale Papers, NRA(S) 832/63/22.

12 Lauderdale Papers, NRA(S) 832/61/68.

Chapter 10

Queensberry House in the time of the first Duke

JOHN LOWREY

10.1 Introduction: the transfer to Queensberry

If Hatton had failed to impress the Duke of York during his sojourn in Edinburgh in the early 1680s, he was even further out of favour when the Duke became James VII and II in 1685. The combined consequences of political failure, allegations of corruption and crippling debt ultimately lay behind Lord Hatton's (now the Earl of Lauderdale) decision to sell the house in 1686 to William, first Duke of Queensberry. Queensberry had been closely associated with the Duke of York since 1682 and had been rewarded by his elevation to the ducal title in 1684 (Douglas 1910, 138). Although it would be a mistake to link the fate of the two men too directly, it is tempting to draw direct comparisons between the two occupants of the house. As the Lauderdale dukedom died with the first Duke in 1682, leaving Hatton to succeed to a mere earldom, William, Earl of Queensberry, was being elevated to a marquisate. In 1684, he was further ennobled with the dukedom of Queensberry. In political terms, Hatton was forced to give up his post in the Treasury and his place on the Privy Council, as Queensberry was elevated to both positions, although as Lord Treasurer rather than Treasurer Depute. However, according to one source, his purchase of Hatton's house in the Canongate was not an indication of his political success, but rather the opposite. Lord Fountainhall recorded that on 21 June 1686:

> By a letter from His majesty, Queenberrie is laid asyde from all his places and offices, as his place in the Treasurie, Privy Council, Session, etc., and desired not to goe out of toune till he cleared his accounts. So he bought Lauderdale's House in the Canongate (Wilson 1891, 106).

While there is little dispute about the timing of Queensberry's political demise,[1] the date of his acquisition of the house from Lauderdale is perhaps slightly more open to question. It is normally given as 1686, as is indicated in the Fountainhall quote, but some of the legal documents relating to the sale suggest that the transaction dragged on until 1688.[2] While there seems little reason to doubt the accuracy

of the secondary sources, especially Boog Watson, the record of the transaction in the Buccleuch Mss, which traces the whole history of the site from 1480 to 1688,[3] suggests a somewhat different timescale and also specifically states that the sale took place in 1688. This document records that the disposition was dated 19 July 1688 and ratified by the Countess of Lauderdale on 2 August 1688. The Instrument of Resignation quickly followed on 29 August, the charter was granted on 12 September and the Instrument of Sasine on 18 September. Even allowing for the time lag between a transaction going through and its official recording, this group of documents of roughly the same date strongly suggests a final handover of the property rather than a confirmatory process. There is no doubt that there was considerable activity stretching back at least as far as 1687. The same source in the Buccleuch Mss includes a Bond of Relief and Assignation by Lauderdale to Sir John Maitland and Sir Robert Milne of Barntoun of £20,000 'as the price of the lodging'.[4] Similarly, there are several references in the Lauderdale Papers to the financial arrangements of the sale, all of them prior to 1688.[5] Whether the date of purchase was 1686 or 1688, the political context was certainly Queensberry's fall from favour and there seems little reason to doubt Fountainhall's explanation of Queensberry's motive, although we may be a little doubtful that there was quite such a strong causal link between his loss of power and the command not to leave town, and his decision to buy a house.

However, from an architectural point of view, what is perhaps more important is that the subsequent alteration and expansion of the house is certainly unlikely to have been started prior to 1688, in other words, before the transaction was completely sealed. Queensberry's fall from favour arose from the fact that he was the victim of petty jealousies that surrounded the Stewart court and as a result lost the ear and confidence of James VII. The Queensberry fortunes did not rise until after the Revolution, and by 1693 the Duke of Queensberry was once again a member of the Privy Council. No evidence of building work survives from this period and, given his commitments at Drumlanrig and various family troubles that assailed him at this time, it is perhaps unlikely that the Duke spent his years in the political wilderness embellishing his Edinburgh house. In other words, the expansion of Queensberry House was undertaken not by William, first Duke of Queensberry, but by James, second Duke, after 1695. This is borne out by the documentation.

10.2 Insights into the first Queensberry House through the 1695 inventory

On 18 February 1695, the first Duke of Queensberry's steward, William Douglas, carried out, 'Ane inventar of the furniture in the severall roumes in My Lord Duke of Queensberry's Lodgeing at Edinburgh …'.[6] The inventory was carried out to take stock of the house at the time the Duke visited Edinburgh early in 1695, apparently to seek medical advice for himself and to deal with a number of matters relating to the death of his wife and his son George, including contracting with James Smith to build a new burial aisle at Durisdeer Kirk (Hume & Boyd 1984, 62). This document is invaluable in that it confirms that the first Duke of Queensberry continued to live in the old Balmakellie/Hatton House and it therefore provides an insight into the planning of the house that tends to confirm what has already been outlined. It also provides detailed information about the way in which the house was furnished and decorated, how it functioned and how it was adapted to suit the particular needs of the Duke at that time, and gives some insight into life in the house in this period. The furnishings of Queensberry House will be dealt with in more detail in Chapter 11, but it is worth considering this issue to some degree at this point because it casts light both on the organisation and functioning of the house, and provides some insight into family life there at an important juncture in the history of the building.

The inventory starts with 'My Lord Duke's Dressing roume'. This appears to have been in the jamb, just as Hatton's accommodation was before (fig 8.10). The room was fairly simply furnished with 'ane little tent bed', that is without a tester but with a suspended canopy, a walnut cabinet and table and a number of chairs. On the walls were two pieces of Arras hangings showing scenes from Ovid. These must have been on the north and east walls of the room, behind the bed and on the partition wall of the closet. There were white serge window curtains and a number of decorative items including two weather glasses (barometers). On

the walls that did not have hangings there were maps of England, Hungary and Ireland and portraits of his children, described as follows:

> My Lord Drumlanrig, Lord William, Lord George and Lady Ann's pictures in the black frame above the chimney with the picture of a black.

Although we do not have precise dates for all of these children, they were certainly grown-up or at least in their teenage years by this time. Lord Drumlanrig was James (1662–1711), the heir to the titles and already married. William (c 1665–1705), who later became Earl of March, was also an adult by this time. Lord George had been a student at Glasgow University, studying Law, in 1682, and died young, in 1693. Finally, Lady Ann seems to have been the apple of her father's eye, at least if the number of portraits of her are any indication. Her portrait in a gilt frame also hung in his dressing room and one of Lady Ann with her mother hung in the best bedchamber. Ann must have been in her teens by the time the inventory was made because she was married two years later to David, Lord Elcho, later Earl of Wemyss (Douglas 1910, 140).

The description in the inventory suggests very strongly that these pictures formed a group portrait and therefore almost certainly showed the children when they were young, possibly around 15 years earlier. The addition of 'the picture of a black' is significant because it suggests that the Queensberrys, as was the fashion of the time, had acquired a black slave/servant, almost certainly as a playmate and servant for the children or a page boy for the Duchess. The former is more likely because he seems to have been part of the group portrait with the children. Elsewhere in the inventory there is a reference to the 'room where the black used to lie', indicating that he was no longer part of the household but had recently been so, because the house had only been acquired in 1688. If the portrait dated from around 1680, it suggests continuous service by the black servant throughout the 1680s and possibly into the early 1690s, that is throughout the childhood of the children. Thereafter, his fate is unknown.

At the north end of the Duke's dressing room was his *valet de chambre's* room. From the contents listed, this does not appear to have been a bedroom for the personal servant but a closet associated with the *toilette* of the Duke. Here he kept his clothes, a washstand and a chamber stool 'with a buff pan and a pewter chamber pott'. A walnut writing desk 'and chair with a cloath cushion of sewed work' suggests that the Duke also used this space as a writing closet. From the point of view of his *toilette*, however, it was certainly easily and discreetly serviced by the valet, who could use the service stair that linked the closet directly to the basement.

The most detailed part of the inventory relates to the state apartment and, on the one hand, confirms the reconstruction of the plan already offered, but on the other, demonstrates the important point that this system of planning was not inflexible and could change according to the circumstances of family life. As will become clear, such flexibility was also to be built into the house in the later expansion of the building.

The state apartment was approached via a sparsely furnished lobby at the top of the stairs (fig 8.10). The dining room was quite simply and rather sombrely furnished, with an oval, wainscot dining table and a folding cedarwood table with drawers that may have functioned as a buffet in the absence of a more permanent piece of furniture. Certainly, the use of folding tables that could be laid aside or removed if the occasion demanded was typical of this period (Thornton 1990, 283). This room was panelled by Lord Hatton but this was supplemented by two pieces of gilded leather hanging, probably both on the west wall (the others being broken up by fireplaces and windows), and it may have been against this wall that the 'buffet' table was positioned when in use. The chairs were also typical of dining rooms of the time: 14 in all, including two with arms and all with cane backs and seats (see endpapers).

Next door was the drawing room. This was furnished in a rather similar, though more comfortable, fashion. It also had cane chairs, but one of these was a 'large resting cane chair', which was possibly a day bed or an easy chair that was more elaborate than merely a chair with arms. There was a triad arrangement of a large looking glass with two stands, placed between the two windows, while a walnut table stood in front. The walls in this room, also panelled by Hatton, were enriched and softened by three large pieces of tapestry depicting Ovid's *History*.

The rest of this set, another three pieces, hung in the adjoining room, which was the climax of the state apartment. The 'fyne Bedchamber' was extremely rich in its decoration. The focus was a grand bed that stood with gilt claws on carpets, with a full set of yellow mohair hangings, with matching chairs and presumably window curtains (although only the rods are mentioned). Complementing this was a set of olivewood furniture, including a cabinet, a triad and a little writing table. In addition, a portrait of the Duke and the portrait of his by (now deceased) wife and their daughter Ann hung on the walls.

The sequence of rooms in this kind of plan has already been discussed but it is interesting to see how the actual usage of this period departs from it. The Duke was a widower by this time, the Duchess having died in 1691 (Hume & Boyd c 1984, 62).[7] The bedchamber would undoubtedly have been hers, albeit she may not always have used it and would, as suggested already, have had generous accommodation in her dressing room and closet that might have included a bed. However, the dressing room in this inventory is labelled 'My Lord Duke's sleeping room'. This was furnished not with one bed, but with two. There was a bed with brown serge hangings, lined with black and yellow watered calico. But there was also a box bed, one of a number in the house, which is a surprising addition to such a room. It seems unlikely that the room was fitted up for two occupants, since the major occupant was the Duke himself. Perhaps in this case the box bed was a fixture in the room, conforming to the panelling and orginally serving as a discreet addition to a room that was mainly used for other functions. Alternatively, it might have been brought in to serve the Duke when he was ill because the box bed was used as a place of confinement during illness.[8] Certainly box beds could be prestigious items, at least in the Edinburgh area, where they were sometimes used as test pieces by the Incorporation of Wrights, with the result that a tradition of elaborate and rather architectural pieces grew up in the area (Jones 1996, 56). In this case, the Duke was content to leave the best bedchamber for show and to spread himself into his deceased wife's quarters so that he had a suite of rooms across the eastern end of the house. As will become clear, in the subsequent phase of the building this use of a number of rooms making up a suite in different parts of the house, rather than directly interconnecting, was to be a feature of the arrangements for the second Duke of Queensberry also and had precedents in the planning of male quarters in other Scottish houses in this period.

The final surprise in this part of the house, however, is that two box beds were also to be found in the closet at the very end of this planning sequence. Box beds in combination like this were almost always built into the structure of the room, in this perhaps for personal servants or even for children.

Given that it has already been established that the main room on the upper floor filled the entire depth of the building, it would be surprising if a full apartment had existed at this time on the first floor of the house, because without the lobby it would have been impossible to access the beginning of the planning sequence without going through another room (fig 8.12). Although the inventory is not precise enough to identify every room on this floor, it is clear that, although the rooms were arranged *enfilade*, there was no sequentially planned apartment, but rather a number of private suites comprising bedchamber and accompanying closets. The large room in the centre seems to have been a common public room, or salon, for these suites.[9] In 1695, the evidence of the inventory suggests that this entire floor was given over to Lord and Lady Drumlanrig. Lord Drumlanrig was particularly well catered for with an outer room with a closet, a bedchamber with two closets (one of them 'dark') and a dressing room. His wife had to make do with a dressing room. The reason for this could simply have been that it was Lord Drumlanrig who most frequently used the house since he was Lord High Treasurer at this time and would have been in Edinburgh frequently. On the other hand, while his political career was flourishing reasonably well, his father's was essentially at an end and it may even have been the case that quarters elsewhere, possibly in the palace, were a more attractive option. At the time the inventory was taken, all of these rooms were pretty poorly furnished, suggesting that they were not often used and tying in, perhaps, with the Duke's letter to the Marquess of Tweeddale (28 February 1695) in which he talks about his son's failure to contact him and asking Tweeddale to persuade him to visit, 'if he understands his interest he would find that my condition requires his presence' (quoted in Hume & Boyd c 1984, 62). The precise positions of the rooms are impossible to ascertain with absolute certainty, but it seems that the largest room should probably be identified as the 'outer room', which could have functioned as a salon, with the private rooms opening off this to east and west.

The floor above seems to have been used for family and higher servants (fig 8.13). By this time only Lady Ann was in residence and she had substantial and well-furnished quarters at this level. It is difficult to see how this plan could have worked for so many suites of rooms without the room that corresponds to the lobby on the principal floor assuming that role here also. If that were the case, it seems most likely that Lady Ann would have taken the finer rooms on the west side of the house. She had a room that was well furnished with a bed with serge and calico hangings, walnut furniture, including a triad, and five chairs with silk cushions, 'that was formerly in the low dining room'. She also had an outer room with blue hangings. A little bed formed part of the same set, along with various bits and pieces apparently gleaned from other rooms and including a parrot's cage – empty. Lady Ann's quarters also include a space simply identified as 'mamie's bed', which, from its contents, seems to have been just that, a bed. Since it is listed as a room, however, we must assume that this was placed in a closet that was otherwise empty and since the frame of the bed is not mentioned it may be, once again, that we are dealing with a built-in box bed.

There is something of a transitional quality to certain aspects of this inventory, which will be discussed in more detail below. It is, however, particularly marked in the case of Lady Ann, who was to be married two years after this date. The 'mamie' mentioned in her quarters was presumably her old nurse, who, with all the older children grown-up and gone and her youngest charge on the brink of adulthood, had found her usefulness outgrown. Similarly transitional in tone is the 'roume called Doctor Faalls', which is marked on the inventory in a later hand. 'The tutor' suggests, once again, a period in the children's lives and specifically in Ann's that was now at or close to an end. The room in question does not seem to have been the personal quarters of the tutor, certainly no bed is mentioned, but with a couple of tables and stamped leather hangings on the walls, it may have been used as a classroom and it is possible therefore that it might have been situated in the 'lobby' position as this would not have involved any issues of privacy.

This floor also contained a suite for Lord William, who had a well-furnished room and closet that may have been in the jamb, which would have allowed him a greater degree of privacy and ease of service.

A number of servants also seem to have been housed at this level, including William Douglas, the steward, and Mrs Gantlet, presumably the housekeeper. Another servant, William Craik, is also mentioned. A room that formerly contained Lord William's equipage was probably also at the same level, with the equipage possibly in the small closet off the south end of the main chamber in the jamb.

The attic floor contained rooms for a number of servants (fig 8.14). Because of the large shaped gables on the garden side of the house, some of the rooms at least had good light and headroom. There had certainly been a nursery at this level at some point, because one of the servant's rooms had formerly belonged to Lady

Ann. In addition, a number of important functions took place here. The inventory mentions 'the stairhead roume which was 'My Lady Dutches wardrop', which had evidently been replaced by a new wardrobe that we can identify on plan because of the way it is described as part of a sequence (fig 8.14). The 'stairhead room' implies the room in the jamb, which was at the head of the timber stair that replaced the main stair at this level. At this time it contained a table, some old chairs and a press with some glasses and pots in it, perhaps suggesting that it was used by the servants as a parlour or dining room.

The wardrobe in this context, and in this position, was not the closet or dressing room in which clothes might be stored, that we would expect to find at the lower and more prestigious levels of the house. Rather, the term applies here in a broader and slightly more old-fashioned sense of a place for the storage of textiles and even furniture (Thornton 1990, 299–300). In this case, the room was used for a great variety of materials, including tapestries, spare bed hangings, blankets and cushions, and even 'a long carpet for the church'. This must refer to the new Canongate kirk, where the Queensberrys had a pew and presumably the carpet was kept for special occasions that involved the family.

To the east of the wardrobe was another room used for storage, this time of slightly bigger items, including window shutters and various things associated with the Duchess. There is then a group of three rooms, including the housekeeper's room, 'the womens' roume' and 'the roume next the women house wher the black us'd to lye'.

The reference to the black servant has been mentioned already and confirms that he certainly lived at Queensberry House, possibly at the time when this level was still used as the nursery for Lady Ann. The terminology used for the other room, 'the women house', is familiar from country house planning where an outer and inner woman house frequently formed part of the offices and were used, unsurprisingly, for female work, including looking after children and the care of materials and textiles. That certainly seems to have been the case at Queensberry House because, in addition to the wardrobe, at this level the inventory also lists the laundry, which must have been on the west side of the house. On the face of it, this seems an unlikely position for such an activity since the transport of clean and dirty water would have presented something of a challenge. However, although a washing board and washing brush are mentioned, the key piece of furniture here was almost certainly the long fir table, which would have been used for repairing and probably ironing linen and which suggests that the room was more concerned with care and maintenance of fabrics rather than the actual washing of them. This arrangement, if not this terminology, was found in other houses, including, perhaps significantly, Ham House, the Lauderdale mansion in Middlesex, where the wardrobe room on the second floor (not the attic) also included long deal tables where repairs and pressing could be carried out (Thornton & Tomlin 1980, 159, 161–74). The picture of the attic that emerges, therefore, is of a place dominated by the female servants, where the children were cared for, and where important and expensive materials were stored and repaired in the wardrobe and laundry, or linen room.[10]

The 1695 inventory also illuminates our understanding of the other service areas of the house. The Duke's equipage included a gilded 'great coach', an old and new travelling coach and a light chariot, all of which are described in minute detail in the inventory, as are the accoutrements that went with them, with everything from old suits of armour to firearms, including a blunderbuss, being stored in a room that seems to have been part of the coach house and had another room above 'where the spiceries used to lye'.

The basement at this stage must have been essentially the same as it was during Hatton's time, although the inventory provides more detail than Hatton's *Instructions* (fig 9.3). Dining seems to have played an even more important part than it did formerly. There is still the distinction between the lower servants' eating room, the latter meat hall ('footman's eating room' on fig 9.3), which contains the draw well, and the upper servants' accommodation, the 'gentlemens' dyneing roume' ('best servants' eating room' on fig 9.3). In 1695, however, there was also a 'laigh dyneing roume', furnished with six cane chairs, including two with arms, a folding table and a white painted table with stands, which suggests a pier table to go between the windows rather than a dining table. This was clearly not a room for the servants since even the gentlemen sat on benches rather than cane chairs. The most likely explanation for this is that the low parlour, where Hatton had installed his marble floor, had been converted to this new use, perhaps for informal dining. Certainly, apart from the furniture mentioned, there are a number of references in other parts of the inventory to things that had been moved from this room, including a considerable number of silk cushions, five pieces of Arras tapestry that adorned the walls and mourning drapes for the entire room and all its furniture, that clearly indicate this was a room of some importance.

The rest of the basement was, of course, given over to service. The kitchen took up the whole of the west end of the house. There was a larder, probably the same room that Hatton had used in the south-east corner, with hooks for hanging meat, a long shelf built into the wall and a long table for preparing meat. To the north of that was a wine cellar and there were also a buttery, possibly alongside the wine cellar, and a pantry, the main contents of which at this time was, surprisingly, a bed with curtains and silk fringes. There was a porter's lodge that must have been close to the door. The only furniture here was a 'close bed', in other words yet another box bed. The location of this is difficult to ascertain, but under the stairs is a distinct possibility.

Outside, as well as the stables and coach house, and the coal house against the west gable that are all mentioned in Hatton's time, there was another porter's lodge at the main gate, and a gardener's house in the garden that may well have existed in the earlier period also.

The 1695 inventory is an excellent source not only for indicating what was in the house but also how the house was being used and who was using it at this time. It also provides an insight into the lives of the occupants, often with implications beyond the simple fact of how a room was furnished. A transitional quality has already been noted in relation to the presence and use of the house by the youngest daughter Ann. The way the Duke used the house was influenced by the fact that the balance of equal status between the male and female occupant, that underpinned the formal plan, no longer applied and we find instead the Duke using the house in a pragmatic way. As noted above, the Duchess had died by this time and there are a number of reminders of that fact throughout the inventory, although nothing that specifically states it. One example is the passing of several of her personal belongings to her daughter, including an olivewood chest of drawers, and an olivewood dressing box, that is not specified as belonging to the Duchess but was almost certainly from the same set as the chest. Even the hangings in Ann's room came from the Duchess's room. Firmer evidence of bereavement is also found in those rooms where items were stored because of the more recent death in the family, that of Lord George, the Duke's youngest son, who had attended Glasgow University in the 1680s. He died in 1693 and the house was hung with black crepe and other cloth for an appropriate period of time afterwards. The wardrobe still contained this material in 1695, including:

> Ane bundle of black cloath being the remnant of the cloath and searge that hung the great dyneing roume and drawing roume the rest being made use of for footman's cloaths and lyneing to the velvet pale and more cloath made use of at Lord George's buriall.

The wardrobe also contained black hangings with white linings for the Duke's bed and black slips for all the furniture in his sleeping room. The same applied to the fine bedchamber and to the drawing room. The low dining room has already been mentioned. Among the Duke's equipage, there were other items that also related to mourning, including a 'mourning black saddle cloath', but, perhaps most important of all, this was where he stored the 'great black velvet cloath of state with its cushion … the cushion having four great silk tassells one at each corner'. No cloth of state is mentioned anywhere else in the inventory so it seems that the Duke did not habitually use one in the state apartment. The use of such items in a period of mourning was normal practice for someone of his rank and it would have hung over a chair of state, along with the cushion, or possibly over the bed, or even a portrait of the deceased (Thornton 1990, 172 & pl. 136). Since the Duke's younger son was not of an elevated rank, it is possible that the cloth of state had been stored since the death of his wife.

But if items like these lend an unexpected poignancy to what would normally be a useful rather than truly interesting document, simply the date of the inventory, 18 February 1695, adds to that feeling. As part of his continuing desire to honour his youngest son, the Duke arranged for his books to be donated to the Advocates' Library in Edinburgh, which was done on 1 March 1695 (Douglas 1910, 140), less than two weeks after the inventory was made. Four weeks after that, on 28 March, the Duke himself died.

The inventory, therefore, is a document that marks the very end of the first stage of the Queensberry ownership of the house. If it hints at a family in transition, with one generation growing up and another passing on, it also presages a period of change for the building itself, as the second Duke of Queensberry began the process of altering it to suit his own needs.

Notes

1 The date is given as some five days earlier by Wood & Armet 1954, 239.

2 The 1686 date is to be found in Gifford *et al* 1984, 217. Grant is very precise, giving the date as June 1686 (1882, vol. 2, 35). Charles Boog Watson is similarly, and typically precise, yet ultimately confusing in *Some Notes on Queensberry House, Canongate, Edinburgh* (1926 typescript in Edinburgh City Library, Edinburgh Room, qYHV 1481 H, p. 4), where he states that the property was disposed to Queensberry in 1686, but goes on to say that the disposition is dated 19 July 1688 and was registered 13 October 1689.

3 Buccleuch Mss, NRA(S) 1275/vol. 16, includes an 'Inventar of the Writs and Evidents of the Duke of Queensberrie's house in the Canongate purchased by his Grace from the Earle of Lauderdale Anno 1688 put now in their proper box in the Charter house at Drumlanrig'. Sadly, these items appear to be no longer 'in their proper box' and none of them has been traced, leaving the detailed list as our main evidence. This item forms part of the basis of the detailed discussion in Chapter 7.

4 Buccleuch Mss, NRA(S)1275/vol. 16, ff.120v–124v, item 113.

5 Lauderdale Papers, NRA(S) 832/61/110, Inventory and vouchers of Charles, Earl of Lauderdale's debts to Gavin Thomson, paid out of part of the price of the great lodginging the Canongate sold to the Duke of Queensberry, 1685–1688. 61/103, Vouchers of Charles Maitland of Hatton's expenditure, mainly discharges for annual rent, 1671–1705, includes at least one reference to the transaction dated April 1687.

6 Edinburgh City Libraries, Edinburgh Room C0012389013/qYHV1481. This is a photocopy of a 19th-century copy of the original inventory at Drumlanrig. The Drumlanrig document has been mislaid, but the Edinburgh copy had previously been made available to the library by the Duke of Buccleuch as part of the project by Margaret Hume and Sydney Boyd (c 1984) that resulted in the book: *Queensberry House Hospital: a History*.

7 Douglas (1910, vol. 7, 140) does not offer a date for her death but simply states that 'she was living 20 December 1688'.

8 I am grateful to David Jones of the University of St Andrews for this information.

9 Boog Watson (1923) suggests that this space was the great gallery of the house, citing Grant (1882, vol. 2, 38) as his main authority. In fact, Grant only says that there was a gallery 70ft long in the house. This corresponds pretty accurately with the gallery in the west wing that the recent archaeological investigations have identified. But the house did not have two galleries and Watson's argument, that the central room could be combined with those to east and west to make a space some 80ft in length, is weak and arithmetically unsound. What is clear, however, is that there was a large space in the centre of the plan at the level above the principal floor, which functioned as the principal public room at this level.

10 Thornton (1990, 328, pl. 320, shows a painting of a Dutch dolls' house of c 1700 which combines the same functions at the same level.

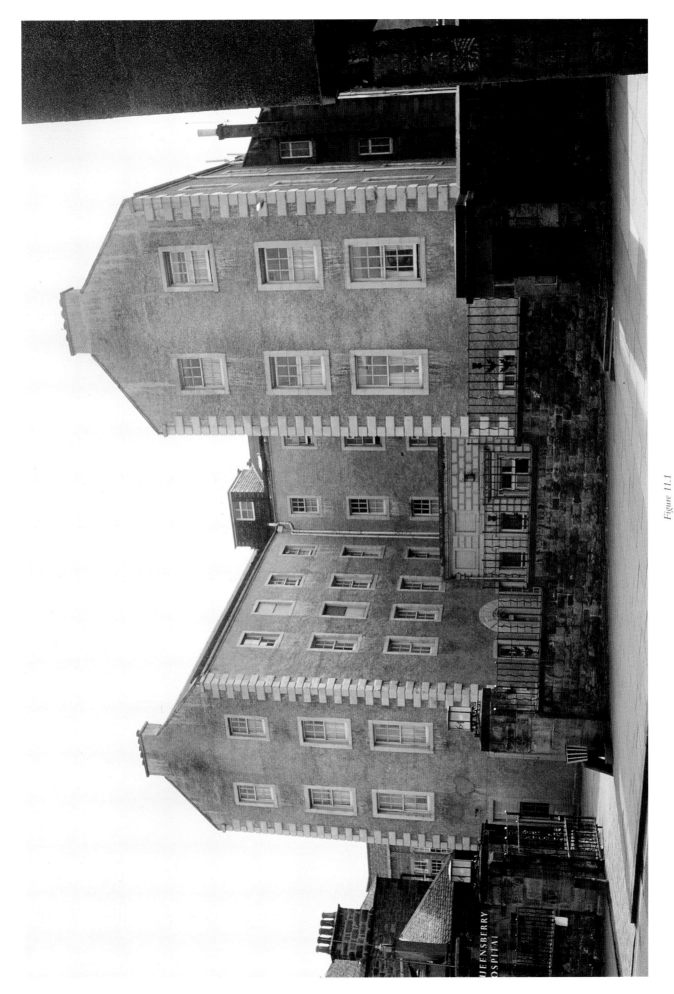

Figure 11.1

Queensberry House with its late seventeenth–century porch, photographed by John Hume in 1979 (© RCAHMS. Licensor www.scran.ac.uk)

Chapter 11

Queensberry House in the time of the second Duke

TOM ADDYMAN and JOHN LOWREY

11.1 Introduction

With the accession of James, second Duke of Queensberry in 1695, Queensberry House entered its most important period as the Edinburgh base of one of the most powerful political figures in Scotland and as a location of some significance in the lead-up to the Act of Union. James had been born in 1662 and since 1684 had embarked on a successful political career. In that year he became a member of the Privy Council and in 1688 took the calculated risk of being the first Scotsman to welcome William of Orange. In the 1690s, along with Argyll, he dominated Scottish politics and held a whole series of important and sometimes lucrative posts, including Commissioner of the Treasury, Lord High Treasurer, Keeper of the Privy Seal and Extraordinary Lord of Session (Douglas 1910, 140–1; Riley 1979, especially Chapters 6 & 7). This success depended not only on his own elevation, but also on his success in having supporters and family elevated to appropriate and useful positions, ensuring that the Queensberry interest as a whole was well provided for. Among his many successes in this area was the elevation of his brother William to the Earldom of March and to the Privy Council in 1697 (Riley 1979, 123).

> It must have been at around this same time that Queensberry turned once again to the family house in Edinburgh in order to provide an appropriate base for his political activities in a house that would suitably reflect his prestige and his sense of his family's importance.

11.2 Background to the rebuilding of the house

JOHN LOWREY

To do this he turned once again to James Smith, the master mason and architect who had been involved with the building ever since Hatton's time and, at that stage, probably as a result of his involvement with the royal works. But Smith also had a long-standing and important connection with the Queensberrys that actually pre-dated his work for Hatton. Since the late 1670s he had been working for the first Duke on the huge task of building Drumlanrig Castle and had

agreed to build a new burial aisle at Durisdeer Kirk for the Duke (Chapter 10.2). The contract for this is dated 20 March 1695, a week before the first Duke's death, with an agreed completion date of 1 May 1698 (MacKechnie 1994, 432). With prestigious commissions like these, by the 1690s Smith had emerged alongside Sir William Bruce as the most important architect working in Scotland at the time.

The political changes that had seen the demise of the Lauderdale interest and the rise of the Queensberrys had also badly affected Bruce, who was a politician as much as an architect and was tainted by suspicions of Jacobitism. That may have excluded him from Queensberry's reckoning, but Bruce's misfortunes worked very much to Smith's advantage because throughout most of the 1690s Bruce was either under house arrest or actually in prison and, as a result, Smith was able to develop his career either as an amanuensis for Bruce or, increasingly, as architect in his own right. By the time he received the Queensberry House commission he was already involved in one of the biggest commissions of this period, the rebuilding of Hamilton Palace (Macaulay 1987, 35–8; 1988, 17–24). By comparison, the work at Queensberry House was a small-scale operation, but nonetheless one that was architecturally significant. Between c 1696 and c 1700, Smith was responsible for a significant remodelling of the existing house, which was to be entirely subsumed within the new building. A detailed account of this work is included below, but in summary, the work involved:

1 A new west wing that corresponded to the old east jamb but extended through the full depth of the house to the gardens. A new staircase was contained within this new wing.

2 The east jamb's north façade was slightly remodelled to bring it into the same line as the west and was given the same architectural treatment as the west.

3 Fenestration throughout the building was regularised. Some old windows were blocked up and new windows were inserted.

4 The courtyard level was raised and a new single-storey vestibule was added between the two wings. This provided a new central entrance and direct access to the state apartment.

5 Two new closet towers with ogee roofs were built at either end of the garden façade. These provided inner closets to the main suites of apartments and extended the *enfilade* along the garden side of the building.

One key document relating to this work survives in the Drumlanrig archive. On 13 December 1697, the Duke, in London, sent James Naismith, one of his servants, north to Edinburgh with a set of instructions regarding the work on both house and gardens (the gardens are dealt with in Chapter 12): *Instructions by his Grace the Lord Duke of Queensberry to James Naithsmith given at London the 13th Dec' 1697.*[1] The following entries refer to works on the house itself:

1 That he [Naithsmith] goe with all convenient speed to Edinburgh and at his arrival there take an account of the progress made in the alterations to the house which Mr Smith had orders for when we parted that he particularly consider the closeness and exactness of the doors and report his opinion of the whole as soon as may be

2 That he applay himself to some Painter and agree with him for painting with white lead some time in the Spring the great outward Gate the great dore at the foot of the Staire that to the Garden and the other towards the Stable yard with the iron rail upon the wall of the Court, and that the whole outsides of the windows meaning the frames of the glass be painted in the like manner both to the street and Garden and that after painting the pullys be soe adjusted that the windows may easily open and shut and that the glasier take care according to contract that there be no defect in the glass

3 That he advise with M' Smith what may be the expense of vaulting over the Court and how soon he can undertake to doe it soe that the entry to the house may fall directly inn upon the Vestibule without goeing up or down stairs

4 That M' Smith be immediately employed to cause pave and so order the syver [sewer] before the gate that both the Court and Stable yard may be secured against water and durt from that cannel and that posts of Stone be sett up before the Gate to prevent the Coach whiles [wheels] breaking in upon the syver

5 That in anay agreement for painting either within or without dores particular inspection be made that there be a sufficient quantity of sise mixed with the colours for in this the painters there are generally deficient

6 That as soon as may be he send up hither the height and bredth of the severall pannels of the wainscoting in the passage betwixt the bedchamber and Closet below staire in the great Apartment and not ommitte the dimentions of thate above the dores and that other above the window

7 That the Roome at Edinburgh where My Lady Ann lay may be cleaned mended in its dores – windows and other necessarys and made every way fitt for furniture

Naismith's job was to liaise with James Smith about the work, but also to work directly with other tradesmen, specifically the painters, about the work they were doing. The most substantial building work that is mentioned is the possibility, 'of vaulting over the court … so that the entry to the house may fall directly upon the vestibule without going up or down stairs'. This was an important decision because, by raising the level of the courtyard, access from the street was made easier and, most important of all, it allowed direct access to the *piano nobile* of the house. The significance of the whole redesign for the planning and the design of the façade of the house is discussed in more detail below, but, for the moment, it is worth stressing simply the implications of the contents of this document for the building history. Given the work that is described in the paper, the main building work was clearly almost complete by this time. The emphasis is on painting, panelling, drainage and the gardens. This strongly suggests that the west wing and the closet towers were already built. The fact that the vestibule is mentioned also suggests that this new single-storey extension on the front of the building was also completed before the decision was taken to raise the courtyard level, meaning, presumably, that the original intention was to approach the main door via a staircase.

Further light is cast on the timing of the building work by a dispute between the Duke and his neighbour to the west, Mungo Malloch, one time Deacon and Treasurer of the Incorporation of Bakers.[2] The dispute centred on a common gable (common because it rested on a 20ft wall erected by Lord Hatton) that overlooked the entry to Queensberry House, which Malloch wanted to re-erect as part of a building project of his own, with windows in the gable overlooking the Duke's property. The Duke took out a complaint of neighbourhood and the Dean of Guild court convened on the site on 13 September 1695.[3] The deliberations of the court make it clear that the Duke's building work had not started at that point because it states, as part of Malloch's case, that:

his having of windows in the said gavell should be without prejudice to the said Duke to build upon his ground adjoining thereto at his pleasure.

In the absence of the Duke's representatives, the court found in favour of Malloch, providing he used frosted glass in the windows. However, the Duke returned to the fray, this time with legal representation and the expert opinion of 'Mr James Smith of Whythill', to have the original decision overturned. Smith's involvement suggests that building work was underway. Certainly, the Duke's complaint that he, 'could not shift himself in his dressing room or do any other thing but he was exposed to the [view?] of Mungo Malloch and his tenants', suggests that by this time the west wing, containing his new dressing room, had been constructed. Although the libel was raised in February 1696, the decision (entirely inconclusive)

was reached at an unspecified time in 1697, tying in with the *Instructions* document and strongly suggesting a building programme that had reached the finishing trades by the end of that year.[4]

11.3 The archaeological evidence

TOM ADDYMAN

Externally the major works of extension that resulted in the creation of Queensberry House project an image of regularity and symmetry that belies the complex and often sophisticated solutions required to adapt and upgrade the pre-existing interior space. From the archaeological evidence the broad sequence of construction was traceable, as were a number of major design modifications during the course of construction.

Phase

☐ *Balmakellie*	*ca. 1667–70*	■ *Military*	*ca. 1803–11*
☐ *Hatton*	*ca. 1680–81*	▦ *Hospital*	*l.C19th–e.C20th*
☐ *Queensberry*	*ca. 1695–1700*	☐ *Modern*	
▦ *Queensberry (secondary)*	*ca. 1700–1705*		

0   *10*
metres

Figure 11.2
North exterior elevation showing the colour-coded extents of the Balmakellie, Hatton and Queensberry phases; original appearance reconstructed c 1700

11.3.1 The Canongate frontage (fig 11.2)

The major element of the exterior works was to regularise and recast the Canongate frontage on the north side of the pre-existing mansion, a radical scheme that brought Queensberry House in line with the prevailing architectural requirements of a major aristocratic urban residence. The frontage was conceived about a three-sided court with symmetrically arranged projecting wings to the north-east and north-west. This operation required the infilling of the *Lower Ground* level entry area and much of the inner courtyard area to the north and the creation of a new entrance area at street (*Upper Ground*) level.

To the north-east the original east jamb was re-ordered, its north gable wall was refaced and brought to the square externally. To the north-west a new projecting wing was erected that mirrored the recast east jamb. Each presented a two-bay gable wall to the street that was fenestrated at *Upper Ground*, *First*, *Second* and *Attic* levels with paired windows of diminishing height. The windows were detailed with tightly rounded arises, the first departure from the chamfer otherwise employed universally at Queensberry House. Most of these windows survive in much modified form. At *Attic* level only the cills and lower jambs of the windows of the east jamb remain, with no indication as to their height. Of the original eight windows on the gable end of the east jamb, six appear to have been blind. There was no indication of internal ingos although this area had seen extensive later disturbance. However, an account of 1723 in the Queensberry papers for Walter Melville, painter, itemises 'painting six blind windows to the front of the east jamb' (NRA(S) 1275/1642/E/5; 22 June 1723). The *Attic* level windows may have been open.

On the east jamb at the new courtyard level a plinth course was let in that extended around the jamb, a detail replicated on the new west jamb. Straight skews were indicated by three probable cope stones incorporated into the later rubble.

Each jamb was detailed with rusticated quoins of polished ashlar at the corners. Each quoin was 12in (30cm) high except the uppermost, which was 13in (32.5cm). The upprmost quoin bore no chamfer on its upper edge and had evidently met a cornice course returning round from the side elevations at that point. The cornice no longer survived and the upper parts of each gable had been rebuilt. In the absence of a contemporary representation of the Canongate frontage, it is only by analogy with other contemporary buildings, particularly those of James Smith, that the suggested appearance of the upper parts of the gable can be reconstructed.

It is probable that the cornice continued across the gable wall without interruption and that the *Attic* level windows had been diminutive, their lintels lying below the cornice. A similar arrangement existed at the now demolished Royal Infirmary building designed by William Adam in c 1736. It is possible that Adam reproduced the Queensberry House design.

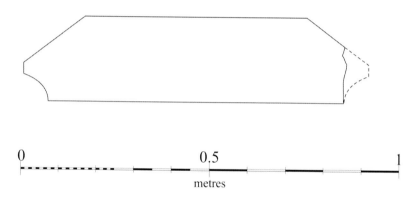

0   0.5   1

metres

Figure 11.3
Profile of chimney cope from the Queensberry phase alterations at the east jamb, recovered from later Military phase stonework in the same area

Here diminutive *Attic* storey windows lie close below a cornice. The upper parts of the gable are simply detailed with straight projecting copes that culminate at a chimney.

Although the gables are now long gone, parts of their chimney stonework were rebuilt into the masonry of the next major phase (fig 11.3). The chimneys were largely reconstructable having been built of polished ashlar and detailed with a projecting cope, the underside of which was formed to a *cavetto* profile. The four-bay arrangement of the east wing was reproduced to the west with the single omission of the earlier mezzanine window arrangement. No evidence survived to demonstrate whether the east jamb dormer windows were retained and indeed reproduced in the opposite jamb to the west at the Queensberry phase.

The focal point of the new entrance frontage was the new entrance vestibule. This structure projects into the entrance court by one bay (fig 11.8) and is entirely constructed of rusticated polished ashlar arranged in five bays, including paired windows on either side of a central entrance. The entrance is detailed with a bolection-moulded surround that is lugged at its upper corners, with a pulvinated frieze and architrave above. The windows are detailed with an internally chamfered raised margin and voussoired rustications forming relieving arches over the lintels. The upper wall contains four squared blind windows arranged in pairs above the windows below. A cornice lies immediately above. Investigations of the single course of parapet stones, which appear not to be of the Queensberry phase, and of the walling on either side failed to identify any evidence that there had been a stone balustrade or other form of parapet ornamentation. Below the main windows at the east and west end of this elevation exist cellar windows

within sunken masonry-lined light wells. The creation of a new porch and entrance necessitated the blocking of all pre-existing windows in the former north wall at *Lower Ground* (basement), *Upper Ground* (new entrance) and *Mezzanine* levels and the creation of new openings into the rooms beyond.

The north façade of the principal range rises above the projecting entrance vestibule. No evidence survived to suggest whether the Queensberry phase saw any rearrangement of the fenestration; it is possible that the smaller windows at the south-east re-entrant with the east jamb were infilled at this stage, rendering the remaining *First* and *Second* floor windows symmetrically disposed. In the absence of surviving evidence it can only be assumed that the original wall-head cornice in this area remained unaffected by the new works.

There were no surviving traces of the original exterior finish on the north frontage area. It is suggested as a possibility that part or all of this area of the exterior

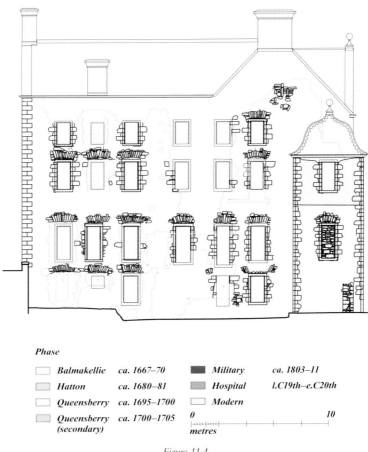

Phase

☐	*Balmakellie*	*ca. 1667–70*	■ *Military*	*ca. 1803–11*
☐	*Hatton*	*ca. 1680–81*	▨ *Hospital*	*l.C19th–e.C20th*
☐	*Queensberry*	*ca. 1695–1700*	☐ *Modern*	
▨	*Queensberry (secondary)*	*ca. 1700–1705*		

0   10

metres

Figure 11.4
West exterior elevation in the Queensberry phase, with overall reconstruction c 1700

had been detailed with a flattened harl or straightened plaster may have been applied and ruled out to imitate ashlar, as had been employed at the near contemporary Newhailes House, Musselburgh, for example (James Smith, after 1686).

The north frontage also extended out beyond the east jamb to the east. However, this area remained unaltered. It was the all-important street frontage that was brought up to date in the currently fashionable mode of the open-courted French urban *hôtel*, with immediate English prototypes such as Clarendon House (1664–7), and contemporary Scottish models at Hamilton Palace.

11.3.2 The west wing (figs 11.4–11.6)

The major element of the Queensberry reordering of the Balmakellie–Hatton mansion was the erection of the west wing. This was conceived as a two-bay westwards extension of the principal range that extended to the north in the form of the large jamb that reproduced the massing of the east jamb as already described. On plan the new wing measured 24m (north/south) by 7.7m. On the south frontage this simply took the form of a two-bay extension built out from the original west gable wall of the principal range and the original roofline taken across to a new gabled wall-head to the west. The latter was surmounted by a substantial chimney. There is a slight change in alignment of the south frontage at the junction where the new work met the old. At this point many of the original quoins were truncated or wholly removed so as to tie in the new masonry.

It is apparent from the mid-18th-century Sandby panorama (fig 8.3) that the original shaped gables on the garden frontage were retained, albeit now asymmetrically placed in relation to the façade.

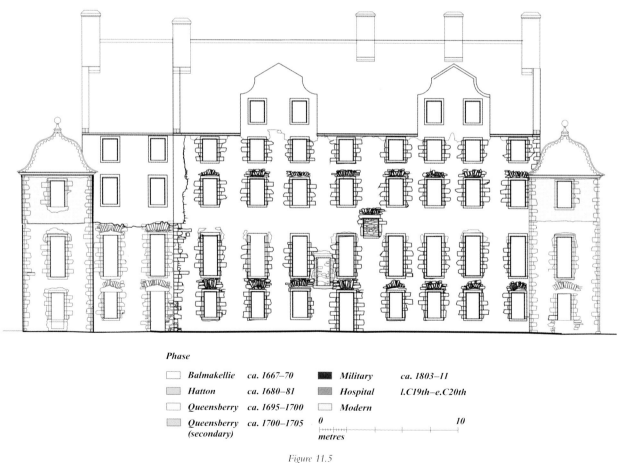

Phase

☐	*Balmakellie*	*ca. 1667–70*	■ *Military*	*ca. 1803–11*
▨	*Hatton*	*ca. 1680–81*	▨ *Hospital*	*l.C19th–e.C20th*
☐	*Queensberry*	*ca. 1695–1700*	☐ *Modern*	
▨	*Queensberry (secondary)*	*ca. 1700–1705*		

0   *10*

metres

Figure 11.5
South exterior elevation showing the surviving extent of Balmakellie, Hatton and Queensberry phase masonry, with original appearance reconstructed c 1700

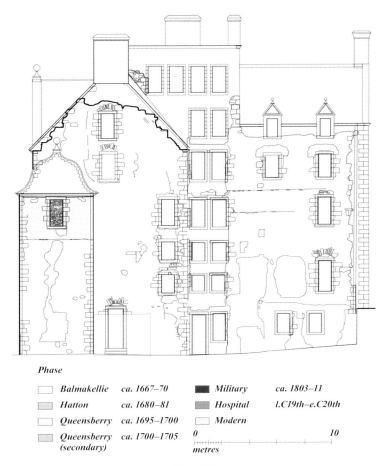

Phase

☐	*Balmakellie*	*ca. 1667–70*	■ *Military*	*ca. 1803–11*
▨	*Hatton*	*ca. 1680–81*	▨ *Hospital*	*l.C19th–e.C20th*
☐	*Queensberry*	*ca. 1695–1700*	☐ *Modern*	
▨	*Queensberry (secondary)*	*ca. 1700–1705*		

0   10

metres

Figure 11.6
East exterior elevation showing surviving extent of Balmakellie, Hatton and Queensberry phase masonry,
with original appearance reconstructed c 1700

Internally the west wing contained chambers arranged on either side of a new stairwell, the west stair. While this stair still remains in use, it was clearly a complex structure and has seen very major subsequent modification. It is best described at each individual level.

The general character of the masonry of the west wing was very similar to that of the previous phases, being of random rubble whose mortar bonding employed a creamy lime and river sand mix and was roughly faced with the edge of the trowel. Indeed, on masonry characteristics alone it was impossible to differentiate the Queensberry phase work from the earlier. Window details closely reproduced the original although the relieving arches employed considerably longer unworked slabs of sandstone than previously. In contrast to the Balmakellie period, oyster shells were not employed as levellers below the cornice or elsewhere; small chips of sandstone and occasional fragments of slate were employed.

Three mason's marks were recorded in the area of the west wing, two *in situ* upon the jamb of a *Lower Ground* floor entrance and one *ex situ* from what may have originally been a coping from the newel of the west stair (fig 11.7). Reused dressed stones were noted periodically within the general masonry fabric of the new west wing although considerably less frequently than within the Balmakellie phase fabric. Many of these stones may well derive from modified parts of the Balmakellie–Hatton mansion.

11.3.3 Closet towers

Two closet towers were added to the now extended principal range, at its south-west and south-east corners. The archaeological evidence has demonstrated that these were initially of only two stories and that

181

they had been constructed around the pre-existing masonry of the garden walls extending out to the east and west from the corners of the original mansion. While their primary purpose was the provision of additional closet chambers at either end of the *Upper Ground* floor *enfilade* of rooms, they also lent further architectural gravitas to the garden frontage, where they slightly broke forward from the general line of the frontage.

However, at two stories the towers may not have balanced the façade very effectively, perhaps appearing as minor appendages dwarfed by the extraordinary scale of the main body. Whatever the reason, an additional *First* floor storey was added to each tower. This is attested by clear horizontal construction breaks at the junction, and by the fact that the upper masonry of the south-west tower abutted that of the west wing. There also exist slight but discernible differences in the character of their general masonry above and below, the masonry above containing a higher proportion of orangey and reddish rubble. The only other instance of masonry of this character in the Queensberry phase work is within the surviving stump of the west gable-head of the principal range. This would appear to demonstrate that the raising of the closet towers occurred in the later stages of the general construction programme.

The towers were detailed with plain raised margins at their angles and a wall-head cornice. The original roof structures are now lost, but the Sandby panorama demonstrates that these had been of bell-cast profile.

11.3.4 *Lower Ground floor level (fig 11.7)*

The erection of the west wing and the raising of the courtyard had major implications for the organisation of the *Lower Ground* floor. The original main entrance into the Balmakellie–Hatton phase mansion was rendered redundant. The area below the new street level entrance vestibule was formed into a vaulted chamber, doubtless the 'vaulting over the Court' referred to in the 1697 *Instructions*; this measured 3.2m by 10.2m (east/west). The chamber was lit by the two basement light well windows at either end of its north wall. The principal entrance to the vault was from the west, where a substantial entrance with a dressed sandstone surround faced onto the lower part of the west stairwell. It was not possible to determine whether an earlier window near the centre of the south wall that formerly admitted light into the kitchen beyond may have been opened further to form a second entrance into the vault at this point.

Whether the original mansion entrance, which now lies at the east end of this new vaulted room, remained open or was blocked off cannot now be known. Perhaps the latter was the case as its bolection-moulded surround was clawed off – had the entrance thus been blocked and plastered over? This has implications for the understanding of the function of the vaulted chamber. If open at each end, it may have functioned as a basement-level circulation route; if closed, the space might more comfortably have functioned as a storeroom and cellar.

The original kitchen was modified to provide access into the new west wing. A 1.45m-wide passage was formed by the insertion of a masonry partition wall along its north side. With a new entrance through the pre-existing masonry to the east and the breaking through of the original kitchen window at the north end of the west wall, this permitted direct passage from east to west without entering the now reduced kitchen. In order to facilitate this access, the floor of the passage was raised by about 1m. Evidence from impressions within the kitchen wall plaster to the north-east indicated that there had been a short wooden stair leading down into the kitchen from an entrance at the east end of the passage. It is not clear whether the original kitchen entrance in the centre of the east wall was blocked off at this stage.

West wing to the north

The northern part of the west wing was subdivided by a substantial east/west masonry cross-wall. The northern, somewhat smaller, chamber was vaulted and contained a single window to the west. Outlines in red limewash suggested preparation of the wall before the fitting of woodwork features to the north-east and north-west. To the north-east this had consisted of a vertical feature, to the north-east a horizontal structure. The room was entered from the south-east, the dressings of the stone entrance surround facing into the chamber to the south. This chamber has a wooden ceiling and was provided with a corner fireplace to the south-west. A large window lit the chamber in the west wall. On the north side of this had existed a much smaller window at high level. The reason for this difference was not determined. The southern chamber was entered from the south-east through a further ashlar-defined entrance opening off the stairwell.

The function of these rooms requires some discussion. The cellar chamber may have functioned as a secure wine cellar and the room on its south side, with its fireplace to the south-west, as accommodation

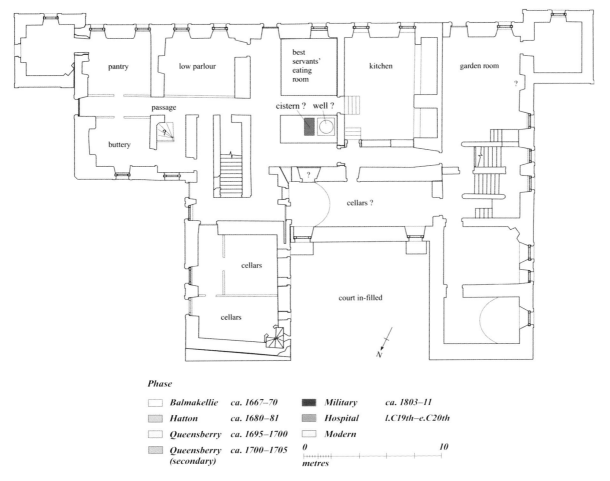

Figure 11.7
Lower Ground floor plan of the Queensberry phase

for the cellarer. The adjacent stairs, leading to both dining rooms of the floor above, may support this. A further possibility is that the rooms provided secure accommodation for Lord Drumlanrig, the second Duke of Queensberry's mentally ill eldest son. This suggestion is perhaps supported by the limewash outlines in the vaulted northern room, the form of which could be taken to suggest a bed below the window to the north-west and some form of press to the north-east.

West stair

The archaeology of the lower level of the west stair was not fully understood because of extensive subsequent modification. At this level the stair contains three bays defined by east/west masonry cross-walls-cum-newels. The first flight of stairs occupied the southern bay and descended east to west from *Upper Ground*

floor level to a half-landing. From the half-landing one passes through an entrance to the north before turning and descending a second flight within the central bay to the east. The half-landing also permitted access to a further entrance if one continued north, into the northern bay of the stairwell arrangement. An area of subsequent refacing on the north wall of this northern bay suggested that the landing extended into the bay, turned to the east then descended to *Lower Ground* floor level to the east where it faced directly opposite the entrance to the large vaulted cellar below the entrance vestibule.

The purpose of this apparent double stair arrangement was not wholly clear. The northernmost bay may have contained a smaller service stair from the floor above that had been constructed of wood above the level of the half-landing. The purpose of a second stair at this point may have been to permit independent service access to and from a second dining room that occupied the northern parts of the west wing at *Upper Ground* floor level. This seems to be the only arrangement that would make sense of the otherwise curious planning of the bays, and there is evidence for a partitioned area at the southern end of the dining room area on the floor above.

The fenestration within the west wall of the stair is equally confusing, having been heavily impacted upon by the insertion of later openings. The southern bay, containing the first flight down, was very well lit by a large window at high level. However, directly below this to the exterior can be seen the jambs of a further opening. Unfortunately this was so heavily truncated that its nature could not be determined, whether relict evidence of an earlier design altered during construction, part of an entrance down to the stable court to the west, or, least likely, a very low window below the first.

Garden room to the south-west

The half-landing of the stairwell also contained a second entrance on its south side. This led by means of a stair down into the garden-facing room occupying the western two bays of the principal range. A single step remained of this stair, seen embedded within the masonry of the north wall of the garden room to the north-west. The riser was detailed with a bottle-nosed moulding and fillet within that returned downwards at the sides. The quality of this stair detail demonstrates that the large room formed part of the family accommodation of Queensberry House as opposed to a further service area; access was also direct to the Duke's chamber on the floor above.

The period of the blocking of the stair entrance was not determined although it may even have been during the original construction process. The only alternative access to the garden room would have been from the base of the main stair, leading into the garden room through an entrance at its north-east corner.

The garden room contained a fireplace in the centre of the west wall, and a window to the north-west. This perhaps suggested that the stair had returned down to the east at the corner of the room, just clear of this window. The chamber was further lit by a large window in the south wall to the south-west and opened directly into the garden by means to an entrance to the south-east.

A broad entrance leading to the base of the stairwell exists to the north-east. The east jamb of this entrance is detailed with a rounded nosing formed of polished

ashlar dressings that represents a vertical extension down of a similar feature at this point on the floor above. The nosing terminates below at an elegantly formed lamb's-tongue stop. If this had functioned as a service entrance, there is little apparent need for such an elaborate detail. A possible explanation is that this is a relict feature from a previous design for the stair, abandoned during the construction process.

This garden room perhaps replaced the considerably smaller Hatton phase 'low parlour' further to the east. It is apparently the room referred in an inventory of 1706 as the 'Apartment below' stairs (*Inventory of Goods disposed of by Robert Cochrane: 10 June 1706.* Drumlanrig Muniments), and can be identified with the 'garden room' mentioned in a 1723 inventory.

11.3.5 Upper Ground floor level (fig 11.8)

Entrance area

As stated in the 1697 *Instructions,* the newly raised courtyard surface was intended so that 'the entry to the house may fall directly inn upon the Vestibule without goeing up or down stairs'. The new vestibule formed an elegant new centrepiece to the Canongate entrance ensemble as well as a highly convenient means of accessing the state apartment. However, the modification to the original *Upper Ground* floor planning was considerable.

The new vestibule was lit by the paired windows on either side of the entrance and was high-ceilinged and commodious. It is unfortunate that the south and east walls have seen extensive subsequent modification, rendering interpretation of the Queensberry phase planning uncertain. Scars in the centre of its south wall suggest that a substantial entrance was newly installed at that point that provided direct access into the state dining room beyond. There may have been lesser entrances to either side, although evidence both to the east and west is now ambiguous. Similarly it is unclear whether an earlier window in the east wall had been reformed into an entrance leading to the eastern stair or had simply been blocked off.

It is only to the west that firm evidence remains, in the form of a broad arched opening into the area of the western stairwell. As one enters the vestibule and looks west through the arch to the stair, the arrangement beyond appears symmetrically designed. The stairwell landing at this point presented a number of options. One could turn to the north and enter a large chamber within the jamb that had functioned as a public dining room. One could ascend the stairs to the west to a

First floor apartment, or descend by a flight down to the south-west, or to the south enter a large apartment overlooking the gardens to the south, the Duke's chamber.

West wing

The majority of the northern part of the west wing was occupied by a large single chamber, referred to in an early 18th-century inventory as the 'public dining room to the street'. This was symmetrically arranged with three windows in the east and west walls, and paired windows on either side of a large fireplace to the north. Horizontal timber lacings at dado level and at 2.2m and 3m above floor level evidently represent fixings for panelling. These lacings stop abruptly to the south and it is clear that there must have been an east/west partition wall that had formed the south wall

of the chamber. It is within the narrow space to the south of this partition that it is suggested there had been a service stair down to the *Lower Ground* floor areas. Preserving the symmetry of the room, the principal entrance from the stairwell area, which must have been to the south-east, would probably have been balanced by an entrance to the south-west that had accessed the service stair.

The chamber saw further modification during the construction process. The central window in the west wall was blocked off and a fireplace inserted (also seen in the corresponding location on the floors above, perhaps relating to the necessity of inserting a flue track). This suggests a change in function and planning of the dining room. Had the original fireplace intended for the centre of the north wall been discarded so as to permit this symmetrically aligned and focal location,

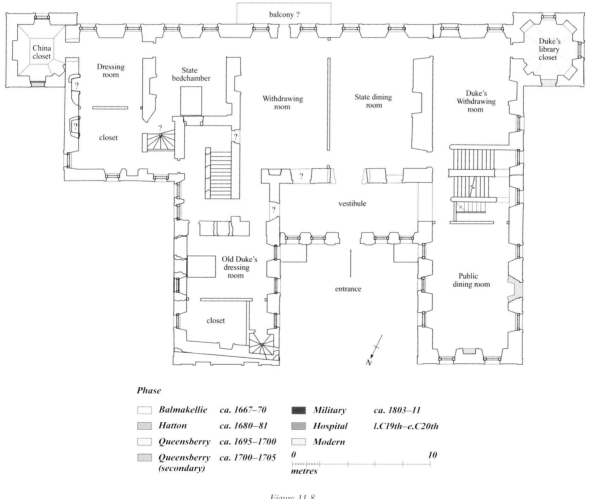

Figure 11.8
Upper Ground floor plan of the Queensberry phase

as seen as one entered the chamber from the south, to be used for other purposes, or was it retained to heat the room more efficiently?

West stair

At the south-west corner of this can be seen part of an original window that was mostly infilled when the north wall of the west stair was constructed. The stair wall runs westwards into the central part of the window. Here the head of the window ingo was lowered and a lintel put in to support the east/west-aligned lintel of an adjacent entrance formed within the stair wall. Is it possible that the lower parts of the window remained open so as to provide light to the stair behind, or were they simply left as a recess?

One of the more curious features of the west staircase is the rounded nosing detail that forms the west jamb of the entrances into the rooms to the north and south. This detail rises from floor to ceiling where it terminates at lamb's-tongue stops at each point. The feature is not repeated for an opposite, east jamb in either case and there is no evidence to suggest that these unusually high entrances were internally framed or had been designed to contain a door.

Duke's withdrawing room

A very substantial single chamber occupies the southern part of the new west wing at *Upper Ground* floor level, the Duke's drawing room. The east end of the north wall contains an entrance off the west stairwell area, its south jamb consisting of a rounded nosing of dressed ashlar that rises from floor to ceiling, detailed with a lamb's-tongue stop at its base and top. This feature is curious in this location, suggesting that there had not been a door at this point. It is possible that a door and doorframe were inserted at a later stage of construction and that the rounded nosing related to the original intention for the stair, which was subsequently modified. The only other feature visible within the north wall is a relieving arch lower down at the north-west corner – relating to the entrance down into the garden room on the floor below.

The south end of the east wall saw the insertion of a new entrance in the area previously occupied by a window of the Balmakellie phase. The south wall contains two substantial windows. A number of horizontal timber lacings exist between and on either side of these windows, the most prominent being at dado level and a little below the window-heads; others exist between these two levels.

The west wall remains largely from the Queensberry phase and contains three principal features, a large central fireplace, a window to the north and an entrance into the south-west closet tower room to the south. Little survives of the fireplace other than truncated lower jamb stones, revealing an apparent width of about 1.6m, and a relieving arch over. Much of the original lintel seems to have been rebuilt in about its original position. The entrance to the south-west had been constructed with coarse masonry jambs and had evidently been intended to be fully lined out with timberwork. Horizontal timber lacings survive at 2.2m above floor level, as do occasional dooks above, at 3.5m above floor level.

South-west closet tower: Duke's library closet

The *Upper Ground* floor level room occupying the south-west closet tower is identified in an inventory of c 1710 as 'the closet wher my Lord Duke's library is' (Drumlanrig Muniments). In contrast to the storey above, the *Upper Ground* floor level of the closet tower seems to have been built during the main phase of Queensberry construction, its masonry fully tied into that of the west wing. The chamber was originally designed with windows to the south, west and north, in the centre of each wall; all of these survive despite subsequent modification. The western window is symmetrically placed to the exterior of the closet tower, but its internal splays are offset to the north, so as to line through to the *enfilade* of entrances further east, as well as to achieve internal symmetry. The interior splays of the north wall window were similarly skewed, to the west, so as to remain symmetrical to the interior.

To the north-east exists a diagonally set chimney breast and fireplace below. The fireplace appears never to have had a bolection-moulded surround integral to the jambs and lintel of the fireplace itself, suggesting that it had had a fascia. The chamber is particularly noteworthy for three intramural recesses diagonally set into the south-east, south-west and north-west corners of the chambers. At the wall face these measured about 0.95m wide (diagonal) and rose to an arched head between 3.4m and 3.8m above floor level, the best preserved to the south-east.

Horizontally set timber lacings exist at dado level and at 2.2–2.3m above floor level to the west, north and north-east. Dooks also exist to the west, north and north-east at 3.6–3.8m above floor level; these may relate to the ceiling structure that may have been coved in a similar manner to the surviving ceiling in the south-east closet tower at this level. Other horizontal lacings occur at dado level to the north, and somewhat higher to the north and east.

It is clear that the library closet had been fully lined out with panelling and wooden shelving. The three recesses can only have been book cabinets. With the shelves and the corner chimney breast to the north-east, the chamber had clearly been octagonal in internal form and most probably had an eight-panel coved plaster ceiling. It is probable that the fireplace to the north-east had been furnished with a coloured marble surround such as the smaller of the surviving examples at Gosford House in East Lothian (a deep red marble with large white inclusions).

At a late stage in the construction process or some time shortly thereafter, the north and west windows were blocked off with rubblework, the ingos remaining to the interior and perhaps acting as additional shelving

areas. The head of the south window was raised to the same height as the south elevation windows at this level, a change most likely coeval with the addition of the *First* floor stories of the closet towers.

The reason for the blocking of the north and west windows may have been to achieve greater privacy in this most intimate of spaces – the interior was overlooked by buildings to the north and west; or simply as a pragmatic means of catering for a larger library collection.

The state apartment

In contrast to the extensive modifications of the surrounding space, the state apartment was little altered in its broad outline at the Queensberry phase. All of the pre-existing *Upper Ground* floor windows overlooking the garden were raised by 0.45m, a modification that must surely relate to the installation

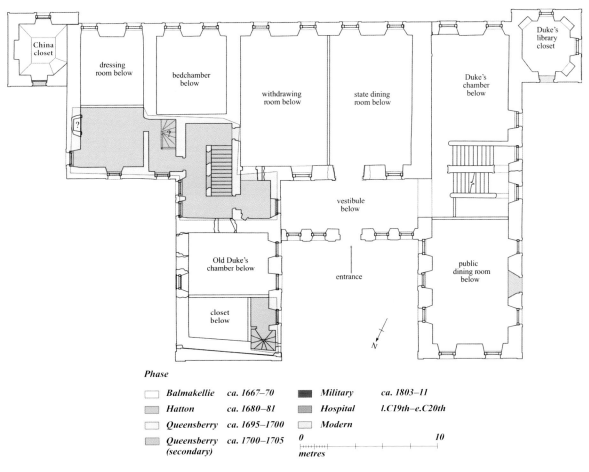

Figure 11.9
Mezzanine level plan in the Queensberry phase

of sash and case windows as described in item 2 of the 1697 *Instructions*.

The state dining room saw a number of alterations. To the south-west the earlier window was reformed into an entrance that extended the *enfilade* into the west wing. The window to the north-west also seems to have been formed into an entrance leading to the stairwell area. The pre-existing windows in the north wall were lost with the addition of the new entrance vestibule. A major entrance seems to have been formed to the north-east, while to the north-west there seems either to have been a subsidiary entrance or a press.

Although the archaeological evidence is somewhat ambiguous, the drawing room on the east side of the state dining room saw alteration. This included the insertion of an entrance to an exterior balcony between the two garden facing southern windows. Unfortunately the exterior elevation at this point had been so defaced by later modifications that it was impossible to identify the extent of the former balcony structure. With the addition of the west wing this feature lay on the architectural centre line of the façade.

The area beyond the original drawing room to the north, the original vestibule leading to the state apartment (fig 8.10), appears to have been extended to the full height of the floor by the removal of the mezzanine apartment above. In the latter area there is a contemporary blocking of the mezzanine level fireplace. With the loss of the windows following the erection of the new entrance vestibule, the original vestibule area no longer had a source of natural light. On this evidence it is probable, although not definitively proven, that the original drawing room was extended northwards into this space, although, admittedly, the fireplace in the east wall would have been rendered off-centre as a consequence (fig 11.9).

11.3.6 First floor level (fig 11.10)

West wing

The western stair extended up to the *First* floor level where it apparently terminated. Round-headed coping stones that may have surmounted the sloping top of the newel had been incorporated into later fabric in the vicinity. It is possible that the *First* floor rooms within the west wing formed a private apartment for the second Duke, and there may have been no connection through to the earlier parts of the mansion to the east at this level.

Northern rooms

A large chamber occupies the northern part of the west wing at *First* floor level. The north wall contains two windows and a central fireplace that is now considerably damaged. Fragments of the clawed-back bolection-moulded surround had been built into a later part-blocking of the fireplace; these were recovered, permitting a reconstruction of its original appearance. With the later blocking of the fireplace removed during works, its interior was revealed; its jamb stones had been checked internally (for a grate?) behind which the cheeks had been hollowed out to a concave profile.

The east wall contains four windows, with the northern three equally spaced. An almost continuous horizontal timber lacing, formed of sections of embedded plank, exists at dado level along the length of the wall, evidently for a dado rail. Multiple dooks exist at the internal angles of each window, fixings for wooden architraves.

The west wall contains two well-preserved original windows between which a further window had originally been formed, the remains of its south and lower north jambs still visible internally. Timber lacings exist at dado level along much of the wall, except to the south-west, as do dooks at the internal splays of the windows. At the south end of the west wall the plastered north jamb of a further window survives but is now blocked.

Between the southern two windows of the east wall there is a vertical alignment of dooks, interpreted as possible fixing points for the framing of an east/west partition wall towards the southern end of the chamber. This is supported by the abrupt termination of the dado-level wooden lacings on the west wall just short of the corresponding junction. The resulting chamber to the north, measuring about 8.6m by 5.85m, would thus have been symmetrically arranged with three equally spaced windows on either long wall (east and west) and a central fireplace to the north with a window on either side. The south (inferred partition) is likely also to have been symmetrically disposed; the principal entrance from the stair that had presumably existed to the south-east may have been balanced by a second entrance to the south-west. This second entrance would probably have provided access to a closet.

The central window in the west wall seems to have been filled in at an early stage, perhaps even during the Queensberry phase construction process; the window dressings were removed and the void infilled with

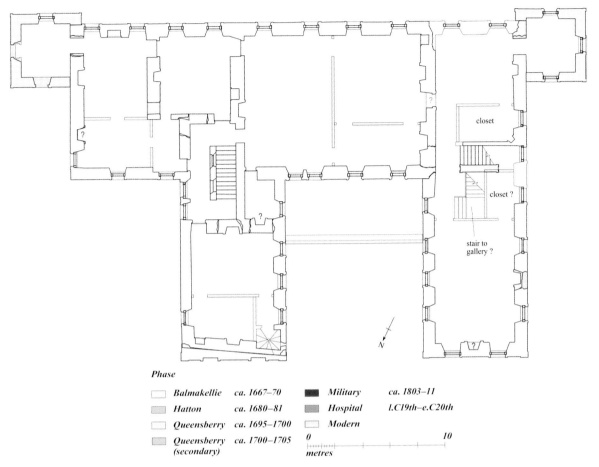

Phase

☐	*Balmakellie*	*ca. 1667–70*	■ *Military*	*ca. 1803–11*
▨	*Hatton*	*ca. 1680–81*	▨ *Hospital*	*l.C19th–e.C20th*
☐	*Queensberry*	*ca. 1695–1700*	☐ *Modern*	
▨	*Queensberry (secondary)*	*ca. 1700–1705*		

Figure 11.10
First floor plan in the Queensberry phase

rubble masonry. A fireplace was formed in its stead, a feature that is still well preserved and with interior features found to be similar to those of the fireplace in the north wall upon removal of a later blocking.

It is possible that the infilling of the central window in the west wall related to modifications relating to the early 18th-century subdivision and letting out of Queensberry House. Could this chamber have been subdivided to form closets to the north (heated by the existing fireplace central to the north wall) and a new fireplace inserted in the north wall to heat the newly formed room to the south? This insertion would have necessitated the creation of a flue to the wall-head within the splay of the existing window and the one on the floor. Supporting this idea, there is no evidence for the blocking off of the north fireplace.

In summary, the northern part of the west wing contained a well-proportioned chamber of three bays by two, defined by the existing north, east and west walls and, internally, by a studwork partition wall to the south – suggested both by the spacing of the various windows and by a line of vertical dooks on the east wall. This would appear to be further confirmed by the presence of an ochre limewash skirting preparation which stops at this point, suggesting that the partition remained at the Military phase. With the partition reinstated, the resulting chamber is symmetrically laid out. In the north gable wall there was a fireplace which may have been blocked in a latter stage of the construction process in order to relocate it to the central bay of the west wall. Here a window had been constructed, but subsequently removed again, leaving only some truncated dressings and its relieving arch over to the exterior, and the south jamb internally.

Horizontal fixing dooks were built into the walls of the chamber at dado level, perhaps indicating a dado rail or dado panelling. Similar dooks were seen at upper wall level on the west side.

The larger chamber can perhaps be identified with a 1706 inventory reference to 'His Grace's upper dressing room' (Drumlanrig Muniments: *Inventory of Goods disposed of by Robert Cochrane: 10 June 1706*), which at that time was being set up with bed furniture for the Earl of March, the Duke's brother. Apparent confirmation comes from the evidence of the 1696 dispute with Malloch, already mentioned, where the Duke complains that he:

> could not shift himself in his dressing room or do any other thing but he was exposed to the [view?] of Mungo Malloch and his tenants …

Neighbouring properties were closest to the new west wing at its northern end, while to the south lay the stables constructed for Lord Hatton.

Southern rooms

The entirety of the southern part of the west wing at this level is occupied by a large chamber, which is accessed from the landing of the west stairwell to the north and in turn provides access into the upper level of the south-west closet tower, and to the central part of the principal range to the east. The north wall is in large part Queensberry phase masonry. A high wooden lintel to the north-east is all that remains of the original entrance off the stair landing at that point. To the north-west survive parts of a corner fireplace, including its much truncated east jamb stone. No Queensberry phase modifications were traced within the masonry of the east wall. No evidence survived to demonstrate whether the existing east entrance, occupying the site of the Balmakellie phase window, had been opened up or blocked off at the Queensberry phase. The existing south wall is wholly of the Military phase although its two large windows must replicate Queensberry phase predecessors.

Except to the south-west, the west wall is largely of the Queensberry phase. At the south-west a subsequently reformed entrance must be in the position of its predecessor, parts of its north jamb apparently surviving, as well as two of its relieving arch stones. Just to the north of the entrance are the remains of a fireplace, the truncated jamb stones of which remain *in situ*. Its original lintel was subsequently raised; this was also truncated, but retains the last vestiges of its bolection-moulded surround. The remains of a window survive further north. Parts of horizontal timber lacings survive at dado level and within the upper wall area towards the south end of the west wall.

This room retains its original width, although it would appear from the evidence of two early fireplaces to have been divided formerly by an east/west partition forming a larger south chamber and a much smaller north chamber (evidence for the partition may still lie behind plaster to the west). The south chamber had a fireplace central to its west wall that had had a stone bolection-moulded surround, evidence for which remains on its displaced lintel. To the south of this, an entrance led into a closet room occupying the uppermost floor of the south-west closet tower.

Two large windows lit the room to the south (subsequently reconstructed). It is not clear whether the former Balmakellie phase gable window in the east wall was turned into an entrance at the Queensberry phase or simply blocked (the latter is perhaps more likely).

The smaller northern chamber may itself have been subdivided into an eastern vestibule providing access from the west stair to the north, and a west chamber, served by a window in its west wall and the corner fireplace to the north-west. The west chamber may have been a servant's room accessed from the east, or an inner chamber or closet accessed from within the south chamber.

South-west closet tower chamber

The upper chamber of the south-west closet tower is accessed by an entrance at the south-west corner of the room and must originally have formed a closet or private chamber for the larger chamber to the east. Externally it was discovered that this storey had been added to the closet tower as a change in the design process. A clear construction break was seen at *First* floor level and the north wall was not tied into the body of the house above this level. There is clear evidence that the walls of the closet tower were constructed against the pre-existing masonry of the west wall and south-west corner of the Queensberry phase west wing. The north and south walls of the chamber clearly abut the west wing to the east. The chamber was lit by three large windows, one in each of the north, south and west walls, although only the window to the south remains open. The room did not contain a fireplace. The chamber most probably had had a coved ceiling, rising into the ogee form roof structure that disappeared at the beginning of the 19th century.

Central parts of the principal range

It is not clear whether there were any Queensberry phase alterations within the space described. Certainly the erection of the west wing obviated the need for the window within the west wall of the south-west chamber. Whether this was blocked or knocked through to form an entrance is not revealed by the evidence, but blocking seems by far the more likely. If a link with the new wing were required, the more obvious candidate would have been the presumed press at the north-west corner of the north-west chamber, which would have provided access direct to the head of the west stair. Again the evidence for such does not survive and it is far from clear whether there was ever a link with the west wing at this level in this phase.

There is further ambiguity with the evidence of the north wall. The extent to which this part of the Canongate façade was modified, if at all, under Queensberry is uncertain. Slezer's view, which shows five windows across this part of the Balmakellie building, has been demonstrated to be untrustworthy and cannot be taken as a guide (fig 8.1). The evidence suggests that at most there had been four windows across the façade and that the arrangement had not been symmetrical, with windows offset at the south-east re-entrant at *First* and *Second* floor levels, while there had been a different arrangement on the floors below. It is probable that the Queensberry phase saw minimal alteration of these apartments.

Closet tower room to the south-east

In common with the *First* floor level of the south-west closet tower, the upper stage of the south-east closet tower appears to have been a secondary addition following the completion of the general Queensberry works. The walls abut the main body of the Balmakellie mansion to the west, and there is a clear horizontal construction break between *Upper Ground* and *First* floor levels. Indeed, so carefully levelled is the upper surface of the *Upper Ground* floor level wall-head that it is probable that the cornice had been installed and then raised up to its final level. For these reasons the upper levels of the closet towers have been assigned a nominal 'Queensberry (secondary)' phase designation.

The chamber was entered by means of a new doorway slapped through from the south-east corner of the room to the west. There is no surviving evidence to demonstrate whether the chamber had had a fireplace: if at the north-west corner, all evidence has now been lost beneath a later replacement. The chamber was furnished with a window central to each of its exterior walls but contained no other features.

A further early development within the tower was the blocking off of the north and east windows. The masonry employed (stone and mortar) is very similar to that of the surrounding walls, and a date in the first half of the 18th century is suggested for this work. The window to the north was wholly infilled, the only feature of its flush interior wall face being a horizontal timber lacing at dado level. In contrast, the blocking of the eastern window was recessed, and the jambs faced up to the perpendicular to form a press. A horizontal timber lacing was built into the upper rear side of this new work.

11.3.7 *Second floor level (fig 11.11)*

West wing (gallery)

Various early-18th-century inventories refer to a long gallery at Queensberry House. It is evident that the entirety of the upper level of the west wing formed such a unified chamber. The existing *Second* floor stage of the western stair, which dates to the beginning of the 19th century, now disrupts the space. The surviving features of the former gallery are confined to its exterior walls.

The upper limit of surviving Queensberry phase masonry to the east and west lies at the existing ceiling level. The east wall within the jamb extending to the north contains four windows. Each of these has had its lintels and overlying masonry (relieving arches?) removed. The west wall originally contained seven windows. The second window from the north was blocked off during the construction process, repeating the situation at this point of the floors below.

The north wall contains two Queensberry phase windows that have seen much subsequent modification, and similarly the south wall must have contained paired windows. The remains of a fireplace survive between the second and third windows from the south end of the west wall. This still retains a substantial lintel, an over-lintel stone and the lower stone of its south jamb, now clawed back.

Further Queensberry phase features include multiple dooks for the fixing of window architraves, and horizontal timber lacings at about 0.85m above floor level, seen particularly on the east wall, but also at the north end of the west wall and to the north. These lacings were clearly intended for affixing a dado rail.

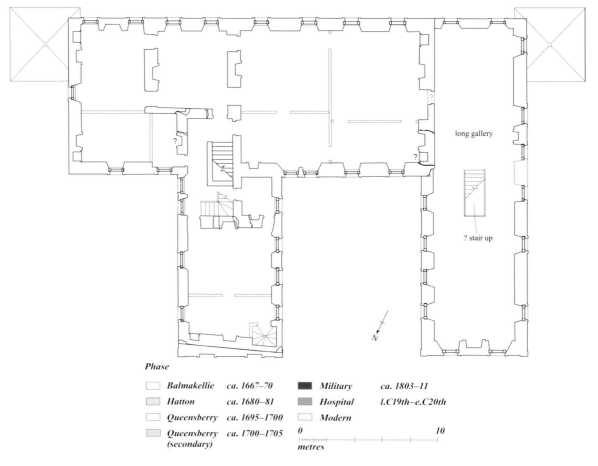

long gallery

? stair up

N

Phase

☐ *Balmakellie*   *ca. 1667–70*   ◼ *Military*   *ca. 1803–11*

▨ *Hatton*   *ca. 1680–81*   ▨ *Hospital*   *l.C19th–e.C20th*

☐ *Queensberry*   *ca. 1695–1700*   ☐ *Modern*

▨ *Queensberry*   *ca. 1700–1705*
   (secondary)

0   *10*

metres

Figure 11.11
Second floor plan in the Queensberry phase

There is no direct evidence as to how the gallery was entered. The two possibilities include an entrance from the earlier parts of the mansion within the east wall to the south or a stair up from the floor below. There are two possible locations for an entrance, a breaking through of the window centrally located in the west gable wall of the Balmakellie phase mansion or a new slapping at the north end of the same wall. Unfortunately, both areas have seen subsequent modification and no direct evidence survives. Alternatively, a wooden stair may have risen from within the *First* floor apartment of the west wing, the most likely location being an extension (presumably wooden) up from the north side of the western stairwell. This location is suggested on the plan (fig 11.11).

It is quite possible that the gallery was never completed. The major use of the mansion by the second Duke of Queensberry's household was confined to a short period leading up to the Union Parliament of 1707. At this date and subsequently, inventories of Queensberry House indicate that the gallery was the main area of the house employed for the storage of furniture and fittings.

11.3.8 Roof structure to the west (fig 11.12)

No direct evidence for the form of the roof structure of the west wing survived. It is probable that the gallery ceiling rose into the roof space and had been coved, if not barrel-vaulted. The south pitch of the roof structure of the principal range dictated that the gallery ceiling must have been coved at its south end, an arrangement that may have been replicated to the north to preserve internal symmetry. Considerable efforts were made during the project works to identify surviving physical evidence and historical records for roofing materials employed at different periods.

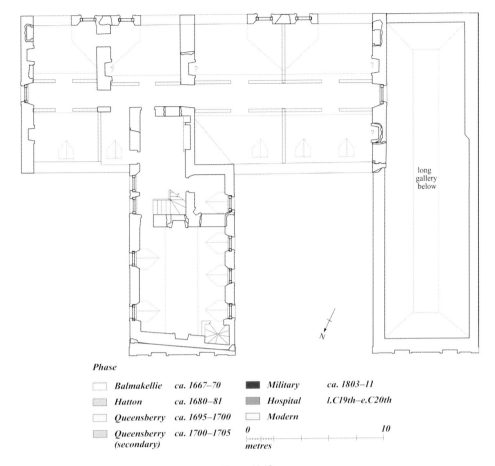

long
gallery
below

N

Phase

☐	*Balmakellie*	*ca. 1667–70*	■ *Military*	*ca. 1803–11*
▨	*Hatton*	*ca. 1680–81*	▨ *Hospital*	*l.C19th–e.C20th*
☐	*Queensberry*	*ca. 1695–1700*	☐ *Modern*	
▨	*Queensberry*	*ca. 1700–1705*		
	(secondary)			

0   10

metres

Figure 11.12
Attic floor plan in the Queensberry phase

11.4 Architectural analysis

JOHN LOWREY

The work carried out by James Smith produced the final form of the building during the Queensberry ownership. On the Canongate side, Smith attempted to bring order, symmetry and balance to Queensberry House. By this stage it was strongly under the influence of the monumental and sometimes rather austere classicism that he was developing in his country house practice. The new west wing, the recasting of the east jamb, the reorganisation of the fenestration of the central portion, the blind windows on the old east jamb to balance the windows in the new west jamb, and the new entrance, with a terrace above, all combined to produce a monumental, essentially classical, street façade.

By the late 1690s, Smith was involved in a number of important projects for various aristocratic patrons.

He also had the work of Sir William Bruce to draw on, including a number of buildings on which he had worked with Bruce. The broad arrangement of the building on its site seems to have conformed to what was being developed in country houses elsewhere. The arrangement of courts towards the street, with an inner court in the centre, a base court to the east and a stable court to the west echoes the arrangements Smith had proposed in 1694 for Raith House near Kirkcaldy, for Lord Raith, brother of the Earl of Melville. By raising the level of the inner court and entering the house directly into the *piano nobile*, Smith created a change in level between front and back. Coincidentally, this occurred naturally at Raith, where the ground level drops away dramatically to the rear of the building. Smith dealt with that by proposing a garden terrace that wrapped around three sides of the building and was accessed from the *piano nobile* by a staircase. A very similar arrangement was put in place at Queensberry

House (although the terrace ran only along the garden front), the broad arrangements of which closely echo those of Raith.

As far as the footprint of the building is concerned, Smith had created an F-plan building but with the emphasis firmly on the inner court, with the two wings projecting forward from the main elevation, giving the impression of a deep U-plan building. This broadly echoed the form of Hamilton Palace, which Smith was building at the same time. It is probably more appropriate, however, to look to rather less grandiose buildings for comparison with Queensberry House, and the urban house, rather than the country palace, is probably a more useful area for exploration. The word *hôtel* has already been used in connection with Scottish aristocratic urban housing in the 17th century (see Chapter 7.2) and there is no doubt that the French aristocratic urban house is relevant in discussing Scottish architecture in this period. The basic form of a *corps de logis* with projecting wings enclosing an inner court, service courts on either side, a closing range or wall sheltering the house from the street and a garden to the rear are the familiar elements of this typology and provided the model not only for Argyll's Lodging in Stirling, which was given its final form only in the 1670s (Fawcett 1996, 19), but also Queensberry House. Significantly, it also forms the basic pattern of the plan of Bruce's remodelled Holyrood Palace, emphasising the connection between royal and aristocratic design in this period. As if to emphasise this point, there is one remarkable project produced for a Scottish nobleman that brings royal and aristocratic, Scottish and French closely together. It has been demonstrated that a series of engravings pasted into the bottom of the drawers of a 17th-century chest at Newhailes (the house of the architect James Smith in the 1680s and 1690s and known as Whitehill) are the design for a townhouse for John Hope of Hopetoun (Rock 1987, 516–18). The design was produced by Claude Comiers, a French polymath with wide interests ranging from architecture to the occult (Rock 1987, 517), and it is, quite straightforwardly, a Parisian, aristocratic *hôtel particulier* designed for the Cowgate rather than the Marais in Paris (Rock 1987, 518). It demonstrates all of the classic features of the type and has above its *porte cochère* a plaque with the legend 'Hostel D'Hopton'. Of course, it was never executed and that was partly related to the fact that the prospective patron, a favourite of the Duke of York (the future James VII and II), died in a shipwreck in 1682, while

accompanying the future king at the end of his three-year stay at Holyrood Palace, as chief commissioner to the Scots Parliament. Whether Hope would ever have managed to build such a house can never be known, but it is significant that he deemed it the appropriate type to employ at the very time his royal master was inhabiting the palace, and it emphasises the connection between the royal and aristocratic and this French building type and the planning that went with it. Part of Hope's motivation was to have a suitably impressive house while he went about his business as a member of the Scottish Parliament. These concerns were shared by Hatton, as already discussed, and were certainly of great importance to the highly ambitious Duke of Queensberry.

Of course, unlike the proposed Hopetoun House, Queensberry House, as it was inherited by the second Duke and his architect, was a very plain building, though impressive in its very size. Smith's work not only involved a regularisation of the old T-plan building, but also, with the sparing use of judiciously applied detail, the classicising of the structure, and in this the use of mouldings and rusticated quoins are important elements of the design. The most significant element in this connection is certainly the single-storey vestibule that fills the inner court between the two wings and provides the new entrance to the house (fig 11.1). Here, Smith designed a highly wrought focal point not only for the entrance but for the whole Canongate façade. The fine ashlar construction contrasts with the harled rubble of the rest of the building and the use of channelled rustication is an unusual feature in Scottish architecture at this period. For the most part, where it had been used, mostly by Sir William Bruce, it was to differentiate the semi-basement from the ashlar of the main wall, as at Kinross House in Perthshire. In the case of Queensberry House, however, it covers the entire one and a half stories of the entrance vestibule and makes a powerful impact on the façade design. Again, Bruce is relevant here, and in a similar situation. At the very time that Smith was working in Edinburgh, Bruce was finishing his son-in-law's house at Craighall, near Cupar, with a dramatic centrepiece of a two-storey arcade beneath a segmental pediment standing on top of a highly rusticated entrance of three bays. However, there is a major difference between Bruce's rustication and that of Smith at Queensberry House. Bruce almost invariably followed the French practice of running the deep groove between the joints only along the horizontal joints, leaving the verticals plain. This has the effect of casting long, horizontal bands of shadow along the rusticated area and reaches its climax in Bruce's work in his design for Hopetoun House, in 1698, where this technique is applied to the whole façade (Macaulay 1987, 21). Later, around 1715, it was also used by Smith at Yester House, East Lothian. However, at Queensberry House all of the joints are emphasised so that each individual block stands out and this type of rustication features in many of Smith's designs even for basement rustication, for example at Raith House, Fife. This type of rustication is more common in Italian architecture, notably in the work of Palladio. It also features heavily in the drawings attributed to James Smith that demonstrate his Italian training and important role as a proto-Palladian (Colvin 1974). This feature of Queensberry House is therefore a useful lesson in drawing a comparison between the strongly French-influenced work of Sir William Bruce and the more modern source of his younger rival's work.

The rusticated stonework is combined with a doorway with a lugged architrave that is typical of Smith's, and indeed Bruce's, work of this time. It can be seen at Smith's own house at Whitehill, Edinburgh, and even on the wings of the far grander work at Hamilton Palace, which was proceeding at the same time as Queensberry House. Above the windows, corresponding to the mezzanine level of the old house, there are panels or blind windows that break up the upper part of the wall, but they also provide a link to the attic windows of the new west wing and the refaced east wing; this is one of the features that link this elaborate centrepiece with the rest of the façade, thus unifying the overall design.

The vestibule structure is of interest also in that it provides a kind of terrace on the front of the building, since it is flat roofed and comes up to *First* floor level. There are a number of contexts in which this feature can be analysed. The first connects the terrace with the entrance; that is, a well-marked entrance feature might also contain a feature that is related to prospect. Again, the relevant building here is Hamilton Palace, the new entrance to which was exercising Smith at the same time that he was working on Queensberry House. At the beginning of 1696, he sent a proposal to the Earl of Arran in London to seek his and others' advice. The description of what he proposed is contained in a surviving letter and it was clearly a projecting portico, with the columns starting at *First* floor level and the entrance through a rusticated ground level. The portico itself opened off the great

gallery and was designed to be used as a viewing platform for a prospect over the new formal landscape to the south.[5] Of course, there was never going to be a portico at Queensberry House, but the idea of the projecting entrance that is also a kind of terrace is similar. Whether Queensberry House was used in this way is unknown, but no evidence of a balustrade, which would tend to suggest the terrace function, has survived. However, the idea of a terrace or other place of prospect is a strong one that had already been addressed by Hatton's belvedere. The lower, flat-roofed terrace that Smith built is of course quite different but also had antecedents in recent Scottish architecture at houses including Panmure, Angus, from the 1660s, and Prestonfield, from the 1680s. A similar idea was picked up at Thirlestane, with a proposed library block by Sir William Bruce that was placed between the two rear towers, overlooking the landscape towards the river. These larger terraces also find validation in the new west quarter of Holyrood Palace, which has an extensive terrace on top of the closing range of the inner court. The source for this arrangement lies in the French antecedents of its plan and this is also relevant to Queensberry House, where the entrance block with its flat roof can be related to the *hôtel* plan, but with the block withdrawn from the street and incorporated into the house itself. This, as discussed below, is not the only detail of the Queensberry House plan that can be linked to the urban *hôtel*.

A connection has been made between the square 'blind' panels above the windows in the vestibule with the attic windows in the two gables that face the street. The probable treatment of these upper-floor windows in the two wings is particularly interesting since it links the house with a tendency seen in Scotland since 1679 at Bruce's Dunkeld and Moncrieffe houses (fig 11.13). This 'squashed' treatment of the windows finds its grandest form at Kinross, in the form of the suppressed attic there, but it persists in a number of other houses in which the upper windows are smaller and sometimes pushed up under the eaves. Melville House, Fife (fig 11.14), in which both Bruce and Smith were involved and which Smith certainly executed, has a number of connections with this new street façade of the contemporaneous Queensberry House, including both the overall composition and this particular feature of the fenestration.

A further issue here is the possible influence of Dutch architecture on Smith. The particular window arrangement discussed above seems to have its origins

Figure 11.13
Moncrieffe House, Perthshire (© Crown copyright: RCAHMS)

in Rubens's *Palazzi de Genova*, published in Antwerp in 1622. Therefore, although the architecture was Italian, the author and publication were from the Low Countries. The idea that the Low Countries, and the Netherlands in particular, could be a source of influence and inspiration to Scottish architects, not simply through the importation of pantiles or the use of curly gables, is an important one in a late 17th-century context (Howard 1992, 33–48; Lowrey 1996, 20–34). Dutch classical architecture was a significant influence in Scotland in the 17th century both through direct contact and through publication. Smith seems to have been particularly impressed by Philips Vingboons, whose book *Tweede Deel Afbeeldsels der Voornaemste Gebouwen* was published in Amsterdam in 1674. The design for Castle Clant illustrated there has an austere monumentality that links it with Melville, but in terms of composition is probably even closer to Queensberry House, not only through the more extended wings but also through the entrance vestibule, which bears very

close comparison with the arrangements of Smith's house.

Of course, both Melville and Castle Clant have hipped roofs, and the treatment of the gables of Queensberry House cannot therefore draw on these or other classical sources. By the 1690s, the use of the hipped roof was becoming increasingly common in Scotland and there are few examples on which to draw to provide a possible source for appropriate gable treatments. Most of the examples discussed in relation to the Balmakellie phase of the house are still relevant here but, Prestonfield and Cammo (Fife) notwithstanding, it is highly unlikely that shaped gables were used at Queensberry House on the Canongate frontage; Dutch influence on James Smith was more sophisticated and simply more classical than that. Panmure House provides one example of a house with a steep gable facing the front with simple moulded skews. Another example of this kind of façade on an otherwise classical frontage is Donibristle, in Fife, by Alexander McGill (a partner of Smith's in some early 18th-century projects). Built in 1719, Donibristle is later than Queensberry, although it was rather old-fashioned by the time it was built. Here McGill combined two gabled wings with a recessed pedimented centre. The skew moulding does not cut across the top, under the chimney; nor does it terminate in an elaborate skew putt. Instead, the simple moulding returns to become the cornice at wall-head level for the rest of the building. This, of course, means that it cannot cross the base of the gable because that would create a very awkward junction. By contrast, the evidence at Queensberry House suggests that this moulding both cut across under the chimneys and cut across the lower end of the gable, immediately above the windows. An example of how this might have been managed by Smith might be found in the later example of William Adam's Edinburgh Royal Infirmary (1738–41), which combines gables, mouldings and windows in a way that is compatible with the archaeology of Queensberry House.

11.5 Planning

JOHN LOWREY

The discussion of the planning of the house at this phase of its development is based on a combination of archival research and archaeological investigation, which allows a reconstruction of the plan to be made. The main archival source, apart from the list of instructions to James Naismith already discussed, is a series of inventories of the early 18th century and, in particular, a very full inventory produced in 1723.[6] Despite the addition of a whole new west wing, the principles of the established planning were not changed in Queensberry's time and he did not take the opportunity to insert a new Duke's apartment to match that of the Duchess, in his new wing. Clearly, neither precisely balanced male and female quarters, nor even family and state apartments were required. Instead, Smith provided a subtly different arrangement, which provided for a series of overlapping public and private

Figure 11.14
Melville House, Fife (© National Archives of Scotland, RHP4093)

spaces, with a great deal of emphasis on the house's function as a place of reception. The inventories suggest that the Duke supplemented his accommodation in the east jamb, which hereafter was usually referred to as 'the Old Duke's dressing room'[7] (ie the first Duke), with new accommodation in the south-west corner of the building. Here his drawing room seems to have been both a public and private space. On the one hand it acted as one of a pair with the principal drawing room, separated by the dining room, indicating that withdrawal from that space could be either along the main apartment route or, in the opposite direction into what is clearly designated as the Duke's space. As part of the west wing, it also linked with a 'large dining room to the street'.[8] In this way it connected two planning sequences: the state apartment itself in the main body of the house, and a new and almost self-contained sequence which is peripheral, in the west wing. The use of the house in the late 17th century is dealt with in more detail below, but what the planning seems to indicate is that the new west wing was so arranged that it could perform two different kinds of function: a domestic one in which the Duke acted as host with his wife, and a separate, more private, but nevertheless quite formal one, related perhaps to business matters. On the other hand, this same drawing room was also a private, intimate space. With its associated closet and possibly a dressing room on the floor above the drawing room (fig 11.10),[9] it seems to have been the Duke's private apartment and was as substantial as that of his wife, whose quarters were also expanded by the addition of the tower closet.

The Duke therefore had rooms in two different areas of the building and that perhaps requires some explanation. The main issue is where he slept. There are a number of possibilities, one of which is that one of the rooms not actually identified as a bedchamber did, in fact, contain a bed. This was certainly a common arrangement in dressing rooms and, as has already been discussed, was the case in the dressing room in the east jamb in 1695. There is evidence among the inventories not only of this common arrangement but also of the Duke and Duchess sharing a marital bedchamber, for example in an inventory of 1708 which refers to 'My Lord Duke and Lady Dutchess's Bedchamber' (Lowrey 2000, 49).[10] Wherever he slept, this separation of the drawing room and closet from the dressing room and sleeping place is slightly unusual but it fits in well with the idea of different zones of the plan fulfilling different functions, and of the need, within the relatively restricted space of a townhouse, to combine grand reception spaces with family and private apartments. Perhaps it also indicates a certain flexibility in the apartment plan which, as the 1695 inventory has shown, could be adjusted to accommodate particular family circumstances. The separation of the various elements of the Duke's accommodation was also not without precedent: the inventories of Panmure House in the late 17th century present a picture of a plan that has elements in common with Queensberry House. In 1695, on one side of the house was an apartment that led to 'My Lord and Lady's chamber', which formed the Countess's apartment, while on the opposite side of the house, the Earl had his antechamber, dressing room and closet.[11] Although on a larger scale, these arrangements were very similar to those at Queensberry House.

These additions by Smith and the second Duke not only produced a sophisticated and complex series of rooms on the principal floor, they also greatly increased the length of the building, east to west. The effect of this was to enhance the great *enfilade* along the south side of the house, increasing it from approximately 25m to approximately 45m in length. There is a possibility that a mirror was placed at the east end of the *enfilade*, in the Duchess's closet, which would have had the effect of doubling the apparent length of the view and would suggest that the development of this aspect of the plan was important to the Duke and his architect.[12] Such an arrangement was not unknown elsewhere, notably in the state apartment of Chatsworth, where the *enfilade* is mirrored in a similar manner, although with the mirror in the dining room rather than the closet (Girouard 1980, fig 11, 155).

Without going into too many of the details of how the rest of the plan functioned, it is worth establishing some of the key characteristics of the rest of the plan at this point. As the major addition to the building, the west wing is the most interesting area of the house and two features stand out in considering this area. The first is that it appears to have been entirely, or almost entirely, self-contained, that is to say, with a link through the vestibule to the rest of the house at *Upper Ground* floor level, but no other links at the upper levels. The self-contained nature of the wing has implications for the functioning of that area during the heyday of the house at the turn of the 18th century but also for its later history as a place for letting to tenants. Architecturally, the major feature of the wing is the great gallery at *Second* floor level, which filled the entire space (fig 11.11). This links the house both with a Scottish tradition and a wider European one. The use of galleries in Scottish houses and palaces can be traced back to the 15th century (Howard 1995, 83–4; McKean 2001). These were often positioned high up in the buildings, so-called 'skied' galleries (McKean 2001; Coope 1986, 54), and were used as a place for exercise, as a place of prospect, as a picture gallery, and even, in the case of Crathes Castle, as a courthouse (McKean 2001, 169). The Queensberry gallery was placed on the top floor and garret space of the west wing, linking with this well-established tradition. In addition, although the long gallery was going out of fashion by the late 17th century (Coope 1986, 59), there were at least two that were directly relevant to Queensberry House. The first of these was the gallery built by James Smith at Drumlanrig, on the principal floor, above the main entrance (incidentally in the same position as the gallery at Hamilton Palace, also built in the 1690s by Smith). The second was the gallery built by Bruce in the 1670s on the principal floor of Holyrood Palace that filled an entire wing of the building and connected the two royal apartments. As has already been discussed, French planning is a source for this arrangement, in both chateaux and urban *hôtels* and its use at Queensberry House links it both with the historic and recent Scottish tradition, both noble and royal, and also with the French.

11.6 Furniture, furnishings and function, 1695–1723[13]

JOHN LOWREY

11.6.1 Introduction: the surviving archival evidence

As a result of the institutional use of Queensberry House since the early 19th century, almost nothing of the original decorative scheme has survived.[14] Although the archival sources are also very incomplete, there is, luckily, a good collection of furniture inventories covering the period in between those of 1695 and 1723, already discussed.[15] Some of these documents are fragmentary and/or undated. However, taken in combination, they provide some very useful insights into the planning, furnishing and decoration of the house in the early 18th century. The 1723 inventory is the most complete and the most well organised in that it lists rooms in sequence and by floor. This allows the plan to be reconstructed for that period, but is more generally useful because it serves as a baseline against which the other documents can be compared. There are a number of inventories made in the crucial years 1706–8, covering the period when the house was being

prepared for its busiest period, around the time of the Act of Union, and then when it was being partially dismantled in the aftermath of the political activity surrounding the Union.[16]

As regards planning, there is a great consistency between all of the inventories from 1695 onwards; however, there is a great contrast between the rather Spartan simplicity found in the furnishings of 1695 and all of the other lists, from 1706 onwards, in which there is great consistency in the decoration and furnishing of the main apartments.

11.6.2 Fixed decoration

Very little is known about the fixed decoration of Queensberry House. Inside the house, only the tiniest fragment of an original cornice (in the east tower closet) survives. Apart from that, a number of fireplaces were sold to the Earl of Wemyss for his house at Gosford in East Lothian at the beginning of the 19th century (Wilson 1891) Three marble fire surrounds of the correct detail still remain on the Gosford Estate, two in upper floor rooms on the east side of the principal block of Gosford House, and one within the Factor's House at Craigielaw. Each fire surround is formed of an exotic marble and detailed with a prominent bolection moulding, the profile of which is entirely correct for the Queensberry phase. The use of exotic marbles is well attested in other Smith buildings and the Gosford examples closely resemble those within the principal apartments at Dalkeith Palace.

Since the partial survival of a Smith period bolection-moulded surround of sandstone in the *First* floor ducal apartment within the west wing of Queensberry House (of similar profile to the Gosford examples) suggests that these fireplaces at Gosford must have originated within even more august chambers, it seems most likely that they must have originated on the principal floor and since the state apartment was largely left as Hatton had completed it, the new west wing seems the most likely location for these fireplaces.

The documentary evidence is also fairly scant, however, it does tell us that from Hatton's time, at least, the main rooms of the house were panelled. The Lauderdale Papers contain references to 'true wainscott' panelling in the drawing room and dining room, as well as in Hatton's own quarters in the east jamb.[17] Similarly, the Queensberry papers at Drumlanrig have a reference to the panelling in the 'passage betwixt the bedchamber and the closet' of the great apartment.[18] Unfortunately, no record survives of the appearance of any of these rooms, although they were clearly of high quality since a third source cites them as a model. In 1710, David Hay of Belton, in East Lothian, instructed his wright, William Tait, to 'line three rooms ... with firr after the manner of the lining of the best rooms in the Duke of Queensberry's house in Canongate'.[19] High quality is also suggested by Hatton's *Instructions* and his reference to 'true wainscott' suggests that the rooms were not simply lined with boards with a moulding applied to the surface to divide it up into panels, but that individual panels were set into a framework. The same document mentions 'Alex Isatt', which must refer to Alexander Eizatt, a master wright associated with Sir William Bruce and the royal works in this period, who executed much of the panelling in Holyrood Palace. The evident excellence of his work on Hatton's house suggests that it is indeed Holyrood and perhaps Bruce's houses at Balcaskie (Fife) and Kinross that provide the most suitable models for the panelling; certainly his presence suggests work of the highest quality. Similarly, in the expansion of the house under James Smith in the 1690s, the contemporary work at Melville House, Hamilton Palace and Dalkeith Palace might provide clues to the appearance of Queensberry's panelled rooms. In some cases, notably Hamilton Palace, not all rooms were completely panelled. In the west wing at Hamilton all of the main rooms in the apartment were panelled only to dado level, except for the fireplace wall which was completely panelled. This allowed tapestries to be hung on the other three walls. That is a possible arrangement at Queensberry House and certainly all of the main rooms, and many others besides, were decorated with hangings of some kind. However, this does not preclude the use of full panelling and there are numerous examples of rooms with large panels above dado level that were decorated with hangings, not least Holyrood Palace.

11.6.3 Decorative hangings (see endpapers)

Tapestry hangings at Queensberry House are always referred to as 'Arras' hangings and crop up in all of the inventories. Most entries provide no detail on the nature of the hangings but some are described as 'forest' hangings, meaning that they had an essentially two-dimensional pattern of foliage (Thornton 1990, 130), which was the most commonly used tapestry in Scotland at this time (Swain 1988, 49). The more prestigious and expensive 'History' tapestries were more elaborate hangings showing scenes from classical mythology,

history or literature and there were a number of such sets in Queensberry House. In 1695, both the drawing room and best bedroom were each adorned with three pieces of Arras depicting 'the History of Ovid', which presumably referred to scenes from *Metamorphosis*. Later, in 1706, as stoic philosophy personified in the Diogenes set was sent from Canongate to the Duke's house in Piccadilly, London, it was replaced by Roman stoicism and imperial triumph, represented in a set of eight tapestries with scenes from the life of Marcus Aurelius. One of the inventories refers to these as 'The procession of Marcus Aurelius', suggesting that it showed a triumphal procession. Cochrane's marginalia show that this set was split between the drawing room and dressing room. While expensive items like these were clearly intended for the more prestigious areas of the house, tapestry hangings were found all over the house, including the bedchambers and closets on the upper floor. Despite their high value and prestige, however, tapestry works in general were not looked after as precious materials and they tended to wear out fairly quickly (Thornton 1990, 131). As a result even expensive items might be recycled to less prestigious areas of the house as they wore out. This certainly seems to be one of the messages of the 1723 inventory, which mentions 'old Arras' in less important rooms and even includes an 'old piece of History arras' in a small room overlooking the street in the west wing. What is certain is that this form of decoration and insulation was widely used by the Duke of Queensberry in his house. When Jean Wardlaw made her inventory in January 1708, quite apart from the hangings in use, she listed 38 pieces in storage on the top floor at that time.

Tapestry, or Arras, was only one kind of hanging that was used in Queensberry House and a number of other materials can be found in the inventories. The most prestigious of these were leather hangings, which were very popular in Scotland in the late 17th and early 18th centuries. They had been used as early as 1623 at Hamilton Palace and were imported directly from Holland for most of the century. By the 1690s there was even a manufactory in Edinburgh, which supplied hangings to households all over Scotland.[20]

At Queensberry House, in every inventory from 1695 to 1723, the main dining room was hung with at least one stamped and gilded leather hanging. Two large pieces were hanging there in 1695, probably on the north and west walls. In 1706, five pieces were brought from the Duke's house in Piccadilly and several of these hangings were to be found in the dining room, along with two black, gilded leather screens.

As the first room in the state apartment, the dining room was an important public space and a high-prestige area of the house, but, whereas tapestry hangings were deemed the most appropriate adornment for the other major rooms, leather hangings were frequently used in dining rooms because they did not hold the smell of food as textiles did (Thornton 1990, 285).

Elsewhere, other types of hanging adorned the walls of the rooms of family and servants, ranging from 'flour'd drogget' (woollen cloth), and various striped hangings mentioned in 1707 and 1708, to a number of different kinds of paper hangings found mainly in servants' quarters on the uppermost floor of the house. In 1723 these included four pieces of green and yellow painted paper in the housekeeper's room, four pieces of stamped paper hangings in the *valet de chambre's* room and red and blue painted paper hangings in the steward's room.

While the hangings discussed so far were almost part of the structure of the rooms, since they were placed against walls and in many cases combined with panelling, other kinds of hangings were also employed. Window curtains, which sometimes matched the other hangings in the room but often did not, and door curtains, which usually matched the wall hangings and provided extra insulation for the room, were widely used, although the latter mainly in the state apartment. Most important of all, perhaps, were the bed hangings, which not only matched the window curtains in many cases but also the coverings of the furniture, and it was this ensemble that gave these rooms their decorative character. In addition, while wall hangings provided an almost permanent element in some of the room schemes, hangings could also be employed for temporary decorations such as the extensive use of black crepe recorded in the 1695 inventory when the family was in mourning for Lord George (see Chapter 8).

11.6.4 Furniture and function

Using the 1723 inventory as the starting point, it is possible to gain quite a good idea of how the house was furnished at that time, but also, by comparing it with the earlier inventories, we can see that the furniture and furnishings were very little changed between c 1708 and 1723. The 1695 inventory (discussed in Chapter 7) is also relevant to this discussion because, although it reflects the house before James Smith's alterations on behalf of the second Duke and before the substantial refurnishing that appears to have taken place in 1706,

it still has interesting connections and contrasts with the later inventories. The most useful way to approach this is through a room by room examination of the house, at least on the principal floor (fig 11.8) and in some of the other important rooms.

State dining room

The 1723 inventory starts with the great dining room and lists not only the leather hangings but also a screen of the same material and 16 'Black Rushia leather chairs'. Inventory 4 (1707/08) indicates not only that this same furniture was in place at that time, but also that the hangings, screen and chairs were all in matching gilded, black leather.[21] This contrasts with 1695, when the room was furnished with cane chairs. In 1723, the other main feature of this room was a 'large wanescot oval table with turned feet'. Large oval tables were a feature of Scottish dining rooms in the late 17th and early 18th centuries, and it is possible that the 'folding wainscott oval table' listed in 1695 was still in use in 1723. In 1695, there was also a folding cedarwood table with a drawer and this use of two tables was relatively common (Carruthers 1996, 128). In none of the inventories is there any indication of a large, permanent dining table; dining tables in this period tended to be made of smaller pieces that could be combined as required and dismantled for storage. That seems to have been the case here, where a set of black tables was to be found in the room, combined with stands and a glass and with matching stands on either side of the fireplace. Some of this furniture was probably placed between the two windows as an ensemble comprising glass, table and two stands, making a classic 17th-century 'triad'. All in all, the room seems to have been rather sombre, relieved only by the brightness of the gilding, the mirror and the white silk lace mountings of the crimson window curtains and cushions.

State drawing room

With the construction of the new vestibule, the state drawing room was able to expand into the space of the old lobby. Thereafter the room was furnished by Robert Cochrane in 1706 and most of the original furniture seems to have been still in place in 1723. In common with most drawing rooms of this period, the furnishings were fairly simple, restricted mainly to chairs.[22] In 1723, the main furniture for the room was a set of 14 chairs: two easy chairs and 12 elbow chairs, 'all covered with aurora tabbie', evidently a form of silk upholstery (Thornton 1990, 116). In 1723, the other major pieces of furniture were a writing desk and a matching gilded mirror, and a 'black table and stands' matching a black-framed looking glass. In 1707/08 there was an ensemble of black japanned table, glass and stands, similar to that in the dining room and probably positioned in the same way, between the windows. It cannot be shown that the table and mirror were the same pieces that were in the room in 1723, although a black writing table was certainly brought to the house in 1706.[23] Certainly, the arrangement would have been broadly similar, although, in the 18th century, the stands have been dispensed with.[24]

Most of the rest of the furnishings do not seem to have changed in this room. In each list, there are the same white, Indian silk damask window curtains, with pands (and also window cushions, in 1723) and the same portrait of the Duke of Douglas. The walls were decorated with two large pieces of Arras hangings, probably the same pieces recorded by Robert Cochrane in 1706, when two of the Marcus Aurelius set were hung in this room.[25] The only significant addition to the room by 1723 is the 'fine India screen consisting of six leaves'.[26] Again, it possible that this is the same item as one recorded in 1706 as having been brought from London.[27]

Principal bedchamber

The main feature of the principal bedchamber was the great bed, which was described in the finest detail in 1695 as 'ane fyne yellow mohair bed consisting of four piece of curtains lyn'd with gold colour's tafety with small mix't silk fringes round bottom and edges'. This was a very elaborate piece of furniture. It was a full tester bed which sat on a bedstall (platform), with gilded claw feet resting on two 'fine carpets'. It had an architectural cornice above the valances and gilded finials on the corners. The inventory also refers to a *tour de lit*, which indicates a further elaboration and confirms the grandness of the bed. The *tour de lit* was a series of curtains that wrapped around the normal series of hangings in order to protect them (Thornton 1990, 177–9). These curtains were suspended on iron rods and the Queensberry inventory shows that some system of pulleys must have been used to open and close them. Clearly, the main bed hangings must have been of the very highest quality to warrant such protection and the yellow silk mohair and gold taffeta of the state bed of the first Duke was of such quality; indeed, even the protective drapes were of gold satin.

In 1695, the furnishings of this room were completed with a set of six chairs in the same upholstery as the bed, a triad in quilted olive wood and a matching cabinet. Portraits of the Duke and the Duchess and Lady Ann, their youngest daughter, completed the room.

Post-1706 decoration was equally luxurious. The bed was hung with blue and white striped mohair hangings and blue silk lining and this same material was used on the eight chairs and the window curtains. In addition, a large carpet under the bed (probably still on the platform recorded in 1695), two looking glasses, one above a writing table, the other above the fireplace, two pairs of black japanned stands, and a portrait of General Ramsay made up the rest of the furnishing in 1723. Once again, this is broadly confirmed by the other evidence, notably in Inventory 4 (1707/08), which is almost identical to the 1723 list. Inventory 5 (1708) is the source for its description as 'My Lord and Lady Dutches's bed chamber'. It also shows that at this date the conjugal chamber included one rather risqué item, 'Rape of Sabine a statue on a pear tree pedestal'.

Dressing room

Beyond the bedchamber lay the Duchess's dressing room. By 1723, this was rather simply furnished, mainly with chairs. This differs slightly from Inventory 4 (1707/08) when there were far more chairs and the whole room was brightened by the use of scarlet and yellow damask upholstery. One item of interest in this inventory was the 'trimming chair', possibly the same item as the 'dressing chair' of 1723 and, in both cases, indicating an item probably used in the toilette, possibly hairdressing.

As a result of the work carried out for the second Duke, the Duchess's quarters had been somewhat refined from the earlier Hatton–Balmakellie phase of the house. The closet to the north of the dressing room was superseded by the new tower closet and the old room is referred to (in 1723) as 'the waiting room at the back of my Lady Dutchess's dressing room', emphasising the alternative approach to the more private end of the planning sequence.

Closet

As a result of James Smith's remodelling of the house in the late 1690s, the two towers on the garden front provided closets for the Duke and Duchess. The combined information from the various inventories allows quite a detailed picture of the way this most private and intimate of spaces was used by the Duchess in the early years of the 18th century. The archaeological evidence indicates an original coved, octagonal ceiling with a simple cornice. The room itself is almost square, but with one corner chamfered with the fireplace. The implication of all of this is that the room was furnished in such a way as to chamfer the other corners, with shelves or with some items of furniture. In this way, the room would have been octagonal in conformity with the ceiling.

The 1723 inventory describes quite a grand but intimate room. It was decorated with forest tapestry and had four chairs covered in red and green mohair, a pier glass, a walnut cabinet, a small, folding cedarwood table, and curtains that matched those in the dressing room. The earlier inventories from the 1706–8 period confirm most of this but add additional detail. The picture that emerges is of a well-furnished room, in which the Duchess might entertain her friends, playing cards and taking tea (one undated inventory in the bundle also lists a chocolate pot and stove). On the walls were tapestry hangings and a great number of paintings, mainly portraits and landscapes. On shelves and in cabinets around the walls, she had arranged her china collection, which is listed in detail in the inventory. This amounted to several hundred items, including five teapots, five or six teasets, some of them missing saucers, and dozens of other dishes, all in a variety of colours. Little precise detail is provided about the collection: there is a mention of 'ane pair of stoups of rope work' and the occasional mention of dishes with gilded covers. In addition to the dishes and cruets, there were also some figurines and small animal pieces, including a hart and '2 beasts that could not be named'. All of this builds up a picture of a classic female closet of this period.

West wing

Most of the undated and fragmentary inventories provide information on the principal apartment and it is impossible to get the same depth of information for the rest of the house. However, given the consistency between 1707 and 1723 already demonstrated, it is perhaps reasonable to assume that the same consistency applied at least in the other major spaces of the house.

Having said that, the simplicity of the furniture of the 'Old Duke's Dressing Room in the east wing' in Inventory 7 (1723) perhaps indicates a room that was very much less important than in 1707. Old Arras

hangings, striped worsted curtains, a table, mirror and six rush chairs do not sound like a very luxurious private apartment, unlike 1695 when it functioned as the first Duke's dressing room (discussed in Chapter 10).

On the west side, the new apartment added by the second Duke contained a drawing room furnished in a very similar manner to that of the Duchess in the main apartment. Tapestry on the walls, a dozen elbow chairs with padded seats in purple and blue velvet, a writing desk and a large mirror made up the main furnishings of this apartment.

The archaeology of the staircase area of this part of the house is almost Piranesian in its complexity and there appears to have been a strong concern with servicing the west wing from the basement in such a way that the principal dining room, the new drawing room and the new dining room could all be served easily and independently, adding to the idea that the west wing could have functioned almost independently of the rest of the house. The 1723 inventory mentions a waiting room between the two main rooms here and that is borne out by the archaeological remains, although the precise arrangement remains unclear.

The furnishing of the 'large dining room to the street', in 1723, seems rather basic, comprising as it did three large tables, the oval one apparently the same as that in the principal dining room.

The Duke's closet, in the tower, corresponding to the elaborately decorated closet occupied by the Duchess, would have functioned in a similar way, as an inner sanctum for relaxation and a place to indulge his interests. Evidence concerning the furniture and furnishings is rather scant. A pier glass and corner cabinet are mentioned in 1723, but are not mentioned in Inventory 5 (1708), which lists instead a tent bed. This was probably some kind of portable field bed, which is perhaps what we would expect to find in a closet, and such a bed is listed in Inventory 1 (1706).[28]

The other items in Inventory 5 (1708) are a clock, a picture of Pope Innocent and a weather glass. Clearly, the picture that emerges here is not nearly as consistent nor as detailed as that for the principal apartment, however, the description of the room as 'the closet where my Lord Duke's library is'[29] provides a vital clue as to the function of the room and it is possible to see it as the western counterpart to the Duchess's closet in the eastern tower. Just as she indulged her interest in collecting china in this private space, so the Duke used his for his books. Scarring in the corners of this room strongly suggests that bookshelves were built into the room and, because they were therefore part of the fabric of the room rather than its removable furniture, these do not feature in the inventories. That the room was used for books is, however, unquestionably the case because a full catalogue of the library survives (Inventory 6, 1707/8). There are almost 300 books in the list, divided into folio and quarto volumes and then into broad subject categories including History, Divinity, 'Prackticks' (which included political works but also Virgil), miscellaneous and pamphlets. Two architectural books are listed: one, simply, a 'Book of Architecture', the other 'The Compleat Architect', which was probably Joseph Moxon's edition of *Vignola*, published in 1655.[30] This gentlemanly interest in architecture on the part of the man who modernised Queensberry House is further attested by the Drumlanrig part of the inventory, which lists Freart de Chambray, Pierre le Muet and Scammozzi.[31]

The service and upper floors of the house have already been discussed above in terms of function and planning; however, it is worth saying a little more about the furnishing and decoration of these areas. This, of necessity, must be a much briefer discussion than for the principal floor because the rooms are difficult to locate (no inventory allocates rooms to a floor level until 1723) and because the furniture was both fairly sparse and fairly unremarkable. There are three areas that are of some interest however: the provisions made for the children; the second apartment on the first floor of the house; and the continuing importance of the upper areas for storage and service, and, as part of that, the role of the gallery at Queensberry House.

Accommodation for the children

In this period, the Duke and Duchess's children were still very young, therefore the nurseries and other accommodation for the children were an important part of the house. It is therefore worth exploring a little more where they fitted into the new building. The eldest surviving child in the late 1690s was James (1697–1715); Charles was born in 1698 (died 1778), followed by Mary in 1699 (died 1703). Two younger daughters were born around 1700, Jean (died 1729) and Anne (died 1741), and the youngest son, George, was born in 1701 (died 1725) (Douglas 1910, 143).

Of these, the only ones who are mentioned consistently in the documentation that relates to the house are the younger children, Jean, Anne and George. In Robert Cochrane's 1706 inventory each of these

children has a room in 'the nurseries' which in each case is combined with either a closet or a 'back room', or, in the case of Lord George, both. These rooms, the contents of which included beds, tables (including a 'playing table'), 'frames for the fire' (presumably fire guards) and even a smoothing iron, were probably for servants who looked after the children, who were only around the ages of six to eight years old. The precise location of these quarters is uncertain, but they were almost certainly at the top of the house, either in the garret or on the floor below, as had been the case in 1695.

By 1708, the children's quarters are described in slightly more elaborate terms.[32] There was clearly a nursery suite, probably on the second floor of the house. This comprised a dining room for the children, with a room off, a chamber and dressing room for Lord George, a chamber and two closets for Lady Jean, and a chamber and outer room for Lady Ann. In the last case, the description of an outer room is reminiscent of the accommodation provided for her namesake and aunt in 1695, which was on the west side of the second floor. It is probably not appropriate to identify this apartment precisely with the earlier one, but it is likely to have been at least on the same floor. As in 1695, this level of the house also seems to have been where some of the more important servants had their quarters, a Mr Barclay and a Mr Naismith, who was presumably the man charged with overseeing the building work for the Duke in 1697.

By 1723, the children had all moved on, with the exception of Lady Ann, for whom quite commodious accommodation was provided. This comprised most, if not all, of the first floor of the west wing of the house (fig 11.10), with a bedchamber, with white linen damask hangings throughout, decorated with silk lace, and a contrasting gilded, japanned table. Beyond that, she had her own drawing room, with green Camlet hangings mounted with green and white lace and a japanned console table and mirror. Her closet also contained a bed: 'an old yellow silk field bed' with additional hangings in green and white on bed and windows. This room also contained a tea table and a number of presses, one with glass doors.

A slightly surprising element of the inventories is that there are two children whose names are never mentioned, namely the two eldest sons, James and Charles. James was the eldest, but, because of his incapacity, Charles was identified as the heir. Charles may not have been mentioned as he was away at school at the time these inventories were made. James is more of a puzzle. According to Chambers, there were quarters for James who 'was always kept confined in a ground apartment, in the western wing of the house, upon the windows of which, till within these few years, the boards still remained by which the dreadful receptacle was darkened to prevent the idiot from looking out or being seen' (Chambers 1868, 337). It would not be surprising if the family tried to hide the fact that they had a child who suffered as he did, but we would surely expect a neutral and workaday document like an inventory to give us some indication of how he was provided for. The fact that he is never mentioned in the inventories might suggest that he was not in the house, although, on the other hand, none of the inventories describe what was at the north end of the west wing, possibly indicating an area that was 'off-limits'. Cochrane's 1706 inventory does refer to 'an apartment below stairs', which was almost certainly in this west wing. This area contains two rooms at the north end, the furthest one vaulted and with a small west-facing window.

Second apartment on the first floor (fig 11.10)

In houses of this period, it would have been normal for the floor above the state apartment, in this case the first floor, to have an apartment plan that echoed the lower floor. As discussed in Chapter 9, this was not the case prior to 1695, when the arrangement of the rooms suggested a salon arrangement with small apartments off on either side. However, the new staircase in the west wing made possible the opening up of a sequence to match the lower state sequence by entering at the west end, rather than in the middle. As previously discussed, the archaeology is inconclusive here and it seems that the west wing may well have functioned as a self-contained area, but, by 1723 at least, the logic of the pattern of the floor plan of the upper floor is confirmed in the inventory, which identifies a series of 'Dining room to the garden, Drawing room, and Bedchamber off the said room'.

The dining room was furnished in a similar manner to the one on the floor below, 12 leather chairs, and a leather screen, but no hangings, and no table. The drawing room was hung with forest Arras and had a console table and mirror in black wood (probably japanned). The bedchamber had no bed but an easy chair in blue upholstery and a black table with green velvet top.

Surprisingly, this was not the only dining room on this floor and the second one, 'to the street' and probably on the east side, was also only partly furnished, although in this case with a full set of leather hangings.

Service areas and the gallery

The concern here is not so much with the furnishing of servants' rooms or with the equipment in the various service areas of the house. The furnishings were fairly mundane, as we would expect, throughout the period covered by the inventories, and the equipment is not the concern of this chapter. Rather the issue is about the use of the upper floors of the house for storage of furniture and furnishings and, to some extent, their care and maintenance. This was certainly a function of the attic prior to 1695 (see Chapter 9) and that continued after the expansion of the house by the second Duke. The linen room, or laundry, is still mentioned in the early 18th-century inventories (although not in 1723, when the attic is not covered by the inventory) and invariably as a general storage space, with furniture as well as upholstery kept there.

Perhaps the most surprising, and slightly disappointing, aspect of the inventories is what they tell us about the gallery. From the outset, or at least from 1706 when Robert Cochrane made his inventory, the gallery was used a storage room and it continued to be used in that way right through until 1723. This may have been due to the fact that the house was well furnished but the family only in residence sporadically and so in between those visits much more was put into storage than would normally have been the case. Whatever the reason, it meant that the gallery seems never to have functioned either as a place for sheltered promenading, or a place in which to show off a picture collection. From the point of view of learning about the furnishing and decoration of the house, however, the inventories of this glorified storeroom are extremely useful and allow the historian to trace much of the furniture from gallery to rooms and back again. The inventories also provide an excellent overview of the furniture as a whole and from this it is clear that the house was lavishly appointed. There were, in total, some 300 chairs in the building over the 20 or so years covered, around a quarter of them elbow or armchairs. They included cane chairs and Dutch chairs (accounting for about half the total number) and a large number of elaborate chairs that formed part of the various suites, including green velvet, yellow mohair, blue velvet, yellow silk damask and red mohair sets, in addition to those discussed already. There were over 60 tables, ranging from black japanned tables to 15 oval tables of different sizes in oak, pine and cedar.

In all of the wealth of materials and furniture that was installed at Queensberry House one major set stands out. In 1706, among the many items sent from Piccadilly to Edinburgh by Robert Cochrane, was a large set of crimson velvet furniture. His inventory includes '12 elbow chairs with gilt frames; 6 chairs without elbows, black frames; 2 stools, ditto frames, all belonging to the Crimson Velvett furniture'.[33] In the rest of the inventory, which mainly lists the contents of boxes stored in the gallery, the details of this set gradually emerge. Box 30 contained the hangings and other furnishings of a great bed, including four curtains, counterpane, valence, all lined with silk and trimmed with gold. The two window curtains that also formed part of this set had the same embellishment. Box 87 contained the bolster boards and tester for this bed and its cornice was to be found in another box. Inventory 4 (1707/08), which includes a relisting of the material stored in the gallery in 1706, confirms that the set was still in the house at that time, and adds 'a crimson velvet safoy and two cushions . . .'.[34]

The complete set, therefore comprised a great bed, with four main hangings in red velvet, lined with silk and trimmed with gold. These were matched by the window curtains. A sofa, or perhaps a day bed, was also included, along with 12 elbow chairs, six plain chairs and two stools. All of this amounted to a set of furniture considerably grander than anything that is actually recorded in use in the house. The principal bedchamber was certainly luxurious, but was not as rich and did not comprise so many pieces as the red velvet set. It is difficult, therefore, to see how this lavish set of furniture could have been used. It was stored in the gallery in 1706 and was evidently still in storage there at the time Inventory 4 was drawn up in 1707/08. It appears again, however, in an undated document listing, 'Goods proposed to be sent from the Duke of Queensberry's Lodging in the Canongait to the house of Drumlanrig in carts'.[35] The author of this list has scored out the word 'from the gallery', indicating that the material in question had been stored there prior to shipment. The dating of this document is uncertain, but it refers to the 'late Duchess', indicating a date after her death in 1709. What all of this suggests, therefore, is that a very grand set of furniture, almost certainly for the principal bedchamber, was brought to Queensberry House, but for some reason was never used and in the end was moved on to the main Queensberry residence at Drumlanrig. It has so far proved impossible to document this furniture at Drumlanrig, although research is continuing to attempt to track it down and

it is possible that at least some of this set survives, in the red velvet furniture, including elbow chairs and a day bed, in the ante-room at Drumlanrig Castle.

11.7 Queensberry House and the Union of 1707

The 1706 inventory certainly suggests that the house was very full at that very busy time for the Duke and his political allies. The inventory is simply a list of items of furniture and furnishings sent from the family house in Piccadilly to Edinburgh to supplement what was already in Queensberry House and is annotated by Robert Cochrane, the servant responsible for organising the house and making sure that the rooms were adequately furnished. These notes include the information that other members of the Duke's family were accommodated and there are a number of references to the Countess and Earl of March and their family. William, Earl of March, was the younger brother of the Duke, a political ally, member of the Scottish Parliament and governor of Edinburgh Castle, 1702–4 (Douglas 1910, 144–6). However, although there are references to the Earl, his wife and their family, there is no doubt that he was dead by the time this inventory was made, because he had succumbed to a surfeit of alcohol at a drinking party in Edinburgh the previous September (Doubleday & de Walden 1932, 456). His widow and six children were all living at Queensberry House at this time and the Earl, who was given accommodation in the Duke's upper dressing room, was actually the second earl, nine or ten years old but separated off from his younger siblings and relatives. Cochrane also noted that some of the things he had listed had been 'moved for the conveniencie of the Earl of March's family and the Earl of Mar's'.

Mar was not a relative of Queensberry, but the inventories make it clear that accommodation was provided for him and his wife and child. He was a very important political ally and, as Secretary of State for Scotland, worked with Queensberry, who, as Queen's Commissioner to the Scottish Parliament, was responsible for conducting the business of the House that saw the Act passed through the Scots Parliament. Mar's letters of this period provide a very detailed picture of the day-to-day business of the preparations for the legislation and the progress through the parliamentary debates (Mar & Kellie Mss). They show that Mar himself came up to Edinburgh in mid-August 1706 and the Duke followed him about a month later. Between October and March 1707, the political business securing the Act was done and Mar, along with most other Scottish politicians, stayed in Edinburgh throughout most of that time.

Apart from the business of the house, the winter was also spent in private negotiation and intrigue and the lodgings of the various Scots noblemen on both sides of the debate became the scenes of much of this activity. Queensberry, of course, was very active in this. He was in the fortunate position of having rather generous accommodation, because he not only had his greatly extended house but also official lodgings in Holyrood Palace. In the context of the Union debates, the fact that the Duke of Hamilton, one of the main opponents of the Act, had substantial quarters in the palace, as hereditary keeper, made it all the more important that Queensberry, who after all was representing Queen Anne, should exercise his right to residence there. Contemporary sources make it clear that the palace was an important base for Queensberry and it became the scene of much of the political intrigue that took place over that winter (Lockhart of Carnwath 1817, 164); Mar's letters certainly mention occasions when he was invited back to Queensberry's quarters, there to follow up the day's debates, while on the other side the Dukes of Hamilton and Atholl were doing the same with their supporters (Mar & Kellie Mss).

Therefore, while the Duke and his cronies plotted in the palace, the Duchess, the extended family and guests lived alongside in Queensberry House. However, notwithstanding the fact that the house was clearly a haven of domesticity, the Duke might still have used it not only as a refuge from the Edinburgh mob (Lockhart of Carnwath 1817, 164, 166) but also as a rendezvous for parliamentary business away from the prying eyes of his adversaries, who shared the palace with him.

Here, the design of the new wing is very important. Its discreet quality has already been noted and this would have allowed the rest of the house to function normally, while the Duke could enter the new wing directly from the vestibule and entertain his allies and friends in his suite of dining room and drawing room. With the only connection between the two parts of the house through the vestibule, the west wing was effectively a separate building and could have functioned independently of the rest of the house. These highly unusual arrangements, whether or not they were designed with a political purpose in mind, certainly connect Queensberry House to the machinations of the Union negotiations and therefore

make it particularly appropriate that this building should form the centrepiece of a new parliament.

Notes

1 Buccleuch Mss, NRA(S) 1275/1124.
2 ECA, Canongate Charters, vol. 5, 1683–1711; Mungo, sometimes known as Kentigern, appears in his official capacity involving property transfers on behalf of the Incorporation of Bakers in 1684 (item 709), and 1691 (item 758). There is also a precept of clair constat in his name of three tenements of land, including one adjacent to Queensberry House, dated 17 July 1700, suggesting that he had died at around this time (item 820).
3 ECA, Dean of Guild Court Book, vol. 7, 86; Duke of Queensberry v Mungo Malloch, 13/6/1695.
4 ECA, Dean of Guild Court Book, vol. 7, 129–35; Duke of Queensberry v Mungo Malloch, 1697.
5 NAS, Hamilton Mss GD406/11221 & 11222.
6 Buccleuch Mss NRA(S) 1275/1103: 1723 inventory.
7 Buccleuch Mss NRA(S) 1275/1103: 1723 inventory.
8 Buccleuch Mss NRA(S) 1275/1103: 1723 inventory.
9 An upper dressingroom is mentioned in an inventory of 10 June 1706, Buccleuch Mss NRA(S) 1275/1103.
10 Buccleuch Mss NRA(S) 1275/1103: 1708 inventory.
11 NAS, Dalhousie Mss GD45/18/864.
12 The mirror is suggested by the archaeologiocal evidence, and there is some support for it in the 1723 inventory, which mentions a pier glass. In this room, the mirror could not have been placed in the normal position, between two windows, and a corner position is a possibility.
13 This section is based on Lowrey 2000, 44–62. The numbering of the inventories adopted in that article is also used here, although reference is also made to an earlier, 1695 inventory and to an inventory of furniture used by a tenant in 1712. These two do not form part of the numbering sequence which is:

Inventory 1 (1706).   The earliest is an 'Inventory of goods disposed of by Robert Cochrane, 10 June 1706'. This takes the form of a list of goods sent to Edinburgh from the Duke's house in Piccadilly, with marginalia indicating in which rooms some of the goods were to be placed.

Inventories 2 and 3 (1707 & 1708).   After the Union, the household was scaled down and there are two dated inventories, one by Mrs Wardlaw (presumably, the housekeeper) made on 26 December 1707 and another made exactly one month later.

Inventory 4 (1707/08).   This is an undated inventory but it is in a small notebook which contains a list of items in the gallery, based on Cochrane's 1706 inventory, suggesting that his list was still extant, and goes on to a detailed listing of the principal floor of the house, room by room; it then concludes with a more general list of the furniture, utensils, etc, in the rest of the house. All of this is in the same handwriting and includes references to children's items, suggesting the beginning of the 18th century when the Queensberry children were still young. For these reasons, this inventory is dated to 1707/08.

Inventory 5 (1708.) The evidence for dating this is very similar to that for Inventory 4. Cochrane's inventory is still referred to but an indication of date is provided by a record of goods being shipped to Drumlanrig on 31 December 1707. The inventory lists items in some of the rooms but things were clearly in a state of flux, the Duchess's dressing room, for example, containing a total of 30 chamber pots, suggesting, perhaps, that goods were being packed up for shipment to Drumlanrig, or at least for storage in the gallery at Queensberry House.

Inventory 6 (1707/08). This is a catalogue of the Queensberry library at Drumlanrig and Queensberry House. It is dated here on the basis that it ties in with Inventory 5, which refers to the Duke's library at Queensberry House.

Inventory 7 (1723). This is the most systematic inventory, organised by floor and by room, giving the most complete picture of the house at that time.

14 One survival in the building is discussed below and a number of fireplaces have been traced by Tom Addyman to Gosford House in East Lothian, having been sold to the Earl of Wemyss by William Aitcheson, c 1803.

15 Buccleuch Mss, NRA(S)1275/1103, is a bundle containing a total of 24 inventories or fragments of inventories. The 1695 inventory has gone astray from the Buccleuch archive, but a copy is available in ECL, Edinburgh Room (C0012389013/qYHV1481H).

16 This chapter is based on those seven inventories identified and numbered in Lowrey 2000, 45–6, along with other fragmentary documents also from around the 1707/08 period in the same bundle (NRA(S)1275/1103) and the 1695 inventory, which had not been discovered at the time the article was written.

17 Lauderdale Papers, NRA(S)832/61/68. 'Instructions for my house in the Canongate, with the costs thereof, etc', 22 March 1681.

18 Buccleuch Mss, NRA(S)1275/1124, 'Instructions by his Grace the Lord Duke of Queensberry to James Naismith given at London the 13th Decr. 1697'.

19 Hay of Belton Mss, GD73/1/12, Agreement between David Hay of Belton and William Tait, wright, 13/4/1710. I am grateful to Dr Tristram Clarke of the National Archives of Scotland for this reference.

20 Alexander Brand was a merchant who, having imported stamped leather hangings into Scotland from Holland, secured a 17-year monopoly on the production of such hangings at a new manufactory in Edinburgh, c 1692. See NAS RH15/53. Hangings from around the same period can still be seen in Prestonfield House Hotel, Edinburgh.

21 This also ties in with the dated evidence of Inventory 1 (1706).

22 The furnishings of this room listed in all of the Queensberry House inventories show that the room was furnished in a similar manner to both Panmure House and Ham House. See Panmure Mss, SRO GD45/18/864, 'Inventar of Household Furniture in the House of Panmure', 1695, and *Furniture History*, 16 (1980), special issue on Ham House, especially 67–71.

23 Inventory 1 (1706).

24 *Furniture History* (1980, 68) discusses the evolution of the 17th-century ensemble of table, glass and stands into the 18th-century pier glass and console table arrangement, in which the stands are dispensed with and replaced by candelabra on the table.

25 Inventory 1 (1706).

26 Probably some kind of oriental screen, not necessarily Indian. See Thornton 1990, 259.

27 Inventory 1 (1706) has a list of screens, including an Indian silk screen.

28 Mentioned as the contents of box 82.

29 Inventory 5 (1708).

30 Moxon 1655, with further editions until 1694.

31 The 1707/08 inventory is identified as Inventory 4 in Lowrey 2000.

32 Inventory 6 (1707/08.)

33 Inventory 1 (1706).

34 Inventory 4 (1707/08).

35 Buccleuch Mss, NRA(S) 1275/1103, item 15.

Chapter 12

The gardens of Queensberry House 1660–1808

JOHN LOWREY

12.1 The urban garden in Edinburgh Old Town

The relationship between town and garden in the medieval burgh was a close one. One of the main reasons for a burgh's existence was to bring about a concentration of people to provide a market for goods and to provide a focus for local agriculture. Many of the burghers were farmers, with lands around the edges of the burgh and tofts, burgage plots or tenements, which included gardens, within. These were also cultivated for food and many were distinctly agricultural in character, with kail, bere (barley) and oats being grown. Livestock such as pigs, cows, horses and chickens were also kept there.

The relationship between the open space of the city and the economic activity that took place there also led to other kinds of usage, including tanning and other small-scale industries, which have been recorded on the Parliament site (see Chapter 3). All of these contributed to the overbuilding of the backlands, so that byres, stables and workshops of various kinds were intermixed with the housing that also sprang up in these areas.

In the Canongate, there were other factors that influenced developments. There is certainly a long history of gardening, of a grander and more specialist kind, and on a more ambitious scale than in the rest of Edinburgh. The more complex typology of the garden in this area is related partly to topography, but mainly to the proximity of Holyrood Palace and its predecessor, Holyrood Abbey. The Augustinian canons of the abbey developed extensive gardens there, including orchards which usually featured in monastic gardens (Robertson 2000, 105), and these were taken over when the monastic institution was superseded by the royal residence and developed as royal gardens, which survived more or less intact into the 17th century (Jamieson 1994; fig 12.1). However, the palace gardens, in the absence of the monarch, were also turned to other purposes that led to both commercial and even academic uses. After the rebuilding of the palace by Sir William Bruce in the 1670s, and the partial reconfiguration of the gardens that went with that, the Quaker gardener, William

Miller, was appointed hereditary kitchen gardener and thus started a long association between the Millers and the palace that saw the function of a large part of the gardens change from royal pleasure and kitchen gardens to specialist nursery gardens. Miller's son, George, started the process before the end of the 17th century, but the real impetus for this new business came from a partnership between William, the royal gardener, and his younger son, also William. Their nursery was eventually to encompass most of the royal gardens, as well as the ground immediately to the south of Queensberry House (fig 12.5) and the business was one of the most dominant in the Scottish nursery trade until the second half of the 18th century (Robertson 2000, 196–7).

Holyrood Palace also formed the backdrop for yet another aspect of the history of gardening that forms part of the context for Queensberry House and that is the establishment of the Physic Garden by Sir Robert Sibbald in 1670 (Cox 1935, 149–51). The Miller family's development of commercial nursery ground was unusual in the late 17th century; a much more common practice at Holyrood was for the keepers of the various gardens or yards to let out ground to market gardeners, who would supply the city with fruit and vegetables. It was from one of these palace gardeners, John Brown, that Robert Sibbald and Andrew Balfour leased a small plot of land on the north side of the palace as the original Edinburgh Physic Garden. This plot was quickly superseded when the first keeper of the garden, James Sutherland, found a new, much larger site alongside Trinity Hospital in 1675 (Fletcher & Brown 1970, 7). However, Sutherland's energetic expansion of the gardens led to new developments around the College (now Old College, Edinburgh University) and in the King's Garden, to the north of the palace forecourt, which he took over in 1695 (Fletcher & Brown 1970, 13). Here he laid out a garden around the great sundial and raised melons as well as the more traditional medicinal plants. He also petitioned the Privy Council for funds to build a greenhouse, 'to preserve oranges, lemons, myrtles with other tender greens and fine exetick and forraigne plants in winter

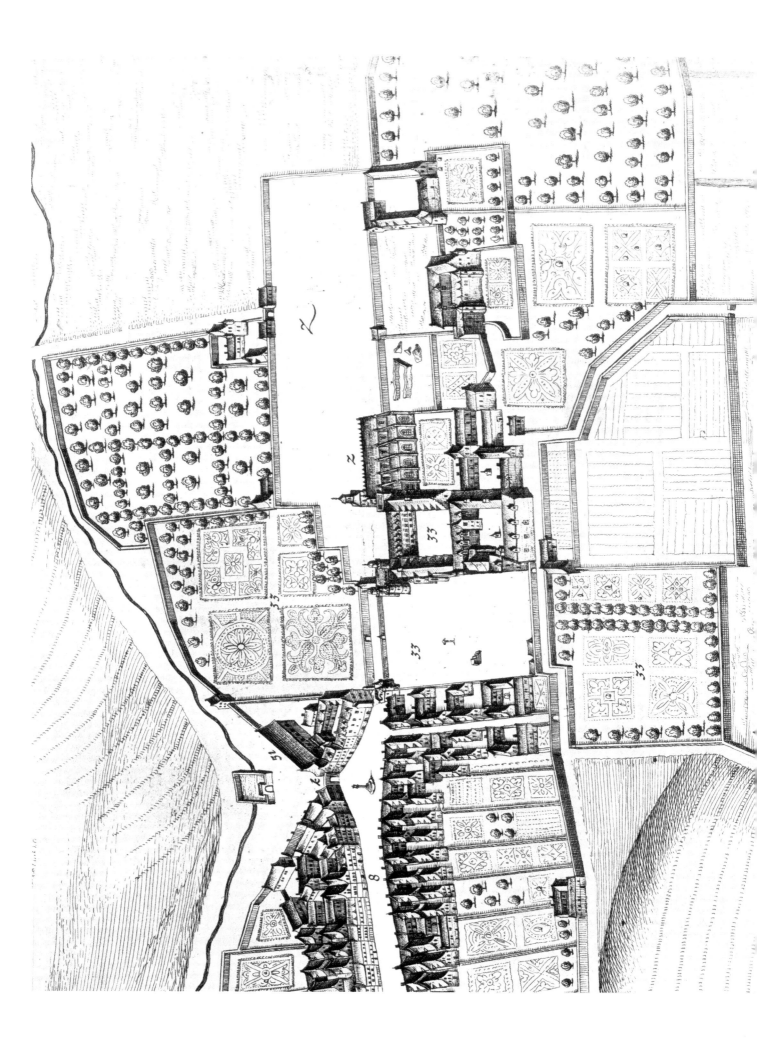

...' (Privy Council Register, 12 December 1695, quoted in Fletcher & Brown, 1970, 13). The site of this garden is clearly identifiable on Gordon of Rothiemay's 1647 plan of Edinburgh (fig 12.1) and the layout of Sutherland's garden, with the space quartered around the sundial, is recorded from Edgar's 1742 plan right through until the mid-19th century. On a number of maps, including Edgar, the area is actually labelled 'Physick garden' (fig 12.5).[1]

The final component in the garden typology of the Canongate in the mid-17th century was the aristocratic garden and the most famous of these was undoubtedly Moray House, where the gardens stepped back in a number of terraces from the house on the street to the South Back of the Canongate. In the early 18th century it was described as having:

> a very large parterre or flower garden behind, with four hanging walks or terraces to the bottom, where there is a bowling green, and a handsome pavilion or pleasure house (Macky 1723, 64).

Another source even suggests that, such was its fame and popularity that it became 'a place of public resort ... a sort of public promenade' (Bonar 1856, 16).

The other important house in the Canongate in the mid-17th century was Winton House, sited almost exactly opposite Queensberry House (fig 12.2). This had been the townhouse of the Earls of Seton (later Winton) from the middle of the 16th century and was noted for the elaborate architecture of the house, which was withdrawn from the street and built around a courtyard, adorned with evergreen trees and shrubs. Beyond the house, sloping down to the North Back of the Canongate, were elaborate formal gardens (Smith 1924, 114–15; Grant 1882, vol. 2, 34–5).

The main source for information about gardens in the city in the period immediately preceding the Balmakellie–Hatton phase of what was to become Queensberry House is James Gordon of Rothiemay's

Figure 12.2
Gordon of Rothiemay's map of 1647, Winton House to the left of the picture, withdrawn from the street and built around a courtyard. The garden is shown with three plots in designs of varying complexity, next to the garden with one large parterre (© NLS)

remarkable map of 1647 (fig 12.3). In broad terms, one of the points this map makes, and was undoubtedly intended to make by Gordon, is the great contrast between the Canongate and the city of Edinburgh itself. Although this contrast is undoubtedly exaggerated, and the precise details of individual buildings and garden designs need to be treated with great caution, nevertheless the plan does show the different character of the royal and aristocratic suburb of the Canongate. It seems likely also that the detailed garden designs, although they are represented by a series of draughtsman's conventions, bear some relation to the reality of the gardens themselves (Cox 1935, 63, concurs on this point). Gordon's treatment of Holyrood Palace indicates three types of garden: the parterre, which is found mainly in the north (king's garden) and south yards; the productive plot, found to the south; and the orchard or plantation, found to the east and north-east, which seem broadly in line with what is known of the functions of the garden (Jamieson 1994). These three basic conventions crop up across the rest of the plan and are almost certainly at least functionally accurate, even though we cannot rely on them for design detail. Certainly there is a consistency between Gordon's treatment of Moray House gardens, through Macky's description (apart

Figure 12.1
Gordon of Rothiemay's map of 1647, showing detail of Holyrood Palace and Gardens (© NLS)

Figure 12.3
Gordon of Rothiemay's map of 1647, detail showing the site of Queensberry House
(© NLS)

emphasising something that has been implicit in this discussion thus far, namely that much of the gardening activity in the area at this time was concerned with the practical and the productive. The emergence of market gardens, commercial nurseries and even the Physic Garden all attest to this, but more generally it ties in with what is known of Scottish gardening in this period, when, on the large estates, it was closely related to improvement schemes and a general desire to improve the economic performance of the estates (Lowrey 1996). The practical and the productive were therefore important elements in the Scottish garden and that comes through strongly in John Reid's *The Scots Gardener*, the first Scottish gardening book, published in 1683, which lays great emphasis on the practical aspects of gardening and advocates this even in the pleasure garden, of which he wrote:

> Plain drafts only are in use, and most preferable; that which I esteem is plain straight borders and paths running all one way …' (Reid 1683, 26).

Elsewhere he writes that 'the kitchen garden is the best of all gardens' (Reid 1683, 22), clearly indicating his preference for the productive garden. This was not simply the opinion of the professional gardener, however, and there is good evidence that the productive garden was held in high esteem in aristocratic circles also. One example of this is the remarkable record left by the Earl of Crawford, whose hobby was fruit tasting around various, mainly lowland Scotland, gardens, providing an insight into what was grown on some of the great estates at the end of the 17th century (1692).[2] This encompassed a tremendous variety of fruits, covering not only native tree fruits and currants but also more exotic items like apricots and even peaches and nectarines. Although town gardens in Edinburgh do not feature in the list, Charles Maitland's garden at Hatton House, near Ratho, does feature as a place notable for its peaches and nectarines (Robertson 2000, 123).

from the bowling green, which would be a surprise in 1647), Edgar's plan of 1742 (fig 6.4) and Sandby's panorama of c 1745 (fig 8.3). The four separate zones of the garden are certainly indicated and even a garden pavilion, albeit in a slightly different position and of a different design from the real one, is indicated. The lowest zone of the garden is indicated by a plantation of trees, almost certainly indicating an orchard and that accords well with the record of 1646 listing 24 apple trees, 60 plums, 80 cherries, damson, quince, apricot and fig trees (Robertson 2000, 128).

As far as Queensberry House is concerned, the relationship between the Rothiemay map and the site of the house has already been discussed (Chapter 7) and shown to be useful. However, it might be open to doubt that the gardens in this area were quite as grand as the series of parterres would tend to suggest, although it does seem that there were some quite prestigious houses here even at this date and pleasure gardens would certainly have featured. Perhaps of more significance is the suggestion of a belt of trees across the bottom of two of the plots that were later to make up the Queensberry Garden and which is certainly in line with what we know was there at a later date.

While the Gordon of Rothiemay plan has some use in giving an insight into the nature of gardening in the Canongate in the mid-17th century, it is worth

Using Gordon of Rothiemay as a starting point, and noting both the limitations of that source but also its consistency with other evidence, it seems that the gardens of the Canongate, and the aristocratic gardens in particular, can be characterised as combinations of pleasure and productivity. The layouts were fairly simple, with different functional zones almost certainly relating to the different levels of the sloping ground of the Canongate. There was a long history of gardening in this area, including a long history of fruit growing, that traced its origins back to the monastic gardens of the Augustinian canons of Holyrood and there is considerable evidence that this activity continued into the 17th century and beyond. The inventory of Moray House makes this clear for the 17th century and another inventory, of 1730, describes a similarly abundant fruit garden at the Duke of Roxburgh's house, immediately to the west of Queensberry House, showing that this activity continued (Robertson 2000, 128).

12.2 House, offices and garden

Although on a fairly restricted site, Queensberry House, in its original Hatton form and certainly in its expanded Queensberry form, was a relatively large structure, as large as many of the country houses that were being erected at the same time. As such, it required fairly sophisticated services both within the house as well as in the offices outside, and in the provision of a garden. Various sources in the late 17th and early 18th centuries provide ample evidence of this, with most of the normal offices being mentioned, including the coach house, stables and stable court; inner court; brew-house and coal house. All of these in fact are mentioned in Charles Maitland of Hatton's *Instructions*.[3] This contains little in the way of direct evidence on the gardens and is also limited because of subsequent alterations made by the Duke of Queensberry, but it does allow us to understand some of the service arrangements around the house, especially those around the stable court.

The stable court lay on the west side of the house, in the north-west corner of the site (fig 9.3). Although the Edgar plan shows the house after alterations by the Duke of Queensberry, which involved not only the house but also the courts, the description by Charles Maitland can still be seen to be relevant in the mid-18th century. He wrote:

As to the stable court the est wall of it is the wall of the inner court, the south wall is the wall of the garden, the north wall runs in a straight leine west from the inner court wall to the street and the back gate in that wall must joyne to Hepburn's land; and this gate must be nothing but plain rebets and must not be arched above but open and to open with two leaves and must be 9 feet wide of daylight to the street. The stables and coach house makes up the west side of this court ... the cotchhouse is nearest the south and the croks of the south side of the doors thereof are to be fixed in the garden wall which is the south gavell of the cotch house. The east side wall of the cotchhouse must be all doors and must not be built of stone being in width just 24 feet ... [the stables were to be at the north end of the coach house] ... The weidness of the cotchhouse and stables within the walls must be 22 futts, the lenth of all ... will be about 73 fut. The height of the cotchhouse and stables to the joists is 12 fut at the lower end or south gavell and the loft is to be 3 fut in height above the joists which is in all 16 fut in height [actually 15 feet] in the said wall above ground ... '[modern punctuation].

The image that comes out of this is of a stable and coach yard lying to the west of the house but separated from it at the northern end at least by a wall which divides stable yard from inner court (fig 12.4). The stable yard is entered by an entrance in the north-west corner of the site, with a separate and narrower gateway entering the inner court. The stable yard was separated from the garden by a wall along its south side which continued the line of the south gable of the coach house, which presented itself to the garden. This point is not only borne out by the Edgar plan but also by the Sandby drawing, although the gable there suggests a slightly larger building than the one described here. The Sandby drawing also shows a doorway connecting the stable yard and the garden (fig 8.3). What all of this suggests is that Queensberry did not have to rebuild the stable block and coach house but retained the one only recently built by Charles Maitland of Hatton. The same was true of most of the other service areas outside the house. In the 1695 inventory, made by the first Duke of Queensberry, there is a mention of a 'porter's house at the gate', and this was certainly retained later; similarly, 'the gardener's roume in the garden' in the same inventory also featured (as the 'gardener's house') later. The only building that was demolished by the second Duke was the coal house, immediately west of the kitchen, because this was the site of the new wing. Subsequently, coal was stored in the open on the opposite side of the house, in the space between Queensberry House and Glen's Land.[4] On the other hand, the 1723 inventory mentions a still house in the garden which tends to underline the unusually sophisticated provision of services at Queensberry House and link it more with the country house than a house in the city.

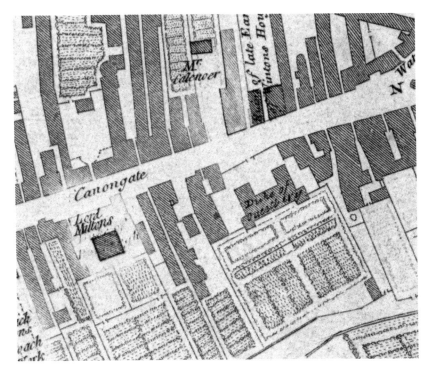

Figure 12.4
Detail of Edgar Survey of 1742 (1765 edition), showing Queensberry House (© NLS)

towards the garden'. The lowering of the floor and of the drain had the added advantage of allowing the drain to pass underneath the garden terrace on the south side of the house (discussed below). The drain, with its various branches, appears to have run through the garden and disgorged itself into the South Back of the Canongate, where William Adam later provided a substantial stone-built sewer to accommodate the outflow from the various Canongate properties.[5] This arrangement is confirmed by the archaeological evidence (see Chapter 3.5).

One further item relevant to the relationship between house, gardens and services is also found in Charles Maitland's *Instructions*. Whereas the *Lower Ground* floor of the building is clearly the locus of all the main services of the house (the kitchens, the well, various servants' quarters, and so on), it also contained 'the low parlour ... to be paived with blackwhait marbles ...' (see Chapter 9.4.1). This was clearly a rather grand space and was almost certainly a garden room, certainly overlooking the gardens and giving easy access to them.

12.3 The arrangement of the gardens in the late 17th and early 18th centuries

In the absence of detailed manuscript material on the gardens at Queensberry House, the illustrative material, particularly the city plans, takes on added importance. Among the cartographic material, William Edgar's 1742 survey is the most important source for the gardens in their heyday, approximately the first third of the 18th century, and may be used as the starting point in any attempt to visualise what the gardens were like (fig 12.4). The Edgar plan shows roughly what we would expect for this time. The garden is strictly formal, with rectangular plots arranged symmetrically about a central axis. The formal plots, which are very much in keeping with those in the other gardens depicted by Edgar, do not suggest very elaborate designs or complicated parterres. Indeed, they are very staid compared with the pretty knots indicated in Gordon of Rothiemay's plan of a century

Many of Maitland's instructions were concerned with the problem of the change of level from the north to the south side of the site. This slope is of some significance for the garden, but it also caused practical problems in the relationship between garden and service areas. The change of level meant that within the coach house/stable block, there was a 3ft (0.9m) drop across the 73ft (22.3m) length of the building. Even more important to Maitland was the problem of flooding in the garden as water and nastier fluids seeped from the stable yard down the slope towards the gardens. For this reason, he insisted that 'the south end of the back court must be half a fut lower than the level of the garden is to be or els the garden will never be dray ... '. That manipulation of the levels not only provided him with a kind of dam to stop liquid flowing into the garden, but also made it easier for him to run a drain out from under the stables There seem to have been at least two branches into this drain, one from the inner court, passing under the stable yard, and the other from the kitchen, which was at ground level on the south side of the house. Again, in this case, we find him manipulating the levels for the purposes of good drainage. The kitchen was sunk 2ft (0.6m) lower than the rest of the ground floor 'having a sayver holl earlier. It might even be said that these gardens look more concerned with production than with pleasure; there is quite a strong similarity, for example, between Queensberry House gardens and the large garden immediately to the south, which was operated as a commercial nursery by William Miller. For a number of reasons that will become apparent this connection between the nursery and the garden is quite relevant to the story of Queensberry House gardens. On the other hand, we should not read too much into the detail of Edgar's plan (or, for that matter, Gordon of Rothiemay's). Even Moray House gardens appear to be a rather plain affair in Edgar's plan at a time when they were still praised by almost all who visited them. The same source provides no detail on Queensberry House but does remark on the 'handsome garden', in contrast to the Duke of Roxburgh's next door which was 'much neglected' (Macky 1723, 63).[6]

There are no documents, drawings or maps that give any information on the gardens of Lady Balmakellie's house, although it can probably be assumed that she did have a garden. From the document already discussed, it is clear that Charles Maitland planned gardens on the south side of the house in 1681 and that is exactly what would be expected of the creator of the extraordinary gardens at Hatton. When he writes about the different levels between stable yard and garden, he says that the yard must be lower 'than the garden *is to be*' [author's emphasis], in other words, the gardens do not exist yet, although it seems that they were being 'roughed out' at that time. Evidence of this can be seen in his instruction to dig the soil out of the basement areas of the house and lay it on the garden, suggesting a certain amount of garden construction at that time. There is, however, nothing else in the Lauderdale Papers on either house or garden. This is perhaps unsurprising since, by the time this was written, Lauderdale fortunes were already on the wane and, although Charles inherited the estates of his brother only one year after this, in 1682 (becoming Earl of Lauderdale), he was already in the deep financial trouble that led to the sale of the house to the Duke of Queensberry in 1686.

If the documentary evidence is scant, though suggestive, the archaeological investigation has added some important detail to our understanding of the gardens in identifying a terrace structure, with a staircase leading down onto the central axis of the garden (fig 3.14). It is also clear that the terrace was built in at least two phases, with a central portion corresponding to the original Hatton–Balmakellie phase of the house (that is, it is the same width as the house) and with two later extensions to east and west. This expansion may well relate to the widening of the house by the second Duke of Queensberry, in which case the most likely sequence of events is that the original terrace was built by Hatton and that this was then extended by Queenberry in his larger reconstruction of the house and garden. It is possible, however, that the original terrace belonged to Lady Balmakellie and that it was Maitland who extended it. Some indirect evidence for this may be found in the fact that the documentary evidence for the acquisition of all the properties on the site of Queensberry House (discussed in Chapter 7) shows that Maitland purchased all the properties that Queensberry House was later to sit on. This is also borne out by the evidence that he built the stables and stable court on the west side of the site, showing that the space for Queensberry's west wing was created by Hatton. If the whole garden space was created by Hatton, it would not make sense for him then to have built a terrace that simply covered the width of the house and not the width of the whole garden.

Whoever built it, it was certainly the Queensberrys who benefited from it. James, second Duke of Queensberry, was the man mainly responsible for the final (pre-1808) form of Queensberry House and the gardens depicted in Edgar's plan. As with Maitland, there is one major source for his activities, the series of instructions, already referred to, that he issued to James Naismith (his factor) from London in December 1697.[7]

The man responsible for the gardens was one Cornelius, who appears to have been the Drumlanrig gardener, brought to Edinburgh for this particular job. Naismith was instructed to, 'sett Cornelius to work on the garden at Edinburgh and furnish him with a sufficient number of workmen for that use'. Cornelius was also to 'employ the greens in Mr Sutherland's custody and some of them in his own for the use of the garden there if needful'. This presumably refers to the planting of the garden, although it is not clear exactly what plants were employed. 'Mr Sutherland' was almost certainly James Sutherland, Intendant of the Physic Garden, and this implies that part of the Physic Garden, perhaps the recently acquired yards at Holyrood, was effectively being used as nursery ground for the Duke. The document is quite a rich source for establishing both the structure and, to a lesser extent, the embellishment of the gardens. Taken in conjunction with the Edgar plan, it is easy to visualise very clearly what is meant by statements like:

Figure 12.5

Thomas Sandby's view of the lower part of Canongate and Holyrood Palace in 1746 (© NGS)

That the back door of the garden be made to answer exactly the midle walk and the dore handsome with jambs of hewen stone.[8]

Similarly, the instruction that 'a wall be built at the foot of the garden where it is now uneven to bring it into a line where the gardener's house stands if Cornelius thinks it fit' seems to tie in with the south wall of the garden, which bulges forward at its eastern end to accommodate a structure which may well have been the gardener's house. This feature of the plan has already been remarked on in connection with Gordon of Rothiemay's plan, but Edgar's plan certainly does not show a building as large as that one. The Sandby drawing (fig 12.5) shows a very small, lean-to structure in that position, which can probably be identified with the gardener's house and perhaps even more with 'the gardener's roume in the garden' mentioned in 1695.

The *Instructions* document also mentions that the Duke wanted to build a greenhouse and instructed Naismith, Smith and Cornelius to look into it. There is a slight possibility that this, rather than the gardener's house, is what Edgar has shown, but the position of the building, in a shady south-east corner of the garden, perhaps makes this unlikely. This proposal comes within two years of Sutherland's petition to the Privy Council to build a greenhouse in the Physic Garden (referred to above), but the Queensberry greenhouse seems to have been intended for a slightly more mundane function, which was 'to keep trees and plants for some time after their first arrival till they can be conveniently transported to Drumlanrig …'. In other words, Queensberry House gardens were being used as nursery ground for the Duke's main gardens at Drumlanrig. This, of course, would make sense, especially if the Duke was importing plant materials from London or from Dutch suppliers that were shipped to Leith then transported overland, via Queensberry House, where they would be hardened off before being sent on to Drumlanrig. Such practical concerns are also reflected in the final instruction that, 'Cornelius be allow'd what glass frames and other things you shall find necessary either for the preservation or propagation of his plants'. In addition, William Miller brought trees into his Holyrood nursery for hardening off before transportation to Dumfriesshire.[9] This evidence, along with the reference to the Physic Garden already mentioned, shows that Drumlanrig was obviously the Duke's main focus, but that the gardens in the Canongate were important in that they could support the larger enterprise.

Having discussed some of the archival evidence along with the archaeological, it is necessary to find out if that is confirmed by the cartographic evidence in order that the basic structure of the garden can be established. The terrace shown up by the excavations is certainly suggested on the Edgar survey, although not definitively illustrated. There is a clear, sharp line drawn across the garden below the first pair of formal plots nearest the house, which strongly suggests a terrace, although it does not show the stairs and is not confirmed by later maps, with one exception. The Kincaid map of 1784 has a very clear indication of a terrace with steps down to the lower garden in the centre of the terrace (fig 12.6). Some supporting evidence can also be found in the Buccleuch Mss. George Anderson's mason account for 1723 includes the item:

For mending the stairs in the garden and furnishing lead, sand and lyme to run the batts with.[10]

Two other features of what might be broadly termed the structure of the garden can also be noted, one of which is indicated on the Sandby drawing, while the other, puzzlingly, is contradicted by it. As to the first, Sandby's panorama of Edinburgh provides an interesting vista of the gardens on the south side of the Canongate, but almost no detail of Queensberry House gardens is visible because of a stand of mature trees that runs along the south side of the garden. It is possible that these are the same trees that run along the same plots in Gordon of Rothiemay's plan and were therefore an established part of the garden before the Duke of Queensberry purchased the property. In a sense, therefore, the trees were part of the structure of the garden and were accommodated within the subsequent design.

One possible problem with the trees is the very one that now frustrates the garden historian, namely that they block the views, not only into the garden but also out of it. That problem may have been offset, however, by the slope of the ground and the terrace at the top of the garden would have allowed views to Salisbury Crags and Arthur's Seat beyond. Indeed, it is even possible that the trees were kept precisely because they blocked the foreground view from the terrace, which was the South Back of the Canongate, a busy thoroughfare, and the functional nursery grounds of William Miller. A view across trees to the wilder landscape beyond would certainly have been desirable and this combination of features once again raises the

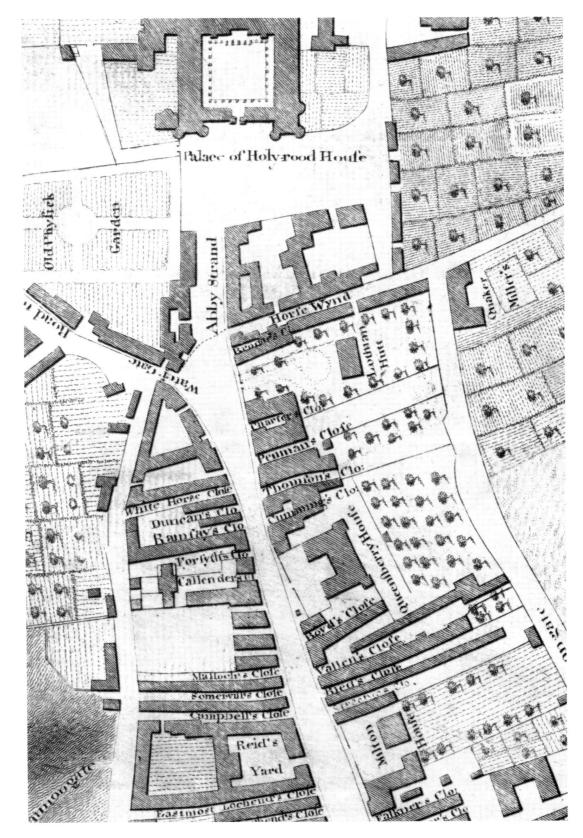

Figure 12.6
Detail of Kincaid map, 1784 (© NLS)

issue of the uniqueness of Queensberry House as a town mansion. Its scale, sophistication and facilities all link it with the emerging formal country houses of the period and the interpretation of Queensberry House in this light also requires it to be withdrawn from its urban surroundings. The house itself withdraws from the street behind a high wall, like the Parisian *hôtel* that is one of its models. The gardens seem to withdraw from their immediate surrounding by screening them out in such a way that the experience of viewing along the main axis becomes mainly a rural one, with formal gardens in the foreground and sublime nature in the background. It is almost as if the experience of Drumlanrig itself was being attempted in Edinburgh.

The final structural element in the garden is actually part of the house. It is suggested by the archaeological analysis of the building but had been removed by the time Sandby made his drawing. This is the opening between the two drawing room windows, which overlook the gardens and are one storey above the terrace. The opening was exposed during the archaeological investigation of the house as, apparently, a doorway. This can only have led out onto some external feature, either a balcony or a stairway down to the gardens themselves. However, whatever the structure was, it does not seem to have left any substantial archaeological remains, which suggests that it was not a stone structure but an easily removable timber one. This might tie in with items like the timber balcony drawn by Isaac Miller (the Duchess of Hamilton's gardener at the time) on the north front of Hamilton Palace in 1677 and which may well have survived the rebuilding of the palace by James Smith in the 1690s. Smith certainly would have known it and perhaps introduced it at Queensberry House, which he was working on at the same time.

So much for the broad structure of the garden. Filling in the detail, however, is rather more difficult. No accounts for seeds or plants have been discovered and Queensberry's 1697 *Instructions* were written at a time when the garden was still under construction; indeed, they include an order that, 'Cornelius be ordered as soon as he comes to a resolution about the garden to send up hither a draft of it'. The one piece of embellishment that is mentioned are flowerpots, 'formerly sent down may be shown to the painters there where it may be enquired first whether they can paint and guild them like to those sent last and then at what rate they will undertake them and to send up an account of it'.

As so often in analysing Queensberry House, the major archival source that really is useful is the furniture inventory. This is perhaps a surprising source

for the gardens, but, just as the gardens were used as nursery ground for Drumlanrig, so the gallery in the house seems to have been used as a storage place both for things in transit to Drumlanrig, especially after 1707, and as storage for things that were not in use when the family was not in residence. This included garden features and the instruction about the lead flowerpots given in 1697 is borne out in some detail in an inventory of c 1707 which describes them:

A pair of large flower pots gilded with stars 23 inches overall

A pair of lesser ditto gilded with faces 18 inches overall

A single pot not gilded 18 inches overall

A single pot with stars not gilded 20 inches overall

A pair of blue potts glass'd [glazed] 13 inches overall

A single blue and white ditto broke in the foot 14 inches overall.[11]

The dimensions given may relate either to the height or to the diameter of the pots (which is the traditional way of measuring flowerpots) and the inventory certainly indicates that there were a number of rather elaborate lead flowerpots of the kind normally found on balustrades and terraces. The two gilded pairs in this case might have been found at each end of the terrace and framing the stairs in the centre. Such items were fairly common in formal gardens and similar pots can still be seen, for example, on the terrace at Balcaskie.

The reference to glazed pots, especially the blue and white one, suggests delftware flowerpots that were also commonly used in aristocratic gardens. Some of these were very large and elaborate, although the Queensberry examples do not seem to have been very large. That may suggest that these items were used indoors, possibly in the garden parlour, rather than outdoors on the terrace or elsewhere in the garden.[12]

The same inventory contains even more important information on the garden with references to:

One box the Statue of Diana with a grayhound standing be her of hard lead metal

In another box the statue of ane Appollo leaning on his harp of the same metal

In two boxes, two pedestals for the said statues.[13]

The Queensberry inventories list other statues elsewhere, including a 'Rape of the Sabines' and a portrait bust of the second Duchess. However, while the material and subject matter of those statues indicate that they were kept in the house, the material, subject matter and the fact that they are listed along with the flowerpots, all suggest that Apollo and Diana were garden statues.

The pairing was appropriate, for Apollo and Artemis (Diana in Roman mythology) were the twin children of Zeus and Leto. Their iconography was highly appropriate to the themes of a garden. Apollo, in particular, was associated with the sun and hence with the driving away of winter and the coming of spring. Diana was associated with the moon and with the seasonal cycle. They were associated with youthful male and female beauty and each had both an active and a more passive personification. In this case, Diana, with her greyhound (and possibly a bow), adopts the role of the huntress and Apollo, with his lyre, adopts the role of the leader of muses.

In a small garden like Queensberry House, they would have been the main decorative feature, set on either side of the main axis of the garden, possibly on a grass plot. The exact siting of statues like these features in a slightly later document relating to the huge formal gardens at Alloa, which might provide a useful source for Queensberry. At Alloa, a proposal for four statues around a central fountain includes a sketch showing how the statues would sit on the ground. In that case, the pedestal sat on a circle of grass, with a border of gravel around that and then finally a further border of tulips and pinks around the whole ensemble.[14]

One further source adds some more useful information to the emerging picture of the garden. In 1749, John Halkerston took over the running of the garden and his proposal for running it was relayed to Lord Shewaltoun by the Duke's factor in Edinburgh, Thomas Goldie, who wrote:

> The bearer proposes to keep the Duke's garden in the Canongate Viz: the grass plots and walks, the gravel walks, the flowers and Jesmin in good order …[15]

So what did the garden look like in this period? The following features can be suggested: starting at the house, there was a door from the south-facing state drawing room giving access to the timber balcony suggested above, with views over the gardens below and Arthur's Seat and the countryside beyond. Below, was a terrace the full width of the garden, probably with a stone balustrade adorned at the ends and on either side of the central staircase with gilded lead flowerpots. Inside the house, at basement level, there was a parlour with a black and white marble floor,

possibly also decorated with blue and white delftware flowerpots for more delicate and exotic plants. This room may also have been used as an informal dining room at some times and, after the expansion of the house in the late 1690s, a further room was used at the west end of the house as a garden room.[16] The terrace could be accessed from a doorway in the basement, though not directly from either of the garden rooms. It is possible that the timber balcony also included a stair to the terrace, but no corroborative evidence has been found on this. Below the terrace the garden was divided into two halves around a central axis. Other paths, as Edgar's plan suggests, also crossed the garden, although all of these ran with or at right angles to the main axis. Some paths were gravel, others were grass. The statues of Apollo and Diana were positioned on either side of the main axis and in the borders and various plots there was a combination of grass, flowers and flowering, scented shrubs, in particular jasmine. At the foot of the garden, in the south-east corner, was the gardener's house. This area was shaded by mature elm trees and it was in this area that the kitchen garden was probably also sited.[17]

There was, therefore, a small but fairly elaborate formal garden that provided a space for relaxation, for promenading and with a somewhat controlled outlook that might have helped the Duke to imagine that he was not in one of the most crowded and dirty cities in Europe, but rather in a pleasant rural retreat overlooking a spectacular natural landscape. It is perhaps significant, however, that some of the key evidence for this garden is also evidence that it was partly dismantled, certainly temporarily and possibly permanently, quite early in the 18th century.

12.4 The development of the gardens, 1730–1800

Most of the evidence on the gardens in the 18th century indicates a fairly simple, even workaday environment. Since the house was only used intermittently by the family after about 1710, it should come as no surprise that elaborate pleasure gardens were not maintained. That is not to say, of course, that the gardens were allowed to go to rack and ruin. A skeleton staff, comprising a housekeeper, Mrs Wardlaw, and a gardener, James Bennett, was retained at Queensberry House. Bennett seems to have worked there from around 1710, when he probably replaced David Redpath, who is recorded as gardener in 1706 (Boog Watson 1996, vol. 7, 81) until around 1730, which means that he was responsible for the gardens at the time that Macky paid his compliments in 1723 (Macky 1723, 63). This date is significant because it coincided with a lengthy visit by the family (discussed in more detail in Chapter 13.2.2). The Buccleuch Mss are very rich on Queensberry House at this time because so many preparations had to be made for what was becoming a fairly rare event. Unfortunately, the papers are less informative on the gardens themselves. Bennett, the gardener, was allowed to bring in help to put the gardens in good order prior to the family's visit.[18] Other snippets, from the smith's account and from the wright's account of the same period, also cast light on the gardens. Thomas Wallace, smith in Canongate, supplied ironwork for a scythe and an iron frame for a rolling stone.[19] At the same time, John Heart, wright, supplied a 'half hunder nails to gardener' along with 'a raik for gras and a reel to the gardener's line'.[20] Taken together, this perhaps suggests a fairly simple garden with well-maintained grass plots and wall trees.

Before considering this further, and in particular considering the later history of fruit growing at Queensberry House, it is worth considering the evidence of a particular episode in the middle of the century that casts some light on the gardens and provides an insight into both gardening practices and general living conditions in the area. In 1756, the Duke brought a case against William Miller, the nurseryman in the palace yards who had ground directly south of Queensberry House.[21] The essence of his case was that Miller had reopened a drainage ditch, sometimes referred to as the torrent running along the north side of the South Back which, through seepage into the Duke's garden, had previously done damage. This ditch was, in fact, the main sewer for this part of the city and had been built as a stone channel by William Adam in the 1720s. Blockage of the channel caused flooding both of the road and of Miller's grounds on the south side of the road. However, by reopening the channel, it was claimed that Miller was undermining the garden wall and was endangering plants in the garden once more. From the Duke's case and Miller's (successful) defence, a number of important pieces of information about the gardens emerge. The case referred to problems stretching back to the 1720s and it was claimed that seepage from the drain had killed old elm trees planted along the south side of the garden, clearly those depicted by Sandby. Miller's defence, essentially that he was providing a public service by keeping the drain clear and thus the road dry, also included a number of telling points about how the drain had been used by the various proprietors

on the south side of the Canongate. The drain had been blocked by people dumping their refuse and this ranged from dead horses at one extreme, to the Duke of Queensberry's own gardeners, 'having been in the practice for many years of wheeling out weeds and kail roots, and other rubbish from the garden, and laying the same upon the road …'. Miller went further, in fact, claiming that far from worrying about the poisonous effect of the fetid waters of the drain, Queensberry's gardeners used it as a liquid fertiliser and actively encouraged it to flow into the garden. To this end they had dug holes in the base of the garden wall (the only damage caused to the wall) and had opened the garden gate (incidentally, the only evidence that there was a gate from the garden to the South Back).

Apart from the rather revolting waste disposal and gardening practice this reveals, it also hints at a rather practical garden. It would be wrong, however, to see Queensberry House simply as a kale yard by this time, for most other evidence suggests that the formal gardens were still broadly intact and that, of course, would include the kitchen garden. It is even possible that the growing of kale was the first step towards an expansion of the fruit production in the garden because, from the mid-17th century, cabbage had been recommended as a crop for cleaning the soil before fruit trees were planted and that practice may have continued in the 18th century (Jacques & van der Horst 1988, 201).

Of course, as has already been suggested, the Scottish garden was very often more concerned with the simple and productive than with the elaborate and expensive and there is good evidence that the productive side of Queensberry House garden was important and, in particular, that fruit production was always a major activity. The Charter in favour of William, first Duke of Queensberry, which confirms the transfer of the property from Lauderdale in 1688, describes, 'that great mansion or tenement with yard, orchard and other pertinents, lately built by Charles Earl of Lauderdale …'.[22] Similarly, in 1706, when the Duke was granted the privilege of making the house and grounds part of the jurisdiction of Drumlanrig rather than Edinburgh (Chapter 13.2.2), the Town Council was very careful to describe its property, and therefore the jurisdiction, in detail. In the minutes there are numerous references to, 'all & haill of that great lodging or tenement of land with the yaird orchyaird lying upon the south side thereof now enclosed with a stone wall, stables and office houses …'.[23] These references to the orchard were not simply a form of words used in legal documents, but described what was actually an important feature of the gardens. In this there was both an historical continuity with the monastic tradition of fruit production in the area, but, more importantly, with the aristocratic tradition that saw fruit production as a horticultural challenge and, when delicate fruits were concerned, a somewhat exotic activity.

The orchard may have been a pleasant, healthy and tasty diversion for the early inhabitants of the house, but in the second half of the century it was the major feature of the garden. When John Halkerston became gardener in 1749, he was not seeking paid employment from the Duke, but was actually offering to tend the gardens in return for the fruit, which he could then sell in the markets in Edinburgh. In addition, he also offered to, 'delve up what part of the garden your lordship desires and lay it into grass', again suggesting a simplification of the grounds. At this time, the orchard was probably a combination of standards and wall trees and the illustrative material, such as it is, lends some support to this. The limitations of Sandby's drawing as a source for the gardens have been noted, but the south-facing walls are visible and the gable of the stable block, for example, does seem to suggest planting of some kind against the wall (fig 8.3). Any other planting in the lower half of the garden is, of course, screened by the trees along the south wall, but later maps, such as Kincaid's of 1784 (fig 12.6), seem to show a simplification of the garden by that time, with an overall planting of trees which might well have been fruit trees. The only exception to this general picture of a garden being turned over to fruit production is the Ainslie map of 1804 (fig 12.7), which shows a garden quartered with paths around a central circular lawn. It is not clear how reliable this plan is; certainly this form is not borne out by any other maps and the house had already been sold by this time, but it is possible that

the new owner, the distiller William Aitchison, laid out the gardens when he first bought the property. Given his subsequent treatment of the house, that is perhaps an unlikely scenario, but the plan at least shows a garden substantially planted with trees and to that extent is consistent with others.

Halkerston had a fall-back position in his proposal, namely that if for some reason he left before the crop was ready, then he would be paid a wage by the Duke. It is not clear from the surviving records what the

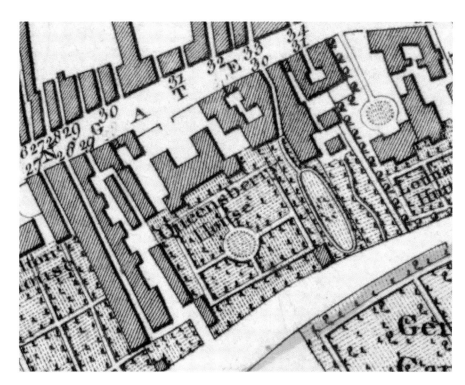

Figure 12.7
Detail of Ainslie map, 1804 (© NLS)

relationship between the Duke and his gardeners was in the later part of the century, although there was certainly still a gardener living at Queensberry House when it was finally sold. By that time, however, it seems that the practice of allowing the gardener to exploit the gardens commercially to some extent had given way to the commercial letting of the gardens. In much the same way that the palace yards had been let out to the Miller family, and in the absence of any domestic interest in Queensberry House from the fourth Duke, the gardens were turned over to a market gardener who leased the land for many years and who allowed people in for sixpence at a time to pick as many gooseberries as they could eat (Hume & Boyd c 1984, 84).

Notes

1 Kincaid's 1784 plan labels it 'Old Physick Garden'.

2 NAS, Dalhousie Mss, GD45/18/746. This document is discussed in relation to Hamilton Palace in Marshall, 1973, 54 and, more generally and in more detail, in Robertson 2000, 108–28.

3 Lauderdale Papers, NRA(S) 832/61/68.

4 This was an arrangement that caused problems in the 18th century as the coal lay below windows of the tenants of Glen's Land and was 'in great measure rendered useless through nestiness being thrown over the window...' Buccleuch Mss, NRA(S) 1275/unnumbered bundle (stored with 1108, 1112, 1110).

5 Buccleuch Mss, NRA(S) 1275/479/A/4–12. This is discussed below.

6 Although, as indicated above, it was clearly producing a substantial amount of fruit within a few years of Macky's dismissal of the gardens.

7 Buccleuch Mss, NRA(S) 1275/1124. NB: according to the NRA(S) survey, this should be in bundle 497.

8 Perhaps not quite as clear as all that. There is a slight ambiguity here as to whether this door was in the south wall of the garden or the south front of the house.

9 Buccleuch Mss, NRA(S) 1275/1531. Estate Accounts, including 'Accompt for Fraught & Ca of trees brought from London the year 1727 for the Duke of Queensberry £77:6 Scots, £6.8.10 Ster'.

10 Buccleuch Mss, NRA(S) 12775/1643. Account of George Anderson, Mason, June 1723. Batts are iron staples used for fixing stone blocks together.

11 Buccleuch Mss, NRA(S) 2175/1104. Undated inventory from c 1707/08.

12 Ceramic pots, including delftware ones, were used in gardens, often for exotica like citrus fruits (see Hunt & de Jong 1988, 308 (cat. 164) and 323 (cat. 181)).

13 Buccleuch Mss, NRA(S) 2175/1104. Undated inventory from c 1707/08.

14 Mar & Kellie Mss, NAS GD124/15/1363/1+2. Letter from Francis Petty concerning 'The Marquis's garden', undated, c 1720. Includes a drawing with the concentric borders and statues all drawn separately then pinned to a plan. The statues are two male and two female. One of the males is certainly Apollo, with his bow. The other male looks like Apollo with his lyre. The two females are more difficult to interpret, but the active and passive personifications of Diana are a possibility.

15 Buccleuch Mss, NRA(S) 1275/unnumbered bundle (stored with 1108, 1112, 1110.). 'Agreement anent the garden in the Canongate March 10 1749'. It is not clear what Lord Shewaltoun's role was (or indeed who he was).

16 This is referred to in the 1723 inventory, but it was barely furnished at all at that time.

17 The trees are identified in a later court case between the Duke and William Miller, the nurseryman. This is discussed below.

18 Buccleuch Mss, NRA(S) 1275/1550.

19 Buccleuch Mss NRA(S) 1275/1556.

20 Buccleuch Mss, NRA(S)1275/1642/E/4.

21 Buccleuch Mss, NRA(S) 1275/479.

22 ECA, Canongate Charters, vol. 5 1683–1711, no. 745 (transcribed).

23 Edinburgh Town Council Minutes, 6 March 1706.

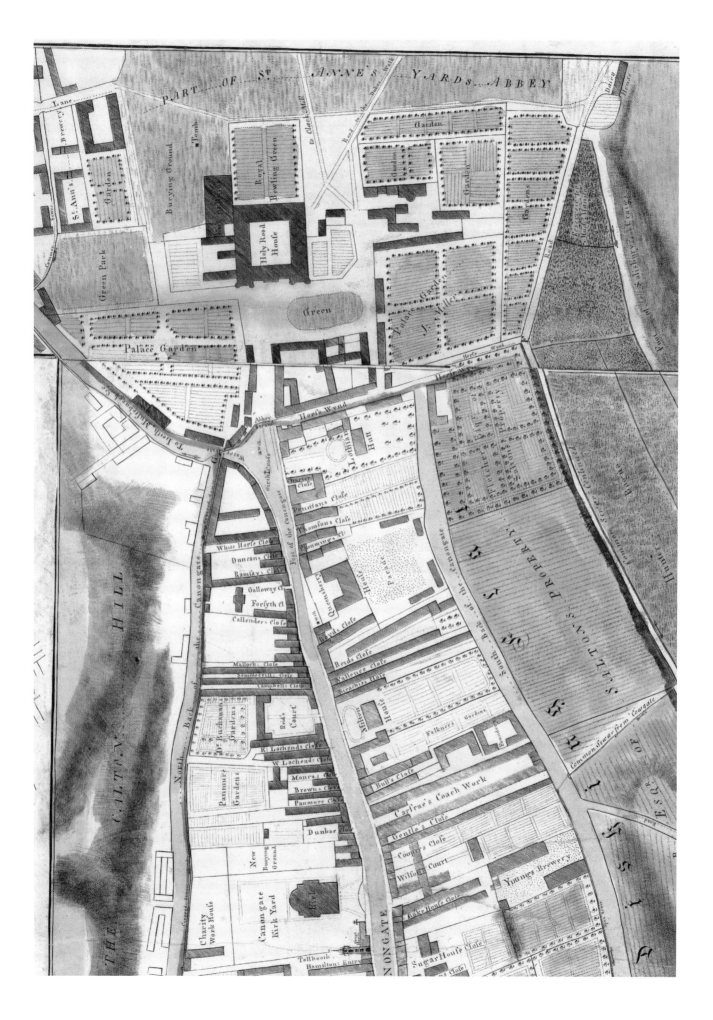

PART OF ST. ANNE'S YARDS ABBEY

Road to the Quarry Walk

Lane

St. Ann's Brewery

St. Ann's Garden

Tomb

Burying Ground

Garden

to Clock Mill

Royal Bowling Green

Garden

Green Park

Holy Rood House

J. Miller

Palace Garden

Green

Palace Garden

To Leith Mill Town

Abbey Strand

Horse Wynd

Horse Wynd

Horse Wynd

Water Gate

Girth Cross

HILL

White Horse Close

Duncans Close

Ramsay's Close

Galloway Cl.

Forsyth Cl.

Callenders Close

Malloch's Close

Sommerville Close

Campbells Close

Dr. Buchanan's Gardens

Reid's Court

E. Lochends Close

W. Lochends Close

Monro's

Browne's Cl.

Panmure Gardens

Dunbar

Panmure Cl.

New Burying Ground

Charity Work House

Canongate Kirk Yard

Kirk

CALTON

THE

Foot of the Canongate

North Back of the Canongate

South Back of the Canongate

Chalmers Close

Paunians Close

Thomson's Close

Cummings Cl.

Queensberry House

Lothian Hutt

Davie's Close

Reids Close

Nallence Close

Brachies Close

Milton House

Falkner's Gardens

Bull's Close

Carfrae's Coach Work

Gentle's Close

Coopers Close

Wilson's Court

Parade

FLEICHER OR FULLER OF SALTONS PROPERTY

Common Sewer from Cowgate

Young's Brewery

Tollbooth

Hamilton's Entry

CANONGATE

Sugar House Close

Dairy House

Reservoir for Holyrood

Fishmarket or Salisbury Crags

Footpath to St John's

Road

Common Sewer Conducted

Common Sewer from

Tunnell

ESQ.

P.

Chapter 13

The site and Canongate in the 18th century

E PATRICIA DENNISON and JOHN LOWREY

13.1 Canongate

E PATRICIA DENNISON

13.1.1 The Union

Little is known of the feelings of the Canongate burgesses about the Union negotiations, and how far the 'pamphlet war' of late 1705 and 1706 actually influenced the Canongate people is unclear. But for many, the influx of politicians and nobility would have been of economic benefit, whether it came from sales of merchandise or paid services, legitimate or otherwise. In 1707, for example, Moray House was occupied by the Lord Chancellor Seafield, who took a prominent part in the negotiations leading to the Union, the signing of which some have argued may have been completed in the summer house of Moray House (Boog Watson 1923, 22).

If the true cost of the loss of Parliament to Westminster crossed the minds of the man and woman in the High Street of Canongate, it is not documented. This probably represented a microcosm of the state of the entire nation. Perhaps most people in Scotland were opposed to political union with England, but bribery and corruption and lack of political debate would secure the necessary votes to force through the agreement. Many were also acutely aware of the potential economic benefits; the burgh of Montrose was not alone in advising its representative to Parliament to vote for Union, for fear of losing trade. Edinburgh would see its last Parliament until 1999.

13.1.2 Later political developments

Political unrest in the 18th century impacted little on Canongate. The 'Fifteen left the town untouched. The occupation of Edinburgh by the Jacobite army in 1745 led to 'all the shops in Edinburgh being closed'. This was possibly the case also in Canongate, but there are very few references in burgh sources to the Jacobites. In,

for example, the cordiners' minutes there is reference to the postponement of an admission 'by reason of the late disturbances'; another was a complaint against the cordiners of Edinburgh for searching hides in North Leith, the prerogative of the Canongate cordiners, 'during the late troblous times' (Malcolm 1932, 142). It was said that after the Battle of Prestonpans a number of officers of the Highland army were accommodated in Queensberry House, but this seemed to bother the populace little if the near-silence in the records is taken as an indicator (Boog Watson 1927, 20; Blaikie 1909, 32). There is no reference at all in, for example, the tailors' minute book to these events, although it is fair to say that the tailors intervened little in public affairs, while supporting good works at home, such as providing £10 towards the new grammar school after its burning and, in 1792, unanimously joining with the other crafts in petitioning for the abolition of the slave trade, thanking Wilberforce and colleagues and voting two guineas to their expenses (Marwick 1938, 122). It is difficult not to conclude that the people of Canongate continued their accustomed routine.

By the 1790s, debating societies and radical political associations were spreading rapidly. Newspapers were proliferating and their contents were increasingly outspoken: in 1782, there were only eight newspapers in the whole of Scotland, giving mainly local news, but by 1790 there were 27, most of which were highly political (Ferguson 1968, 251). 'Everything rung, and was connected with the Revolution in France; which for above 20 years was, or was made, the all in all. Everything, not this or that thing, but literally everything, was soaked in this one event' (Cockburn 1910, 73). But many of the avowedly political societies of Edinburgh showed little desire for extreme radical change. In 1790, the Edinburgh Revolution Society, while pledging the cause of liberty throughout the world, failed to make specific reference to France. The following year, vague grievances, possibly fuelled by such publications as Tom Paine's *The Rights of Man*, which advocated democracy and deism; the rejection of the petition in favour of repeal of the Test Act, which imposed a religious assessment of those holding civic

Figure 13.1
Bell's 1810 plan of the east end of Canongate (© NLS)

225

office; the Corn Law of 1790, which increased prices and was meant to be permanent, unlike its predecessors; opposition by the government to burgh reform and to the abolition of slavery; and the issue of a proclamation against seditious writing, resulted in supporters of the French Revolution meeting in Edinburgh to celebrate, but this passed off sufficiently quietly that it gave little anxiety to the authorities. A three-day riot in June 1792 in Edinburgh, however, had to be controlled by the reading of the Riot Act and the firing of troops; and the following month the first Society of the Friends of the People in Scotland met in Edinburgh. The use by the government of paid spies and the sentencing of Thomas Muir, the self-appointed tribune of the people in the Friends of the People, to 14 years' transportation to Botany Bay in 1793 highlighted the government's fear of radical subversiveness (Meikle 1912, 53, 67, 71, 81; Ferguson 1968, 253–6). Such political events, so close to Canongate, must have had an impact on the thinking of many.

13.1.3 The people of Canongate

It was estimated that by 1775 there were approximately 4500 people in Canongate. By the 1790s this figure had risen to about 6200 (Withrington & Grant 1975, ii, 6–7). The Canongate people were of varied social background; a telling comment was made in the 1790s that:

> a considerable change has taken place with respect to the rank and the opulence of the inhabitants. It was formerly remarkable for the number of noble and genteel families residing in it. But of late … the number of these has considerably diminished (Withrington & Grant 1975).

Queensberry House was by far the most prestigious dwelling. The restoration of Charles II to the thrones of Scotland and England had brought renewed activity to the east end of Canongate, with the partial rebuilding of Holyroodhouse in the 1670s and 1680s (see Chapter 6.7.1). The construction work at Queensberry House involved a clash with the Canongate craftsmen, noted for their skills. Hatton employed country masons, who had no rights to labour in the burgh. The Canongate freemen, protesting that they would not even permit Edinburgh masons, never mind other outsiders, to work in their burgh, took their tools (Fountainhall 1928, 106). The Privy Council deemed that Hatton could employ whom he pleased. Whether the fact that Hatton was a member of the Privy Council was of influence in this decision is not documented, but the

craftsmen were cleared of the charge of rioting. The dwelling was completed, in spite of such setbacks.

When an assessment was made for a window tax in 1710–11, it is not surprising that Queensberry House features as having 30 windows or more, one of only 14 such properties in Canongate. This compares with 55 such properties in the much larger burgh of Edinburgh. Canongate had 22 other houses liable to tax, since they had 20 windows or more, compared with Edinburgh's 147. As would be expected, given the difference in size, Edinburgh had more substantial houses than Canongate, but, significantly, Canongate had, at this time, proportionately a higher concentration of dwellings at the quality end of the market.[1]

The Hearth Tax records of 1691[2] give a further clue to the quality and size of properties in Canongate. Hatton's, later Queensberry House, had 52 hearths, compared with Moray House which had 18, but these were exceptional. If three 'lands' are considered as test cases, individual dwellings were relatively commodious. In Ramsay or Reid's Land, 11 homes had an average of 3.7 hearths, one having seven (Sir John Cochrane), four having six and only three possessing single hearths. At Thomson's Land there were six dwellings. Their average number of hearths was 2.8, one having six hearths (Widow Maxwell) and two having single hearths. In Chalmer's Land, ten properties averaged 2.5 hearths each, as many as five having single hearths, but one, that of Widow Gibb, having as many as eight hearths. For these three lands, 37 per cent of properties had single hearths, although the percentage of single hearths for the whole of Canongate rose to be as high as 62 per cent. When compared with an Annuity Roll for Canongate taken in 1687,[3] however, it is clear that, while properties with multiple hearths might raise the highest rentals, the rents paid for single- and two-hearth properties might vary greatly, suggesting that wealthier tenants were prepared to pay more for good-quality, smaller properties than for multi-hearthed properties of inferior quality (Dingwall 1994, 90). Although too much should not, therefore, be inferred from hearths, when compared with other towns the standing of Canongate becomes clearer. In Musselburgh, for example, 72.5 per cent of properties were single-hearthed and in its suburb of Fisherrow the figure was as high as almost 78 per cent; Stranraer had almost 64 per cent of dwellings with single hearths; Linlithgow almost 70 per cent; Kirkcaldy 58 per cent; and Dumfries 63 per cent.[4]

It was claimed in 1753 that Canongate:

has suffered more by the union of the kingdoms than all the other parts of Scotland: for having, before that period, been the residence of the chief of the Scottish nobility, it was then in a flourishing condition; but being deserted by them, many of their houses are fallen down, and others in a ruinous condition; it is a piteous case! (Grant 1881–3, iii, 15)

Queensberry House, in spite of such complaints, was not, immediately, to suffer such ignomy (see 13.2.3 below).

The continued investment in property in Canongate during this century is also clear indication that all was not decay. Milton House, for example, was built east of Moray House in the garden of Lord Roxburgh, by a nephew of Fletcher of Saltoun in c 1754 (Grant 1881–3, iii, 23). Fletcher of Saltoun would eventually own much of the land to the south of the Strand, according to Bell's map (fig 13.1). Lothian Hut was also constructed in 1750 by William, third Marquis of Lothian. In spite of its name, Lothian Hut was an elegant townhouse, described as 'finely built' (Wilson 1891, 301) and 'small but magnificently finished' (Grant 1881–3, iii, 38). It had a dining room that measured some 75ft by 26ft (23m by 8m).[5] It had a double access, from both Canongate and Horse Wynd, and an imposing circular driveway (see 13.2.5 below). Although closes would begin to proliferate, Canongate still had sufficient space for imposing large gardens and yards at the rear of many properties.[6] The records also indicate clearly that, even after the building of their elegant townhouse, the Lothians were still interested in purchasing property on what is now the Parliament site: dispositions were made, for example, in favour of the Marquis of Lothian in 1764,[7] to the Marchioness of Lothian in 1771 and 1775,[8] and to the marchioness as dowager in 1777.[9] A further property, Lothian Vale, was added at the southern end of the site on the corner of Horse Wynd and Holyrood Road, with entry by the Marquis of Lothian's Close.[10] Bell's fine map (fig 13.1) of the Canongate shows the site clearly before the major change that would come in the 19th century.

The 17th- and early 18th-century titles of properties that ultimately were all bought up and formed the residential complex of Lothian Hut show that people of a variety of occupations, some in prestigious professions and some craftsmen, once occupied the site. The regular disposal of tenements and land in this confined area over a period of less than 80 years offers an interesting case study into the type of people living at the east end of Canongate at this time, and also into the service industries attracted to Holyrood.

Archibald Campbell, a brewer, for example, lived next door to Bailie Robert Deans, a merchant, in 1700.[11] The property of Deans was then to pass, via Alexander Deans, to Thomas Smith, writer (lawyer) in Edinburgh; his heir, Anna Smith, also an heir of Thomas Ruddiman, a well-known publisher and keeper of the Library of the Faculty of Advocates, then disposed of the land in favour of Andrew Chalmers in 1762.[12] He, in turn, sold the land to the Marquis of Lothian in 1764.[13] Land in Chancellor's Close, once owned by James Ross, merchant, was sold by his daughter to the Marchioness of Lothian in 1771.[14] Four years later, the Marchioness came into possession of nearby property with the disposition of Mrs Margaret Watt of lands once belonging to James Yorston, the brewer and distiller. Tenements close by and, from 1658 to 1716, in the possession of the church of Holyroodhouse, were disponed to a slater, Robert Jack, burgess of Edinburgh, and in due course passed to James Gibson, surgeon, who sold to the Marchioness of Lothian in 1771.[15] In 1742, Katherine Penman inherited from her father, William Mitchell, a baxter burgess. Her brother, Edward Penman, was a goldsmith and in 1771, this property passed to his son James, who had been the surgeon major to the garrison hospital at Gibraltar. James then sold to John McArthur, writer, who in 1777, in his turn, sold to the dowager Marchioness of Lothian.[16] Another parcel of land and property passed in 1688 from the bailies of Canongate to a Canongate baxter, then to his daughter and son-in law, a merchant burgess of Edinburgh, and from this family to a Canongate merchant, whose wife disposed of the property to a candlemaker and soap boiler in Canongate; he, in turn, in 1775 sold to the dowager Marchioness in 1775.[17] Another pocket of property that would be subsumed within the Lothian Hut policies was sold to William Henry, Marquis of Lothian in 1766. This transaction required the assent of one James Reid, coachmaker in Canongate, so he had at least some interest in the property. In 1714, this same subject had been disponed to Robert Lauder, a harnessmaker in Canongate, by the heir of Bartholomew Gibson, farrier in the abbey of Holyroodhouse.[18] This same man in 1695, when he was defined as 'Her Majesty's master farrier', came into possession of some adjacent land; this passed to James Ross, a brewer, also in the abbey of Holyrood in 1708 and stayed in the Ross family until sold by his daughter to the Marquis of Lothian in 1765.[19] Other parcels of land sold to the Marquis in the 1760s came from a mason who had purchased his property from the incorporation of baxters; from the heir of a writer; and from Francis Brodie, a wright.[20] This man built a large tenement on the west side of Horse Wynd for his brother, William, a tailor. When he died in 1782 he passed the wadset to his son, William Brodie, the notorious Deacon of the Wrights. This man led a remarkable life as a pillar of society during the day and the leader of a gang of thieves at night. He was ultimately executed for burglary by his own invention, an improved hanging machine, and his story is said to have inspired Robert Louis Stevenson to write *The Strange Case of Dr Jekyll and Mr Hyde*.

People of very varied backgrounds from wealthy gentry to people of quite humble social origins were living in close proximity to each other. On the sale of some of the hammermen's property in 1762, an interesting mix of tenants, 17 in all, is revealed. They included Lord Adam, son of the Dowager Duchess of Gordon, four weavers, a plumber, a painter, a merchant, a blacksmith, a staymaker, a letter-carrier, a stabler and a gardener (Wood 1935, 82). Interestingly, when compared with two other Edinburgh parishes, Canongate parish in the 1690s showed a higher percentage of families without resident servants, which suggests a lower socio-economic status for the smaller burgh (Dingwall 1994, 52).

It is clear, moreover, that not all properties were substantial. A complaint by one David Bowie, cowfeeder, against a Mrs Straiton over the state of a thatch roof of a byre in the Canongate, and another by Alex Campbell, a brewer, against the widow of Hugh Cleghorn, distiller, for damage to his malt and maltbarn by the 'stopping' of the sewers are reminders that routine life in the Canongate was sometimes still very rudimentary.[21] The Hanoverian kings had little interest in Holyroodhouse. It was permitted to fall into decay and many tenants sub-let. Even the debtors living there for sanctuary complained in 1753 to the Duke of Hamilton, the hereditary keeper of Holyroodhouse, that the common sewer was stopped up, not having been cleaned since the Union of the two crowns [sic] and that if it was not soon cleaned, the palace would be under water (Forbes Gray 1940, 42). The Minute Book of Magistrates and Stent Masters for 1724 to 1742, listing monies received for poor relief, is merely a further small reminder that the less fortunate were rubbing shoulders with the moneyed classes.

Lothian Hut, however, was evidence that, in spite of the departure of many Scots, Canongate still attracted some wealthy residents. Much of this was due to the continuing importance of the Scottish law courts and

the flowering of the 'Golden Age', when Edinburgh became, briefly, a centre for literature, philosophy and architecture. It was in Canongate, for example, that Robert Burns was inaugurated as the poet-laureate of Canongate Kilwinning Freemasons Lodge, no. 2, in 1787 (Forbes Gray 1933, 220). This particular lodge was a favourite of the Edinburgh artists and architects of the 18th century.[22] Panmure House was the residence of the economist Adam Smith from 1778 to 1790 (Home 1908, 12). He was visited here by Edmund Burke, the statesman and orator, in 1784 and 1785 (Forbes Gray 1924, 16). David Hume, the philosopher, was one of the tenants in Jack's Land from 1753 (Kerr 1922, 29). The graveyard of Canongate Church testifies to the many 'worthies' who stayed in Canongate, including Adam Smith, Robert Fergusson, the poet, Dugald Stewart, philosopher, and 'Grecian Williams', the artist. The sanctuary of Holyrood even became the home of the exiled Comte d'Artois, later to become Charles X of France, brother of Louis XVI. He arrived in January 1796, three years after his brother was guillotined. A debtors' sanctuary was considered by some to be suitable accommodation, as it was believed that he was sufficiently poor because he had only one carriage (Hannah 1927, 95).

Holyroodhouse was also occupied for other purposes. In 1742, the constable of Holyroodhouse informed Canongate kirk session that David Paterson, formerly a trainee minister who fell foul of the authorities for sexual misdemeanours and was already under the sentence of lesser excommunication and admonished of the sentence of greater excommunication, had hired a room there, 'where he continued the practice to marry persons irregularly, and sometimes three or four Coupel in a Day'. The rise of irregular marriages, often conducted by ministers unemployed after the establishment of Presbyterianism or by laymen, was one aspect of urban life that made kirk session control of the populace extremely difficult. Regular marriage meant the reading of banns on three successive Sundays and a ceremony performed by a minister in the parish church. This very public form of marriage tended to deter bigamy and protected women in particular. The use of a room in Holyroodhouse by Paterson was merely one further flaunting of the church's code of conduct. By the 1790s Paterson was in prison, from where he continued to perform irregular marriages. Indeed, after further dubious actions, it was deemed that:

> the said David Paterson had been for many years not only a Reproach to the Ministeriall orders but had been

and still continues to be a perfect Nuisance in the Town and City of Edinr and suburbs thereof while he still lurked notwithstanding of a Sentence of Banishment pronounced against him by the high Court of Justiciarie (Leneman & Mitchison 1998, 130).

The Canongate remained, however, in many respects, one of Edinburgh's dignified and elegant social centres. When St John Street was constructed, its first residents were mainly aristocratic (Forbes Gray 1953, 61). Canongate became, in effect, both the home of the wealthy and reputable – noblemen, judges, generals, writers, doctors, bankers and the like – and, equally, the resort of the poorer elements of society.

The presence of the wealthier classes continued to offer opportunities for the services of others, including women. Mantua-makers, who became called dressmakers by the end of the 18th century, were a new breed of women, usually from the upper and middle classes. Their production of mantuas, a woman's garment, to some extent superseded the role of tailors in making women's clothes. Miss Euphemia Elphinstone, a single lady, and her partner were advertising in the *Caledonian Mercury* in 1764 to the effect that they made garments without fittings, to the newest fashions from London, in their house in Canongate opposite the parish church. Louisa Cleghorn, spouse of Archibald Russell, a weaver in Canongate, worked as a sick-nurse in 1775; it was 'her business to wait upon sick persons'. In 1750, Margaret Yorston, wife of James Yorston, the brewer, was functioning as a grocer in her own right, sending out bills for such commodities as candy, sugar, vinegar and whisky (Sanderson 1996, 187, 90, 204, 211).

An 18th-century house, still partially standing until the new Parliament site was developed, was called Haddington House, later known as 8 & 10 Haddington Entry. This was reputedly built around 1700 as a townhouse for the Earl of Haddington, leading off Haddington's Entry to the east of Reid's Close, the latter so named after a brewer alive in the 1730s. Adjoining this property and possibly also forming part of it was 12 Haddington Entry, later known as 99 Holyrood Road, built by Alexander Bredin of Rosemount, who is recorded as 'Captain Alexander Bredin late Fort Major of Edinburgh Castle' in 1766.[23] A Major Bredin was a feuar in this area in 1740, and in 1780 Reid's Close seems to have been (probably briefly) referred to as 'Bryden Close'.[24] The land at the foot of Haddington Entry was previously held by George Hogg, brewer, and before that by the weavers' incorporation.[25] None of this appears on

the extant early 18th-century maps, however, other than on Kerr's 1750 map, which specifically shows a property on the site of what is traditionally called 'Haddington House', although it is possible that the name 'Haddington House' is a later addition. Edgar's 1765 plan, however, shows nothing on site, but from 1775 maps onwards it is delineated, although there is a variation on how far south the property extended. According to *Williamson's Directories* of 1775 to 1779, for private postal deliveries, one James Bryden did live in the close to the west of Queensberry House, but by 1777 he is specified to be a shoemaker and is not, because of profession and age, the same person as Major Bryden, although he may have been a relative.[26] The standing remains of the property, before demolition for the new Parliament building, indicate that this was originally a quality building (see Chapter 3.6).

In spite of its name, documentary evidence makes it clear that the Earl of Haddington's House, for which permission to be built was given in 1782,[27] was not, in fact, on this site. Various records of the neighbours to Haddington's property indicate that the lands on which Haddington built were the 'yards and gardens once owned by William Wilson of Sourhope, or Soonhope, writer'. Philip Wilson of St Christopher, West Indies, inherited his father's property on 8 March 1782. The whole property was called 'Wilson's Court' and it extended right down to the Strand (South Back of Canongate – Holyrood Road); it stood opposite Canongate Church and it already had one tenement built on it. Exactly where on this plot Haddington built is not stated; but in *Williamson's Directory* in 1782–3 the Earl is specified to be 'opposite Canongate Church' and in 1786/7 as at 'Wilson's Court', thus it may have been on a frontage site, or perhaps set back a little. Here is further firm indication that people of standing in society were still content to invest and live in Canongate. The tenement was passed to Robert Walker, minister in Canongate and his spouse Jean Fraser in 1787,[28] and by 1790–2, the Earl had moved to the newly built George Street,[29] a portent of things to come for Canongate.

13.1.4 Culture and leisure

Edinburgh, as the leading city in Scotland, became the fashionable role model for cultural activities. The city had its own school of artists, which included such prestigious persons as Allan Ramsay, Henry Raeburn and David Wilkie (Smout 1975, 455–6). The Norrie family, well-known as interior house painters, lived close to Canongate, at the head of Blackfriars' Wynd.[30] Poets and philosophers frequented the elegant salons of Canongate and Edinburgh. And the sophisticated liked to be seen. They went to Leith to watch horse racing and archery contests (Topham 1776 , 38, 51, 84, 256) or, later in the century, travelled to the farms between Edinburgh and Leith to eat curds and whey. Promenading, according to a contemporary, became customary for the well-to-do; they would 'drive in their carriages to the sands at Leith and Musselburgh, and parade back and forwards, after the manner of Scarborough' (Topham 1776, 94). The same observer noted of the capital in the 1770s that 'we have an elegant playhouse and tolerable performers; assemblies, concerts, public gardens and walks, card parties and a hundred other diversions' (Topham 1776, 90). Playhouse Close, opposite New Street, took its name from the first theatre opened there in 1747, although visiting companies had previously met in the Taylors' Hall (Mackay 1879, 118). As early as 1664 there is mention in the records, as their costumes were impounded to pay for their debts, of a dancing master, a principal dancer, a trainee comedian and others in the entertainment industry (Houston 1994a, 205).

Societies proliferated, there being over 200 including about 40 different types ranging from literary, to masonic, scientific, learned and political (Clark & Houston 2000, 588). There was also organised music-making in Edinburgh by the 1720s (Clark & Houston 2000, 580). Outdoor activities gained interest. Edinburgh had two golf societies by the 1740s; skating was a popular pastime; Canongate had a bowling green at the end of Shoemakers' Close, to the north of the High Street; and fishing tackle, shooting gear and children's toys could be bought at Thomas Henderson's shop at Cross Well in Edinburgh by 1759 (Gray 1935, 111–60).

There developed also a fashionable interest in gardening and botany. The growing number of gardeners being entered as burgesses of Canongate attests to this (eg Armet 1951, 8, 24, 27, 32, 35, 44). The *London Chronicle* of 3 September 1778 recorded the Quakers of Edinburgh, one of whom was a 'Mr Miller who lives on a beautiful piece of ground near Holyroodhouse'. William Miller originally came from Hamilton to Holyrood as a nurseryman in 1689 (Chapter 12.1). His son and grandson continued the highly successful family business with extensive lands at Craigentinny. Their Canongate home was at St Ann's Yard, Holyrood, from 1760 to 1790, and, according to

Kincaid's map of 1784, they also possessed land further west, to the south of Lothian Hut and the Strand (fig 12.5). Their stock included 'prickly spinage', 'field turneep', 'cowcumber' and flowers such as sweet william, Chinese hollyhock, French marigold, lupins and asters. More adventurous still was the importation from Canada in 1775 of Canadian tree seeds, such as Canada oaks (Minay 1991, 15–16).

Newspapers, printers and booksellers were commonplace after the end of censorship in 1695. Although Edinburgh was well behind London in its output, it produced more than three times the number of printed works produced by its nearest rival, Oxford. By the 1760s there were more than 15 libraries in Edinburgh (Clark & Houston 2000, 596–7) and the upper classes had an extensive range of periodicals, newspapers, novels and histories from which to choose. The principal booksellers were Bell and Bradfute, and Manner and Miller in Parliament Close, Elphinstone Balfour, Peter Hill and William Creech in High Street, and William Laing in Canongate. Laing was particularly noted as a collector of old books (Cockburn 1910, 162). The French Revolution produced a mushroom growth of periodicals and journals. As already indicated, where there had been eight Scottish newspapers in 1782, 27 were being produced by 1790, with even more in 1791 and 1792. The first to claim to be as a direct result of the French situation was the *Edinburgh Herald* (Meikle 1912, 86).

Adam Ferguson, the philosopher and historian, commented in 1759 that 'the wit and ingenuity of this place is still in a flourishing way, and with a few corrections … is probably the best place for education in the island' (Clark & Houston 2000, 597). Edinburgh University (the college) had approximately 1000 students in 1700, and this figure had risen to 4400 a century later. The Scottish enlightenment was firmly entrenched in the universities and academics took a prominent role among the literati. In particular, medicine was dominated by Scottish institutions, which produced as many as nine out of ten doctors academically trained in Britain (Clark & Houston 2000, 599).

By the end of the 17th century, Canongate's grammar school was in the first-floor flat of a tenement in Leith Wynd, but this burned down in 1696. From 1704 it was sited further east, set back from Canongate High Street, almost midway between Leith Wynd and New Street. There it stayed until 1822. By 1799 Canongate had 150 scholars, compared with Edinburgh's 489 (Law 1966, 110).

In the *Edinburgh Courant* of 12 September 1778 it was stated that the school's grounds were 'in a very extensive area surrounded by walls which affords an ample space for the school games and exercise without being exposed to the danger of the public street' (Anderson 1935, 13, 15, 19). This gives an interesting insight into the growing realisation of the necessity of exercise and fresh air, as well as book work.

The Comte d'Artois, while staying at Holyrood, was given English lessons by the current grammar school master, William Ritchie (Anderson 1935, 20). Other schools began to proliferate in Edinburgh, some boarding, others charity, English, or sewing schools. Many of these were run by women (Sanderson 1996, 36, 76–81, 87–8, 94, 102–4, 121, 136, 138, 141–2). It is highly significant, however, that by 1760 there were still only 5–15 per cent of women and the poorer working classes who could sign their names (Clark & Houston 2000, 598), although it is possible that many more could read. The capital consisted of divided societies.

One section of Edinburgh society on the increase was prostitutes. In 1763, it was claimed, there were only five or six brothels in the whole of Edinburgh; one might have walked the entire length of the roadway from the castle to Holyroodhouse without being 'accosted by a single street walker'. Within 20 years the number of brothels had allegedly increased 20 times, 'and the women of the town more than a hundred fold. Every quarter of the city and suburbs was infested with 'multitudes' of prostitutes (Withrington & Grant 1975, 51). It is doubtful, however, whether this virtuous account of only five or six brothels in 1763 would stand up to much scrutiny (Leneman & Mitchison 1998, 28); privately published in 1775, *Ranger's Impartial List of the Ladies of Pleasure in Edinburgh* suggests a different story. Also probably masking the full truth were the difficulties the Church faced when dealing with sexual services and the upper classes, resulting in lack of recording. One such unpleasant case in 1743 involved a girl of 12 in Canongate, who was procured by one Isobell Ivie, forced to drink ale and wine and then raped by a 'Sir William'. The kirk session deemed the offence a 'scandalous and heinous Iniquity', ordered the prosecution of Ivie by the civil magistrates for banishment from the town, but brought no action against Sir William, who was never named in full (Leneman & Mitchison 1998, 30).

The level of concern over sexual misdemeanours resulted in Scotland's first non-statutory female penitentiary, or magdalene home, being opened in Canongate in 1797 by the Philanthropic Society. Named the Edinburgh Magdalene Asylum, it originally housed all ages of women recently discharged from prison, but after four years it was concluded that a better success rate would be achieved if younger women were focused upon. Older women failed to turn 'from their inveterate habits' and younger women had probably not been on the streets long enough to develop serious drinking problems and contacts with the criminal underworld. It was also believed that they might benefit more from a strict regime of 'mild, wholesome, paternal and Christian discipline'. The only specification for admission to the asylum in Canongate was that the inmate 'be sincerely sorry for her past delinquencies and desirous of being reformed'. The clientele was, therefore, not professional prostitutes with long criminal records, but rather young female misdemeanants, vagrants and paupers. Women under 24, with no disease and not pregnant, were favoured, but the records show that many could hoodwink the authorities, being subsequently sent to hospital for a 'course of mercury', the treatment for venereal disease, or to the poorhouse when pregnancy became obvious (Mahood 1990, 75–8).

Drinking continued to be a popular pastime for all classes. Many of the drinking establishments were now larger and more commercial, with their landlords financing and marketing much of the entertainment. Inns became the prime venue for new entertainments, such as lectures, exhibitions, scientific experiments, sports, concerts and society meetings, as well as displays of animals, birds, human freaks, and acts by jugglers and magicians.

The White Horse Inn or White Horse Stables stood at the foot of Canongate, near the Watergate, and dated to 16–3 (the middle number was missing from the lintel). It was approached by Ord's Close, later called Davidson's Close, and then White Horse Close. The whole of the ground floor was originally used as stables, such was the demand for horse-drawn traffic.

One of the earliest inns on record is the Coach and Horses, standing in 1712 at the head of Canongate. From here the stagecoach left for London. The journey took 13 days and the fare was £4 10s. One of the most famous inns at the head of Canongate was the White Horse (not to be confused with that at the foot of Canongate). In the second half of the 18th century this was owned by James Boyd, and here it was that Samuel Johnson stayed in August 1773 on his tour to the Hebrides. The White Horse would become the starting point for the Edinburgh–London Fly,

Edinburgh–Aberdeen Fly and the stagecoaches to Leith and Kelso. Another inn at the head of Canongate was the Black Bull Inn, standing in either Bell's or Gullan's Close. From here the Edinburgh and Newcastle flying post coach set off every Monday, Wednesday and Friday at 6am. It carried six passengers inside, at a fare of 31s 6d. In March 1772 it was announced that 'by this speedy convenience' passengers passed 'from Edinburgh to London in only four days at only five pounds stg per seat'. It was also advertised that at the Black Bull travellers could 'depend on clean beds and good entertainment and civil treatment'. John Somervell in the mid-18th century had an inn at the foot of Canongate. He then opened a coaching business advertising, in 1754, a London stagecoach as, 'a new genteel two-end glass machine … drawn by six horses, with a postillion on one of the leaders'.

James Clark, once 'farrier to his majesty' and owner of repository stables, proved even more entrepreneurial: in 1781 he opened 'for the reception of the Nobility and gentry Clark's Hotel, Chessel's Buildings' – probably the first hotel in the Old Town. Contiguous to the hotel were stables with 'a great number of stalls for horses, sheds and coach-houses for carriages etc…. But the better class of patron was resorting to the luxurious establishments in the New Town' and in 1783 it was advertised to be let (Jamieson 1925, 126–34). Canongate was becoming a less desirable area.

The ordinary man and woman of Canongate was excluded from much of this entertainment and cultural activity. But traditional pastimes linked to the home and drinking houses remained. Celebrations and festivities meant bonfires, bells, flags and noise. Skittles, quoits, football, cards, gaming, gambling and boxing did not necessarily require great funds, and there was a new sport at which the spectator might bet – cock fighting. The first book on the subject in Scotland was published in 1705, and thereafter it proved very popular.

13.1.5 The changing townscape

Apart from the impressive dwellings that graced Canongate, probably the outstanding feature of the 18th-century townscape was the multiplicity of closes that grew up in the backlands behind the street frontages. One of the principal reasons for this was that the capital remained very much confined to the narrow limits of the medieval burghs of Canongate and Edinburgh. The net result was congestion and uncomfortable accommodation for the growing professional classes, including the rapidly expanding

class of lawyers who concentrated in the capital to administer criminal justice and civil jurisdiction. New streets were introduced into Canongate – New Street, for example, originally called Young Street, from the house of Dr Thomas Young, which appears as one of the additions to Edgar's map in 1765 (Boog Watson 1923, 95). It was intended initially as a private thoroughfare and remained so until 1786. Described as 'the boldest scheme of civic improvement effected in Edinburgh before the construction of North Bridge' (Bonar 1856, 16), the new streets were designed for the wealthy – to avoid the lack of privacy and squalor of the main street.

Being cramped into a narrow site, one solution to accommodation, as in Edinburgh, was to develop upwards. This tended to add to social stratification, with the poorer elements of society occupying attics and cellars. Closes were an alternative.[31] Reid's Close, which forms the western boundary of the Holyrood Parliament site, Vollen's Close, Boyd's Close, Cumming's Close, Thomson's Close, Penman's Close, Charter Close, Brodie's Close and Horse Wynd are all clearly visible on Kincaid's map of 1784 (fig 12.5). All feature a measure of development, particularly Reid's Close (off which ran Haddington's Close, Vollen's Close, Brodie's Close and Horse Wynd. Apart from Reid's Close and Horse Wynd, the two determining thoroughfares for the Holyrood Parliament site, all have now disappeared under more recent development. But closes were not confined to the Parliament site; they were a feature of all of Canongate.

The names of some of the closes give clues to the occupations of the residents and are a further indication of the multiplicity of people, craftsmen and professionals, who huddled together in Canongate. Boyd's was called after James Boyd, a stabler. Both Cumming's and Thomson's Closes probably owed their names to brewers (Boog Watson 1923, 122–4). The name of Vollen's or Vallen's Close could go back to c 1610, when one John Vallange, a master hammerman, is on record (Harris 1996, 614). Brodie's Close was once called 'Little's Close'. This close and Horse Wynd offer interesting insights into the jumble of properties and owners who could exist, sometimes cheek by jowl, in one close. Brodie's Close had two entrances, one from Horse Wynd and one from Canongate, reflected in some cartographic and documentary sources in the additional name of 'Brodie's Back Entry'. The name came from Francis Brodie, the wright, who built a large tenement on the west side of Horse Wynd for his brother, William, a tailor. Francis' nephew and son of William, also William, was a barber and periwig maker in Holyroodhouse. The close was also called Baxters' Close, after baker brothers called Greig, one of whom, Thomas, was baker to the abbey. In consequence, Greig's Close was also its name (Boog Watson 1923, 122–4). Thomas Greig acquired further ground on the west side of Horse Wynd from William Miller, the seed merchant at the abbey, in 1796.[32] It was said that Miller had built a 'house or chapel' here, which Greig converted into a dwelling house. In fact, the Quaker meeting house built by Miller may have stood to the east of Horse Wynd or south of the Strand and Lothian Hut. This may, then, be an allusion to a property described in the Dean of Guild Records when a complaint was laid by James Ramsay, a mason, against the Marquis of Lothian. The marquis was, apparently, pulling down the dyke, arch and wall of a cellar that was a back land and east tenement 'of the chapel of the Virgin Mary lying at the end of the church of the monastery of the holycross of old possessed by John Eiston vicar of the said monastery lying near the foot of the Canongate on the south side'.[33] There was probably not a chapel on the site, but rather a property that financially supported a chapel. The close also had the names of Kinloch's Close and Chancellor's Close (Boog Watson 1923, 122–4); and it is known that in 1773 some of the buildings here were to be demolished by the Marquis of Lothian, presumably to open up his new property, Lothian Hut.[34]

These closes with the general name of Brodie's Close were further subdivided into 'lands', and in the property records sometimes as 'subjects'. Sasines and accompanying plans indicate that the backlands off the fore-tenements on Canongate and the west frontage of Horse Wynd were highly developed, housing not only dwellings but also associated yards, stairs, coal houses, cow byres, coach houses and stables.

Congestion was also creeping into the land to the east side of Horse Wynd – in areas that had once formed part of the policies of the palace. The home of Miller, the nurseryman, was in this area; another tenement was bounded by Horse Wynd on the west and by the property of Thomas Crawford, merchant burgess on the east in 1676.[35] By March 1685, a dwelling house, malt kiln and barn stood at the head of Horse Wynd.[36] By 1739, a 'laigh house and cellar or baikhous and chamber above the samen' was 'lying within the precinct of the Abbay of Holyroodhouse'.[37] The plan drawn of the palace of Holyroodhouse and precincts in 1770, taken from a plan of James Turnbull, to show the changes that had taken place since the map

of Edinburgh was made in 1742 by William Edgar (fig 12.4), shows graphically the colonising of this area.

Attempts were made to improve the quality of house structures. In c 1676, it was laid down that houses were not to be constructed of inflammable material, as wood and thatch posed too much of a fire risk, particularly given the increasingly close proximity of dwellings. To enforce this new ruling, a 500 merk penalty for non-conformity might be incurred. Chimneys were to be cleaned at least four times a year; and, in 1707, it was enacted that it was:

> strickly prohibited the keeping and using of privat furnices … made use of in brewing distilling and melting of mettells and the like especially where the floor of these rooms … are laid with daills … without a speciall licence from the Dean of Guild.[38]

Much of the head of the Canongate, including the school, burned down in 1696 (Armet 1951, 208). Rebuilding after conflagrations did, however, give an excellent opportunity to upgrade, and rebuilding and reoccupation usually took only one year. A fire of 1700 was exceptionally fierce, but even that damage had been repaired by 1704. The disadvantage to the residents, apart from the loss of possessions and homes, was probably the resultant increased rentals (Houston 1994b, 33).

Market days inevitably brought greater congestion. Canongate's market was still held at the head of Canongate where there was a variety of stands selling numerous types of goods. The market cross, however, was moved in 1737 from the centre of the road to the churchyard wall 'for the convenience of passage in the street' (Maitland 1753, 156). The need for space on the thoroughfare was accentuated by the proliferation of horses and coaches, and the records, both documentary and cartographic, throughout indicate the build-up of coach houses.[39] The head of Canongate, it was said, was particularly congested, with butchers selling their wares. 'Coaches and carts [could not] go one by another' and doors to houses were ' almost stopped by crowds of people and multitudes of fleshers' dogs' (Wood 1935b, 103). This congestion continued after the construction of a new north–south axis at Trongate, via the newly constructed North Bridge over the old streets to the New Town of Edinburgh. Although this must have impacted on the traffic east–west along Edinburgh and Canongate's High Streets, the problem was not resolved.

A visitor to the capital in 1705 made an interesting comment that Canongate was easier to navigate than

Edinburgh, as all the houses in the lower part of the town had the names and trades of the occupants written on the doors (Taylor 1903, 103). But overcrowding was causing problems on public occasions even in Canongate. From 1675, the place for public execution in Canongate was moved from the High Street to Gallowlee (Houston 1994a, 125–6).

New public buildings also joined the tolbooth, market cross, school and new church. Canongate Charity Workhouse was built in 1761 and was located at the foot of the tolbooth. Built through public subscriptions, it was occupied by the infirm and destitute of the parish (Mackay 1900, 180). Contributions to a charity workhouse in Canongate were made by the cordiners and other crafts from 1761 (Malcolm 1932, 113). The workhouse regulations included provision for nurses to tend both children and the sick.[40] The workhouse in large measure superseded the chapel and almshouse of St Thomas at the Watergate, which had been converted into a hospital for the poor of the burgh. Over the entrance were inscribed the Canongate arms, supported by an old man and an old woman (both disabled), with the inscription, 'Help here the poore, as ze wald God did zow. June 19, 1617'. The town magistrates had sold the patronage in 1634 to the kirk session, by whom, it was claimed, its revenues 'were entirely embezzled'. By 1747 the buildings were turned into coach houses and in 1787 pulled down and replaced with 'modern houses of hideous aspect' (Grant 1881–3, ii, 39). The kirk treasurer's accounts suggest that approximately 30 to 45 poor received weekly financial support, as well as possibly ten or so being in receipt of monthly charity and a few individuals of one-off donations (Dingwall 1994, 259). The itinerant and begging poor would not have benefited, however, from temporary accommodation in the charity workhouse nor from regular handouts. Their numbers are difficult to calculate and the back alleys probably supplied homes to far more than are recorded. The poor, many of whom, particularly children, were vulnerable to smallpox, were to be an increasingly growing problem in Canongate. But the town was relatively fortunate in the 1690s. Famine hit Scotland, but the effects in Canongate were minimised by importation of foodstuffs via the harbour at Leith.

For certain sections of society, there were rising standards of living and a desire to display this growing wealth (Maver 1998, i, 160–1). Conspicuous consumption and restricted urban space sat ill together. With a certain inevitability arising from this desire for improved living conditions and economic aspiration for

profit, the greatest change on the capital's townscape would be set in motion from 1767. It was perhaps understandable that the New Town, Nicolson Street and George Square attracted many of Canongate's more notable residents away from the congestion of the Old Town. With the development and establishment of the New Town, life in the old burgh of Canongate was to be irrevocably changed. Those who could not afford to move were the poorer elements of society, and it was they who, with the development of the New Town and exodus of many of the upper classes, would come to dominate Canongate in the 19th century (Kinnear 1969, 6–7).

13.2 Queensberry House in its urban context, 1708–1801

JOHN LOWREY

13.2.1 Introduction

The history of Queensberry House in the 18th and 19th centuries has been characterised by one Victorian author as 'a descent in the scale of degradation' (Wilson 1891, 108), that is, from the most important aristocratic townhouse in Scotland, from both an architectural and political point of view, to a House of Refuge for the lowest and most unfortunate stratum of society. That process was largely related to the social and economic changes that affected Edinburgh in general and the Canongate in particular in the 18th and 19th centuries. The very suburban character that had made the Canongate such a pleasant place to live for some in the later 17th and 18th centuries provided the space required for quite dense industrialisation in the 19th. Along with that was an influx of immigrants that made the 19th-century Canongate one of the most overcrowded and insalubrious parts of the city.

After the Act of Union, Queensberry House lost its political significance and much of its importance as a base for the Queensberry family, who, thereafter, were more concerned with their Drumlanrig and English estates and their London townhouse than their Edinburgh mansion. The 18th century saw their gradual disengagement from the Canongate house until its sale in 1803, its use by the army, and its eventual conversion to a House of Refuge. In urban and architectural terms, a broad pattern is very clear over this period, for, whereas in the late 17th and early 18th century, the creation of the house was partly concerned with the creation of space within the fabric of the city that could allow the house, in a sense, to function independently of the city, as the 18th century progressed the issue was about preserving and defending that independence against encroachments. Encroachment occurred nonetheless, until the house was absorbed into the social and industrial milieu of the 19th-century Canongate (see Chapter 14).

13.2.2 The Queensberry family and Edinburgh in the 18th century

The independence of Queensberry House has already been outlined in previous chapters. It was a matter of architectural design, setting and servicing which linked the house, on the one hand, to the discreet and aloof architecture of the Parisian *hôtel particulier* and, on the other, to the country house. In the case of Queensberry House it was also a matter of the legal framework through which the relationship between house and city was defined. From an early stage the aristocratic owners of the house worked hard to secure rights for themselves that cut across the normal protocols that operated within the city. Thus, Lord Hatton successfully broke the monopoly held by burgh craftsmen when he brought in his own workmen to convert the Balmakellie mansion to his own use in 1681, despite the intervention of the disgruntled Canongate guilds (Wilson 1891, 106).[41] The unusual rights accorded to James, second Duke of Queensberry were, however, even more significant. In 1706, in the months leading up to his extended stay in Edinburgh to oversee the demise of the Scottish Parliament, the Duke undertook a series of legal moves, that were also honorific, that seem to have been concerned with simplifying his feudal relationships. Thus, in June 1706, he resigned all of his titles in favour of Queen Anne who duly resigned them back in his favour a few days later, confirming the transaction with a charter under the Great Seal at Windsor on 17 June 1706, meaning that James held his lands directly from the Crown.[42] Shortly before this, in March 1706, Edinburgh Town Council ratified an act of the previous month in which it renounced its right of regality within the defined bounds of Queensberry House and its gardens. Instead, the Duke and his heirs were made 'heretable baillies of regalitie within the bounds of the said lodging and pertinents with power to him and them to exercise the said baillerie with all the jurisdiction and priviledges, fees, emoluments and casualities which might belong to us as principal baillies of the said regalitie … as if the said Duke and his forsaids were made and constitute heretable baillies within the bounds forsaid immediately by her majesty'.[43] The

city retained some rights, mainly concerned with the Duke's obligations to pay certain public burdens, but in terms of legal jurisdiction Queensberry House was effectively part of the Regality of Drumlanrig, and it is a very good example of the Duke's success in distancing himself and his family from at least some of the cares of urban living.[44]

There were limits to this, not least when the rights and privileges accorded to the Duke and his family in 1706 were swept away when heritable jurisdictions were abolished in 1747. However, having lost this power of jurisdiction, it is possible that the Duke continued to derive some financial benefit from the Council Act of 1706 because in the same year, 1747, the third Duke disputed an Annuity Tax assessment of £1400 on the grounds that the original Act of Council in February 1706 had fixed the assessment for Queensberry House at £700; in other words he argued for the benefit of a perpetual assessment for his property based on that Act, an interpretation of the Act that was not shared by the city stent masters. It seems likely that the Duke would eventually have had to capitulate on this (Boog Watson 1923, 10–11) but, for a time at least, he was able to resist the authorities and as late as 1762/3 he was still paying the old valuation (Hume & Boyd c 1984, 77).

By this time, Queensberry House was far less important to the family than it had been in the heady days of the Act of Union. However, the house continued to be used as a residence by both the second and third Dukes for much of the 18th century. It has been noted elsewhere (see Chapter 11.5.3) that, although the Duke left Edinburgh in 1707, and a lot of material was removed from the house, Queensberry House was retained as a fully furnished residence. There is a great continuity between the furnishings and decoration in 1707 and those in 1723, when a detailed inventory was made at the end of a visit to the house by the third Duke, Charles, and his wife, and this is well documented in the archives.[45] From June 1723, a large number of tradesmen were at work in the house preparing for the family's visit. Walter Melville, the painter, painted the windows and exterior doors and whitewashed all of the service areas of the house. In addition, he painted some of the grander spaces, including a bedchamber in 'pearl blew', Lady Jean's apartment and a number of fireplaces in imitation black marble.[46] Other work included minor masonry repairs by George Anderson, the most important of which was the lowering of some of the window sills in the house,[47] and wright work by both George Hay and John Heart.[48] Hay's work included the repair of a number of pieces of furniture in the house and also 'the loan of twinty Rushia leather chairs at the time of the Duke's aboad in the Canongate at 6d per chair'.[49] John Heart's account went back to 1722, when he carried out maintenance in and around the house. In 1723, his workload increased enormously and the account gives a very good idea of the kind of work a man of his skills was expected to carry out, ranging from straightforward joinery work to cabinetmaking and even encompassing tasks normally associated with the upholstery profession. Thus, he spent a lot of time repairing floors, making a new door for the belvedere, repairing timber work in the stables, gardens and gardener's house and repairing or replacing windows in the main house. At the same time, he repaired furniture, mainly chairs and tables, and even turned a new handle for a warming pan. Heart was also greatly involved both in the transit of furniture, including making the packing cases for things that were to leave Queensberry House, unpacking boxes as they arrived, and setting up furniture and furnishings all over the house. It was this latter activity that brought him into the upholsterer's realm, and he was to be found not only setting up beds for the visiting family but also putting up their hangings. Similarly, he was responsible for the window curtains and even for putting up the wall hangings, both tapestry and paper. Upholstery work of this kind formed a major part of the preparations for the 1723 visit and Heart's contribution was merely to supplement the main work carried out by William Schaw, an Edinburgh upholsterer, whose accounts itemise cushions, hangings and drapes in a vast array of colours and materials.[50] Alongside him was William Oliphant, the dyer, who cleaned and dyed a number of sets of bed hangings, including one that was dyed yellow.[51] Other trades also played a part in preparing the house for the visit: locksmiths, glaziers and blacksmiths all worked hard in the spring and early summer of 1723 to set up rooms, repair windows, supply lanterns and candle sconces and fireplace equipment.[52] Kitchen utensils were supplied by the coppersmith, Alexander Miller, who also supplied tea kettles and a chocolate pot for the Duchess.[53]

All of this feverish activity was overseen by the permanent fixture at Queensberry House, Jean Wardlaw, who was the housekeeper who oversaw the departure of the family in 1707 and who was still there to welcome them back in 1723. To help her, she recruited some extra staff, including two housemaids, Margaret Smail and Isobel McIntosh, who each worked for seven weeks in the house. Janet Clark, an assistant, and Thomas Swinton, the porter, were each employed for four months, while Jean Somerville was apparently an occasional employee who worked a total of 13 days 'stearing the speets' (turning the spits) in the kitchen.[54]

Even allowing for the distortions in the history of the house that are an inevitable result of the haphazard survival of archival material, the 1723 visit seems to have been an important and unusual event. The enormous amount of repair work alone suggests that such a visit had not taken place in the immediate past and an obvious reason for that is that the Duke and Duchess preferred their London townhouse in Piccadilly to their Canongate house. However, in 1723, the third Duke and Duchess were involved in architectural activity on a large scale in their other properties, notably at Amesbury in Wiltshire (by Henry Flitcroft) and, more importantly, on Lord Burlington's estate in London, where in 1722 they purchased the shell of an impressive Palladian townhouse, designed by Giacomo Leoni for Lord Clifton. The fitting up and completion of this London Queensberry House lasted until about 1725 and the result was a house that could hardly have been more different from the Canongate mansion, although the inclusion in the London building of a long gallery running through the depth of the building on the right-hand side of the plan may indicate some connection with the older residence in Edinburgh (*Survey of London* 1963, vol. 32, 458; Sykes, 1989, 87). As far as the visit itself was concerned, it seems likely that the special preparations made in Edinburgh, coupled with the extensive building work in London, suggest that Edinburgh was chosen as their summer residence that year because their London house was not in a useable state.

The third Duke and Duchess (Charles and Catherine) are best known as sophisticated patrons of the arts, associated in particular with Alexander Pope, Jonathan Swift and John Gay. Despite the rather eccentric Duchess's apparent antipathy to the Scots (Chambers 1868, 340; Grant 1881–3, vol. 2, 38), the pair seem to have been quite frequent visitors to Edinburgh, most notably after falling from favour at court over the Duchess's support for Gay in 1729 (Burgess 1966, 79). Gay was a house guest of the Queensberrys for several years after this, staying mainly at their London house and at Amesbury (Burgess 1966), but he also spent some time in Scotland and was certainly in Edinburgh in May/June 1729 (Nokes 1995, 471), when he seems to have divided his time between Alan

Ramsay's bookshop and Jenny Ha's tavern, opposite Queensberry House, with accommodation supplied by the Queensberrys not in the house itself but in an apartment close to the tavern (Wilson 1891, 107–8).

Precise details of how the Duke and his family used the house in this period are hard to come by and, although there is clear evidence from a number of secondary sources of the family being in residence, as well as the main primary source (the Buccleuch archive), there is equally evidence of the Duke attempting to find another use for the house when the family were not in residence.

13.2.3 18th-century tenants in Queensberry House

The third Duke's attempts to keep the house in use even when the family were elsewhere can be dated back to as early as 1712, only one year after he had inherited the title. In that year, part of the house was let to Major General Whelham,[55] 'General of the forces in Scotland'. An inventory made at the time does not precisely accord with any earlier one but has some overlap with the 1723 inventory and, whilst being mindful of the possibility of items being moved around the house, seems to suggest that Whelham's quarters took up most of the second floor of the house, that is above the state floor. This is perhaps what one might expect and ties in with a pattern that emerges over at least the first half of the 18th century in which the Duke is willing to let out part of the house, in this case furnished, but is also keen to retain part for the family's use and, at least in this case, is not willing to let out the state apartment or make available the best furniture that was situated there. It raises at least the possibility that the house could have been shared by family members and tenants and that possibility is certainly acknowledged in other documents that refer to renting out the property. Probably the most important of these was the attempt to lease the house to the Board of Customs in 1732. John Clerk of Penicuik, the Duke's commissioner in Edinburgh, successfully negotiated a tack with Commissioners for Customs in February 1732, which was ratified and due to come into effect at the beginning of April.[56] Under this arrangement, the house and its gardens, offices, etc, were let on a 19-year tack for £125 sterling, plus all public burdens. The Board of Customs was allowed to make internal alterations so long as the house was made good at the end of the lease, and the Board was also responsible for looking after the interior. The Duke was responsible for structural maintenenace and was allowed to keep a

large room and two closets in the east jamb, as well as the garret above, for the storage of furniture that was not otherwise disposed of. There was no suggestion that the family would use the accommodation in any other way. At this time, the Board of Customs was located in Customs House Stairs, off the north side of Parliament Close, on part of what became the Merchants' Exchange (incorporating a new Customs House) in 1753. However, it appears that the Customs officers never took up residence in Queensberry House because the city was keen to keep them where they were and made a plea to that effect, after the agreement had been made with Queensberry. According to a later document, the Duke 'was generously pleased to release them from the obligement in the Tack' and did not hold them to their contract, as he might well have done.[57] In 1749, the Duke was forced to revisit this episode because the Commissioners, although they never paid any rent, sub-let part of the house to a Brigadier Moyle, Commander General of the army in Scotland, who 'continued to possess for some years and particularly would not remove but kept his possessions when the Duke and his family went down to Scotland in 1734 and they were obliged to content themselves with the possession of a part of their own house'. The result of this plea for restitution of the rent is unknown, but the episode confirms both the tendency to rent out to the military, already seen in the case of General Whelham, and also another family visit. Both of these also feature in the record of a tack of 1741 in which the house was set to Major General Joshua Guest, who rented:

> the west end of his Grace's house in the Canongate with the large kitchen and cellar belonging thereto and as many of the rooms in the upper part of the house as he shall have occasion for, for the accommodation of his servants together with stables and a hay loft over the same and room in the coach house for a coach as also his Grace's garden at the yearly rent of £40 sterling.

However, to avoid the inconvenience of not having an Edinburgh base if it proved necessary, the Duke had a right to take his house back at a month's notice, for as long as necessary, with reversion to the general afterwards.[58]

By the mid-1740s the redoubtable Jean Wardlaw had been replaced as resident housekeeper by Mary Mackenzie. She was responsible for making preparation for the last recorded instance of the family using Queensberry House in the summer of 1747. The arrangements were broadly similar to those of 1723, although the documents serve to confirm that the earlier preparations were more thoroughgoing and more unusual. In 1747, there was a great deal of spring cleaning rather than construction and the records are full of references to sweeping chimneys, cleaning the forecourt and the apartments in the house, repairing bedding and supplying goods like firewood, coal and beer.[59] As in 1723, a number of servants were taken on for the duration of the visit, including two porters (one for the lodge and one for the house), an assistant chambermaid, a stable boy, a turnspit and a butler.[60]

Throughout the first half of the 18th century, clearly, Queensberry was keen to find a tenant for the house, but, in the absence of a long-term institutional tenant like the Board of Customs, he was perfectly content to make other arrangements that on the one hand kept the house occupied and possibly provided an income and, on the other, provided an Edinburgh base for himself and his family. The evidence for the second half of the century is much scarcer, but some of it suggests that the main concern for the Duke was not so much using the house as a source of income but simply keeping it occupied. By the middle of the century another factor was that his sons might also have been interested in using the house and may have had some say in how it was occupied. In 1747, the eldest son, Henry, Lord Drumlanrig, was first to use the house, with the Duke and other members of the family coming afterwards. Drumlanrig may also have had a say in organising the tenancy of John, second Earl of Stair, who used the house in the winter of 1746/47 while seeking treatment in Edinburgh for what turned out to be his last illness. Stair was a famous soldier and diplomat, with great successes in the reigns of both Queen Anne and George I, and in 1744, he was appointed Commander in Chief of the British Army. He had been Lord Drumlanrig's commander during his military service abroad in the early 1740s (Grant 1881–3, vol. 1, 103–5). It is possible, therefore, that his use of the house was by way of a favour from an admiring, younger officer rather than as a paying tenant.

Both Henry and his younger brother Charles died young (1754 and 1756 respectively), and the Duke and Duchess seem to have been less interested in visiting Edinburgh in their later years. The little information available for the second half of the century suggests fairly straightforward tenancies of the kind that were quite common in the Canongate at the time, when larger aristocratic houses were let to, and sometimes split between, high-ranking tenants. In the case of Queensberry House, the shared tenancy of the Earl of Glasgow and the Duke of Douglas in 1761 is an example (Boog Watson 1932, 12). However, it is still possible that the financial interest was not uppermost in the mind of the Duke, and the final tenant, who was by far the longest continuous resident of Queensberry House, was Sir James Montgomery, Lord Chief Baron of the Exchequer. He lived in the house from 1773 until his death in 1803 and, according to one source, he was given the use of the house for no rent (Grant 1881–3, vol. 2, 38).

Although the evidence for how the house was used in this period is fairly scant, there is enough here to suggest firstly that the family continued to have an interest in the building, at least in the first half of the century, and that when it was tenanted, some at least of those tenants (including the main one who lived there for 30 years) did so on a grace and favour basis. That being the case, it is not surprising that there is very little evidence of substantial architectural activity of the kind that would have been necessary to convert the house effectively into a tenement. Thus, the arched, rusticated doorways on the inside walls of the two wings are very unlikely to have been connected with the subdivision of the house at this time and, as the archaeological evidence confirms, are part of the later alterations by the army. The only recorded building work in the 18th century involved reharling the building and all the garden and office house walls, repairing cracked sills and lintels and repairing chimneys and vents.[61] This was fairly run of the mill repair work and of little significance in the building history of the house. Apart from that, it seems that the well in the basement of the house, activated by a pump from Hatton's time, was eventually superseded in the late 18th century when the tenant James Montgomery applied for permission to bring in a piped water supply from the water main in the Canongate, in 1784.[62]

13.2.4 Queensberry and his neighbours in the 18th century: troublesome tradesmen

While the creation of what was virtually a country house in the city gave the Duke of Queensberry a highly unusual and privileged position even within the Canongate (where there were other grand houses), Queensberry House cannot be viewed entirely in isolation, and there are two aspects that are particularly important in understanding the house in its wider urban context. The first of these is the relationship between Queensberry House and its immediate neighbours, and the second is the relationship between

Queensberry House as a grand aristocratic townhouse and the other grand houses in the vicinity.

The archival sources are quite rich in information about the Duke's relationship with his neighbours, although the focus, inevitably, is on legal disputes. One of these has already been dealt with in the discussion of the Duke's garden, which brought him into conflict with William Miller, the nurseryman at Holyrood Palace, whose attempts to drain the fetid stank in the South Back of the Canongate apparently caused damage to the Queensberry Gardens (Chapter 12). But the Duke had other, sometimes less considerate, neighbours than Quaker Miller to deal with.

A major issue for the Dean of Guild Court in both the 17th and 18th centuries was complaints of neighbourhood which, in terms of buildings, usually meant encroachment by one neighbour on another (Bailey 1996, 171). This could involve not only the actual building on another's property, or perhaps more commonly usurping the boundary wall as part of a new building, but also encroaching on the privacy of a neighbour by inserting new windows so that they overlooked another property. In the case of the Duke of Queensberry, with neighbours on the east and west sides of his property, this was obviously an encroachment to be defended against. At Queensberry House there was also the added complication of neighbours on the north-east and north-west whose property overlapped with that of the Duke: that is Glen's Land on the north-east and what was in the 17th-century Hepburn's Land on the north-west, which by the end of the century was owned, or partly owned, by the Mallochs, a family of bakers.[63]

The first dispute between the Duke and his neighbours actually goes back to 1695 when Mungo Malloch proposed to rebuild the gable of his property that overlooked the entry into the courtyard of Queensberry House.[64] The basis of the dispute was Malloch's intention to slap windows out through a gable to overlook the Duke's property[65] (Chapter 11.2).

There were several similarities between this dispute and those the third Duke had with his neighbours in the mid-18th century, demonstrating that the same kinds of issues caused problems between neighbours and that encroachment could either be physical usurpation of part of someone else's property or it could be a matter of encroaching on their privacy. In 1750, the Duke was successful in persuading Robert Reid to remove completely a lean-to construction against the west wall

of the stable block, as a physical encroachment on his property.[66] In this case it is also very likely that the Duke's objection was not simply to the use of his stable wall as part of the structure of someone else's building, but also that the building was just too close. Certainly, that seems to have been the motivation in a provisional objection made by Alexander Goldie, the Duke's representative, in 1755, when he wrote to the Dean of Guild in connection with the southward extension of a tenement owned by George Hog, a brewer, on the west side of Queensberry House. The objection was not to the building itself but to the possibility that it might deviate from the existing building line. There was an 11ft gap between Hog's building and the Duke's property and Goldie's intention was to see that such a gap was maintained.[67]

On the same side, at around the same time, the Duke took action against a weaver, George Rae, who was a tenant in a property owned by the Incorporation of Wrights, that was either very close to or identical with the property, owned by Mungo Malloch, about which the second Duke had complained. And the complaint was very similar. Rae had slapped a 5ft by 3ft window in his east gable, directly overlooking the Duke's courtyard 'and thereby intends to appropriate a servitude of light into the complainer's said area or enclosed court, an encroachment neither allowable nor desirable'.[68] To make matters worse, like Malloch 60 years before, Rae had allowed the debris of his illegal demolition to fall into the Duke's courtyard and left it there. In this case, the outcome appears to have been satisfactory from the Duke's point of view. The wrights had been unaware of their tenant's activities and undertook to restore things to their previous condition.

While the western boundary was thus troublesome to successive Dukes, the eastern boundary also had its problems and, as in the west, a particular difficulty attended the area of overlap between Queensberry House and Glen's Land, the southern as well as the western elevations of which overlooked the Queensberry property. By 1747, the Duke had had so much trouble from the tenants in Glen's Land that he took out a complaint and secured an act against them. The problem was very basic and very typical of 18th-century Edinburgh, namely that:

> they had been in a constant tract and custom for these several years bypast of throwing over the windows on the southside of the said tenement into an area belonging to his Grace for keeping his coalls; wash, excreaments and fowl water which rendered the same useless.[69]

Previously, the landlord had put spars on the windows to prevent such use but this: had no effect by reason of their pulling off the said spars and throwing over their nastiness in the said area which appeared to the said Baillies by ocular inspection upon a visit thereof upon application by his Grace.

The solution, which the Duke insisted be made personally known to the tenants, was for wire mesh to be fixed over the windows, with fines of £10 for anyone who removed them. It seems doubtful that this was entirely effective, especially since an irate John Halkerston, the Duke's gardener, found it necessary to take out an Instrument of Intimation against the Glen's Land tenants in 1751, re-emphasising the original act and spelling out the penalties once more.[70]

13.2.5 Queensberry and his neighbours in the 18th century: quality

By the middle of the 18th century, even with the court and Parliament gone, Canongate continued to attract some of the upper echelons of society, who wanted to build their houses there, presumably because it was relatively uncongested compared with Edinburgh proper. From the 1730s onwards, there had been a number of developments, mainly south of the Cowgate, that allowed the remaining aristocratic and professional classes of the city to experience the unique pleasure of living in a house, based on the established pattern of London townhouses, rather than a flat. The first of these was Argyle Square, built in the 1730s, and, after a number of others in the same area (present day Chambers Street), this southern expansion culminated in the construction of George Square in the 1760s. At the same time, there was also expansion in the Canongate, where two new streets of houses were laid out. The first at New Street, laid out by Dr Thomas Young from 1765, not as a thoroughfare but as a private and possibly gated community. The second was St John's Street, built from 1768, again as a private community (Harris 1996, 461, 545), 'guarded by an ancient seneschal in faded uniform who banned entrance of all carriages except those of residents' (quoted in Catford 1975, 88–9). In both developments, people of quality and resources were able to have spacious townhouses within the city but at a distance from hoi polloi. The architecture of the houses was a specifically urban typology developed from late 17th- and early 18th-century townhouses in London that were adapted for use in Edinburgh and elsewhere in the mid-18th century, most notably in the New

Town of Edinburgh.[71] However, Queensberry House belongs to a different tradition of grand housing in the city, which, as has been shown, had its roots both in the urban hôtel (a different urban typology) and the country house, and which demanded both more space and more privacy than the terraced urban house. This tradition continued in the Canongate in the 18th century, especially in the area around Queensberry House itself.

Pre-18th-century houses, such as Panmure, Winton and Moray House, have been discussed elsewhere. Most of these continued to be used; others were redeveloped, among them Roxburgh House, which lay slightly to the west of Queensberry House. Nothing is known about this building, although its productive gardens have already been commented on (see Chapter 12), and it is mentioned but not described by Daniel Defoe in 1724 as one of the major houses in the Canongate (Defoe 1724, Letter 11). It is equally marked by its absence on Edgar's 1742 map of Edinburgh, which indicates a site with buildings around the edge and substantial gardens to the south but with no house and simply the legend 'Duke of Roxburgh' where one would expect the house to be. By 1765, however, when the Edgar plan was reissued, a new house had been built on the site for Lord Milton (fig 12.4). This was the townhouse of Andrew Fletcher of Milton, nephew of the famous anti-Unionist Andrew Fletcher of Saltoun and politically as far from his esteemed uncle as it was possible to be. Fletcher was associated with John, second Duke of Argyll and his brother, the Earl of Islay,

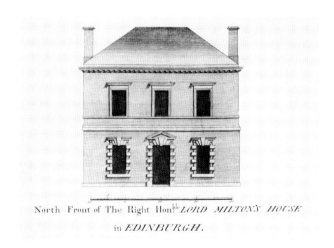

Figure 13.2
John Adam's Milton House, Canongate, c 1754
(© Crown copyright: RCAHMS)

who succeeded as third Duke of Argyll (Lindsay & Cosh 1973, 8). Through the latter's influence Fletcher was appointed Lord Justice Clerk in 1743, in which capacity he had to deal with the defeated Jacobites after 1746 (Grant 1882, 34). His house in the Canongate was built some time around 1754, almost certainly by John Adam (Simpson 1980, 30). It was essentially a small, suburban villa, almost square on plan, with a hipped roof and a very plain façade, relieved only by Gibbsian surrounds on the openings of the ground floor (fig 13.2). On plan, a porter's lodge lay to the left of the main door, while Lord Milton's dressing room or business room lay to the right. At the back of the house were the two main public rooms with views out over the gardens and towards Salisbury Crags. Although it was somewhat smaller and less elaborate in its planning, Milton House seems to be closely related to an earlier Adam townhouse: Minto House, designed by William Adam for Gilbert Elliot of Minto around 1738 (sited in what is now Chambers Street).

The main public rooms of Milton House were lavishly decorated by William Delacour, the first master of the Trustees Academy (Macmillan 2000, 118; Simpson 1980, 30). When James Grant was writing just a few years before the 1887 demolition of the house, he indicated that:

> its walls are still decorated with designs and landscapes, having rich floral borders painted in distemper, and rich stucco ceilings are among the decorations and 'interspersed amid the ornamental borders there are various grotesque figures, which have the appearance [says Wilson] of being copies from an illuminated missal of the 14th century. They represent a cardinal, a monk, a priest, and other churchmen, painted with great humour and drollery of attitude and expression' (Grant 1882, 34).

Delacour evidently was admired by the Adams, since he also worked for John at Hawkhill in Edinburgh and for Robert at Yester. More locally, some idea of the decorative style that embellished Milton House can still be seen within the school building

that replaced it, where four of the landscape panels adorn the main staircase. Similar work can also be seen at Moray House, where the 18th-century work is almost certainly by Delacour.[72]

A somewhat similar pattern of overbuilding occurred on the opposite side of the street, that is an existing older house was replaced by a new one in the 18th century. Winton House, directly opposite Queensberry House (see Chapter 12.1), was ruinous by the time Edgar's map was published in 1742, having been abandoned by the Earl of Winton when he fled to Europe after his part in the Jacobite uprising of 1715 (Grant 1882, 35). The first development of the site was not in fact domestic, but business, and also linked to both Queensberry House and Milton House. As part of a general attempt to improve the economy

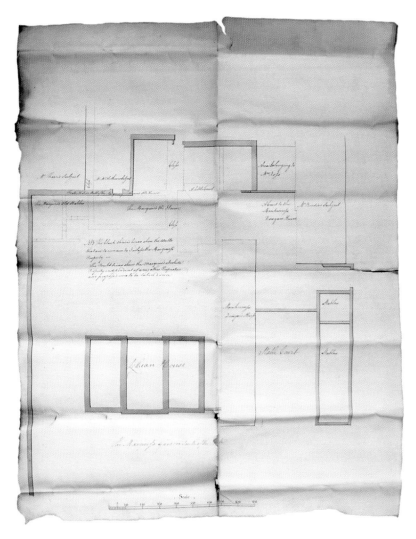

Figure 13.3
Dean of Guild plan of Lothian Hut and its surroundings, 1773 (© ECA)

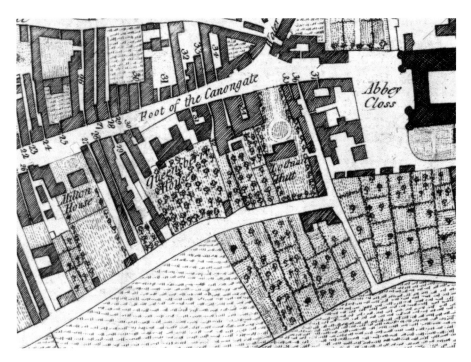

Figure 13.4
Detail of Ainslie's map, 1780 (© NLS)

of post-Union Scotland, a number of companies were set up with the aim of encouraging activity in various sectors of the economy. Among these was the British Linen Company, established in Edinburgh in 1740 under the governorship of the Duke of Argyll and the Duke of Queensberry. The real moving force behind this, however, was Lord Milton, who was also appointed deputy governor (Lindsay & Cosh 1973, 145; Smith 1924, 115). The original premises for the new company was Winton House, which was acquired in 1744 (Smith 1924, 115) and seems to have served adequately despite its ruinous condition, which was still recorded on Edgar's revised map of 1765 (fig 12.4). In the 1750s, the accommodation was expanded into Moray House and the decrepit premises at the foot of the Canongate were finally demolished in the late 1760s to be replaced by a house for Sir John Whitefoord, the advocate and friend of Robert Burns. Whitefoord House was designed by Robert Mylne (Gifford *et al* 1984, 216). The house was a simple harled, classical box, three stories over a basement with an extra storey on the north side because of the slope of the ground (Smith 1924, 116) and a single-storey Doric porch on the front. As in the case of Milton House, the new building sat within the grounds of what had originally been a considerably larger house and in

this case a smaller house was evidently added at around the same time. Callender House, built for Sir John Callender of Craigforth, is built against the east gable of the slightly larger Whitefoord House.

The other major new house built in the vicinity of Queensberry House in this period was Lothian Hut.[73] This was situated to the east of Queensberry House, immediately behind the buildings on Horse Wynd. Most secondary sources give the date of the house as c 1750, making it roughly contemporary with Milton House. However, while Milton House appears on Edgar's revised map of 1765, Lothian Hut does not. The most recent research suggests that the house was not actually built until c 1765 and that the building work was unfinished at the Marquis's death in 1767. It seems clear, however, that William, fourth Marquis of Lothian, certainly owned a property on the site already and his petition to the Dean of Guild in 1766, to rebuild a gable 'in a very crazy condition' contiguous to his lodging, certainly suggests two buildings, one of them perhaps older and in a more dilapidated condition.[74] This appears to be borne out by a Dean of Guild petition in 1773, submitted by John, fifth Marquis, which includes a site plan, which shows both the new house and, on the north of the site, partly hemmed in by other properties, 'The Marquis's old house' (fig 13.3). The old Marquis had spent time and money trying to do for Lothian Hut what Lord Hatton had done for the house that became Queensberry over 80 years before, namely, to acquire surrounding properties to create space around his premises and, thereafter, as Queensberry continued to do in the 18th century, to protect his interests against encroaching neighbours.

Figure 13.5
Painting by G Walker of Edinburgh from St Anthony's Chapel, c 1823; detail showing Lothian Hut, Queensberry House, Milton House and Crichton's Coach Works (© City Art Centre)

In fact, the site plan actually indicates three Lothian buildings: the old house to the north, which appears to butt against the property of a Mr McArthur, the new house, and, immediately to the east of that, a long building running north/south, labelled 'Marchioness Dowager's House'. Through a process of gradual acquisition and rebuilding, the Lothians managed to achieve something similar to the Queensberrys. The Ainslie map of 1780 (fig 13.4) indicates the new house about halfway back along the deep site, with gardens to the south and a courtyard or garden to the north, with a drive and turning circle for carriages. The Marquis had achieved his aim of opening the site up to the street, but the courtyard is nonetheless framed by buildings to both east and west and, indeed, the entire site is overlooked from the west by the buildings on Horse Wynd. While relations with most of the other proprietors were cordial and the transactions passed off with little trouble, two proprietors, in particular, did cause problems for the Marquis, and vice versa. They were James Ramsay, whose property lay to the north-west of the site, and Francis Brodie, whose property lay to the north-east of Lothian Hut. In each case, the difficulties were mainly over boundaries and encroachment and of the two, the dispute with Brodie was possibly the more significant in that the marquis managed to delay Brodie's redevelopment of his site from 1768 until 1772, when work finally started.[75] His building was a five-storey tenement of good-quality flats built to a new building line that allowed Horse Wynd to be widened and overlooked the Marquis's property from the east.

Little information has survived on Lothian Hut itself, although there are some clues as to its appearance. The site plan clearly indicates a simple, tripartite classical box, with the central bays projecting to the south but recessed on the north, entrance front. That certainly suggests a pediment on the south front, although the arrangement of the entrance front is more difficult to work out. This interpretation is borne out by an early 19th-century view of Edinburgh from St Anthony's Chapel which clearly shows a seven-bay Palladian villa with a pedimented centrepiece on the south side (fig 13.5). Some indication of the interior and planning of the house is provided by the advertisement at the public roup of contents (when the house itself was also offered for let) in 1788:

> Lothian New and East Houses, adjoining to one another
> – The new house, consisting of dining and drawing room, parlour, six bed chambers, servants' hall, laundry, kitchen, three garrets and cellars, with coach house, stables and offices; and the east house, consisting of dining and drawing rooms, parlour, five bed chambers, laundry, servants' hall, kitchen, garrets, cellars, and other conveniencies …[76]

The east house was presumably the building identified as the 'Marchioness Dowager's House' in 1773, although it is slightly puzzling that there is no sign of this on Ainslie's 1780 map. Armstrong and Mostyn's map of the Lothians, published in 1773, includes an inset map of Edinburgh, based on Edgar but updated, and this does show Lothian Hut with a long east wing stretching back towards the Canongate and actually linking with the buildings on the street. This would tend to suggest that the east wing was demolished prior to 1780, when Ainslie's map was published; however, since the wing seems to reappear on Kirkwood's 1817 map, questions are again raised about the building pattern in this area. Leaving that mystery aside, however, what does seem clear from this discussion is that Lothian Hut, or house, forms part of a small group of what were essentially villas erected in the Canongate at around this time, including the extensions to the slightly earlier Reid's Court, lying opposite Milton House. Of the whole ensemble, however, it is Lothian Hut and Milton House, which is also visible in the Walker painting, that really stand out as the two most refined and commodious houses, apart, of course, from Queensberry House itself. Lothian Hut was the last of the aristocratic townhouses built in the Canongate and was arguably something of an anachronism even as it was built. It was a house that is now more famous for its tenants, notably Dugald Stewart, than for its architecture and even this cursory glance at the archival evidence for the house indicates that the Canongate was beginning to change. Not only were the great houses not occupied by their original patrons, and instead were taking single or even multiple tenants, but also, as the Brodie petition indicates, more specialist, specifically urban housing, designed with tenants in mind, was also erected in the area. Brodie was by no means alone in this and his intention, judging from the accommodation his flats provided, was certainly for professional and well-to-do tenants.[77] This links it with developments like Chessel's Court, dating back as early as the 1740s. Later tenement development in the 19th century was not always of such quality.

Notes

1 ECA, 'Burgh of Canongate, Window Tax, 1710–1711', shelf ref. 64; indexed at page 74.

2 NAS, Hearth Tax records, E69.

3 ECA, Annuity Roll 1687.

4 NAS, Hearth Tax, E69/16/3. ff. 53 & 62. Figures calculated for other towns from manuscript sources are quoted in Dennison & Coleman 1996, 34; Torrie & Coleman 1995, 18–19; Dennison & Coleman 2000, 35; Torrie & Coleman 1995, 17.

5 Archives and Business Record Centre (ABRC), University of Glasgow, Ms, 'Messrs Wm Younger & Co., Ltd, Abbey and Holyrood Breweries Ltd, report' (undated), 15.

6 Bell 1994, 240.

7 ABRC, Ms, 'Inventory of titles and properties belonging to Messrs William Younger & Co, Ltd.', 5, no. 20; 7, no. 30, for example.

8 ABRC, Ms, 'Inventory of titles and properties belonging to Messrs William Younger & Co, Ltd.', 8, no. 38; 9, no. 40.

9 ABRC, Ms, 'Inventory of titles and properties belonging to Messrs William Younger & Co, Ltd.' 11, no. 54, for example.

10 ECA, Ms, 'Black Index Book, no. 1/5', 84, no. 37.

11 ABRC, Ms, WY 2/1, 'Inventory of titles of properties belonging to Messrs William Younger & Co. Ltd.', 2, nos 1 & 3; 4, no. 14.

12 As 11 above, 5, nos 19 & 20.

13 As 11 above, 7, no. 30.

14 As 11 above, 8, no. 38.

15 As 11 above, 9, nos 42–4; 10, no. 45.

16 As 11 above, 10, nos 49, 51, 53, 54.

17 As 11 above, 12, nos 59 & 62; 13, nos 64, 66, 69; 14 nos 71, 72, 73, 74.

18 As 11 above, 16, nos 86, 87, 90.

19 As 11 above, 17, nos 91, 92, 94 96–8, 99.

20 As 11 above, 19, nos 101 &103; 20, nos 105, 106; 20, nos 108, 109.

21 ECA, Ms, 'Dean of Guild Records', xv, 1 October 1746 and 14 January 1747.

22 E Patricia Dennison is grateful to Dr J Rock for this information.

23 NAS, Protocol Book of George Lindsay, B22/2/63, fo. 137v–139.

24 Williamson 1780, 58; Ms, 'Roll of the Superiorities of the City', 11.1.1740. ECA.

25 Ms, 'Notarial Instrument in favour of Agnes Gunion Brotherston and others', 1896. ECA.

26 Williamson 1889, 1773–4; 1774–5; 1775–6; 1776–7; 1778–9.

27 NAS, Ms, Minutes of the Town Council of Edinburgh, 11 September 1782.

28 NAS, Register of Sasines, P.R. 322.245 (2797; 21.May.1787; 30.May.1788).

29 Williamson 1889, 1790–2; 1793–4; 1794–5; 1794–6; 1796–7; 1797–8; 1798–9.

30 E Patricia Dennison is grateful to Dr J Rock for this information.

31 RCAHMS, Ms, 'Design for the Canongate which was ratified by Parliament and dated 22 March 1661'.

32 Ms, 'Inventory of titles', 35, nos 201–3. ECA.

33 ECA, Ms, 'Dean of Guild Records', 18 September 1766.

34 ECA, Ms 'Dean of Guild Records', 13 November 1773.

35 ECA, Moses Bundle IV – bun 85/3696; 24 August 1680, vol. III, bun 73/3256.

36 ECA, Moses Bundle, vol. IV – bun 82/3594.

37 NAS, Minute Book, Particular Register of Sasines, 1733–1739 (RS71/11), fo. 155; Lib. 123, fo. 112.

38 *Register of the Privy Council*, iv (1673–76), 182; Armet, *Extracts from the Records of the Burgh of Edinburgh, 1689–1701*, 83; Armet, *Extracts from the Records of the Burgh of Edinburgh, 1701–1718*, 144.

39 NAS, Minute Book, Particular Register of Sasines, 1726–1733 (RS71/10), fo. 133v; Lib.109, fo. 394.

40 *Regulations for the Canongate Workhouse, 1761*, quoted in Houston 1994a, 24.

41 The original source for this is 'Fountainhall's Historical Notices', see *Book of the Old Edinburgh Club*, XVI, 1928, 106–7.

42 Buccleuch Mss, NRA(S) 1275/vol. 16, 157: 'Inventory of the New Writs of the Whole Estate in the person of the deceas'd James Duke of Queensberry & Dover'.

43 ECA, Town Council Minutes, 6 March 1706, 494–500.

44 Until this point, Queensberry House had fallen under the jurisdiction of the burgh of Broughton, with both civil and criminal cases heard in the Canongate courts.

45 Buccleuch Mss, NRA(S) 1275/1103, 'Inventory of the Furiture of his Grace the Duke of Queensberry's House in Canongate taken up this thirtieth day of August 1723'.

46 Buccleuch Mss, NRA(S) 1275/1642/E/5, 'Accompt due by his Grace the Duke of Queensberry to Walter Melvill, Painter, 1723' (Discharged February 1724).

47 Buccleuch Mss, NRA(S) 1275/1643.

48 Buccleuch Mss, NRA(S) 1275/1553 & 1642/E/4.

49 Buccleuch Mss, NRA(S) 1275/1553.

50 Buccleuch Mss, NRA(S) 1275/1642/A/11.

51 Buccleuch Mss, NRA(S) 1275/1537.

52 Buccleuch Mss, NRA(S) 1275/1642/A/2, E/1, E/2.

53 Buccleuch Mss, NRA(S)1275/1537.

54 Buccleuch Mss, NRA(S)1275/1642/A/4.

55 Buccleuch Mss, NRA(S) 1275/1103. His apartment included the yellow damask room, dressing room, dining room, drawing room, red room, Lady Jean's room, dressing room and closet.

56 Buccleuch Mss, NRA(S) 1275: unnumbered bundle in box with 1108. Includes a minute of tack between John Clerk of Penicuik and Commissioners for Customs, Edinburgh, 15 February 1732, two copies of signed tack by the Duke of Queensberry and witnesses, London, 24 February 1732, Schedule of Requisition and Intimation to the Commissioners of the Board of Customs, 15 May 1732.

57 Buccleuch Mss, NRA(S) 1275/479. 'Copy Representation for the Commissioners [of Customs] of his Grace the Duke of Queensberry and Dover, 1749'.

58 Buccleuch Mss, NRA(S) 1275/vol. 20: Sederunt book of commissioners of Charles, Duke of Queensberry, 1738–50, 178–80, Minute of Tack of west part of Canongate lodging to Major General Joshua Guest, 1 July 1741.

59 Buccleuch Mss, NRA(S) 1275/1668.

60 Buccleuch Mss, NRA(S) 1275/1550.

61 Buccleuch Mss, NRA(S) 1275/479/A/13. 'Estimate of the Duke of Queensberry's house in the Canongate of roughcasting, year 1758'.

62 ECA, Macleod Bundles A4/Bay D/bundle 21/shelf/11/ item 8.

63 For detailed discussion of this complex western boundary, see Chapter 8.3 on the history of the site.

64 ECA, Dean of Guild Court Book, vol. 7, 86, Duke of Queensberry against Mungo Malloch, 13/9/1695.

65 ECA, Dean of Guild Court Book, vol. 7, 129–35, Duke of Queensberry against Mungo Malloch.

66 Buccleuch Mss, NRA(S)1275/479/A/2, 'Obigatory letter by Baillie Reid for removing a toofall to the Duke of Queensberry's stable when desired', 23 March 1750.

67 Buccleuch Mss, NRA(S) 1275/479/A/1, 'Memorial by Alexr. Goldie writer to the signet for his Grace the Duke of Queensberry', 1755.

68 Buccleuch Mss, NRA(S) 1275: unnumbered bundle in a box with bundle 1108. 'Petition and Complaint for the Duke of Queensberry 1754. Anent a window struck out in the wrights' land in Canongate. With judicial declaration for building up the same again when desired.'

69 Buccleuch Mss NRA(S) 1275: unnumbered bundle in a box with bundle 1108. 'Act in favour of His Grace the Duke of Queensbery 1747. Anent tirlessing windows in Canongate.' Another copy of the same document is also in ECA, Macleod Bundles/A3/Bay D/Shelf 2/Bundle 108, item 19.

70 Buccleuch Mss, NRA(S) 1275: unnumbered bundle in a box with bundle 1108. 'Instrument of Intimation Charles Duke of Queensberry against Anne Watson and others tenants in Glen's Land in Canongate', 28 December 1751.

71 Chambers (1868, 296) emphasises the importance of the Canongate as a salubrious 'faubourg' and lists the persons of quality and rank who lived there in 1769. This list included two dukes, 16 earls, two countesses, seven lords, seven lords of session, 13 baronets, four commanders in chief, five 'eminent men' and one banker.

72 RCAHMS, NMRS, Architecture Catalogue IG6/12/82. Notes on Milton House also record pencil sketches of the original Delacour panels.

73 I am indebted to Dr Dorothy Bell, who made her researches on Lothian Hut available to me, including the relevant text from her forthcoming book on the Old Town in the 18th century.

74 Information from Dr Dorothy Bell.

75 ECA, Dean of Guild Records, Petition of Francis Brodie, wright in Edinburgh, 4 March 1772.

76 *Edinburgh Evening Courant*, 18 February 1788.

77 His plans show two-bedroom flats, one of them with a box bed, suggesting a degree of flexibility in the room use, as well as kitchen, dining room and parlour, and a number of closets.

PART 4

Social changes in the Canongate in the
19th and 20th centuries

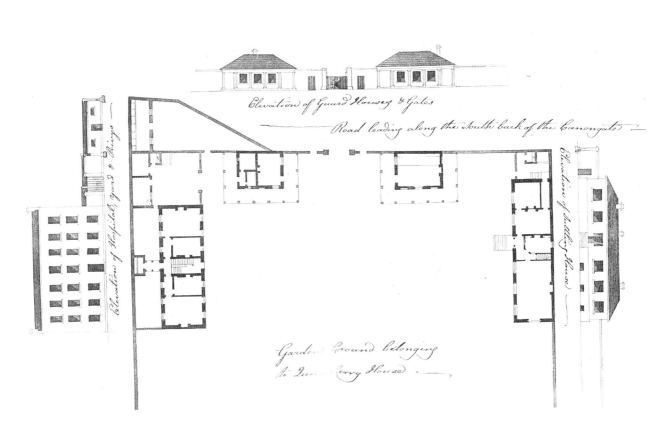

Figure 14.1
Plan of army barracks and hospital at Queensberry House, 1810 (© ECA)

Chapter 14

Queensberry House and the Canongate in the 19th century

TOM ADDYMAN, E PATRICIA DENNISON and JOHN LOWREY

14.1 Introduction

JOHN LOWREY

The 19th century saw the hastening of a number of trends that were already evident in the 18th. In domestic architecture, the age of the great aristocratic townhouse was over. Subdivision, demolition or non-domestic use was the fate that awaited most of these great mansions. New housing was tenemental and, as the century wore on, often of very poor quality. One reason for that was the intensification of industrialisation in the area and the influx of workers, often immigrants from Ireland or the Highlands, needed to supply these industries. The social profile of Canongate changed enormously over the 19th century and nowhere was this better illustrated than Queensberry House, which began its 'descent in the scale of degradation' in 1803 (Wilson 1891, 108). The story of this process starts with the conversion of the house into a barracks and hospital at the beginning of the century, but, in order to understand it in its wider social, urban and architectural contexts, this chapter, having sketched out that transfer process, will go on to explore the built environment of the Parliament site and the wider Canongate in relation to the key themes of hospitals and refuge, trade and industry and, finally, housing.

The third Duke of Queensberry, who died in 1778, was succeeded by his nephew, William Douglas, third Earl of March and fourth Duke of Queensberry. The fourth Duke evidently had little interest in his Scottish estates, other than as a source of income, and certainly had no interest in visiting his Edinburgh mansion. In 1801, he decided to sell the house by public auction at an upset price of £900. Francis Brodie, a local lawyer, purchased the house on behalf of William Aitchison, distiller at St Clement's Wells in East Lothian (Hume & Boyd c 1984, 79) for £1170, including rights to the Duke's seat in Canongate kirk and with the sitting tenant, Sir James Montgomery of Stanhope.[1] Montgomery died in 1803 and thereafter, for a brief period, the house was inhabited by a number of people, including James Lorimer, a spirit agent, a Mr Curtis, a Mrs Williamson, and an unnamed gardener (Hume

& Boyd c 1984, 85). Thereafter, Aitcheson set about realising the true value of his asset by stripping the house and selling on the valuable decorations, most notably the marble fireplaces, some of which went to the Earl of Wemyss for his newly enlarged house at Gosford, which was still under construction (Wilson 1891, 108).

Aitcheson did not retain the house very long; in 1803, he sold it, along with the by now ruinous Glen's Land, to the army, but retained for himself the right to the Queensberry seat in Canongate Kirk (Hume & Boyd c 1984, 86). The army's requirement was mainly for a military hospital to help deal with the large numbers of wounded men returning from the Napoleonic Wars. It was at this time that the building was drastically altered to accommodate the army's needs, with an extra storey being added (causing the suppression of the belvedere), a new stair in the centre of the building, new entrances in the east and west wings and a reconfiguration of some of the interior spaces (see 14.3 below). The original cost of the property was £3150 and it seems that there was an immediate renovation of the house itself to fit it up as a hospital, costing a further £1950. From the army's costings, it seems that most of the new building work was delayed until 1808, when £12,970 was spent or at least budgeted for the work.[2] The plans were certainly drawn up in 1808, but most of the work does not seem to have started until 1810, although some was certainly completed in the same year, when the rainwater goods showing that date were installed.[3] In January 1810, a petition was lodged with the Dean of Guild 'to execute certain works on the premises in erecting an hospital, scuttling house, guard rooms, privies and part of the boundary walls and gates ... and also in fitting up the centre part and east wing ... as a barrack'.[4] The petition identifies the centre and east wing of Queensberry House as the barracks, implying perhaps that the west wing was reserved for officers. The plan provides no details on the house itself, only a block plan of the property, but it does provide elevations and main floor plans of the new buildings (fig 14.1). The hospital building was on the east side of the site, on

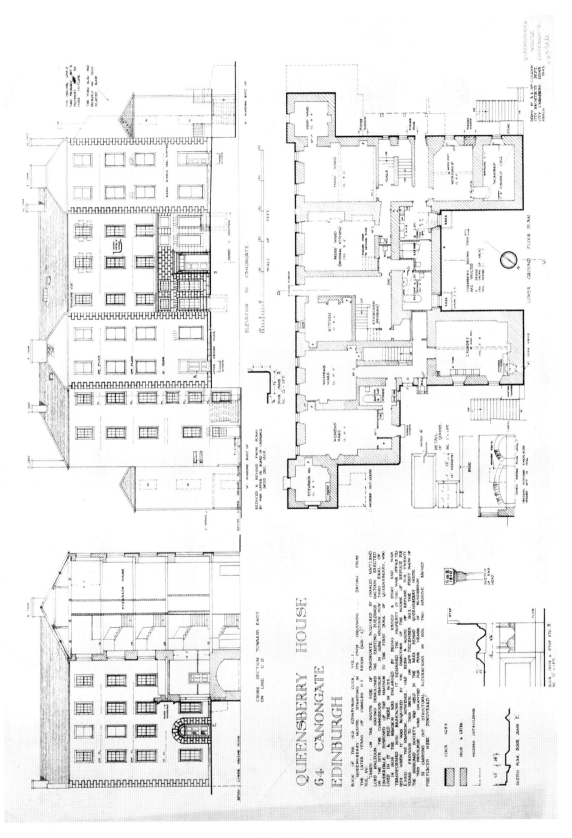

Figure 14.2
Copy (1943) of Board of Ordnance Drawings, dated December 1808 (© ECA)

three floors, with privies alongside on the site of the old gardener's house. The floor plan probably indicates a typical floor, with a central stair, two large rooms at the northern and southern extremities and two smaller ones in the centre. On the ground floor that is shown in the petition plan, a short covered walk connects the hospital block to the mortuary, behind the main building. Opposite the hospital block was the scuttling house, or canteen. This is shown on the plan as a single-storey building over a considerable semi-basement. It contained not only the canteen and kitchen but also stores and even a bar (Hume & Boyd c 1984, 86). A new gateway was slapped through to the South Back, with pedestrian entries on either side of a vehicular entrance. To either side were guardhouses, each with a verandah on its exposed three sides, and within the gardens were replaced by a parade ground.

14.2 William Aitchison (1801–3)

TOM ADDYMAN

Aitchison's principal significance for Queensberry House is that he was responsible for the removal of fine interior features such as panelled rooms and fireplaces. The extent of Aitchison's stripping out is not attested in historical sources. It is now only from the negative archaeological evidence within Queensberry House that inferences can be made. The extent to which the Board of Ordnance had to refurbish the shell of the mansion permits an estimate as to what was no longer in the building. Aitchison clearly did not perform extensive structural dismantling. For example, a large number of the early floor structures still existed, which in turn would indicate that the roof structures remained – there is a gap of some five years before the Board of Ordnance building works commenced. Rather it appears that any saleable non-structural interior fixtures and fittings, which for the large part would amount to internal panelling, other decorative woodwork such as entrance and window architraves, fireplaces and the like, were comprehensively stripped

The absence of surviving decorated plaster ceilings, with the single minor exception of the *Upper Ground* floor chamber within the south-east closet tower, perhaps suggests that these were also dismantled. The absence of any pre-Board of Ordnance period windows at Queensberry House is very notable and it must surely be the case that these were also removed for resale. As previously suggested, there appears to have been minimal removal of masonry features, even

decorative features such as sandstone fire surrounds (ie those that did not have marble fascias) or entrance surrounds. One notable exception may be the entrance that faced one as one came into the porch. Here a very substantial ragged void was subsequently infilled by the military.

During the archaeological project, following the removal of internal plasterwork which was found to be almost entirely of the Board of Ordnance period, only very minimal traces of earlier plaster-onto-the-hard were revealed. It is probable that large zones of the building had been plastered out and it seems likely that the absence of plaster-onto-the-hard indicates further stripping out, and not by Aitchison.

14.3 Board of Ordnance (1803–25): the Military phase

TOM ADDYMAN

14.3.1 Historical and physical evidence

On acquiring the house in 1803, along with the ruinous remains of Glen's Land, the Board of Ordnance's first priority was to convert it for use as a hospital. Certainly the military appear to have started with a blank canvas, little more than an extensive gaunt shell of a building, albeit roofed. The exact architectural outcome of that is unknown, but by 1808 more substantial facilities were required and it seems to have been in the 1808–11 period that the major work on the house and grounds was carried out.

Unfortunately, there is no surviving documentary detail as to what the army actually did at Queensberry House and the original plans for the alterations were not located. However, copies of plans dated December 1808 were made by the City Architect's Department in 1943 and these still survive in the Edinburgh Dean of Guild Records (EDD/32/2: fig 14.2) They evidently delineate the proposed Military phase alterations and are broadly comparable to the recorded modifications. However, in some areas there are individual discrepancies with what was actually constructed. The plans significantly show locations of many early fireplaces, most of which no longer exist, and also illustrate the majority of the upper floor partitions that were inserted in the central part of the building, and other major interventions such as a new central stair. Other sources for this period include Dean of Guild plans of 1811 and Board of Ordnance general site plans of 1823. The latter show that there had been no modification to the general outline of the building.

The stripped-out Queensberry House was extensively remodelled in preparation for its use as a hospital, barracks and officers' quarters. In summary this involved removal of the pre-existing *Attic* level rooms and features of the roofscape and the raising of the wall-heads to form a full additional storey in place of the existing attics, the *Third* floor. The interior was substantially reorganised and, as demonstrated by the 1943 plans, arranged into three discrete units in the east, west and central portions of the building, each segregated from its neighbour and accessible by its own staircase.

The new work was characterised by austerity of detail and emphasis on the strictly functional. The interior space was rationalised on utilitarian lines. The whole effect was to transform Queensberry House into a building with a severe and appropriately institutional bearing.

There is direct physical evidence that the major masonry works involved had progressed in stages, perhaps over three years or so, presumably 1809–11 as suggested by the documentation. The first involved raising the west wing by a full storey and associated works to the interior, particularly the extension of the western staircase. The second stage saw the continuation of works to the east, with the addition of the full *Third* floor level to the remainder of the principal range and the east jamb, and the formation of a central stairwell.

A major construction break was recorded between the episodes of masonry construction at *Third* floor level on the line of the west gable wall of the original Balmakellie mansion. This is most apparent on the south exterior elevation, although two phases of construction were also recorded in the masonry built upon the former Balmakellie phase gable wall within (fig 14.5). Externally the cast iron rainwater hopper heads bear the date of 1810 and the monogram of George III, suggesting that the major masonry works were complete by that date. It is possible, however, that the fitting out of the interior continued into the following year. The phased approach to the programme of construction suggests that the parts of the structure not being worked on remained in use.

The masonry of the new work was of distinctive character, notable for the employment of large unworked slabs of purplish and orange sandstone, visually a more regular rubblework than previously employed. The bedding mortar used throughout was of a light brownish-grey hue containing flecks of charcoal or coal, in contrast to the creamy mortar employed in all earlier phases. Internally all masonry interventions were finished off with a distinctive struck pointing detail not seen previously.

While there was some reuse of earlier dressings, most of the windows inserted at this stage, new quoining at the corners of the jambs to the north and other such features employed a readily identifiable fine–medium grained, light tan-brown sandstone. These dressings were universally tooled and not polished. The arrises of the windows within the additional *Third* floor were left squared within a raised margin. Wall-head copes were newly formed of simple projecting slabs bearing no moulded detail.

All earlier windows had been removed, presumably under the auspices of William Aitchison. They were replaced throughout with new sash and case windows of six-over-six panes, the astragals of which were of narrow *fillet and ovolo* profile. Very often masonry repairs were associated with the windows, such as replacement of cills and lintels. It was often found that where the inner wooden lintels were replaced, the new timbers derived from the earlier roof structures. Many retained significant structural information.

Almost all of the pre-existing fireplaces were blocked off and their surrounds clawed back to the surrounding wall face. Replacement fireplaces were inserted in each newly formed or remodelled chamber. These fireplaces are generally smaller than their predecessors and are universally formed of two vertically-set jamb stones with a lintel above. Each fireplace is splayed internally and detailed with a plain, squared projecting surround. Remarkably, only one of these remained wholly intact, a survivor of yet further works in the 1950s.

Following the removal of panelling, all interior masonry wall surfaces were replastered. It seems likely that substantial areas of pre-existing plaster-onto-the-hard were removed at this stage. In other areas such as the eastern stair existing lime plaster was pecked so that an overlying coat would adhere.

Irregular wall surfaces were made good by packing them out, most commonly with fragments of slate (occasional pantile fragments were also recorded) to form an even plastering surface. The slate may represent building debris deriving from the slating of the new roof structures or residue from the stripping of the pre-existing roof structure. The wall plaster then employed was of similar character to the bedding mortar used at this period, with the addition of cow hair as a binder. A high lime or gypsum skim coat was applied over the general plaster to form a finished surface.

Many of the floor structures in the west wing and at the east end of the principal range were renewed at this stage at *Upper Ground* and *First* floor levels. The existing floors within the east jamb were provided with additional support following the removal of pre-existing partitions at the lower levels. Here the original east/west aligned common joists were supported by the insertion of a large north/south principal joist which was in turn supported by a central vertical post at each level.

Raising the Second *floor*

Second floor ceiling levels were raised by about 0.35–0.4m throughout to provide additional clearance. This involved the systematic removal of the early ceiling structures (the *Attic* level floor structures) and their replacement, as elsewhere, with sawn pine common joists of a narrow rectangular scantling. Externally the *Second* floor window-heads were raised by 0.3m, an operation that involved the insertion of additional

upper jamb stones and, in most cases, the reuse of the pre-existing lintels. Relieving arches were not reinstated; structural relief was in the form of a large horizontal over-lintel stone.

Addition of a full storey at Third *floor level*

All former wall-head details including the shaped gables to the south, cornices in all areas and the gabled heads of the two northwards-projecting jambs were removed. The exterior walls were then built up off the former wall-heads to a uniform height, with the exception of the north gables of the jambs, which were reformed. For the principal range this involved 3.8m of additional masonry and for the sidewalls of the jambs an additional 2.15m. The dressed stone from the former wall-heads, chimneys and other features was built into the masonry of the new *Third* floor. Once recovered and recorded, many of these provided key evidence for the details of the earlier roofscape. The new wall-heads were finished with a plain projecting

Phase

Balmakellie	ca. 1667–70	Military	ca. 1803–11	
Hatton	ca. 1680–81	Hospital	l.C19th–e.C20th	
Queensberry	ca. 1695–1700	Modern		
Queensberry (secondary)	ca. 1700–1705			

0   10
metres

Figure 14.3
North exterior elevation of Queensberry House showing surviving extent of Balmakellie, Queensberry and Military phases

wall-head course. The quoining at the south-west, south-east and north-east corners of the principal range employed large face-bedded dressed slabs, some up to 1.3m long.

Roof structure

The roof structure of Queensberry House that survived until 2000 wholly dated to the Military phase of reconstruction. The new roof structure was formed at a considerably lower pitch than its predecessor. The gabled wall-heads at either end of the principal range were removed and the walling built up to a level wall-head as described and the new roof formed with hipped ends. The gables of the northwards-projecting jambs were reconstructed at a similarly low pitch, as were the roofs behind. At the south end of the east jamb the belvedere tower was reduced to just below the level of the new roof structure.

The roof structures were formed of sawn softwood of very heavy scantling. Low trusses consisting of rafter couples rising from a tie were built off embedded wall plates. The roofs were then sarked and slated. Truncated stumps of major horizontal timbers, lying upon the wall plates and embedded in the wall-head masonry, were also recorded. These must represent the remains of some form of scaffold or construction platform at wall-head level, perhaps required for the lifting and erection of the roof timbers.

The tie beams form the principal support for the *Third* floor ceiling structures. Perpendicular common joists were affixed between these, and lath and plaster laid upon them, as elsewhere within the building at this phase.

North frontage (fig 14.3)

In preparation for the addition of the *Third* floor, the street-facing gable-heads of the east jamb and the west wing were taken down and rebuilt. Large new windows were formed in alignment with those below, and the quoining of the angles extended up to a plain projecting stringcourse at wall-head level. The new gables above were of shallow pitch and detailed with

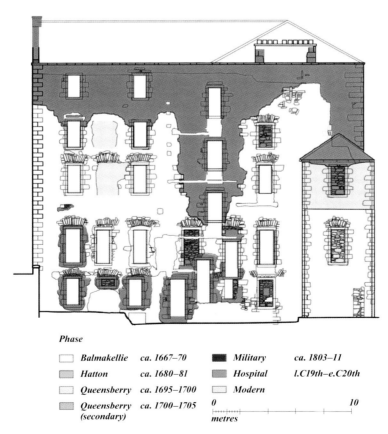

Phase

☐	*Balmakellie*	*ca. 1667–70*	■ *Military*	*ca. 1803–11*
▨	*Hatton*	*ca. 1680–81*	▨ *Hospital*	*l.C19th–e.C20th*
☐	*Queensberry*	*ca. 1695–1700*	☐ *Modern*	
▨	*Queensberry* *(secondary)*	*ca. 1700–1705*		

0   10

metres

Figure 14.4
West exterior elevation of Queensberry House showing surviving evidence for Queensberry and Military phases, to c 1811

Phase

☐	*Balmakellie*	*ca. 1667–70*	■ *Military* *ca. 1803–11*
▨	*Hatton*	*ca. 1680–81*	▨ *Hospital* *l.C19th–e.C20th*
☐	*Queensberry*	*ca. 1695–1700*	☐ *Modern*
▨	*Queensberry* (*secondary*)	*ca. 1700–1705*	

0   10

metres

Figure 14.5
South exterior elevation of Queensberry House, showing surviving extents of all phases

plain projecting copes that extended up to and across the base of a low chimney at the apex, the latter itself detailed with a plain cope.

The north elevation of the principal range was regularised, with new windows inserted to the east to form a broadly symmetrical arrangement of three bays. The existing plain coping upon the entrance vestibule parapet appears to date from this time.

The fenestration of the east jamb and west wing was regularised where the windows faced into the entrance court; the mezzanine window at the north-east corner of the east jamb was removed and the similar half-height window directly below was extended upwards to match those further south. With the addition of the *Third* floor, the dormer windows of the east jamb were obliterated (if they had not already been removed by this period).

West elevation (fig 14.4)

Many of the lower windows of the west elevation, particularly to the north, were reconstructed at this period. The Queensberry phase windows in the area of the western stairwell were removed as will be described below. At *Lower Ground* floor level an entrance was opened out to the west in the area of the stairwell. The only original *Second* floor level window not to be raised on the west elevation – the second from the south – was blocked with rubblework.

The west gable-head of the principal range was substantially deconstructed and the new wall-head of the west wing simply extended across. A low chimney was erected directly upon the plain wall-head course/coping to the south-west.

South elevation (fig 14.5)

The western two bays of the south elevation of the principal range were wholly rebuilt at *First* and *Second* floor levels, a major operation that suggests that the Queensberry phase masonry in this area was in poor repair or structurally unstable. There are many minor repairs to existing windows, principally the replacement of lintels and cill stones. The pre-existing

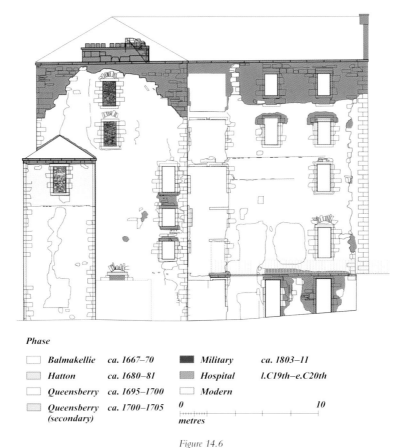

Phase

☐ *Balmakellie*	*ca. 1667–70*	■ *Military*	*ca. 1803–11*
☐ *Hatton*	*ca. 1680–81*	▨ *Hospital*	*l.C19th–e.C20th*
☐ *Queensberry*	*ca. 1695–1700*	☐ *Modern*	
☐ *Queensberry (secondary)*	*ca. 1700–1705*		

0   10

metres

Figure 14.6
East exterior elevation, showing surviving extent of Balnakellie, Hatton, Queensberry and Military phases

shaped gables were dismantled down to little more than small stumps in advance of the formation of the new *Third* floor.

The bell-cast roofs of the two closet towers were removed, along with the cornice below, and a plain projecting wall-head course substituted. The new roofs were simply constructed structures with slated roofs that were hipped to the west and east respectively.

East elevation (fig 14.6)

All early window openings in the east gable wall of the principal range were blocked off. The upper parts of the gable were removed and a flat coping extended across at the level of the *Third* floor wall-head. A broad, low chimney was erected directly upon this.

East side of the east jamb

With one apparent exception, the paired windows lighting the east stairwell were retained. However, the belvedere tower above was substantially reduced to

below the level of the new *Third* floor wall-head. The former dormer windows on its north side were also removed. At *Lower Ground* floor level a new entrance was opened up to the north-east and a second formed in the centre of the wall. Directly above, the remains of what appears to have been a cantilevered exterior walkway run along much of the wall-face from the north-east corner of the jamb. This had been formed of substantial interlocking horizontal slabs let into the earlier wall-face. To the north-east these lie at the level of the entrance courtyard and evidently provided direct pedestrian access from that level to an entrance newly formed by the extending down of the cill of the northern stairwell window.

14.3.2 Interior arrangements

Stairwells

Major modifications were made to both of the existing stairs, and an additional masonry stair was created. In each case the new work was less elaborate than the earlier. Individual steps were formed without moulded detail and dressed with a tooled rather than a polished finish. Their undersides were dressed to a flat profile. Each stair, both the existing and the new, was provided with heavy but plain wrought iron handrails, many of which survive.

The west stair was extended to the full height of the range. This necessitated the removal of the paired Queensberry phase windows in this area of the west elevation and their replacement with single windows at the half-landings. A new entrance was broken through to the western exterior at the *Lower Ground* level of the stairwell following the removal of the pre-existing service stair on its north side.

The most significant intervention to the interior was the insertion of the present central stairwell on the north side of the central part of the principal range,

its east wall shared by the east stair. The new stair was formed of interlocking cantilevered steps countersunk into the surrounding walls and arranged around an open central well. From each floor, flights rose to the east and north before returning back to the west. The stair was lit by the newly reformed windows at the east end of the north elevation above the entrance court.

The creation of the central stair necessitated major masonry subdivision of the central part of the principal range – at *Upper Ground* floor level this corresponds to the area of the Queensberry phase drawing room. The south wall of the stair was newly created and, running south from the west end of this, a further masonry subdivision was erected; both rise for the full height of the building. These walls in effect created a new room on the south side of the central stairwell at each level, defined by pre-existing walls to the south and east and the new partitions to the north and west.

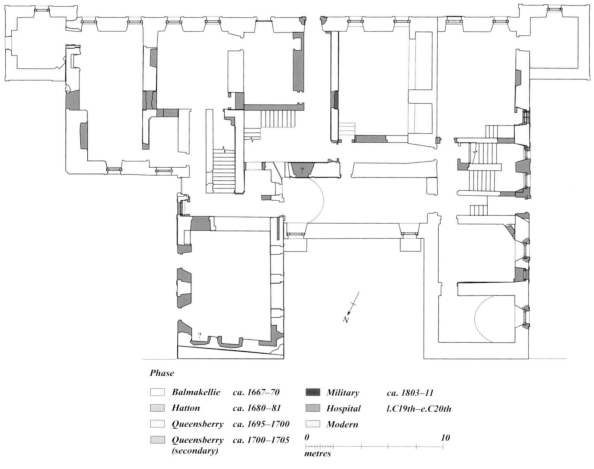

Phase

☐ *Balmakellie*	*ca. 1667–70*	■ *Military*	*ca. 1803–11*
☐ *Hatton*	*ca. 1680–81*	▨ *Hospital*	*l.C19th–e.C20th*
☐ *Queensberry*	*ca. 1695–1700*	☐ *Modern*	
▨ *Queensberry (secondary)*	*ca. 1700–1705*		

0   10

metres

Figure 14.7
Lower Ground floor level plan at the Military phase, 1808–11

The insertion of the stair also necessitated the blocking off of all the entrances that formerly led into the west parts of the principal range from the landings of the original east stair.

The Balmakellie phase eastern stair, the masonry components of which only rose to *Second* floor level, was extended upwards into the new *Third* floor. This necessitated the removal of the wooden stair that had formerly extended up into the belvedere tower. The floor structures within the tower were removed and a new *Third* floor ceiling inserted; the internal features of the tower chambers were clawed back and/or blocked off. The details of the earlier masonry stair newel were reproduced, including the openings for borrowed light and the raised margins at the angles. At *Third* floor level the extended stair terminated at a low masonry balustrade detailed with rounded stone copes.

Lower Ground floor (fig 14.7)

Much of the pre-existing arrangement of space at *Lower Ground* floor level was retained and it is clear that the functional/utilitarian nature of this area of the former mansion was perpetuated, the requirements of a large household being not dissimilar to the running of an institution.

It is possible that the vaulted chamber beneath the entrance vestibule was formed into an east/west connecting passage at this stage. The insertions of new masonry walls on the south side of the central stair created a new chamber and a passage leading from the south-west corner of the stair to a newly formed external entrance in the south exterior elevation. The west wall of the passage retained wall plaster ruled out to imitate ashlar. The new entrance lay one bay to the west of the original exterior entrance, and the original

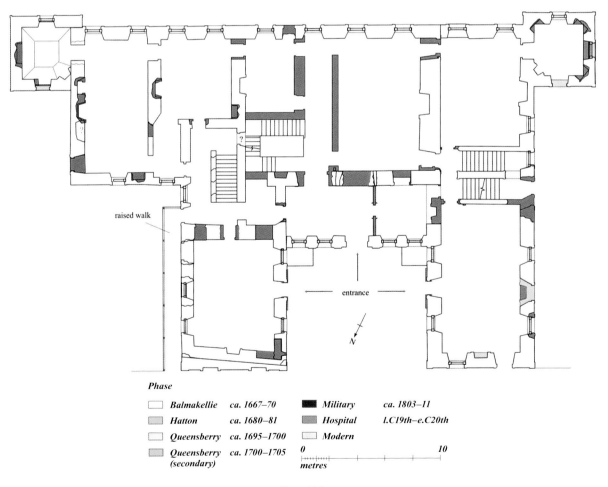

Phase

☐ *Balmakellie*	*ca. 1667–70*	■ *Military*	*ca. 1803–11*
▨ *Hatton*	*ca. 1680–81*	▨ *Hospital*	*l.C19th–e.C20th*
☐ *Queensberry*	*ca. 1695–1700*	☐ *Modern*	
▨ *Queensberry (secondary)*	*ca. 1700–1705*		

0   10
metres

Figure 14.8
Upper Ground floor level plan in the Military phase, 1808–11

was formed into a window. The Queensberry phase garden entrance from the west wing was also turned into a window.

The other major intervention at this period was the removal of the axial east/west service corridor running along the centre-eastern parts of the principal range. Following the removal of the studwork passage partition walls, the associated entrances within the north/south masonry cross-walls were blocked off with masonry. In this way the room on the south side of the eastern stair was extended northwards, the eastern two bays of the range formed into a unified space and the exterior door in the east gable wall blocked off.

The *Lower Ground* cellar rooms within the east jamb saw substantial modification. The back stair to the north-west was removed and the associated wall cavity infilled. The north wall of this former cellar area saw the insertion of what appears to be one or two large fireplaces or similar features, suggesting use as a kitchen or laundry. Unfortunately, subsequent modification was so extensive in this area that it was impossible to determine their nature.

Upper Ground *floor (fig 14.8)*

The *Upper Ground* floor was very substantially rearranged. The entrance vestibule was partitioned into two by a single-skin brick wall offset to the west, and a new, lowered ceiling was inserted. The large entrance into the former state dining room was blocked off, as was the archway leading to the west stairwell. The masonry infill of the latter contained a new fireplace and a smaller entrance on its south side. The entrance is an apparent discrepancy with the 1943 plans, where no such feature appears. These plans also omit an entrance that was formed within the east wall of the vestibule, that provided access to the east stair and the eastern parts of the building. A major new entrance was opened to the south to permit direct access to the central stair. The space beyond the stair to the south was subdivided into three, a small vestibule to the north-west, and a somewhat larger vestibule to the south-west, which in turn led into a larger room to the east.

Within the northern part of the west wing the partitioned service stair at the south end of the public dining room was removed and floored over, creating a single unified space.

The library recesses within the interior of the south-west closet tower were infilled and the window recess in the north wall turned into a press.

The original east wall of the state dining room, which was timber-framed, was removed and replaced with a new masonry wall with an entrance at each end.

The closet rooms and mezzanine arrangement on the north side of the former dressing room (eastern two bays of the principal range) were wholly removed. The space within was unified and the mezzanine windows either blocked off (to the north-east) or reformed (to the north).

A similar process occurred within the east jamb, with the closets and mezzanine chambers removed. The back stair to the north-west was also removed at this stage.

Upper floors *(figs 14.9–14.11)*

The interior space of the three upper floors saw the creation of similar internal arrangements at each level and can be characterised as an exercise in the creation of as much standardised accommodation as possible by the comprehensive rationalisation of the existing space. All pre-existing timber partitions were removed and the service stair at the north-west corner of the east jamb dismantled and its associated wall cavity infilled with masonry at each level. The central part of the principal range was subdivided with internally braced studwork partitions that were then lathed out and plastered. These formed a landing area at each level of the central stair. An entrance on the south side of this provided access to a short east/west-aligned hall or passage from which further entrances led into four rooms, to the south, south-east, south-west and north-west.

There was some reorganisation of the entrance arrangements of the eastern stair. Entrances into the east jamb and into the rooms on the south side of the stair were now centrally placed within the rooms beyond. The arrangement of rooms at the east end of the principal range was considerably modified. The axial east/west passage was removed at each level and the area occupying the eastern two bays of the range formed into a unified space. The remaining, westwards-projecting area to the north-west was formed into new closet-like chambers by means of newly erected north/south masonry partition walls provided with an entrance to the north at each level. The latter permitted a direct connection through to the east stair. The southern part of each of these closet areas was further partitioned and, without natural light, perhaps functioned as large presses.

Phase

Balmakellie	ca. 1667–70	Military	ca. 1803–11
Hatton	ca. 1680–81	Hospital	l.C19th–e.C20th
Queensberry	ca. 1695–1700	Modern	
Queensberry (secondary)	ca. 1700–1705		

0   10

metres

Figure 14.9
First floor plan in Military phase, 1808–11

The internal features of each room were simply appointed and standardised, with the creation of the plainly detailed fireplaces previously described, plastered walls and ceilings with skirtings, dado rails and simple run cornices (where evidence for these survived). All windows were provided with internal wooden architraves. Considerable efforts were made to provide each room with a press. Where these survived, their plaster-lined interior was provided with three shelves. The new presses often occupied earlier openings, stool closets and window recesses. Only one original press door survived within Queensberry House; this was peg-jointed and of plain four-panelled construction; the exterior side of each panel was detailed with a quarter-*ovolo* moulding. Paint traces on this and many of the architraves revealed that a buff or stone colour had been employed, apparently almost universally.

14.4 Hospitals and refuge

JOHN LOWREY

14.4.1 Introduction

The conversion of Queensberry House into a military hospital and the subsequent plans for its future after the end of the war in 1815 highlights a wider context that is relevant to the whole area, namely that of hospital care and the idea of refuge generally. This was not simply, nor indeed mainly, a matter of medical treatment but also of charity and relief of poverty. This is an important theme in the history of the Canongate and Queensberry House's later history ties it very firmly into that historical context.

At its broadest, it might be linked with the general expectation and requirement that the medieval abbey of Holyrood was a place of refuge and hospitality to travellers and pilgrims. This, of course, was hardly directly relevant in the 19th century except that the precincts of the abbey provided sanctuary for debtors from the mid-16th century right up until 1816 (Mackie 1825).

More specifically, the area around the lower Canongate has a history of charity and care and, indeed, of military involvement and military medicine. St Thomas's Hospital was founded in 1541 at the Water Gate, directly opposite the girth cross, by George Crichton, Bishop of Dunkeld and former Abbot of Holyrood. It consisted of a chapel and almshouse for the aged and infirm poor. It passed into the hands of the burgh magistrates in 1617 (Wilson 1891, 115; Mackay 1900, 207), who ran it until the mid-18th century, by which time, it was, according to one contemporary source, in a semi-ruinous condition (Maitland 1753, 156). At around this very time, in 1747, the hospital did finally fall into complete disuse and was demolished to make way for a coach house and stables, built to

serve the growing demand for stagecoach transport from Canongate in this period (Mackay 1900, 207). Although charitable institutions like St Thomas's Hospital and Trinity Hospital survived in the 18th century, other arrangements were being made for the poor and in 1761 Canongate followed Edinburgh by opening its own Charity Workhouse, accommodating some 90 persons, with a further 40 'outpensioners' (compared with 660 in Edinburgh Workhouse) (Arnot 1779, 559–60). This introduces a reformatory element to the charity and the possibility of redemption, or at least rehabilitation, through useful work. This is a theme that certainly re-emerges in Queensberry House itself.

The military were also involved in the Canongate long before 1803. The earliest mention of a military hospital goes back to Cromwellian times, when sick and wounded troops were quartered in Heriot's Hospital. In an effort to get rid of them, in 1652, the hospital and

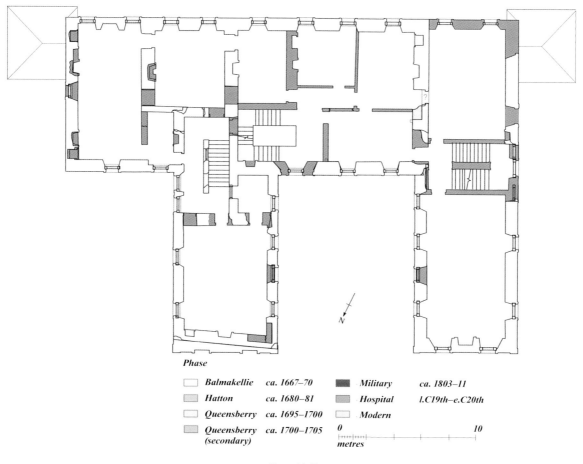

Phase

☐	*Balmakellie*	*ca. 1667–70*	■ *Military*	*ca. 1803–11*
▨	*Hatton*	*ca. 1680–81*	▨ *Hospital*	*l.C19th–e.C20th*
☐	*Queensberry*	*ca. 1695–1700*	☐ *Modern*	
▨	*Queensberry (secondary)*	*ca. 1700–1705*		

Figure 14.10
Second floor plan in Military phase, 1808–11

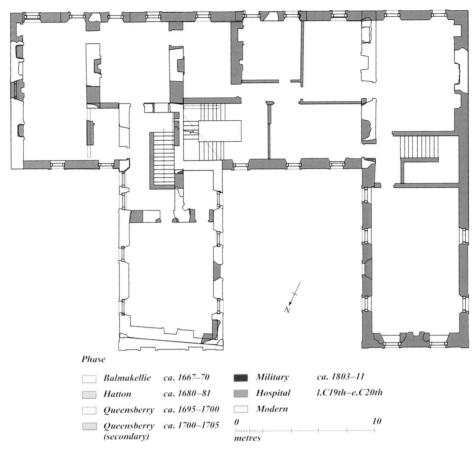

Phase

☐ *Balmakellie*   *ca. 1667–70*   ■ *Military*   *ca. 1803–11*

▨ *Hatton*   *ca. 1680–81*   ▨ *Hospital*   *l.C19th–e.C20th*

☐ *Queensberry*   *ca. 1695–1700*   ☐ *Modern*

▨ *Queensberry*   *ca. 1700–1705*
    (secondary)

0   10

metres

Figure 14.11
Third (attic) floor plan in Military phase, 1808–11

the town offered to find and maintain other suitable accommodation. They provided Kinloch's Land at the foot of the Canongate on the site of what became in the 18th-century Brodie's Close. This Cromwellian military hospital was, therefore, also on the site of the new Scottish Parliament building (Thin 1927, 138), although it seems to have been 1658 before the move took place.[5] While this location does appear to be backed by some original documentation,[6] there is another tradition that identifies barracks, infirmary and even a house for the Protector himself, further up the Canongate near Playhouse Close (Barnard 1891, vol. 4, 383).

It was not only the trustees of Heriot's who were unwilling to have troops on their premises, for throughout the 17th century and later the billeting of troops within the civilian population was seen as a considerable burden and something to be avoided if at all possible. Even Queensberry House suffered this

indignity when officers of the Jacobite army used it in 1745 (Hume & Boyd c 1984, 79). However, when, in 1717, a Doctor Robert Brown 'Chirurgeon to Montague's regiment' proposed building a new hospital in Canongate rather than billeting the sick soldiers on members of the civilian population, there was fierce resistance, partly on the grounds that he was making the proposal for his own convenience and partly because of the expense to the city both in setting up the establishment and in its maintenance, especially if the regiments moved on, leaving their sick and wounded behind as 'a burden upon the neighbourhood of the Canongate, who as men and Christians could not suffer them to starve'.[7] What became of this proposal is uncertain, although it seems most likely that the good doctor's petition went unheeded.

Detailed information on the functioning of Queensberry House as a military hospital and barracks is somewhat vague, partly because some of the

Board of Ordnance records treat Edinburgh Castle and Queensberry House as one establishment, with the latter at least under the management of barrack master Scrymgeour.[8] In 1826, the barrack returns mention 150 patients at Queensberry House and a later document lists the officer establishment as '1 F.O. [senior officer], 4 captains, 6 subalterns'. But goes on 'they do not appear to have been occupied since 1817, except whilst His Majesty was at Edinburgh last year'[9] (presumably 1822, the year of George IV's visit). In fact, with the end of the war, the hospital and barracks were redundant and the army immediately tried to sell them, with an unsuccessful attempt in 1816, for an upset price of £10,000.[10] In the early 1820s, the army returned to this matter, having by this time already found other uses for the building, albeit on a temporary and emergency basis. Two of these are referred to in the report quoted above, which mentions that 'the magistrates and inhabitants of Edinburgh will have an opportunity of purchasing it either as an Asylum for Juvenile Delinquents or as a place for the reception of fever patients, or for both those purposes'. Of these two uses, the asylum was a proposal, but the fever hospital had been set up as early as February 1818 to deal with a serious outbreak of disease in the city at that time that lasted for several years.

By far the best documentation of Queensberry House as a hospital comes from this period of use as a fever hospital. This was quite different from the military hospital in that, after the 1808–10 construction, the military seem to have used the house as barracks and the new building as hospital. In 1818, it was part of the house itself that was converted for hospital use (the proposal for the asylum identifies this as the east wing, with a further room in the body of the house) and a very detailed record of the arrangements of the building, as well as the treatment regime, have been left by the house doctor, Benjamin Welsh (Welsh 1819). Welsh was impressed by Queensberry House. Its situation allowed good ventilation and it provided good accommodation for patients and staff. Welsh described the accommodation:

> The occupied wing consists of five floors. The ground floor is below the level of the street, but quite open in the rear, – like many other buildings in this town situated on the side of the ridge. On this floor are the kitchen, store rooms, apartments for the matron, one of the clerks and the porter, with a waiting room for the physicians. The accommodation for the patients is on the four upper floors, which communicate with each other by an ample staircase. On each floor there are three wards, one of 18 feet by 18; one of 21 feet by 18; and one of 30 feet by 15.... Besides this accommodation for the sick, there is on each floor a good room for the day nurse; and a bed closet for those employed at night. There are no more than fifteen beds in each floor, viz. six in each of the two largest wards, and three in the small ... the wards have fireplaces in each, and are amply supplied with windows and doors, extremely well placed for affording ventilation (Welsh 1819, 2–3).

With the knowledge that this was in the east wing of the house, it is possible to identify fairly precisely where the fever hospital was situated. The three rooms can be identified as those corresponding at each level with the duke's dressing room in the east jamb, the state bedchamber and the adjoining dressing room and waiting room (combined as one room). Any subdivisions of these rooms in the Queensberry phase had been swept away by the army's conversion, creating large spaces, suitable for barrack or hospital ward use. This arrangement indicates that all of the eastern side of the house, rather than just the jamb itself, was used as hospital and the smaller subsidiary spaces, like the tower closet, must have provided the nurses' quarters and other auxiliary spaces.

Welsh's book provides a great deal of detailed information on the system operated at the hospital. It appears to be a classic example of the activities of one of those middle-class philanthropic and charitable institutions that were so important to the running of 19th-century Scottish society (Morton 1999). The hospital was backed up by the Society for the Destitute Sick, which operated a system of inspectors across 16 sectors of the city. They were responsible for identifying, at this time, fever victims, and reporting them to the Society's Medical Officer, who arranged for them to be transferred to hospital (Welsh 1819, 7–8). Ninety per cent of the fever hospital's patients were admitted in this way; the remainder presented themselves at the hospital for assessment at one o'clock each day. This coincided with the physicians' rounds and they, rather than Dr Welsh, would make the decisions about admission. Having been admitted, the patients gave up their own clothes, which were taken away to the laundry in the west wing (indicating that at basement level, the hospital spread beyond the east side of the building), and put to bed. The hygiene regime in the hospital was very strict, with careful cleaning as well as fumigation and ventilation. The patients presented with symptoms of fever, vomiting and diarrhoea and were treated mainly through bleeding, using leeches and lancet, and with an appropriate diet for nursing the invalids back to health. In the period covered by Welsh's book (February 1818 – January 1819) 743 patients were treated, of whom 34 died and the rest made a full recovery (Welsh 1819, Appendix, 129–31). Another source, giving a slightly different time frame, provides more detail but also rather different figures. In the period 1 March 1818 to 28 February 1819, 1676 patients were referred to Queensberry House and 71 died (Turner 1937, 158). The same source also provides more detailed information on the fever itself, indicating that the illness was typhus. The disparity in numbers is hard to account for unless Welsh was only basing his figures on those who received the bloodletting treatment that his book advocated. Of course, this was part of a far wider problem; Queensberry House was being used as overspill from the infirmary proper and the epidemic went on, albeit sporadically, for a number of years. The problem had started in October 1817, when 54 cases were admitted to the infirmary and by December, when 99 cases were admitted, the main hospital was full. When Queensberry House was opened two months later, the two buildings had enough capacity to cope and the numbers tailed off in the summer months. However, the same pattern repeated the following year, with the cases increasing over the winter of 1818–19, averaging 160 per month, and an annexe was needed once more. Queensberry House closed after that epidemic passed, but was then reopened in December 1826, when the fever returned with renewed vigour and an average monthly intake to both hospitals of over 200 patients continued right through until April 1827.[11]

The establishment of the fever hospital by the Royal Infirmary was one of a series of measures taken by the city to counteract problems of disease that were associated with poverty and overcrowding, and which were becoming an increasing problem in the early 19th century. Sanitary measures, such as hosing down the streets, removal of dung and the cleaning of common stairs were the responsibility of an official appointed in 1822 by the body with ultimate responsibility, the Edinburgh Police Commissioners (Rodger 2001, 417). Over the period 1817–30, over 6500 people were treated in the fever hospitals (Rodger 2001, 417–18), which made an immense contribution to the public health of the city.

Queensberry House fever hospital was one of a number of organisations and institutions that were established in the early 19th century for the relief of the sick poor. This point was made quite clear by

Dr Welsh in his description of the operation of the hospital:

> As this hospital ... was designed chiefly for the relief of the needy, instances of poverty and dejection were of course frequently found amongst them; but by far the greater number, at least of the males, appeared to be Irish or Highlanders, engaged in the numerous public works of this city (Welsh 1819, 16).

This raises an important element in the history of Edinburgh, and specifically the history of the Old Town, in this period, namely that the city was an important centre for Irish immigration, long before the Famine brought about the mass migration of the mid-century. In 1819, the attraction of Edinburgh, as Welsh indicates, was the labouring work available on the large number of building projects around the city. Welsh's book also introduces another aspect of concern for the poor in 19th-century Britain, namely a moral concern that saw the victims as being at least partly responsible for their own lot, through failings like drunkenness. The Irish immigrant population was particularly prone to this kind of critical scrutiny. Welsh certainly identified them as the source of disease in Edinburgh and links the spread of disease into the local population with the mendicant ways of the wives of the labourers, which was barely held in check by the Society for the Suppression of Begging within the city (Welsh 1819, 52). More generally, it was 'the labouring Irish, who, without doubt, by their habits of filth and debauchery, have tended much to spread the disease, if not to introduce it in its present form into this city ... as the present epidemic, no doubt, first made its appearance in Ireland' (Welsh 1819, 51).

14.4.2 Agricultural interlude

By the early 1820s, with the established use of Queensberry House as a hospital and with the continuing trend towards industrialisation and immigration within the Canongate, the likely future of the house lay in the charitable or industrial sectors. However, it was still owned by the army, which had been unable to sell it in 1816 and was keen to find a new use for it. While the leasing of part of the premises to the Royal Infirmary was clearly in keeping with its established function, the temporary renting of the parade ground to the Royal Highland Society is perhaps a little more surprising, at least on the face of it. The society had been set up in 1784 with the aim of improving the Highlands. The main focus was on economic improvement, including fisheries, manufactures and agriculture, and in 1821

Sir John Sinclair proposed an annual agricultural show as a means by which members might get together to compare their fatstock and to publicise the activities of the society more generally (Davidson 1984, 26). The first show was held on the parade ground at Queensberry House barracks, with sheep presented up against the house itself and at the guardhouses; competing cattle were penned along the east side of the square, show cattle on the opposite side. Prize-winning animals were penned in the centre (Davidson 1984, 28).

The society continued to hold its shows in Edinburgh for a further three years, always at the end of the year when farmers from across the country could come to Edinburgh (Davidson 1984, Appendix 5, 55).

14.4.3 Care of the poor – disposal of the house by the army

By 1823 the army was looking seriously at the disposal of the property. A report written in August of that year again proposed sale, but this time making it available in three lots. Preparations for the sale included the removal of the fever hospital furniture, which had actually been supplied by the army and to whom it was to be returned.[12] The same source also shows that Queensberry House had been used as the headquarters of the 'Principal Medical Officer in North Britain' from May 1817 and that he was still in residence at the time the report was written in 1823.

This sale also ended in failure, but before it took place, the barrack master, Major Nairne, was approached by the city, seeking to purchase it privately as a replacement for the Edinburgh Charity Workhouse;[13] however, the offer was almost immediately withdrawn along with the suggestion of an alternative use, which was to lease part of the building as a reform school for juvenile delinquents.[14] This reform school idea was to reappear as a serious proposal about a year later, when, in October 1824, a memorial from the city to the Duke of Wellington, as Master General of the Board of Ordnance, and a report of a sub-committee of the city Police Commissioners, made the case for using part of the house as a home for juvenile delinquents.[15] The report is very clear about what was required. The city was suffering from the criminal activities of teenage boys who, for one reason or another, had not had the benefit of a proper moral and religious upbringing. The idea was to take about 30 of these delinquents, aged between 12 and 18, and provide them not only with the moral framework that was evidently lacking

in their lives but also with training in a useful trade, in this case weaving. The preferred premises were the military hospital at Queensberry House; the house itself was to be used as dormitories for the boys. By the time that the city actually asked the army for the premises, the demands had been modified somewhat, with a proposal to take over the space occupied previously by the fever hospital, along with one of the officer's rooms in the centre of the building and a detached kitchen block.[16]

In the meantime, Queensberry House was pressed into service as an emergency shelter for people made homeless in the great fire that raged in the High Street between St Giles and the Tron on 15–17 November 1824. While the Board of Ordnance was clearly content to provide charitable support in such a case, it was less interested in providing rent-free accommodation for an institutional charity of the kind proposed by the city. The search for a buyer for Queensberry House went on, but it was decided to make an offer to the city of the parts of Queensberry House they wanted, but for a rent of £50, plus one-quarter of the public burdens. The proposed use of the house was also of interest to the army and Lord (previously 'Major') Nairne wrote in his report that 'should the endeavour now making of introducing manufactures into this place be successful it may hereafter be sold to advantage'.[17]

In the end, the weaving school for delinquent boys came to nothing simply because, after yet another failed attempt to sell the building at the end of 1825, the army decided that a long-term lease of the whole of Queensberry House to the Royal Infirmary was a better deal than a short-term lease to the city for an experimental enterprise involving only part of the house but of a kind that would probably make the rest of the property unleasable. On 25 January 1825, therefore, the army agreed to a ten-year lease from Whit 1825 and the house became part of the Royal Infirmary.[18] In that capacity it was used as a fever hospital in the typhus outbreaks of the mid-1820s and then, from 1832, as the typhus threat receded, as an outstation of the Infirmary when the new danger of cholera, which claimed 600 lives in the city, was confronted (Hume & Boyd c 1984, 88).

14.4.4 The House of Refuge

The move from medical provision for the poor to charitable provision and education for the poor came about at Queensberry House in the early 1830s and it was connected to the terrible trauma of the cholera epidemic of that time. In a bid to stop the spread of the disease, the Board of Health was given powers to stop vagrants entering the city and to deny them the right to accommodation. The only problem with that was that it left a large number of people destitute and homeless and the House of Refuge was set up to deal with them. The idea was to provide temporary accommodation, basic education for the children and training in various crafts and trades, including shoemaking and tailoring, for the adults (Morton 1999, 85). It allowed the city to control a potentially dangerous population and to provide some rehabilitation for them that could produce useful, productive and morally upright citizens. It was, in fact, rather similar to the municipal initiative for the weaving school for juvenile delinquents. The original building was in Morrison's Close, 117 High Street (Morton 1999, 85), but, as the cholera epidemic receded, the Infirmary decided it no longer needed the army buildings and in 1834, having negotiated an acceptable rent with the Board of Ordnance,[19] the House of Refuge moved into Queensberry House and all of the other army buildings. Despite an occasional threat from the Board of Ordnance that the buildings might be repossessed for army purposes, or sold from under the House of Refuge, the institution eventually managed to acquire the whole establishment from the Board in 1853, for the sum of £5000 (Hume & Boyd c 1984, 29–30). This was considerably less than the £10,000 the Board had been seeking since 1816, but perhaps the inclusion of Queen Victoria among the list of benefactors who contributed to the appeal helped the army to make up its mind to accept the lower offer (Hume & Boyd c 1984, 30).

The regime imposed in the House of Refuge was not dissimilar to that of the fever hospital and that proposed by the House of Refuge for young delinquents and in particular it combined that use of charity, education and training found in the latter with the same emphasis on cleanliness and care found in the former. Similarly, the moral condition of the inmates was also a concern and a chaplain was provided along with, for a time at least, a Mr John Smith from the City Mission, whose job was specifically to see to the 'moral instruction of the inmates'.[20]

The institution quickly began to expand, so great was demand for its services. In 1840 a night shelter for emergency accommodation was set up on the site of the old stables and around the same time a soup kitchen was established in the front courtyard (Hume & Boyd c 1984, 22–3). The public were encouraged to buy penny tickets for the soup kitchen and pass them on to the poor, rather than giving money, which might have been used in other, less wholesome ways (Hume & Boyd c 1984, 24). Other facilities were also added in these early years. A chapel was built alongside the old gatehouse in 1853 and, for the further edification of the inmates, a library was installed in the house in 1840 and expanded over the following years (Hume & Boyd c 1984, 28). Clearly the moral well-being of the inmates was of great concern to the directors and, partly to that end, the regime also strictly segregated the sexes, with men and boys in one wing of the house and women and young children in another. That segregation even extended to the grounds and the garden ground to the south was divided up by high stone walls to keep both sexes and also some categories of inmates quite separate (Hume & Boyd c 1984, 21).

Part of the moral concern that was one of the motivations of those involved in charities like this was related to the evils of begging and the perceived fecklessness of the poor. This was one of the reasons for the training offered and also one of the reasons why people were encouraged to buy meal tickets rather than give money to beggars. The particular concern there was that they would only spend money on drink and the vice of drunkenness was clearly of great concern to the House of Refuge almost from the beginning. In the annual report for 1836–7 the author identified a growing activity that had gradually developed in the first five years of the institution's history:

> This is the reception of a number of individuals, principally females, who, from the predominance of one overpowering vice, have become so utterly regardless of every tie of morality, religion, or even of natural affection, as to bring misery of every description on all who were in any way connected with them. From the accommodation obtained in Queensberry House, the managers have been able to carry this to a very considerable extent …[21]

The vice in question was alcoholism and the report makes it clear that, from this early period, there was a specific concern with treating at least women who suffered from this condition. These women were useful to the institution in that they paid for their treatment, either directly, or as 'nurses and servants'. There are no details of treatment, but the simple fact of institutionalisation kept them 'away from temptation and prevents ruin and destitution for them and their families'. There is a clear implication in this that some at least of this category of inmate were not actually

Figure 14.12
Queensberry Lodge (after Hume & Boyd c 1984, pl 11)

destitute, but were saved from becoming so by the intervention of the House of Refuge. Indeed, there are stories of people being sent to the Canongate not only from within Edinburgh but from considerably further afield, including England. One woman reportedly arrived on the train in a drunken state and had to be given 'such accommodation as could be contrived' (Hume & Boyd c 1984, 42). This aspect of the activities of the House of Refuge was developed in the 1860s, when, between 1861 and 1865, the old military canteen was developed and transformed into Queensberry Lodge, a somewhat understated Scots Baronial pile, set up for the care of female inebriates (fig 14.12). This was a separate institution from the House of Refuge proper and charged its patients for their treatment. This remained a characteristic of Queensberry Lodge throughout its history, and even when National Health patients were being treated in the main building, the Lodge was for private patients (Hume & Boyd c 1984, 46). Of course, by that time, it was not concerned with the treatment of alcoholics; from around the 1920s it was Queensberry Lodge that introduced what was to be the future for the whole institution after 1949, the care of geriatric patients (Hume & Boyd c 1984, 45–6).

Before that, and certainly by the time of its centenary in 1932, a certain amount of reappraisal of the role of the House of Refuge was undertaken. By this time, despite the indignity of the Means Test, social legislation had provided a measure of provision for the poor that was at least more generous than what had been available when the House of Refuge was first set up. Consequently there was less need for its basic services and gradually its concerns became more those of a modern hospital for the care of the elderly. Facilities like the night shelter were little used and it eventually closed in 1949. The directors even looked out of the city for a more salubrious suburban location and in 1945 purchased the Ingliston estate (Hume & Boyd c 1984, 36). However, the House of Refuge was not defined as a hospital under the new National Health Service legislation in 1948, and therefore did not qualify for central funding. The Ingliston venture was cancelled and the estate sold,[22] and the House of Refuge continued to operate as a charitable institution concerned with the care of the elderly. The redundant night shelter was disponed to the city in 1968 as part of a general scheme of improvement to the Canongate and was replaced by a hall, or day centre, for Queensberry House, with three council

267

flats above (Hume & Boyd c 1984, 40).[23] It was in this same year that the name of the institution was finally changed, from the House of Refuge to Queensberry House Hospital.

This phase of the history of Queensberry House lasted until 1998, when it was subsumed within the Scottish Parliament site. Arguably, its role as a refuge from disease and poverty forms the most important, and certainly the longest, part of its history. As such, as this section has shown, it formed part of a wider context in the Canongate that is associated with care and with charity. That aspect of Canongate history did not end, however, in 1998 and the combination of care for the elderly and military history can still be found at Whitefoord House which, since 1909, combined with Callender House and greatly added to over subsequent years, has functioned as a home for army and navy veterans. The Canongate also provided refuge for merchant seamen and, in 1934, the Old Sailors' Ark was built in New Street to provide accommodation for them (Gifford *et al* 1984, 211). This building became a night shelter for homeless people, demonstrating, on the one hand, that the long history of the Canongate as a place of sanctuary continues into the new millennium, but, on the other hand, that poverty and deprivation are inextricably part of that history also.

14.4.5 The House of Refuge – the evidence of the structure (fig 14.13)

TOM ADDYMAN

19th century

Various minor modifications seem to have taken place throughout the building in the 19th century. The roof seems to have been reordered at an unknown (probably 19th-century) stage. The two entrances on the east and west sides of the entrance court seem also to be features of this period. Here original windows were extended and new exterior surrounds, rusticated and with an arched head, were formed in plaster. At the end of the 19th century a major lean-to extension was erected against the central part of the west façade. The intention was to provide a suite of water closets (lavatories) at each level. The structure was brick-built with reinforced concrete floors that were let in to the earlier wall fabric. Earlier windows and doors were extensively modified to provide access to the new extension, further altering an already complicated archaeological record in this area.

Early–mid-20th century

In both c 1926 and c 1950 extensive modernisation programmes were carried out. The City Architect's department plan (fig 14.2) refers to the discovery of two kitchen fireplaces while 'structural alterations' were taking place in 1926. Hume and Boyd (c 1984, 39) refer to a massive renovation in 1952 that included opening up the blind windows in the north gable wall of the east jamb. Many cemented brickwork or cinderblock blockings and extensions can be attributed to this general early–mid-20th-century period, as can the destruction and blocking of numerous early fireplaces that had apparently survived the military phase. The formerly blind windows within the north gable walls of the east jamb and west wing were reopened causing very extensive disruption of the interior wall areas. New courtyard-level entrances were also formed in the gable walls. The iron doors for the early kitchen fireplaces in the basement were apparently installed at this stage following the raising of the floor.

Later 20th century

A further series of interventions can be dated to the earlier 1980s that included the application to the exterior of the cementitious harl that was removed during the building of the new Parliament, various isolated blockings of doorways in the interior, and repairs to lintels and cills of entrances and windows throughout. However, the principal interventions at this stage were the insertion of two lift shafts, the first within the well of the central stair and the second at the eastern re-entrant of the east jamb and the principal range. The former caused little direct impact on the existing structure except at roof level where the winding apparatus required a housing that rose above the roof itself. However, the exterior lift shaft was erected against the paired windows that had hitherto lit the east stair. At each level the windows were broken away so that new entrances into the lift area could be formed. The remaining upper eastern parts of the belvedere were heavily impacted at this stage. The adjacent principal range windows at the re-entrant were blocked off.

14.5 The lives and homes of the people in the first half of the 19th century

E PATRICIA DENNISON

Although there had been an exodus of the wealthier classes, Canongate was not deserted. St John Street,

Figure 14.13

Henry Duguid, watercolour view of Queensberry House from the north-east, mid-19th century (© NGS) in particular, remained, for some time, a little haven, for it was not a public thoroughfare and was regularly cleaned, supplied with water and had a communal green and a street porter to guard the entrances against all but residents and their guests (Forbes Gray 1953, 59–75). Haddington House continued to be so called until 1861, but people of mixed social class lived nearby. In 1832–4, a John Ranken, letter carrier, was resident at Haddington Entry. In Reid's close, at the same time, there were, for example, two teachers, a bricklayer and a letter carrier. In Queensberry House itself were a manufacturer, a married lady of no stated profession and one Alexander Mackay, esquire. He would remain an occupant until at least the mid-1840s, by which time Queensberry House had also functioned as the House of Refuge for some ten years or so and presumably the property was partitioned in some manner. The Edinburgh and Leith Post Office Directories also give an insight into other neighbours, providing a small case study of the type of people living on the street frontage, the better-quality housing. In Cumming's Close were a victual dealer, a haberdasher and a dressmaker. In 1835/36, property no. 56 was occupied by Mrs Stevenson as an 'eating house' and by Miss Menzies, a milliner.[24] For only two years is there a reference to a no. 50 (1835–7), which was lived in by Miss Peat, a dressmaker.[25] John Lauder, victual dealer, lived at no. 48 in the 1830s and 1840s, with, nearby, at no. 44, James Alison (1830–3) and David Harley (from 1834), haberdashers, and at no. 42, A & J Crabbie, dressmakers. Number 40 Canongate was the premises of a surgeon from at least 1835. Another of this profession, Hugh Alexander, resided at no. 46 from 1839 until 1872.[26] There was also a 'John Cuming of Gayswood, Haslemere, Surrey' who owned property in the close in 1835, but he does not appear in most records, presumably as he did not live there. The occupations of those living on the frontage of Canongate suggest, if not a certain level of gentility, at least people of modest means still in the old burgh.

In 1906, the local Charity Organisation Society published a *Report on the Physical Condition of Fourteen Hundred Schoolchildren*, based on a survey conducted over the winter of 1904–5. While its main purpose was to cover such details as heights, weights and general health of the children, information about family background was also noted. North Canongate School was one such analysed. It was noted that while the school was in the old working-class area and served the poorest in the city, 'yet it has also an admixture of the children of the substantially comfortable and thoroughly respectable

working class'. Recent analysis of this report concluded that the less prosperous sections of the working class were almost certainly heavily represented, and that, apart from shoemakers, all of the skilled trades of the city were underrepresented compared to the industrial population of the city generally as at the 1901 census (Gray 1976, 83–4).

By the turn of the century the traditional drinking habits of the Canongate were rejected. Temperance societies such as the Good Templars, the Band of Hope, the Independent Order of Rechabites and the Scottish Alliance – Edinburgh Council drew Canongate people into their ranks. Many of the skilled workers joined volunteer organisations which helped to promote their claim to be admitted to the ranks of civic respectability – a claim that would play a role in the Reform agitation of 1866–7. Allied to this went a belief in thrift and it was this group in its associations that supported such ventures as savings banks and cooperative societies. They, too, were the class of people who would benefit from shorter working hours after 1868. Walking, visits to the sea, golf, swimming, cricket and, in particular, football were soon popular pastimes (Gray 1976, 102). From the late 1860s, football developed as a mass spectator sport, with Heart of Midlothian even owning its own ground by 1881.

In the early years of the century, Queensberry House introduced a new social element into the neighbourhood. Not only did the house itself function as a hospital, but also accommodated, at right angles to Holyrood Road, on the east of the gateway, the officers' guardroom, and on the west the soldiers' guardroom (quartermasters). There were also, separate from these, a canteen with a taproom and a large beer cellar, a bar, a kitchen, and a staffroom (Hume & Boyd c 1984, 86).

Some notion of the close proximity of living in the Canongate may be gained from the 1841 census returns. Number 3 Horse Wynd, for example, contained 16 households and 70 persons; no. 10, 11 households and 44 persons; no. 12 contained nine households and 29 persons. There were 12 households in Reid's Close, eight in Haddington Entry and 14 in Cumming's Close. Significantly, none of these 14 households in the close is merited as needing a postal address. Indeed, from 1845, Cumming's Close is not even referred to in the postal directories. The close is, however, delineated and named specifically on the 1852 Ordnance Survey plan. All this suggests very strongly that Cumming's Close was becoming the resort of the poorer elements of Canongate society. Added to this, its near neighbour, Queensberry House, had become a House of Refuge and by 1853 sheltered 255 persons.[27] Lord Cockburn described the once 'brilliant abode of rank and fashion and political intrigue' as 'now one of the asylums of destitution' (Cockburn 1910, 176). By the middle of the century, throughout Canongate, formerly spacious, well-furnished accommodation for persons of substance had become so subdivided that even one room might function as a home for one family.

It is difficult to imagine the destitution of some of these people. The density of occupation inevitably led to slum conditions in certain areas. The highest floors, it was said, contained hovels 'as destitute of furniture as the habitation … of an inmate of a wigwam' (Kinnear 1969, 7). Of Horse Wynd it was commented that where 'previously genteel families in most excellent houses' once lived, it now became the haunt of 'auctioneers and pawnbrokers' (Cockburn 1910, 99; Clive 1974, 99).

14.6 Industry in the Canongate

JOHN LOWREY & E PATRICIA DENNISON

14.6.1 Introduction

Both the historical and archaeological aspects of this study have shown how a great number of trades and crafts were practised in the Canongate throughout its history and how these coexisted with and impinged upon the other activities that took place there. In the 19th century, however, the scale of some of these operations hugely increased as industrial processes began to take over and large-scale production began to have an effect on both the architectural and the social patterns of the Canongate. For the aristocratic housing in the Canongate, the process of absorption into the new, industrial urban fabric of the area was hastened and reached its peak in the 19th and early 20th centuries. At the beginning of the 19th century, the industries were still fairly small-scale and fairly traditional. Brewing was very important and is discussed separately, but industries such as tanning and coach building were well established; tanning, an ancient industry that had traditionally taken place on a small scale in the backlands,[28] and coach building, a more modern activity, but one that was certainly found in the 18th century. The 1765 edition of Edgar's plan shows Crichton's Coachworks, just west of Bull's Close, which date back to 1762, when Alexander Crichton built a substantial series of workshops and

stables between the Canongate and the South Back.[29] Crichton expanded his holdings at the expense of a rival, William Jamieson, who set up his own coachworks in 1774 but sold to Crichton four years later.[30] By 1807, the Jamieson property was being built on by John Carfrae, who also acquired the Crichton coachworks and subsequent maps of the area indicate that Carfrae had a coachworks there, probably until around 1830.[31] Eventually, the brewing industry was to dominate this area and for a time Carfrae's works sat alongside Mr Berwick's brewery, but, after this was acquired by Younger's, the brewery expanded to take over the whole area.

14.6.2 Brewing

Foremost amongst the industries of the Canongate was brewing, which traced its roots back to the activities of the Augustinian canons of Holyrood, but, perhaps more importantly, owed its success to the presence of excellent water through artesian wells. This supply was to dictate the predominance of breweries around the Canongate, although much later expansion of the industry to Craigmillar, on the opposite side of Arthur's Seat, exploited the same water source. It was not until the 18th century that brewing in Scotland began to take on a truly industrial scale and the major developments took place in the first half of the 19th century. Small brewers could be found in every town and private individuals, especially in the larger aristocratic establishments, even carried out brewing for their own domestic consumption. Such was certainly the case at Queenberry House, which had its own brew-house in the 17th and 18th centuries. The increase in population, and in particular the growth of the towns, made the development of larger-scale enterprises necessary and this trend was assisted by legislation, like the Sale of Beer Act (1795), which required licensing for the brewing and selling of beer and which tended to discourage the very smallest-scale operators (Shaw 1984, 149).

Ultimately, the purity and reliability of the water supply was what underpinned the Edinburgh brewing industry and what allowed it to dominate the Scottish industry as the 19th century progressed (Barnard 1890, vol. 3, 109; Donnachie 1998, 103).

The major company was Younger's, whose Abbey Brewery comprised most of what is now the Parliament site. The original William Younger, who arrived in Leith from West Linton in 1749 – giving that date for the foundation of the company – in fact, had nothing to do with the Abbey Brewery site, nor with brewing in the Canongate (Ritchie 1999, 9–12). It was William's three sons who took their brewing skills into the Canongate. Archibald set up a brewery in the grounds of Holyrood Abbey in 1777 and expanded to Croft an Righ Brewery in 1786 before opening an even larger one in the North Back of the Canongate in 1793 (Ritchie 1999, 13–15). Richard also starting brewing, slightly farther west up the Canongate in Gentle's Close (between Queensberry House and Moray House), from 1788 (Ritchie 1999, 16). The major figure, however, was William Younger II. He started brewing in the Abbey precinct in 1796 and in 1803 took over a brewery belonging to James Blair in Horse Wynd. This was the brewery that was to become the famous Abbey Brewery. In 1806, he also inherited his brother Richard's brewery in Gentle's Close and by 1821 had inherited both his brother Archibald's concerns and those of his mother, Grizel, who had kept a core family business going in Leith. Therefore, by that date, all of the Younger family concerns were in the hands of one man. Many of those concerns were located in the Canongate and, although William initially sold off the brewery in Gentle's Close (Ritchie 1999, 21), Younger's were nevertheless the largest brewing concern in the area by the 1820s,

and the business was to grow even further, eventually reabsorbing the Gentle's Close premises as well.

Lothian Hut, with its stables, byre and courtyard, was bought in 1825, for £5000,[32] and by 1831, Younger had erected a huge malt barn on the site of Lothian Hut, although it is possible that the house was absorbed into the larger fabric, rather than demolished. John Wood's map of Edinburgh, published in the same year, indicates very little development on the site and certainly Lothian Hut is readily identifiable and, indeed, is labelled. In that year, Younger had a dispute with James Fairley, who owned property on the Canongate, about access through the space cleared by the Marquis of Lothian to connect his house to the street. Younger wanted to erect new cellarage and a tun room within the space, once again closing up the gap to the street.[33] The block plan that accompanied Younger's petition shows a large area of malt barn and the whole open area to the north of that being filled with the proposed new building. The erection of this building almost certainly would have meant that Younger's premises filled the entire depth of the site from Canongate to South Back. This is suggested by another Dean of Guild petition, in 1836, to expand an existing building containing malt barn and cellars facing the South Back. The proposal was to raise the

Figure 14.14
Lothian House Maltings (© SBA)

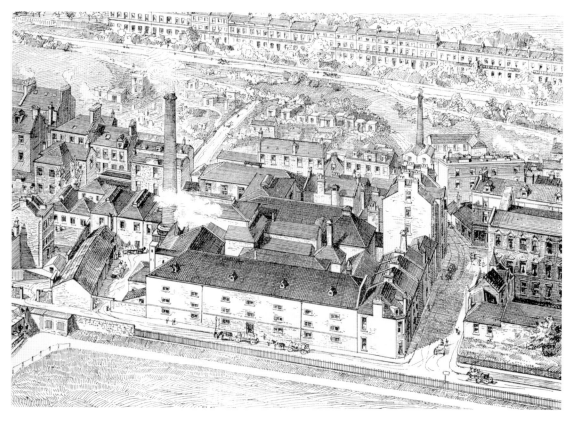

Figure 14.15
The Abbey Brewery, 1887 (© SBA)

building by a storey, to three stories and this was granted.[34] The drawing accompanying the proposal accords very closely with later views of the brewery. Whatever had happened to Lothian Hut itself by this time, this large development on the south of the site is also borne out by James Kay's map of the city of 1836, which shows two large buildings dominating what had been the gardens of the Marquis of Lothian's house. By the time of the first Ordnance Survey map of 1843–50, the site was completely taken over by the brewery and no obvious vestige of its earlier aristocratic history is left, apart from one. Having had the confusion of both Lothian Hut and Lothian House, the OS map adds the further detail of Lothian Vale, a house that stopped just short of the corner of Horse Wynd and South Back, and part of the brewery at this time. This seems to have survived until 1880, when Younger's renovated the house and extended it to the corner.[35]

Some properties on the site remained in private hands, but the Youngers systematically bought whenever the opportunity arose. In 1863, they completed the purchase of Brodie's Land (Keir 1951, 54). This was merely one further step in the buying up of Canongate property throughout much of the century: at the start of the 20th century, the Abbey Brewery, with the Holyrood Brewery, purchased in 1858, further west up the road near where the St Mary's Brewery had stood at the back of Chessel's Court, covered some 27 acres, and their output accounted for a quarter of the entire quantity of ale produced in Scotland.[36]

The new Parliament site was transformed. Contemporary illustrations reveal graphically the altered nature of the site. The core of the site, the erstwhile Lothian Hut, became the Lothian House maltings (fig 14.14), the magnificent dining room functioning as a growing floor for malt.[37] The *Guide to the Great Northern Railway* of 1861 extolled the virtues of Edinburgh ale, explaining that the success of Younger ale was 'partly owing to the adoption of all mechanical and other improvements, and also to the chemical properties of the water of which, by sinking to an immense depth, they get an abundant supply'.[38]

The site was served by a series of wells supported by an integrated network of feeders and cisterns. By 1872, there were five wells in existence, the most recently sunk being 130ft (40m) deep, and 400ft (122m) of mines, most of the boring being through solid rock 150 to 300ft (91.5m) below ground level. Andrew Smith, partner in the growing Younger empire, kept a notebook on aspects of brewing, for he recorded in 1858 that the notebook was to become the property of his two sons. Of Blair's Brewery he noted, 'water not good; they always thought there was some connection with the gas tank' – a telling comment on the closeness of other industrial activities.[39] Two 19th-century views of the Abbey Brewery from Salisbury Crags are clear indication of the level of 'mechanical and other improvements' and industrialisation of the site, which housed all the accommodation necessary for the malting process, the brewing procedures, cooperage, and stabling and smithies for the horses and drays (fig 14.15).[40] On 5 March 1870 the *Scottish Standard* reported that 'The South Back of the Canongate of Edinburgh is more famous for breweries than any street in the United Kingdom'.[41]

Unfortunately, business archives reveal little about the labourers in the brewing industry. Presumably, much of the unskilled labour, as well as more skilled work such as coopering, would come from the local Canongate people. For the majority, work in the brewery meant long hours and considerable physical effort, and there is no evidence of shift work before the 20th century. Labouring for the brewing industry also meant periods of no work. Brewing being a seasonal activity, labourers were often laid off from late spring until early autumn (Donnachie 1979, 94–5).

Although housing will be dealt with in a separate section, it is impossible to avoid some discussion here about the relationship between the brewery property and its neighbours, many of which were eventually swallowed up. The Brodie tenement (Chapter 13.2.5) was built to a new building line, intended to allow Horse Wynd to develop as a proper street. Gradually that line was imposed all along the street and certainly Younger's buildings had to comply with it. A crucial part of this was the corner building on the

Canongate, which controlled the width of the street at its entry and which was replaced in 1828 by a new block, with flats above and shops below.[42] Further up the Canongate, on a site that included the property of James Fairley, the tenement was altered in 1875 (16 Canongate) for James Dickson. The drawing shows this building up against the cellarage to which Fairley had objected in 1831, and the renovated tenement incorporates a shop and, of all things in this situation, a coffee shop. The drawing is signed by Peter L Henderson, who was Peter Lyle Barclay Henderson, an architect who specialised in breweries and pubs (he designed the Central Bar in Leith Central Station, 1899). He does not seem to have worked for Younger's, but, in this case, he certainly worked alongside.[43]

Not long afterwards, Younger's did expand their property in this area. In 1887, the brewery building adjoining Dickson's property was heightened by one storey and a tenement to the east of that seems to have been absorbed into the brewery complex, when the partition walls between the brewery fermentation room and shop on the ground floor of the property were removed to expand the fermentation facility. Alongside this, a further tenement owned by the

Figure 14.16
Detail of J Sulman's Panoramic View of Edinburgh, 1868 (© NLS)

brewery, probably for some of its workers, was upgraded by the insertion of communal water closets, on the advice of the city architect.

The major expansion of Younger's within the Canongate happened slightly further west at Gentle's Close. In 1855, the brewery that had formerly been owned by Richard Younger was bought back from Alexander Berwick's family, who had purchased it from Younger in 1819 (Ritchie 1999, 36). This developed into a substantial part of Younger's business, with an important, existing export trade and, with improvements made to production by the new owners, a local trade that developed over subsequent years (Ritchie 1999, 37). As the expansion of the Abbey Brewery was taking shape in 1887, the Holyrood Brewery, the name for the Gentle's Close establishment, was also expanded and Gentle's Close itself was effectively closed off as a public route, becoming instead the Canongate entrance to the brewery complex.[44] Younger's dominating presence in the South Back reached its climax in 1900, when an existing brewery behind the site of Milton House was taken over by Holyrood Brewery as a storage facility.[45] By this time, Younger's owned premises all along the South Back, or Holyrood Road as it was officially called by then, from Holyrood Palace to Moray House. On the south side of the street, opposite Queensberry House, the Park Ale stores were built, and in 1903 the old malt barn that had sat on the gardens of Lothian Hut made way for a new head office in the Scots Renaissance style.

As Younger's grew over the 19th century, other breweries also flourished and maps of the whole area show that brewing dominated the Canongate on both sides and beyond Moray House. In the new areas, like the Dumbiedykes, developed in the 19th century, brewing was once again the major industry and eventually dominated the industrial scene all around the royal park, from Canongate to Craigmillar. In terms of the effect it had on the Old Town, the pattern that emerges in the example of Younger's also seems to have been replicated elsewhere, although to a lesser extent. Old buildings, and sometimes rather grand old buildings, were at first subsumed within the brewing complex and put to new use by the brewers. However, gradually, as the scale of operations increased, the old buildings were often removed and replaced by new purpose-built structures. Inevitably, as the scale of operations increased so the old pattern of small-scale enterprises growing up along the closes also changed and large areas, like the Abbey Brewery and the

Holyrood Brewery, that were formerly penetrated by a system of closes, in the latter case right through the site, became closed off to the Canongate.

Younger's of course was not the only operator. The Edinburgh and Leith Brewery might also be mentioned as one of the other, fairly large operators in the area. This lay immediately west of St John's Street, between Old Playhouse Close and Milne's Close. By the 1890s it covered a 3-acre site (Barnard 1891, vol. 4, 378), but, despite a large amount of new building, mostly by Peter Henderson, it still incorporated a patchwork of older buildings, including parts of the old playhouse and the buildings, already mentioned, associated with Cromwell. In addition, there was a fine old house still used by the head brewer and others (Barnard 1891, vol. 4, 384).

14.6.3 Other industries

If brewing was the major industry in the Canongate, it is arguable that, notwithstanding the huge impact it had on the townscape of the area, the gas industry had an even bigger visual and olefactory effect. The Edinburgh Gas Light Company was formed as early as 1817 and grew to fill a huge site on the north-west side of the Canongate. However, by the end of the century, its presence was felt along towards Holyrood both on the north side, with a large gas tank behind Reid's Court, and on the South Back, in the vicinity of the Parliament site, with the huge gas tanks next to the Park Ale stores. It was in 1890 that the chemicals involved in the production of gas were contaminating brewery wells, as Andrew Smith had predicted earlier.[46]

On a much smaller scale, other industries also made their presence felt within the complex fabric of the Canongate. In the vicinity of the Parliament site, the effects of industrial and social changes have been charted in detail on Queensberry House and outlined for Lothian Hut. Other great houses that have been dealt with in this chapter were also subject to the effects of industrialisation. Whitefoord House has been commented on as a place of refuge for pensioners from the various armed services; however, it did not acquire that role until the early 20th century and it passed from its grand, domestic function after 1833. Like Queensberry House in the same period, there was some debate about its future function and a number of ideas were put forward 'such as an industrial factory, or an infirmary, a reformatory, or a public home for teaching laundry work' (Smith 1924, 117). After many years of deterioration, it was let to the Marr

Typefounding Company, who operated their business from there between 1876 and 1899.[47] Their lease came to an abrupt end when their machinery fell through the floor of the house, causing immense damage and demonstrating one of the difficulties of adapting ancient premises to modern industrial practices (Smith 1924, 117).

If anything, Milton House had an even more chequered career before its eventual demolition in 1886. Its industrial past actually pre-dates Milton House itself because, prior to its construction in the 1750s, the old house belonging to the Duke of Roxburgh was used as a linen manufactory by William Cheape and two of his partners. Cheape was so energetic in working up his weaving business that he went on within a few years to take a lease of the royal tennis courts by Holyrood Palace as a carpet factory (Dingwall, 1994, 6). Milton House itself, by the early 19th century, was redundant as an aristocratic townhouse. Grant (1882, 34), writing around 1880 lists a number of uses the house was put to, including a Roman Catholic school run by the Sisters of Charity, a school for the deaf and dumb, a maternity hospital and, by the 1880s, an engineering firm. One usage he seems to have overlooked was its very first industrial usage, again in the textile trade, by James Page & Co. as a shawl manufactory, at least in 1834–5.[48] Much of Grant's list is borne out by other sources. Mother Superior St Paul opened the Roman Catholic school in May 1835, after the house was bought by St Margaret's Convent, and it seems to have lasted until the late 1830s at least.[49] No evidence for the deaf school has been found here, but, if it was a predecessor to Donaldson's, it might have lasted until the late 1840s, when Playfair's new building opened. The maternity hospital certainly receives some corroboration in the form of a label ('Royal Maternity Hospital') on Lancefield's 1851 plan of the city. Sometime before 1858, the house passed into industrial use when James Milne & Son acquired it.[50] This period of the house's history is quite well documented, both in maps and in the Dean of Guild Records. The first Ordnance Survey was carried out at just about this time and the sheet that shows Milton House is based on a survey of 1852. It differs from Lancefield in that a large building has been inserted immediately behind the house, suggesting perhaps that the Milne family involvement can be dated to the early rather than the late 1850s. John Milne, presumably the son, was responsible for a considerable expansion of the works from the 1860s. In 1866, he is described as a gas meter manufacturer and at that time applied

to extend his works to the south, with a large, three-storey building, the full width of the site, entered from the South Back.[51] In 1872, he applied to extend the smith's shop on the east side of the property, alongside Milton House itself.[52] By this time, Milne described himself as 'engineer and brassfounder'. Whether he was still involved in making gas meters is not entirely clear and the plan of the works showing the 'old meter-proving shop' is somewhat ambiguous. In 1880, Milne's expansion continued, when he sought approval for a new, three-storey workshop, also on the east side of the property. From the drawings, this appears to have been a masonry, cast-iron and glass construction, with large open floor plan at each level.[53] Milton House itself does not feature in any of these proposals, but the maps of the period show a building gradually being absorbed into the new industrial complex. The 1876/77 Ordnance Survey map shows the site before many of these developments have taken place, but with the house firmly embedded in the factory. A similar sense of the way in which the industrial developments were overwhelming the existing architecture of the Canongate can be gained from Sulman's 1868 panorama of the Old Town from Calton Hill, and, in particular, Milton House can be seen among the chimneys and furnaces of Milne's growing works (fig 14.16).

After 20 years of gradual expansion, the Milne foundry and engineering works finally closed in the mid-1880s and the site was sold: the southern portion to Younger's and the northern half to the Edinburgh School Board.[54] Younger's absorbed the site into their Holyrood Brewery and, in 1886, Robert Wilson designed Milton House School, which still serves the area as the Royal Mile Primary School.[55]

The rather precarious situation of Milton House amidst the belching smoke and fire of the foundry was not particularly unusual among the industrial buildings of the Canongate in the 19th century. Early in the century there was a pottery alongside Carfrae's coachworks,[57] and by 1815 there was certainly an established iron foundry to the west of the gardens of Milton House. In that year, the premises were taken over by William Ford, who converted it into a glassworks. His Dean of Guild petition gives some idea of the effect such relatively heavy industry had in a confined setting like the backlands of the Canongate. A potential objector was John Hume, agent for the Fletchers of Saltoun who owned Milton House. To reassure him, Ford argued that his glassworks would not be 'one hundred part so bad as the former foundry where blast furnaces, coals furnaces, smelting furnaces, steam engines and no less than eighteen smith's forges were kept constantly going at one time'.[58] The accompanying drawing combined the industrial and the elegant, with a plan for a 55ft-high glass furnace and a refined, pedimented Georgian house as the office for Ford's business.

Good-quality architecture seems to have been a feature of Ford's Glassworks. By 1852 (when the OS plan was made) the substantial works included a long frontage to the South Back, filling the whole width of the site between Milne's foundry at Milton House and Bull's Close, with a central pend into the works yard. In 1871, the eastern side of this building was raised by one storey and the rather plain and unassuming public face of the building was hugely enhanced by the very rich Franco-Scots Gothic architecture of the fourth floor, comprising a spiky skyline of triangular pediments with finials, a central gablet attached to a tall chimney and a meandering string-course that held three relief panels, one with the company arms and two showing glass-blowers at work. The extra space appears from the plan to have been a single room, perhaps intended as a boardroom for the successful company.[59]

While beer was the distinctive Edinburgh manufacture, the city's industrial base was also strongly linked to another area of excellence, namely medicine. When James Simpson carried out his experiments with chloroform as an anaesthetic in 1847, he turned to the Canongate chemists Duncan, Flockhart & Co. to produce the drug, which they did with great success. The subsequent development of chloroform for industrial production was the work of another Edinburgh academic, William Gregory, Professor of Chemistry at the university. It was due to that quality of research background that Edinburgh became a centre of excellence not only for academic chemistry but also for drug production and Duncan, Flockhart & Co. were one of the main producers in the city. As Ford's elaborate new glassworks façade was rising in the 1870s, a no less important though more mundane structure had just been erected on the opposite side of the street, where Duncan, Flockhart & Co. built their first chloroform factory, between the working class housing of Holyrood Square and the gas tanks of the Edinburgh Gas Light Company. Their assurances that 'The manufacture of chloroform is by no means injurious to health' seem to have been accepted by the Dean of Guild.[60] Indeed, so successful was this plant that within 20 years they approached the city once again to rebuild and greatly extend the chloroform works.[61] By this time they had already greatly extended

their premises and had added soda water production to the same site in 1875.[62]

14.7 The 'Age of Reform'?

E PATRICIA DENNISON

14.7.1 Material improvements in the care of the poor

Some attempts were made to improve the squalid and unhealthy conditions that were home for the majority of the Canongate inhabitants. The Edinburgh Institution for the Education of Deaf and Dumb Children was founded in 1810. In 1814, part of Chessel's Building was purchased to house the children. There were initially about 45 children being cared for, the boys being taught shoemaking and the girls sewing. By 1824, however, the institution had moved as the accommodation proved too restrictive (McCallum 1997, 14). For many people, moral, mental and physical disorder – the disintegration of the personality – represented in microcosm the symbolic disorder of society, and control could best be effected by institutional care and restraint (Markus 1982, 26). Social order, moreover, mirrored housing conditions; drunkenness was merely one manifestation. While the Edinburgh literati might consume astonishing amounts of ale and claret, by the late 18th century whisky had begun to be, along with stout and porter, the drink of the masses – a potent combination that quickly and efficiently inebriated the drinker (Fraser 1990, 240). The *Edinburgh News* of 1853 commented on the 'irrational expenditure' of 'constitutional drunkards' (Rodger 1999, 11).

The year before Queensberry Lodge was opened, 1864, the Magdalene Asylum, which had been built on the site of the 18th-century Bowling Green, was moved to Dalry (Boog Watson 1923, 97–8), partly as a result of the suggested reforms of Dr William Tait. An attack on women's penitentiaries had begun in 1840 with the publication of his *Magdalenism*. Recently appointed as the secretary of the Edinburgh branch of the newly formed Society for the Protection of Young Females and the Prevention of Juvenile Prostitution, he launched an offensive on the administration of the asylum in Canongate for both its punitive management practices and its location. Violent control methods, such as head shaving, solitary confinement and corporal punishment were practised which Tait believed led to loss of self-respect and depression and resulted in a high percentage of runaways. His comments on the location add an interesting insight into Canongate in the mid-19th century. The asylum itself he likened more to a madhouse or a prison than a refuge for the penitent. Its location in the centre of the city greatly curtailed its ability to perform its purpose: there were temptations in a crowded town; it was impossible to institute a full service laundry because smoke from the surrounding factories contaminated the clothes; and the privacy of the yard was non-existent as it was surrounded by dwellings and the inmates might be watched as they walked in the yard. Tait argued that inmates should be free of the temptations of the city and have 'free exercise and employment in the open air'. Dalry, then a rural location, was the solution (Mahood 1990, 103–4).

Such well-meaning efforts were, however, incapable of dealing with the basic problem confronting Canongate and its inhabitants – abject poverty and all that it brought in its wake. Overcrowding, poverty and high mortality rates were exacerbated by the influx of Highlanders and Irish into the Old Town, in all accounting for 66 per cent of the population increase between 1801 and 1831 (Rodger 1999, 13). The population of Edinburgh and its suburbs rose from 69,000 in 1801 to 161,000 in 1851, many coming to find employment in the expanding breweries of both Canongate and Fountainbridge (there were 40 breweries in greater Edinburgh by the 1880s/90s), in the legal and insurance offices of the New Town, and in the growing printing and publishing industries (Morris 1998, 140). 1832 was to be a bleak year for the destitute, for they were the group of society most affected by a wave of cholera that killed almost 600 people in Edinburgh between January and August. Inadequate efforts were made to counteract the attack: pigs were to be removed from homes; flannel clothing, woollen stockings and soup were provided for some of the poor; very basic facilities for washing and drying clothes were organised; and vagrants and beggars were excluded from the town. The treasurer of Canongate Kirk reported that there were insufficient coffins to bury the cholera victims, and because they were so overworked, gravediggers were given one shilling per burial (Selby Wright 1965, 34).

A German visitor to Edinburgh and Canongate in 1842, one Johann Kohl, was told of events during the outbreak of cholera (Kohl 1844). His account gives an interesting insight into the lifestyles and associated problems of some of the Canongate residents. The closes, he recounts, were so inaccessible to the sun that they were always wet. Moreover, they were almost equally inaccessible to the police, called in during the cholera epidemic to rid the town of pigs. Many

Irishmen lived in these closes, or 'ruins' as Kohl calls them, and they were very fond of their pigs. With no ground to graze them, they were kept in the homes. When ordered to remove them, the owners discovered that the pigs had grown too fat to be driven down the stairs; they were lowered on ropes, sometimes from fourth-floor windows.[63]

This onslaught of cholera was merely one of a number of major epidemics: influenza and typhoid came in 1837; the famine fever, typhus, brought by refugees from the Irish famine, in 1847, and cholera again in 1849. Attempts were made in 1839 to clean up the environment of Canongate: sewers were causing problems and were likened to marshes; the preparing, by drying on the ground, and selling of manure was prohibited; and it was proposed to move the slaughterhouse from the vicinity.[64] But by the time of the publication of Edwin Chadwick's *Report on the Sanitary Condition of the Labouring Population* in 1842, Edinburgh's closes were considered the most debased living conditions in the country. His discussions of death rates, drainage and sewerage, housing conditions, lodging houses and water supply are vivid indication of the abject poverty and filth that many wretched souls had to support (Chadwick 1842, 13, 233, 247, 78, 106, 282, 59–60, 120–4, 97–9, 198, 277, 281–2, 397, 366, 416, 138, 162).

Two years later Friedrich Engels wrote in *The Condition of the Working Class* of the 'foul wretchedness of the poor' of the Old Town of Edinburgh (Engels 1844, 41–3, 113), the death rate by 1831, for example, being as high as one in 22 (Engels 1844, 119). Other contemporary comments were equally damning: 'From their smoky beehives ten storeys high, the unwashed look down upon the open squares and gardens of the wealthy. Social inequality is nowhere more ostentatious than in Edinburgh'; 'Excrementitious matter of some forty or fifty thousand individuals is daily thrown into the gutters ... or poured into carts which are sent about the principal streets' (Rodger 1999, 11).

Gradually, many became certain that there was a clear link between high death rates and certain areas of the large towns – the areas that were crowded, poorly drained, inadequately supplied with water and inhabited by the poor. It was also suggested that when certain predisposing causes were linked with certain environmental conditions, disease would inevitably result. The predisposing causes were felt to include drink, immoral habits and poverty, while the environmental conditions were linked to vapours and smells from putrid waste and sewage (Morris 1998, 141).

Poverty and inadequate housing, and the social problems these brought, became inevitably a concern of the Church, many radical Presbyterian ministers believing that through religious leadership would come economic, social and educational benefits for the people. It was disagreement on the exact method of how to deal with the poor, particularly in Edinburgh, that was one of the factors leading to the Disruption of 1843 and the founding of the Free Church of Scotland, in schism with the Church of Scotland. One of the most forceful and vocal campaigners was Reverend Dr James Begg. In collaboration with other radical ministers, measures to alleviate poor housing conditions had been published in *The Witness*, and in 1849 and 1851 Begg published two further pamphlets: *Pauperism and the Poor Laws* and *Drunkenness and Pauperism*, his intention to deal specifically with improvements in Edinburgh. Following along very much the same lines as the evangelical leader Thomas Chalmers, formerly Moderator of the Church of Scotland, Begg proposed an eight-point charter: improvement in the quantity and quality of education; suppression of drunkenness; better homes for working people; public washing houses and bleaching greens; reform of the land laws; simplification of the transference of land; different treatments for crime and pauperism; and greater justice for Scotland in Parliament (Rodger 1999, 16).

The 1840s were to see a further influx of Irish immigrants into Edinburgh, exacerbating the overcrowding and potential for disease. By 1851, of the population aged between 16 and 60, 29 per cent in the Old Town were born in Ireland (Gray 1976, 11). Many Irish would continue to choose to live in Canongate and Cowgate throughout this century and the next not merely because rents were cheaper, but also because they were near their place of worship, St Patrick's (affectionately still called St Pat's), the Catholic church at the foot of St Mary's Wynd.

The Irish immigrants, it has been argued, were 'in the almost impossible position of being unable to become Scottish.... The essence of Scottishness was Protestantism and its culture of work, thrift and sobriety' (Aspinwall & McCaffrey 1985, 130). George Bell, a doctor, noted that, in 1847, 379 out of 511 fever victims in Edinburgh Royal Infirmary were Irish. He opined that the 'migratory Irish are a pestilence as well as a pest', but admitted that the

most destitute Scots were worse off than the Irish poor, for one very simple reason – the Irish had a lifeline in the form of a greater attachment to religion (Aspinwall & McCaffrey 1985, 143). In reality, the only organisation that could give the Irish cultural cohesion was their Church (Aspinwall & McCaffrey 1985, 139). They tended to find employment where cheap labour had previously attracted Highlanders, in general service, domestic service, portering and cleansing. A small but significant section moved into small-scale retailing, dealing in provisions, spirits and old clothes (Aspinwall & McCaffrey 1985, 134). In fact, only once in the 19th century did the Irish-born figure as the largest 'outsider' or 'alien' group, and that was in the unusual census years of 1851 and 1861, after the Famine, when they accounted for 6 per cent of the Edinburgh population, compared with 4.5 per cent English. Otherwise, the English immigration overshadowed the Irish. Particularly under Bishop Gillis, self-help societies were established which provided such assistance as funeral and sickness benefit and savings societies. This went far to allay fears of the Irish as a radical disruptive force, even though, during the tension of the threatened Chartist outburst of 1848, many Irish sided with the Edinburgh suffrage radicals and took part in the ensuing riots (Aspinwall & McCaffrey 1985, 141, 145). But their culture, religion, appearance (which was reputedly very slovenly and illkempt) and nationality set them apart and made them an easily identifiable group. They also lived in certain identifiable areas (Aspinwall & McCaffrey 1985, 140). 'They were in the Scottish Victorian city, but hardly of it, and yet adapted to it' (Aspinwall & McCaffrey 1985, 149).

George Bell produced two reports (1849, *Day and Night in the Wynds of Edinburgh*, and 1850 *Blackfriars' Wynd Analyzed*) on the almost inhuman conditions and destitution of many, particularly in Blackfriars' Wynd and nearby areas, where overcrowding was worse than in the town's prisons. He cited the case of one family at the foot of the High Street of Canongate which succumbed to typhus and starvation and, because of abject poverty, they were forced to leave their miserable home and disappeared. Bell opined that there could have been few cheaper places to stay, other than possibly lodging houses, 'in themselves all horror and ... situated in the vilest parts of the city' (Bell 1849; 1850, 4–5).

Begg's address at the founding of the Scottish Social Reform Association the following year summed up the views of many, 'You will never get the unclean heart of Edinburgh gutted out until you plant it all around with new houses' (Rodger 1999, 16). Such statements, reports and publications began to influence public opinion and there gradually developed an acquiescence, if not more, that the Town Council had the duty to take a more pro-active role in the state of the urban environment.

The Royal Commission on the Scottish Poor Law, which in a masterly understatement found the Poor Law 'not adequate', resulted in a new Poor Law in 1845, with responsibility now shifted from the Church to the State. Overseen by a Board of Supervision in Edinburgh, parochial boards were compelled to levy funds to assist the poor. But the Act gave no right of relief to the able-bodied and did not require parishes to build poor houses, and it increased the residence qualification for help from three years to five, at which level it would remain until 1898 (Dupree 2000, 367–8). The system thus left huge gaps in the provision of relief.

In 1861, the Canongate Registration District had 47 per cent of families in one-room dwellings and, not surprisingly, the Royal Commission on Housing (1884–5) recorded that those living in one room were 'labourers and people of the poorer classes (Gray 1976, 14, 96). In 1862, Dr Littlejohn was appointed as Edinburgh's first medical officer for health. His report (1865) gives a stark picture of Canongate. Canongate had 220 people per inhabited acre, compared with Morningside's eight, or 140,000 per square mile. Between 100 and 200 people might share a common stair with no water and, in consequence, no water closets or sinks. Many improvements were proposed by Littlejohn: clean supplies of water were essential; the abandonment of the old cesspits was advocated; and public hygiene education was proposed (Kinnear 1969, 8). Most of all he criticised the foul burn system which was peculiar to Edinburgh. The sewage of the Old Town was still used to irrigate meadows and open areas around the town, in particular fields just beyond Holyrood Palace. The stench, apart from the foulness, must have been appalling, and it was one of the reasons that Queen Victoria disliked staying in Holyrood Palace (Morris 1998, 142–3).

In spite of attempts at cleanliness, by 1887 the area was still described as the 'nursery of disease and haunt of vagrants'.[65] The hospital sections of the poorhouses of Edinburgh were dirty, overcrowded and staffed by untrained, pauper personnel. Some of the poor might receive treatment in the Royal Infirmary, which was intended for this group of society, being attached to the medical school and served by eminent medical men who worked without a fee, in the knowledge that prestige would bring students and private patients (Crowther 1990, 276–7). In general, however, the sick were inadequately treated. While cholera, typhus and smallpox were being brought under control, the greatest causes of death were scarlet fever, diptheria, measles, pneumonia and tuberculosis (TB). Indeed, TB was to remain a constant threat with slow advances in its control, well into the 20th century. Even in the late 1920s cows were kept in dark barns in the middle of the city, and little was understood of how dangerous milk could be, until such innovations as tubercule-free cows were brought into Colinton Mains Farm in the 1930s. The net result for the infant born towards the end of the 19th century was that, with child mortality continuing to rise, by 1899 one child in five died before reaching the age of one year.[66]

Improvements were effected, however, at the west end of Canongate, as in other parts of the Old Town, largely as a result of the Improvement Act of 1867. By 1879, the 'wretched old buildings' on the east side of St Mary's Wynd and adjacent closes, such as Home's, Boyd's and Gullane's, had been swept away and the ground rebuilt upon, with 'commodious tenements of an architectural character suited to the "Auld Toune"'. Leith Wynd, likewise, and the closes to the east, Old Fleshmarket Close, Shepherd's Close, Ramsay Court, Midcommon Close and Coull's Close, had all been demolished and were in the process of being replaced with decent housing. Leith Wynd was also at this time renamed Cranston Street, after one of the bailies (Mackay 1879, 110–11). Increased urbanisation on the peripheries of the city created new working-class industrial districts; slum clearance reduced the density in the older slum areas; and some chose to move 'spontaneously'. In consequence, while the population increased throughout the city at 78 per cent in the period 1861 to 1901, the increase in Canongate was only 49 per cent. The resultant alleviation of pressure meant that the percentage of families in only one room fell from 47 per cent to 37 per cent (Gray 1976, 14–15). By the end of the century the women of Canongate could avail themselves of the facility of the 'steamie', opened nearby in South Gray's Close, and of the community spirit associated with these once well-loved establishments.

In 1897, the management of some of the housing at Chessel's Court was taken over by the Edinburgh Social Union, a philanthropic organisation, founded after Patrick Geddes visited Octavia Hill in London to learn about her work in slum clearance. The aim was not merely to provide decent living accommodation but also to promote craft activities. The Union did not purchase the properties, but by agreement with proprietors ensured that rents were ploughed back into property maintenance. Chessel's Court was merely one such property (McCallum 1997, 14), which was also furnished with gardens and a children's playground at the back under the same scheme. Another such initiative took place at White Horse Close, which, in 1902, was restored by the Social Union, after purchase by Dr Barbour and his sister, both active members of the Union. Fitted up as commodious dwellings for the 'humbler classes of the community' (Hope 1902, 13), it was also the aim of Geddes to attract new residents into the Old Town and diversify the social mix.

14.7.2 Politics

The General Election of 1830 brought the Whigs back to power after 50 years. One of the main aims of the prime minister, Lord Grey, was to carry his Reform Bill into law. Throughout the country, various reform meetings were convened. That for Edinburgh was called on 26 April 1832 and was held in St Ann's Yards. The Trades assembled in the Meadows and walked to St Ann's Yards in procession with banners and music. It was calculated that there were between 20,000 and 60,000 present, although Cockburn reckoned the latter was nearer the mark. 'No one thing occurred throughout the whole day to excite regret. All sorts of Reformers sunk their differences in the common object ... not the slightest disorder either at the meeting or in the town' (Cockburn 1874, vol. 1, 28). Another meeting at the same venue was held on 15 May, with about 30,000 present (Cockburn 1874, vol. 1, 29). The resultant Reform Act, in reality, gave little further suffrage to the men of Canongate. By the Act, the vote was given to ten-pound ratepayers, a level far beyond the means of the vast majority in the Old Town.

A small extension of franchise, and a major symbolic victory for the working class vote, was gained with the Reform Act of 1867, the Scottish version being passed in January 1868, when household suffrage was established, although the influence of the 'Irish vote', particularly in Canongate Ward was deplored, especially in 1873 and 1875 (Marwick 1969, 35). Considerable support for the issue of votes for women had been growing. The contemporary feminist movement was represented in Edinburgh by the Women's Suffrage Society in 1867 and by the attempt of the 'Seven Against Edinburgh' to obtain admission to medical study (Marwick 1969, 32). A lot of energy was put into petitioning the House of Commons for the extension of the franchise, and in the nine years from 1867 two million signatures were collected in Scotland. Campaigners were encouraged by the gain of some ground in certain representational capacities: the Education (Scotland) Act of 1872 established elected School Boards and permitted women to participate both as voters and Board members. The role of women on such welfare boards was becoming acceptable and suitable for females, women, for example, officiating on the governing board of the Magdalene Asylum. In 1882, women were enfranchised for municipal elections (although in practice only unmarried women and widows might take advantage of this right), and in 1895, women gained the right to stand and be elected to county councils and parish councils, although they were excluded from standing for town councils until 1907. The only working-class women's organisation formally affiliated to the suffrage movement was the Women's Cooperative Guild, the first socialist and labour organisation to show such support (Gordon 1990, 229). By the 20th century the suffrage movement would resort to sabotage, but the war efforts of such women as Dr Elsie Inglis, the founder of the Scottish Women's Suffrage Federation, went far to ensure that in an ambitious post-war reconstruction programme, which included electoral reform, women were given the parliamentary vote. Essentially a middle-class reform movement, the impact on working-class Canongate women was probably not immediately obvious.[67]

Probably of more importance to Canongate were local affairs. Legally, Canongate ceased to exist as a burgh in 1856, when Canongate and Portsburgh were absorbed into Edinburgh. But the signs of the times were already present. The incorporation of tailors had already resolved that they no longer felt it necessary to 'become burgesses of the Canongate before entering the incorporation or even after they become members, unless they reside within the burgh' (Marwick 1938, 109–10). Although technically unconstitutional, clearly many members lived and worked outwith the burgh, and this was merely a confirmation of the change of times and attitudes – the building of the New Town and other suburbs and the encroachment of the railway and factories impacted particularly on Canongate. These factors, allied with the influx from the Highlands and, in particular, Ireland, went far to undermine the sense of identity of Canongate and destroy the old sense of community and oneness of the old crafts. Complaints about electoral apathy, dilatoriness in settling municipal matters such as the choice of site of the Usher Hall, criticism of municipal salaries, the cost of water supply and civic improvements (1867), and the civic debt (Marwick 1969, 34) became the commonplace political comment for those sufficiently non-destitute to have the luxury of political thought.

14.7.3 Education

With the gradual exodus out of the Old Town of the more genteel classes, the old grammar school began to suffer. As early as 1788 an academy had been opened in Hanover Street where, according to the *Edinburgh Evening Courant*, 'the method of education so successfully practiced [sic] in the English Academies' was adopted and the New Town Grammar School was opened in Register Street in the same year (*Evening Courant*). The master of the Canongate Grammar School was forced to supplement his slender income by taking in as boarders pupils to the High School or university. He further offered to tutor them in classical studies and at their 'leisure moments their attention will be directed to the study of geography and history … by way of recreation and amusement'!

The Disruption in the Church of Scotland in 1843 was also to have far-reaching consequences. The Free Church initiated a programme of setting up a second network of churches, ministers, manses and schools. With its resources thus curtailed the established Church found difficulties dealing not only with the provision of poor relief, but also of parish schools. Gradually this role would pass to the burgh authority and out of Church control. By 1850 New College had been erected in a dominant position at the head of the Mound. Thus was provided the focus for the alternative Church, the Free Church, to train its own ministers, and 150 years later, the first, temporary home for the new Scottish Parliament.

With the sale of Trinity Hospital and College Church, the North British Railway Company acquired the site for Waverley Station. Francis, tenth Earl of Moray sold Moray House as a place of accommodation for the former inmates of the hospital. Subsequently making other arrangements, the governors of Trinity Hospital sold the house to the Free Church of Scotland in 1846. They, in turn, with the assistance of Geddes, converted it from its dilapidated state into a Normal

College for training teachers (Boog Watson 1923, 23). The Normal Training College of the Church of Scotland was first established in Chambers Street. The precursor of Moray House Teacher Training College, it would move location to Canongate (Morris 1998, 139).

Further education was not to be, even within the most fanciful of dreams, for the vast majority of the Canongate populace. The desire for the advancement of medical knowledge in the college and associated institutions would, however, impact on Canongate. William Burke and William Hare began their notorious search for bodies for medical research and, by initially searching out victims who were nomadic, disappearance went unnoticed (Edwards 1993, 76). The poor, unknown and unwanted in the Canongate provided rich pickings.[68]

A new school, Milton House Public School, was built on the site of Milton House, run by the Sisters of Charity in 1842,[69] and in due course a modern burgh school was set up just to the east of the parish church. The Edinburgh Free Kindergarten was established in Reid's Court, Canongate, but could cater for few children. Most working-class children before compulsory education was laid down in 1872 received their basic schooling through the Sunday School. Just how much education, in reality, the average child in Canongate received is very much open to question. It is known that many parents in this period of industrialisation realised the potential of their children as a workforce. Of those who did attend school, many did not stay until they could write, although some achieved a basic reading ability.

14.8 Housing improvements in the 19th century

JOHN LOWREY

'The Canongate, once the abode of the Scottish nobility, is now inhabited by some of the most destitute of Edinburgh, who reside in numerous alleys, called "closes", running out of the High Street'.[70] The anonymous author who made these fairly unremarkable observations on life in the Old Town in the mid-19th century was one of many who observed the same phenomenon at that time. What made his comments slightly different, however, was that his regret was not about the 'descent in the scale of degradation' (Wilson 1891, 108) of the great aristocratic houses but about the conditions which the new occupants of these

Edinburgh 'rookeries' endured. As such, he was one of a number of philanthropic writers concerned with the plight of the poor, who saw the Canongate, and the Old Town in general, as a giant slum and, increasingly, a problem for the city as a whole.

The House of Refuge escaped such censure, but the Destitute Sick Society certainly was one of the means by which patients were referred to the fever hospital and presumably the House of Refuge also, suggesting that perhaps not everyone who needed help was given the opportunity of obtaining it. The reasons seem to have been twofold: first that there were 'no-go' areas in the city, into which the inspectors dared not venture, and secondly (and connected with the first) that certain areas and places were deemed to be full of people of bad character, that is, the undeserving poor, whose own failings had brought them to their current condition. Often what lay behind this censorious attitude was disapproval of drinking, and that moral element was a very important conditioning factor in the city's attitude to the poor and to the housing of the poor, at least in the 19th century.

In architectural terms, the history of housing in the Canongate in the 19th and most of the 20th century has been the history of working-class housing. It has been an unusual history for reasons already suggested, namely that for much of the period, much of the housing was within existing and often important, earlier architecture. That factor has been of great importance in the 20th century and up to the present day, when decisions about housing have also had to take into account the existing historic fabric and pattern of development. To a large extent, therefore, the history of housing in the area has also been related to the history of conservation. Overall, a number of distinctive features and phases characterise working-class housing in the Canongate. An important element is the reuse and subdivision of existing houses, some of them very grand. There is the construction of new tenements in the 19th century, often aimed specifically at the poorest sorts of tenants. Associated with that, the effect of the Sanitary Reform Movement in the mid-19th century has to be considered. With the 20th century, a whole series of interests and concerns started to affect the housing picture. A Geddesian concern for 'conservative surgery' and the creation of open spaces, combined for the first time with a municipal responsibility for housing, started to have an effect. This was also combined with a legal framework for historic buildings and also for planning that started to influence official approaches to housing before the middle of the

century and led to decisions in the immediate postwar period, the effect of which can still be seen today. To give some sense of these developments, a brief overview of their effect on the architecture, and particularly the housing of the Canongate, will be the subject of this final section of the chapter.

With the departure of the well-to-do classes from the late 18th century onwards, combined with the development of large-scale industry already charted and the rise in a working-class population that went with that, many of the old buildings in the Canongate and elsewhere in the old town were effectively colonised by these new inhabitants. A good example of this is Acheson House, in Bakehouse Close, which was built in the 1630s and restored by the Marquis of Bute in the 1930s. By that time, this single, not very large, aristocratic *hôtel*, housed 14 families and 'nearly every room of the original mansion house had been divided and subdivided, and each subdivision housed a family' (Hurd 1952, 5). This was not an unusual arrangement and all along the Canongate historic buildings were reused in this way. Of course, many were not ancient aristocratic townhouses but were later developments, like New Street and St John Street, and some were themselves tenements that were subsequently further subdivided, as in the case of Chessel's Court.

One of the main reasons why the plight of the poor and their housing conditions became a matter of general concern in the 19th century was because of the danger of disease. The typhus that affected the city from 1817 and through the 1820s seems to have been confined to the Old Town, but the cholera epidemics that ravaged the city from the 1830s affected the whole city, New Town and Old Town, rich and poor alike. As late as 1847/48, over 6000 cases of cholera were recorded in Edinburgh. The problems of poor water supply and sanitation that lay behind the epidemics of this period, as well as the more general problem of appalling housing conditions, were by no means confined to Edinburgh, and part of the general solution within the United Kingdom was provided by the Sanitary Reform Movement which grew out of Edwin's Chadwick's shocking 1842 *Report on the Sanitary Condition of the Labouring Population*. What was shameful for Edinburgh, however, was that in all of Chadwick's nationwide survey of housing conditions, Edinburgh emerged as among the very worst and worst of all was Edinburgh Old Town. That was compounded by the contrast between the filth and squalor of the Old Town, on the one hand, and, on the other, the beauty of the New Town and the very public works that so many of the immigrant Irish had been brought in to build, allowing the city its self-proclaimed accolade as the 'Athens of the North'.

A number of initiatives were taken to try to deal with this problem and what they amounted to by the 1860s was a combination of sanitary reform, which mainly meant slum clearance, and tenement construction, although these two activities were not always coordinated. The starting point for the city was the 1862 Burgh Police Act, which was the first attempt to use sanitary reform for slum clearance and, as part of that, the appointment of a medical officer of health, who advised on sanitary matters. In 1862, Dr Henry Littlejohn was appointed to this post, the first in the country, and three years later published his *Report on the Sanitary Condition of Edinburgh* (Littlejohn 1865). Littlejohn's analysis highlighted overcrowding and lack of sanitary provision as two major and related problems. One Canongate example was Birtley buildings, a modern development aimed specifically at the poor. On four floors, this tenement had a total of 35 rooms for 33 families. A total of 125 people lived there, or 3.57 persons per room. For that population, there was no internal water supply and no provision of water closets (Littlejohn 1865, 35). This was typical of the Canongate and the Old Town in general. Littlejohn's analysis of population statistics showed that the Old Town was the most populous part of the city, the most overcrowded and had the worst death rates by far. Canongate and Abbey are the relevant areas for the purposes of this study and Littlejohn's figures showed a population of 12,200 for Canongate and 2237 for Abbey. The death rates were 31.23 and 36.65 per thousand respectively (Littlejohn 1865, 13). Of the very few areas outwith the Old Town that were worse than that, all had some special circumstances, such as the presence of the workhouse or a large asylum. Leaving those aside, Abbey had the worst death rate in the city and Canongate was only marginally better than other central Old Town areas.[71] By comparison with the New Town, which was divided into upper and lower, each with roughly similar populations to Canongate, the death rate figures were 17.38 and 15.47 per thousand, which means a person had roughly twice as much chance of dying in the Canongate area than in the New Town (Littlejohn 1865, 8–9).

Birtley Buildings was one of a great number of developments across the city that were aimed at the very poorest members of society but, in order to get a return on their investment, landlords made these buildings as basic as possible, with conditions that started bad and ended up atrocious. Littlejohn also highlighted examples of good practice – none of them in the Canongate. These included Ashley Buildings at 15 High Street, built on sound sanitary principles and aimed at the 'industrious workman'. This was beyond the reach of the poorest, but was nevertheless of general good to the community because, according to Littlejohn, it provided an example to all (1865, 38). Another was in Warden's Close, Grassmarket, this time aimed at poorer tenants, who were given accommodation and were taught how to keep it clean; they were kept under close supervision, 'and should a newcomer not be susceptible of the lesson, after patient trial, he quickly leaves' (Littlejohn 1865, 40).

This requirement for education and supervision was deemed to be important by Littlejohn, who firmly believed that simply providing the properly equipped accommodation was not sufficient and, without education, could end up undermining the public health benefit that was supposed to accrue. Such a paternalistic approach had architectural consequences, one of which was a predisposition against the existing, subdivided properties that were used by the poor. Littlejohn recommended that all wooden additions should be 'peremptorily removed', on sanitary grounds rather than on the traditional grounds of fire hazard. Returning to the basic business of WCs, he also argued that older properties were not suitable for new plumbing technology, and for new buildings, he recommended one WC between two tenants because that would allow mutual supervision, 'little risk of derangement of the mechanism, and a greater certainty of fixing upon the offender' (Littlejohn 1865, 80).[72]

But the sanitary approach to housing amounted to more than just the basics of paved streets, stair lighting and a clean water supply. Littlejohn was greatly impressed by the development of Cockburn Street in the 1850s. This had nothing to do with sanitary reform but, because it cut through the closes, making them easier to clean and service, and it allowed light and air into a densely built-up part of the Old Town, Littlejohn identified it as a model for other parts of the city. In his report he actually proposed a new street cutting through the closes between Niddry Street and St John Street in the Canongate. Fourteen closes would have been divided by this measure, opening up the area to sanitary reform, allowing new houses to be built for the working classes and by incorporating laundries into the basements on the downward slope, allowing the people to keep themselves clean more easily (Littlejohn 1865, 112–14).

New streets were to be a crucial part of Littlejohn's legacy to the city, but perhaps not quite in the way he imagined. The Edinburgh approach became one of slum clearance and the construction of new streets, but rarely streets aimed at the people displaced by the clearance. The major outcome of the 1867 Improvement Act in Edinburgh was Chambers Street, a street of grand public buildings and institutions, which incorporated only a very few working-class houses in the adjoining Guthrie Street. In the Old Town, more was achieved, although not in the Canongate itself. Blackfriars' Street, near the Tron, St Mary's Street and Jeffrey Street, on the boundary between Edinburgh and Canongate, and Cranston Street, just inside the Canongate, all date from this period. The Canongate itself, however, was virtually untouched and, given the displacement of the poorest in other parts of the city as the slum clearance programme continued, it is quite likely that the conditions in the Canongate actually deteriorated. Most people continued to live in older, and certainly pre-sanitary-reform, buildings. Since Littlejohn had established that these were not suitable for modern plumbing, the alternative was the construction of public toilets across the Old Town. In the Canongate these become a feature of the street furniture, if not the townscape, from this period onwards, the most notable being the urinal situated almost exactly where the girth cross had been. This started something of a tradition in the area and when Scottish & Newcastle built their new office block on the corner of Canongate and Horse Wynd in 1971, it incorporated a public convenience. Earlier, in the early 1950s, Younger's had actually proposed such a building, in what was undoubtedly thought of as an appropriate castellated style, right in the middle of the Canongate, at the entrance to the Holyrood Brewery.[73]

In 1886, the centrepiece of the Edinburgh International Exhibition was the Old Edinburgh Street, designed by the architect Sidney Mitchell and composed of the frontages of Edinburgh buildings that had been demolished since the 18th century. To Patrick Geddes this street took on a symbolic role: symbolic of the subjection of the Old Town by the social and economic forces that had shaped the New Town, and symbolic as the catalyst for his subsequent extensive work in the Old Town. Its importance for Geddes was not simply antiquarian, that is that these were examples of interesting, ancient architecture that had been swept away, but rather that it represented a way forward for the Old Town that would bring about not simply a material regeneration but a renaissance that was social,

intellectual and spiritual.[74] In practical terms, his approach was characterised by 'conservative surgery'. He rejected what he saw as the facile and rather brutal approach of the Sanitary Reform Movement, opting instead for a more sensitive and artistic approach to the regeneration of the city and the people who worked there. Most of his work was done outside the Canongate, in particular in the Lawnmarket and Ramsay Gardens, but his influence was felt throughout the rest of the 20th century, throughout the Old Town, and his work did have some direct effect on the Canongate from quite an early stage. One of his early initiatives was the Edinburgh Social Union, which sought to assist the poor in the slums of the Old Town. Through this he encouraged two of the members, a Dr Barbour and his sister, to take over the historic buildings at Whitehorse Close, at the foot of the Canongate, opposite the Parliament building and to adapt them for working-class housing (RCAHMS 1951, 158). This Barbour Trust housing survived until the 1950s, when the buildings were taken over by the city. In 1925, Frank Mears, partner and son-in-law of Patrick Geddes, had prepared plans for restoring the property and this eventually happened in the 1960s.

An important aspect of Geddes's work in Edinburgh was his attitude to the tenement. The tenement in the modern sense of a group of more or less identical flats within one building is the characteristic Scottish urban building type and its roots lay in the overcrowded conditions of Edinburgh in the 17th century (Robinson 1985, 59). Geddes himself worked with some of the very earliest of the modern-type tenement in the Lawnmarket, in places like Mylne's Court, and, of course, developed it in his own academic community at Ramsay Gardens. But the tenement was not inevitable. Particular circumstances had caused its development in the city, but in earlier times, before the population had been overcrowded within the city walls, a type of domestic building much lower in height had been used. This was actually illustrated by Frank Mears in Geddes's *Civic Survey* and commented on by Geddes:

> My able colleague, Mr F C Mears, has here reconstructed, by help of surviving fragments as well as of tradition, the type of dwelling of Edinburgh in the Middle Ages – long before the days of its high piled tenements – as a dwelling with arcaded ground-level and galleried first floor (Geddes 1910, 549).

Mears's drawing is juxtaposed with Whitehorse Close, which is given as a surviving example of this kind of building, and linked by Geddes with the cottages of the garden suburbs that were so fashionable at the time. In the context of the Canongate, it highlights once again the distinction between the royal suburb and the city proper. To Geddes, tenements were appropriate to the Lawnmarket, whereas in the Canongate, other solutions were possible and Whitehorse Close was the historic survival that proved this.

Many years later, in 1970 (Mears died in 1953), the Mears practice was able to return to the same area and expound essentially the same ideas in the rebuilding of Robertson's Court (1–9 Canongate). Here, by a mixture of judicious demolition, restoration and rebuilding on a smaller and more human scale, although still in tenements, something approaching Geddes's idea of the scale and variety of the medieval street scene was achieved.

In Geddes's reduction in building scale as well as in his 'conservative surgery', and in Littlejohn's cutting of the closes, there was a concern with a reduction in density, the opening up of areas and the creation of space around buildings. A continuing concern from at least Geddes's time right through to the Abercrombie Report in 1949 (discussed below) there was also a concern with the creation of useable open space. Just as he argued for lower-density housing in places where the historic justification for the tenement was not present, so Geddes argued that the medieval city had also been a place full of garden terraces, that had later formed the basis for defensive walls and had then been built over as pressure of overcrowding was brought to bear within the walls in later times. In other words, the loss of urban garden space was due to the same pressures that had brought about the rise of the tenement and, just as the tenement could in places be scaled down or even removed, so the garden terraces could be reinstated. Geddes identified over 10 acres of potential urban garden within the Old Town and, in some places, he reinstated small, productive gardens. For him, this was not simply an urban improvement, but a holistic exercise in which education, health and history came together:

> Thus after long ages of warlike history, our women and children are returning to their gentler tasks of old, their setting of herb and tending of flower. This is a small example, yet, I venture to say, a vital one, of the renewing modern life and use of even what may have been a forgotten past: in this case the very longest forgotten (Geddes 1910, 548).

Geddes's gardens were set up mainly around the Grassmarket and he did not open one in the Canongate, but, of course, he was not alone in advocating the importance of fresh air and garden ground, at least to the young. There was one such garden in the Canongate before the end of the 19th century: St Saviour's Child Garden was a nursery and garden behind Chessel's Court. Around 1900, someone connected with the garden produced a remarkable document *The Life of a Slum Child*,[75] which is a photo-story, illustrating the degradation of slum life in the Canongate, from the poverty of the home environment to the dangers of street life. The emphasis here is very much on the dangers of gambling and drink and, once again, there is a very strong moralistic tone to what is essentially a promotional piece for the nursery and garden. Amidst the poverty and vice of the area, the only green space available to children was the Canongate Kirkyard. But the remedy to all of this was the free kindergarten at St Saviour's in Chessel's Court. Here the very young would be given a different start in life, 'and the childish glee and merriment which echoes from the sand patch tell their own story – the joy of life is not filtered through the filth of the streets or the sordidness of the home'.

Notes

1 NAS, Register of Deeds (CS) 1803, RD3/297/ff.121–7. Disposition in favour of Aitcheson is dated 1 June 1802 (London). Registered in Edinburgh 14 March 1803.

2 PRO WO 44/454/54590 Ordinary Correspondence, Barracks GB E/1826.

3 The starting date is taken from 1944 copies of army plans made in 1808, in ECA, City Architect's department plans of Queensberry House.

4 ECA, Dean of Guild Petition, 10 January 1810.

5 NAS, Records of George Heriot's Trust, GD421/1/7/66.

6 NAS, Records of George Heriot's Trust, GD421/1/7/68, shows that the premises at Kinloch's Lodging was owned by the Trust.

7 ECA, Macleod Bundles A2/Bay d, Shelf 7, Bundle 92, Item 64.

8 Typical records seen at PRO WO40/25, which includes 'Barrack Department, List of Barrack Masters 1806', which names Scrymgeour as barrack master at Queensberry House.

9 PRO, WO 44/545/54590 Ordinary Correspondence, Barracks GB E/1826.

10 PRO, WO 44/545/54590 Ordinary Correspondence, Barracks GB E/1826.

11 *Report Respecting the Affairs and management of the Royal Infirmary of Edinburgh for the period 1 October 1836 to 1st October 1837.*

12 PRO, WO 44/545/54590 Report, Barrack Office 18 August 1823. The blankets were also supplied by the army but the writer of the report suggests that it might not be appropriate to take these back. Plan associated with the

sale is also at NAS RMP2688 with other documents at E 886/50.

13 PRO, WO 44/545/54590, Letter from Major Nairne to AIG of barracks, 30 October 1823.

14 PRO, WO 44/545/54590, Report by Captain Nairne to Board of Ordnance on letting of Queensberry House, 8 November 1823. A letter from Lord Provost of 15 November confirms the city's loss of interest in the purchase of the building as a replacement for the workhouse but does not mention the other proposal.

15 PRO, WO 44/545/54590 'Memorial for the Lord provost of Edinburgh', October 1824 and a printed 'Report of a Committee of general and resident Commissioners of Police Respecting the practicability of establishing a House of Refuge in Edinburgh for Male Juvenile Delinquents, and if teaching them a trade, whereby they may be enabled to gain an honest livelihood'. Edinburgh 15th October 1824.

16 PRO, WO 44/545/54590 Letter from Lord Provost to 'Lord Nairne, Assistant Inspector General of barracks' 9 November 1824.

17 PRO, WO 44/545/54590. Edinburgh Barrack Office report, Lord Nairne to Secretary of Board of Ordnance, London, 17 December 1824.

18 PRO, WO 44/545/54590 Letter from Treasurer of Royal Infirmary to Lord Nairne, 18 January 1825; and, annotated Report from Lord Nairne, Edinburgh Barrack Office, to Secretary of Board of Ordnance, 25 January 1825.

19 A detailed history of the House of Refuge is given in Hume & Boyd c 1984 and the following brief resumé given here is based on that publication.

20 *Fifth Report of the House of Refuge for the Destitute, Edinburgh 1st October 1836 – 30th September 1837*, Edinburgh 1838, 9.

21 *Fifth Report of the House of Refuge for the Destitute, Edinburgh 1st October 1836 – 30th September 1837*, Edinburgh 1838, 8.

22 In 1958, it was sold on to the Royal Highland Society and became the permanent home of their organisation and their annual show – which of course had started at Queensberry House in 1822 (Davidson 1984, 41).

23 Edinburgh City Library, Edinburgh Room, 'Miscellaneous documents relating to Queensberry House' qYHV1481H/C0012162841: 'Disposition by the Trustees of Queensberry House in favour of the Corporation of the City of Edinburgh … 1968'. This bundle of material seems to have formed part of the research project that resulted in the Hume & Boyd book.

24 *Edinburgh and Leith Directory, 1836 –37*.

25 *Edinburgh and Leith Directory, 1835–36*, 160; *Edinburgh and Leith Directory, 1836–37*, 169.

26 *Edinburgh and Leith Post Office Directories*, 1830–50.

27 ECA, 'Census 1841, district no. 685–3; area nos 11 & 12'.

28 For example, Archibald Hamilton's retrospective application for approval for new building he erected in Haliburton's Close, defines his boundaries and shows that there were tanneries both to the west and the north of his property. ECA, Dean of Guild Petition, Archibald Hamilton, 19 April 1815.

29 ECA, Dean of Guild Petition to build three workshops and a stable, Alexander Crichton, 14 April 1762.

30 ECA, Dean of Guild Records: Account of costs in building coach house and stables, William Jamieson, 1 June 1774. Sale to Crichton is mentioned in later document outlining dispute between William Thomson and John Carfrae (see note below).

31 ECA, Dean of Guild Records, William Thomson V John Carfrae, 28 May 1807. Confirms the position of Carfrae's coachworks which appears on maps up to Kirkwood's 1821 plan of Edinburgh.

32 ABRC, Ms, 'Outer House', 7 March 1826.

33 ECA, Dean of Guild Records, Younger V Fairley, 14 November 1831. The petition makes a distinction between Lothian House, which had been demolished, and Lothian Hut, which possibly had not.

34 ECA, Dean of Guild, Petition William Younger, 22 August 1836.

35 ECA, Dean of Guild, Petition, William Younger, for renovation and expansion of Lothian Vale, 19 February 1880.

36 The authors are indebted to Mr Alistair Knowles for much of the information about the 20th-century Abbey Brewery.

37 ABRC, Ms, 'Abbey and Holyrood Breweries Report', 15.

38 ABRC, *Guide to Great Northern Railway* (1861, 217).

39 ABRC, 'Notebook of Andrew Smith'.

40 ABRC, William Younger Collection, *Licensed Victuallers Guardian*, x, no. 337 (London, Saturday 15 June, 1872). The notebook of Andrew Smith, partner of William Younger, which includes notes on brewing and was bequeathed to his two sons, gives clear insight into the brewing practices at Abbey Brewery and elsewhere. *The Scottish Standard*, 5 March 1870, also includes as 'Trade Sketches, no. 32' a sketch of Reid's Close Brewery (British Library Newspaper Collection, Colindale, London). E Patricia Dennison is indebted to Mrs Alma Topen for her assistance.

41 *The Scottish Standard*, 5 March 1870, British Library Newspaper Collection, Colindale, London.

42 ECA, Dean of Guild, Greig V Chambers, 5 September 1828. Greig required to replace old tenement. Chambers was representative of Robert Playfair, owner of Brodie's Land.

43 ECA, Dean of Guild application to make alterations to existing proposal, James Dickson, 30 January 1875.

44 ECA, Dean of Guild Petition, 10 March 1887, to demolish tenement on Gentle's Close and other buildings to form entrance to brewery.

45 ECA, Dean of Guild Petition to erect cellarage behind Milton House, 14 June 1900.

46 ECA, Black Index Book, no. 1/5; 84, no. 27.

47 NLS, online resources, *Scottish Book Trade Index:* www.nls.uk/catalogues/resources/sbti

48 *Gray's Directory 1834–5*.

49 RCAHMS, NMRS, Architecture Catalogue IG6/12/82.

50 RCAHMS, NMRS, Architecture Catalogue IG6/12/82, quoting Trade Directory of 1858/9.

51 ECA, Dean of Guild Petition to build workshops, John Milne, Milton House, 27 April 1866.

52 ECA, Dean of Guild Petition to extend smith's shop, John Milne, 17 May 1872.

53 ECA, Dean of Guild Petition to build new three storey workshop, 26 August 1880.

54 RCAHMS, NMRS, Architecture Catalogue IG6/12/82.

55 ECA, Dean of Guild Petition to demolish Milton House and build new school, Edinburgh Scool Board, 2 September 1886.

56 *New Statistical Account of Scotland, Edinburgh* (Edinburgh, 1845, 650–68).

57 ECA, Dean of Guild Petition by John Carfrae for new buildings in his works, 24 March 1814. In description of his boundaries he mentions a Mr Yule, potter, to the west.

58 ECA, Dean of Guild Petition by William Ford, to convert iron foundry for use as glassworks, 21 December 1815.

59 ECA, Dean of Guild Petition by William Ford to add a fourth storey to factory, 14 March 1871. The architect was R Thornton.

60 ECA, Dean of Guild Petition to erect chloroform works, Duncan, Flockhart & Co., 15 April, 1871. Their existing premises were at 52 North Bridge.

61 ECA, Dean of Guild Petition to rebuild chloroform works, Duncan, Flockhart & Co., 16 January 1890.

62 ECA, Dean of Guild Petition to erect a soda water factory, Duncan, Flockhart & Co., 29 January 1875

63 Kohl 1844, part i, 53. E Patricia Dennison is indebted to Martin Rackwitz for this information.

64 ECA, Ms 'Journal of correspondence regarding slaughter houses', shelf ref. 48, page index 54.

65 ECA, Ms, 'Dean of Guild Records, burgh engineer's drawings', 14. vii, 1887.

66 Information from The People's Story Museum, Canongate.

67 E Patricia Dennison is indebted to Dr Irene Maver for her views.

68 Macnee, J, 1829, writer, taken in shorthand, 'Trial of William Burke and Helen McDougal before the Justiciary at Edinburgh on Wednesday, December 24, 1828 for the Murder of Margery Campbell or Docherty'.

69 *Edinburgh Pictorial*, 19 March 1954.

70 *The Poor of Edinburgh; or, Reflections of the Canongate 1842*, London 1842.

71 Tron, at 34.55, and Grassmarket, at 32.52, were both worse than Canongate. St Giles, at 28.8, was slightly better.

72 Littlejohn was not alone in his unwillingness to advocate more than the absolute minimum in the way of plumbing provision. In 1885, Octavia Hill, who with her army of women collectors had taken over, cleaned up and, in a superficial way, improved many existing slums in London, from the 1840s onwards, gave evidence at the Royal Commission into state of working class housing: 'I should not carry the water and drains all over the place; I think that is ridiculous. If you have water on every floor, that is quite sufficient for working people'.

73 The design was by Dick, Peddie, Mackay & Jamieson, 1949–53. ECA, Dean of Guild Petition, William Younger & Co., to erect public convenience at 124 Canongate, 28 October 1949.

74 Geddes is a complicated character whose achievements and importance lie well beyond the scope of this study. For a good grounding in Geddes's work see Geddes 1910, 537–74; Geddes 1915; Meller 1990; Welter 2002.

75 *The Life of a Slum Child*, c 1900, NMRS ED/9683–93. The original was with Robert Hurd & Partners, who later renovated this area.

Chapter 15

Canongate in the 20th century

E PATRICIA DENNISON and JOHN LOWREY

15.1 Transformation in the Canongate

E PATRICIA DENNISON

The people of Canongate were a depleted number throughout the 20th century. Two World Wars and the savage force of the Depression took their toll as in other areas, but Canongate became increasingly a backwater of Edinburgh, of largely less economically robust members of society. Rationalisation of Younger's brewing empire had a profound effect on the area. In 1931 William Younger's combined with William McEwan's to form Scottish Brewers Ltd. In the same year, the old brewery buildings on the north side of the site were demolished, to be replaced with a new brewhouse and tunrooms, in typically contemporary style, with granite plinth, red brick superstructure and narrow mullioned windows. Further impact on the townscape and the life of the locality came in the 1950s, with the ceasing of brewing operations, and by 1961 the general offices were extended eastwards and northwards up Horse Wynd, culminating in the mid-1960s with conversion of the brew-house, in 1968 with completion of a new computer block and in the 1970s with modifications and alterations along Horse Wynd.

Ambitious housing programmes had two main impacts: rehousing outwith the central core of the Old Town helped to reduce the reality of poverty, while renovation and rebuild improved, though did not totally remove, the air of depredation. Common water closets (lavatories) and water supplies were for many still the norm. But new council housing in the 1920s and 1930s did provide, for some, water closets inside individual homes rather than on common stairs, and private double sinks for washing, thus overcoming the need to go to the communal wash-house. Many women, however, missed the community spirit that such contacts with neighbours provided. Although by 1946 many had been re-housed outwith Canongate, of the remaining families, 80 per cent were still housed in one or two rooms (Kinnear 1969, 9). Glasgow had over 70 per cent dwellings of single or two rooms in 1901 and was stigmatised as the most overcrowded city

in the United Kingdom, while Paris and Berlin had 57 and 35 per cent respectively in this category (Cameron 2000, 126). Compared with these cities, the miserable state of Canongate becomes clearer. By 1949, there were 4369 people still resident in Canongate, making it the highest net residential density in the whole of Edinburgh, while also having the highest industrial area per percentage total area, apart from only Granton, Newhaven and Leith (Abercrombie & Plumstead 1949, 86). By the 1951 census, 20.6 per cent of the people of Holyrood lived at a level of more than two per room. St Giles, Central Leith and Craigmillar were only marginally worse. The equivalent percentages for Morningside and Murrayfield–Cramond were 1.9 and 1.5 respectively (Census 1951). The middle classes had inevitably relocated into more commodious suburbs, leaving the Canongate to be claimed by the working classes (Morris 2000, 425–6). Power and wealth now firmly resided elsewhere in Edinburgh.

15.2 Housing improvements in the 20th century

JOHN LOWREY

The first major figure in 20th-century development of housing in the Canongate was Ebenezer Macrae, the City Architect in the inter-war period who was responsible both for the creation of most of Edinburgh's pre-World War II council house schemes and for the rehabilitation of parts of the central area. These two things were closely related. Macrae was in many ways an unreconstructed sanitary reformer, notwithstanding an undoubted awareness of Geddes's ideas. He was certainly responsible for much slum clearance in the city, with the inhabitants being decanted to the new peripheral schemes like Niddrie and Craigmillar. Within the city, he adopted a ruthless approach to the slums, including some of those that were also part of the historic fabric of the city. In the Canongate his very distinctive, chunky rubble façades are a prominent feature of the townscape, especially in the central area around Moray House. In some cases,

Figure 15.1
Holyrood and the Canongate from Calton Hill

in dealing with subdivided properties, his approach was to demolish, but to record the historic fabric he was destroying. Thus Craig's Close was recorded for posterity, but was demolished to make way for the new municipal offices that Macrae built next to the City Chambers (Macrae 1934, 37–8), and Elphinstone Court, in the area behind St Patrick's Church, was demolished as an unsaveable slum, but its ornate lintel carrying the date of its construction (1679) was retained and built into the renovated Acheson House a few years later (Macrae 1929, 12–15; Gifford *et al* 1984, 215). In a lecture delivered to the Edinburgh Women's Citizens' Association (housing committee) in 1934, Macrae spoke in great detail about the criteria he employed in deciding which buildings should survive and which could not. In this he was guided by the requirements of modern standards of space, light and sanitary arrangements and conservation issues seem to have taken a secondary role. However, it would be wrong to portray Macrae simply as a destroyer of historic buildings, for, in fact, he was greatly involved, according to his lecture, in a number of important restorations of this period, including Huntly House (Macrae 1934).[1]

In the pre-war period Macrae worked under the 1927 Canongate/Corstorphine Improvement Scheme in which hundreds of houses were condemned by the Chief Sanitary Inspector, Allan Watt Ritchie, who described conditions that were hardly different from those outlined by Littlejohn 80 years earlier.[2] Among the results of that was the demolition of two groups of tenements on opposite sides of the street. One of these was 100–?110 Canongate (2–4 Bull's Close) and the other was 221–229 Canongate, in the area known as Big Jack's Close, both rebuilt from 1930. The latter was mentioned in Macrae's 1934 lecture, in which he talks about how the building was condemned and emptied, but the tenants broke back in and reoccupied it. The reasons for this are not clear and seem not to have been of much interest to Macrae. It may be that it says something about community life in the Canongate despite the appalling conditions people were forced to live under, or it may say even more about the peripheral schemes to whch they had been decanted (Macrae 1934, 4). In any case, the buildings were soon emptied and demolished. Here and elsewhere in the historic centre of the city, Macrae developed a particular language for his modern tenements that was broadly sympathetic to the vernacular burgh architecture around. He used unharled, deeply pointed rubble work, often with dressed margins. This was sometimes combined with

moulded doorcases bearing date stones, in response to some of their 17th-century neighbours. Elevations were plain but enlivened very often with wall-head dormers in substantial gablets that broke up the outline of the building. Most of these features were to be found both at Bull's Close and at Big Jack's Close, which had the added refinement of balconies on the back of the houses, looking towards the north and the views over Calton Hill. This linked them with earlier council and other working-class housing in the city from the late 19th and early 20th century, where such features had been used for the purposes of cross-ventilation, but also perhaps linked in with Macrae's interest in Continental apartment blocks, that culminated in his combination of the same Canongate, Scots vernacular, with cantilevered balconies on the front of the buildings at Piershill in 1937.

Macrae's final contribution to the Old Town came during the war, when he put together a plan for the future development of the area (Macrae 1945; 1947). Macrae's focus was on the historic buildings in the Old Town, the strategy for future planning, including the balance of industry and other uses, the creation of green space within the Canongate and the development of the road system. As for the first of these, Macrae identified a considerable number of historic buildings, all of them pre-19th century and most pre-18th century in date. Some were identified as candidates for restoration as housing, including Nisbet of Dirleton's house, slightly west of Queensberry House and dating from 1624. This was acquired by the city in 1949 and renovated a few years later. Similarly, Whitehorse Close was earmarked by him for repair and reuse, and this was done by the Frank Mears practice in the postwar period. Queensberry House was categorised among buildings that were 'capable of use for some other purpose, or unsuitably used, or in disrepair' (Macrae 1945, 1). In terms of planning, he identified Queensberry House as suitable for industrial usage, although the firm 'should retain the exterior of the building, using it for some suitable purpose such as stores or offices' (Macrae 1945, Appendix). This was partly because he believed that Younger's owned the building already, having entered an agreement with the directors of the House of Refuge, who had been anticipating a move to Ingliston (Hume & Boyd c 1984, 36), but it also fitted in with his general ideas for the Canongate, which was that the population should be greatly decreased. He identified 1400 occupied houses, many of which, he argued, were in poor condition and could not be directly replaced because modern planning rules would not allow the same densities and 'the total number of future houses can therefore only be a fraction of the present' (Macrae 1945, 9). He argued that most new housing should be on the north side of the street because the south side, so dominated by the breweries, should be retained for industry.

Macrae also sought to improve access from the Old Town and city centre to Leith and London Road without putting undue pressure on the High Street and Canongate itself. His solution to this was to build on the long-established route through the Cowgate and South Back, redeveloped in the 19th century as Holyrood Road, with a new link to Abbeyhill and beyond. This new link was a redeveloped Horse Wynd, a wider road slightly west of the existing. This would have involved the partial demolition of the Abbey brewery, but perhaps he thought that that loss would have been offset by the acquisition of Queensberry House. Along with this, and as part of the strategy to decrease density and increase open space, Macrae proposed more open space at the foot of the Canongate to increase the general amenity, but, more specifically, to improve the environs of Holyrood Palace, pointing out that 'a public convenience commands the main entrance from the Canongate' (Macrae 1945, 5). This and other inappropriate buildings such as the public wash-house at Abbeyhill and Croft an Righ brewery also represented activities that should not impinge upon the consciousness of the monarch and should therefore be removed. Most of the ground freed by this and by the realignment of Horse Wynd, along with demolition of almost everything around Queensberry House (with the exception of Nisbet of Dirleton's house), was to be turned into parkland and garden ground.

Overall, Macrae's strategy for the Canongate was to retain industry on the south and develop the north for such new housing as was to be allowed. Cultural and educational activities were to be encouraged; this partly harked back to pre-war initiatives like Huntly House, but also included a new museum at Abbeyhill. Communications were to be improved, relieving traffic pressure on the Bridges and, finally, the setting of the royal palace was to be greatly enhanced.

By 1947, when he issued the second report, Patrick Abercrombie and Derek Plumstead had already started their work on a city-wide development plan, finally published in 1949 (Abercrombie & Plumstead 1949). Abercrombie was clearly aware of what Macrae was proposing and is mentioned twice in Macrae's second report: once in connection with industry in the

Canongate and once in relation to road layout, both of which subjects were being appraised by Abercrombie at the time that Macrae was writing (Macrae 1947, 3–4). The relationship between these two strong individuals seems to have been an interesting one. Macrae had been responsible for the development of the city and for creating a policy for its historic buildings since the mid-1920s. He was well thought of by the elected representatives for his commonsense approach and he is certainly a distinct presence in the Abercrombie report. But, from the evidence of that report, it seems that he and Abercrombie did not see eye to eye, especially over the historic centre of the city. Macrae actually wrote the historical background chapter which formed the introduction to the report (Abercrombie & Plumstead 1949, 5–16). Although the work is labelled 'A Civic Survey', the role of the historical chapter was not one that Geddes would have recognised because the historical overview was not, as it was for Geddes, the device that would allow the reader to understand the evolution of the city and the intimate connection between present and past. Macrae, in fact, stressed its independence, writing that 'this chapter has been written independently and its inclusion does not necessarily indicate the writer's agreement with the conclusions or recommendations of the main report' (Abercrombie & Plumstead 1949, 5). It is quite clear that Abercrombie completely disagreed with Macrae's analysis of the Canongate. Time after time there is implied or quite explicit contradiction of Macrae's 1945 proposals. Abercrombie argued that the logic of clearing certain unsavoury activities from around the Palace, especially the demolition of Croft an Righ brewery, was not followed through because the Abbey brewery was even closer and surely just as insalubrious a neighbour (Abercrombie & Plumstead, 1949, 64). In fact, Abercrombie argued, industry should be completely removed from the Canongate and rather than running down the domestic architecture, the industrial land should be rezoned for housing, albeit at fairly low density, but at a level that would make the Canongate sustainable as a community. Abercrombie's other main disagreement with Macrae was over road layout. This is largely outside the scope of this study, but the most relevant aspect of his ideas was the argument that Macrae's proposal for relieving the traffic on the Bridges was inadequate. Instead, he proposed a complex system of roads, including a tunnel through the west end of Calton Hill, a bridge over Waverley Station, a tunnel under the High Street, and a bridge over the Cowgate, all to accommodate a new road running parallel with South Bridge, that would link north and south of the city and made Macrae's realigned Horse Wynd look pretty puny by comparison.

The removal of industry was, of course, a big step and not at that time favoured by the industries concerned. Abercrombie's idea was that the breweries could be relocated to London Road and Craigmillar and the land thus freed up would allow housing for around 4000 people. This would be mainly in addition to the 3800 people who already lived there and was in stark contrast to Macrae's envisaged Canongate population of 1300.[3] Of course, it meant that Queensberry House would have to be found another function and here Abercrombie struck a slightly prophetic note:

> Queensberry House, it is suggested, should be retained for institutional or cultural uses with some modification to the present building to restore it to its original size and character. The garden space on the south side should be retained (Abercrombie & Plumstead 1949, 64).

In the end, however, it was Macrae's pragmatism rather than Abercrombie's logic that won the day. On Monday 3 July 1950, both reports were considered by the planning committee in order to establish the basis for the future of the Canongate. Macrae's report won by ten votes to two mainly because of the problems associated with moving the breweries, who clearly did not want to go.[4] Abercrombie was not present at the Planning Committee meeting but Plumstead gamely argued his case, even suggesting that compensation costs to the brewery could be met by government assistance and by building a block of luxury flats in the area, as private housing that would raise revenue for the city.

The only victory Abercrombie won was on Queensberry House, which was to be retained 'as an institution or for residential use'.[5] It was to be another 50 years, however, before it was restored 'to its original size', as he recommended. The future development of the Canongate, and of housing in particular, was to follow Macrae's recommendations. By 1950, when the report was approved, Macrae had retired and the work that was carried out over the next 20 or so years was, for the most part, not carried out by the City Architect's Department, built up so carefully by Macrae over his 25 years in post. Instead, most of the subsequent developments in the area went to architects in private practice, working with the City. Apart from those already mentioned at the foot of the Canongate, there were four main developments, three of which were by Robert Hurd. Hurd had been

a pupil of Frank Mears and was strongly influenced by the Geddesian philosophy of conservative surgery and traditionalism in infill, burgh architecture. Hurd's approach was influenced partly by the general need to produce an architecture that was sympathetic to its surroundings but also, in two cases out of the three, his developments were directly juxtaposed with historic setpiece buildings (Glendinning et al 1996, 424). The earliest was in the vicinity of the Canongate Tolbooth, at 171–197 Canongate, built from 1954–8. Here Hurd introduced what was to be a characteristic of his work in the Canongate of combining new and old buildings and, on the new buildings, using traditional finishes, from coloured render to timber. He also introduced the idea of an arcade, linking his work with the Scottish 17th-century tradition of the 'piazza', that can be seen at Gladstone's Land, but at one one time was also seen on a larger scale within the Old Town. A similar approach was adopted in the 1956–8 development of the area around Morocco Land (249–263 Canongate), where the informal mix of materials is complemented by a reduction in scale (from five stories in the original buildings to four in the new ones) and an irregular building line. Almost opposite, at Chessel's Court, the now familiar Hurd approach was again adopted in the last of his big Canongate projects, this time with Ian Begg as architect, in 1958–66. The important aspect of this site was not only the creation of a new architecture to the street but also the development of the area behind, in a manner that would incorporate the 18th-century building and retain the open nature of the space (this was the area where St Saviour's nursery garden had been situated). In this case, the wider, flatter arcades do not simply provide cover for shoppers, but provide access to the square beyond and break the line of the street by allowing glimpses into the open space beyond the severe line of the street.

Further east, almost opposite Queensberry House, a rather different approach was taken in the development and, if Hurd represented the traditionalist approach, Basil Spence, Glover and Ferguson's work at 65–103 Canongate represents the Modernist. This is the latest of the main housing developments (1966–9), but perhaps there was some indication of a change of attitude in the 1958 proposal for the same site by the city architect, Alexander Steele, whose design incorporated a nine-storey tower block behind Reid's Close.[6] The buildings actually executed by Spence combine traditional, rubble finishes, associated with a particular Scottish identity in architecture, with rough concrete Brutalism, that linked with the wider currents of international architecture of the time, but perhaps most pertinently in the Scottish context, with his work in the Gorbals. Spence's work has been dismissed as 'aggressive' with the 'clumsy concrete balconies' attracting particular criticism (Gifford *et al* 1984, 215), but it certainly does not represent an alien, Modernist imposition on the street. Spence was not interested in historical pastiche, of either the Macrae or the Hurd variety, but he was certainly trying to create a suitably modern, and Scottish, response to the historical context in which he was working. This is to be found not only in the materials, the combination of domestic and commercial and the variation on Hurd's arcading, but, arguably, even in the north elevations. Here, he did not adopt the vernacular of the circular stair tower and the harled frontage, as others did, but a Brutalist concrete composition of detached stairs and projecting balconies. There was a context for this, seen for example in Macrae's work at Big Jack's Close, where the balconies are slightly at odds with the vernacular of the street front and pick up on a theme in early 20th-century public housing. Spence provides another version of that, but his motives almost certainly had nothing to do with the sanitary concern with cross-ventilation, and had far more to do with the more romantic notion of exploiting and controlling the stupendous views available on the north side of his tenements.

It would be dangerous to read too much into Spence's motives, and indeed sources, in the Canongate, but perhaps it is appropriate to conclude that his work demonstrates that, by 1966, there was more to historical context than traditional burgh architecture or aristocratic housing. As a postscript to this section on housing, and to take the story beyond the now outdated proposals of both Macrae and Abercrombie, it is worth very briefly highlighting the huge changes that have taken place in the area since the breweries and the other industries finally did leave the Canongate. The major achievement of the John Hope Masterplan of 1993, and of the architecture that has been built on the south side of the street since

then, is that it recognises that the historic context is important, but that the context is complex and varied and includes the more recent history of the site, as well as the traditional. This has meant that the work there has not simply been a matter of 'reinstating' a medieval street pattern, far less about zoning any single use for the area. Instead, there is a mixture of densities and a mixture of scale that recalls the suburban/industrial history of the site. Historical pastiche is not necessary or appropriate, except in those few instances where the new work breaks through to the Canongate itself. Strangely, although Ebenezer Macrae, in his proposals of 1945, was concerned with open space in the Canongate, it was not so much landscape as Palace garden that seemed to concern him. By contrast, in the present remodelling of the area, there is, on plan and execution, a very strong awareness of the views to the south, towards Salisbury Crags and Holyrood Park. And this, finally, allows us to move from housing to the one building that neither Macrae, Abercrombie, nor, for that matter, the third Duke of Queensberry, had envisaged for this site, the Scottish Parliament, which, in Miralles words, 'sits in the land', looking towards and integrating with the landscape around, concerned not only with its immediate locale, but with symbolising the country as a whole.

Notes

1 John Lowrey is grateful to Dr John Frew, University of St Andrews, for this information on Macrae and, in particular for the three references discussed here.

2 ECA, Precognition of Allan Watt Ritchie in *Acts, Reports, Bylaws etc.* (1928) Q10.

3 The *Scotsman*, Tuesday 4 July 1950: 'Macrae Plan for the Canongate'.

4 *Edinburgh Evening News*, Wednesday 4 May 1949: 'An Editor's causerie. 200 years of brewing: Edinburgh firm's record: Burns' Howff link'. Article on Younger's, which includes a clear statement from one of the directors that they had no wish to depart their historic site.

5 The *Scotsman*, Tuesday July 4 1950: 'Macrae Plan for the Canongate'.

6 Illustrated in both the *Scotsman* and the *Edinburgh Evening News*, 29 January 1958.

Glossary

ashlar	a square hewn stone for building	*merk*	a unit of Scots money
base court	an inferior court, usually at the rear of the house	*mortcloth*	a pall or cloth covering a coffin on its way to the grave
baxter	baker	*pand*	a pledge
bolection moulding	a moulding raised above the plane of the main surface area	*precept*	Written order from court for its representative to carry something out
burgage plot	a medieval term for a property of land in a burgh	*precept of clare constat*	An order in which a feudal superior acknowledges the heir to landed property held of the superior, and which authorises the giving of sasine.
cavetto	concave moulding of quarter-round section		
coble	Either a vat for steeping malt in brewing or a cess pit (don't mix them up!)	*porte cochère*	porch large enough to admit wheeled vehicles
coomb	a sloping or curved element between a wall and a ceiling	*pulvinated frieze*	frieze of bold convex profile
		quoin	a corner-stone
corps de logis	the main building as distinct from the wings	*retour*	the part of a wall or moulding that turns away (usually at right angles) from the previous direction
cyma recta profile	classical moulding with double curve		
daills	boards	*rybat*	a side-piece of dressed stone in a window or door
decreet	Final judgement of a court	*sarking*	boards laid on the rafters to support the covering slates
decreet of apprysing	Judgement whereby a debtor's heritable property could be sold to settle a debt	*sasine*	Both the symbolic act of taking possession of a piece of heritable property and the legal instrument which proved that possession had taken place.
dook	wooden peg		
enfilade	reception rooms in a formal series		
farriery	the art of shoeing horses	*scantling*	sawn wood
feuferme	a perpetual lease	*skew*	the slope of a gable head
indweller	A resident	*skewputt*	bracket at the bottom end of a skew
infeftment	Act of giving symbolic possession of heritable property	*stent*	rate; tax
ingo	the return face of a wall, usually where it forms the inner side of a doorway or window-opening	*tack*	a lease, usually of landed property
		thackstane	a stone used as a weight to hold down thatch
lorimer	a maker of small metalwork		

thirled	bound as a tenant to grind grain at a certain mill; under a legal obligation	*wall press*	shelved alcove
toft	a homestead and its land	*yett*	a grated iron door or gate with interlacing bars
wadset	mortgage; deed from debtor to creditor assigning rents of land until debts are paid	*vennel*	a narrow alley or lane between houses
		voussoir	stone forming part of an arch

References

Abbreviations used in the end notes and references

ABRC	Archives and Record Centre, University of Glasgow
APS	Innes, C & Thomson, T (eds) 1854 *Acts of the Parliament of Scotland*, 12 vols. London.
BGS	British Geological Survey
BOEC	*Book of the Old Edinburgh Club*
CSPScot	*Calendar of the State Papers relating to Scotland and Mary, Queen of Scots, 1547–1603*, eds J Bain and others (Edinburgh, 1898–)
BL	British Library
ECA	Edinburgh City Archives
Mar & Kelly	Mss *Report on the manuscripts of the Earl of Mar & Kellie preserved at Alloa House, N B*. London, [s.n.], 1904.
NAS	National Archives of Scotland
NLS	National Library of Scotland
OS	Ordnance Survey
PRO	Public Record Office
RCAHMS	Royal Commission on the Ancient and Historical Monuments of Scotland
RMS	Thomson J M *et al* (eds) 1882–1914 *Registrum Magni Sigilli Regum Scotorum*. Edinburgh.
RRS	Barrow, G W S, Duncan, A A M & Webster, B (eds) 1960– *Regesta Regum Scottorum, 1153–1406*. Edinburgh.
SBA	Scottish Brewers Association
SNH	Scottish National Heritage
SRO	Scottish Record Office
TA	Dickson, T & Balfour Paul, Sir J (eds) *Accounts of the Lord High Treasurer of Scotland*, 1877–1914. Edinburgh.
MW	Paton, H M (ed.) 1957 *Accounts of the Masters of Works for building and repairing royal palaces and castles*, vol. 1, 1529–1615. Edinburgh.

References

Abercrombie, P & Plumstead, D 1949 *A Civic Survey and Plan for the City of Edinburgh*. Edinburgh.

Adam, W 1980 *Vitruvius Scoticus*, facsimile edition. Edinburgh.

Addyman, T 2001 *Gallery House, Angus: analytical notes*. Unpubl. typescript.

Anderson, A H 1949 *The Burgh of the Canongate and its Court*. University of Edinburgh, PhD thesis.

Anderson, A O (ed.) 1938 *The Chronicle of Holyrood*. Edinburgh.

Anderson, H M 1935 The grammar school of the Canongate. *Book of the Old Edinburgh Club* 20, 1–25.

Armet, H (ed.) 1951 *Register of the Burgesses of the Burgh of Canongate, 1622–1733*. Scot Rec Soc.

Armet, H (ed.) 1962 *Extracts from the Records of the Burgh of Edinburgh, 1689–1701*.

Armet, H (ed.) 1967 *Extracts from the Records of the Burgh of Edinburgh, 1701–18*.

Aspinwall, B & McCaffrey, J 1985 A comparative view of the Irish in Edinburgh in the nineteenth century. In Swift, R & Gilley, S (eds) *The Irish in the Victorian City*, 130–49. London.

Atkinson, D R & Oswald, A 1969 London Clay Tobacco Pipes. *J Brit Archaeol Assoc* 32, 171–227.

Bailey, R 1996 *Scottish Architects' Papers: a source book*. Edinburgh.

Baillie, H M 1967 Etiquette and the Planning of State Apartments in Baroque Palaces. *Archaeologia* 101, 169–99.

Bain, S 1998 Excavation of a medieval cemetery at Holyrood Abbey, Edinburgh. *Proc Soc Antiq Scot* 128, 1047–78.

Baird, W 1898 *Annals of Duddingston & Portobello*. Edinburgh.

Balcarres, C Earl of 1841 *Memoirs Touching the Revolution in Scotland, MDCLXXXVIII – MDCXC*. Bannatyne Club, Edinburgh.

Ballard, A 1916 The theory of the Scottish burgh. *Scot Hist Rev* 13.

Barnard, A 1890–1 *The Noted Breweries of Great Britain and Ireland* (1890 vols 1–3, 1891 vol. 4). London.

Barrow, G W S (ed.) 1999 *The Charters of King David I*. Woodbridge.

Barrow, G W S 1981 *Kingship and Unity. Scotland 1000–1306*. London.

Bateson, M 1904 *Borough Customs*. Selden Society.

Begg, J 1849 *Pauperism and the Poor Laws*. Edinburgh.

Begg, J 1851 *Drunkenness and Pauperism*. Edinburgh.

Bell, D 1994 *The discernment of merit: a review of Georgian Edinburgh, 1756–93*. Heriot Watt University, PhD thesis.

Bell, G 1849 *Day and Night in the Wynds of Edinburgh*. Edinburgh, reprinted Leicester, 1973.

Bell, G 1850 *Blackfriars' Wynd Analyzed*. Edinburgh, reprinted Leicester, 1973.

Bensen, R A 1978 *South-west Fife and the Scottish revolution: the presbytery of Dunfermline, 1633–52*. University of Edinburgh, MLitt thesis.

Beveridge, E (ed.) 1917 *The Burgh Records of Dunfermline*. Edinburgh.

Blaikie, W B 1909 Edinburgh at the time of the occupation of Prince Charles. *Book of the Old Edinburgh Club* 2, 1–60.

Blanchard, L 1987a Kirk Close. In Holdsworth 1987, 18–46.

Blanchard, L 1987b The excavated buildings. In Holdsworth 1987, 84–7.

Boardman, S 1996 *The Early Stewart Kings; Robert II and Robert III, 1371–1406*. East Linton.

Bonar, A 1856 *The Canongate, Ancient and Modern*. Edinburgh.

Boog Watson, C B 1923 Notes on the names of the closes and wynds of old Edinburgh. *Book of the Old Edinburgh Club* 12, 1–156.

Boog Watson, C B 1927 Lectures, VI, Queensberry House, Canongate. *Book of the Old Edinburgh Club* 15, appendix, 19–21.

Boog Watson, C B 1932 *The Aged Poor: Centenary of the House of Refuge 1832–1932*. Edinburgh.

Boog Watson, C B 1996 *The Notes of Charles Boog Watson: history and derivations of Edinburgh street names*. Edinburgh.

Brooks, N P & Whittington, G 1977 Planning and growth in the mediaeval Scottish burgh: the example of St Andrews. *Trans Inst Brit Geographers* 2(2).

Bullough, D A & Storey, R L (eds) 1971 *The Study of Medieval Records*. Oxford.

Burgess, C F (ed.) 1966 *The Letters of John Gay*. Oxford.

Calderwood, A B (ed.) 1961 *The Buik of the Kirk of the Canagait*. Scot Rec Soc.

Cameron, A I 1925 The Canongate crafts: an agreement of 1610. *Book of the Old Edinburgh Club* 14, 25–44.

Cameron, A S & Stones, J A 2001 *Aberdeen: an in-depth view of the city's past*. Edinburgh: Soc Antiq Scot Monograph 19.

Cameron, E A 2000 Civil society, protest and parliament: housing and land in modern Scotland. In Dickinson, H T & Lynch, M (eds) *The Challenge to Westminster: sovereignty, devolution and independence*, 123–32. East Linton.

Carruthers, A (ed.) 1996 *The Scottish Home*. Edinburgh.

Catford, E F 1975 *Edinburgh, the Story of a City*. London.

Catford, E F (ed.) 1984 *Queensberry House and Hospital. A history*. Edinburgh.

Census 1841, district no. 685–3; area nos 11 & 12, ECA.

Census 1951, Report on the Fifteenth Census of Scotland, vol. 1, part 1, City of Edinburgh.

Chadwick, E 1842 *Report on the Sanitary Condition of the Labouring Population*. Edinburgh.

Chambers, R 1868 *Traditions of Edinburgh*. Edinburgh.

Charters and Other Documents Relating to the City of Glasgow, 1894–7, Glasgow.

City of Edinburgh Charity Organisation Society 1906 *Report on the Physical condition of Fourteen Hundred Schoolchildren in the City*. Edinburgh.

Clark, P & Houston, R A 2000 Culture and leisure, 1700–1840. In Clark, P (ed.) *Cambridge Urban History of Britain*, vol. 2. Cambridge.

Clive, J (ed.) 1974 *Henry Cockburn's Memorial of His Times*. London.

Cockburn, H A (ed.) 1910 *Memorials of his Time*. Edinburgh.

Cockburn, H A 1874 *Journal of, being a continuation of Memorials of His Time, 1831–54*, vols 1 & 2. Edinburgh.

Colvin, H 1978 A Scottish origin for English Palladianism? *Architect Hist* 17, 5–13.

Coope, R 1986 The 'Long Gallery': its origins, development, use and decoration. *Architect Hist* 29, 43–86.

Cowan, E J 1995 *Montrose: for Covenant and King*. Edinburgh.

Cowan, I B 1995 (ed. J Kirk) *The Medieval Church in Scotland*. Edinburgh.

Cowan, I B & Easson, D E (eds) 1976 *Medieval Religious Houses. Scotland*. London.

Cowan, W 1924 Bearford's Parks. *Book of the Old Edinburgh Club* 13, 79–91.

Cox, W 1935 *A History of Gardening in Scotland*. London.

Crowther, M A 1990 Health and welfare. In Fraser, W H & Morris, R J (eds) *People and Society in Scotland, vol II (1830–1914)*, 265–89. Edinburgh.

Dalyell, J (ed.) 1798 *Fragments of Scotish [sic] History*. Edinburgh.

Daniel, W S 1854 *History of the Abbey and Palace of Holyrood*. Edinburgh.

Daunton, M (ed.) 2000 *Cambridge Urban History of Britain*, vol. 3. Cambridge.

Davidson, J 1984 *The Royal Highland and Agricultural Society of Scotland. A Short History 1784–1984*. Ingliston.

Daunton, M (ed.) 2000 *Cambridge Urban History of Britain*. Cambridge.

Defoe, D 1724 *A Tour Through the Whole Island of Great Britain*. London.

Dennison, E P & Coleman, R 1996 *Historic Musselburgh*. Scottish Burgh Survey.

Dennison, E P & Coleman, R 2000 *Historic Linlithgow*. Scottish Burgh Survey.

Dennison, E P & Ewart, G 1998 *An Archaeological and Historical Assessment of the Proposed New Parliament of Scotland Site*. Unpublished Historic Scotland Report.

Dickinson, W C 1946 Burgh life from burgh records. *Aberdeen University Review* 21, 1945–6.

Dickinson, W C (ed.) 1949 *John Knox's History of the Reformation in Scotland*. Edinburgh.

Dingwall, H M 1994 *Late Seventeenth-Century Edinburgh*. Aldershot.

Donaldson, G 1971 *Scotland, James V–James VII*. Edinburgh.

Donnachie, I 1979 *A History of the Brewing Industry in Scotland*, 2nd edn 1998. Edinburgh.

Doubleday, H A & de Walden, H 1932 *The Complete Peerage*, vol. 8. London.

Douglas, D 1908 *The Scots Peerage*, vol. 5. Edinburgh.

Douglas, D 1910 *The Scots Peerage*, vol. 7. Edinburgh.

Driscoll, S T & Yeoman, P A 1997 *Excavations within Edinburgh Castle in 1988–91*. Edinburgh: Soc Antiq Scot Monograph 12.

Dunbar, J G 1964 The Palace of Holyroodhouse during the first half of the sixteenth century. *Archaeol J* 120, 242–54.

Dunbar, J G 1966 *The Historic Architecture of Scotland*. London.

Dunbar, J G 1975 The building activities of the Duke and Duchess of Lauderdale, 1670–82. *Archaeol J* 132, 202–13.

Dunbar, J G 1984 Some Aspects of the planning of Scottish royal palaces in the sixteenth century. *Architect Hist* 27, 15–24.

Dunbar, J G 1999 *Scottish Royal Palaces: the architecture of the royal residences during the late medieval and early Renaissance periods*. East Linton.

Dunbar, J G & Davies, C 1990 Some late seventeenth-century building contracts. *Miscellany* 11, *Scottish History Society* 3, 269–328.

Dunbar, J G & Davies, K 1981 Some late seventeenth-century building contracts. *Misc Scotl Hist Soc* 11, 269–324.

Duncan, A A M 1978 *Scotland. The making of the kingdom*. Edinburgh.

Dupree, M 2000 The provision of social services. In Daunton (ed.) 2000, vol. 3.

Easson, D E (ed.) 1947 *Charters of the Abbey of Coupar Angus*. Edinburgh.

Edington, C 1995 Court and Culture in Renaissance Scotland. Sir David Lindsay of the Mount, 1486–1555. East Lothian.

Edwards, O D 1993 *Burke and Hare*. Edinburgh.

Engels, F 1844 *The Condition of the Working Class in England*. Stanford.

Ewan, E 1990 *Townlife in Fourteenth-Century Scotland*. Edinburgh.

Extracts from the records of the burgh of Canongate near Edinburgh, MDLXI–MDLXXVIII, 1840. Miscellany of the Maitland Club, 2.

Fawcett, R 1994 *Scottish Abbeys and Priories*. London.

Fawcett, R 1996 *Argyll's Lodging, Stirling*. Edinburgh.

Ferguson, W 1968 *Scotland: 1689 to the present*. Edinburgh.

Fergusson, R 1905 *The Poetical Works of Robert Fergusson*. Paisley.

Fletcher, H R & Brown, W H 1970 *The Royal Botanic Garden, Edinburgh 1670–1970*. Edinburgh.

Flinn, M (ed.) 1977 *Scottish Population History from the Seventeenth Century to the 1930s*. Cambridge.

Forbes Gray, W 1924 Panmure House, Canongate. *Book of the Old Edinburgh Club* 13, appendix, 11–17.

Forbes Gray, W 1933 The musical society of Edinburgh and St Cecilia's Hall. *Book of the Old Edinburgh Club* 19, 189–245.

Forbes Gray, W 1940 Gleanings from Scottish exchequer rolls. *Book of the Old Edinburgh Club* 23, 38–62.

Forbes Gray, W 1953 St John Street: an early civic improvement. *Book of the Old Edinburgh Club* 28, 59–75.

Forbes, Hon. Mrs A 1897 *Curiosities of a Scots Charta Chest*. Edinburgh.

Fountainhall, Sir John Lauder of 1928 Historical notices of Scotish [sic] affairs, 1661–1688. *Book of the Old Edinburgh Club* 16, 77–167.

Fraser, W 1890 *The Melvilles, Earls of Melville and the Leslies, Earls of Leven*. Edinburgh.

Fraser, W H & Morris, R J (eds) 1990 *People and Society in Scotland*, vol. 2, 1830–1914. Edinburgh.

Fraser, W H 1990 Developments in leisure. In Fraser & Morris 1990.

Gallagher, D B 1987 Pipes for the Company of Scotland: the documentary evidence. In Davey, P J *The Archaeology of the Clay Tobacco Pipe, vol. 10, Scotland*, 233–8. Oxford.

Gallagher, D B 1998 Holyrood Abbey: the disappearance of a monastery. *Proc Soc Antiq Scot* 128(2), 1079–99.

Geddes, P 1910 'The Civic Survey of Edinburgh', *RIBA Town Planning Conference, London, 10–15 October 1910, Transactions*, 1910, 537–74.

Geddes, P 1915 *Cities in evolution: an introduction to the Town Planning Movement and to the Study of Civics*. London.

Geddie, J 1930 Sculptured stones of the 'Royal Mile'. *Book of the Old Edinburgh Club* 17, 22–48.

Gifford, J, McWilliam, C & Walker, D 1984 *The Buildings of Scotland: Edinburgh*. Harmondsworth.

Girouard, M 1978 *Life in the English Country House*. Second edition 1980. Harmondsworth.

Glendinning, M, MacInnes, R & MacKechnie, A A 1996 *History of Scottish Architecture from the Renaissance to the Present Day*. Edinburgh.

Gooder, J 1999 Archaeological Excavation at Plot N, Holyrood North Development Area, Edinburgh: Data Structure Report. Unpublished AOC Archaeology Group Report.

Grant, J 1881–3 *Old and New Edinburgh*, vols 1–3. London.

Gray, R Q 1976 *The Labour Aristocracy in Victorian Edinburgh*. Oxford.

Gray, W F 1935 An 18th-century riding school. *Book of the Old Edinburgh Club* 20, 111–59.

Grieve, M 1931 *Modern Herbal*. London.

Hannah, H 1927 The sanctuary of Holyrood. *Book of the Old Edinburgh Club* 15, 55–98.

Hannay, R K (ed.) 1932 *Acts of the Lords of Council in Public Affairs, 1501–54*. Edinburgh.

Harris, S 1996 *Place Names of Edinburgh and Their Origins and History*. Edinburgh.

Harrison, J 1919 *The History of the Monastery of the Holy-Rood and of the Palace of Holyrood House*. Edinburgh & London.

Holdsworth, P (ed.) 1987 *Excavations in the Medieval Burgh of Perth 1979–81*. Edinburgh: Soc Antiq Scot Monogr Series 5.

Home, B J 1908 Provisional list of old houses remaining in High Street and Canongate of Edinburgh. *Book of the Old Edinburgh Club* 1, 1–30.

House of Refuge for the Destitute, The 1835 *Second Report by the Committee of the House of Refuge for the Destitute, July 1835*. Edinburgh.

House of Refuge for the Destitute, The 1841 I: *Eighth Annual Report of the House of Refuge for the Destitute in Edinburgh from 1st October 1839, to 30th September 1840. II: Ninth Annual Report of the House of Refuge for the Destitute in Edinburgh, from 1st October 1840, to 30th September 1841.* Edinburgh.

Houston, R A 1994a *Social Change in the Age of Enlightenment: Edinburgh, 1660–1760.* Oxford.

Houston, R 1994b Fire and filth: Edinburgh's environment, 1660–1760. *Book of the Old Edinburgh Club* new series 3, 25–36.

Howard, D 1992 Dutch influence of Scottish architecture. In Lloyd Williams, J (ed.) *Dutch Art in Scotland, a Reflection of Taste.* Edinburgh, 33–48.

Howard, D 1995 *The Architectural History of Scotland: Scottish architecture from the Reformation to the Restoration, 1560–1660.* Edinburgh.

Hunt, J D & de Jong, J 1990 'For profit and ornament: the function and meaning of Dutch garden art in the period of William and Mary', in Hunt, J D (ed.) *The Dutch Garden in the Seventeenth Century*, 13–48. Dumbarton Oaks Colloquium on the History of Landscape Architecture, XII. Washington.

Hume Brown, P (ed.) 1891 *Early Travellers in Scotland.* Reprinted 1978. Edinburgh.

Hume, M & Boyd, S C 1984 *Queensberry House Hospital: a history.* Edinburgh.

Hurd, R 1952 *A History of Acheson House.* Edinburgh.

Hutton, R 1997 The triple-crowned islands. In Glassey, L K J (ed.) *The Reigns of Charles II and James VII and II.* London.

Innes, C (ed.) 1869 *Ancient Burgh Laws.* Scot Burgh Rec Soc.

Innes, C (ed.) 1867 *Ledger of Andrew Halyburton, 1492–1503.* Edinburgh.

Jacques, D & van der Horst, A J (eds) 1988 *The Gardens of William and Mary.* London.

Jamieson, F 1994 The Royal gardens of the Palace of Holyroodhouse, 1500–1603. *J Garden Hist Soc* 22(1), 18–36.

Jamieson, J H 1925 Some inns of the 18th century. *Book of the Old Edinburgh Club* 14, 121–46.

Keir, D 1951 *The Younger Centuries.* Edinburgh.

Kerr, H F 1922 Map of Edinburgh in the mid-18th century. *Book of the Old Edinburgh Club* 11, 1–20.

Kinnear, W 1969 The Canongate, Edinburgh. In Salmon, R B (ed.) *Field Excursions in Eastern Scotland.* Edinburgh.

Kirk, J 1989 *Patterns of Reform, Continuity and Change in the Reformation Kirk.* Edinburgh.

Kirkwood, R 1817 *This Plan of the City of Edinburgh and its Environs.* Edinburgh.

Kohl, J G 1844 *Reisen in Schottland.* Dresden/Leipzig, 2 Thle (in 1 Bd).

Laing, D 1854 On the state of the abbey church of Holyrood subsequent to the devastations committed by the English forces in the years 1544 and 1547. *Proc Soc Antiq Scot* 1, 1951–4, 101–15.

Law, A 1966 Teachers in Edinburgh in the 18th century. *Book of the Old Edinburgh Club* 22, 108–57.

Lawrie, A C 1905 *Early Scottish Charters Prior to 1153.* Glasgow.

Leneman, L & Mitchison, R 1998 *Sin in the City, 1660–1780.* Edinburgh.

Lewis, J H 1996 Excavations at St Andrews, Castlecliffe, 1988–90. *Proc Soc Antiq Scot* 126, 605–88.

Lindsay, I & Cosh, M 1973 *Inveraray and the Dukes of Argyll.* Edinburgh.

Littlejohn, J 1865 *Report on the Sanitary Condition of the City of Edinburgh.* Edinburgh.

Lockhart of Carnwath, G 1817 *The Lockhart Papers*, vol. 1. London.

Lowrey, J 1996 The influence of the Netherlands on Early Classicism and the Formal Garden in Scotland. *J Scot Soc Art Hist* 1, 20–34.

Lowrey, J 1999 Archive and archaeology: the prehistory of Queensberry House, Edinburgh. *Scottish Archives (J Scot Records Assoc)* 5, 29–40.

Lowrey, J 2000 The Furnishings of Queensberry House. *Regional Furniture. J Regional Furniture Soc* 14, 44–62.

Lynch, M 1981 *Edinburgh and the Reformation.* Edinburgh.

Lynch, M (ed.) 1987 *The Early Modern Town in Scotland.* London.

Lynch, M 1987 Introduction. In Lynch 1987, 1–35.

Lynch, M 1991 *Scotland. A new history.* London.

Lynch, M (ed.) 1987 *The Early Modern Town in Scotland.* London.

Lynch, M, Spearman, M & Stell, G (eds) 1988 *The Scottish Medieval Town.* Edinburgh.

Macaulay, J 1987 *The Classical Country House in Scotland, 1660–1800.* London.

MacDonald, A A 1991 Mary Stewart's entry to Edinburgh: an ambiguous triumph. *Innes Rev* 42(2), 101–10.

MacIvor I & Peterson, B 1984 Lauderdale at Holyrood, 1669–70. In Breeze, D J (ed.) *Studies in Scottish Antiquity presented to Stewart Cruden*, 249–68. Edinburgh.

Mackay, J 1879 *History of the Burgh of Canongate, with notes of the Abbey and Palace of Holyrood.* Edinburgh.

Mackay, J 1900 *History of the Burgh of Canongate, with notes of the Abbey and Palace of Holyrood.* Edinburgh. Second edition.

MacKechnie, A 1994 *Scots Court Architecture of the Early Seventeenth Century.* University of Edinburgh, PhD thesis.

Mackie, A 1963 *An Industrial History of Edinburgh.* Glasgow.

Mackie, C 1825 *The History of the Abbey, Palace, and Chapel Royal of Holyrood House including a description of the buildings as they now exist; with an account of the sanctuary for insolvent debtors.* Edinburgh.

Macky, J 1723 *A Journey through Scotland: in Familiar Letters from a Gentleman Here, to His Friend Abroad. Being the third volume which compleats Great Britain.* London.

Macmillan, D 2000 *Scottish Art 1460–2000.* Edinburgh.

MacQueen, H L & Windram, W J 1988 Laws and courts in the burghs. In Lynch *et al* (eds) 1988, 208–27.

Macrae, E J 1929 Details from Old Edinburgh: Elphinston House. *RIAS Quarterly* 41, 12–15.

Macrae, E J 1934 Craig's Close, High Street, Edinburgh. *RIAS Quarterly* 46, 37–8.

Macrae, E J 1934 The Manner in which Edinburgh deals with their ancient and historic buildings when these have to be reconstructed or adapted to modern requirements. Unpublished lecture notes delivered to the Housing Committee of the Edinburgh Women's Citizens Association, 16 November 1934. Typescript in Edinburgh Room, Edinburgh City Library.

Macrae, E J 1945 *City of Edinburgh. The Royal Mile. Report by the City Architect 1945*. Edinburgh.

Macrae, E J 1947 *City of Edinburgh. The Royal Mile. Second Report*. Edinburgh.

Mahood, L 1990 *The Magdalenes. Prostitution in the 19th century*. London.

Maitland, F W 1897 *Domesday Book and Beyond*. Cambridge.

Maitland, W 1753 *The History of Edinburgh from its Foundation to the Present Times*. Edinburgh.

Makey, W 1987 Edinburgh in mid-seventeenth century. In Lynch 1987, 192–218.

Malcolm, C A 1932 Incorporation of the cordiners of Canongate, 1538–1773. *Book of the Old Edinburgh Club* 18, 100–50.

Markus, T A 1982 Buildings for the sad, the bad and the mad in urban Scotland, 1780–1830. In Markus, T A (ed.) *Order in Space and Society*. Edinburgh.

Marshall, R K 1973 *The Days of Duchess Anne*. London.

Marwick, W H 1938 The incorporation of the tailors of Canongate. *Book of the Old Edinburgh Club* 22, 91–131,

Marwick, W H 1969 Municipal politics in Victorian Edinburgh. *Book of the Old Edinburgh Club* 33, 31–41.

Maule, H 1874 *Registrum de Panmure*. Edinburgh.

Maver, I 1998 Urbanisation. In Cooke, A, Donnachie, I, Macsween, A & Whatley, C A (eds) *Modern Scottish History, 1707 to the Present*, vol. 1. East Linton.

McCallum, I 1997 Historical notes on Chessels Court. *Book of the Old Edinburgh Club* new series, 4, 1–22.

McGladdery, C 1990 *James II*. Edinburgh.

McKean, C 2001 *The Scottish Chateau*. Stroud.

McNeill, P G B & MacQueen, H L (eds.) 1996 *Atlas of Scottish History to 1707*. Edinburgh.

Meikle, H W 1912 *Scotland and the French Revolution*. Glasgow.

Meller, H 1990 *Patrick Geddes, Social Evolutionist and City Planner*. London & New York.

Merriman, M 2000 *The Rough Wooings: Mary Queen of Scots, 1542–51*. East Linton.

Minay, P 1991 18th and early 19th-century Edinburgh seedsmen and nurserymen. *Book of the Old Edinburgh Club* new series, 1, 7–27.

Morris, R J 1998 Death, Chambers Street and Edinburgh corporation. In Cooke, A, Donnachie, I, MacSween, A & Whatley, C A (eds) *Modern Scottish History, 1707 to the Present*, vol. 4: *Readings, 1850 to the present*. East Linton.

Morris, R J 2000 Structure, culture and society in British towns. In Daunton, M (ed.) *The Cambridge Urban History of Britain, vol III (1840–1950)*, 395–426.

Morton, G 1999 *Unionist Nationalism: Governing Urban Scotland, 1830–1860*. East Linton.

Moxon, J 1655 *Vignola: Or the Compleat Architect*. London.

Murdoch, A 1998 *British History 1660–1832: National identity and local culture*. London.

Mylne, R S 1893 *The Master Masons to the Crown of Scotland and their works*. Edinburgh.

New Statistical Account of Scotland, vol. 1: List of Parishes: Edinburgh. 1845.

Noad, R 1928 The influence of the Low Countries on the architecture of Scotland. *Quarterly Inc Archit Scot* 28, 101–22.

Nokes, D 1995 *John Gay: A Profession of Friendship*. Oxford.

O'Sullivan, J 1995 Abbey, market and cemetery: topographical notes on Coupar Angus in Perthshire, with a description of archaeological excavations on glebe land by the parish church. *Proc Soc Antiq Scot* 125, 1045–68.

Ouston, H 1982 York in Edinburgh: James VII and the patronage of learning in Scotland, 1679–88. In Dwyer, J, Mason R A & Murdoch, A (eds) *New Perspectives on the Politics and Culture of Early Modern Scotland*, 133–55. Edinburgh.

Pryde, G S 1965 *The Burghs of Scotland: a critical list*. Oxford.

Ranger's Impartial List of the Ladies of Pleasure in Edinburgh. Edinburgh, 1775 (reprinted Edinburgh, 1978).

RCAHMS 1951 *An Inventory of the Ancient and Historical Monuments of the City of Edinburgh*. Edinburgh.

Reed, D & Lawson, J 1999 Ronaldson's Wharf, Sandport Street, Leith. *Discovery Excavation Scot*, 40.

Reed, D 1999 20 Calton Road, post-medieval urban settlement and burial ground. *Discovery Excavation Scot*, 35.

Reid, J 1683 *The Scots Gardener*. Edinburgh.

Riley, P W J 1979 *King William and the Scottish Politicians*. Edinburgh.

Ritchie, B 1999 *Good Company: the story of Scottish & Newcastle*. Edinburgh.

Robertson, F W 2000 *Early Scottish Gardeners and their Plants, 1650–1750*. East Linton.

Robinson, P 1985 'Tenements: A Pre-Industrial Urban Tradition', *Review of Scottish Culture*, 1, 52–64.

Rock, J 1987 The Hopetoun Chest at Newhailes House. *Burlington Magazine* 129(1013), 516–18.

Rodger, R 1999 *Housing the People*. Edinburgh.

Rodger, R 2001 *The Transformation of Edinburgh: Land, Property and Trust in the Nineteenth Century*. Cambridge.

Ross, T 1922 The Tailors' Hall, Canongate. *Book of the Old Edinburgh Club* 11, 125–71.

Sanderson, E C 1996 *Women and Work in 18th-Century Edinburgh*. Edinburgh.

Schofield, J 1976 Excavations south of Edinburgh High Street, 1973–74. *Proc Soc Antiq Scot* 107, 155–241.

Scottish Natural Heritage & British Geological Survey 1993 *Edinburgh, a Landscape Fashioned by Geology*. Edinburgh.

Selby Wright, R 1965 *An Illustrated Guide to the Canongate Kirk, Parish and Churchyard*. Edinburgh.

Selby Wright, R 1992 The School of the Royal College of Holyrood House. *Book of the Old Edinburgh Club* new series, 2, 133–5.

Shaw, M 1984 Northampton: excavating a 16th century tannery. *Curr Archaeol* 91, 241–4.

Simpson, J (ed.) 1980 Adam, William, *Vitruvius Scoticus*, facsimile publication. Edinburgh.

Simpson & Brown Architects 1997 *Queensberry House: a study for the Scottish Office: 22–31 December 1997*. Unpubl. report.

Sinclair, J 1905 Notes on the Holyrood 'Foir-yet' of James IV. *Proc Soc Antiq Scot* 39 (1904–5), 352–63.

Smith, J & Paton, H M 1940 St Leonards lands & hospital. *Book of the Old Edinburgh Club* 23, 111–46.

Smith, J S 1924 *Historic Stones and Stories of Bygone Edinburgh*. Edinburgh.

Smout, T C 1975 *A History of the Scottish People, 1560–1830*. Glasgow.

Spearman, R M 1988a The medieval townscape of Perth. In Lynch *et al* (eds) 1988, 42–59.

Spearman, R M 1988b Workshops, materials and debris: evidence of early industries. In Lynch *et al* (eds) 1988, 134–47.

Stevenson, S, Simpson, A T & Holmes, N 1981 *Historic Edinburgh, Canongate and Leith: the archaeological implications of development*. Scottish Burgh Survey.

Stones, J A (ed.) 1987 *A Tale of Two Burghs*. Aberdeen.

Survey of London 1963 *Survey of London, vol. 32, The Parish of St James Westminster, Part 2, North of Piccadilly*. London.

Sykes, C S 1989 *Private Palaces: Life in the Great London Houses*. London.

Swain, M 1988 *Tapestries and Textiles at the Palace of Holyroodhouse*. Edinburgh.

Taylor, J 1903 *A Journey to Edenborough in Scotland, 1705*.

Thin, R 1927 The old infirmary and earlier hospitals. *Book of the Old Edinburgh Club* 15, 135–65.

Thompson, A, Grew, F & Schofield, J 1984 Excavations at Aldgate, London, 1974. *Post-Medieval Archaeol* 18, 1–148.

Thornton, P 1990 *Seventeenth-Century Interior Decoration in England, France and Holland*. Yale, Newhaven & London.

Thornton, P & Tomlin, M 1980 The furnishing and decoration of Ham House. *Furniture History*, 16.

Topham, E 1776 *Letters from Edinburgh Written in the Years 1774 and 1775*. London.

Torrie E P D & Coleman, R 1995 *Historic Kirkcaldy*. Scottish Burgh Survey.

Torrie, E P D & Coleman, R 1995 *Historic Stranraer*. Scottish Burgh Survey.

Torrie, E P D (ed.) 1986 *Gild Court Book of Dunfermline, 1433–1597*. Scottish Record Society, new series 12.

Torrie, E P D 1990 *Medieval Dundee: a town and its people*. Dundee.

Torrie, R J D 1988 Central Dunfermline: an analysis of the 1988 road network and the geographical factors that determined its layout. Unpublished typescript.

Turner, A L 1937 *History of a Great Hospital. Edinburgh Royal Infirmary, 1729–1929*. Edinburgh.

Turner Simpson, A & Holmes, N 1981 *Historic Canongate: the archaeological implications of development*. Scottish Burgh Survey.

Walker, B 2001 The use of 'skailie' in medieval and post-medieval Scotland. *Antiquity* 75, 163–71.

Watson, C B B (ed.) 1929 Roll of Edinburgh Burgesses & Guild Brethren 1406–1700. Edinburgh.

Watt, D E R (ed.) 1987 *Scotichronicon* by Walter Bower. Aberdeen.

Welsh, B 1819 *A Practical Treatise on the Efficacy of Bloodletting in the Epidemic Fever of Edinburgh*. Edinburgh.

Welter, V 2002 *Biopolis, Patrick Geddes and the City of Life*. London.

Williamson, P 1875–89 *Edinburgh Directories*. Edinburgh.

Wilson, D 1891 *Memorials of Edinburgh in the Olden Times*. Edinburgh.

Withrington, D J & Grant, I R (eds) 1975 *Statistical Account of Scotland, 1791–99*. Edinburgh.

Wodrow, R 1836 *The History of the Sufferings of the Church of Scotland from the Restoration to the Revolution*. Glasgow.

Wood, E S 1982 A 16th-century glasshouse at Knightons, Alfold, Surrey. *Surrey Archaeol Collect* 73, 1–47.

Wood, M & Armet, H 1954 Extracts from the Records of the Burgh of Edinburgh, 1681–89. Edinburgh.

Wood, M (ed.) 1937 *Court Book of the Regality of Broughton and the Burgh of Canongate, 1569–73*. Edinburgh.

Wood, M 1933a The hammermen of the Canongate: part I. *Book of the Old Edinburgh Club* 19, 1–30.

Wood, M 1935b The hammermen of the Canongate, part 2. *Book of the Old Edinburgh Club* 20, 78–110.

Wood, M 1950 Extracts from the Records of the Burgh of Edinburgh, 1665–80. Edinburgh.

Wood, M 1956 *Book of Records of the Ancient Privileges of the Canongate*. Edinburgh: SRS.

Wood, M 1974 Survey of the development of Edinburgh. *Book of the Old Edinburgh Club* 34 (1), 23–56.

Yeoman, P 1995 *Medieval Scotland*. London.

Index